MONTANA, WYOMING & IDAHO CAMPING

FOGHORN OUTDOORS

MONTANA, WYOMING & IDAHO CAMPING

The Complete Guide to More Than 1,200 Campgrounds

FIRST EDITION

Judy Kinnaman

AVALON
TRAVEL

FOGHORN OUTDOORS:
MONTANA, WYOMING
& IDAHO CAMPING
The Complete Guide to More
Than 1,200 Campgrounds
1st EDITION
Judy Kinnaman

Published by
Avalon Travel Publishing, Inc.
5855 Beaudry St.
Emeryville, CA 94608, USA

Please send all comments, corrections,
additions, amendments, and critiques to:
FOGHORN OUTDOORS: MONTANA,
WYOMING & IDAHO CAMPING
AVALON TRAVEL PUBLISHING
5855 BEAUDRY ST.
EMERYVILLE, CA 94608, USA
email: info@travelmatters.com
www.travelmatters.com

ISBN: 1-56691-283-0
ISSN: 1532-1142

Editor: Karen Bleske
Series Manager: Marisa Solís
Copy Editor: Carolyn Perkins
Index: Karen Bleske
Graphics: Erika Howsare
Production: David Hurst
Map Editors: Karen Bleske, Mike Balsbaugh
Cartography: Landis Bennett, Mike Morgenfeld

Front cover photo: Wind River Mountains,
© Cheyenne Rouse, 2001.

Printing History
1st edition—June 2001
5 4 3 2 1

Distributed in the United States and Canada by Publishers Group West
Printed in the USA by R.R. Donnelley

TABLE OF CONTENTS

HOW TO USE THIS BOOK. x

INTRODUCTION. 1

CAMPING TIPS 3

  Who Puts the Wild in Wildlife?. 3

  Wilderness Areas 4
    National Parks: America's Favorite Destinations;
    Other Protected Lands

  More Fun in the Great Outdoors. 12
    Places to Visit; Camping with Kids without Losing Your
    Mind; Floating; Fly-fishing; Photography

  Health, Safety, and Common Sense 17
    Watch Out for Wildlife; Getting In (and Staying Out) of Hot
    Water; Fire; Obeying the Laws of the Land; Ready to Ramble:
    Other Things You Need To Know; Guided Adventures:
    Learning the Easy Way

SPECIAL TOPICS

Keep It Wild **4**; *Keep It Wild Tip 1: Campfires* **5**; *Keep It Wild
Tip 2: Travel Lightly* **10**; *Keep It Wild Tip 3: Camp with Care*
12; *Keep It Wild Tip 4: Sanitation* **16**; *Keep It Wild Tip 5: Keep
the Wilderness Wild* **18**; *Keep It Wild Tip 6: Respect Other
Users* **22**; *Camping Gear Checklist* **26**

MONTANA 28
  Chapter MT1 31
  Chapter MT2 45
  Chapter MT3 79
  Chapter MT4 91
  Chapter MT5 99
  Chapter MT6 105

Chapter MT7 113
Chapter MT8 119
Chapter MT9 141
Chapter MT10 171
Chapter MT11 195
Chapter MT12 205
Chapter MT13 211
Chapter MT14 215
Chapter MT15 219

WYOMING 230
Chapter WY1 233
Chapter WY2 259
Chapter WY3 277
Chapter WY4 285
Chapter WY5 291
Chapter WY6 301
Chapter WY7 311
Chapter WY8 325

IDAHO 334
Chapter ID1 337
Chapter ID2 367
Chapter ID3 383
Chapter ID4 389
Chapter ID5 423
Chapter ID6 447
Chapter ID7 465
Chapter ID8 469
Chapter ID9 481

RESOURCE GUIDE. 496

Montana 496
National Forests; National Parks; Bureau of Land
Management; U.S. Army Corps of Engineers; State and
Federal Offices; Other Valuable Resources

Wyoming 500
National Forests; State Parks; National Parks; Bureau of
Land Management; State and Federal Offices; Other
Valuable Resources

Idaho 503
National Forests; State Parks; National Parks; Bureau of
Land Management; U.S. Army Corps of Engineers; State and
Federal Offices; Other Valuable Resources

GENERAL INDEX 509
CAMPGROUND INDEX 511

MAPS

Montana, Wyoming & Idaho Overview Map ix

MONTANA STATE	29	WYOMING STATE	231
Map MT1 32		Map WY1 234	
Map MT2 46		Map WY2 260	
Map MT3 80		Map WY3 278	
Map MT4 92		Map WY4 286	
Map MT5 100		Map WY5 292	
Map MT6 106		Map WY6 302	
Map MT7 114		Map WY7 312	
Map MT8 120		Map WY8 326	
Map MT9 142			
Map MT10 172			
Map MT11 196		IDAHO STATE	335
Map MT12 206		Map ID1 338	
Map MT13 212		Map ID2 368	
Map MT14 216		Map ID3 384	
Map MT15 220		Map ID4 390	
		Map ID5 424	
		Map ID6 448	
		Map ID7 466	
		Map ID8 470	
		Map ID9 482	

Montana, Wyoming & Idaho Overview Map

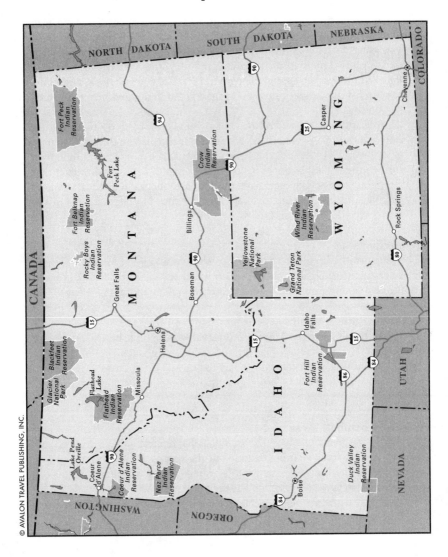

HOW TO USE THIS BOOK

Finding a Campground

This book is organized to help you in a couple of different ways, depending on how you like to plan your trip. Each of the three states is divided into a grid; each map corresponds to a section on the grid. Each map is also divided into a grid, using the letters a–h and the numbers 1–8 for a total of 64 sections, to make it easy for you to locate the area in which you are interested.

1. If you know the name of the campground you'd like to visit, look it up in the campground index, beginning on page 511, to find it and turn to the corresponding page.
2. If you want to visit a general area but are not committed to a particular location, turn to the Montana, Wyoming, and Idaho map on the previous page or in the back of this book. Find the zone where you'd like to camp and then turn to the corresponding chapter. Each chapter opens with a map that clearly numbers every campground in that area. Locate individual camping destinations on the map and then turn to those numbered sites in the chapter for detailed descriptions.

About the Maps

The maps in this book are designed to show the general location of each campground. Readers are advised to buy a detailed state map before heading out to any campground, particularly when venturing into remote areas.

What the Ratings Mean

Every camping spot in this book is designated with a scenic beauty rating of **1** through **10**. Other factors that can influence a trip, such as noise or restroom cleanliness, can change from day to day and do not affect the ratings. That is why it is possible to have a great trip at a campground that is rated a **1** or a **2**.

What the Symbols Mean

Listings in this book feature activity symbols that represent the recreational offerings at or within walking distance of the campground. Other symbols identify whether there are sites for RVs or tents or any wheelchair-accessible facilities. Wheelchair accessibility has been indicated when it is mentioned by campground managers, and concerned campers should call the contact number to ensure that their specific needs will be met.

ACTIVITY SYMBOLS

 hiking

biking

swimming

fishing

boating

hot springs

 pets permitted

playground

 wheelchair access

RV sites

tent sites

Our Commitment

We are committed to making *Montana, Wyoming & Idaho Camping* the most accurate, thorough, and enjoyable camping guide to the region. Every camping spot in this book has been carefully reviewed and accompanied by the most up-to-date information available. However, with the change of seasons, you can bet that some of the fees listed herein have changed and that camping destinations may have opened, closed, or changed hands. If you have a specific need or concern, it's a good idea to call the campground ahead of time.

If you would like to comment on the book, whether it's to suggest a tent or RV spot we overlooked or to let us know about any noteworthy experience—good or bad—that occurred while using *Montana, Wyoming & Idaho Camping* as your guide, we would appreciate hearing from you. Please address correspondence to:

Foghorn Outdoors: Montana, Wyoming & Idaho Camping, 1st Edition
Avalon Travel Publishing
5855 Beaudry Street
Emeryville, CA 94608
USA

email: info@travelmatters.com

ACKNOWLEDGMENTS

The information for this book came from research and the helpful information provided by the Forest Services; Bureau of Land Management; Departments of Fish, Wildlife, and Parks; chambers of commerce; campground and resort owners; and others. Your enthusiasm and interest in the book added greatly to the content. Thanks to Katie, who is recovering from "phone ear," and Ron at B. Dalton, who saved a spot at the signing table.

Thank you to Craig, Jennifer, Caty, Barb, and Chris,
who put up with my fits and starts. Thanks to Wayne,
who remained calm throughout, and to Marisa, whose
support and encouragement made this book possible.
Last, but not least, Sunny, Max, and Speedo,
who kept their noses to the ground.

INTRODUCTION

Backcountry of Yellowstone National Park

INTRODUCTION

Montana, Wyoming, and Idaho: The very names conjure images of open spaces and western spirit, and you won't be disappointed. Here the animals easily outnumber the people, and western hospitality isn't a trite catchphrase.

These states offer many unique natural wonders. Yellowstone National Park, in Wyoming, was the world's first national park. Frank Church–River of No Return, in the heart of Idaho, is the largest wilderness area in the lower 48 states. Flathead Lake, in northern Montana, is the largest freshwater lake west of the Mississippi. And Glacier National Park, a land of breathtaking scenery, is adjacent to Waterton Lakes National Park in Canada.

The region boasts designated Wild and Scenic Rivers, blue-ribbon trout streams, spectacular forests, and pristine alpine lakes. Uncrowded hiking trails, excellent fishing, a variety of wildlife, and magnificent scenery define these states.

The territory is dotted with natural mineral waters. Once thought to have restorative powers and health benefits, hot springs are enjoyed today for simply being a relaxing environment.

If you like history, there are ghost towns, dinosaur digs, and battlegrounds. Lacking the push of population, many of the historical sites remain much as they were in their heyday.

If you are looking for a new adventure, but you still want the comfort of being in experienced hands, there are guest ranches, cattle drives, white-water guides, and wilderness pack trips.

If you are used to camping in a more metropolitan area, don't hesitate to ask questions. While the great outdoors in Montana, Wyoming, and Idaho may resemble the camping situations you are used to, there are some very serious differences of which you need to be aware.

After all, you don't want to be one of *those* visitors who does something unbelievably ignorant, such as posing the wife next to a bison or sending the husband to stand next to the boiling waters of Yellowstone to get a better picture. When the lethargic-looking bison gores the woman or the man falls in the deadly waters and dies, the locals simply shake their heads.

What were they thinking? becomes the rhetorical question of the day. Maybe they just didn't know, someone offers. No excuse, another's bound to say, this ain't Disneyland.

The moral of this tale? You can't be too well prepared or too knowledgeable when you travel through the wild west.

Of course, the biggest danger is one you might not want to avoid. That's the danger of falling in love with the magnificent wildlife, open spaces, fragrant forests, and breathtaking scenery that you'll find in Montana, Idaho, and Wyoming. Let this book introduce you to this special land, and guide you to adventures you won't soon forget.

CAMPING TIPS

Who Puts the Wild in Wildlife?

Computers and technology are taking over the world! Well, maybe, but what do you think is the fastest-growing recreational activity in the great outdoors today?

Give up?

Watching wildlife. It seems, in our modern world, that the soaring flight of an eagle or the dainty first steps of a fawn still hold a special magic.

According to statistics gathered for the state of Montana, more people visit to view wildlife than to hunt or fish combined. Nationally, people interested in photographing or viewing wildlife increased nearly 50 percent in five short years.

Wildlife watching can be even more rewarding with some preparation. Several guides on the market can help you find and identify native animals, and a good strong pair of binoculars can bring you up close and personal in a way that's safe for both you and the wildlife. A camera with a telephoto lens can capture your experiences forever.

Montana, Wyoming, and Idaho are the best states anywhere to eavesdrop on these creatures in their natural environment. However, as with any visit to a foreign country, it helps to understand the culture and the language of this new world.

To be a good wildlife observer, you need to stay quiet, keep your distance, and blend in—no loud clothing or heavy perfume. Animals are highly sensitive to their space, and their very survival depends on being aware of changes in their surroundings. When they sense your presence and take off, it not only upsets their normal activity, it squanders their energy.

Don't stress the wildlife. If you have small children and they can't contain themselves, wait until they are a little older to watch wildlife. Chasing or pursuing animals is considered harassment and is against federal and state laws. This includes you and your dogs, so keep your pets on a leash so they don't get themselves or the wildlife in trouble.

Common warning signs of distress in animals are panting, pointing their ears toward you, raising their heads abruptly, sounding alarm calls, or exhibiting other nervous movements. If you see these signs, you are too close.

Another rule: don't interfere. This can be a tough one. If you see an animal struggling, your impulse is to save it. But don't forget, you are in another country, and the situation may not be what it looks like. The worst thing you can do is meddle. If an animal feels cornered, it can become desperate, and a desperate animal could be dangerous. If you think an animal is in real trouble, note the location and report to the Fish and Game or appropriate agency immediately.

The best time to see wildlife is early morning or early evening until dark, because animals are more active during the cool hours.

The national parks, wilderness areas, and forests are good choices for wildlife viewing. Some other interesting places in Montana include, but aren't limited to, Mount Haggin Wildlife Management Area (Anaconda), Cliff and Wade Lakes (Ennis), Gates of the Mountains (Helena), and Lewis and Clark Caverns (Three Forks). In Wyoming, visit Bighorn Sheep Reserve (Dubois), National Elk Refuge (Jackson), and Pryor Mountain Wild Horse Range (Lovell). Idaho offers Massacre Rocks State Park (American Falls), Bear Lake National Wildlife Refuge (Montpelier), and Cherry Springs Nature Area (Pocatello).

This is just a sample of the selection, and you may discover others. The Fish, Wildlife, and Parks departments and related agencies have information available on places to go and animals to see.

Wilderness Areas

National Parks: America's Favorite Destinations

People flock to the national parks during the peak months of June, July, and August. If you plan your trip for before or after those months, you can avoid the biggest single drawback to a visit, crowds.

Yellowstone National Park

Designated as the first national park in 1872, this 2.2-million-acre park is often called the crown jewel of our national park system. Born of volcanic activity, Yellowstone offers sights and sounds that are duplicated nowhere else. The spectacular hot pots and geothermal features terrified early explorers, who had never seen or heard of such wonders. Today even generations raised on the magic of special effects can find something captivating about water shooting from the center of the earth into the sky above their heads.

And the land continues changing as we watch. At Mammoth Hot Springs, the superheated water percolates up through the ancient limestone to deposit nearly an inch a month of travertine on Opal Terrace. The encroaching travertine threatens a historic home, built in the early 1900s, and a dirt wall and sandbags have been erected to prevent the house from damage.

Besides its 300 geysers and colorful hot springs, Yellowstone National Park boasts mudpots and fumaroles. Mudpots are bubbling brown pools of silica and clay; interesting to look at, their smell is memorable. The bubbling mud combines with sulfuric acid, giving off a "rotten egg" odor that defines them as mudpots. Fumaroles, or steam vents, send hissing steam and gases into the air.

Names such as Grand Prismatic and Sapphire testify to the colorful nature of the hot springs, as the superheated water carries a variety of minerals along with it as it travels to the earth's surface. The unique results are beautiful, but they can be fatally attractive. Hot doesn't begin to describe the intensity of these waters; for example, Emerald Spring, in Norris Geyser Basin, reaches temperatures of over 400 degrees.

Inevitably, someone will ignore the warnings or misjudge the terrain, fall into the waters, and boil to death. Make sure this doesn't happen to you, your loved ones, or your pets. People have died trying to save their pets from this tragic end, when such tragedy can be avoided by following all park rules. The dangers are not always obvious to those unfamiliar with Yellowstone's geology, so you don't want to rely on your own judgment, but instead treat the cautions and rules of the park seriously. There is no second chance with heat like that, so respect it and keep your distance. And remember, while the presence of lots of other people might lull you into thinking Yellowstone is a controlled environment designed for human entertainment, nothing could be further from the truth. Yellowstone is home to wild animals, and in it they are king. Treat them with the caution and respect they deserve.

Keep It Wild Tip 1: Campfires

1. Fire use can scar the backcountry. If a fire ring is not available, use a lightweight stove for cooking.
2. Where fires are permitted, use existing fire rings away from large rocks or overhangs.
3. Don't char rocks by building new rings.
4. Gather sticks from the ground that are no larger than the diameter of your wrist.
5. Don't snap branches of live, dead, or downed trees, which can cause personal injury and also scar the natural setting.
6. Put the fire "dead out" and make sure it's cold before departing. Remove all trash from the fire ring and sprinkle dirt over the site.
7. Remember that some forest fires can be started by a campfire that appears to be out. Hot embers burning deep in the pit can cause tree roots to catch fire and burn underground. If you ever see smoke rising from the ground, seemingly from nowhere, dig down and put the fire out.

If you choose to fish in Yellowstone National Park, you need a fishing license, which you can obtain, along with the rules and regulations, at ranger stations and visitor centers throughout the park.

Glacier National Park

Glacier National Park was established in 1910. Situated on the northern border of Montana, it is often overlooked, which only adds to its appeal. The views are spectacular: towering mountain ranges carved by prehistoric ice rivers, alpine meadows, wildflowers, deep forests, waterfalls, glaciers, and sparkling lakes.

Few roads exist in the park's 1,600 square miles, thus preserving its primitive and unspoiled beauty. Glacier National Park joins Waterton Lakes National Park in Alberta, Canada.

One experience not to be missed is the Going-To-The-Sun Road, a popular drive over a 52-mile highway that takes you through some of the most beautiful alpine scenery anywhere. The road crosses the Continental Divide at Logan Pass and runs along the towering Garden Wall. Vehicle restrictions apply for traversing Logan Pass; the maximum length is 20 feet and the maximum width is eight feet (including mirrors). Oversize vehicles may be parked at various points, and rental cars are available. The park may have shuttle service, but call ahead for current information. Because of the elevation, Going-To-The-Sun Road is open only when the weather allows, which is usually the entire summer, but check ahead to be sure.

Glacier has more than 700 miles of hiking and horse trails, providing many opportunities for short hikes and extended backpacking trips. The Trail of the Cedars, Huckleberry Mountain, Hidden Lake, Sun Point, and Swiftcurrent Nature Trails are five self-guided walks you can take at your own pace to learn about the area. The Trail of the Cedars is wheelchair accessible. The park offers many good day hikes, and visitor center staff can offer suggestions and provide free maps of popular trails in the park.

If you plan to camp overnight in Glacier's backcountry, you must stop at a visitor center or ranger station and obtain a backcountry permit. It's important for hikers and backcountry visitors to assume individual responsibility for planning trips and hiking safely. Before leaving on your hike, stop by a park visitor center to obtain needed warnings and recommendations. This will increase your odds of a safe hike, decrease your disturbance to park wildlife, and lessen damage to resources. Trail guides, topographic maps, and field guides are available in the visitor center bookstores. You can also order them by mail from the Glacier Natural History Association. Call 406/888-5756 to request a catalog. You may also visit its backcountry website: www.nps.gov /glac/activities/bcguide1.htm.

Blackfeet, Salish, and Kootenai tribal members offer special campfire talks on native life and culture at locations throughout the park. Native dance troupes perform weekly during July and August at the St. Mary Visitor Center.

If you bring your pet to the park, be aware that pets are not allowed on any park trails. They must be on a leash or caged at all times. Kennels are available in neighboring communities if you need to board your pet during your visit.

Grand Teton National Park

This park near Yellowstone often doesn't get its due, but it is well worth visiting. The spectacular Tetons rise from the valley floor, and the six summits offer excellent climbing and hiking opportunities. Nearly 200 miles of hiking trails in Grand Teton National Park provide access to backcountry lakes, streams, and canyons. Trail difficulty varies from easy to very strenuous, and hikes take a few minutes or several days. Self-guided trails with booklets describe the features that border the two-mile Colter Bay Nature Trail and the three-mile Taggart Lake Trail and discuss the history of the .5-mile Menor's Ferry and the .5-mile Cunningham Cabin Trail. The Cascade Canyon Trail begins at the south end of Jenny Lake, and the booklet explains natural features up to Lake Solitude, nine miles from the trailhead.

Grand Teton has some of the most accessible and diverse climbing opportunities in the country, from easy outings to extremely difficult undertakings. Many inherent risks and hazards are associated with climbing and hiking. Risks include, but are not limited to lightning, rock fall, avalanches, crevasses, and extreme weather conditions (even during the summer). If you plan to take part in these activities, remember you are responsible for all risks and any injury, including death, that may result. You must have a competent technique, plenty of experience, well-maintained safety equipment, excellent physical fitness, and good judgment before you even consider climbing or hiking. If you're planning an overnight stay, you must have a backcountry permit to camp or bivouac. Current and detailed information is available at the Jenny Lake Ranger Station; in the summer call 307/739-3343; in the winter call 307/739-3309.

Other Protected Lands

Frank Church–River of No Return Wilderness

This wilderness area in the center of Idaho comprises 2.3 million acres, the largest wilderness area in the lower 48 states. As you might imagine, this territory includes a variety of habitats, from the forests to the plains. Deer, moose, elk, mountain goats, bighorn sheep, black bears, and mountain lions share this land with a variety of songbirds, raptors, and waterfowl.

Congress created the River of No Return Wilderness with the passage of the Central Idaho Wilderness Act on July 23, 1980. The wilderness area lies in the Challis, Salmon, Nez Perce, Payette, and Boise National Forests in Idaho and the Bitterroot National Forest in Montana. The name of Frank Church, the U.S. senator from Idaho who was key in its creation, was added in 1983, one month before his death.

The Frank Church–River of No Return Wilderness includes some of Idaho's most famous white-water rivers: the Middle Fork of the Salmon Wild and Scenic River and the Salmon Wild and Scenic River, and the source of the Selway. The Salmon River and the Middle Fork of the Salmon River offer water adventures of truly national proportions and draw enthusiasts from all over the United States. Permits are required to raft on the Main Salmon and the Middle Fork; their popularity means it would be wise to get your permits the winter before your intended raft trip. Obtain these from the Middle Fork Ranger District in the Challis National Forest for the Middle Fork River and the North Fork Ranger District in the Salmon National Forest for the Main Salmon River.

Numerous hiking trails lead to spectacular vistas, alpine lakes, and hot springs. If you want to experience nature firsthand and get away from it all, this is the place to be. Of course, the remoteness, combined with mechanical and motorized ban, means that you need to be especially prepared and definitely experienced in exploring and surviving the wilderness.

Contact: Besides the national forests, a small swath of land is managed by the Bureau of Land Management.

Bitterroot National Forest, Supervisor, 1801 N. 1st St., Hamilton, MT 59840; 406/363-3131

Boise National Forest, Cascade Ranger District, Highway 55, P.O. Box 696, Cascade, ID 83611; 208/382-4271

Nez Perce National Forest, Red River Ranger District, Elk City Ranger Station, P.O. Box 416, Elk City, ID 83525; 208/842-2245, fax 208/926-2245

Nez Perce National Forest, Slate Creek Ranger Station, HC 01, Box 70, Whitebird, ID 83554; 208/839-2211, fax 208/839-2211

Payette National Forest, Krassel District Office, P.O. Box 1026, 500 N. Mission St., McCall, ID 83638; 208/634-0600

Salmon-Challis National Forest, Salmon-Cobalt Ranger District, RR2, Box 600, Salmon, ID 83467; 208/756-5100

Salmon-Challis National Forest, Middle Fork Ranger District, P.O. Box 750, Highway 93, Challis, ID 83226; 208/879-4101

Salmon-Challis National Forest, North Fork Ranger District, P.O. Box 180, North Fork, ID 83466; 208/865-2700

Salmon-Challis National Forest, Yankee Fork Ranger District, HC 67 Box 650, Highway 75, Clayton, ID 83227; 208/838-2201

Bureau of Land Management—Upper Columbia–Salmon/Clearwater District, 1808 N. 3rd St., Coeur d'Alene, ID 83814-3407; 208/769-5000 (information)

Craters of the Moon National Monument

Craters of the Moon National Monument was designated in 1924 to preserve its unique volcanic features, including lava flows, cinder cones, spatter cones, rafted blocks, and lava caves. The Craters of the Moon Lava Field is the largest basaltic lava field in the United States, with the West's most unusual displays of volcanic phenomena. The lava field sits on a large fissure in the earth's crust called the Great Rift Zone. The Great Rift was active about 15,000 years ago, and most activity ceased here about 2,000 years ago. The land shows many small craters and fissures. Craters form a line above the fissure, and the lava flows run from most of the craters. Basalt lava flows are of two types: "a'a" and "pahoehoe" (Hawaiian terms). Pahoehoe lava begins in a liquid state and hardens smoothly. The dissolved gas in it is associated with spectacular "lava fountain" displays during eruptions in Hawaii. Several fascinating caves, actually "lava tubes," are created by large flows of pahoehoe lava. The liquid form of lava cools into a crust; the interior lava flows within the crust and creates tunnels. The gaseous lava explosions collapse the tunnels in places, creating openings through which people can enter. A'a lava comes out thick and viscous during eruption, and it creates short, jagged flows. A'a is razor sharp and can cut shoes, hands, and exposed areas. The park has a network of easy trails to the craters, lava flows, and the caves. Most of the park is also a designated wilderness area.

Contact: Craters of the Moon National Monument, Superintendent, P.O. Box 29, Arco, ID 83213; 208/527-3267.

Fossil Butte National Monument, Kemmerer, Wyoming

Fossil Butte National Monument, one of the richest fossil fields in the world, has 50 million-year-old fish, insects, birds, reptiles, and plants. More than 75 fossils are on display, including a 13-foot crocodile and the oldest known bat.

You can participate in paleontology and geology programs and watch fossil preparation demonstrations. Kids can learn to clean fossils and make crayon replicas of fossils. You can hike two park trails: the quarry trail is a 2.5-mile loop to the fossil quarry, and Fossil Lake Trail shows you plants and animals in the park.

Contact: Fossil Butte National Monument, P.O. Box 592, Kemmerer, WY 83101-0592; 307/877-4455 (headquarters), fax 307/877-4457; email: FOBU_Superintendent@nps.gov.

Vore Buffalo Jump, Sundance, Wyoming

Plains Indians chased bison over the rim of this natural sinkhole to their deaths, and today this buffalo jump is considered an excellent archeological site. Because of the nature of the dirt, much material has been preserved. You can tour ongoing excavations and visit the museum.

Contact: Vore Buffalo Jump Foundation, P.O. Box 369, Sundance, WY 82729; 307/283-1192, 307/766-2208, or 307/766-5136.

Dry Creek Petrified Tree Environmental Education Area, Buffalo, Wyoming

This .8-mile interpretive trail takes you back 60 million years to see petrified trees and plants from the Early Eocene era.

Contact: Dry Creek Petrified Tree Environmental Education Area, Buffalo, WY 82834; Bureau of Land Management, 5353 Yellowstone Rd., P.O. Box 1828, Cheyenne, WY 82003-1828; 307/775-6256 (general information), fax 307/775-6129.

Cottonwood Creek Dinosaur Trail, Alcova, Wyoming

The self-guided hiking trail has interpretive signs to help you find the fossils of small Mesozoic reptiles still in the ground.

Contact: Cottonwood Creek Dinosaur Trail, Alcova, WY 82620; Bureau of Land Management, 5353 Yellowstone Rd., P.O. Box 1828, Cheyenne, WY 82003-1828; 307/775-6256. (general information), fax 307/775-6129

Tynsky's Fossil Fish, Kemmerer, Wyoming

You can dig in the quarry, tour the dig site, and visit the gift shop. Fossils found here include the herringlike Diplomystus, the spined Priscacara (see fish fossil descriptions below under Ulrich's Fossil Gallery), and crocodile, turtle, and stingray.

Contact: Tynsky's Fossil Fish, 201 Beryl St., Kemmerer, WY 83101; 307/877-6885.

Ulrich's Fossil Gallery, Fossil, Wyoming (10 miles west of Kemmerer)

For a fee, Ulrich's supplies transportation, tools, and a staff member for digs. You can collect and keep all sizes of *Diplomystus, Priscacara, Mioplosis, Phareodus, Knightia, Notogoneus,* and all others, excluding those declared rare and unusual by the state. Ulrich's has been featured in *National Geographic,* and there are specimens on display at the Smithsonian Institute.

Diplomystus is an extinct fish from the Eocene period that resembles a herring; it's found in Wyoming's Green River Formation. *Priscacara* is a 55 million-year-old extinct fish from the Green River Formation. It had spines to keep predators from eating it. *Mioplosis* is an extinct fish that had a long, strong body, similar to that of a modern-day perch. *Mioplosis* was a major predator of the Green River system. *Phareodus* is an extinct fish that had large pointed teeth, a long pectoral fin, and large median fins set close to the tail fin. *Knightia* is the most abundant extinct fossil fish in the Green River Lake system and has been designated the Wyoming state fossil. *Notogoneus* is an extinct sucker fish that is about 50 million years old.

Contact: Ulrich's Fossil Gallery, Fossil Station #308, Fossil, WY 83101; 307/877-6466.

Warfield Fossils, Thayne, Wyoming (12 miles west of Cody)

You can learn to dig, and Warfield Fossils will provide tools to collect your own fossils. Hobbyists are welcome to bring their collections to the preparatory studio in Thayne to trade.

Contact: Warfield Fossils, 2072 S. Muddy String Rd., Thayne, WY 83127; 307/883-2445.

The Wyoming Dinosaur Center, Thermopolis, Wyoming

You can visit the Dinosaur Museum, tour the dig site, or dig yourself (all bones found stay at the center) at the Wyoming Dinosaur Center. Dinosaur giants such as the *Camarosaurus, Apatasaurus,* and *Diplodocus* are the most common on the Warm Springs Ranch where the digs take place. Kid and Teen Digs are available in the summer.

Contact: Wyoming Dinosaur Center, 110 Carter Ranch Rd., P.O. Box 868, Thermopolis, WY 82443; 800/455-DINO (3466); website: www.wyodino.org.

Big Cedar Ridge, Worland/Ten Sleep, Wyoming

There are no fees or guides, but you can find nearly 150 different types of plants here. Dr. Scott Wing has a display in the Smithsonian on plant fossils from this site.

Contact: Big Cedar Ridge, Bureau of Land Management, 101 S. 23rd St., P.O. Box 119, Worland, WY 82401-0119; 307/347-5100, fax 307/347-6195; email: worland_wymail@blm.gov, website: www.wy.blm.gov.

Jurassic Digs, Greybull, Wyoming

The most complete *Aurosuarus* skull in the world was found here and is now on display at the Tate Museum in Casper. For a fee, you can dig here and discover fossils of both plant- and meat-eating dinosaurs.

Contact: Jurassic Digs, 1445 Lane 43, Otto, WY 82434; 307/762-3290.

Keep It Wild Tip 3: Camp with Care

1. Choose an existing, legal site. Restrict activities to areas where vegetation is compacted or absent.
2. Camp at least 75 steps (200 feet) from lakes, streams, and trails.
3. Always choose sites that won't be damaged by your stay.
4. Preserve the feeling of solitude by selecting camps that are out of view when possible.
5. Don't dig trenches or build structures or furniture.

Red Gulch Dinosaur Tracksite, Shell, Wyoming

Rare fossil footprints from the Middle Jurassic Period are visible near the Red Gulch/Alkali National Back Country Byway. You can collect petrified wood, invertebrates, and plant fossils, but vertebrates are kept in the public trust through the Bureau of Land Management. The Red Gulch Dinosaur Tracksite is changing how scientists view the geology of this area.

Contact: Red Gulch Dinosaur Tracksite, Bureau of Land Management, 101 S. 23rd St., P.O. Box 119, Worland, WY 82401-0119; 307/347-5100, fax 307/347-6195; email: worland_wymail@blm.gov, website: www.wy.blm.gov.

More Fun in the Great Outdoors

Places to Visit

The Museum of the Rockies, Bozeman, Montana

The Willow Creek Anticline, on the eastern slope of the Rocky Mountains near Choteau, is the site of the Paleontology Field Program. This is where Dr. Jack Horner discovered the remains of dinosaur nesting colonies. Fossil finds here include dinosaur eggs, embryos, nests of several species, and a massive bone-bed of *Maiasaura peeblesorum* fossils.

The Paleontology Field Program offers different sessions depending on your interest and energy. One-day sessions, popular with families, include fossil identification, fossil discovery, and a tour of the paleontological sites. A weeklong session features rock excavation, fossil prospecting, and geologic data collection.

In the Judith River area, paleontologist Nate Murphy of the Judith River Dinosaur Institute offers a hands-on dinosaur experience at an established dinosaur site.

The Old Trail Museum in Choteau displays fossils, dinosaurs, and Native American artifacts. You can take two- to 10-day hands-on paleontology field classes, for adults and children, with the professional paleontology staff.

Contact: Museum of the Rockies, 600 W. Kagy Blvd., Bozeman, MT 59715; 406/994-2251.

Hagerman Fossil Beds National Monument, Hagerman, Idaho
Idaho has no dinosaurs, but it does have Pliocene Epoch fossils dating from 3.5 million years ago. Hagerman Fossil Beds National Monument is most famous for the horse, *Equus simplicidens,* which is Idaho's state fossil. Complete and partial skeletons of this zebralike ancestor of today's horse have been found here, along with 140 animal species of both vertebrates and invertebrates and 35 plant species. Eight species are found nowhere else, and 44 were found here first. More than 200 published scientific papers focus on the Hagerman fossil species.

Contact: Hagerman Fossil Beds, 221 N. State St., P.O. Box 570, Hagerman, ID 83332; 208/837-4793; website: www.nps.gov/hafo.

Passage to the Past: History Surrounds You
Lewis and Clark's historic expedition took place nearly 200 years ago, yet today you can visit many of the places they stopped and the routes they took through Montana and Idaho.

William Clark carved his name into Pompey's Pillar, east of Billings, in July 1806. You can trace the path the explorers took along the Missouri River below Fort Benton, passing land that has remained virtually unchanged for 200 years. The Corps of Discovery found the headwaters of the Gallatin, Madison, and Jefferson Rivers, which form the Missouri River in Three Forks. The Lewis and Clark National Historic Trail Interpretive Center in Great Falls describes the month Lewis and Clark spent in the area, along with additional historical facts.

U.S. 12 in Idaho is known as Lewis and Clark Highway, and many historical sites lie along this drive. A section of it, east from Lewiston, is the Clearwater Canyon Scenic Byway, a beautiful drive to Kooskia.

The Oregon and California Trails stretch across Wyoming and Idaho. You can still see the wagon ruts from the settlers who traveled the South Pass in central Wyoming on their way west. Fort Hall, in Idaho, was a well-known fur trade settlement and popular stop along the Oregon and California Trails.

The Fossil Butte National Monument in Wyoming rises 1,000 feet and contains impressive paleontological artifacts and geological formations. On these 8,000-plus acres are a visitor center and walking trails, and park rangers offer interpretive programs.

Old bones are not the only treasures that the land here holds. Philipsburg, in Montana, is a National Historic District and was voted Montana's 1998 Tourism Community of the Year. This old mining town still has much to offer. Ghost towns are nearby, and in once place in town you can mine concentrate and find rough Montana sapphires that can be made into jewelry, all in one place.

Wine (Yes, Wine!) Country
When you hear the words "wine country," Idaho is probably not the first place that leaps to mind. However, Idaho winegrowers are working hard to

change that. The first vineyard in Idaho was planted in 1864, and today more vineyards are being planted than ever before. In 1999, Corus Brands, through its affiliate, Winemakers L.L.C., planted more than 230 acres at Skyline Vineyards and Sawtooth Vineyards, and it planted another 370 acres in 2000. The Idaho Grape Growers and Wine Producers Commission is working with the University of Idaho to research which varieties of wine grapes will thrive in Idaho. The majority of Idaho's vineyards are in the southwest corner of the state, near the Snake River. The combination of long growing days, moderate climate, and unique soil makes this region favorable to growing wine grapes.

Not to be left behind, Montana has its own vineyards. Mission Mountain Winery, a family-owned winery on the west shore of Flathead Lake (there's even access by boat), was started 19 years ago, and its first vintage was in 1984. It is the first bonded winery in Montana. The winery produces approximately 6,500 cases of wine a year, including Johannisberg Riesling, chardonnay, a "blush" wine called Sundown, an exceptional muscat canelli dinner wine, cabernet sauvignon, merlot, pinot noir, and a port. Mission Mountain Winery is not alone in the quest to grow grapes in Montana. Over the years others have started vineyards around Flathead Lake and in the Flathead Valley and have banded together to form the Montana Winegrowers Institute. Pinot noir and other varieties are being grown on Finley Point, pinot noir has been planted above the eastern shores of Flathead Lake, gewurztraminer and pinot noir are being grown in Flathead Valley, and Partridge Hill Vineyard, in Polson, is growing a variety of clones of pinot noir as well as experimenting with many other varieties of *vinifera* grapes.

Wyoming has the Terry Ranch Cellars at Terry Bison Ranch in Cheyenne.

Camping with Kids without Losing Your Mind

Two words: plan ahead.

One of the hurdles you face is the contrast between passive activities, such as TV and computer games, and the active involvement required when camping. Many kids are used to being entertained, as opposed to entertaining themselves, and if that's the case, then start there.

If you introduce them with some structured activity, it won't be long until their natural curiosity and interest will take over.

The approach you take depends on the age of your kids. Try to imagine the experience from their point of view. Young children are interested in the touch and feel of things. They can be entertained for hours by exploring the immediate area, including flora, fauna, and even simple dirt.

Older kids like games and competitions, and fortunately you can make up games to suit almost any situation. Animals that frequent the area leave clues to their identities, and a field guide (available at most book stores) can aid in discovering who has been visiting. This works with birds, fish, and plant life, too. Have a contest to see who can come up with the longest list. If you are ambitious, take plaster or sand casts of footprints or leaves. Budding artists will enjoy sketching their favorite landscape. You can begin or expand a bug collection, hold a fishing contest, or pursue that old favorite, cloud study. Nothing beats a leisurely analysis of drifting clouds, and, once the mood is set, stories to fit the shapes and descriptions are sure to follow. History also plays a big part in the attraction of the West. Ghost towns hold a certain allure, and rock hounding can be a consuming hobby.

The key to enjoying the outdoors with children is to see the potential the way a child might. Open your eyes and your mind to the possibilities, and don't be afraid to use your imagination. Allow yourself to be silly, innovative, and even impossible. Daydream. You'll be surprised how much fun you can have.

Hiking

If you want to take your kids hiking, be sure the trip is short and suitable for your children's abilities. This way you can avoid those trip-ruining situations in which you have to rush them to get to your destination before dark (in case you haven't noticed, ha ha, the faster you push them, the slower they go).

Make it fun. Show them the map of where you are going and refer to it along the way. Bring snacks and take time for breaks. This is a great opportunity to point out the natural features and animals in the area. Make it a learning experience—explain how you are making safe choices when crossing a stream, following a trail, or avoiding a danger. Keep the mood light but factual.

And last, but not least, dress the children appropriately. Nothing is worse than an overheated child, unless it's one who is too cold. This isn't the time to try the new hiking boots, and experienced parents might bring a change of clothes. The misery of a wet, cold child, with miles to go is indescribable.

Floating

Floating is a term that might be unfamiliar to some, but it is simply another way to describe rafting. Spending time on the water helps us appreciate the primal, restorative aspects of nature. Rocking gently on a pond, drifting in the easy current of a mountain stream, or gliding between the banks of an ageless river creates enchantment like nothing else.

Floating offers an unparalleled opportunity for wildlife watching, as the quiet passage of a raft doesn't disturb the animals and birds as they go about their business. The development of disposable waterproof cameras makes it easy to capture these images.

Often you can float through areas you would not be able to reach any other way. Thick trees and underbrush, along with posted private lands, might make foot travel impossible, but you can float by with great ease.

June–September are the most popular months for family float trips. The most common vessels are rafts, canoes, small boats, or drift boats. On some of the calmer stretches, large inner tubes provide group fun.

Here again, and it can't be repeated enough, situations can change unexpectedly, and it is your responsibility to know the condition of the waterway you intend to explore. Even if you have floated a section of river before, it always makes sense to find out the current conditions. Weather can be a factor, and spring runoff can turn a leisurely stream into a raging torrent. Be informed.

Fly-fishing

If fishing for you has always been about hooking a squirming worm, you might be surprised to see the number of fly-fishing enthusiasts casting in Montana, Wyoming, and Idaho waters. Boasting some of the best trout streams in the United States, these three states provide a challenge to beginning and expert anglers alike.

Fly-fishing is taken very seriously here, but beginners are welcome. As in golf, you can never learn enough about technique, but classes, books, and guides are available to instruct you in the ways of the sport. Check with the local sporting goods stores for information on all three.

Licenses are a must and are available from the Fish and Wildlife Department in each state, as well as from many sporting goods stores and even gas stations.

Keep It Wild Tip 4: Sanitation

If no refuse facility is available:
1. Deposit human waste in "cat holes" dug six to eight inches deep. Cover and disguise the cat hole when finished.
2. Deposit human waste at least 75 paces (200 feet) from any water source or camp.
3. Use toilet paper sparingly. When finished, carefully burn it in the cat hole, then bury it.
4. If no appropriate burial locations are available, such as in popular wilderness camps above tree line in granite settings, then all human refuse should be double-bagged and packed out.
5. At boat-in campsites, chemical toilets are required. Chemical toilets can also solve the problem of larger groups camping for long stays at one location where no facilities are available.
6. To wash dishes or your body, carry water away from the source and use small amounts of biodegradable soap. Scatter dishwater after all food particles have been removed.
7. Scour your campsites for even the tiniest piece of trash and any other evidence of your stay. Pack out all the trash you can, even if it's not yours. Finding cigarette butts, for instance, provides special irritation for most campers. Pick them up and discard them properly.
8. Never litter. Never. Or you become the enemy of all others.

The Fish and Wildlife Departments issues fishing regulations and current lists of where and how to get your license. The regulations are available at the department offices, and usually at chambers of commerce, sporting goods stores, and tourist shops.

A number of areas are designated catch-and-release, which, as the term implies, requires you to return any fish caught to the water. Nevertheless, more is involved than simply tossing the fish back. Specific methods help the fish survive the experience, and plenty of sources are available to teach them to you. Fishing is a year-round activity in most places, but limits can and will be placed on areas where the fish need protecting. These restrictions change as the situations change, so be sure to check with the Fish and Wildlife Department in each state to make sure you have the most current information.

This book includes many campgrounds that are perfect for camping and fishing alike, and it lists the popular species found at those locations.

Photography

As you explore, don't forget your camera. The spectacular mountains, abundant wildlife, and beautiful alpine streams and lakes are worth preserving on film. In fact, your friends back home might not believe it unless you document some of the breathtaking scenery and majestic creatures you encounter. And if you make it to the top of that mountain, or get up on skis for the first time, you'll want a picture to commemorate the accomplishment. If you're not interested in lugging a lot of equipment around, you can buy disposables that offer a wide variety of features, from zoom lenses to panoramic views. There are waterproof varieties, too. If you enjoy more challenging photography, this is the place to use a wide-angle or telephoto lens to capture images of wild animals or scenic panoramas, and special filters and settings enhance the natural beauty of your subjects.

Health, Safety, and Common Sense
Watch Out for Wildlife

Of course, you don't want to be out in the wilderness watching wildlife only to discover the wildlife watching you. Certain animals are prudent to avoid under any circumstances. These are the animals that consider you prey, and they are the ones that aren't intimidated by your presence.

Using common sense and adhering to the basic rules will eliminate most of the problems that occur when people encounter wildlife. Many of the horror stories heard each year, such as charging bison in Yellowstone National Park, are caused by such foolishness as tourists attempting to pose with or even climb on the animals. Unbelievable, you say? Yes, but sadly true. It's hard to fault the wild animal when the humans behave with such stupidity. (If you wonder why I mention this more than once, it's that this actually happens at least once every summer.)

Mountain Lions

Where you see deer, mountain lions could very well be, too. Deer are the primary prey of mountain lions, and things that attract deer to an area can lure a lion to the same place. A mountain lion's attacking a human is still a rare event, with only eight attacks and one fatality in the past 10 years. Nevertheless, the experts say the frequency of such attacks is increasing. The potential for increased attacks corresponds with the growing number of times the paths of people and lions cross. It used to be that humans rarely saw the lions, but it isn't uncommon now to hear of such sightings.

Mountain lions, also called pumas or cougars, are adaptable, finding ways to accommodate themselves to areas humans frequent, which results in a familiarity that bodes no good for lion or human. The natural progression of this escalating comfort level is to aggression. Lions that demonstrate dominant behavior toward humans are one step away from considering their former adversary a handy dinner. Although a lion attack is still very unlikely, it's good to know what experts recommend for behavior, based on experiences of people who have survived lion encounters.

Make noise and stay together. Never corner a lion, even inadvertently. Most lions will try to avoid confrontation, so be sure they have an escape route. Stay calm and don't run, because hysteria and quick movements provoke lions, much as a fleeing, squealing mouse tantalizes a house cat. Along these same lines, don't turn your back on the lion and do everything you can to project a large, confident image. Never lie on the ground or play dead with a mountain lion. According to the experts, survivors have often repelled an attack by standing and fighting back. Dogs are not good deterrents, unless you consider using your best friend as a decoy a good backup plan.

Moose

Moose can appear deceptively docile and even sluggish. They don't have the predatory instincts of cougars and bears, but the moose can move quickly and deliver an ugly surprise to an unprepared person. A female with calves can behave very aggressively, and it's wise to keep a far distance, with objects between you, if you don't want to experience maternal rage first-hand. Moose and bison are both larger than grizzly bears, but their slow, deliberate manner causes people to underestimate them. Never try to get close for a photo opportunity, and never make contact with these wild animals. They can charge quickly and fatally if given motivation and opportunity.

Grizzly Bears

Grizzly bears have a majestic image, and few people would be foolish enough to approach one on purpose, let alone lure one into camp. Most encounters occur from not taking the basic precautions outlined by bear authorities. Make noise, stay on the trails, and travel in groups. Bears are not anxious to meet a human crowd, and they hate to be surprised by silent stalkers. If you meet a bear, don't run away and don't yell or jump at the bear. Speak calmly, the experts advise, and leave, but don't run. Backing down is not in the grizzly lexicon, and challenging the bear is the last thing you want to do—in fact, it could be the last thing you do.

Sound confusing? It's really simple. The best way to avoid trouble is to avoid an encounter.

Don't attract trouble. Keep a clean camp. Separate cooking equipment and supplies from the area where you plan to sleep, hang all food and garbage, or use a bear-proof container. The idea is to keep your identity as removed from that of food as possible.

Here again, a female with cubs is bad news, and your best defense is to follow the basic rules: make noise, stay on established trails, and travel in groups. Always check with the local agency for current information about the status of animal activity in the area and pay close attention to closed trails and posted warnings.

Use your head, but also remember to keep things in perspective. You have a greater chance of being killed by lightning than being attacked by a bear. In general, animals in the wild are not interested in human interaction, and they will take steps to avoid meeting you at all. If you take the free, but priceless, advice offered by the federal or state agency where you intend to visit, you'll likely have a delightful, safe, and uneventful experience.

Getting In (and Staying Out) of Hot Water

You'll find numerous natural mineral springs in Montana, Wyoming, and Idaho. They vary from highly developed, commercial resorts to remote little spots where clothing is optional.

Some people design their entire vacation going from hot spring to hot spring. At the turn of the century, hot springs were touted as cure-alls with magical healing properties. Responding to the demand of evolving civilization, entrepreneurs developed hotels, restaurants, and other services around the popular springs. Today it's the esthetic rather than the medicinal that draws people to soak in the hot waters.

Not all hot water is desirable, however, and it's staggering the number of people who fail to understand the dangers of hot pots and thermal pools, such as those found in Yellowstone National Park.

As I mentioned in the section on Yellowstone, hot doesn't begin to describe the intensity of these waters. The temperature in the Norris Geyser was tested at 459 degrees Fahrenheit, which will literally boil one to death. There is no chance when we are talking about heat like that, so respect it and keep your distance.

These hot pots don't always bubble and boil like water in your pan on the stove at home. Sometimes they lie there and push out a lazy mud-covered bubble occasionally, but don't be fooled. These waters are deadly, and best seen from a distance, so stay on the trails and walkways. This means you, your kids, and your pets (who should always be on leashes if they are with you).

Fire

Campfires go with camping like ants go with a picnic. But the forest is a terrible place to be careless with fire. Be sure to follow a few simple rules to keep yourself and the woods out of danger. Since most wildfires are caused by human negligence, we all have a part in preventing them. A little extra care could prevent a fire, and encouraging others to do the same will help reach the goal of fewer uncontrolled wildfires.

The West recently experienced one of the worst fire seasons ever. Forest fires are a natural occurrence in the woods, but people start four out of every five fires in the forest (lightning is the other cause). Careless human behavior, such as smoking in forested areas or improperly extinguishing campfires, is the cause of many fires (see guidelines below).

The forest is designed to weather natural fires, and the experience usually rejuvenates the flora and fauna, resulting in spectacular spring wildflowers and strong new tree growth. But people can minimize their detrimental impact on the fire season by observing a few basic rules:

- **Use spark arresters.** Chain saws, portable generators, cross-country vehicles, and trail bikes—to name a few—require spark arresters if used in or near grass, brush, or wooded areas. To make sure that the spark arrester is functioning properly, check with the dealer or contact your local forest service or state forestry office.
- **Put out cigarettes.** When smoking is permitted outdoors, safe practices require at least a three-foot clearing around the smoker. It is unsafe to smoke while walking or riding a horse or trail bike. Use your ashtray while

in your car. Grind out your cigarette, cigar, or pipe tobacco in the dirt. Never grind it on a stump or log.

- **Douse charcoal.** After using the burning charcoal briquettes, "dunk 'em!" Don't sprinkle. Soak the coals with lots of water; stir them and soak again. Be sure they are out cold! Carefully feel the coals with your bare hands to be sure.

It's always a good idea to check with Forest Service representatives about local OHV or camping and fire restrictions before going to the forest. Every agency has guidelines about fire-building free for the asking.

Building and Putting Out a Campfire

Developed campgrounds usually have fire-rings or fire pits, designed especially to contain campfires. If the camping site has a fire ring, use that and only that. If not, make sure campfires are allowed where you are. Once you confirm they are legal, build your campfire away from overhanging branches or flammable items nearby such as dead stumps, dry logs, withered grass, or leaves. Avoid steep slopes. Clear the area of litter and any burnable material for about a 10-foot radius. Keep your woodpile away from the fire. Flying sparks can cover a wide area, and even a small breeze can mean trouble.

Keep a good-sized container of water handy and have a shovel nearby in case you have to throw dirt on the fire.

Start your fire with dry twigs and small sticks, and add larger sticks as the fire builds up, using the largest pieces of wood last. Keep the campfire small. If you surround it with rocks, even a small fire can give off plenty of heat.

Never leave your campfire unattended. When it's time to put out the campfire, make sure the fire is completely out. This means dumping water on it, stirring it, checking under the rock pile for hot spots and adding more water if that's what it takes. If you're short on water, dirt smothers fires pretty effectively. Don't simply bury coals; they may smolder and flame up later, when no one's around to extinguish them.

Obeying the Laws of the Land

Trespassing

The term "public lands" stirs emotions in almost every outdoor enthusiast. After all, we're all members of the public, so this land is my land. But is it your land?

If you look at a map of Montana, Wyoming, and Idaho, you will see the checkerboard pattern of public and private lands. Public lands, managed by agencies such as the U.S. Forest Service, Bureau of Land Management, Bureau of Reclamation, Fish and Game, land designated as Indian reservations, and private lands come together in a way that doesn't always look logical on a piece of paper.

Private lands include ranches, farms, and individual acreage, and the property lines can be hard to find when you're actually there. Private property owners have the right to keep you off their land, and if you enter it anyway,

Keep It Wild Tip 6: Respect Other Users

1. Horseback riders have priority over hikers. Step to the downhill side of the trail and talk softly when encountering horseback riders.
2. Hikers and horseback riders have priority over mountain bikers. When mountain bikers encounter other users even on wide trails, they should pass at an extremely slow speed. On very narrow trails they should dismount and get off to the side so hikers or horseback riders can pass without having their trip disrupted.
3. Mountain bikes aren't permitted on most single-track trails and are expressly prohibited in designated wilderness areas. Mountain bikers breaking these rules should be confronted and told to dismount and walk their bikes until they reach a legal area.
4. It's illegal for horseback riders to break off branches that may be in the path of wilderness trails.
5. Horseback riders on overnight trips are prohibited from camping in many areas and are usually required to keep stock animals in specific areas where they can do no damage to the landscape.

you're as guilty of trespassing as if you were caught in the backyard of your neighbor in a residential subdivision.

Occasionally people trespass by accident, but that's not the case when they open gates to get on to the property. Many large sections of land are home to cattle, and leaving a gate open could create havoc. Thoughtless trespassing and irresponsible actions are the reason so many private property owners simply don't want to bother with the public anymore. Many landowners who used to be accommodating have literally shut their doors. If you find an exception, remember it's in your power to ruin this generosity with carelessness.

Always know where you are, and be sure to stay on public land. If you want to cross private land, be sure to get permission.

Knowing where you are can save you money, too. If you stray into a wilderness area on a mechanized vehicle, you will be subject to big fines from the government. It is prudent to get those maps and study them.

Always check with local state and federal agencies before exploring the backcountry. Circumstances change frequently in the great outdoors and they have the most up-to-date information, advice, and warnings.

Treading Lightly and Getting Along

Summer in the Rockies is beautiful, with clear sunny days and cool, star-studded nights. The forests seem like one, big, inviting playground for camping, hiking, and exploration. However, you have a responsibility, at the very least, to do no harm to the public lands and wildlife as you pursue your activities.

In the wilderness, the watchwords are "Tread Lightly," reinforced by the acronym, TREAD: Travel only where permitted; Respect the rights of others; Educate yourself; Avoid streams, meadows, wildlife areas, etc.; and Drive and travel responsibly. To that I would add tolerance. Public lands are available to all of us, and our duty is to behave responsibly, not to censor others who participate in approved pursuits that might differ from our preferred activities.

When you're camping in a designated area, you are creating a temporary community. If you want to get along, avoid these five things and you'll make a much better impression on those around you. Don't:

(1) Arrive at the campsite at midnight or later, with radio blaring and lights ablaze;

(2) Set up your gear with abandon, encroaching on the camping spot of everyone around you;

(3) Bring two or three unleashed big male dogs, who proceed to visit every campsite and lift their legs on chairs, occupied or not

(4) Party into the wee hours and shout obscenities at the grumpy neighbors when they complain; and finally

(5) Send your kids around to ask for pop, beer, eggs, matches, or any of the other things you forgot to pack when you left the house.

Ready to Ramble: Other Things You Need To Know

You're not in Kansas anymore, Dorothy, and a cell phone might not get you the help you need. In addition, you should know that search-and-rescue organizations take a dim view of launching an operation for someone who ran out of gas or developed a debilitating blister. They also have taken to charging for frivolous rescues, so prepare yourself appropriately.

Nature's playground has much to offer in beauty, challenge, respite, and education, but unlike structured entertainment such as theme parks, exploring the great outdoors requires you to take an active role in your preparations and activities. To avoid some of the rookie mistakes made by uninformed campers, start by researching the area you plan to visit. Contact the appropriate state and federal agencies. This book is intended to be as accurate as possible, but conditions and circumstances change constantly. The state and federal agencies make it their business to be up-to-date on these changes, and they are your best source for current information.

The geographical area included in this book is huge, and the light population leaves a lot of land sparsely populated. In many sections, animals outnumber people with ease. This is one of the reasons Montana, Wyoming, and Idaho are desirable destinations, but it also requires you to become your own travel expert.

Weather

Every campground is subject to the whims of Mother Nature. When you see opening and closing dates, remember that weather and resulting conditions are important factors in determining when the campground will be open, so it's always best to verify this information if you don't want to be disappointed.

Mountain weather is erratic, and it can vary dramatically. You can be basking in sunshine in the morning and by evening be wearing every stitch of clothing in your bag. Factors such as altitude and whether an area is exposed or sheltered all contribute to the weather's effects.

Lightning can be deadly. When lightning is flashing, rain is usually falling, and many people instinctively head for shelter. Unfortunately, they might duck under trees to stay dry, and that can be a real mistake. You don't want to be in a high spot during a storm or next to a lightening rod such as a tall tree or on the water.

Road Conditions

The saying goes in Montana (and probably in Wyoming and Idaho, too) that we have nine months of winter and three months of construction. And there's no way around it—road repair and building must be done when the weather cooperates.

What this means to the traveler is frustration, delays, and detours if you don't find out ahead of time what awaits you on the open road.

A simple phone call can ease your mind. All three states have road report numbers, accessible through their departments of transportation. For Montana, call 800/332-6171 or 800/226-7623. Or get on the website: mdt.state.mt.us and click on Road and Weather Report. For Wyoming, call 888/996-7623 (in Wyoming), or 307/772-0824 (outside Wyoming) or get on the website: wydotweb.state.wy.us and click on WYDOT Road Report. For Idaho, call 208/376-8028, 800/432-7623, or go to the website: www.state.id.us/itd/itdhmpg.htm and click on Road/Weather Conditions and Construction Information. The national parks aren't immune to roadwork, either, so if they are on your agenda, a call to them would be prudent, too. Information on current construction activities is available by mail or from park visitor centers and entrance gates.

If you intend to leave the well-traveled road, a four-wheel drive vehicle is a prudent choice, as clearance on some of the back roads can stop a two-wheel drive in its tracks. Many of these suffer from the effects of harsh weather, and maintenance can be little to none. Even some boat ramps are steep enough or bumpy enough to require a four-wheel drive to launch or retrieve your boat. Use caution and plan ahead, because road conditions can deteriorate rapidly and you don't want to find yourself stranded in a remote place with no help available.

The very qualities that draw people to the wilderness can work against them if they don't know what they're getting into. The wilderness is remote and secluded. If you run into difficulties, you are pretty much on your own. If you aren't familiar with wilderness survival, you could be in serious, possibly fatal, trouble. If you don't know if you're ready for the wilderness, you probably aren't. Fortunately, there are licensed experienced guides to take you into the backcountry if you have your heart set on it.

Maps

If you think you have the knowledge to strike out into the backcountry, be sure to stop by the forest ranger station or appropriate agency office to pick up topographical maps, guidelines, and the latest word on conditions. Spend a few minutes talking with a ranger about your plans. Circumstances can change, and roads, trails, and access can open or close unexpectedly.

Take responsibility for your own safety. Wilderness areas have very strict guidelines on what is allowed. Motorized and mechanical transportation is prohibited on the ground or in the air. That includes search-and-rescue vehicles, and it means you must be doubly cautious and prepared when you enter the wilderness.

Remember, you should undertake wilderness exploration only if you are knowledgeable about orienteering and experienced in survival skills. If you aren't, but want the wilderness experience, this is an excellent time to use the services of a licensed guide.

Guided Adventures: Learning the Easy Way

If you're hungry for adventure, but not willing to bet your life on your own skills, a licensed guide could be the answer.

The Shoshone Sacajawea was one of the first guides for Lewis and Clark, and the service is still in demand, and for much the same reason.

Guides, or outfitters, know both the man-made and natural laws governing the wilderness, so you can stay out of trouble in more ways than one. Plus they know the best places to go and where to find what you're looking for.

But how do you find one of these experts?

In Montana, contact the Montana Outfitters and Guides Association, P.O. Box 1248, Helena, MT 59624; 406/449-3578, fax 406/443-2439. Or contact Montana Board of Outfitters, Department of Commerce, 111 N. Jackson St., Helena, MT 59620; 406/444-3738. For fishing guides, try the Fishing Outfitters Association of Montana, P.O. Box 67, Gallatin Gateway, MT 59730.

In Idaho, contact the Idaho Outfitters and Guides Association, P.O. Box 95, Boise, ID 83701; 800/847-4843; website: www.ioga.org.

In Wyoming, contact Wyoming Outfitters & Guides Association, P.O. Box 2284, Cody, WY 82414; 307/527-7453, fax 307/587-8633; email: wyoga@wtp.net.

Outfitters and guides are trained professionals who provide the benefit of their knowledge to make your experience a good one.

CAMPING GEAR CHECKLIST

Everybody has his or her own indispensables. These lists are guides to help you remember and to get you thinking about what you want to have with you on your trip.

BASIC EMERGENCY KIT

Batteries
Candle or lantern
Canteen
Compass
Eating utensils
Emergency blanket
First aid kit
Flashlight
Flare
High energy food

Knife, scissors
Poncho or rain gear
Sewing kit
Signaling mirror
Tea bags, broth or soup mix
Water bottle
Waterproof matches in waterproof container
Water purifying tablets or filtering system
Whistle

CLOTHING

Hat
Fleece wear
Good socks
Layered clothing

Long underwear
Rain gear
Sunglasses
Swimsuit

GENERAL GEAR

Air mattress or foam pad
Sleeping bag

Tent
Towel

DON'T FORGET

Aspirin
Binoculars
Biodegradable soap
Camera
Extra shoelaces
Extra set of prescription glasses
Games, books, or other entertainment
Insect repellent

Maps
Moleskin for feet
Prescription drugs
Sunscreen
Toiletries and hygiene products
Toothbrush and toothpaste
Vitamins

If you plan to fish, bring your fishing gear. Depending on your cooking plans, bring appropriate supplies.

MONTANA

Chapter MT1 31
Chapter MT2 45
Chapter MT3 79
Chapter MT4 91
Chapter MT5 99
Chapter MT6 105
Chapter MT7 113
Chapter MT8 119
Chapter MT9 141
Chapter MT10 171
Chapter MT11 195
Chapter MT12 205
Chapter MT13 211
Chapter MT14 215
Chapter MT15 219

MONTANA STATE   29

Map MT1 32   Map MT9 142
Map MT2 46   Map MT10 172
Map MT3 80   Map MT11 196
Map MT4 92   Map MT12 206
Map MT5 100   Map MT13 212
Map MT6 106   Map MT14 216
Map MT7 114   Map MT15 220
Map MT8 120

MONTANA STATE MAP

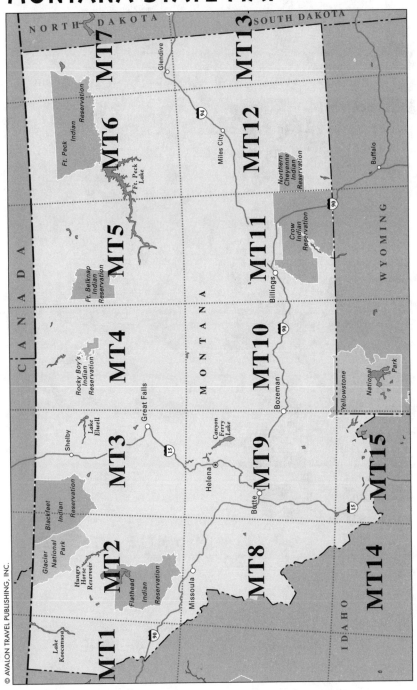

MONTANA
CHAPTER MT1

Lakeside campsite

MAP MT1

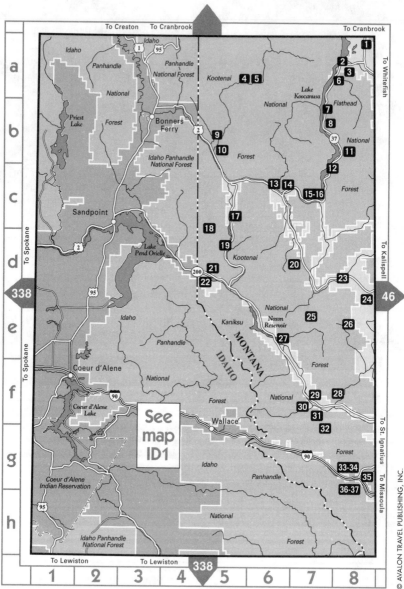

© AVALON TRAVEL PUBLISHING, INC.

CHAPTER MT1

1 Blue Mountains RV Park.....33		**21** Bull River 39	
2 EZ-K RV Park...................33		**22** Cabinet Gorge RV Park	
3 Rexford Bench 34		& Campground 39	
4 Whitetail.....................34		**23** Happy's Inn 40	
5 Pete Creek....................34		**24** Logan State Park.............40	
6 Mariners Haven 35		**25** Willow Creek...................40	
7 Peck Gulch....................35		**26** Fishtrap Lake 40	
8 Rocky Gorge 35		**27** North Shore...................41	
9 Yaak Falls....................36		**28** Copper King...................41	
10 Kilbrennan Lake..............36		**29** Thompson Falls	
11 Koocanusa Resort 36		State Park 41	
12 McGillivray 36		**30** The Riverfront Motel	
13 Woodland RV Park 37		& Cabins........................41	
14 Meadowlark Campground...37		**31** Birdland Bay RV Resort......42	
15 Sportsman's RV Park........37		**32** Gold Rush.......................42	
16 Big Bend RV Park.............37		**33** Cabin City......................42	
17 Dorr Skeels....................38		**34** Campground St. Regis 42	
18 Spar Lake 38		**35** St. Regis KOA 42	
19 Bad Medicine..................38		**36** St. Regis Riding Stables......43	
20 Howard Lake 39		**37** Sloway..........................43	

1 Blue Mountains RV Park

       5

Location: Near Eureka; map MT1, grid a8.

Campsites, facilities: There are 36 RV or tent campsites. Showers, laundry facilities, water, electricity, and a sanitary disposal facility are available.

Reservations, fees: No reservations are needed; the fee is $9–15 per night. Open May 1–October 30.

Directions: From Kalispell, go north on U.S. 93 through Whitefish to Eureka. From Eureka, go 5.5 miles north on U.S. 93; the campground is on the left.

Contact: Blue Mountains RV Park, Eureka, MT 59917; 406/889-3868, fax 406/296-2890.

Trip notes: You can swim, boat, and fish for rainbow and cutthroat trout in Lake Koocanusa and hike in the Kootenai National Forest. You can fish the rivers, streams, and lakes for rainbow, cutthroat, and brook trout, and kokanee salmon, mountain whitefish, sturgeon, ling, perch, bass, and sunfish. Bald eagles, osprey, and harlequin ducks can be seen seasonally.

2 EZ-K RV Park

      5

Location: Near Lake Koocanusa; map MT1, grid a8.

Campsites, facilities: There are 10 RV or tent campsites. Fire pits, water, and electricity are available.

Reservations, fees: No reservations are needed; the fee is $15 per night. Open April 1–September 30.

Directions: From Libby, go north on Highway 37 to Rexford. The campground is the first RV park on the left as you enter Rexford.

Contact: EZ-K RV Park, 101 Kootenai, Rexford, MT 59930; 406/296-2000.

Trip notes: This campground is about ten miles south of the U.S./Canada border and near Lake Koocanusa, where you can swim, boat, and fish for rainbow and cutthroat trout and hike in the Kootenai National Forest. You can fish the rivers, streams, and lakes for rainbow, cutthroat, and brook trout, and kokanee salmon, mountain whitefish, sturgeon, ling, perch, bass, and sunfish. Bald eagles, osprey, and harlequin ducks can be seen seasonally.

3 Rexford Bench

 5

Location: Northwest of Kalispell; map MT1, grid a8.

Campsites, facilities: There are 153 RV or tent campsites, which can accommodate a maximum RV length of 75 feet. A wheelchair-accessible restroom and trailer boat launch are available.

Reservations, fees: No reservations are needed; the fee is $9–50 per night. Open May 15–October 1. The stay limit is 14 days.

Directions: From Kalispell, go north on U.S. 93 to Eureka; then go seven miles northwest on Highway 37 and turn left; the campground is the first right.

Contact: Kootenai National Forest, Eureka Ranger Station, 1299 Hwy. 93 North, Eureka, MT 59917; 406/296-2536.

Trip notes: This campground is near Lake Koocanusa, where you can swim, boat, and fish for rainbow and cutthroat trout. Lake Koocanusa is 90 miles long with a 370-foot-deep reservoir formed by Libby Dam, backing water 42 miles into Canada. Lake Koocanusa Bridge is the longest and highest in Montana and provides the only crossing of the lake in the United States. The bridge is 2,437 feet long. You can hike in the Kootenai National Forest.

4 Whitetail

 4

Location: In Kootenai National Forest; map MT1, grid a5.

Campsites, facilities: There are 12 RV or tent campsites, which can accommodate a maximum RV length of 32 feet.

Reservations, fees: No reservations are needed; the fee is $5 per night. Open May 20–September 30. The stay limit is 14 days.

Directions: From Libby go 18 miles west on U.S. 2 to Troy. At Troy, take U.S. 2 10 miles west to Highway 508 (Yaak River Road), turn right and drive 24 miles to the Whitetail campground; the campground is on the right.

Contact: Forest Service, Troy Ranger Station, 1437 N. Hwy. 2, Troy, MT 59935; 406/295-4693.

Trip notes: The old mining community of Sylvanite is at mile marker 11. In its heyday it was home to three mining companies, stamp mills, a three-story hotel, two newspapers, and a mercantile store. They all burned in a huge forest fire in 1910. You can hike in the Kootenai National Forest and fish the rivers, streams, and lakes for rainbow, cutthroat, and brook trout and kokanee salmon, mountain whitefish, sturgeon, ling, perch, bass, and sunfish. Bald eagles, osprey, and harlequin ducks can be seen seasonally.

5 Pete Creek

 5

Location: In Kootenai National Forest; map MT1, grid a6.

Campsites, facilities: There are 13 RV or tent campsites, which can accommodate a maximum RV length of 35 feet.

Reservations, fees: No reservations are needed; the fee is $5 per night. Open May 20–September 30. The stay limit is 14 days.

Directions: From Libby go 18 miles west on U.S. 2 to Troy. From Troy, go 10 miles northwest on U.S. 2 to Highway 508 (Yaak River Road), turn right and go 26 miles to the Pete

Creek campground sign. The campground is on the right.

Contact: Forest Service, Troy Ranger Station, 1437 N. Hwy. 2, Troy, MT 59935; 406/295-4693.

Trip notes: The town of Yaak has a small mercantile store and the Dirty Shame Saloon. Yaak comes from the Native American word "Ahk" meaning the arrow, and the word "Kootenai" means bow. You can hike in the Kootenai National Forest. You can fish the rivers, streams, and lakes for rainbow, cutthroat, and brook trout and kokanee salmon, mountain whitefish, sturgeon, ling, perch, bass, and sunfish. Bald eagles, osprey, and harlequin ducks can be seen seasonally.

6 Mariners Haven

     4

Location: Near Rexford; map MT1, grid a8.

Campsites, facilities: There are 61 RV or tent campsites. Showers, laundry facilities, a sanitary disposal facility, electricity, water, store, playground, and marina are available.

Reservations, fees: No reservations are needed; the fee is $19.50 per night. Open year-round.

Directions: From Kalispell, go north on U.S. 93 through Whitefish to Highway 37, take this west to Rexford, and then go one mile south to the campground.

Contact: Mariners Haven, 101 Mariner Dr., Rexford, MT 59930; 406/296-3252, fax 406/296-3311.

Trip notes: This campground is near Lake Koocanusa, where you can fish for rainbow and cutthroat trout, and hike in the Kootenai National Forest.

7 Peck Gulch

     4

Location: In Flathead National Forest; map MT1, grid b7.

Campsites, facilities: There are 75 RV or tent campsites, which can accommodate a maxi-

mum RV length of 32 feet. A wheelchair-accessible restroom and trailer boat launch are available.

Reservations, fees: No reservations are needed; the fee is $7 per night. Open May 15–October 1. The stay limit is 14 days.

Directions: From Eureka, go 23 miles southwest on Highway 37 to the campground.

Contact: Forest Service, Eureka Ranger Station, 1299 Hwy. 93 North, Eureka, MT 59917; 406/296-2536 or 800/280-2267.

Trip notes: The Flathead National Forest lies adjacent to Glacier National Park and west of the Continental Divide. You can hike glaciated peaks and fish alpine lakes in this beautiful setting.

8 Rocky Gorge

    5

Location: In Kootenai National Forest; map MT1, grid b7.

Campsites, facilities: There are 120 RV or tent campsites, which can accommodate a maximum RV length of 32 feet. A wheelchair-accessible restroom and trailer boat launch are available.

Reservations, fees: No reservations are needed; the fee is $8–8.50 per night. Open June 1–September 30. The stay limit is 14 days.

Directions: From Kalispell, go north on U.S. 93 through Whitefish to Eureka. From Eureka, go 30 miles on Highway 37; follow the signs to the campground on the right.

Contact: Forest Service, Eureka Ranger Station, 1299 Hwy. 93 North, Eureka, MT 59917; 406/296-2536 or 800/280-2267.

Trip notes: You can hike in the Kootenai National Forest. You can fish the rivers, streams, and lakes for rainbow, cutthroat, and brook trout and kokanee salmon, mountain whitefish, sturgeon, ling, perch, bass, and sunfish. Bald eagles, osprey, and harlequin ducks can be seen seasonally.

9 Yaak Falls

 5

Location: In Kootenai National Forest; map MT1, grid b5.

Campsites, facilities: There are seven RV or tent campsites, which can accommodate a maximum RV length of 32 feet.

Reservations, fees: No reservations are needed; there is no fee charged. Open May 20–September 30. The stay limit is 14 days.

Directions: From Libby go 18 miles west on U.S. 2 to Troy. From Troy, go 10 miles northwest on U.S. 2, then six miles northeast on Highway 508 (Yaak River Road) to the campground.

Contact: Forest Service, Troy Ranger Station, 1437 N. Hwy. 2, Troy, MT 59935; 406/295-4693.

Trip notes: On Highway 508 (Yaak River Road) is a two-mile stretch called Stonecrest Grade, a scenic drive that overlooks a 700-foot deep canyon. You can hike in the Kootenai National Forest. You can fish the rivers, streams, and lakes for rainbow, cutthroat, and brook trout and kokanee salmon, mountain whitefish, sturgeon, ling, perch, bass, and sunfish. Bald eagles, osprey, and harlequin ducks can be seen seasonally.

10 Kilbrennan Lake

 5

Location: In Kootenai National Forest; map MT1, grid b5.

Campsites, facilities: There are seven RV or tent campsites, which can accommodate a maximum RV length of 32 feet.

Reservations, fees: No reservations are needed; the fee is $7 per night. The stay limit is 14 days.

Directions: From Libby go 18 miles west on U.S. 2 to Troy. From Troy, go three miles northwest on U.S. 2, then 10 miles northeast on Forest Service Road 2394 to the campground.

Contact: Kilbrennan Lake, Troy Chamber of Commerce, Troy, MT 59935; 406/295-1064.

Trip notes: You can boat and fish here.

11 Koocanusa Resort

 6

Location: On Lake Koocanusa; map MT1, grid b8.

Campsites, facilities: There are 55 RV campsites with full hookups, and many tent campsites. Boat rentals, a restaurant, and a general store are available.

Reservations, fees: No reservations are needed; the fee is $9–15.75 per night. Open April 15–December.

Directions: From Libby, go north on Highway 37 for 23.8 miles and look for the sign on the left.

Contact: Koocanusa Resort, 23911 Hwy. 37, Libby, MT 59923; 406/293-7474; website: www.koocanusa.com.

Trip notes: This is a full-service resort. The name came from a woman in Libby who chose KOO for the Kootenai Indians, CAN for Canada, and USA for the United States. The resort covers 65 acres on the shore of Lake Koocanusa, which is known for kokanee salmon, rainbow, brook trout, sunfish, and perch. You can bike, boat, hike, swim, water-ski, and horseback ride nearby.

12 McGillivray

 5

Location: In Flathead National Forest; map MT1, grid c7.

Campsites, facilities: There are 50 RV or tent campsites, which can accommodate a maximum RV length of 32 feet. A wheelchair-accessible restroom and trailer boat launch are available.

Reservations, fees: No reservations are needed; the fee is $6 per night. Open May 23–September 15. The stay limit is 14 days.

Directions: From Libby, go 15 miles east on Highway 37, then 10 miles north on Forest Service Road 228 to the campground.

Contact: Forest Service, Eureka Ranger Station, 1299 Hwy. 93 North, Eureka, MT 59917; 406/296-2536 or 800/280-2267.

Trip notes: The Flathead National Forest lies adjacent to Glacier National Park and west of the Continental Divide. You can hike glaciated peaks and fish alpine lakes in this beautiful setting.

13 Woodland RV Park

   5

Location: Near Libby; map MT1, grid c6.

Campsites, facilities: There are 65 RV or tent campsites. Laundry facilities, showers, water, a sanitary disposal facility, and electricity are available. Pets are allowed on leashes.

Reservations, fees: No reservations are needed; the fee is $15–20 per night. Open April 15–October 15.

Directions: From Libby city limits, this campground is .25 mile west. Turn left on Woodland Boulevard to the campground.

Contact: Woodland RV Park, P.O. Box 1152, 185 Woodland Blvd., Libby, MT 59923; 406/293-8595 or 406/293-8395.

Trip notes: This campground has trees and a creek and is just outside Libby. You can fish for trout here.

14 Meadowlark Campground

    5

Location: In Libby; map MT1, grid c6.

Campsites, facilities: There are 25 RV or tent campsites, some with full hookups, cable TV, and pull-through sites. Showers and a sanitary disposal facility are available.

Reservations, fees: No reservations are needed; the fee is $12–20 per night. Open year-round.

Directions: From Whitefish, go four miles north on U.S. 93 to Twin Bridges Road. Turn left and go 1.5 miles to the Tally Lake campground sign, where you turn right (it's still Twin Bridges Road), go to Farm To Market Road and turn left. Go two miles to Tally Lake Road, turn right (this is a dirt road), and the campground is nine miles ahead on the right.

Contact: Meadowlark Campground, 716 Hwy. 2 West, Libby, MT 59923; 406/293-8323.

Trip notes: This campground has grassy sites and trees, and it is close to shopping. You can hike in the Kootenai National Forest and fish the rivers, streams, and lakes for rainbow, cutthroat, and brook trout and kokanee salmon, mountain whitefish, sturgeon, ling, perch, bass, and sunfish. Bald eagles, osprey, and harlequin ducks can be seen seasonally.

15 Sportsman's RV Park

    5

Location: Near Lake Koocanusa; map MT1, grid c7.

Campsites, facilities: There are 21 RV or tent campsites. Water and electricity are available.

Reservations, fees: No reservations are needed; the fee is $10 per night. Open year-round.

Directions: From Libby, take Highway 37 for 12 miles toward Libby Dam (east); the RV park is between mile markers 11 and 12, on the left.

Contact: Sportsman's RV Park, 11741 Hwy. 37, Libby, MT 59923; 406/293-2267, fax 406/293-7365.

Trip notes: This campground is near Lake Koocanusa, where you can swim, boat, and fish for rainbow and cutthroat trout and hike in the Kootenai National Forest. Lake Koocanusa is 90 miles long with a 370-foot-deep reservoir formed by Libby Dam, backing water 42 miles into Canada. Lake Koocanusa Bridge is the longest and highest in Montana and provides the only crossing of the lake in the United States. The bridge is 2,437 feet long.

16 Big Bend RV Park

      5

Location: Near Lake Koocanusa; map MT1, grid c7.

Campsites, facilities: There are 50 RV or tent campsites. Showers, laundry facilities, electricity, a sanitary disposal facility, water, and restaurant are available.

Reservations, fees: No reservations are needed; the fee is $15 per night. Open April 1–November 1.

Directions: From Libby, go 13 miles on Highway 37 to the campground, which is on the right.

Contact: Big Bend RV Park, 13068 Hwy. 37, Libby, MT 59923; 406/293-4536.

Trip notes: This campground sits on 10 acres on the Kootenai River and is near Lake Koocanusa, where you can swim, boat, and fish for rainbow and cutthroat trout and hike in the Kootenai National Forest. Lake Koocanusa is 90 miles long with a 370-foot-deep reservoir formed by Libby Dam, backing water 42 miles into Canada. Lake Koocanusa Bridge is the longest and highest in Montana and provides the only crossing of the lake in the United States. The bridge is 2,437 feet long.

17 Dorr Skeels

 5

Location: On Bull Lake; map MT1, grid c5.

Campsites, facilities: There are six RV or tent campsites, which can accommodate a maximum RV length of 32 feet. A trailer boat ramp is available.

Reservations, fees: No reservations are needed, and no fee is charged. Open May 20–September 15. The stay limit is 14 days.

Directions: From Troy, go three miles southeast on U.S. 2, then 18 miles south on Highway 56 to the campground.

Contact: Montana Fish, Wildlife & Parks, Region 1, 490 N. Hwy. 2, Troy, MT 59935; 406/295-4693.

Trip notes: This campground is on Bull Lake, where you can boat, swim, and water-ski. North of the campground, on Highway 56, is Savage Lake, a good family fishing spot. You can hike in the Kootenai National Forest and

fish the rivers, streams, and lakes for rainbow, cutthroat, and brook trout and kokanee salmon, mountain whitefish, sturgeon, ling, perch, bass, and sunfish. Bald eagles, osprey, and harlequin ducks can be seen seasonally.

18 Spar Lake

 6

Location: In Kootenai National Forest; map MT1, grid c5.

Campsites, facilities: There are eight RV or tent campsites. A trailer boat launch is available.

Reservations, fees: No reservations are needed; no fee is charged. Open May 20–September 30. The stay limit is 14 days.

Directions: From Libby go 18 miles west on U.S. 2 to Troy. From Troy, go three miles southeast on U.S. 2, then 16 miles south on Forest Service Road 384 to Little Spar and the campground.

Contact: Kootenai National Forest, Troy Ranger Station, 1437 N. Hwy. 2, Troy, MT 59935; 406/295-4693.

Trip notes: You can fish, boat, and hike in the area.

19 Bad Medicine

 5

Location: In Kootenai National Forest; map MT1, grid d5.

Campsites, facilities: There are 16 RV or tent campsites, which can accommodate a maximum RV length of 32 feet. A trailer boat launch is available.

Reservations, fees: No reservations are needed; the fee is $7 per night. Open May 30–September 30.

Directions: From Troy, go three miles southeast on U.S. 2, 22 miles south on Highway 56, one mile west on Forest Service Road 398, and one mile north on Forest Service Road 7170 to the campground.

Contact: Kootenai National Forest, Troy

Ranger Station, 1437 N. Hwy. 2, Troy, MT 59935; 406/295-4693.

Trip notes: This campground is along the route to the 100-acre scenic area where the western red cedars are preserved. The .9-mile self-guided nature trail loops through the forest among the giant cedars, flowers, and native ferns. You can boat, swim, and water-ski on Bull Lake. Savage Lake is a good family fishing spot. You can hike in the Kootenai National Forest and fish the rivers, streams, and lakes for rainbow, cutthroat, and brook trout and kokanee salmon, mountain whitefish, sturgeon, ling, perch, bass, and sunfish. Bald eagles, osprey, and harlequin ducks can be seen seasonally.

20 Howard Lake

 5

Location: In Kootenai National Forest; map MT1, grid d7.

Campsites, facilities: There are 10 RV or tent campsites, which can accommodate a maximum RV length of 20 feet. A wheelchair-accessible restroom and trailer boat launch are available.

Reservations, fees: No reservations are needed; the fee is $6 per night. Open May 26–October 1. The stay limit is 14 days.

Directions: From Libby, go 12 miles south on U.S. 2, then 14 miles southwest on Forest Service Road 231 to the campground.

Contact: Kootenai National Forest, Troy Ranger Station, 1437 N. Hwy. 2, Troy, MT 59935; 406/295-4693.

Trip notes: This campground is in the Libby Creek gold-panning area. You can hike in the Kootenai National Forest and fish the rivers, streams, and lakes for rainbow, cutthroat, and brook trout and kokanee salmon, mountain whitefish, sturgeon, ling, perch, bass, and sunfish. Bald eagles, osprey, and harlequin ducks can be seen seasonally.

21 Bull River

 4

Location: In Lolo National Forest; map MT1, grid d5.

Campsites, facilities: There are 26 RV or tent campsites, which can accommodate a maximum RV length of 32 feet. A wheelchair-accessible restroom and trailer boat ramp are available.

Reservations, fees: No reservations are needed; the fee is $6 per night. Open May 15–September 30. The stay limit is 14 days.

Directions: From Thompson Falls, go west on Highway 200 to Noxon. From Noxon, go six miles northwest on Highway 200 to the campground.

Contact: Lolo National Forest, Trout Creek Ranger Station, 2693 Hwy. 200, Trout Creek, MT 59874; 406/827-3533 or 406/752-5501.

Trip notes: You can fish for trout in the Clark Fork River and hike in Lolo and Kootenai National Forests.

22 Cabinet Gorge RV Park & Campground

 4

Location: In Cabinet Mountains; map MT1, grid d5.

Campsites, facilities: There are 45 RV or tent campsites. Showers, laundry facilities, electricity, water, boat docks, and canoe rentals are available.

Reservations, fees: No reservations are needed; the fee is $10–16 per night. Open May 1–November 15.

Directions: From Libby, go west on U.S. 2 to Highway 56 south. Continue south to the intersection of Highway 56 and Highway 200; turn south on Blue Jay Lane (follow the signs) to the campground.

Contact: Cabinet Gorge RV Park & Campground, 30 Blue Jay Lane, Noxon, MT 59853; 406/847-2291.

Trip notes: This campground is near the Clark

Fork River, where you can fish for rainbow, cutthroat, brown, and cutthroat trout; and you can hike in Kootenai National Forest.

23 Happy's Inn

 4

Location: Southeast of Libby; map MT1, grid d8.

Campsites, facilities: There are 41 RV or tent campsites. Showers, laundry facilities, a store, electricity, water, a restaurant, and cabins are available.

Reservations, fees: No reservations are needed; the fee is $7–15 per night. Open year-round.

Directions: From Libby, go 41 miles southeast on U.S. 2 to Happy's Inn, which is right on the highway.

Contact: Happy's Inn, 39704 Hwy. 2 South, Libby, MT 59923; 406/293-7810.

Trip notes: You can hike in the Kootenai and Lolo National Forests and fish the rivers, streams, and lakes for rainbow, cutthroat, and brook trout and kokanee salmon, mountain whitefish, sturgeon, ling, perch, bass, and sunfish. Bald eagles, osprey, and harlequin ducks can be seen seasonally.

24 Logan State Park

 7

Location: West of Kalispell; map MT1, grid e8.

Campsites, facilities: There are 44 RV or tent campsites, which can accommodate a maximum RV length of 40 feet. Water, a restroom, a trailer boat launch, and a sanitary disposal facility are available. Pets are allowed on leashes.

Reservations, fees: No reservations are needed; the fee is $12 per night. Open May 1–September 30. The stay limit is 14 days.

Directions: From Kalispell, go 45 miles west on U.S. 2 to milepost 77 and the park.

Contact: Montana Fish, Wildlife & Parks, Region 1, 490 N. Meridian, Kalispell, MT 59901; 406/752-5501.

Trip notes: This is a forested, scenic park where you can boat, swim, and fish.

25 Willow Creek

 8

Location: North of Thompson Falls; map MT1, grid e7.

Campsites, facilities: There are four RV or tent campsites, which can accommodate a maximum RV length of 20 feet.

Reservations, fees: No reservations are needed, and no fee is charged. Open May 15–September 30. The stay limit is 14 days.

Directions: From Thompson Falls, go west on Highway 200; as soon as you cross the bridge, turn right and stay right on Blue Side Road for about seven miles; turn left on Roughly for 14 miles to the campground.

Contact: Lolo National Forest, Trout Creek Ranger Station, 2693 Hwy. 200, Trout Creek, MT 59874; 406/827-3533 or 406/752-5501.

Trip notes: This is a beautiful campground, where you can fish and hike.

26 Fishtrap Lake

 5

Location: Near Thompson Falls; map MT1, grid e8.

Campsites, facilities: There are 11 RV or tent campsites, which can accommodate a maximum RV length of 32 feet. There is a trailer boat launch.

Reservations, fees: No reservations are needed; no fee is charged. Open June 1–September 30. The stay limit is 14 days.

Directions: From Thompson Falls go five miles east on Highway 200, 13 miles northeast on Forest Service Road 516, and two miles west on Forest Service Road 7593; follow the signs to the campground.

Contact: Lolo National Forest, Plains Ranger Station, P.O. Box 429, Plains, MT 59859; 406/824-3821.

Trip notes: You can boat, fish, and hike here.

Scenic Thompson Falls has easy access for a family picnic.

27 North Shore

 6

Location: Near Thompson Falls; map MT1, grid e6.

Campsites, facilities: There are 12 RV or tent campsites, which can accommodate a maximum RV length of 32 feet. A trailer boat launch is available.

Reservations, fees: No reservations are needed; the fee is $6 per night. Open May 15–September 30. The stay limit is 14 days.

Directions: From Thompson Falls, go west on Highway 200 to Trout Creek, then continue past Trout Creek nearly three miles and you will see the North Shore campground sign. Take a left at the sign, go about half a mile to the stop sign and another campground sign. The campground is ahead to the left.

Contact: Lolo National Forest, Trout Creek Ranger Station, 2693 Hwy. 200, Trout Creek, MT 59874; 406/827-3533 or 406/752-5501.

Trip notes: You can boat, swim, and fish here. Scenic Thompson Falls has easy access for a family picnic.

28 Copper King

 4

Location: In Lolo National Forest; map MT1, grid f8.

Campsites, facilities: There are five RV or tent campsites, which can accommodate a maximum RV length of 16 feet.

Reservations, fees: No reservations are needed; no fees are charged. Open June 1–September 30. The stay limit is 14 days.

Directions: From Thompson Falls, go five miles east on Highway 200, then four miles northeast on Forest Service Road 56 to the campground.

Contact: Lolo National Forest, Plains Ranger Station, P.O. Box 429, Plains, MT 59859;

406/824-3821.

Trip notes: You can fish here.

29 Thompson Falls State Park

 5

Location: Northwest of Thompson Falls; map MT1, grid f7.

Campsites, facilities: There are 17 RV or tent campsites, which can accommodate a maximum RV length of 30 feet. A vault toilet, water, grills, picnic tables, and a trailer boat launch are available.

Reservations, fees: No reservations are needed; the fee is $9 per night. Open May 1–September 30. The stay limit is 14 days.

Directions: From Thompson Falls, go one mile northwest on Highway 200 and then follow signs to the park.

Contact: Montana Fish, Wildlife & Parks, 490 N. Meridian, Kalispell, MT 59901; 406/752-5501.

Trip notes: You can boat, swim (at your own risk), and fish here. There is a golf course in Thompson Falls.

30 The Riverfront Motel & Cabins

 4

Location: Near Missoula; map MT1, grid f7.

Campsites, facilities: There are 11 RV or tent campsites. Showers, a store, a large group fire pit, a sanitary disposal facility, electricity, and water are available.

Reservations, fees: No reservations are needed; the fee is $19 per night. Open April–November. The motel is open year-round.

Directions: From Thompson Falls, go one mile west on Highway 200; the campground is on the right.

Contact: The Riverfront Motel & Cabins, 4907 Hwy. 200 W., Thompson Falls, MT 59873; 406/827-3460.

Trip notes: There is fishing access here.

31 Birdland Bay RV Resort

   5

Location: Near Thompson Falls; map MT1, grid f7.

Campsites, facilities: There are 35 RV or tent campsites. Boat docks, showers, laundry facilities, electricity, and water are available.

Reservations, fees: No reservations are needed; the fee is $10.40–19.25 per night. Open May 1–October 1.

Directions: From Thompson Falls, go right one mile on Blue Slide Road. One mile past Thompson Falls State Park, take a left to the resort.

Contact: Birdland Bay RV Resort, 171 Blue Slide Rd., Thompson Falls, MT 59873; 406/827-4757 or 800/735-2531.

Trip notes: You can fish here, and a golf course is in Thompson Falls.

32 Gold Rush

   4

Location: Near Thompson Falls; map MT1, grid g7.

Campsites, facilities: There are seven RV or tent campsites, which can accommodate a maximum RV length of 32 feet.

Reservations, fees: No reservations are needed; there is no fee charged. Open June 1–October 30. The stay limit is 14 days.

Directions: From Thompson Falls, go nine miles south on Forest Service Road 352 to the campground.

Contact: Lolo National Forest, Plains Ranger Station, P.O. Box 429, Plains, MT 59859; 406/824-3821.

Trip notes: You can fish here.

33 Cabin City

    5

Location: In Lolo National Forest; map MT1, grid g8.

Campsites, facilities: There are 24 RV or tent campsites, which can accommodate a maximum RV length of 22 feet.

Reservations, fees: No reservations are needed; the fee is $6 per night. Open May 23–September 6. The stay limit is 14 days.

Directions: From Superior, go west on I-90 toward De Borgia, then take Exit 22 northeast for 2.5 miles on Camel's Hump Road and .2 mile north on Forest Service Road 352 to the campground.

Contact: Lolo National Forest, Building 24A, Fort Missoula, Missoula, MT 59802; 406/329-3814.

Trip notes: You can fish and hike here.

34 Campground St. Regis

     6

Location: In Lolo National Forest; map MT1, grid g8.

Campsites, facilities: There are 75 RV or tent campsites. Showers, laundry facilities, a store, and a sanitary disposal facility are available. A pool, game room, horseshoes, and golf are on-site.

Reservations, fees: No reservations are needed; the fee is $6 per night. Open April 1–November 30.

Directions: From Superior, go west on I-90 to St. Regis. From St. Regis, go west 1.5 miles on Frontage Road to the campground.

Contact: Campground St. Regis; 44 Frontage Rd. W, St Regis, MT 59866; 406/649-2470 or 888/247-8734.

Trip notes: There are two golf courses in St. Regis. The Taft Tunnel Bike Trail is 15 miles of challenging converted rails. You can fish and raft on the Clark Fork River and hike at the Lookout Pass.

35 St. Regis KOA

    5

Location: In Lolo National Forest; map MT1, grid g8.

Campsites, facilities: There are 87 RV or tent campsites, some with hookups. Showers, laundry facilities, a store, and a sanitary disposal station available.

Reservations, fees: No reservations are needed; the fee is $8–19 per night. Open April 1–November 11.

Directions: From Superior, go west on I-90 to St. Regis. From I-90, take St. Regis exit; go one mile east, take a right at the four-way stop; the campground is up the hill.

Contact: St. Regis KOA; 105 Old U.S. Hwy. 10 E, St. Regis, MT 59866; 406/649-2122, 800/562-4670.

Trip notes: This campground has beautiful views and it's near a golf course. There are two golf courses in St. Regis. The Taft Tunnel Bike Trail is 15 miles of challenging converted rails. You can fish and raft on the Clark Fork River and hike at the Lookout Pass.

36 St. Regis Riding Stables

     5

Location: In Lolo National Forest; map MT1, grid g8.

Campsites, facilities: There are 40 RV or tent campsites.

Reservations, fees: No reservations are needed; the fee is $10–18 per night. Open May–Labor Day.

Directions: From Superior, go west on I-90 to St. Regis. From I-90, take Exit 33 to the campground.

Contact: St. Regis Riding Stables; St. Regis, MT 59866; 406/649-2110, 406/822-3384.

Trip notes: Trail rides on horseback can be arranged. There are two golf courses in St. Regis. The Taft Tunnel Bike Trail is 15 miles of challenging converted rails. You can fish and raft on the Clark Fork River and hike at the Lookout Pass.

37 Sloway

   6

Location: In Lolo National Forest; map MT1, grid g8.

Campsites, facilities: There are 16 RV or tent campsites, which can accommodate a maximum RV length of 22 feet.

Reservations, fees: No reservations are needed; the fee is $10 per night. Open May 30–September 4. The stay limit is 14 days.

Directions: From St. Regis, go seven miles east on I-90 to Exit 43, then three miles west on Dry Creek Road on the Clark Fork River to the campground.

Contact: Lolo National Forest, Building 24A, Fort Missoula, Missoula, MT 59802; 406/329-3814.

Trip notes: You can fish in the Clark Fork River for brown, bull, cutthroat, rainbow, whitefish, and bass.

No reservations are needed; the fee is $8

CHAPTER MT2

Lake McDonald, Glacier National Park

MAP MT2

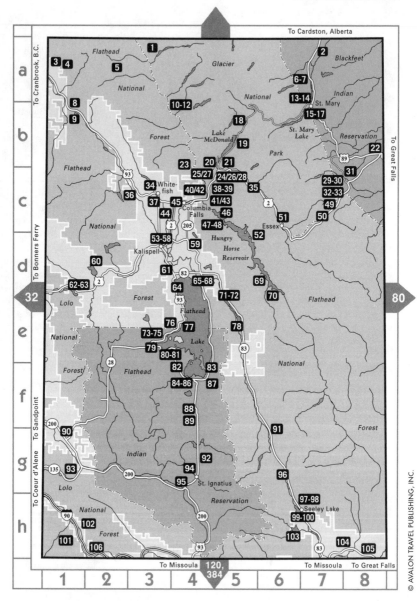

CHAPTER MT2

1	Kintla Lake	48
2	Chief Mountain Junction	49
3	Little Therriault	49
4	Big Therriault	49
5	Tuchuck	49
6	Old North Trail Campground	50
7	Many Glacier	50
8	Jerry's RV Park	50
9	North Dickey Lake	50
10	Quartz Creek	51
11	Bowman Lake	51
12	Logging Creek	51
13	Johnson's of St. Mary	51
14	St. Mary-Glacier Park KOA Kampground	52
15	Two Medicine	52
16	St. Mary Lake	52
17	Rising Sun	53
18	Avalanche	53
19	Sprague Creek	53
20	Fish Creek	53
21	Apgar	54
22	Sleeping Wolf Campground & RV Park	54
23	Big Creek Campground	54
24	Lake Five Resort	55
25	Glacier Campground	55
26	North American RV Park & Campground	55
27	Sundance RV Park & Campground	56
28	Coram RV Park	56
29	Cut Bank	56
30	Sears Motel & Campground	56
31	Y Lazy R RV Park	57
32	Smiley's RV Park	57
33	Firebrand Pass Campground	57
34	Whitefish Lake State Park	58
35	Stanton Creek Lodge	58
36	Tally Lake	58
37	Whitefish KOA	58
38	San-Suz-Ed RV Park & Campground	59
39	Canyon RV & Campground	59
40	West Glacier KOA	59
41	The Timber Wolf Resort	60
42	Emery Bay	60
43	Mountain Meadow RV Park & Campground	60
44	Glacier Peaks RV Park	60
45	Columbia Falls RV Park	61
46	Lost Johnny Point	61
47	Doris Point	61
48	Lid Creek	62
49	Summit	62
50	Three Forks Campground	62
51	Devil Creek	62
52	Murray Bay	63
53	LaSalle RV Park & Campground	63
54	White Birch RV & Campground	63
55	Glacier Pines RV Park	64
56	Greenwood Village RV Park	64
57	Spruce Park RV Park	64
58	Rocky Mountain "Hi" RV Park & Campground	64
59	Lake Blaine Resort	65
60	Lion's Bitterroot Youth Camp	65
61	Edgewater Motel & RV Resort	65
62	McGregor Lake	65
63	McGregor Lake Resort	66
64	West Shore	66

(continues)

65 Woods Bay Marina
& RV Park 66
66 Timbers RV Park 66
67 Outback Montana 67
68 Wayfarers 67
69 Handkerchief Lake 67
70 Spotted Bear 68
71 Deer Lick Resort 68
72 Swan Village Market
& Campground 68
73 Lake Mary Ronan
State Park 68
74 Mountain Meadows
Resort & Golf Course 69
75 Lake Mary Ronan Lodge
& Resort 69
76 Big Sky RV Resort
& Marina 69
77 Camp Tuffit 69
78 Swan Lake 70
79 Arrowhead Resort 70
80 Big Arm 70
81 Big Arm Resort & Marina ... 71
82 Snowberg Port & Court 71
83 Yellow Bay 71
84 Polson/Flathead Lake KOA .. 71
85 Eagle Nest RV Resort 72

86 Rocking C Ranch 72
87 Finley Point 72
88 Mission Meadow
Campground 72
89 Diamond 'S' RV Park 73
90 Crossroads Motel
& RV Park 73
91 Holland Lake 73
92 Willow Creek
Campground 73
93 Cascade 74
94 Hostel of the Rockies
at St. Ignatius Camping 74
95 Ravalli Store 74
96 Lake Alva 74
97 Big Larch 75
98 River Point 75
99 Seeley Lake 75
100 Jocko Hollow
Campground 76
101 Trout Creek 76
102 Quartz Flat 76
103 Placid Lake State Park 76
104 Salmon Lake State Park ... 77
105 Russell Gates Memorial ... 77
106 Big Pine 77

1 Kintla Lake

  7

Location: In Glacier National Park; map MT2, grid a3.

Campsites, facilities: There are 13 RV or tent campsites, which can accommodate a maximum RV length of 18 feet. A boat launch is available, but no motorized boats are allowed.

Reservations, fees: No reservations are needed; the fee is $12 per night. Open seasonally; call for specific dates. The stay limit is seven days.

Directions: From Columbia Falls, go north on County 486 to Polebridge. From Polebridge, go 15 miles north on North Fork Road (an unpaved road that can get narrow and that is not recommended for large RVs or trailers), past Bowman Lake; watch for signs.

Contact: Glacier National Park Headquarters, Building 25, Mather Dr., West Glacier, MT 59936; 406/888-7800.

Trip notes: Glacier National Park offers a wide variety of recreational activities, including hiking, boating, fishing, and sightseeing.

2 Chief Mountain Junction

 7

Location: Near Glacier National Park; map MT2, grid a7.

Campsites, facilities: There are 56 RV or tent campsites. Showers, water, electricity, a store, propane gas, and a sanitary disposal station are available.

Reservations, fees: No reservations are needed; the fee is $10–16 per night. Open year-round.

Directions: From St. Mary, go north nine miles on U.S. 89 to Babb. From Babb, go four miles north at the junction of Highway 17 and U.S. 89 to the campground.

Contact: Chief Mountain Junction, Hwys. 17 & 89, Babb, MT 59411; tel./fax 406/732-9253.

Trip notes: Glacier National Park offers a wide variety of recreational activities, including hiking, boating, fishing, and sightseeing.

3 Little Therriault

 5

Location: In Flathead National Forest; map MT2, grid a1.

Campsites, facilities: There are six RV or tent campsites, which can accommodate a maximum RV length of 32 feet.

Reservations, fees: No reservations are needed; the fee is $3–3.50 per night. Open May 20–October 15. The stay limit is 14 days.

Directions: From Kalispell, go north on U.S. 93 through Whitefish to Eureka. From Eureka, go seven miles southeast on U.S. 93, three miles northeast on County Road 114, 11 miles northeast on Forest Service Road 114, and 13 miles west on Forest Service Road 319 to the campground.

Contact: Forest Service, Eureka Ranger Station, 1299 Hwy. 93 North, Eureka, MT 59917; 406/296-2536 or 800/280-2267.

Trip notes: The Flathead National Forest lies adjacent to Glacier National Park and west of the Continental Divide. You can hike glaciated

peaks and fish alpine lakes in this beautiful setting.

4 Big Therriault

 5

Location: In Flathead National Forest; map MT2, grid a1.

Campsites, facilities: There are 10 RV or tent campsites, which can accommodate a maximum RV length of 32 feet. A trailer boat launch is available.

Reservations, fees: No reservations are needed; the fee is $3 per night. Open July 1–November 15. The stay limit is 14 days.

Directions: From Kalispell, go north on U.S. 93 through Whitefish to Eureka. From Eureka, go seven miles southeast on U.S. 93, three miles northeast on County Road 114, 11 miles northeast on Forest Road 114, and 13 miles west on Forest Service Road 319 to the campground.

Contact: Forest Service, Eureka Ranger Station, 1299 Hwy. 93 North, Eureka, MT 59917; 406/296-2536 or 800/280-2267.

Trip notes: The Flathead National Forest lies adjacent to Glacier National Park and west of the Continental Divide. You can hike glaciated peaks and fish alpine lakes in this beautiful setting.

5 Tuchuck

 6

Location: In Flathead National Forest; map MT2, grid a2.

Campsites, facilities: There are seven RV or tent campsites, which can accommodate a maximum RV length of 22 feet.

Reservations, fees: No reservations are needed; there is no fee. Open June 15–September 30. The stay limit is 14 days.

Directions: From Martin City, which is northeast of Kalispell on U.S. 2, go 53 miles north on Forest Service Road 210, then 10 miles west on Forest Service Road 114 to the campground.

Contact: Forest Service, Eureka Ranger Station, 1299 Hwy. 93 North, Eureka, MT 59917; 406/296-2536 or 800/280-2267.

Trip notes: The Flathead National Forest lies adjacent to Glacier National Park and west of the Continental Divide. You can hike glaciated peaks and fish alpine lakes in this beautiful setting.

6 Old North Trail Campground

 6

Location: Near Glacier National Park; map MT2, grid a7.

Campsites, facilities: There are 40 RV or tent campsites. Showers, laundry facilities, water, electricity, cabins, and tepees are available.

Reservations, fees: No reservations are needed; the fee is $5–10 per night. Open June 1–September 15.

Directions: From St. Mary, go north nine miles on U.S. 89 to Babb. From Babb, go four miles west on Many Glacier Road, next to Glacier National Park.

Contact: Old North Trail Campground, Volley Reed, P.O. Box 21, Babb, MT 59411; 406/732-4182.

Trip notes: There is a wide variety of recreational activities in Glacier National Park, including hiking, boating, fishing, and sightseeing.

7 Many Glacier

 6

Location: In Glacier National Park; map MT2, grid a7.

Campsites, facilities: There are 110 RV or tent campsites, which can accommodate a maximum RV length of 35 feet. A wheelchair-accessible restroom and a boat launch are available.

Reservations, fees: No reservations are needed; the fee is $14 per night. Open seasonally; call for specific dates. The stay limit is seven days.

Directions: From St. Mary, go north nine miles on U.S. 89 to Babb. From Babb, go 12 miles on Many Glacier Road to campground.

Contact: Glacier National Park, Superintendent, West Glacier, MT 59936; 406/888-7800; website: www.nps.gov/glac.

Trip notes: There are many recreational activities in Glacier National Park, including hiking, boating, fishing, and sightseeing.

8 Jerry's RV Park

 4

Location: North of Kalispell; map MT2, grid b1.

Campsites, facilities: There are 28 RV or tent campsites. A restaurant, golf course, water, electricity, store, and a sanitary disposal facility are available.

Reservations, fees: No reservations are needed; the fee is $12 per night.

Directions: From Kalispell go north on U.S. 93 to Fortine; drive to the post office, turn left, and look for a big blue building.

Contact: Jerry's RV Park, 205 1st St. South, Fortine, MT 59918; 406/882-4474.

Trip notes: There is a golf course here, and the town of Fortine is between the Flathead and Kootenai National Forests, where you can fish and hike. The section of highway between Kalispell and Fortine is a designated scenic route.

9 North Dickey Lake

 4

Location: In Flathead National Forest; map MT2, grid b1.

Campsites, facilities: There are 25 RV or tent campsites, which can accommodate a maximum RV length of 50 feet. A wheelchair-accessible restroom and trailer boat launch are available.

Reservations, fees: No reservations are needed; the fee is $7 per night. Open May 15–September 18. The stay limit is 14 days.

Directions: From Eureka, take U.S. 93 south

for 15 miles to the North Dickey Lake campground sign and turn right. A short distance ahead you'll see another campground sign and the campground is on the left.

Contact: Forest Service, Troy Ranger Station, 1437 N. Hwy. 2, Troy, MT 59935; 406/295-4693.

Trip notes: The Flathead National Forest lies adjacent to Glacier National Park and west of the Continental Divide. You can hike glaciated peaks and fish alpine lakes in this beautiful setting.

10 Quartz Creek

    6

Location: In Glacier National Park; map MT2, grid b4.

Campsites, facilities: There are seven RV or tent campsites, which can accommodate a maximum RV length of 18 feet.

Reservations, fees: No reservations are needed; the fee is $12 per night. Open seasonally; call for specific dates. The stay limit is seven days.

Directions: From Polebridge, go 5.5 miles southeast on Inside North Fork Road. The campground is on the left; watch for signs.

Contact: Glacier National Park, Superintendent, West Glacier, MT 59936; 406/888-7800; website: nps.gov/glac.

Trip notes: There are many recreational activities in Glacier National Park, including hiking, boating, fishing, and sightseeing.

11 Bowman Lake

     7

Location: In Glacier National Park; map MT2, grid b4.

Campsites, facilities: There are 48 RV or tent campsites, which can accommodate a maximum RV length of 22 feet.

Reservations, fees: No reservations are needed; the fee is $12 per night. Open seasonally; call for specific dates. The stay limit is seven days.

Directions: From Apgar, go north on Inside North Fork Road 27 miles to Polebridge. From Polebridge, go seven miles east on a dirt road, and the campground is on the right side.

Contact: Glacier National Park, Superintendent, West Glacier, MT 59936; 406/888-7800; website: www.nps.gov/glac.

Trip notes: Bowman Lake is accessible by a secondary road. Trailers are permitted, but the access roads are unimproved, and large units are not recommended. Primitive camping is allowed until closed by snow. You can fish for cutthroat, Dolly Varden, and whitefish. Boat access is nearby, but there are some restrictions on powerboats, based on boat's engine size.

12 Logging Creek

   6

Location: In Glacier National Park; map MT2, grid b4.

Campsites, facilities: There are eight tent campsites; RVs are not recommended. This is a primitive campground with pit toilets.

Reservations, fees: No reservations are accepted; the fee is $12 per night. Open seasonally (usually July–Labor Day); call for specific dates. The stay limit is seven days.

Directions: From Polebridge, go eight miles southeast on Inside North Fork Road, a dirt road.

Contact: Glacier National Park, Superintendent, West Glacier, MT 59936; 406/888-7800; website: www.nps.gov/glac.

Trip notes: Glacier National Park offers a wide variety of recreational activities, including hiking, boating, fishing, and sightseeing.

13 Johnson's of St. Mary

    7

Location: Near Glacier National Park; map MT2, grid a7.

Campsites, facilities: There are 112 RV or tent campsites. Showers, laundry facilities, a store, water, electricity, and a sanitary disposal facility are available. A restaurant is on-site.

Reservations, fees: No reservations are needed; the fee is $15–22 per night. Open April 1–October 31.

Directions: From St. Mary, go north on U.S. 89; the campground is on the right, on the outskirts of town. Watch for signs. St. Mary is on the east side of Glacier National Park at Going-To-The-Sun Road and St. Mary Lake.

Contact: Johnson's of St. Mary, HC 72-10 Star Route, St. Mary, MT 59417; 406/732-5565, 406/732-4207.

Trip notes: Glacier National Park offers a wide variety of recreational activities, including hiking, boating, fishing, and sightseeing.

14 St. Mary-Glacier Park KOA Kampground

 5

Location: Near Glacier National Park; map MT2, grid a7.

Campsites, facilities: There are 219 RV or tent campsites. Laundry facilities, showers, a store, water, electricity, a sanitary disposal facility, Kamping Kabins, hot tubs, and canoe rentals are available.

Reservations, fees: No reservations are needed; the fee is $21–33 per night. Open May 15–October 1.

Directions: From St. Mary, go one mile northwest to the campground. St. Mary is on the east side of Glacier National Park at Going-To-The-Sun Road and St. Mary Lake.

Contact: Glacier National Park, Superintendent, W. Shore, St. Mary, MT 59417; 406/732-4122 or 800/562-1504.

Trip notes: This campground is on the Going-to-the-Sun Road, a popular scenic mountain byway. You can fish and boat on St. Mary Lake. Be sure to visit the St. Mary Visitor Center. There are many varied recreational activities in Glacier National Park, including hiking, boating, fishing, and sightseeing.

15 Two Medicine

 6

Location: In Glacier National Park; map MT2, grid b7.

Campsites, facilities: There are 99 RV or tent campsites, 13 of which can accommodate a maximum RV length of 32 feet. A wheelchair-accessible restroom and a trailer boat launch are available.

Reservations, fees: No reservations are needed; the fee is $14 per night. Open seasonally, usually May 27–September 14; call for specific dates. The stay limit is seven days.

Directions: From East Glacier, go three miles north on Highway 49, then 12 miles west on Two Medicine Road to the campground.

Contact: Glacier National Park, Superintendent, West Glacier, MT 59936; 406/888-7800; website: www.nps.gov/glac.

Trip notes: Glacier National Park offers a wide variety of recreational activities, including hiking, boating, fishing, and sightseeing.

16 St. Mary Lake

 7

Location: In Glacier National Park; map MT2, grid b7.

Campsites, facilities: There are 156 RV or tent campsites, which can accommodate a maximum RV length of 30 feet. A wheelchair-accessible restroom is available.

Reservations, fees: campgrounds may be reserved through the National Park Service Reservations System by calling 800/365-CAMP (800/365-2267) or through the website: www.reservations.nps.gov. The fee is $17 per night. Open seasonally; call for specific dates. The stay limit is seven days.

Directions: From St. Mary, go one mile west on Going-To-The-Sun Road; the campground is on the right. St. Mary is on the east side of Glacier National Park at Going-To-The-Sun Road and St. Mary Lake.

Contact: Glacier National Park, Superintendent, West Glacier, MT 59936; 406/888-7800; website: www.nps.gov/glac.

Trip notes: You can fish and boat on St. Mary Lake and learn about the area at St. Mary Visitor Center. Glacier National Park offers a wide variety of recreational activities, including hiking, boating, fishing, and sightseeing.

17 Rising Sun

 7

Location: In Glacier National Park; map MT2, grid b7.

Campsites, facilities: There are 83 RV or tent campsites, which can accommodate a maximum RV length of 30 feet. A wheelchair-accessible restroom and a trailer boat launch are available.

Reservations, fees: No reservations are needed; the fee is $14 per night. Open seasonally; call for specific dates. The stay limit is seven days.

Directions: From St. Mary, go six miles west on Going-To-The-Sun Road; the campground is on the right. St. Mary is on the east side of Glacier National Park at Going-To-The-Sun Road and St. Mary Lake.

Contact: Glacier National Park, Superintendent, West Glacier, MT 59936; 406/888-7800; website: www.nps.gov/glac.

Trip notes: This campground is on St. Mary Lake, where you can fish. Glacier National Park offers a wide variety of recreational activities, including hiking, boating, fishing, and sightseeing.

18 Avalanche

 7

Location: In Glacier National Park; map MT2, grid b5.

Campsites, facilities: There are 87 RV or tent campsites, 50 of which can accommodate a maximum RV length of 26 feet. A wheelchair-accessible restroom is available.

Reservations, fees: No reservations are ac-

cepted; the fee is $14 per night. Open seasonally, usually mid-June–Labor Day; call for specific dates. The stay limit is seven days.

Directions: From Lake McDonald, go five miles northeast on Going-To-The-Sun Road, and the campground is on the right. Lake McDonald is on the west side of Glacier National Park.

Contact: Glacier National Park, Superintendent, West Glacier, MT 59936; 406/888-7800; website: www.nps.gov/glac.

Trip notes: Glacier National Park offers a wide variety of recreational activities, including hiking, boating, fishing, and sightseeing.

19 Sprague Creek

 7

Location: In Glacier National Park; map MT2, grid b5.

Campsites, facilities: There are 25 campsites for tents only, no towed units. A wheelchair-accessible restroom is available.

Reservations, fees: No reservations are needed; the fee is $14 per night. Open seasonally; call for specific dates. The stay limit is seven days.

Directions: From West Glacier, the west entrance to Glacier National Park, go eight miles northeast on Going-To-The-Sun Road.

Contact: Glacier National Park, Superintendent, West Glacier, MT 59936; 406/888-7800; website: www.nps.gov/glac.

Trip notes: You can boat and fish on Lake McDonald. Glacier National Park offers a wide variety of recreational activities, including hiking, boating, fishing, and sightseeing.

20 Fish Creek

 7

Location: In Glacier National Park; map MT2, grid b4.

Campsites, facilities: There are 180 RV or tent campsites, 80 of which can accommodate a maximum RV length of 26 feet. A wheelchair-accessible restroom is available.

Reservations, fees: Reservations are accepted; campgrounds may be reserved ahead of time through the National Park Service Reservations System by calling 800/365-CAMP (800/365-2267) or through the website: www.nps.gov. The fee is $17 per night. Open seasonally; call for specific dates. The stay limit is seven days.

Directions: From West Glacier, the west entrance to Glacier National Park, go five miles northwest on Camas Road; the campground is on the right, on the northwest shore of Lake McDonald.

Contact: Glacier National Park, Superintendent, West Glacier, MT 59936; 406/888-7800; website: www.nps.gov/glac.

Trip notes: Glacier National Park offers a wide variety of recreational activities, including hiking, boating, fishing, and sightseeing.

21 Apgar

     7

Location: In Glacier National Park; map MT2, grid b5.

Campsites, facilities: There are 196 RV or tent campsites, which can accommodate a maximum RV length of 35 feet. Wheelchair-accessible restrooms and water are available.

Reservations, fees: No reservations are needed; the fee is $10–15 per night. Open year-round, but services are only available mid-May–mid-October. The stay limit is seven days.

Directions: From Going-To-The-Sun Road, go one mile northwest to the campground, which is at the foot of the south shore of Lake McDonald. Apgar is two miles north of West Glacier, the west entrance to Glacier National Park.

Contact: Glacier National Park, Superintendent, West Glacier, MT 59936; 406/888-7800; website: www.nps.gov/glac.

Trip notes: Seasonal dates are subject to change, so call first. There are hiking trails, and swimming, boating, and fishing at Lake

McDonald. Glacier National Park offers a wide variety of recreational activities, including hiking, boating, fishing, and sightseeing.

22 Sleeping Wolf Campground & RV Park

     5

Location: Near Glacier National Park; map MT2, grid b8.

Campsites, facilities: There are 21 RV or tent campsites. Showers, laundry facilities, water, electricity, and a sanitary disposal facility are available.

Reservations, fees: No reservations are needed; the fee is $10–19 per night. Open May 1–October 1.

Directions: From Browning, go half a mile west on U.S. 89 and turn north at the first county road to the campground. Browning is east of Glacier National Park, 13 miles east of East Glacier Park on U.S. 2.

Contact: Sleeping Wolf Campground & RV Park, P.O. Box 607, Browning, MT 59417; 406/338-7933; email: k3papa@3rivers.net; website: www.sleepingwolf.com.

Trip notes: This campground is quiet and off the highway near Glacier Park. Glacier National Park offers a wide variety of recreational activities, including hiking, boating, fishing, and sightseeing.

23 Big Creek Campground

    6

Location: Near Glacier National Park; map MT2, grid b4.

Campsites, facilities: There are 22 RV or tent campsites. A boat launch and water are available. Group-use areas can be reserved. Pets are allowed on leashes.

Reservations, fees: No reservations are needed; the fee is $9 and up per night. Open May 30–September 1. The stay limit is 14 days.

Directions: From Kalispell, go north on U.S. 2 to Columbia Falls. From Columbia Falls, take

Highway 486 north for 20.5 miles (last 12.6 miles is dirt); the campground is on the right. It's 2.5 miles from the Camas Creek entrance to Glacier National Park.

Contact: Big Creek Campground, 1935 3rd Ave. East, Columbia Falls, MT 59912; 970/224-0375, fax 970/484-6151; email: lcarter@verinet.com; website: www.fs.fed.us/r1/flathead.

Trip notes: This is a pack-in, pack-out campground. It's at the North Fork of the Flathead River, a designated Wild and Scenic River, popular for floating. A map can be picked up at the Hungry Horse Ranger District Office. The Big Creek Outdoor Education Center of the Glacier Institute is across from the campground. The center explains the diverse natural and cultural resources of Glacier National Park, and the institute offers field seminars, including guided hikes in the Glacier National Park. Glacier National Park offers a wide variety of recreational activities, including hiking, boating, fishing, and sightseeing.

24 Lake Five Resort

     7

Location: Near Glacier National Park; map MT2, grid c5.

Campsites, facilities: There are 14 RV and 36 tent campsites. Showers, laundry facilities, water, electricity, a store, boat rentals, and barbecue pits are available.

Reservations, fees: No reservations are needed; the fee is $16.50–22 per night. Open April 1–October 15.

Directions: From West Glacier, the west entrance to Glacier National Park, go three miles west on U.S. 2, then .75 mile north on Belton Stage Road to the campground.

Contact: Lake Five Resort, 540 Belton Stage Rd., P.O. Box 338, West Glacier, MT 59936; 406/387-5601; email: lakefive@digisys.net.

Trip notes: This is a spring-fed lake, and you can swim, boat, and water-ski here. Glacier National Park offers a wide variety of recreational activities, including hiking, boating, fishing, and sightseeing.

25 Glacier Campground

 5

Location: Near Glacier National Park; map MT2, grid c4.

Campsites, facilities: There are 160 RV or tent campsites. Showers, laundry facilities, water, electricity, propane gas, and a sanitary disposal facility available. Cabins, a playground, and a volleyball court are on-site.

Reservations, fees: Reservations are accepted; the fee is $15–20 per night. Open June 1–September 15.

Directions: From West Glacier, the west entrance to Glacier National Park, go one mile west on U.S. 2 to milepost 206, where you will see the sign. The campground is .25 mile on the left.

Contact: Glacier Campground, P.O. Box 447, West Glacier, MT 59936; 406/387-5689 or 888/387-5689.

Trip notes: Glacier National Park offers a wide variety of recreational activities, including hiking, boating, fishing, and sightseeing.

26 North American RV Park & Campground

    6

Location: Near Glacier National Park; map MT2, grid c5.

Campsites, facilities: There are 108 RV sites, some pull-through, and tent sites. Showers, laundry facilities, stores, water, electricity, a sanitary disposal station, and a telephone are available.

Reservations, fees: No reservations are needed; the fee is $23 per night. Open year-round.

Directions: From Glacier National Park, go five miles on U.S. 2 to the campground.

Contact: North American RV Park & Campground, 10784 Hwy. 2 East, P.O. Box 130449, Coram, MT 59913; 406/387-5800, 800/704-4266, fax 406/387-5888; email: narvpark@montana.com; website: www.northamericancamp.com.

Trip notes: This campground is next to Glacier National Park and close to the Bob Marshall Wilderness. Glacier National Park offers a wide variety of recreational activities, including hiking, boating, fishing, and sightseeing.

27 Sundance RV Park & Campground

   5

Location: Near Glacier National Park; map MT2, grid c4.

Campsites, facilities: There are 58 RV or tent campsites. Showers, a store, water, electricity, and a sanitary disposal facility are available.

Reservations, fees: No reservations are needed; the fee is $13–16 per night. Open May 1–October 1.

Directions: From West Glacier, the west entrance to Glacier National Park, drive six miles southwest on U.S. 2; the campground is at milepost 147.

Contact: Sundance RV Park and Campground, 10545 Hwy. 2 East, P.O. Box 130037, Coram, MT 59913; 406/387-5016.

Trip notes: Lake McDonald is to the north, Glacier National Park is to the north, and Hungry Horse is to the south.

28 Coram RV Park

     5

Location: Near Glacier National Park; map MT2, grid c5.

Campsites, facilities: There are nine RV and 12 tent campsites, some with cable hookups. Showers, water, electricity, and a sanitary disposal facility are available.

Reservations, fees: No reservations are needed; the fee is $12–15 per night. Open May 15–September 15.

Directions: From West Glacier, the west entrance to Glacier National Park, go seven miles west on U.S. 2; the campground is one block off U.S. 2, behind Stoner's Inn.

Contact: Coram RV Park, 97 Corbett Lane, P.O. Box 130314, Coram, MT 59913; 406/387-5552.

Trip notes: This campground is close to the water slides, the maze, and Beaver Park. Coram is home to the North American Wildlife Museum and the Great Bear Adventure, where visitors can observe bears in their natural habitat. The Big Sky Waterslide in Columbia Falls is eight miles away. The west entrance to Glacier National Park is seven miles away and there are many recreational activities in Glacier National Park including hiking, boating, fishing, and sightseeing.

29 Cut Bank

    6

Location: In Glacier National Park; map MT2, grid c7.

Campsites, facilities: There are 19 tent campsites, but RVs are not recommended.

Reservations, fees: No reservations are needed; the fee is $12 per night. Open seasonally; call for specific dates. The stay limit is seven days.

Directions: From East Glacier Park, at the southeast corner of Glacier National Park, go 17 miles north on Highway 49, then four miles west on Cut Bank Creek Road to the campground.

Contact: Glacier National Park, Superintendent, West Glacier, MT 59936; 406/888-7800; website: www.nps.gov/glac.

Trip notes: Glacier National Park offers a wide variety of recreational activities, including hiking, boating, fishing, and sightseeing.

30 Sears Motel & Campground

     5

Location: Near Glacier National Park; map MT2, grid c7.

Campsites, facilities: There are 17 RV or

tent campsites. Showers, a store, electricity, water, a gift shop, motel, and car rentals are available.

Reservations, fees: No reservations are needed; the fee is $11–16 per night. Open May 15–September 30.

Directions: From East Glacier, at the southeast corner of Glacier National Park, go half a mile north of U.S. 2 on Highway 49 to the campground.

Contact: Sears Motel & Campground, 1023 Hwy. 49 North, P.O. Box 275, East Glacier Park, MT 59434; 406/226-4432, fax 406/226-4432; email: eglacier@aol.com.

Trip notes: Glacier National Park offers a wide variety of recreational activities, including hiking, boating, fishing, and sightseeing.

31 Y Lazy R RV Park

     5

Location: Near Glacier National Park; map MT2, grid c8.

Campsites, facilities: There are 30 RV and 10 grassy tent campsites. Showers, laundry facilities, water, electricity, and a sanitary disposal facility are available.

Reservations, fees: Reservations are accepted; the fee is $10–15 per night. Open June 1–September 15.

Directions: From East Glacier, at the southeast corner of Glacier National Park, go two blocks east and south of U.S. 2. If you are coming from the east, turn left at the Exxon gas station, go two blocks, then turn right. If you are coming from the west, turn right at the Exxon gas station, drive two blocks, and turn right.

Contact: Y Lazy R RV Park, P.O. Box 146, East Glacier Park, MT 59434; 406/226-5573.

Trip notes: This campground has a beautiful view. It's convenient to services; a playground is a half block away, and the restaurant is two blocks away. Glacier National Park offers a wide variety of recreational activities, including hiking, boating, fishing, and sightseeing.

32 Smiley's RV Park

   5

Location: Near Glacier National Park; map MT2, grid c7.

Campsites, facilities: There are 14 RV campsites for self-contained units only. Laundry facilities, water, electricity, and a sanitary disposal station are available.

Reservations, fees: No reservations are needed; the fee is $10–22 per night. Open May 15–October 15.

Directions: From East Glacier go two blocks east and turn east at Glacier Avenue (which is two blocks south of the Exxon service station or two blocks east of Dawson Avenue).

Contact: Smiley's RV Park, 411 Meade St., P.O. Box 282, East Glacier, MT 59434; 406/226-4105.

Trip notes: This campground has large shade trees in a quiet setting. Glacier National Park offers a wide variety of recreational activities, including hiking, boating, fishing, and sightseeing.

33 Firebrand Pass Campground

   7

Location: West of East Glacier; map MT2, grid c7.

Campsites, facilities: There are 29 RV or tent campsites. Showers, laundry facilities, water, electricity, and a restaurant are available.

Reservations, fees: No reservations are needed; the fee is $15 per night. Open June 1–September 15.

Directions: From East Glacier go three miles west on U.S. 2 to milepost 206.

Contact: Firebrand Pass Campground, P.O. Box 146, East Glacier Park, MT 59434; 406/226-5573.

Trip notes: This campground is in a clean, beautiful setting, with fishing available in the nearby creek.

34 Whitefish Lake State Park

 5

Location: North of Flathead Lake; map MT2, grid c3.

Campsites, facilities: There are 25 RV or tent campsites, which can accommodate a maximum RV length of 35 feet. Grills, picnic tables, water, and a trailer boat launch are available.

Reservations, fees: No reservations are needed; the fee is $12 per night. Open May 1–September 30. The stay limit is seven days.

Directions: From Kalispell, go north on U.S. 93 14 miles to Whitefish. From Whitefish, go one mile west on U.S. 93, then one mile north on State Park Road to the campground.

Contact: Department of Fish, Wildlife & Parks, 490 N. Meridian Rd., Kalispell, MT 59901; 406/862-3991, 406/752-5501, fax 406/257-0349.

Trip notes: You can fish, swim, boat, and water-ski on Whitefish Lake. There are golf courses in Whitefish, Kalispell, and Columbia Falls.

35 Stanton Creek Lodge

 6

Location: Near Glacier National Park; map MT2, grid c5.

Campsites, facilities: There are 10 full-hookup RV sites and unlimited tent campsites. Showers, restrooms, water, a store, and electricity are available. Six cabins, a restaurant, and a bar are on-site.

Reservations, fees: Reservations are accepted; the fee is $7.50–12.50 per night. Group sites are $4 per person. Open year-round.

Directions: From West Glacier, go 16 miles east on U.S. 2 to milepost 170, where the lodge is. East Glacier is at the southeast corner of Glacier National Park.

Contact: Stanton Creek Lodge, HC 36 Box 2C, Essex, MT 59916; 406/888-5040, fax 406/888-5040; email: kencard@cyberport.net

Trip notes: The Flathead Range is to the west,

and the Flathead River, to the east, has fishing. Walton Goat Lick overlook is to the southeast. Glacier National Park offers a wide variety of recreational activities, including hiking, boating, fishing, and sightseeing. You can arrange golf, floating trips, and helicopter rides at the lodge.

36 Tally Lake

 5

Location: In Flathead National Forest; map MT2, grid c3.

Campsites, facilities: There are 39 RV or tent campsites, which can accommodate a maximum RV length of 22 feet. A trailer boat launch is available.

Reservations, fees: No reservations are needed; the fee is $10 per night. Open year-round. The stay limit is 14 days.

Directions: From Whitefish, go four miles west past Spencer Lake. Turn left onto Twin Bridges Road, continue until it joins Farm to Market Road, then turn right on Forest Service Road 913 and follow signs to the campground.

Contact: Flathead National Forest, Whitefish Ranger Station, 1335 Hwy. 93W, Whitefish, MT 59937; 406/863-5400.

Trip notes: The Flathead National Forest lies adjacent to Glacier National Park and west of the Continental Divide. You can hike glaciated peaks and fish alpine lakes in this beautiful setting. You can boat and swim here.

37 Whitefish KOA

 5

Location: North of Flathead Lake; map MT2, grid c3.

Campsites, facilities: There are 60 RV and 25 tent campsites. Showers, laundry facilities, water, electricity, and a store are available. Ten Kamping Kabins, a lodge, restaurant, and game room are on-site.

Reservations, fees: Reservations are recommended; the fee is $21–29 per night. Open year-round.

Directions: From Whitefish, go a little over two miles south on U.S. 93, or from Kalispell, go eight miles north on U.S. 93 to the campground.

Contact: Whitefish KOA, 5121 Hwy. 93 South, Whitefish, MT 59937; 406/862-4242, 800/562-8734, fax 406/862-8967; email: whitefishkoa@netscape.net.

Trip notes: You can fish, swim, boat, and water-ski on Whitefish Lake. There are golf courses in Whitefish, Kalispell, and Columbia Falls.

38 San-Suz-Ed RV Park & Campground

 5

Location: Near Glacier National Park; map MT2, grid c5.

Campsites, facilities: There are 68 RV or tent campsites. Showers, laundry facilities, a store, water, and electricity are available.

Reservations, fees: No reservations are needed; the fee is $16.64–23.92 per night. Open year-round.

Directions: From West Glacier, the west entrance to Glacier National Park, go two miles west on U.S. 2. The campground is on the right between mileposts 150 and 151.

Contact: San-Suz-Ed RV Park & Campground, P.O. Box 387, West Glacier, MT 59936; 406/387-5280.

Trip notes: Glacier National Park offers a wide variety of recreational activities, including hiking, boating, fishing, and sightseeing.

39 Canyon RV & Campground

 5

Location: Near Glacier National Park; map MT2, grid c5.

Campsites, facilities: There are 51 RV and tent campsites, which can accommodate a maximum RV length of 75 feet. Wheelchair-accessible restrooms, showers, a store, mini-golf, water, electricity, a sanitary disposal facility, and cabins are available. Pets are allowed on leashes.

Reservations, fees: Reservations are accepted; the fee is $18–21 per night. Open May 1–September 30.

Directions: From the west entrance of Glacier National Park, go eight miles to Hungry Horse, where the campground is. Look for a white rail fence and sign on Highway 2.

Contact: Canyon RV & Campground, P.O. Box 7, 9540, Hwy. 2 East, Hungry Horse, MT 59919; 406/387-9393 or 800/337-9393, fax 406/387-9394; email: canyonrv@montanacampground.com; website: www.montanacampground.com.

Trip notes: The U.S. #2 bike path is across Highway 2. Glacier National Park offers a wide variety of recreational activities, including hiking, boating, fishing, and sightseeing.

40 West Glacier KOA

 5

Location: Near Glacier National Park; map MT2, grid c4.

Campsites, facilities: There are 148 RV or tent campsites. Water, electricity, showers, laundry facilities, a store, and sanitary disposal station are available. Kamping Kabins, a lodge, and game rooms are on-site.

Reservations, fees: Reservations are accepted; the fee is $21.95–29.95 per night. There's a 10 percent discount with a KOA card. Open May 1–October 1.

Directions: From West Glacier, the west entrance to Glacier National Park, go 2.5 miles west on U.S. 2, then one mile south on Half Moon Flats; the campground is on the right.

Contact: West Glacier KOA, P.O. Box 215, West Glacier, MT 59936; 406/387-5341, or 800/562-3313.

Trip notes: Glacier National Park offers a wide variety of recreational activities, including hiking, boating, fishing, and sightseeing.

41 The Timber Wolf Resort

 6

Location: Near Glacier National Park; map MT2, grid c5.

Campsites, facilities: There are 44 RV or tent campsites. Showers, laundry facilities, a store, water, electricity, and cabins are available.

Reservations, fees: Reservations are strongly suggested; the fee is $16–22 per night. Open year-round.

Directions: From Kalispell, go north on U.S. 2 to Hungry Horse. From Hungry Horse, go east on U.S. 2; this is the first campground on the right at the corner of Hungry Horse Dam Road and U.S. 2.

Contact: The Timber Wolf Resort, 9105 U.S. Hwy. 2 East, P.O. Box 190800, Hungry Horse, MT 59919; 406/387-9653, 877/846-9653, fax 406/387-9654; email: elek@timberwolfresort.com; website: www.timberwolfresort.com.

Trip notes: This campground is wooded, with scenic views. Hungry Horse Reservoir is to the southeast, and the west entrance of Glacier National Park is nine miles to the east. You can boat and fish at Hungry Horse Reservoir.

42 Emery Bay

 6

Location: In Flathead National Forest; map MT2, grid c4.

Campsites, facilities: There are eight RV or tent campsites, which can accommodate a maximum RV length of 22 feet. A boat launch is available.

Reservations, fees: No reservations are needed; no fee is charged. Open June 1–September 15. The stay limit is 14 days.

Directions: From Kalispell, go north on U.S. 2 to Hungry Horse. From Hungry Horse, take U.S. 2 for nearly a mile to the East Side Hungry Horse Reservoir sign, where you turn right. At the Y, go right for nearly six miles to the campground sign. At this Y, stay right; the campground is about .5 mile ahead.

Contact: Flathead National Forest, 1935 3rd Ave. East, Hungry Horse, MT 59919; 406/387-3800; website: www.fs.fed.us/r1/flathead.

Trip notes: This campground overlooks the Hungry Horse Reservoir, where you can boat and fish. Hungry Horse Dam is close to Glacier National Park, where you can hike, boat, fish, and sightsee. This campground is in bear country, so use precautions.

43 Mountain Meadow RV Park & Campground

 5

Location: At Hungry Horse; map MT2, grid c5.

Campsites, facilities: There are 62 RV or tent campsites. Showers, laundry facilities, a store, water, electricity, a sanitary disposal facility, and a trout pond available. Pets are allowed on leashes.

Reservations, fees: Reservations are strongly suggested (especially July and August); the fee is $5-24.50 per night. Open May 1–October 1.

Directions: From West Glacier, go nine miles east on U.S. 2; this campground is .25 mile east of Hungry Horse Ranger Station.

Contact: Mountain Meadow RV Park & Campground, P.O. Box 190442, 9125 Hwy. 2 East, Hungry Horse, MT 59919; 406/387-9125, fax 406/387-9126; email: camp@mmrvpark.com.

Trip notes: This campground has spacious wooded sites and beautiful views. It's four miles from Hungry Horse Reservoir, where you can fish, and behind the reservoir are the Bob Marshall and Great Bear Wildernesses. There are seven golf courses, in Kalispell, Bigfork, and West Glacier. Glacier National Park is 10 minutes away.

44 Glacier Peaks RV Park

 5

Location: Near Glacier National Park; map MT2, grid c3.

Campsites, facilities: There are 60 RV and

some tent campsites, some with pull-throughs and room for slide-outs. Showers, laundry facilities, a store, water, electricity, and a sanitary disposal facility are available.

Reservations, fees: No reservations are needed; the fee is $19 per night. Open year-round.

Directions: From Kalispell, go north on U.S. 2 13 miles to Columbia Falls. From Columbia Falls, go three miles west on U.S. 2; the campground is one-eighth mile from the junction of Highway 40 and U.S. 2.

Contact: Glacier Peaks RV Park, 3185 Hwy. 40, P.O. Box 492, Columbia Falls, MT 59912; 406/892-2133, 800/268-4849.

Trip notes: Big Sky Waterslides in Columbia Falls has a wading pool, mini-slide, straight slides, and giant slides with twists and turns, as well as a river ride with inner tubes. Glacier National Park offers a wide variety of recreational activities, including hiking, boating, fishing, and sightseeing.

45 Columbia Falls RV Park

  5

Location: Near Glacier National Park; map MT2, grid c4.

Campsites, facilities: There are 60 RV or tent campsites, some with cable hookups. Showers, laundry facilities, water, electricity, and a gift shop are available.

Reservations, fees: No reservations are needed; the fee is $70–120 per night. Open June 1–October 15.

Directions: From Highway 2, take 3rd Avenue East exit; the RV park is right there.

Contact: Columbia Falls RV Park, 1000 3rd Ave., P.O. Box 2031, East Columbia Falls, MT 59912; tel./fax 406/892-1122, 888/401-7268.

Trip notes: Columbia Falls has the Meadow Lake Golf Course and Big Sky Waterslide. The town serves as Glacier National Park's west entrance, and County Road 486, also called North Fork Road, is a scenic drive along the North Fork of the Flathead River. This river is

the western boundary of the park and has been designated a Wild and Scenic River. The road is about 20 miles to the national park entrance,; the last nine miles are dirt. Glacier National Park offers a wide variety of recreational activities, including hiking, boating, fishing, and sightseeing.

46 Lost Johnny Point

 6

Location: In Flathead National Forest; map MT2, grid c5.

Campsites, facilities: There are two sections; one has 21 RV or tent campsites, which can accommodate a maximum RV length of 22 feet. A wheelchair-accessible restroom and a boat launch are available. The other section has five undeveloped campsites with no water and no fee.

Reservations, fees: No reservations are needed; the fee in the developed section is $9 per night. Open June 1–September 15. The stay limit is 14 days.

Directions: From Kalispell, go north on US2 to Hungry Horse. From Hungry Horse, go nine miles southeast on Forest Service Road 895 to the campground.

Contact: Flathead National Forest, 1935 3rd Ave. East, Hungry Horse, MT 59919: 406/387-3800; website: www.fs.fed.us/r1/flathead.

Trip notes: This campground is in two sections on the shore of Hungry Horse Reservoir. There are many hiking trails in the area.

47 Doris Point

 6

Location: In Flathead National Forest; map MT2, grid c4.

Campsites, facilities: There are 18 tent campsites.

Reservations, fees: No reservations are needed; no fee is charged. Open June 15–September 30. The stay limit is 14 days.

Directions: From Kalispell, go north on US2 to

Hungry Horse. From Hungry Horse, go eight miles southeast on Forest Service Road 895 to campsite.

Contact: Flathead National Forest, 1935 3rd Ave. East, Hungry Horse, MT 59919; 406/387-3800; website: www.fs.fed.us/r1/flathead.

Trip notes: Flathead Lake is nearby, where you can fish, boat, swim, water-ski, and hike interpretive trails.

48 Lid Creek

 6

Location: In Flathead National Forest; map MT2, grid c4.

Campsites, facilities: There are 22 RV or tent campsites, which can accommodate a maximum RV length of 16 feet. A boat launch is available.

Reservations, fees: No reservations are needed; the fee is $7 per night. Open June 1–September 15. The stay limit is 14 days.

Directions: From Kalispell, go north on U.S. 2 to Hungry Horse. From Hungry Horse, go 15 miles southeast on Forest Service Road 895 to the campground.

Contact: Flathead National Forest, 1935 3rd Ave. East, Hungry Horse, MT 59919; 406/387-3800; website: www.fs.fed.us/r1/flathead.

Trip notes: There are six golf courses nearby, and you can fish, boat, swim, and water-ski Flathead Lake.

49 Summit

 6

Location: In Lewis and Clark National Forest; map MT2, grid c7.

Campsites, facilities: There are 17 RV or tent campsites, which can accommodate a maximum RV length of 36 feet. A wheelchair-accessible restroom is available.

Reservations, fees: No reservations are needed; the fee is $12 per night. Open seasonally; call for specific dates. The stay limit is 14 days.

Directions: From East Glacier, at the southeast corner of Glacier National Park, go 13 miles southwest on U.S. 2 to the campground.

Contact: Lewis and Clark National Forest, Rocky Mountain Ranger District, P.O. Box 340, Choteau, MT 59422; 406/466-5341; website: www.fs.fed.us/r1/lewisclark.

Trip notes: This campground is on the edge of Glacier National Park, near Marias Pass in Lewis and Clark National Forest. Glacier National Park offers a wide variety of recreational activities, including hiking, boating, fishing, and sightseeing.

50 Three Forks Campground

 5

Location: Near Glacier National Park; map MT2, grid c7.

Campsites, facilities: There are 25 RV and 16 tent campsites. Showers, laundry facilities, water, electricity, a sanitary disposal facility, and a playground are available. A group pavilion can be reserved.

Reservations, fees: No reservations are needed; the fee is $13–16 per night. Open May 20–September 15.

Directions: From East Glacier, go 16 miles west on U.S. 2.

Contact: Three Forks Campground, P.O. Box 124, East Glacier Park, MT 59434; 406/226-4479.

Trip notes: Near Bear Creek, in Flathead National Forest. Glacier National Park offers a wide variety of recreational activities, including hiking, boating, fishing, and sightseeing.

51 Devil Creek

 6

Location: In Flathead National Forest; map MT2, grid c6.

Campsites, facilities: There are 13 RV or tent campsites, which can accommodate a maximum RV length of 30 feet. A stock unloading ramp and feed troughs for horses are available. This is a pack-in, pack-out campground.

Reservations, fees: No reservations are needed, and no fee is charged. Open June 1–September 15. The stay limit is 14 days.

Directions: From West Glacier, the west entrance to Glacier National Park, go 35 miles southeast on U.S. 2 to the campground.

Contact: Flathead National Forest, 1935 3rd Ave. East, West Glacier, MT 59936; 406/758-5200; website: www.fs.fed.us/r1/flathead.

Trip notes: This is a heavily wooded area with some privacy. This is bear country, so use precautions. The Devil Creek Trail is for horse and foot use. This seven-mile trail accesses the Spotted Bear Wilderness.

52 Murray Bay

      6

Location: In the Flathead National Forest; map MT2, grid d6.

Campsites, facilities: There are 18 RV or tent campsites, which can accommodate a maximum RV length of 22 feet. A trailer boat launch is available.

Reservations, fees: No reservations are needed; no fee is charged. Open June 1–September 15. The stay limit is 14 days.

Directions: From Martin City, go 22 miles southeast on Forest Service Road 38 to the campground. Martin City is northeast of Kalispell on U.S. 93.

Contact: Flathead National Forest, Hungry Horse Ranger District, P.O. Box 190340, Hungry Horse, MT 59919; 406/387-3800; website: www.fs.fed.us/r1/flathead.

Trip notes: This campground is along the Hungry Horse Reservoir, where you can fish, swim, and boat.

53 LaSalle RV Park & Campground

     5

Location: Near Flathead Lake; map MT2, grid d3.

Campsites, facilities: There are 35 RV campsites with full hookups, and eight tent sites. Showers, laundry facilities, water, electricity, and a sanitary disposal station are available.

Reservations, fees: No reservations are needed; the fee is $18.72 per night. Open year-round.

Directions: From Kalispell, go north 11 miles on U.S. 2, then one mile south at the intersection of Highway 40; the campground is on the west.

Contact: LaSalle RV Park & Campground, 5618 Hwy. 2 West, Columbia Falls, MT 59912; 406/892-4668; email: vvcap@sisna.com; website: www.sisna.com/trailhuts/lasalle.htm.

Trip notes: This campground is among mature trees and has a view of the mountains. There are six golf courses nearby, and you can fish, boat, swim, and water-ski Flathead Lake.

54 White Birch RV & Campground

    4

Location: Near Flathead Lake; map MT2, grid d3.

Campsites, facilities: There are 45 RV or tent campsites. Showers, laundry facilities, water, and electricity are available. Pets are allowed on leashes.

Reservations, fees: No reservations are needed; the fee is $12.48–15.60 per night. Open May 1–October 1.

Directions: From Kalispell, go north on U.S. 2 to the junction of U.S. 2 and Highway 35, and then go east .75 mile to Shady Lane and campground.

Contact: White Birch RV & Campground, 17 Shady Lane, Kalispell, MT 59901; 406/752-4008, 888/275-2275, fax 406/752-1106; email: joanie@whitebirchmotel.com; website: www.whitebirchmotel.com.

Trip notes: You can fish, boat, swim, water-ski, and hike interpretive trails at Flathead Lake.

55 Glacier Pines RV Park

 5

Location: Near Flathead Lake; map MT2, grid d3.

Campsites, facilities: There are 140 RV and 30 tent campsites. Showers, laundry facilities, a store, electricity, water, sanitary disposal station, and a swimming pool are available.

Reservations, fees: No reservations are needed; the fee is $22 per night. Open May 1–October 1.

Directions: From Kalispell, at the junction of Highway 35 and U.S. 2, go one mile east on Highway 35 to the RV park.

Contact: Glacier Pines RV Park, 1850 Hwy. 35 East, Kalispell, MT 59901; 406/752-2760 or 800/533-4029.

Trip notes: This campground is in a forested setting near Kalispell (five minutes' drive), with paved roads. You can fish, swim, boat, water-ski at Flathead Lake, golf in Flathead, and hike in the national forest.

56 Greenwood Village RV Park

 5

Location: Near Flathead Lake in Kalispell; map MT2, grid d3.

Campsites, facilities: There are 40 RV campsites with full hookups, and no tent sites. Showers, laundry facilities, a store, water, electricity, a sanitary disposal station, and cable TV are available.

Reservations, fees: Reservations are recommended; the fee is $18–22 per night. Open April 1–October 1.

Directions: From the junction of U.S. 93 and U.S. 2, go seven blocks east, turn left onto 7th Avenue E., go two blocks and turn right on Oregon Street and follow signs.

Contact: Greenwood Village RV Park, 1100 E. Oregon, Kalispell, MT 59901; 406/257-7719.

Trip notes: Flathead Lake is nearby, where you can fish, boat, swim, and hike interpretive trails.

57 Spruce Park RV Park

 5

Location: Near Flathead Lake; map MT2, grid d3.

Campsites, facilities: There are 100 RV and 60 tent campsites. Showers, laundry facilities, water, electricity, a sanitary disposal facility, and a playground are available.

Reservations, fees: Reservations are accepted; the fee is $10–15 per night. Open year-round.

Directions: From Kalispell, go north on U.S. 2 to Highway 35, then three miles east to the Flathead River Bridge and the campground.

Contact: Spruce Park RV Park, 1985 Hwy. 35, Kalispell, MT 59901; 406/752-6321, 406/756-8288 or 888/752-6321, fax 406/756-0480; email: sprucepk@digisys.net.

Trip notes: You can fish, boat, swim, water-ski, and hike at Flathead Lake.

58 Rocky Mountain "Hi" RV Park & Campground

 5

Location: Near Flathead Lake; map MT2, grid d3.

Campsites, facilities: There are 60 RV or tent campsites, which can accommodate a maximum RV length of 45 feet. Hookups, showers, laundry facilities, a store, water, electricity, wheelchair-accessible restrooms, and other facilities are available. Pets are allowed on leashes. A playground is on-site, and group facilities can be arranged.

Reservations, fees: Reservations are accepted; the fee is $18.50 per night. Open year-round.

Directions: From Kalispell, go five miles north on U.S. 2, then east on Reserve Drive to Helena Flats Road.

Contact: Rocky Mountain "Hi" RV Park & Campground, 825 Helena Flats Rd., Kalispell, MT 59901; 406/755-9573, 800/968-5637, fax 406/755-8816; email: rmhc@bigsky.net; website: kalispell.bigsky.net/rmhc.

Trip notes: There are shady sites and easy access in this campground. Flathead Lake is nearby, where you can fish, boat, swim, water-ski, and hike interpretive trails.

59 Lake Blaine Resort

     6

Location: Near Flathead Lake; map MT2, grid d4.

Campsites, facilities: There are 87 RV or tent campsites. Showers, laundry facilities, a store, water, electricity, a sanitary disposal station, and playground are available.

Reservations, fees: No reservations are needed; the fee is $12–17 per night. Open June 1–September 5.

Directions: From Kalispell, go 11 miles east on Highway 35, then three miles on Lake Blaine Road.

Contact: Lake Blaine Resort, 1700 Lake Blaine Rd., Kalispell, MT 59901; tel./fax 406/755-2891.

Trip notes: You can swim, boat, water-ski, and fish on Flathead Lake.

60 Lion's Bitterroot Youth Camp

    4

Location: In Flathead National Forest; map MT2, grid d2.

Campsites, facilities: There are 29 RV or tent campsites. Showers, electricity, a swimming area, and a playground are available.

Reservations, fees: No reservations are needed; the fee is $8 per night. Open May 1–September 30.

Directions: From Kalispell, go west on U.S. 2 to Marion. From Marion, go five miles north along Bitterroot Lake; the road turns into Pleasant Valley Road after two miles. Go right at the fork in the road; continue two miles, take a left at Lodgepole, and the campground is on the left.

Contact: Lion's Bitterroot Youth Camp, 1650 Pleasant Valley Rd., Marion, MT 59925; 406/854-2744.

Trip notes: The Flathead National Forest lies adjacent to Glacier National Park and west of the Continental Divide. You can hike glaciated peaks and fish alpine lakes in this beautiful setting.

61 Edgewater Motel & RV Resort

      6

Location: Near Flathead Lake; map MT2, grid d3.

Campsites, facilities: There are 46 RV or tent campsites. Showers, laundry facilities, water, cable, electricity, and a sanitary disposal station are available. A restaurant and lounge is nearby.

Reservations, fees: No reservations are needed; the fee is $12–20 per night. Open May 1–October 30.

Directions: From Kalispell, go 13 miles south on U.S. 93 to the resort.

Contact: Edgewater Motel & RV Resort, 7145 U.S. Hwy. 93 South, P.O. Box 312, Lakeside, MT 59922; 406/844-3644, 800/424-3798, fax 406/844-3840.

Trip notes: This campground is on Flathead Lake, where you can fish, boat, swim, and hike interpretive trails nearby.

62 McGregor Lake

     5

Location: In Lolo National Forest; map MT2, grid d1.

Campsites, facilities: There are 15 RV or tent campsites, which can accommodate a maximum RV length of 32 feet. There is a trailer boat launch.

Reservations, fees: No reservations are needed; the fee is $7 per night. Open May 23–September 30. The stay limit is 14 days.

Directions: From Kalispell, go 32 miles west on U.S. 2 to the campground.

Contact: Lolo National Forest, Trout Creek Ranger Station, 2693 Hwy. 200, Trout Creek, MT 59874; 406/827-3533, 406/752-5501, or 406/293-7773.

Trip notes: You can boat, swim, fish, and hike here.

63 McGregor Lake Resort

 4

Location: On McGregor Lake; map MT2, grid d1.

Campsites, facilities: There are 25 RV or tent sites. Showers, a store, electricity, water, restaurant, cabins, and boats are available.

Reservations, fees: No reservations are needed; the fee is $7–50 per night. Open year-round.

Directions: From Kalispell, go 30 miles west on U.S. 2, and you will see the resort, which is right on the highway.

Contact: McGregor Lake Resort, 12250 Hwy. 2W, Marion, MT 59925; 406/858-2253, fax 406/858-2251.

Trip notes: You can fish, water-ski, boat, and swim at McGregor Lake, and hike and bike in Lolo National Forest.

64 West Shore

 6

Location: On Flathead Lake; map MT2, grid d4.

Campsites, facilities: There are 26 RV or tent campsites, which can accommodate a maximum RV length of 35 feet. A trailer boat launch is available.

Reservations, fees: No reservations are needed; the fee is $8 per night, but the site is day-use-only October 1–April 30. Open May 1–September 30 for overnight use. The stay limit is seven days.

Directions: From Kalispell, go 20 miles south on U.S. 93 to the campground.

Contact: Flathead Lake State Park, Department of Fish, Wildlife & Parks, 490 N. Meridian Rd., Kalispell, MT 59901: 406/844-3901, 406/752-5501, fax 406/257-0349; website: www.fs.fed.us /r1/flathead.

Trip notes: This is a forested campground along a rocky shoreline at Flathead Lake. There are a boat launch and interpretive displays. You can fish, swim, boat and hike in the area and enjoy scenic views of Flathead Lake and the Mission and Swan Mountains. There are golf courses in Kalispell.

65 Woods Bay Marina & RV Park

 5

Location: On Flathead Lake; map MT2, grid d4.

Campsites, facilities: There are 21 RV and six tent campsites. Showers, a store, water, electricity, marine service, and boat slips are available.

Reservations, fees: Reservations are recommended; the fee is $12–19 per night. Open May 1–September 1.

Directions: From Bigfork, at the northeast corner of Flathead Lake, go three miles south on Yenne Point Road to the campground.

Contact: Woods Bay Marina & RV Park, 624 Yenne Point Rd., Bigfork, MT 59911; 406/837-6191, fax 406/837-1474; email: dbaroo@montana .com; website: www.woodsbay.com.

Trip notes: This campground is on Flathead Lake; Swan Lake is to the east. You can fish, boat, swim, water-ski, and hike interpretive trails at Flathead Lake.

66 Timbers RV Park

 5

Location: Near Flathead Lake; map MT2, grid d4.

Campsites, facilities: There are 35 RV or tent campsites, some with hookups. Showers, laundry facilities, water, electricity, a sanitary disposal facility, swimming pool, hot tub, and sauna are available. There are wheelchair-accessible facilities, but please call ahead to make arrangements. Pets are allowed on leashes.

Reservations, fees: Reservations are accepted; the fee is $18 per night. Open March 1–October 31.

Directions: Bigfork is at the northeast corner

of Flathead Lake. South of Bigfork, the campground is on the left side of Highway 35, 100 yards south of the junction of Highway 35 and Highway 209.

Contact: Timbers RV Park, P.O. Box 757, Big Fork, MT 59911; 406/837-6200, 800/821-4546, fax 406/837-6203.

Trip notes: You can fish, boat, swim, water-ski, and hike interpretive trails at Flathead Lake.

67 Outback Montana

 6
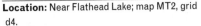

Location: Near Flathead Lake; map MT2, grid d4.

Campsites, facilities: There are 50 RV and tent campsites, some with hookups and pull-through sites. Showers, water, electricity, and a sanitary disposal station are available. Pets are allowed on leashes.

Reservations, fees: Reservations are accepted; the fee is $11–15 per night. Open May 1–October 1.

Directions: From Kalispell, go south on U.S. 93 for eight miles to Highway 82, east on Highway 82 seven miles to Highway 35, turn south to Bigfork. From Bigfork, go four miles south on Highway 35 to the campground, on the left. From Missoula, take Highway 93 north to Highway 35 (just south of Polson), and the campground is 30 miles north on the right.

Contact: Outback Montana, Inc., 27202 E. Lakeshore, Bigfork, MT 59911; 406/837-6973 or 888/900-6973; email: outback@cyberport.net.

Trip notes: Flathead Lake is one mile away, where you can fish, boat, swim, and water-ski. Jewel Basin hiking area is close enough for a day trip.

68 Wayfarers

Location: Near Flathead Lake; map MT2, grid d4.

Campsites, facilities: There are 30 RV or tent campsites, which can accommodate a maximum RV length of 40 feet. A wheelchair-accessible restroom and a trailer boat launch are available. Pets are allowed on leashes.

Reservations, fees: No reservations are needed; the fee is $9 per night. Open May 1–September 30. The stay limit is seven days.

Directions: From Kalispell, go south on U.S. 93 for eight miles to Highway 82, east on Highway 82 seven miles to Highway 35, turn south to Bigfork. From Bigfork, go west to milepost 31, near the junction of Highways 35 and 209.

Contact: Fish, Wildlife & Parks, Wayfarers State Recreation Area, 490 N. Meridian, Kalispell, MT 59901; 406/837-4196, 406/752-5501.

Trip notes: This campground is in a forested site on a beach at the northeast shore Flathead Lake, where you can fish, swim, boat, water-ski, and hike.

69 Handkerchief Lake

 7

Location: In Flathead National Forest; map MT2, grid d6.

Campsites, facilities: There are nine RV or tent campsites, which can accommodate a maximum RV length of 22 feet.

Reservations, fees: No reservations are needed, and no fee is charged. Open June 1–September 15. The stay limit is 14 days.

Directions: From Kalispell, go north on US2 to Hungry Horse. From Hungry Horse, go 35 miles southeast on Forest Service Road 892, then two miles northwest on Forest Service Road 897 to the campground.

Contact: Flathead National Forest, 1935 3rd Ave. East, Hungry Horse, MT 59919; 406/387-3800; website: www.fs.fed.us/r1/flathead.

Trip notes: This campground is a mile from Hungry Horse Reservoir, and there are many hiking trails nearby. You can fish in Handkerchief Lake.

70 Spotted Bear

 7

Location: In Flathead National Forest; map MT2, grid d6.

Campsites, facilities: There are 13 RV or tent campsites, which can accommodate a maximum RV length of 22 feet.

Reservations, fees: No reservations are needed; no fee is charged. Open June 20–September 10. The stay limit is 14 days.

Directions: From Martin City, go 55 miles southeast on Forest Service Road 38 to the campground. Martin City is northeast of Kalispell on U.S. 2.

Contact: Flathead National Forest, 1935 3rd Ave. East, Kalispell, MT 59901; 406/758-5200, fax 406/758-5363; website: www.fs.fed.us/r1/flathead.

Trip notes: This campground is on the South Fork of the Flathead River. A nearby trail leads to the Great Bear Wilderness. This is a very remote campground.

71 Deer Lick Resort

 6

Location: On Swan Lake; map MT2, grid d5.

Campsites, facilities: There are 47 RV or tent campsites. Showers, cabins, electricity, water, and a sanitary disposal station are available.

Reservations, fees: No reservations are needed; the fee is $12–18 per night. Open May 1–October 15.

Directions: From Kalispell, go south on U.S. 93 for eight miles to Highway 82, east on Highway 82 seven miles to Highway 35, turn south to Bigfork. From Bigfork, go 15 miles east on Highway 83 to the campground.

Contact: Deer Lick Resort, P.O. Box 5158, Swan Lake, MT 59911; 406/886-2321; email:

marilynroberts@montana.com.

Trip notes: This campground is on Swan Lake, where you can boat, fish, and swim.

72 Swan Village Market & Campground

 6

Location: Near Swam Lake; map MT2, grid d5.

Campsites, facilities: There are four RV and 15 tent campsites. Showers, laundry facilities, a store, water, and electricity are available.

Reservations, fees: No reservations are needed; the fee is $12–17 per night. Open year-round, but fully operational May 1–September 30.

Directions: From Kalispell, go south on U.S. 93 for eight miles to Highway 82, east on Highway 82 seven miles to Highway 35, turn south to Bigfork. From Bigfork, go 17 miles southeast on Highway 83 to the campground.

Contact: Swan Village Market & Campground, 70712 Hwy. 83, Swan Lake, MT 59911; 406/886-2303.

Trip notes: This campground is one mile from Swan Lake, near Swan River National Wildlife Refuge. The Swan River State Forest is an old-growth coniferous forest with trees 20–50 inches in diameter, and as tall as 100–170 feet. You can boat, fish, and swim at Swan Lake.

73 Lake Mary Ronan State Park

 6

Location: On Lake Mary Ronan; map MT2, grid e3.

Campsites, facilities: There are 27 RV or tent campsites, which can accommodate a maximum RV length of 35 feet. Pets are allowed on leashes.

Reservations, fees: No reservations are needed; the fee is $12 per night. Open May 15–September 30. The stay limit is 14 days.

Directions: From Kalispell, go south on U.S.

93 to Dayton and take Lake Mary Ronan Highway seven miles northwest to the park.

Contact: Montana Fish, Wildlife & Parks, Region 1, 490 N. Meridian, Kalispell, MT 59901; 406/752-5501.

Trip notes: You can boat, swim, and fish here for trout, bass, and kokanee salmon. Fir trees shade this campground.

74 Mountain Meadows Resort & Golf Course

 5

Location: Near Lake Mary Ronan; map MT2, grid e3.

Campsites, facilities: There are 50 RV or tent campsites. Showers, a sanitary disposal facility, water, docks, and a lodge are available. Pets are allowed on leashes.

Reservations, fees: No reservations are needed; the fee is $14 and up per night. Open April 1–October 31.

Directions: From Kalispell, go south on U.S. 93 to Dayton and take Lake Mary Ronan Highway seven miles west to the campground.

Contact: Mountain Meadows Resort & Golf Course, Lake Mary Ronan, Proctor, MT 59929; 406/849-5459 or 406/849-5134; website: www.montanaweb.com/mmresort; email: mmresort@digisys.net.

Trip notes: You can boat, swim, and fish here for trout, bass, and kokanee salmon. The resort boasts the "best worst golf course in the last best place."

75 Lake Mary Ronan Lodge & Resort

 6

Location: West of Flathead Lake; map MT2, grid e3.

Campsites, facilities: There are 45 RV or tent campsites. Showers, water, electricity, a sanitary disposal facility, a restaurant, and a marina are available.

Reservations, fees: No reservations are needed; the fee is $8–18 per night. Open May 15–September 15.

Directions: From Kalispell, go south on U.S. 93 to Dayton; take the Dayton off ramp, turn right on Mary Ronan Highway and go nine miles to the campground.

Contact: Lake Mary Ronan Lodge & Resort, 2216 Lake Mary Ronan Rd., Proctor, MT 59929; 888/845-7702 or 406/849-5483; website: www.hotyellow98.com; email: lmaryron@digisys.net.

Trip notes: You can boat, swim, and fish here for trout, bass, and kokanee salmon.

76 Big Sky RV Resort & Marina

 5

Location: On Flathead Lake; map MT2, grid e4.

Campsites, facilities: There are 50 RV and 12 tent campsites. Showers, laundry facilities, a store, water, electricity, and a sanitary disposal station are available. A boat launch, boat slips, restaurant, and miniature golf are on-site.

Reservations, fees: Reservations are suggested; the fee is $15–17.50 per night. Open year-round.

Directions: From Kalispell, go south on U.S. 93 about 18 miles to Rollins. From Rollins, go one mile south on U.S. 93 to the campground. This campground is 25 miles north of Polson, and 25 miles south of Kalispell on the west shore of Flathead Lake.

Contact: Big Sky RV Resort & Marina, Hwy. 93 South, Rollins, MT 59931; 406/844-3501, 888/841-5324.

Trip notes: You can fish, boat, and swim on Flathead Lake, and hike interpretive trails nearby.

77 Camp Tuffit

 6

Location: On Lake Mary Ronan; map MT2, grid e4.

Campsites, facilities: There are 25 RV and 10 tent campsites. There are showers, laundry facilities, a store, water, electricity, restaurant, and boat rentals available.

Reservations, fees: Reservations are required; the fee is $12–19 per night. Open May 15–September 30.

Directions: From Polson, go north on U.S. 93 for about 22 miles to Dayton. From Dayton, go five miles west off U.S. 93 to the campground, follow signs.

Contact: Camp Tuffit, Lake Mary Ronan, P.O. Box 196, Proctor, MT 59929; 406/849-5220.

Trip notes: This campground is on the shore of Lake Mary Ronan, and Flathead Lake is to the east. You can fish, boat, and swim on Flathead Lake, and hike interpretive trails nearby.

78 Swan Lake

 6

Location: In Flathead National Forest; map MT2, grid e5.

Campsites, facilities: There are 42 RV or tent campsites, which can accommodate a maximum RV length of 55 feet. A wheelchair-accessible restroom is available. There are facilities for groups, but reservations are needed.

Reservations, fees: No reservations are needed for individuals, but reservations are required for groups (call 406/837-3577). The stay limit is 14 days. The fee is $10 per night. Open May 15–September 30. The stay limit is 14 days.

Directions: From Polson, go north on Highway 35 for 33 miles to Bigfork, then go east five miles on Highway 209 to Highway 83 (there is a Swan Lake sign). Turn right on Highway 83 and go 11 miles. There will be a campground sign; turn left to campground.

Contact: Flathead National Forest, Swan Lake Ranger District, 200 Ranger Station Rd., Big Fork, MT 59911; 406/837-7500; website: www.fs.fed.us/r1/flathead.

Trip notes: On Swan Lake you can fish and

boat. The Swan River National Wildlife Refuge is to the south.

79 Arrowhead Resort

 6

Location: On Flathead Lake; map MT2, grid e3.

Campsites, facilities: There are 45 RV or tent campsites. Showers, water, electricity, and boat ramps and slips are available.

Reservations, fees: No reservations are needed; the fee is $13–19.50 per night. Open May 1–September 30.

Directions: From Polson, go northwest on U.S. 93 to Elmo, and then at the junction of Highway 28 and U.S. 93 go one mile south to the campground on left. This campground lies along the highway and lake.

Contact: Arrowhead Resort, P.O. Box 118, Elmo, MT 59915; tel./fax 406/849-5545.

Trip notes: You can boat, fish, swim, water-ski, and canoe on Flathead Lake.

80 Big Arm

 6

Location: In Flathead State Park; map MT2, grid e3.

Campsites, facilities: There are 52 RV or tent campsites, which can accommodate a maximum RV length of 40 feet. Grills, picnic tables, water, a trailer boat launch, and seasonal interpretive programs are available.

Reservations, fees: No reservations are needed; the fee is $12 per night. Open May 1–September 30. The stay limit is seven days.

Directions: From Polson, go 15 miles north on U.S. 93; from Kalispell, go south on U.S. 93 to the campground.

Contact: Department of Fish, Wildlife & Parks, 490 N. Meridian Rd., Kalispell, MT 59901; 406/849-5255; website: www.fs.fed.us/r1/flathead.

Trip notes: Wild Horse Island, a 2,163-acre wilderness area on the west shore of the lake, is home to bald eagles, bighorn sheep, and wild horses. Polson has a golf course. You can fish, boat, swim, water-ski, and hike at Flathead Lake.

81 Big Arm Resort & Marina

 6

Location: On Flathead Lake; map MT2, grid e3.

Campsites, facilities: There are 12 RV campsites. Hookups, water, boat slips, rental boats, dock fishing, and swimming are available.

Reservations, fees: Reservations are suggested; the fee is $20 per night. Open May 1–September 1.

Directions: From Polson, go 12 miles north on U.S. 93 to the marina.

Contact: Big Arm Resort & Marina, P.O. Box 99, Big Arm, MT 59910; 406/849-5622.

Trip notes: You can fish, boat, and swim on Flathead Lake and hike interpretive trails nearby. This is a popular departure point for tours of Wild Horse Island, one of the largest inland islands in the United States. The hilly terrain is home to herds of bighorn sheep, deer, and wild horses. Bald eagles and osprey frequent the area. You can fish, swim, boat, and water-ski on Flathead Lake.

82 Snowberg Port & Court

 5

Location: Near Flathead Lake; map MT2, grid f4.

Campsites, facilities: There are 14 RV campsites. Showers, water, electricity, boat dock spaces, and pedal boat rentals are available.

Reservations, fees: No reservations are needed; the fee is $17.50–22 per night. Open May 30–October 1.

Directions: From Polson, go 11.5 miles north on U.S. 93.

Contact: Snowberg Port & Court, P.O. Box 38, Big Arm, MT 59910; 406/849-5838, or 406/849-5754.

Trip notes: Flathead Lake is nearby, where you can fish, boat, swim, water-ski, and hike interpretive trails.

83 Yellow Bay

 7

Location: At Flathead Lake; map MT2, grid f4.

Campsites, facilities: There are four tent campsites, grills, picnic tables, water, and a trailer boat launch. Pets are allowed on leashes.

Reservations, fees: No reservations are needed; no fee is charged. Open May 1–September 30 for overnight camping; day-use-only from October 1–April 30. The stay limit is seven days.

Directions: From Polson, go 15 miles north on Highway 35 to milepost 17 and the campground.

Contact: Department of Fish, Wildlife & Parks, 490 N. Meridian Rd., Kalispell, MT 59901; 406/752-5501, fax 406/257-0349; website: www.fs.fed.us/r1/flathead.

Trip notes: This campground is in the cherry orchard region. There is a gravelly beach and several interpretive trails. You can fish, boat, swim, water-ski, and hike at Flathead Lake. A joint state/tribal fishing license is required to fish. Polson has a golf course.

84 Polson/Flathead Lake KOA

 5

Location: Near Flathead Lake; map MT2, grid f4.

Campsites, facilities: There are 80 RV or tent campsites, some with pull-through sites. Showers, laundry facilities, a store, water, electricity, a sanitary disposal facility, a swimming pool, and a spa are available.

Reservations, fees: No reservations are needed; the fee is $15–25 per night. Open April 17–October 17.

Directions: From Polson, go one mile north on U.S. 93.

Contact: Polson/Flathead Lake KOA, 200 Irvine Flats Rd., Polson, MT 59860; 406/883-2151, 800/562-2130, fax 406/883-0151.

Trip notes: Flathead Lake is nearby, where

you can fish, boat, swim, water-ski, and hike interpretive trails.

85 Eagle Nest RV Resort

 5

Location: Near Flathead Lake; map MT2, grid f4.

Campsites, facilities: There are 60 RV or tent campsites. Showers, laundry facilities, a store, cable, electricity, water, swimming pool, and spa are available.

Reservations, fees: No reservations are needed; the fee is $10 and up per night. Open April 15–October 1.

Directions: From Polson, go east to the junction of Highway 35 and U.S. 93; the RV resort is a quarter of a mile east on Highway 35.

Contact: Eagle Nest RV Resort, 259 Eagle Nest Dr., Hwy. 35, Polson, MT 59860; 406/833-5904; email: eaglerv@cyberport.net; website: www.polsonchamber.com/eaglerv.

Trip notes: Flathead Lake is nearby, where you can fish, boat, swim, water-ski, and hike interpretive trails.

86 Rocking C Ranch

 5

Location: Near Flathead Lake; map MT2, grid f4.

Campsites, facilities: There are 85 RV or tent campsites. Showers, laundry facilities, a store, water, electricity, and a sanitary disposal station are available. A restaurant, casino, lounge, outdoor stage, and miniature golf course are on-site. Pets are allowed on leashes.

Reservations, fees: No reservations are needed; the fee is $12.48–18.72 per night. Open year-round.

Directions: From Polson, go seven miles north on Highway 35 to mile marker 7 and the ranch.

Contact: Rocking C Ranch, 6913 E. Shore Route, Polson, MT 59860; 406/887-2537, fax 406/887-2386; email: rockcbp@digisys.net; website: www.clubmontana.com.

Trip notes: Flathead Lake is nearby, where you can fish, boat, swim, water-ski, and hike interpretive trails.

87 Finley Point

 7

Location: In Flathead Lake State Park; map MT2, grid f4.

Campsites, facilities: There are 16 RV and four tent campsites, which can accommodate a maximum RV length of 40 feet. Grills, picnic tables, a boat launch, wheelchair-accessible restrooms, and water are available. Pets are allowed on leashes.

Reservations, fees: No reservations are needed; the fee is $15 per night. Open May 1–September 30. The stay limit is seven days.

Directions: From Polson, go 11 miles north on Highway 35; then go four miles west on the county road to the campground.

Contact: Flathead Lake State Park, 490 N. Meridian Rd., Kalispell, MT 59901; 406/887-2715; website: www.fs.fed.us/r1/flathead.

Trip notes: This campground is in a secluded forest site near the south end of Flathead Lake, where you can fish, boat, swim, and water-ski. A joint state/tribal license is required to fish.

88 Mission Meadow Campground

 5

Location: Near Flathead Lake; map MT2, grid f4.

Campsites, facilities: There are 50 RV and 50 tent campsites. Showers, laundry facilities, a store, water, electricity, and a sanitary disposal station are available. A swimming pool, horseshoes, fire pits, and hot tub are on-site.

Reservations, fees: Reservations are recommended; the fee is $12 per night. Open April 1–October 30.

Directions: From Missoula, go north on U.S. 93 to Ronan. Continue three miles north on U.S. 93, then take a left and go about a half-

mile on county paved road to the campground.
Contact: Mission Meadow Campground, Mission Meadow Dr., P.O. Box 298, Ronan, MT 59864; 406/676-5182

Trip notes: You can fish here in the pond. Flathead Lake is ten miles to the north, and you can fish, boat, swim, water-ski, and hike interpretive trails nearby.

89 Diamond 'S' RV Park

 5

Location: Near Flathead Lake; map MT2, grid f4.

Campsites, facilities: There are 33 RV or tent campsites, 22 of them pull-through sites and some with full hookups. Showers, laundry facilities, restrooms, picnic tables, water, electricity, and a sanitary disposal facility are available. Tepees can be rented, and tours of the working ranch can be arranged.

Reservations, fees: No reservations are needed; the fee is $12–19 per night. Open April 1–November 1.

Directions: From Missoula, go north on U.S. 93 to Ronan. From Ronan city center, go .5 mile north on Highway 93 to the campground.

Contact: Diamond 'S' RV Park, P.O. Box 792, Ronan, MT 59864; 406/676-3641.

Trip notes: This campground is centrally located near Flathead Lake, the Bison Range, and Glacier Park. You can fish, boat, and swim on Flathead Lake, and hike interpretive trails nearby.

90 Crossroads Motel & RV Park

 4

Location: In Plains; map MT2, grid g1.

Campsites, facilities: There are 50 RV or tent campsites. There are showers, water, electricity, and a sanitary disposal facility available.

Reservations, fees: No reservations are needed; the fee is $15–18 per night Open year-round.

Directions: From Plains, this campground is on the east side on Highway 200.

Contact: Crossroads Motel & RV Park, 401 RR East, Plains, MT 59859; 406/826-3623.

Trip notes: A swimming pool and restaurant are nearby.

91 Holland Lake

 7

Location: In Flathead National Forest; map MT2, grid g6.

Campsites, facilities: There are 40 RV or tent campsites, which can accommodate a maximum RV length of 22 feet. A trailer boat is available. Pets are allowed on leashes.

Reservations, fees: Reservations area accepted; the fee is $10 per night. Open May 15–October 1. The stay limit is 14 days.

Directions: From Missoula, go east on I-90 for six miles to Highway 200. Go east on Highway 200 33 miles to Highway 83, go north on Highway 83 about 30 miles to Holland Lake, then three miles east on Forest Service Road 44 (Holland Lake Road) to the campground.

Contact: Flathead National Forest, Swan Lake Ranger District, 200 Ranger Station Rd., Big Fork, MT 59911; 406/837-7500 or 406/837-3577 (for group site reservations); website: www.fs.fed.us/r1/flathead.

Trip notes: You can swim, boat, and fish at Holland Lake, and there are access trails into the Bob Marshall Wilderness.

92 Willow Creek Campground

 3

Location: North of Charlo; map MT2, grid g4.

Campsites, facilities: There are 10 RV or tent campsites. Restrooms and water are available.

Reservations, fees: Reservations strongly suggested; the fee is $12 per night. Open May 15–September 20.

Directions: From Missoula, go west on I-90 six miles to U.S. 93, then north on U.S. 93 to County Road 212, and then go two miles west to the campground.

Contact: Willow Creek Campground, 14954 Hwy. 212, Charlo, MT 59824; 406/644-2356.

Trip notes: This campground has lawns, a creek, and weeping willows. The National Bison Range is to the south; Ninepipe National Wildlife Refuge is a wetlands waterfowl refuge east of Charlo. You can fish near here, but because this is on the Flathead Indian Reservation, you need to check locally for permits and restrictions.

93 Cascade

     5

Location: In Lolo National Forest; map MT2, grid g1.

Campsites, facilities: There are 10 RV or tent campsites, which can accommodate a maximum RV length of 22 feet. A wheelchair-accessible restroom and hand boat launch are available.

Reservations, fees: No reservations are needed; the fee is $6 per night. Open May 15–October 31.

Directions: From Thompson Falls, go south on Highway 200 for 32 miles to Paradise. From Paradise, go nine miles south to the campground.

Contact: Lolo National Forest, Building 24A, Fort Missoula, Missoula, MT 59802; 406/329-3814.

Trip notes: You can boat, fish and hike in the Lolo National Forest.

94 Hostel of the Rockies at St. Ignatius Camping

   5

Location: On the Flathead Indian Reservation; map MT2, grid g4.

Campsites, facilities: There are 37 RV or tent campsites. Showers, laundry facilities, water, and electricity are available.

Reservations, fees: No reservations are needed; the fee is $12.48–20.80 per night. Group rates are available. Open April 1–November 1.

Directions: From Missoula, go north on U.S. 93 for about 32 miles to St. Ignatius. From St. Ignatius, go north to the corner of U.S. 93 and Airport Road; the campground is on the northeast corner.

Contact: Hostel of the Rockies at St. Ignatius Camping, 33076 Hwy. 9, St. Ignatius, MT 59865; 406/745-3959; website: www.tenting-hostels .com.

Trip notes: This campground is near the National Bison Range, St. Marys Lake, and many other lakes. Because this is on the Flathead Indian Reservation, you need to check locally for permits and restrictions.

95 Ravalli Store

   5

Location: In Ravalli; map MT2, grid g4.

Campsites, facilities: There are 15 RV or tent campsites, some with hookups. Showers, laundry facilities, and a store are available.

Reservations, fees: No reservations are needed; the fee is $6–17 per night. Open year-round.

Directions: From Missoula, go north on U.S. 93 to the junction of Highway 200 and U.S. 93, go .5 mile south, and the campground is on the left.

Contact: Ravalli Store, 205 Buffalo St., P.O. Box 630223, Ravalli, MT 59863; 406/745-4554 or fax 406/745-4658; email: sti4658@montana.com.

Trip notes: This campground is near a restaurant, and the National Bison Range, rivers, and fishing areas are nearby.

96 Lake Alva

     6

Location: Near Seeley Lake; map MT2, grid g6.

Campsites, facilities: There are 43 RV or tent campsites, which can accommodate a maximum RV length of 22 feet. A wheelchair-accessible restroom and trailer boat launch are available, but no hookups.

Reservations, fees: No reservations are needed; the fee is $8 per night. Open May 24–September 1. The stay limit is 14 days.

Directions: From Missoula, go east six miles on I-90 to Highway 200, then northeast 33 miles to Highway 83, then north 15 miles on Highway 83 to Seeley Lake. From Seeley Lake, go 12 miles north on Highway 83 to the campground.

Contact: Lolo National Forest, Seeley Lake Ranger District, Hwy. 83, HC 31, Box 3200, Seeley Lake, MT 59868; 406/677-2233, fax 406/677-2073; website: www.fs.fed.us/r1/lolo.

Trip notes: You can boat, fish, swim, and hike in Lolo National Forest.

97 Big Larch

 6

Location: In Lolo National Forest; map MT2, grid h7.

Campsites, facilities: There are 50 RV or tent campsites, which can accommodate a maximum RV length of 32 feet. Wheelchair-accessible restrooms and a trailer boat launch are available.

Reservations, fees: No reservations are needed; the fee is $8 per night. Open May 24–September 1. The stay limit is 14 days.

Directions: From Missoula, go east six miles on I-90 to Highway 200, then northeast 33 miles to Highway 83, then north 15 miles on Highway 83 to Seeley Lake. From Seeley Lake, go one mile north on Highway 83, then .5 east on Forest Service Road 2199 to the campground.

Contact: Lolo National Forest, Seeley Lake Ranger District, Hwy. 83, HC 31, Box 3200, Seeley Lake, MT 59868; 406/677-2233, fax 406/677-2073; website: www.fs.fed.us/r1/lolo.

Trip notes: You can boat, fish, swim, and hike in Lolo National Forest.

98 River Point

 5

Location: In Lolo National Forest; map MT2, grid h7.

Campsites, facilities: There are 27 RV or tent campsites, which can accommodate a maximum RV length of 22 feet. A wheelchair-accessible restroom is available.

Reservations, fees: No reservations are needed; the fee is $8 per night. Open May 24–September 1. The stay limit is 14 days.

Directions: From Missoula, go east six miles on I-90 to Highway 200, then northeast 33 miles to Highway 83, then north 15 miles on Highway 83 to Seeley Lake. From Seeley Lake, go .3 mile south on Highway 83, then 2.2 miles northwest on Boy Scout Road and campground.

Contact: Lolo National Forest, Seeley Lake Ranger District, Hwy. 83, HC 31, Box 3200, Seeley Lake, MT 59868; 406/677-2233, fax 406/677-2073; website: www.fs.fed.us/r1/lolo.

Trip notes: You can boat, fish, and swim at Seeley Lake and hike in Lolo National Forest.

99 Seeley Lake

 6

Location: In Lolo National Forest; map MT2, grid h6.

Campsites, facilities: There are 29 RV or tent campsites, which can accommodate a maximum RV length of 32 feet. A wheelchair-accessible restroom and hand boat launch are available.

Reservations, fees: No reservations are needed; the fee is $9 per night. Open May 24–September 1. The stay limit is 14 days.

Directions: From Missoula, go east six miles on I-90 to Highway 200, then northeast 33 miles to Highway 83, then north 15 miles on Highway 83 to Seeley Lake. From Seeley Lake, go .3 mile south on Highway 83, then 3.3 miles northwest on Boy Scout Road to the lake.

Contact: Lolo National Forest, Seeley Lake

Ranger District, Hwy. 83, HC 31, Box 3200, See-ley Lake, MT 59868; 406/677-2233, fax 406/677-2073; website: www.fs.fed.us/r1/lolo.

Trip notes: You can boat, fish, and swim at Seeley Lake and hike in Lolo National Forest.

100 Jocko Hollow Campground

    6

Location: In Arlee; map MT2, grid h7.

Campsites, facilities: There are 16 RV or tent campsites. Showers, laundry facilities, a store, electricity, a sanitary disposal facility, and a playground are available.

Reservations, fees: No reservations are needed; the fee is $12–15 per night. Open May 1–October 1.

Directions: From Missoula, go west eight miles on I-90 to Exit 96 (U.S. 93) and go north for 19 miles, and then go one mile north of Arlee to the campground, which is on the right; watch for signs.

Contact: Jocko Hollow Campground, P.O. Box 645, Arlee, MT 59821; 406/726-3336, fax 406/726-3334.

Trip notes: There are five private fishing ponds here.

101 Trout Creek

   6

Location: In Lolo National Forest; map MT2, grid h1.

Campsites, facilities: There are 12 RV or tent campsites, which can accommodate a maximum RV length of 30 feet.

Reservations, fees: No reservations are needed; there is no fee. Open May 23–September 6. The stay limit is 14 days.

Directions: From Superior, go seven miles southeast on Forest Service Road 269, then three miles southwest on Forest Service Road 250 to the campground.

Contact: Lolo National Forest, Building 24A, Fort Missoula, Missoula, MT 59802; 406/329-3814.

Trip notes: You can fish in the Clark Fork River for brown, bull, cutthroat, and rainbow trout, whitefish, and bass.

102 Quartz Flat

    4

Location: In Lolo National Forest; map MT2, grid h2.

Campsites, facilities: There are 52 RV or tent campsites, which can accommodate a maximum RV length of 32 feet. A wheelchair-accessible restroom is available.

Reservations, fees: No reservations are needed; the fee is $12 per night. Open May 23–September 6. The stay limit is 14 days.

Directions: From Superior, go 11 miles east on I-90; the campground is near the I-90 rest area.

Contact: Lolo National Forest, Building 24A, Fort Missoula, Missoula, MT 59802; 406/329-3814.

Trip notes: You can fish in the Clark Fork River for here brown, bull, cutthroat, and rainbow trout, whitefish, and bass.

103 Placid Lake State Park

     5

Location: Southwest of Seeley Lake; map MT2, grid h6.

Campsites, facilities: There are 40 RV or tent campsites, which can accommodate a maximum RV length of 25 feet. Some sites have picnic tables and grills. A wheelchair-accessible restroom, water, and trailer boat launch are available.

Reservations, fees: No reservations are needed; the fee is $12 per night. Open May 1–September 30. The stay limit is 14 days.

Directions: From Missoula, go east six miles on I-90 to Highway 200, then northeast 33 miles to Highway 83, then north 15 miles on Highway 83 to Seeley Lake. From Seeley Lake, go three miles south on Highway 83, then three miles west on Placid Lake Road (Forest Ser-

vice Road 349) to the park, which is on the left.
Contact: Fish, Wildlife & Parks, 3201 Spurgin Rd., Missoula, MT 59802; 406/542-5500.

Trip notes: You can boat, fish, and swim here. There are interpretive displays depicting early logging in the area. Seeley Lake has a golf course.

104 Salmon Lake State Park

 7

Location: Near Seeley Lake; map MT2, grid h8.
Campsites, facilities: There are 25 RV campsites, which can accommodate a maximum RV length of 25 feet. Some sites have picnic tables and grills. A wheelchair-accessible restroom and trailer boat launch are available.

Reservations, fees: No reservations are needed; the fee is $10 per night. Open May 1–November 30. The stay limit is 14 days.

Directions: From Missoula, go east six miles on I-90 to Highway 200, then northeast 33 miles to Highway 83, then north 15 miles on Highway 83 to Seeley Lake. From Seeley Lake, go five miles on Highway 83 to the state park. There are signs on the right.

Contact: Fish, Wildlife & Parks, 3201 Spurgin Rd., Missoula, MT 59802; 406/542-5500.

Trip notes: You can boat, fish, hike, water-ski, and swim here, surrounded by pine trees. A golf course is at Seeley Lake.

105 Russell Gates Memorial

 6

Location: On Blackfoot River; map MT2, grid h8.

Campsites, facilities: There are 12 RV campsites, which can accommodate a maximum RV length of 20 feet. A wheelchair-accessible restroom and hand boat launch are available. Pets are allowed on leashes.

Reservations, fees: No reservations are needed; the fee is $4–10 per night. Open year-round. The stay limit is seven days.

Directions: From Missoula, go east six miles on I-90 to Highway 200, then east on Highway 200 to Bonner. From Bonner, go 35 miles east on Highway 200 to milepost 35; the campground is on the right.

Contact: Fish, Wildlife & Parks, 3201 Spurgin Rd., Missoula, MT 59802; 406/542-5500.

Trip notes: You can boat and fish on the Blackfoot River.

106 Big Pine

 6

Location: In Lolo National Forest; map MT2, grid h2.

Campsites, facilities: There are 10 RV or tent campsites.

Reservations, fees: No reservations are needed; no fee is charged. Open year-round. The stay limit is seven days.

Directions: From Superior, go 18 miles east on I-90 to Fish Creek exit, then five miles southwest on Fish Creek Road to the campground.

Contact: Montana Fish, Wildlife & Parks, Region 2, Missoula, MT 59802; 406/542-5500.

Trip notes: You can fish for brook, brown, cutthroat, and rainbow trout and mountain whitefish.

Aspen grove

MAP MT3

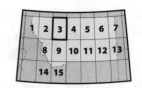

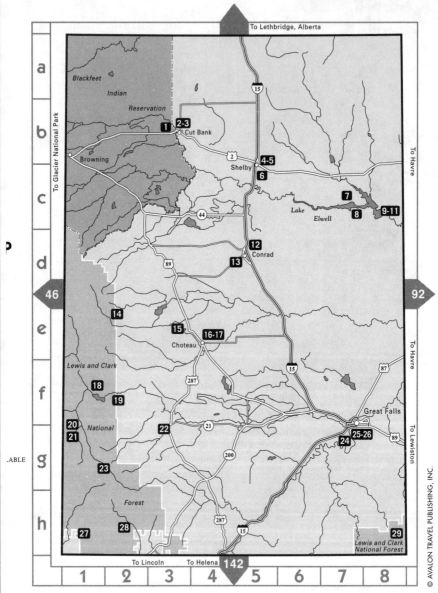

To Lethbridge, Alberta

a
Blackfeet
Indian
Reservation

To Glacier National Park

b
1
2-3
Cut Bank
Browning
2
Shelby
4-5
6

c
44
7
Lake
Elwell
8
9-11

To Havre

d
89
12
Conrad
13

46
92

e
14
15
16-17
Choteau

To Havre

f
Lewis and Clark
18
19
287
15
87

To Lewiston

g
20
21
National
22
21
200
24
25-26
89
Great Falls
23

To Lewiston

h
Forest
27
28
287
15
29
Lewis and Clark
National Forest

To Lincoln   To Helena   142

1   2   3   4   5   6   7   8

© AVALON TRAVEL PUBLISHING, INC.

CHAPTER MT3

1 Shady Grove Campground..81
2 Gary Smith Memorial........81
3 Riverview Campground 81
4 Lake Shel-oole
  Campground...................82
5 Lewis & Clark RV Park 82
6 Williamson Park
  Campground...................82
7 North Bootlegger.............82
8 South Bootlegger............83
9 Willow Creek..................83
10 Island Area 83
11 VFW Campground 83
12 Sunrise Trailer Court........84
13 Pondera RV Park 84
14 West Fork........................84
15 Cave Mountain.................84

16 Choteau KOA....................84
17 Choteau Park
  & Campground 85
18 Mortimer Gulch...............85
19 Home Gulch 85
20 Benchmark 86
21 South Fork......................86
22 Wagons West...................86
23 Wood Lake 87
24 Dick's RV Park 87
25 L'n Eve Travel Trailer Park ..87
26 Great Falls KOA
  Campground....................88
27 Big Nelson 88
28 Cooper Creek..................88
29 Logging Creek 88

1 Shady Grove Campground

    3

Location: On the Blackfeet Indian Reservation; map MT3, grid b3.
Campsites, facilities: There are 30 RV or tent campsites. Showers, water, electricity, a horseshoe pit, and playground are available.
Reservations, fees: No reservations are needed; the fee is $16 per night.
Directions: From Cut Bank, go six miles west on U.S. 2 to the campground.
Contact: Shady Grove Campground, P.O. Box 691, Cut Bank, MT 59427; tel./fax 406/336-2475.
Trip notes: Fishing is only four miles away.

2 Gary Smith Memorial

    3

Location: In Cut Bank; map MT3, grid b3.
Campsites, facilities: There are five RV or tent campsites, which can accommodate a maximum RV length of 30 feet.
Reservations, fees: No reservations are needed; no fee is charged. Open May 1–October 1.
Directions: From U.S. 2, take the Cut Bank exit; the campground is on 5th Avenue Northwest.
Contact: Gary Smith Memorial, Cut Bank Area Chamber of Commerce, 715 E. Main St, Cut Bank, MT 59427; 406/873-4041
Trip notes: You can fish on the Marias River.

3 Riverview Campground

   3

Location: In Cut Bank; map MT3, grid b3.
Campsites, facilities: There are 45 RV or tent campsites. Laundry facilities, showers, a spa, a store, water, electricity, and a sanitary disposal facility are available.
Reservations, fees: No reservations are needed; the fee is $11–14 per night. Open May 1–October 3.
Directions: From U.S. 2, take the Cut Bank exit; the campground is at the end of 4th Avenue Southwest.

Contact: Riverview Campground, P.O. Box 1235, Cut Bank, MT 59427; 406/873-4151, fax 406/873-5546.

Trip notes: You can fish on the Marias River.

4 Lake Shel-oole Campground

 4

Location: In Shelby; map MT3, grid b5.

Campsites, facilities: There are 56 RV or tent campgrounds. Showers, water, electricity, and a sanitary disposal facility are available. Picnic tables and grills are provided.

Reservations, fees: No reservations are needed; the fee is $7–12 per night. Open May 1–September 30.

Directions: From I-15, take the Shelby business loop (exit 364) north for half a mile. Take a right and the campground is 1.5 miles ahead on the left.

Contact: Lake Shel-oole Campground, City of Shelby, P.O. Box 743, Shelby, MT 59474; 406/434-5222.

Trip notes: An 18-hole golf course is nearby, and you can enjoy fly-fishing and hiking around the Tiber Dam.

5 Lewis & Clark RV Park

 4

Location: In Shelby; map MT3, grid b5.

Campsites, facilities: There are 65 RV or tent campsites. Showers, laundry facilities, a store, water, electricity, and a sanitary disposal facility are available.

Reservations, fees: No reservations are needed; the fee is $18.72–22.88 per night. Open May 1–September 30.

Directions: From I-15 at Shelby, take Exit 364 and go .25 mile south to the campground on the right.

Contact: Lewis & Clark RV Park, P.O. Box 369, Shelby, MT 59747; 406/434-2710, 888/434-2710.

Trip notes: There is an 18-hole golf course nearby. Tiber Dam and Lake Elwell are east of Shelby, with 50 miles of shoreline, and you can

boat, swim, and fish for walleye, northern and sauger pike, native trout, ling, and perch. Tiber has sandstone formations and Indian rings and one of the largest earthen dikes in the world, which is over three miles long.

6 Williamson Park Campground

 4

Location: In Shelby; map MT3, grid c5.

Campsites, facilities: There are 25 RV or tent campsites. Picnic tables, a playground, horseshoe pits, and water are available.

Reservations, fees: No reservations are needed; the fee is $8 per night. Open May 1–September 30.

Directions: From I-15 at Shelby, take Exit 358 and drive seven miles south on Frontage Road to the campground.

Contact: Williamson Park Campground, City of Shelby, P.O. Box 743, Shelby, MT 59474; 406/434-5222.

Trip notes: This campground is on the Marias River, popular for floating, but for information on river levels and water variations, call Shelby City Hall, 406/434-5222. The Marias Valley Golf and County Club has an 18-hole course, and you can hike in the Sweetgrass Hills outside of Sunburst.

7 North Bootlegger

 4

Location: South of Chester; map MT3, grid c7.

Campsites, facilities: There are RV and tent campsites, wheelchair-accessible restrooms, and a trailer boat ramp.

Reservations, fees: No reservations are needed; no fee is charged. Open year-round. The stay limit is 14 days.

Directions: From U.S. 2, go 12 miles south at Chester on County Road 223, then seven miles west on the county road to the campground.

Contact: U.S. Bureau of Reclamation, P.O. Box 220, Chester, MT 59522; 406/247-7313,

406/456-3228, fax 406/456-3238.

Trip notes: There is a public marina here, and you can fish.

8 South Bootlegger

  4

Location: South of Chester; map MT3, grid c7.

Campsites, facilities: There are campsites, wheelchair-accessible restrooms, and a trailer boat ramp.

Reservations, fees: No reservations are needed, and no fee is charged. Open year-round. The stay limit is 14 days.

Directions: From U.S. 2, go 12 miles south at Chester on County Road 223, then seven miles west on the county road to the campground.

Contact: U.S. Bureau of Reclamation, P.O. Box 220, Chester, MT 59522; 406/247-7313, 406/456-3228, fax 406/456-3238.

Trip notes: There is a public marina here, and you can fish.

9 Willow Creek

  3

Location: At Lake Elwell; map MT3, grid c8.

Campsites, facilities: There are five RV or tent campsites, a wheelchair-accessible restroom, and a trailer boat ramp.

Reservations, fees: No reservations are needed; there is no fee. Open year-round. The stay limit is 14 days.

Directions: From Chester, go 12 miles south on Route 223, then seven miles west on the county road to the campground.

Contact: U.S. Bureau of Reclamation, P.O. Box 220, Chester, MT 59527; 406/247-7313, 406/456-3228, fax 406/456-3238.

Trip notes: Major game fish in Lake Elwell (or Tiber Reservoir) include northern pike, walleye, and rainbow trout. You can swim and boat here.

10 Island Area

 3

Location: Southwest of Chester; map MT3, grid c8.

Campsites, facilities: There are campsites, wheelchair-accessible restrooms, and a trailer boat ramp.

Reservations, fees: No reservations are needed; there is no fee. Open year-round. The stay limit is 14 days.

Directions: From Chester, go 12 miles south on Route 223, and seven miles west on the county road to the campground.

Contact: U.S. Bureau of Reclamation, P.O. Box 220, Chester, MT 59527; 406/247-7313, 406/456-3228, fax 406/456-3238.

Trip notes: Major game fish in Lake Elwell (or Tiber Reservoir) include northern pike, walleye, and rainbow trout. You can swim and boat here.

11 VFW Campground

 3

Location: Southwest of Chester; map MT3, grid c8.

Campsites, facilities: There are six RV or tent campsites, a wheelchair- accessible restroom, and trailer boat ramp.

Reservations, fees: No reservations are needed; there is no fee. Open year-round. The stay limit is 14 days.

Directions: From Chester, go 12 miles south on Route 223, then seven miles west on the county road to the campground.

Contact: U.S. Bureau of Reclamation, P.O. Box 220, Chester, MT 59527; 406/247-7313, 406/456-3228, fax 406/456-3238.

Trip notes: Major game fish in Lake Elwell (or Tiber Reservoir) include northern pike, walleye, and rainbow trout. You can swim and boat here.

12 Sunrise Trailer Court

 3

Location: In Conrad; map MT3, grid d5.

Campsites, facilities: There are 20 RV or tent campsites. Water, electricity, and a sanitary disposal facility are available.

Reservations, fees: No reservations are needed; the fee is $10 per night. Open year-round.

Directions: From Conrad city center, go 3.5 blocks east of the stoplight to the campground.

Contact: Sunrise Trailer Court, 309 S. Minnesota, Conrad, MT 59425; 406/278-5901.

Trip notes: Lake Valier is northwest of Conrad, and you can boat, water-ski, windsurf, or fish for walleye, northern pike, and perch.

13 Pondera RV Park

 3

Location: In Conrad; map MT3, grid d5.

Campsites, facilities: There are 55 RV or tent campsites. Showers, laundry facilities, water, electricity, a swimming pool, playground, and sanitary disposal station are available.

Reservations, fees: No reservations are needed; the fee is $10–19 per night. Open year-round.

Directions: From I-15 at Conrad, take Exit 339, go south on Main Street, right on 7th Street, and left at the alley before Maryland to the campground.

Contact: Pondera RV Park, 510 S. Maryland, Conrad, MT 59425; 406/949-3090, fax 406/278-7644; website: www.conradrv.com.

Trip notes: There is a nine-hole golf course at the Pondera Golf Club, and a park, pool, playground, stores, and a restaurant are all within one block.

14 West Fork

 5

Location: In Lewis and Clark National Forest; map MT3, grid e2.

Campsites, facilities: There are RV and tent campsites, with a toilet and water available.

Reservations, fees: No reservations are needed; no fee is charged. Open May 1–September 1. The stay limit is 14 days.

Directions: From Choteau, go six miles north on U.S. 89, then 33 miles northwest on County Road 144 (wilderness access) to the campground.

Contact: Lewis and Clark National Forest, Rocky Mountain Ranger District, 1102 N. Main Ave., Choteau, MT 59422; 406/466-5341.

Trip notes: You can fish and hike here.

15 Cave Mountain

 5

Location: In Lewis and Clark National Forest; map MT3, grid e3.

Campsites, facilities: There are 14 RV or tent campsites, which can accommodate a maximum RV length of 22 feet. A boat launch and water are available.

Reservations, fees: No reservations are needed; the fee is $5 per night. Open May 1–October 1. The stay limit is 14 days.

Directions: From Choteau, go five miles north on U.S. 89, then 23 miles west on Forest Service Road 144 (wilderness access) to the campground.

Contact: Lewis and Clark National Forest, Rocky Mountain Ranger District, 1102 N. Main Ave., Choteau, MT 59422; 406/466-5341.

Trip notes: Lake Elwell is behind Tiber Dam four miles to the northeast, Lake Frances is 30 miles to the northwest. A nine-hole golf course is nearby in Choteau.

16 Choteau KOA

 5

Location: In Choteau; map MT3, grid e4.

Campsites, facilities: There are 75 RV or tent campsites. Laundry facilities, showers, a store, a sanitary disposal facility, electricity, and water are available. Dinosaur digs are nearby.

Reservations, fees: No reservations are needed; the fee is $12–25 per night. Open April 15–October 15.

Directions: From Choteau, go .75 mile east on County Road 221 to the campground.

Contact: Choteau KOA Kampground, Rt. 2, Box 87 KOA, Choteau, MT 59422; 406/466-2615, 800/562-4156, fax 406/466-5635.

Trip notes: Eureka Reservoir, where you can fish, swim, boat, and water-ski, is northwest of Choteau. A nine-hole golf course is nearby, and the Rocky Mountain Front and Bob Marshall Wilderness is a one-hour drive to the west.

⁍ Choteau Park & Campground

   4

Location: In Choteau; map MT3, grid e4.

Campsites, facilities: There are 60 RV and tent campsites. Water and a sanitary disposal facility are available.

Reservations, fees: No reservations are needed; the fee is $5 per night. Open May 1– September 1.

Directions: From Great Falls, go 52 miles northwest on U.S. 89, turn off 89 at the blinking light, and follow the road to the park and campground.

Contact: Choteau Park & Campground, City of Choteau, P.O. Box 619, Choteau, MT 59422; 406/466-2510, fax 406/466-2531.

Trip notes: Egg Mountain, where the first dinosaur egg sites in the western hemisphere were discovered, is west of Choteau. There is a nine-hole golf course nearby, as well as a park, playground, and swimming pool.

⁍ Mortimer Gulch

       6

Location: In Lewis and Clark National Forest; map MT3, grid f1.

Campsites, facilities: There are 26 RV or tent campsites, which can accommodate a maximum RV length of 22 feet. This is a pack-in, pack-out campground. A trailer boat launch (four-wheel drive only) and wheelchair-accessible restrooms are available.

Reservations, fees: No reservations are needed; the fee is $6 per night. Open seasonally; call for specific dates. The stay limit is 14 days.

Directions: From Choteau go 26 miles south on U.S. 287 to Augusta. In Augusta, take Manix Street west toward Gibson Reservoir, for four miles. Turn right at the Gibson Reservoir sign (Forest Service Road 106) and drive 22 miles (mostly dirt road, end section is paved) to the Mortimer Gulch campground sign, and the campground is on the left.

Contact: Rocky Mountain Ranger District, P.O. Box 340, Choteau, MT 59422; 406/466-5341, fax 406/466-2237; website: www.fs.fed.us/r1/lewisclark.

Trip notes: You can swim, boat, and water-ski on Gibson Reservoir and fish for rainbow and cutthroat trout. You can hike and horseback ride in the area. This is bear country, so use proper precautions.

⁍ Home Gulch

     4

Location: Near Gibson Reservoir; map MT3, grid f2.

Campsites, facilities: There are 12 RV or tent campsites, which can accommodate a maximum RV length of 16 feet. A wheelchair-accessible restroom and trailer boat launch access are available.

Reservations, fees: No reservations are needed; the fee is $5 per night. Open seasonally; call for specific dates. The stay limit is 14 days.

Directions: From Choteau go 26 miles south on U.S. 287 to Augusta. From Augusta, go 20 miles northwest on Sun River Canyon Road, then two miles west on Forest Service Road

108 to the campground.

Contact: Lewis and Clark National Forest Service, Rocky Mountain Ranger District, 1102 N. Main Ave., Choteau, MT 59422; 406/466-5341.

Trip notes: Gibson Reservoir has 15 miles of shoreline, and you can boat and fish for rainbow trout, cutthroat trout, and brown trout. You can hike in the area, too.

20 Benchmark

 7

Location: In Lewis and Clark National Forest; map MT3, grid g1.

Campsites, facilities: There are 25 RV or tent campsites, which can accommodate a maximum RV length of 22 feet, and grills and picnic tables. The camp is a pack-in, pack-out campground, and has wide, grassy sites for large RVs or horse trailers. There are stock troughs at some of the sites.

Reservations, fees: No reservations are needed; the fee is $5 per night. Open seasonally; call for specific dates. The stay limit is 14 days.

Directions: From Choteau go 26 miles south on U.S. 287 to Augusta. From Augusta, take County Road 435 to Bean Lake fishing access (Eberl Street) and turn right. From here on, the road is mostly dirt. Eberl Street becomes Laurel Street and then turns into Forest Service Road 235. Stay on this for almost 15 miles to the Y, and go left. Fifteen miles ahead is the Benchmark campground sign. Turn left to the campground.

Contact: Rocky Mountain Ranger District, P.O. Box 340, Choteau, MT 59422; 406/466-5341, fax 406/466-2237; website: www.fs.fed.us/r1/lewisclark.

Trip notes: The drive to this campground is long, but it is scenic. Bears frequent the area, so use precautions. You can hike here. Straight Creek Trail 212 (for horses or walking) is 15.2 miles long and provides access to a network of trails, including the Scapegoat Wilderness.

21 South Fork

 6

Location: Lewis and Clark National Forest; map MT3, grid g1.

Campsites, facilities: There are seven RV or tent campsites, which can accommodate a maximum RV length of 22 feet. A wheelchair-accessible restroom is available.

Reservations, fees: No reservations are needed; the fee is $9 per night. Open seasonally; call for specific dates. The stay limit is 14 days.

Directions: From Choteau go 26 miles south on U.S. 287 to Augusta. From Augusta, go 31 miles west on Benchmark Road 23 to the campground.

Contact: Lewis and Clark National Forest, 1102 Main Ave. NW, P.O. Box 340, Choteau, MT 59422; 406/466-5341, fax 406/466-2237; website: www.fs.fed.us/r1/lewisclark.

Trip notes: Gibson Reservoir is to the northeast, and the Choteau Country Club has an 18-hole public golf course. Egg Mountain, 12 miles west of Choteau, has yielded more information about dinosaur biology during the Cretaceous period than any other paleontology dig in the world. Dinosaur eggshell fragments, nests, and babies were discovered here for the first time in North America. Paleontology programs are available for adults and children.

22 Wagons West

 4

Location: In Augusta; map MT3, grid g3.

Campsites, facilities: There are 36 RV or tent campsites. Hookups, showers, water, electricity, picnic area, restaurant, and a sanitary disposal station are available. Pets are allowed on leashes.

Reservations, fees: No reservations are needed; the fee is $10–15 per night. Open May 1–November 1.

Directions: From Choteau go 26 miles south

on U.S. 287 to Augusta. Take the Augusta exit. At the flashing light, turn right, and the campground is on the left at the end of town.

Contact: Wagons West, 76 Main St., Augusta, MT 59410; 406/562-3295.

Trip notes: The Willow Creek Reservoir offers fishing for rainbow trout and kokanee salmon. The Sun River is also nearby.

23 Wood Lake
     6

Location: In Lewis and Clark National Forest; map MT3, grid g1.

Campsites, facilities: There are nine RV or tent campsites, which can accommodate a maximum RV length of 22 feet. Restrooms and water are available.

Reservations, fees: No reservations are needed; the fee is $5 per night. Open seasonally; call for specific dates. The stay limit is 14 days.

Directions: From Choteau, go south on U.S. 287 for 26 miles to Augusta. From Augusta, go 24 miles west on Benchmark Road (Forest Service Road 235) on the right.

Contact: Lewis and Clark National Forest Service, Augusta Ranger Station, 1102 Main Ave. NW, P.O. Box 340, Choteau, MT 59422; 406/562-3247.

Trip notes: You can fish, swim, and hike at Wood Lake.

24 Dick's RV Park
    3

Location: In Great Falls; map MT3, grid g7.

Campsites, facilities: There are 150 RV or tent campsites, some with hookups. Showers, laundry facilities, a store, propane gas, sanitary disposal station, and a game room are available.

Reservations, fees: No reservations are needed; the fee is $14.75–23.10 per night. Open year-round.

Directions: From I-15 in Great Falls, take Exit 278 (10th Avenue South), go 100 yards to Exit 0 (14th Street Southwest) and follow the small blue camping signs; go under the train bridge to the RV park.

Contact: Dick's RV Park, 1403 11th St. SW, Great Falls, MT 59404; 406/452-0333, fax 406/727-7340.

Trip notes: The Giant Springs State Park in Great Falls was discovered by the Lewis and Clark Expedition in 1805 and is one of the largest freshwater springs in the world. The water stays at a temperature of 54 degrees and has been carbon dated to be about 3,000 years old. You can see a variety of birds and visit the nearby Rainbow Falls Overlook, the visitor center, and the fish hatchery. There are golf courses in Great Falls and you can hike and bike in Lewis and Clark National Forest.

25 L'n Eve Travel Trailer Park
   3

Location: In Great Falls; map MT3, grid g7.

Campsites, facilities: There are 11 RV campsites, self-contained units only. hookups and a sanitary disposal facility are available.

Reservations, fees: Reservations are suggested; the fee is $20 per night. Open April 1–October 1.

Directions: From Great Falls, take Exit 276 off I-15, go by Dick's RV; at Central, turn left and go up a hill; the campground is on the right in front of a school.

Contact: L'n Eve Travel Trailer Park, 11 12th St. NW, Great Falls, MT 59404; 406/452-5217.

Trip notes: The Giant Springs State Park in Great Falls was discovered by the Lewis and Clark Expedition in 1805 and is one of the largest freshwater springs in the world. The water stays at a temperature of 54 degrees, and has been carbon dated to be about 3,000 years old. You can view a variety of birds and visit the nearby Rainbow Falls Overlook, the visitor center, and the fish hatchery. There are golf courses in Great Falls, and you can hike and bike in Lewis and Clark National Forest.

26 Great Falls KOA Campground

     4

Location: In Great Falls; map MT3, grid g8.

Campsites, facilities: There are 150 RV or tent campsites, some with hookups. Laundry facilities, showers, a store, a sanitary disposal facility, playground, and water park are available.

Reservations, fees: No reservations are needed; the fee is $23.95–39 per night. Open year-round.

Directions: From I-15 in Great Falls, take Exit 278 (10th Avenue South) and go east to 51st Street and the campground.

Contact: Great Falls KOA Campground, 1500 51st St. South, Great Falls, MT 59405; 406/727-3191, 800/562-6584.

Trip notes: The Giant Springs State Park in Great Falls was discovered by the Lewis and Clark Expedition in 1805 and is one of the largest freshwater springs in the world. The water stays at a temperature of 54 degrees, and has been carbon dated to be about 3,000 years old. You can view a variety of birds, and visit the nearby Rainbow Falls Overlook, the visitor center, and the fish hatchery. There are golf courses in Great Falls and you can hike and bike in Lewis and Clark National Forest.

27 Big Nelson

      6

Location: In Lolo National Forest; map MT3, grid h1.

Campsites, facilities: There are four RV or tent campsites, which can accommodate a maximum RV length of 16 feet. A hand boat launch is available.

Reservations, fees: No reservations are needed; there is no fee. Open June 15–September 15. The stay limit is 14 days.

Directions: From Ovando, go eight miles east on Highway 200, then 11 miles northeast on Forest Service Road 500 to the campground.

Contact: Lolo National Forest, Seeley Lake Ranger District, Hwy. 83, HC 31, Box 3200, Seeley Lake, MT 59868; 406/677-2233, fax 406/677-2073; website: www.fs.fed.us/r1/lolo.

Trip notes: You can boat, fish, swim, and hike in Lolo National Forest.

28 Cooper Creek

   5

Location: In Lolo National Forest; map MT3, grid h2.

Campsites, facilities: There are 20 RV campsites.

Reservations, fees: No reservations are needed; the fee is $5 per night. Open May 24–September 1. The stay limit is 14 days.

Directions: From Missoula, go east six miles on I-90 to Highway 200, then go east 73 miles to Lincoln. From Lincoln, go 6.5 miles east on Highway 200, then eight miles northwest on Forest Service Road 5721 to the campground.

Contact: Lolo National Forest, Lincoln Ranger District, 7269 Hwy. 200, Lincoln, MT 59639; 406/362-4265.

Trip notes: You can fish and hike in Lolo National Forest.

29 Logging Creek

    6

Location: In Lewis and Clark National Forest; map MT3, grid h8.

Campsites, facilities: There are 26 RV and tent campsites, which can accommodate a maximum RV length of 22 feet. A wheelchair-accessible restroom and water are available.

Reservations, fees: No reservations are needed; the fee is $6 per night. Open May 1–November 1. The stay limit is 14 days.

Directions: From Great Falls take U.S. 89 south 3.2 miles to Highway 227, turn right. Go five miles to Y intersection and bear left toward Stockett. Go 8.7 miles, past Stockett, to another Y intersection and bear left onto Evans-Riceville Road (dirt and gravel). Continue 15.4 miles to still another Y intersection and bear right (single-lane dirt and gravel with turnouts), then go 4.4 miles to Logging Creek Campground/Forest Service Road 839 sign. Turn right onto Forest Service Road 839 and go 2.2 miles to the campground sign. Turn left into the campground.

Alternative directions (not recommended for RVs): From Monarch, take U.S. 89 north three miles to the Forest Access sign (County Road 427). Turn left onto County Road 427 and go 11.2 miles to a Y intersection and Logging Creek campground sign. Bear left and go 2.2 miles to the campground sign. Turn left into the campground. NOTE: Much of this alternative route is single-lane without turnouts, dirt, steep and very rocky.

Contact: Lewis and Clark National Forest, Belt Creek Station, 4234 Hwy. 89 N., Neihart, MT 49465; 406/236-5511.

Trip notes: You can fish and hike here.

RV camping

MAP MT4

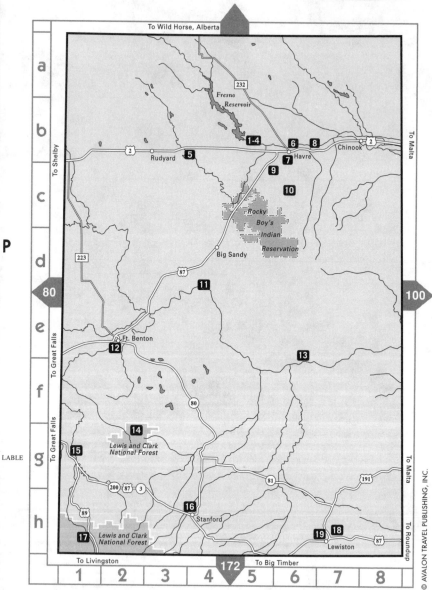

To Wild Horse, Alberta

232

Fresno
Reservoir

To Shelby

2

Rudyard

1-4

6

8

Chinook

To Malta

2

5

7 Havre

9

10

Rocky
Boy's
Indian
Reservation

80

223

Big Sandy

87

100

11

To Great Falls

12 Ft. Benton

13

80

To Great Falls

14

Lewis and Clark
National Forest

LABLE

15

200 87 3

81

191

To Malta

89

16

Stanford

19 18

To Roundup

17 Lewis and Clark
National Forest

Lewiston

87

To Livingston

172

To Big Timber

1 2 3 4 5 6 7 8

a b c d e f g h

P

© AVALON TRAVEL PUBLISHING, INC.

CHAPTER MT4

1 Kiehns Bay 93
2 River Run 93
3 Kremlin...........................93
4 River Fresno Beach..........94
5 Hi-Way Bar & Quick Stop....94
6 Great Northern Fair
  & Campground 94
7 Havre RV Park &
  Travel Plaza 94
8 Havre KOA Campground 95
9 Evergreen Campground.....95
10 Beaver Creek Park
  Campground 95

11 Coalbanks Landing...........95
12 Benton RV Park................96
13 Judith Landing 96
14 Thain Creek 96
15 Fort Ponderosa RV Park.....96
16 J & M RV Park.................97
17 Rocking J Cabins
  & Campground 97
18 Mountain Acres RV Park
  & Campground 97
19 Kiwanis Campground 97

1 Kiehns Bay

 3

Location: At Fresno Dam; map MT4, grid b5.
Campsites, facilities: There are four RV or tent campsites. A wheelchair-accessible restroom is available.
Reservations, fees: No reservations are needed; there is no fee. Open year-round. The stay limit is 14 days.
Directions: From Havre, go west on U.S. 2 to Fresno Dam exit, then two miles north on the county road to the campground.
Contact: U.S. Bureau of Reclamation, P.O. Box 220, Chester, MT 59527; 406/247-7313, 406/456-3228, fax 406/456-3238.
Trip notes: Fresno Dam and Reservoir has 65 miles of shoreline, and you can fish for walleye, northern pike, and perch. You can swim and boat here.

2 River Run

 3

Location: At Fresno Dam; map MT4, grid b5.
Campsites, facilities: There are six RV or tent campsites and a trailer boat ramp.
Reservations, fees: No reservations are needed; there is no fee. Open year-round. The stay limit is 14 days.
Directions: From Havre, go west on U.S. 2 to Fresno Dam exit, then two miles north on the county road to the campground.
Contact: U.S. Bureau of Reclamation, P.O. Box 220, Chester, MT 59527; 406/247-7313, 406/456-3228, fax 406/456-3238.
Trip notes: Fresno Dam and Reservoir has 65 miles of shoreline, and you can fish for walleye, northern pike, and perch. You can swim and boat here.

3 Kremlin

 3

Location: At Fresno Reservoir; map MT4, grid b5.
Campsites, facilities: There are six RV or tent campsites and a trailer boat ramp.
Reservations, fees: No reservations are needed; there is no fee. Open year-round. The stay limit is 14 days.
Directions: From Havre, go west on U.S. 2 to

Fresno Dam exit, then two miles north on the county road to the campground.

Contact: U.S. Bureau of Reclamation, P.O. Box 220, Chester, MT 59527; 406/247-7313, 406/456-3228, fax 406/456-3238.

Trip notes: Fresno Dam and Reservoir has 65 miles of shoreline, and you can fish for walleye, northern pike, and perch. You can swim and boat here.

₄ Fresno Beach

 3

Location: At Fresno Dam; map MT4, grid b5.

Campsites, facilities: There are five RV or tent campsites, wheelchair-accessible restrooms, and a trailer boat ramp.

Reservations, fees: No reservations are needed; there is no fee. Open year-round. The stay limit is 14 days.

Directions: From Havre, go west on U.S. 2, then two miles north on the county road to the campground.

Contact: U.S. Bureau of Reclamation, P.O. Box 220, Chester, MT 59527; 406/247-7313, 406/456-3228, fax 406/456-3238.

Trip notes: Fresno Dam and Reservoir has 65 miles of shoreline, and you can fish for walleye, northern pike, and perch. You can swim and boat here.

₅ Hi-Way Bar & Quick Stop

 3

Location: In Hingham, map MT4, grid b4.

Campsites, facilities: There are 26 RV or tent campsites, some with pull-through sites. Showers, laundry facilities, a store, water, electricity, a sanitary disposal facility, and a restaurant and bar are available.

Reservations, fees: No reservations are needed; the fee is $15 per night. Open year-round.

Directions: From Havre, go 35 miles west on U.S. 2 to the campground.

Contact: Hi-Way Bar & Quick Stop, P.O. Box

95, Hingham, MT 59528; 406/397-3211.

Trip notes: Fresno Dam and Reservoir has 65 miles of shoreline, and you can fish for walleye, northern pike, and perch. You can swim and boat here.

₆ Great Northern Fair & Campground

 4

Location: Near Havre; map MT4, grid b6.

Campsites, facilities: There are 38 RV or tent campsites. Showers, water, electricity, and a sanitary disposal facility are available.

Reservations, fees: No reservations are needed; the fee is $6–17 per night. Open April 15–October 15.

Directions: From Havre, go one mile west on U.S. 2 to the campground.

Contact: Great Northern Fair & Campground, Hill County Fairgrounds, 1676 U.S. Hwy. 2 West, Havre, MT 59501; 406/265-7121, 888/265-7121.

Trip notes: You can fish, swim, and boat at the Fresno Reservoir, to the west, and fish in the Milk River for bass, perch, pike, and sturgeon.

₇ Havre RV Park & Travel Plaza

 4

Location: In Havre; map MT4, grid b6.

Campsites, facilities: There are 105 RV or tent campsites. Laundry facilities, showers, a store, water, electricity, a sanitary disposal facility, gift shop, swimming pool, fuel, and a restaurant are available.

Reservations, fees: No reservations are needed; the fee is $24.99 per night. Open year-round.

Directions: From U.S. 87 North at Havre, turn right onto U.S. 2, which becomes U.S. 2/1st Street West, and the RV park is there.

Contact: Havre RV Park & Travel Plaza, 1415 1st St., Havre, MT 59501; 406/265-8861, 800/278-8861, fax 406/265-4448.

Trip notes: You can fish, swim, and boat at the Fresno Reservoir, to the west, and fish in the Milk River for bass, perch, pike, and sturgeon. Havre-Beneath-the-Streets is a historical re-creation, and the Ulm Piskin buffalo jump is 20 miles away.

8 Havre KOA Campground

 4

Location: In Havre; map MT4, grid b6.

Campsites, facilities: There are 90 RV or tent campsites. Laundry facilities, showers, a store, electricity, water, a sanitary disposal facility, game room, playground, and swimming pool are available.

Reservations, fees: No reservations are needed; the fee is $10–18 per night. Open May 15–September 30.

Directions: From Havre, go eight miles east on U.S. 2.

Contact: Havre KOA Campground, P.O. Box 410 Malta, Havre, MT 59501; 406/265-9722.

Trip notes: You can fish, swim, and boat at the Fresno Reservoir to the west and fish in the Milk River for bass, perch, pike, and sturgeon. Havre-Beneath-the-Streets is a historical re-creation, and the Ulm Piskin buffalo jump is 20 miles away.

9 Evergreen Campground

 3

Location: In Havre; map MT4, grid c5.

Campsites, facilities: There are 47 RV or tent campsites. Showers, laundry facilities, water, electricity, a sanitary disposal facility, playground, laundry facilities, and fire pits are available.

Reservations, fees: No reservations are needed; the fee is $13.48–15.60 per night. Open year-round.

Directions: From Havre, drive to three miles to the junction of U.S. 2 and U.S. 87 and go four miles south on U.S. 87 to the campground at milepost 107.5, between mile markers 107 and 108.

Contact: Evergreen Campground, 7350 U.S. Hwy. 87 West, Havre, MT 59501; 406/265-8228.

Trip notes: Fresno Dam and Reservoir is to the north, and you can fish for walleye, northern pike, and perch. You can swim and boat here.

10 Beaver Creek Park Campground

 4

Location: South of Havre; map MT4, grid c6.

Campsites, facilities: There are primitive campsites, picnic tables, and fire grates.

Reservations, fees: No reservations are needed; the fee is $5 per night. Open year-round.

Directions: From Havre, go 20 miles south on Highway 234.

Contact: Beaver Creek Park Campground, P.O. Box 368, Shambo Route, Havre, MT 59501; 406/395-4565.

Trip notes: You can fish, swim, and boat at the Fresno Reservoir, to the west, and fish in the Milk River for bass, perch, pike, and sturgeon. Havre-Beneath-the-Streets is an historical re-creation, and the Ulm Piskin buffalo jump is 20 miles away.

11 Coalbanks Landing

 4

Location: On Missouri River; map MT4, grid d4.

Campsites, facilities: There are 10 RV or tent campsites, which can accommodate a maximum RV length of 24 feet. A toilet and a trailer boat ramp are available.

Reservations, fees: No reservations are needed; there is no fee. Open year-round. The stay limit is 14 days.

Directions: From Havre, go three miles west on U.S. 2, then south on U.S. 87 to Big Sandy. From Big Sandy, go 11 miles south on U.S. 87, then south at the sign for Upper Missouri Wild and Scenic River to the campground.

Contact: Lewis and Clark National Forest, P.O. Box 869, 1101 15th St. North, Great Falls, MT 59403; 406/791-7700.

Trip notes: You can float and fish in the Missouri River.

12 Benton RV Park

   4

Location: Near Missouri River; map MT4, grid e2.

Campsites, facilities: There are six RV or tent campsites. Water, electricity, and full hookups are available.

Reservations, fees: No reservations are needed; the fee is $15 per night. Open May 1–September 31.

Directions: From U.S. 87, take the Fort Benton exit and follow signs to the campground.

Contact: Benton RV Park, P.O. Box 803, 2411 St. Charles, Fort Benton, MT 59442; 406/622-5015.

Trip notes: This campground is close to the city pool and the Missouri River, where you can float and fish.

13 Judith Landing

   4

Location: Northwest of Winifred; map MT4, grid e6.

Campsites, facilities: There are 10 RV or tent campsites, which can accommodate a maximum RV length of 48 feet. A toilet, water, and trailer boat ramp are available.

Reservations, fees: No reservations are needed; no fee is charged. Open May 15–October 15. The stay limit is 14 days.

Directions: From Winifred, go 26 miles northwest on County Road 236 to the campground.

Contact: Bureau of Land Management, Airport Rd., Lewistown, MT 59457; 406/538-7461.

Trip notes: You can fish here.

14 Thain Creek

     6

Location: In Lewis and Clark National Forest; map MT4, grid g2.

Campsites, facilities: There are 20 RV or tent campsites, which can accommodate a maximum RV length of 22 feet. A wheelchair-accessible restroom and water are available.

Reservations, fees: No reservations are needed; the fee is $6 per night. Open May 1–September 1. The stay limit is 14 days.

Directions: From Great Falls, go six miles east on U.S. 89, then 13 miles east on County Road 228, 16 miles east on County Road 121, and two miles east on Forest Service Road 8840 to the campground.

Contact: Lewis and Clark National Forest, Judith Ranger District, P.O. Box 484, Stanford, MT 59479; 406/566-2292.

Trip notes: You can fish and hike here.

15 Fort Ponderosa RV Park

    4

Location: Southeast of Great Falls; map MT4, grid g1.

Campsites, facilities: There are 66 RV or tent campsites. Hookups, showers, a store, a sanitary disposal facility, electricity, water, laundry facilities, propane gas, playground, and gift shop are available. Pets are allowed on leashes.

Reservations, fees: No reservations are needed; the fee is $14.75–18.75 per night. Open March 1–December 1.

Directions: From Great Falls, go 20 miles southeast on U.S. 89 to Belt, then take Armington Road south one mile to the campground.

Contact: Fort Ponderosa RV Park, 568 Arlington Rd., Belt, MT 59412; 406/277-3232, fax 406/277-3309.

Trip notes: Creeks in the area offer good trout fishing. Sluice Boxes State Park, 10 miles north of Monarch, has hiking, biking, and wildlife viewing. Nearby Neihart also has good creek fishing and hiking opportunities. Be sure to visit Memorial Falls and take the nature trail, which is wheelchair accessible.

16 J & M RV Park

   4

Location: In Stanford; map MT4, grid h4.

Campsites, facilities: There are 10 RV and tent campsites. Showers, laundry facilities, electricity, and water are available.

Reservations, fees: No reservations are needed; the fee is $10–12 per night. Open year-round.

Directions: From U.S. 87, take the Stanford exit, go west; the park is on the left on U.S. 87.

Contact: J & M RV Park, Hwy. 87, Stanford, MT 59479; 406/566-2289.

Trip notes: You can fish near here.

17 Rocking J Cabins & Campground

 4

Location: In Monarch, map MT4, grid h1.

Campsites, facilities: There are seven RV or tent campsites. Showers, electricity, and water are available. Creekside cabins are for rent.

Reservations, fees: No reservations are needed; the fee is $10–16 per night. Open May 1–October 31.

Directions: From Great Falls, go 45 miles south on U.S. 89 to Monarch. Take the Monarch exit, and the campground is on the right on Cascade Street.

Contact: Rocking J Cabins & Campground, P.O. Box 24, Monarch, MT 59463; tel./fax 406/236-5535.

Trip notes: Creeks in the area offer good trout fishing. Sluice Boxes State Park, 10 miles north of Monarch, has hiking, biking, and wildlife viewing. Nearby Neihart also has good creek fishing and hiking opportunities. Be sure to visit Memorial Falls and take the nature trail, which is wheelchair accessible.

18 Mountain Acres RV Park & Campground

  4

Location: In Lewistown; map MT4, grid h7.

Campsites, facilities: There are 50 RV campsites. Showers, laundry facilities, water, and a sanitary disposal facility are available.

Reservations, fees: No reservations are needed; the fee is $17–79 per night. Open May 1–October 31.

Directions: From Lewistown, go .25 mile north on U.S. 191.

Contact: Mountain Acres RV Park & Campground, 103 Rocklyn Ave., Lewistown, MT 59457; 406/538-7591.

Trip notes: This campground is within the city limits of Lewistown and walking distance of main street shopping. Good fly-fishing is close by on Spring Creek.

19 Kiwanis Campground

  3

Location: Near Lewistown; map MT4, grid h7.

Campsites, facilities: There are RV campsites, but no tents are allowed. Water is available.

Reservations, fees: No reservations are needed; there is no fee. Open May 1–September 1.

Directions: From Lewistown, go half a mile west on U.S. 87. The campground is on U.S. 87 west, about 150 feet northeast of the junction of U.S. 87 and U.S. 191, across from Torguson Tires.

Contact: Kiwanis Campground, Kiwanis Clubs, c/o Ron Combs, Route 2, Box 2198, Lewistown, MT 59457; 406/538-5436.

Trip notes: Good fly-fishing is close by on Spring Creek.

Neighborly tents

MAP MT5

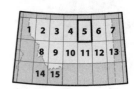

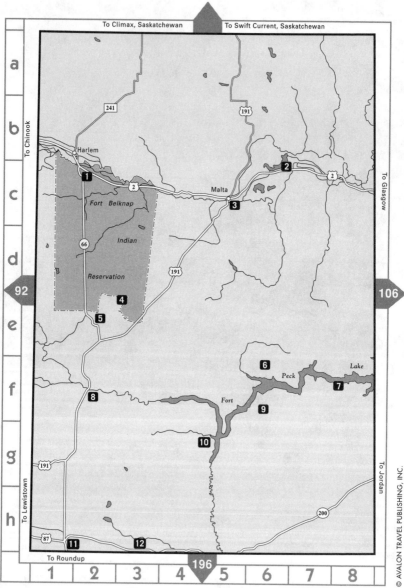

To Climax, Saskatchewan

To Swift Current, Saskatchewan

To Chinook

241

191

Harlem

1

2

Malta

Fort Belknap

2

3

66

Indian

Reservation

191

4

5

To Glasgow

6

Peck

Lake

7

8

Fort

9

10

191

To Jordan

200

To Lewistown

87

11

12

To Roundup

92

106

196

a b c d e f g h

1 2 3 4 5 6 7 8

© AVALON TRAVEL PUBLISHING, INC.

CHAPTER MT5

1 Fort Belknap Rest Area 101
2 Nelson Reservoir............101
3 Trafton Park.................101
4 Camp Creek 102
5 Montana Gulch..............102
6 Fourchette Creek 102
7 Bone Trail 102
8 James Kipp 102
9 Devils Creek.................103
10 Crooked Creek..............103
11 Little Montana Truck Stop & Café.........................103
12 Hilltop Campgrounds 103

1 Fort Belknap Rest Area

   4

Location: In Harlem; map MT5, grid c2.

Campsites, facilities: There are 15 RV or tent campsites. Laundry facilities, showers, a store, electricity, and water are available.

Reservations, fees: No reservations are needed; the fee is $6–10 per night. Open year-round.

Directions: From Harlem, go three miles east on U.S. 2 and Highway 66.

Contact: Fort Belknap Rest Area, P.O. Box 66, Rail Route 1, Harlem, MT 59526; 406/353-2205, 800/859-2794.

Trip notes: This campground is near a swimming pool.

2 Nelson Reservoir

    4

Location: East of Malta; map MT5, grid c6.

Campsites, facilities: There are five RV or tent campsites, restrooms, water, and a trailer boat launch.

Reservations, fees: No reservations are needed; the fee is $12 per night. Open year-round. The stay limit is 14 days.

Directions: From Malta, go 17 miles east on U.S. 2 to the campground. This is easy access on a paved road.

Contact: U.S. Bureau of Reclamation, Montana Area Office, P.O. Box 30137, Billings, MT 59107-0137; 406/247-7314, 406/654-1776.

Trip notes: Nelson Reservoir lists itself as the number-one place to catch walleyes. You can also find yellow perch, and northern pike.

3 Trafton Park

    3

Location: In Malta; map MT5, grid c5.

Campsites, facilities: There are 20 RV or tent campsites, and restrooms and water are available.

Reservations, fees: No reservations are needed; the fee is $3 per night. Open year-round.

Directions: At the junction of U.S. 191 and U.S. 2 at Malta, go north; Trafton Park is directly north of the new rest stop at the intersection.

Contact: Trafton Park, P.O. Box 1420, Malta, MT 59538; 406/654-1776.

Trip notes: There are basketball and volleyball courts, softball fields, playground equipment, and a horseshoe pit. Fishing access is provided along the Milk River, which surrounds the park on two sides. A museum, store, food, and fuel are available within a mile. Bowdoin National Bird Refuge is just seven miles east, and the C. M. Russell Wildlife Refuge is 40 miles south.

4 Camp Creek

  3

Location: Near Zortman; map MT5, grid e3.
Campsites, facilities: There are 21 RV or tent campsites, which can accommodate a maximum RV length of 24 feet. A toilet and water are available.
Reservations, fees: No reservations are needed; there is no fee. Open year-round. The stay limit is 14 days.
Directions: From Malta, go south on U.S. 191 to Seven Mile Road, and take this north to Zortman. From Zortman, go one mile northeast on the county road to the campground.
Contact: Bureau of Land Management, Airport Rd., Lewistown, MT 59457; 406/538-7461.
Trip notes: There is a large mining operation near here.

5 Montana Gulch

  3

Location: Near Landusky; map MT5, grid e2.
Campsites, facilities: There are 15 RV or tent campsites, which can accommodate a maximum RV length of 24 feet. A toilet is available.
Reservations, fees: No reservations are needed; there is no fee. Open year-round. The stay limit is 14 days.
Directions: From Landusky, go one mile south on the county road to the campground.
Contact: Bureau of Land Management, Airport Rd., Lewistown, MT 59457; 406/538-7461.
Trip notes: There is a large mining operation near here.

6 Fourchette Creek

 4

Location: At Fort Peck Lake; map MT5, grid f6.
Campsites, facilities: There are primitive campsites. There is a toilet, and trailer boat ramp available.
Reservations, fees: No reservations are needed; there is no fee charged. Open year-round. The stay limit is 14 days.
Directions: From Malta, go 60 miles south on the county road to the campground.
Contact: Army Corps of Engineers, P.O. Box 208, Fort Peck, Montana 59223; 406/526-3411.
Trip notes: You can fish, boat, water-ski, swim, hike, and bike in and around Fort Peck Lake.

7 Bone Trail

 4

Location: At Fort Peck Lake; map MT5, grid f8.
Campsites, facilities: There are primitive campsites, which can accommodate a maximum RV length of 16 feet. A toilet and a trailer boat ramp are available.
Reservations, fees: No reservations are needed; there is no fee. Open year-round. The stay limit is 14 days.
Directions: From Fort Peck, go 60 miles southwest on Willow Creek Road to the campground.
Contact: Army Corps of Engineers, P.O. Box 208, Fort Peck, Montana 59223; 406/526-3411.
Trip notes: You can fish, boat, water-ski, swim, hike, and bike in and around Fort Peck Lake.

8 James Kipp

 4

Location: In the C. M. Russell National Wildlife Refuge; map MT5, grid f2.
Campsites, facilities: There are 34 RV or tent campsites, which can accommodate a maximum RV length of 48 feet. Wheelchair-accessible restrooms, a toilet, water, and a trailer boat ramp are available.
Reservations, fees: No reservations are needed; the fee is $6 per night. Open April 1–December 1. The stay limit is 14 days.
Directions: From Lewistown, go 64 miles northeast on U.S. 191 to the campground.
Contact: Bureau of Land Management, Airport Rd., Lewistown, MT 59457; 406/538-7461.
Trip notes: You can fish and hike here.

9 Devils Creek

 4

Location: At Fort Peck Lake; map MT5, grid f6.

Campsites, facilities: There are primitive campsites, which can accommodate a maximum RV length of 16 feet. A toilet and a trailer boat ramp are available.

Reservations, fees: No reservations are needed; there is no fee. Open year-round. The stay limit is 14 days.

Directions: From Jordan, go 48 miles northwest on County Road 245 to the campground.

Contact: Army Corps of Engineers, P.O. Box 208, Fort Peck, Montana 59223; 406/526-3411.

Trip notes: You can fish, boat, water-ski, swim, hike, and bike in and around Fort Peck Lake.

10 Crooked Creek

 4

Location: Near Fort Peck Reservoir; map MT5, grid g5.

Campsites, facilities: There are 45 RV and tent campsites, and a wheelchair-accessible toilet is available.

Reservations, fees: No reservations are needed; the fee is $6–12 per night. Open April 15–November 15. The stay limit is 14 days.

Directions: From Winnett, go 48 miles northeast on the county road.

Contact: P.O. Box 128, Winnett, MT 59087; 406/429-2999, 406/429-2900.

Trip notes: This campground has access to Fort Peck Reservoir, where you can fish for walleye, northern pike, paddlefish, sauger, lake trout, small mouth bass, and chinook salmon. You can hike nearby.

11 Little Montana Truck Stop & Café

 3

Location: U.S. 87 and Grass Range; map MT5, grid h1.

Campsites, facilities: There are 24 RV or tent campsites. Showers, a store, café, rock shop, and water are available.

Reservations, fees: No reservations are needed; the fee is $10.40 per night. Open year-round.

Directions: From Lewistown, go east on U.S. 87 about 34 miles to Grass Range and the campground is right there.

Contact: Little Montana Truck Stop & Café, 530 Hwy. 87 S., Grass Range, MT 59032; 406/428-2270.

Trip notes: You can fish here.

12 Hilltop Campgrounds

 4

Location: In Winnett; map MT5, grid h3.

Campsites, facilities: There are eight RV and tent campsites.

Reservations, fees: No reservations are needed; the fee is $10 per night. Open April 1–December 1.

Directions: From Lewistown, go 55 miles east to Winnett on Highway 200 (this road is also U.S. 87 for about 31 miles before they split at Grassrange); the campground is at the junction of Highway 200 and County Road 244.

Contact: Hilltop Campgrounds, P.O. Box 32, Winnett, MT 59087; 406/429-5321.

Trip notes: The War Horse National Wildlife Refuge is near here. It was established as a refuge and breeding ground for migratory birds and other wildlife in 1958. This refuge consists of three units: War Horse Lake, Wild Horse Lake, and Yellow Water Reservoir. All offer good wildlife observation opportunities, and Yellow Water Reservoir has boating and fishing.

WAYNE SCHERR

MAP MT6

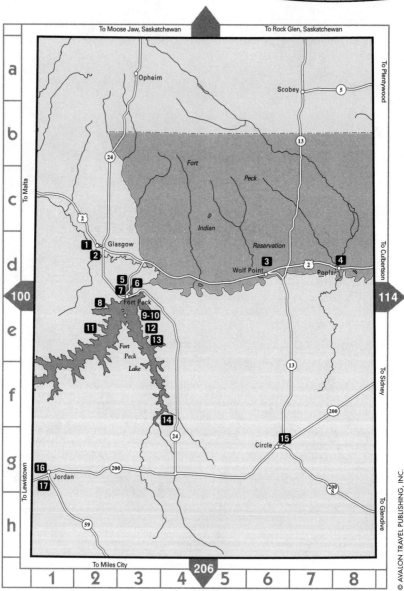

To Moose Jaw, Saskatchewan

To Rock Glen, Saskatchewan

To Plentywood

Opheim

Scobey

5

13

To Malta

24

Fort

Peck

2

Indian

Glasgow

Reservation

1

Wolf Point

3

2

Poplar

4

To Culbertson

5

6

7

Fort Peck

8

9-10

11

12

13

Fort
Peck
Lake

To Sidney

13

200

14

24

200

Circle

15

To Lewistown

16

200

Jordan

17

200
S

To Glendive

59

To Miles City

206

© AVALON TRAVEL PUBLISHING, INC.

100

114

CHAPTER MT6

1	Trails West Campground ..107	**9**	Flat Lake........................109
2	Shady Rest RV Park.........107	**10**	Bear Creek.....................109
3	Rancho Motel &	**11**	The Pines Campground 109
	Campground 108	**12**	Rock Creek Marina..........109
4	Smith's Mobile Park 108	**13**	Mcguire Creek 110
5	Trout Pond.....................108	**14**	Nelson Creek.................110
6	West End 108	**15**	Scheer's Trailer Court 110
7	Downstream 108	**16**	Kamp Katie 110
8	Bear Creek.....................109	**17**	Jordan RV Park...............111

1 Trails West Campground

4

Location: In Glasgow; map MT6, grid d2.
Campsites, facilities: There are 50 RV or tent campsites. Laundry facilities, water, electricity, a sanitary disposal facility, a store, playground, and a swimming pool are available. Pets are allowed on leashes.
Reservations, fees: No reservations are needed; the fee is $15 and up per night. Open year-round.
Directions: From downtown Glasgow on U.S. 2, go 1.5 miles west. Turn north on Skylark Road.
Contact: Trails West Campground, Route 14404 Skylark Rd., Glasgow, MT 59230; 406/228-2278.
Trip notes: You can fish, boat, water-ski, swim, hike, and bike in and around Fort Peck Lake. The Charles M. Russell National Wildlife Refuge is to the south. Be sure to check conditions and directions at the Glasgow Chamber of Commerce, the Bureau of Land Management in Glasgow, or the Fort Peck CMR Refuge Office on Highway 117. The South Valley Wildlife Viewing area provides an opportunity to see antelope, deer and other animals. The road route is about 65 miles long and can take three

hours or more. The Trails West Campground is .25 mile from Sunnyside Golf Course.

2 Shady Rest RV Park

4

Location: In Glasgow; map MT6, grid d2.
Campsites, facilities: There are 48 RV or tent campsites, some with pull-through sites. Laundry facilities, showers, a store, water, and electricity are available.
Reservations, fees: No reservations are needed; the fee is $13.57–16.38 per night. Open year-round.
Directions: From U.S. 2 at Glasgow, go two blocks north on Lasar Drive to the campground at the east end of town.
Contact: Shady Rest RV Park, 8 Laser Drive, P.O. Box 442, Glasgow, MT 59230; 406/228-2769, 800/422-8954.
Trip notes: You can fish, boat, water-ski, swim, hike, and bike in and around Fort Peck Lake. The Charles M. Russell National Wildlife Refuge is to the south. Be sure to check conditions and directions, at the Glasgow Chamber of Commerce, the Bureau of Land Management in Glasgow, or the Fort Peck CMR Refuge Office on Highway 117. The South Valley Wildlife Viewing area provides an opportunity to see antelope, deer and other

animals. The road route is about 65 miles long and can take three hours or more. You can golf at Sunnyside Golf Course.

3 Rancho Motel & Campground

 3

Location: In Wolf Point; map MT6, grid d6.
Campsites, facilities: There are 49 RV or tent campsites. Showers, laundry facilities, water, and electricity are available.
Reservations, fees: No reservations are needed; the fee is $15 per night. Open April 1 –October 1.
Directions: From Wolf Point, go two miles west on U.S. 2, pass the bridge; the campground is on the left side.
Contact: Rancho Motel & Campground, Hwy. 2 West, Wolf Point, MT 59201; 406/653-1940.
Trip notes: You can fish in the Missouri River or at Fort Peck Lake for walleye, northern, lake trout, and salmon. This 245,000-acre lake is popular for boating, swimming, water-skiing, and other water sports.

4 Smith's Mobile Park

 3

Location: In Poplar; map MT6, grid d8.
Campsites, facilities: There are 12 RV or tent campsites. Water, electricity, and a sanitary disposal facility are available.
Reservations, fees: No reservations are needed; the first night is free; the fee is $50 per week. Open April 1–October 1.
Directions: From Wolf Point go 22 miles east on U.S. 2 to Poplar. From Poplar, go one mile east on U.S. 2 to the campground.
Contact: Smith's Mobile Park, P.O. Box 729, Poplar, MT 59255; 406/768-3841.
Trip notes: You can fish in the Missouri River for lake trout, sturgeon, walleye, and sauger.

5 Trout Pond

 4

Location: North of Fort Peck Lake; map MT6, grid d3.
Campsites, facilities: There are 10 primitive RV or tent campsites.
Reservations, fees: No reservations are needed; there is no fee. Open year-round. The stay limit is 30 days.
Directions: From Fort Peck, go three miles north on Highway 117 to the campground.
Contact: Montana Fish, Wildlife, & Parks, Route 1, Box 210, Fort Peck, MT 59223; 406/228-3700.
Trip notes: You can fish, boat, water-ski, swim, hike, and bike in and around Fort Peck Lake.

6 West End

 4

Location: At Fort Peck Lake; map MT6, grid d3.
Campsites, facilities: There are 12 RV or tent campsites, which can accommodate a maximum RV length of 35 feet. Wheelchair-accessible restrooms, water, and a trailer boat ramp are available.
Reservations, fees: No reservations are needed; the fee is $12 per night Open May 31–September 6. The stay limit is 14 days.
Directions: West End campground is two miles southwest of Fort Peck. Take National Wildlife Road 108 off Highway 24 to the campground.
Contact: Army Corps of Engineers, P.O. Box 208, Fort Peck, MT 59223; 406/526-3411.
Trip notes: You can fish, boat, water-ski, swim, hike, and bike in and around Fort Peck Lake.

7 Downstream

 4

Location: At Fort Peck Lake; map MT6, grid d3.
Campsites, facilities: There are 69 RV or tent

campsites. Wheelchair-accessible restrooms, water, and a trailer boat ramp are available.

Reservations, fees: No reservations are needed; the fee is $12 per night. Open May 1–October 30. The stay limit is 14 days.

Directions: From Fort Peck, go .5 mile east on Highway 117 to the campground.

Contact: Army Corps of Engineers, P.O. Box 208, Fort Peck, MT 59223; 406/526-3411.

Trip notes: You can fish, boat, water-ski, swim, hike, and bike in and around Fort Peck Lake.

8 Bear Creek

 4

Location: At Fort Peck Lake; map MT6, grid e2.

Campsites, facilities: There are primitive campsites, a toilet, tables, and firepits.

Reservations, fees: No reservations are needed; there is no fee. Open year-round. The stay limit is 14 days.

Directions: Bear Creek campground is four miles southwest of Fort Peck. Take National Wildlife Refuge Road 108 off Highway 24 to the campground.

Contact: Army Corps of Engineers, P.O. Box 208, Fort Peck, MT 59223; 406/526-3411.

Trip notes: You can fish, boat, water-ski, swim, hike, and bike in and around Fort Peck Lake.

9 Flat Lake

 4

Location: At Fort Peck Lake; map MT6, grid e3.

Campsites, facilities: There are campsites, a toilet, and a trailer boat ramp.

Reservations, fees: No reservations are needed; there is no fee charged. Open year-round. The stay limit is 14 days.

Directions: From Fort Peck, go six miles east on Highway 24 to the campground.

Contact: Army Corps of Engineers, P.O. Box 208, Fort Peck, MT 59223; 406/526-3411.

Trip notes: You can fish, boat, water-ski, swim, hike, and bike in and around Fort Peck Lake.

10 Bear Creek

 4

Location: At Fort Peck Lake; map MT6, grid e3.

Campsites, facilities: There are primitive campsites and a toilet available.

Reservations, fees: No reservations are needed; there is no fee charged. Open year-round. The stay limit is 14 days.

Directions: From Fort Peck, go 14 miles southeast on Highway 24, then seven miles west on the county road to Bear Creek Campground.

Contact: Army Corps of Engineers, P.O. Box 208, Fort Peck, MT 59223; 406/526-3411.

Trip notes: You can fish, boat, water-ski, swim, hike, and bike in and around Fort Peck Lake.

11 The Pines Campground

 4

Location: At Fort Peck Lake; map MT6, grid e2.

Campsites, facilities: There are primitive RV or tent campsites, restrooms, water, and a trailer boat launch.

Reservations, fees: No reservations are needed; the fee is $12 per night. Open year-round. The stay limit is 14 days.

Directions: From Fort Peck, go north on Highway 24 five miles to Willow Creek Road, take Willow Creek Road west 12 miles to Pines Road, and go approximately 12 miles southeast to the campground.

Contact: Army Corps of Engineers, P.O. Box 208, Fort Peck, Montana 59223; 406/526-3411.

Trip notes: You can fish, boat, water-ski, swim, hike, and bike in and around Fort Peck Lake.

12 Rock Creek Marina

 4

Location: At Fort Peck Lake; map MT6, grid e3.

Campsites, facilities: There are 20 RV and numerous tent campsites, which can accommodate a maximum RV length of 40 feet. This is a full-service marina, with a sanitary disposal facility, shower, water, store, and playground.

Reservations, fees: Reservations are strongly suggested; the fee is $5–14 per night. Open May–October. The stay limit is 30 days.

Directions: From Fort Peck, go 45 miles southeast on Highway 24, then seven miles west on the county road to the campground, which is on Big Dry Arm.

Contact: Rock Creek Marina, 652 S. Rock Creek Rd., Fort Peck, MT 59223; 406/485-2560, fax 406/485-2760.

Trip notes: You can fish, boat, water-ski, swim, hike, and bike in and around Fort Peck Lake.

13 Mcguire Creek

 4

Location: At Fort Peck Lake; map MT6, grid e3.
Campsites, facilities: There are 12 primitive RV or tent campsites (no water, no boat ramp).

Reservations, fees: No reservations are needed; there is no fee. Open year-round. The stay limit is 14 days.

Directions: From Fort Peck, go 41 miles southeast on Highway 24, then seven miles west on the county road to the campground.

Contact: Army Corps of Engineers, P.O. Box 208, Fort Peck, MT 59223; 406/526-3411.

Trip notes: This campground has shoreline access, and you can fish, boat, water-ski, swim, hike, and bike in and around Fort Peck Lake.

14 Nelson Creek

 4

Location: At Fort Peck Lake; map MT6, grid f4.
Campsites, facilities: There are primitive campsites, a toilet, and a trailer boat ramp available.

Reservations, fees: No reservations are needed; there is no fee. Open year-round. The stay limit is 14 days.

Directions: From Fort Peck, go 45 miles southeast on Highway 24, then seven miles west on the county road to the campground.

Contact: Army Corps of Engineers, P.O. Box 208, Fort Peck, MT 59223; 406/526-3411.

Trip notes: You can fish, boat, water-ski, swim, hike, and bike in and around Fort Peck Lake.

15 Scheer's Trailer Court

 3

Location: In Circle; map MT6, grid g6.
Campsites, facilities: There are five RV or tent campsites. Showers, laundry facilities, electricity, and water are available.

Reservations, fees: No reservations are needed; the fee is $12 per night. Open April 1–September 30.

Directions: From Circle, go to the north end of 1st Avenue North to the campground.

Contact: Scheer's Trailer Court, 120 B Drive, P.O. Box 356, Circle, MT 59215; 406/485-2285.

Trip notes: You can fish, boat, water-ski, swim, hike, and bike in and around Fort Peck Lake.

16 Kamp Katie

 4

Location: In Jordan; map MT6, grid g1.
Campsites, facilities: There are 20 RV or tent campsites. There are showers, water, and a café nearby. Pets are allowed on leashes.

Reservations, fees: No reservations are needed; the fee is $7–8 per night. Open June 15–September 1.

Directions: From Highway 200 at Jordan, Kamp Katie is on the southern outskirts of town. There are signs, but Kamp Katie is not visible from the highway because of hill and trees.

Contact: Kamp Katie, P.O. Box 44, Jordan, MT 59337; 406/557-2851.

Trip notes: Hell Creek State Park is 25 miles north, and you can swim, fish, boat, and water-ski.

17 Jordan RV Park

   4

Location: In Jordan; map MT6, grid g1.

Campsites, facilities: There are 12 RV or tent campsites. Water and electricity are available.

Reservations, fees: No reservations are needed; the fee is $12 per night. Open May 1–December 1.

Directions: This campground is at the east end of Jordan, just off Highway 200.

Contact: Jordan RV Park, P.O. Box 317, Hwy. 200 E., Jordan, MT 59337; 406/557-6116.

Trip notes: Hell Creek State Park is 25 miles north, and you can swim, fish, boat, and water-ski.

Mountain biking in Coalridge Ghost Town

MAP MT7

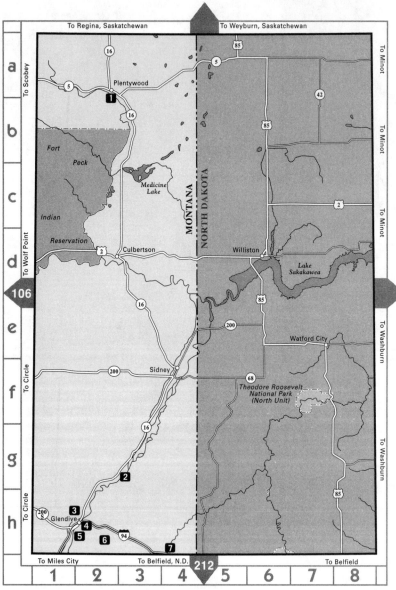

© AVALON TRAVEL PUBLISHING, INC.

CHAPTER MT7

1 Bolster Dam
   Campgrounds...............115
2 Intake........................115
3 Green Valley
   Campground................115
4 Glendive Campground....116
5 Spring Grove Trailer
   Court........................116
6 Makoshika State Park.....116
7 Beaver Valley Haven.......116

1 Bolster Dam Campgrounds

 5

Location: Near Plentywood; map MT7, grid a2.
Campsites, facilities: There are primitive campsites, and a boat launch is available. Water is not available, but there are a few electrical outlets by the streetlights.
Reservations, fees: No reservations are taken; there is no fee. Open year-round.
Directions: In Plentywood, go north at the stoplight (only one in town) on Main Street as far as you can, then east on Laurel for about 1.5 blocks; turn left on Box Elder (there is a dip at the end of the road), and you will see the campground sign.
Contact: Bolster Dam Campgrounds, Plentywood City Clerk, 205 W. 1st Ave., Plentywood, MT 59254; 406/765-1700, fax 406/765-2738.
Trip notes: You can fish here at the Bolster/Box Elder Dam for perch and walleye. Medicine Lake National Wildlife Refuge south of here includes over 31,000 acres of wetlands, lake, and prairie. The refuge is home to ducks, geese, herons, cranes, and pelicans. There are many hiking trails throughout the refuge. No motorized boats are allowed on the lake.

2 Intake

 3

Location: North of Glendive, map MT7, grid g3.
Campsites, facilities: There are 40 RV or tent campsites. Restrooms, water, and a trailer boat ramp are available.
Reservations, fees: No reservations are needed; the fee is $5 per night. Open May–September. The stay limit is seven days.
Directions: From Glendive, go 16 miles north on Highway 16, then south on the county road to the campground.
Contact: Montana Fish, Wildlife & Parks, P.O. 1242, Glendive, MT 59330; 406/365-6256 or 406/247-2940.
Trip notes: You can fish the Yellowstone River for paddlefish and other species. Glendive is an excellent location for agate hunting. Makoshika State Park, south of Glendive, has hiking, fishing, wildlife, and fossils. Glendive has a golf course.

3 Green Valley Campground

 3

Location: North of Glendive; map MT7, grid h1.
Campsites, facilities: There are 67 RV or tent campsites. Showers, laundry facilities, a store, water, electricity, a playground, game room, and a sanitary disposal facility are available.
Reservations, fees: No reservations are needed; the fee is $12–16.55 per night, plus $3 per child. Open April 1–November 1.
Directions: From Glendive, take Exit 213 off I-94 and go .5 mile north to campground.
Contact: Green Valley Campground, P.O. Box 1396, Glendive, MT 59330; 406/365-4156.
Trip notes: You can fish here for a fee or try the Yellowstone River. Glendive is an excellent location for agate hunting. Makoshika State Park, south of Glendive, has hiking, fishing, wildlife, and fossils. Glendive has a golf course.

4 Glendive Campground

 3

Location: In Glendive; map MT7, grid h2.

Campsites, facilities: There are 65 RV or tent campsites. Showers, laundry facilities, a store, a playground, restaurant, swimming pool, electricity, water, and a sanitary disposal facility are available.

Reservations, fees: No reservations are needed; the fee is $18.51–25.99 (which includes cable) per night. Open April 1–October 1.

Directions: From I-94 at Glendive, take Exit 215 and go north of I-94 to campground.

Contact: Glendive Campground, 201 California, Glendive, MT 59330; 406/377-6721.

Trip notes: You can fish the Yellowstone River for paddlefish and other species. Glendive is an excellent location for agate hunting. Makoshika State Park, south of Glendive, has hiking, fishing, wildlife, and fossils. Glendive has a golf course.

5 Spring Grove Trailer Court

 3

Location: In Glendive; map MT7, grid h2.

Campsites, facilities: There are 12 RV or tent campsites. Showers, laundry facilities, electricity, and water are available.

Reservations, fees: No reservations are needed; the fee is $10–19.50 per night ($5 extra charge per second person or more). Open year round.

Directions: From I-94 at Glendive, take the business loop exit; the campground is across from the mall.

Contact: Spring Grove Trailer Court, 1720 Crisafulli Drive, Glendive, MT 59330-3246; 406/377-2018.

Trip notes: A mall, parks, and grocery store are close by. You can fish the Yellowstone River for paddlefish and other species. Glendive is an excellent location for agate hunting. Makoshika State Park, south of Glendive, has

hiking, fishing, wildlife, and fossils. Glendive has a golf course.

6 Makoshika State Park

 4

Location: Near Glendive; map MT7, grid h2.

Campsites, facilities: There are eight RV or tent campsites. Wheelchair-accessible restrooms, picnic areas, and water are available.

Reservations, fees: No reservations are needed; the fee is $11 per night. Open year-round. The stay limit is 14 days.

Directions: From I-94 at Glendive, take Exit 215 to Towne Street, take Towne Street over the Yellowstone River to Merrill Avenue, and turn right on Merrill Avenue. Continue south, and go under the railroad underpass onto Barry. Go east on Barry four blocks, turn right on Taylor Avenue, go six blocks to Snyder Avenue and turn left to the park. Makoshika State Park signs and *Tyrannosaurus rex* tracks will help you find your way.

Contact: Montana Fish, Wildlife & Parks, Region 5, 2300 Lake Elmo Drive, Billings, Montana 406/247-2940.

Trip notes: There are nature trails and interpretive displays in this badlands area. Pine and juniper trees dot the badlands formations, and there are fossil remains of dinosaurs in the park. Glendive has a golf course. You can fish the Yellowstone River for paddlefish and other species. Glendive is an excellent location for agate hunting.

7 Beaver Valley Haven

 3

Location: East of Glendive; map MT7, grid h4.

Campsites, facilities: There are 38 RV and tent campsites. Showers, laundry facilities, water, electricity, and a sanitary disposal facility are available.

Reservations, fees: No reservations are needed; the fee is $8–10 per night. Open April

1–November 1.

Directions: From Glendive, go 27 miles east on I-94 to Wibaux, then go two blocks on Highway 7 to Main Street, cross a bridge, go two blocks, and turn right to a brown house.

Contact: Beaver Valley Haven, HC 71, P.O. Box 7111, Wibaux, MT 59353; 406/796-2280.

Trip notes: This campground is within walking distance of town. The Town House Museum Complex in Wibaux includes a "town house" fully restored to its original condition, antique furniture of the homestead era, a barbershop, a livery stable, gardens, and a railroad caboose. There is a walking tour with a brochure available from the Centennial Car Information Center. Glendive, 27 miles west, has a golf course. You can fish the Yellowstone River for paddlefish and other species.

MONTANA
CHAPTER MT8

Georgetown Lake Recreation Area, Anaconda

MAP MT8

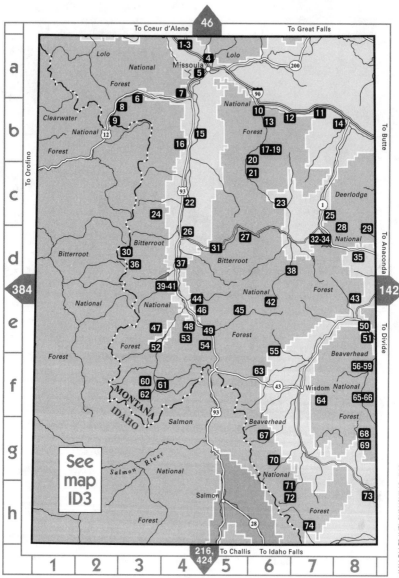

To Coeur d'Alene   46   To Great Falls

1-3
4
Missoula
5
Lolo
National
Forest
200
90
6
7
Lolo
National
8
9
Forest
10
13
12
11
14
Clearwater
National
12
Forest
16
15
17-19
20
21
To Orofino
93
22
23
Deerlodge
24
25
28
29
National
32-34
30   Bitterroot
36   37
31   27   35
39-41   Bitterroot   38
384   142   To Anaconda
44   National   43   To Divide
46   45   42
National   50
47   48   53   49   Forest   51
52   54   55   Beaverhead
63   56-59
60   61   43   Wisdom   National   65-66
62   64
MONTANA   68
IDAHO   Beaverhead   69
See   Salmon   67
map   70
ID3   Salmon   River   National   71   73
National   72   Forest
Salmon   74
28
Forest
216,   To Challis   To Idaho Falls
424

© AVALON TRAVEL PUBLISHING, INC.

120 Montana

CHAPTER MT8

1	Out Post Campground	122
2	Jim & Mary's RV Park	122
3	Jellystone RV Park	122
4	Mountain View Trailer Court	122
5	Missoula KOA	123
6	Lewis & Clark	123
7	Square & Round Dance Center	123
8	Lolo Hot Springs Resort	123
9	Lee Creek	124
10	Ekstrom Stage Station	124
11	Chalet Bearmouth Campground	124
12	Beavertail Hill State Park	124
13	Elkhorn Guest Ranch	125
14	Good Time Camping & RV Park	125
15	Chief Looking Glass	125
16	Charles Waters	125
17	Norton	126
18	Grizzly	126
19	Dalles	126
20	Harry's Flat	126
21	Bitterroot Flat	127
22	Tucker Crossin' RV Park Campground	127
23	Racetrack	127
24	Blodgett Canyon Campground	127
25	Flint Creek	128
26	Angler's Roost	128
27	Crystal Creek	128
28	Cable Mountain	128
29	Lost Creek State Park	128
30	Schumaker	129
31	Black Bear	129
32	Denton's Point	129
33	East Fork	129
34	Spillway	130
35	Spring Hill	130
36	Bear Creek Pass	130
37	Bitterroot Family Campground	130
38	Copper Creek	131
39	Lick Creek Campground	131
40	Lake Como Lower	131
41	Lake Como Upper	131
42	Martin Creek	132
43	Seymour	132
44	Spring Gulch	132
45	Jennings Camp	132
46	Moosehead Campground, Store, & Rock Shop	133
47	Sam Billings Memorial	133
48	Warm Springs	133
49	Sula Country Store, Campground, & RV Park	133
50	East Bank	134
51	Dickie Bridge	134
52	Rombo	134
53	Crazy Creek	134
54	Indian Trees	135
55	Mussigbrod	135
56	Fourth of July	135
57	Boulder	135
58	Lodgepole	136
59	Beaverhead	136
60	Painted Rock	136
61	Slate Creek	136
62	Alta	137
63	May Creek	137
64	Steel Creek	137
65	Mono Creek	137
66	Price Creek	138
67	Twin Lakes	138
68	Grasshopper	138
69	Maverick Mountain RV Park	139

(continues)

70 Miner Lake	139	73 Bannack	140
71 North Van Houten	139	74 Reservoir Lake	140
72 South Van Houten	139		

1 Out Post Campground

 5

Location: In Missoula; map MT8, grid a4.

Campsites, facilities: There are 43 RV or tent campsites, some with hookups. Showers, laundry facilities, a store, and a playground are available.

Reservations, fees: No reservations are needed; the fee is $10–12 per night. Open year-round.

Directions: From Missoula, go west on I-90 to Exit 96, then two miles north on U.S. 93 to the campground on the right.

Contact: Out Post Campground, 11600 Hwy. 93, Missoula, MT 59808; 406/549-2016.

Trip notes: You can fish and swim in the Clark Fork River.

2 Jim & Mary's RV Park

 5

Location: In Missoula; map MT8, grid a4.

Campsites, facilities: There are 45 RV campsites; no tents are allowed. Showers, laundry facilities, water, and electricity available.

Reservations, fees: No reservations are needed; the fee is $19 per night. Open April 1–October 31.

Directions: From Missoula, go five miles west to Exit 96, then one mile north on U.S. 93 to the campground.

Contact: Jim & Mary's RV Park, 9800 Hwy. 93 N., Missoula, MT 59808; 406/549-4416.

Trip notes: You can hike, fish, swim, bike, and raft in Lolo National Forest.

3 Jellystone RV Park

 4

Location: In Missoula; map MT8, grid a4.

Campsites, facilities: There are 110 RV sites, which can accommodate a maximum RV length of 70 feet. There are complete facilities for family RVs, a playground, swimming pool, game room, and horseshoe pit. Showers, water, electricity, a store, and a sanitary disposal station are available. Group facilities are available, and there are some wheelchair-accessible facilities.

Reservations, fees: Reservations are accepted; the fee is $21–26 per night. Open May 1–October 31.

Directions: From Missoula, go west on I-90 to Exit 96, then .25 mile north on U.S. 93; the campground is on the left.

Contact: Jellystone RV Park, 9900 Jellystone Drive, Missoula, MT 59808; tel./fax 406/543-9400, 800/318-9644; website: www.campjellystonemt.com.

Trip notes: You can golf nearby, river raft, and fish here.

4 Mountain View Trailer Court

 5

Location: In Hamilton; map MT8, grid a5.

Campsites, facilities: There are 26 RV and tent campsites, some with hookups. Showers, laundry facilities, and a sanitary disposal station are provided, and fishing is available on the property.

Reservations, fees: Reservations are accepted; the fee is $8–12 per night. Open year-round.

Directions: From Highway 93 at Hamilton, take

the Hamilton exit to 1st Street.

Contact: Mountain View Trailer Court, 1420 N. 1st, Hamilton, MT 59840; 406/363-1848, fax 406/363-4355.

Trip notes: This quiet, peaceful campground has great views. You can hike and fish in Bitterroot National Forest.

5 Missoula KOA

   5

Location: In Missoula; map MT8, grid a4.

Campsites, facilities: There are 200 RV or tent campsites, some with hookups. Showers, laundry facilities, a store, hot tub, swimming pool, and a petting zoo are available.

Reservations, fees: Reservations are accepted; the fee is $18–28 per night. Open year-round.

Directions: From I-90 at Missoula, take the Reserve Street exit (Exit 101) and go 1.5 miles south to the campground on the right.

Contact: Missoula KOA, 3450 Tina Ave., Missoula, MT 59808; 406/549-0881, 800/562-5366, fax 406/549-0594.

Trip notes: You can hike and fish in Bitterroot National Forest.

6 Lewis & Clark

   7

Location: West of Lolo; map MT8, grid a3.

Campsites, facilities: There are 18 RV or tent campsites, which can accommodate a maximum RV length of 30 feet.

Reservations, fees: No reservations are needed; the fee is $6 per night. Open May 20–September 30. The stay limit is 14 days.

Directions: From Missoula, go south on U.S. 93/12 to Lolo. From Lolo, go 15 miles west on U.S. 12 to the campground.

Contact: Lolo National Forest, Building 24A, Fort Missoula, Missoula, MT 59802; 406/329-3814.

Trip notes: This campground is on Lolo Creek, where you can fish. There are numerous hiking trails in the Bitterroot Mountains.

7 Square & Round Dance Center

     4

Location: In Lolo; map MT8, grid a4.

Campsites, facilities: There are 60 RV or tent campsites, some with hookups. There are showers, a sanitary disposal facility, fishing stream access, and a square dance center.

Reservations, fees: No reservations are needed; the fee is $12–18 per night. Open May 1–September 1.

Directions: From Missoula, go south on U.S. 93/12 to Lolo. From Lolo, go 2.5 miles west on U.S. 12; the campground is on the left.

Contact: Square & Round Dance Center, 9955 Hwy. 12, Lolo, MT 59847; 406/273-0141.

Trip notes: You can hike, fish, swim, bike, and raft in Lolo National Forest.

8 Lolo Hot Springs Resort

     6

Location: In Lolo National Forest; map MT8, grid b2.

Campsites, facilities: There are 130 RV or tent campsites, some with hookups. There are showers, a restaurant, and hot springs pools.

Reservations, fees: No reservations are needed; the fee is $8–25 per night. Open May 1–October 1.

Directions: From Missoula go 10 miles south on U.S. 93 and 25 miles west on U.S. 12 to the hot springs.

Contact: Lolo Hot Springs Resort, 38500 Hwy. 12, Lolo, MT 59847; 406/273-2294, 800/273-2290.

Trip notes: You can soak and swim in the natural hot springs pools here. This campground is on Lolo Creek, where you can fish. Numerous hiking trails are in the Bitterroot Mountains.

9 Lee Creek

 6

Location: In Lolo National Forest; map MT8, grid b2.

Campsites, facilities: There are 22 RV or tent campsites, which can accommodate a maximum RV length of 30 feet.

Reservations, fees: No reservations are needed; the fee is $6 per night. Open May 20–September 30.

Directions: From Missoula, go south on U.S. 93/12 to Lolo. From Lolo, go 26 miles west on U.S. 12 to the campground.

Contact: Lolo National Forest, Building 24A, Fort Missoula, Missoula, MT 59802; 406/329-3814.

Trip notes: This campground is on Lolo Creek, where you can fish. There are numerous hiking trails in the Bitterroot Mountains.

10 Ekstrom Stage Station

 6

Location: On Rock Creek; map MT8, grid b6.

Campsites, facilities: There are 59 RV and numerous tent campsites. Showers, laundry facilities, a store, water, electricity, a sanitary disposal facility, swimming pool, restaurant, playground, and tepees are available.

Reservations, fees: No reservations are needed; the fee is $10–20 per night. Open May 1–September 30.

Directions: From Missoula, go east on I-90 to Exit 126. Go .75 mile south on Rock Creek Road; the campground is on the right.

Contact: Ekstrom Stage Station, 81 Rock Creek Rd., Clinton, MT 59825; 406/825-3183.

Trip notes: Ekstrom Stage Station is a collection of historic log buildings reassembled to serve as a campground, with the amenities housed in the log buildings. You can fish in Rock Creek and hike the surrounding area. Saddle horses are available for trail rides.

11 Chalet Bearmouth Campground

 5

Location: In Clinton; map MT8, grid b7.

Campsites, facilities: There are 66 RV or tent campsites. Showers, laundry facilities, a store, water, electricity, a motel, restaurant, and sanitary disposal station are available.

Reservations, fees: No reservations are needed; the fee is $19–25 per night. Open year-round.

Directions: From Missoula, go 33 miles east on I-90 to Exit 138; go about .25 mile to the campground on the right.

Contact: Chalet Bearmouth Campground, P.O. Box 975, Clinton, MT 59825; 406/825-9950, 406/825-9950.

Trip notes: You can fish, hike, and bike in the national forest.

12 Beavertail Hill State Park

 5

Location: Southeast of Missoula; map MT8, grid b6.

Campsites, facilities: There are 28 RV or tent campsites, some with grills and picnic tables, and can accommodate a maximum RV length of 28 feet. Water and a hand boat launch are available.

Reservations, fees: No reservations are needed; the fee is $12 per night. Open May 1–September 30. The stay limit is 14 days.

Directions: From Missoula, go 26 miles southeast on I-90 to milepost 130, Beavertail exit; then go .25 mile south on the county road to the park.

Contact: Fish, Wildlife & Parks, 3201 Spurgin Rd., Missoula, MT 59801; 406/542-5500.

Trip notes: The campsites have cottonwood trees and a half mile of Clark Fork River frontage for fishing and floating. Boating is carry-in only. Missoula has golf courses and shopping.

13 Elkhorn Guest Ranch

 6

Location: In Clinton; map MT8, grid b6.

Campsites, facilities: There are 58 RV and 62 tent campsites. Showers, laundry facilities, a store, water, electricity, a sanitary disposal facility, swimming pool, restaurant, and cabins are available.

Reservations, fees: No reservations are needed; the fee is $15–25 per night. Open May 1–September 1.

Directions: From Missoula, go 20 miles east on I-90, then four miles south to Exit 126. The campground is on the left.

Contact: Elkhorn Guest Ranch, 408 Rock Creek Rd., Clinton, MT 59825; 406/825-3220, fax 406/825-3224; website: www.montana.com /elkhorn; email: cln3224@montana.com.

Trip notes: Elkhorn Guest Ranch has two miles of Rock Creek frontage for fishing and floating.

14 Good Time Camping & RV Park

 5

Location: Near Garnet Ghost Town; map MT8, grid b8.

Campsites, facilities: There are 28 RV or tent campsites. Showers, laundry facilities, a store, water, electricity, and propane gas are available.

Reservations, fees: No reservations are needed; the fee is $12–15.60 per night. Open April 1–October 1.

Directions: From Butte, go west on I-90 about 68 miles to e Exit 154 at Drummond, make a left, and go through town. At the stop sign (Hwy. 1), turn right and follow Frontage Road for two miles; the campground is on the left. From I-90 eastbound take Exit 153 at Drummond, go left at the stop sign, and follow Frontage Road for two miles to the campground on the left.

Contact: Good Time Camping & RV Park, 239 Frontage Rd. West, Drummond, MT 59832; tel./ fax 406/288-3608; email: turtle@montana.com.

Trip notes: This campground has grassy sites and is near Garnet Ghost Town. You can hike and fish in the national forest.

15 Chief Looking Glass

 5

Location: South of Missoula; map MT8, grid b4.

Campsites, facilities: There are 10 RV and 25 tent campsites and a hand boat launch.

Reservations, fees: No reservations are needed; the fee is $10 per night. Open May 1–November 30. The stay limit is seven days.

Directions: From Missoula, go 14 miles south on U.S. 93 to milepost 77, then one mile east on the county road to the campground.

Contact: Fish, Wildlife & Parks, 3201 Spurgin Rd., Missoula, MT 59801; 406/542-5500.

Trip notes: You can boat and fish here, and golf in nearby Missoula.

16 Charles Waters

 6

Location: In Bitterroot National Forest; map MT8, grid b4.

Campsites, facilities: There are 18 RV or tent campsites, which can accommodate a maximum RV length of 45 feet. A wheelchair-accessible restroom is available.

Reservations, fees: No reservations are needed; the fee is $9 per night. Open May 25–September 10. The stay limit is 14 days.

Directions: From Missoula, go south on U.S. 93 to Stevensville. From Stevensville, go two miles northwest on County Road 296, then four miles north on U.S. 93 and two miles west on County Road 22, and finally one mile west on Forest Service Road 1316 to the campground.

Contact: Bitterroot National Forest, Stevensville Ranger District, 88 Main St., Stevensville, MT 59870; 406/777-5461, fax 406/777-5461; website: www.fs.fed.us/r1/bitterroot.

Trip notes: You can fish and hike in Bitterroot National Forest.

17 Norton

 5

Location: Near Missoula; map MT8, grid b6.

Campsites, facilities: There are 10 RV or tent campsites, which can accommodate a maximum RV length of 16 feet.

Reservations, fees: No reservations are needed; the fee is $5 per night. Open year-round. The stay limit is 14 days.

Directions: From Missoula, go 22 miles east on I-90 to Rock Creek Exit, then 11 miles south on Forest Service Road 102 to Norton campground.

Contact: Lolo National Forest, Missoula Ranger District, Bldg. 24A, Fort Missoula, MT 59804; 406/329-3814.

Trip notes: You can fish and hike here.

18 Grizzly

 5

Location: In Lolo National Forest; map MT8, grid b6.

Campsites, facilities: There are nine RV or tent campsites, which can accommodate a maximum RV length of 35 feet.

Reservations, fees: No reservations are needed; there is no fee. Open year-round. The stay limit is 14 days.

Directions: From Missoula, go 22 miles east on I-90 to Rock Creek Exit, then 11 miles south on Forest Service Road 102, one mile east on Ranch Creek Road to Grizzly campground.

Contact: Lolo National Forest, Bldg. 24A, Fort Missoula, Missoula, MT 59801; 406/329-3814, 406/329-3750, fax 406/329-1049; website: www.fs.fed.us/r1/lolo.

Trip notes: You can hike and fish in Lolo National Forest.

19 Dalles

 5

Location: In Lolo National Forest; map MT8, grid b6.

Campsites, facilities: There are 10 RV or tent campsites, which can accommodate a maximum RV length of 32 feet.

Reservations, fees: No reservations are needed; no fees are charged. Open year-round. The stay limit is 14 days.

Directions: From Missoula, go 22 miles east on I-90 to Rock Creek Exit, then 13 miles south on Forest Service Road 102 to the campground on the right.

Contact: Lolo National Forest, Bldg. 24A, Fort Missoula, Missoula, MT 59801; 406/329-3814, 406/329-3750, fax 406/329-1049; website: www.fs.fed.us/r1/lolo.

Trip notes: You can hike and fish in Lolo National Forest.

20 Harry's Flat

 5

Location: In Lolo National Forest; map MT8, grid b6.

Campsites, facilities: There are 18 RV or tent campsites, which can accommodate a maximum RV length of 32 feet.

Reservations, fees: No reservations are needed; the fee is $5 per night. Open year-round. The stay limit is 14 days.

Directions: From Missoula, go 22 miles east on I-90 to Rock Creek Exit, then 18 miles south on Forest Service Road 102 to the campground on the right.

Contact: Lolo National Forest, Bldg. 24A, Fort Missoula, Missoula, MT 59801; 406/329-3814, fax 406/329-1049.

Trip notes: You can hike and fish in Lolo National Forest.

21 Bitterroot Flat

 6

Location: In Lolo National Forest; map MT8, grid c6.

Campsites, facilities: There are 15 RV or tent campsites, which can accommodate a maximum RV length of 32 feet.

Reservations, fees: No reservations are needed; the fee is $5 per night. Open May 20–September 30. The stay limit is 14 days.

Directions: From Missoula, go 22 miles east on I-90 to Rock Creek Exit, and then go 24 miles south on Forest Service Road 102.

Contact: Lolo National Forest, Bldg. 24A, Fort Missoula, Missoula, MT 59801; 406/329-3814, 406/329-3750, fax 406/329-1049; website: www.fs.fed.us/r1/lolo.

Trip notes: You can hike and fish in Lolo National Forest.

22 Tucker Crossin' RV Park Campground

 6

Location: Near Hamilton; map MT8, grid c4.

Campsites, facilities: There are 25 RV or tent campsites, some with hookups. Showers, laundry facilities, and a sanitary disposal station are available.

Reservations, fees: No reservations are needed; the fee is $10 and up per night. Open May–October.

Directions: From Hamilton, go seven miles north on U.S. 93 to Tucker Crossing fishing access and the campground.

Contact: Tucker Crossin' RV Park Campground, 1714 U.S. Hwy. 93, Victor, MT 59875; tel./fax 406/642-3089.

Trip notes: There are stocked trout ponds, river access, and excellent wildlife viewing opportunities. You can hike, float, and golf nearby.

23 Racetrack

 5

Location: In Deerlodge National Forest; map MT8, grid c6.

Campsites, facilities: There are 13 RV or tent campsites, which can accommodate a maximum RV length of 22 feet. A wheelchair-accessible restroom is available.

Reservations, fees: No reservations are needed; the fee is $5 per night. Open May 25–September 15. The stay limit is 16 days.

Directions: From Butte, go west on I-90 about 70 miles to Exit 195 (Racetrack), then go west one mile, then south .75 mile, then westerly on Forest Service Road 169 to the campground.

Contact: Deerlodge National Forest, 1 Hollenback Rd., Deer Lodge, MT 59722; 406/846-1770; website: www.fs.fed.us/r1/bdnf.

Trip notes: You can fish here. Be sure to visit the historic Grant-Kohrs Ranch, which was the home of one of Montana's largest cattle barons. The original furnishings are in the house, and there is horse-drawn equipment that was used in the 1800s.

24 Blodgett Canyon Campground

 6

Location: In Lolo National Forest; map MT8, grid c3.

Campsites, facilities: There are six RV or tent campsites, which can accommodate a maximum RV length of 30 feet.

Reservations, fees: No reservations are needed; there is no fee. Open May 15–September 15. The stay limit is five days.

Directions: From Hamilton, go five miles northwest to the campground.

Contact: Lolo National Forest, Building 24A, Fort Missoula, Missoula, MT 59802; 406/329-3814.

Trip notes: You can fish and hike here.

25 Flint Creek

 5

Location: In Deerlodge National Forest; map MT8, grid c7.

Campsites, facilities: There are 16 RV or tent campsites, which can accommodate a maximum RV length of 16 feet. A wheelchair-accessible restroom is available.

Reservations, fees: No reservations are needed; no fee is charged. Open May 1–October 30. The stay limit is 16 days.

Directions: From Philipsburg, go eight miles south on Highway 1 to the campground.

Contact: Deerlodge National Forest, 8810A Business Loop, P.O. Box H, Philipsburg, MT 59858; 406/859-3211, fax 406/859-3689; website: www.fs.fed.us/r1/bdnf.

Trip notes: You can hike and fish in Deerlodge National Forest.

26 Angler's Roost

 5

Location: Near Hamilton; map MT8, grid d4.

Campsites, facilities: There are 69 RV and tent campsites. Showers, laundry facilities, a store, water, electricity, and a sanitary disposal station are available.

Reservations, fees: No reservations are needed; the fee is $10.40–16.64 per night. Open year-round.

Directions: From Hamilton at U.S. 93, go three miles south to the campground on the right.

Contact: Angler's Roost, 815 Hwy. 93 South, Hamilton, MT 59840; 406/363-1268.

Trip notes: You can hike and fish in Bitterroot National Forest.

27 Crystal Creek

 6

Location: In Deerlodge National Forest; map MT8, grid d5.

Campsites, facilities: There are three primitive RV or tent campsites, which can accom-

modate a maximum RV length of 16 feet.

Reservations, fees: No reservations are needed; no fee is charged. Open July 1–September 30. The stay limit is 16 days.

Directions: From Philipsburg, go six miles south on Highway 1, then west on Highway 38 for 25 miles to the campground.

Contact: Deerlodge National Forest, 8810A Business Loop, P.O. Box H, Philipsburg, MT 59858; 406/859-3211, fax 406/859-3689; website: www.fs.fed.us/r1/bdnf.

Trip notes: This is a primitive campsite. The Crystal Creek Trail begins here, a 3.4-mile hike (the first half mile is a primitive road).

28 Cable Mountain

 5

Location: In Deerlodge National Forest; map MT8, grid d8.

Campsites, facilities: There are 11 RV or tent campsites, which can accommodate a maximum RV length of 22 feet.

Reservations, fees: No reservations are needed; the fee is $8 per night. Open May 29–September 15. The stay limit is 14 days.

Directions: From Philipsburg go south on Highway 1 for 12 miles to Forest Service Road 65, then north on Forest Service Road 65 for three miles, then east on Forest Service Road 242 .2 mile to the campground.

Contact: Deerlodge National Forest, 8810A Business Loop, P.O. Box H, Philipsburg, MT 59858; 406/859-3211, fax 406/859-3689; website: www.fs.fed.us/r1/bdnf.

Trip notes: You can fish and hike in Deerlodge National Forest.

29 Lost Creek State Park

 7

Location: Near Anaconda; map MT8, grid d8.

Campsites, facilities: There are 25 RV or tent campsites, which can accommodate a maximum RV length of 23 feet. Grills, picnic tables, water, and restrooms are available.

Pets are allowed on leashes.

Reservations, fees: No reservations are needed; the fee is $12 per night. Open May 1–November 30. The stay limit is 14 days.

Directions: From Anaconda, go 1.5 miles east on Highway 1 at milepost 5, then two miles north on Route 273 and six miles west to the park.

Contact: Fish, Wildlife & Parks, 3201 Spurgin Rd., Missoula, MT 59802; 406/542-5500.

Trip notes: There are nature trails, fishing and excellent opportunities to view wildlife, such as mountain goats and bighorn sheep. The gray limestone cliffs and pink and white granite towers reach a height of 1,200 feet. Lost Creek Falls tumbles 50 feet, and is in the northwest corner of the 25-acre park. Anaconda has golf courses.

30 Schumaker

 7

Location: In Bitterroot National Forest; map MT8, grid d3.

Campsites, facilities: There are five tent sites and a hand boat launch available.

Reservations, fees: No reservations are needed; no fee is charged. Open July 15–September 15. The stay limit is 14 days.

Directions: From Salmon, Idaho, go 77 miles north on U.S. 93 to Darby. From Darby, go seven miles north on U.S. 93, two miles west on the county road, 16 miles west on Forest Service Road 429, and two miles north on Forest Service Road 5505 to the campground.

Contact: Bitterroot National Forest, 1801 N. 1st St., Hamilton, MT 59840; 406/363-7161.

Trip notes: The Bitterroot River has good fishing, and Bitterroot National Forest has hiking trails. You can fish, swim, and boat on Lake Como.

31 Black Bear

 6

Location: In Bitterroot National Forest; map

MT8, grid d5.

Campsites, facilities: There are six RV or tent campsites, which can accommodate a maximum RV length of 18 feet. A wheelchair-accessible restroom is available, but no water. This is a pack-in, pack-out campground.

Reservations, fees: No reservations are needed; there is no fee. Open June 1–September 1. The stay limit is 14 days.

Directions: From Hamilton, go two miles south on U.S. 93, then 13 miles east on Highway 38 to the campground.

Contact: Bitterroot National Forest, Darby Ranger District, 712 Hwy. 93 North, P.O. Box 388, Darby, MT 59829; 406/821-3913, fax 406/821-3675; website: www.fs.fed.us/r1/bitterroot.

Trip notes: You can hike and fish in Bitterroot National Forest.

32 Denton's Point

 8

Location: At Georgetown Lake; map MT8, grid d7.

Campsites, facilities: There are 24 RV and 15 tent campsites. Showers, laundry facilities, a sanitary disposal facility, restaurant, marina, and boat rentals are available.

Reservations, fees: No reservations are needed; the fee is $12.48–21.84 per night. Open May 1–September 20.

Directions: From Anaconda, go west on Highway 1 and then two miles to the campground, which is on the south shore of Georgetown Lake.

Contact: Denton's Point, Denton's Rd., Anaconda, MT 59711; 406/563-6030.

Trip notes: You can fish, boat, and swim at Georgetown Lake.

33 East Fork

 6

Location: In Deerlodge National Forest; map MT8, grid d7.

Campsites, facilities: There are 10 RV or tent

campsites, which can accommodate a maximum RV length of 22 feet.

Reservations, fees: No reservations are needed; no fee is charged. Open May 1–September 30. The stay limit is 16 days.

Directions: From Philipsburg, go six miles south on Highway 1, then six miles southwest on Highway 38, five miles southeast on Forest Service Road 672, and one mile southeast on Forest Service Road 9349 to the campground.

Contact: Deerlodge National Forest, 8810A Business Loop, P.O. Box H, Philipsburg, MT 59858; 406/859-3211, fax 406/859-3689; website: www.fs.fed.us/r1/bdnf.

Trip notes: You can fish and hike in Deerlodge National Forest.

34 Spillway

 6

Location: In Beaverhead Deerlodge National Forest; map MT8, grid d7.

Campsites, facilities: There are 13 RV or tent campsites, which can accommodate a maximum RV length of 22 feet. A wheelchair-accessible restroom is available.

Reservations, fees: No reservations are needed; there is no fee. Open May 25–September 30. The stay limit is 16 days.

Directions: Go south on Highway 1 for six miles to Highway 38, then go west on Highway 38 for six miles, south on Forest Service Road 672 for five miles and south on Forest Service Road 5141 for a mile to the campground.

Contact: Beaverhead Deerlodge National Forest, 8810A Business Loop, P.O. Box H, Philipsburg, MT 59858; 406/859-3211, fax 406/859-3689; website: www.fs.fed.us/r1/bdnf.

Trip notes: You can fish and hike here.

35 Spring Hill

 5

Location: In Deerlodge National Forest; map

MT8, grid d8.

Campsites, facilities: There are 15 RV or tent campsites, which can accommodate a maximum RV length of 22 feet.

Reservations, fees: No reservations are needed; the fee is $8 per night. Open May 25–September 5. The stay limit is 16 days.

Directions: From Anaconda, go 11 miles northwest on Highway 1 to the campground.

Contact: Deerlodge National Forest, 91 N. Frontage Rd., Deer Lodge, MT 59722; 406/846-1770, fax 406/846-2127; website: www.fs.fed.us/r1/bdnf.

Trip notes: You can fish and hike in Deerlodge National Forest. At Georgetown Lake, eight miles to the west, you can fish, swim, boat, and water-ski.

36 Bear Creek Pass

 7

Location: In Bitterroot National Forest; map MT8, grid d3.

Campsites, facilities: There are seven tent campsites.

Reservations, fees: No reservations are needed; there is no fee. Open July 15–September 15.

Directions: From Salmon, Idaho, go 77 miles north on U.S. 93 to Darby. From Darby, go seven miles north on U.S. 93, then 18 miles west on Forest Service Road 429 (Lost Horse Road) to the campground.

Contact: Bitterroot National Forest, 1801 N. 1st St., Hamilton, MT 59840; 406/363-7161.

Trip notes: The Bitterroot River has good fishing. The Bitterroot National Forest has hiking trails. You can fish, swim, and boat on Lake Como.

37 Bitterroot Family Campground

 5

Location: Near Hamilton; map MT8, grid d4.

Campsites, facilities: There are 51 RV or tent

campsites. Showers, laundry facilities, a store, water, electricity, restrooms, and a sanitary disposal station are available. A playground and trout pond are on-site.

Reservations, fees: No reservations are needed; the fee is $10.40–16.64 per night. Open year-round.

Directions: From Hamilton, go eight miles south on U.S. 93 to milepost 39; the campground is on the east side.

Contact: Bitterroot Family Campground, 1744 S. U.S. 93, Hamilton, MT 59840; 406/362-2430, 800/453-2430.

Trip notes: There is river access for fishing, and you can hike in the national forest.

38 Copper Creek

 5

Location: In Deerlodge National Forest; map MT8, grid d6.

Campsites, facilities: There are seven RV or tent campsites, which can accommodate a maximum RV length of 22 feet. A wheelchair-accessible restroom is available.

Reservations, fees: No reservations are needed; there is no fee. Open May 15–September 30. The stay limit is 16 days.

Directions: From Philipsburg, go six miles east on Highway 1, then nine miles southwest on Highway 38 and 10 miles south on Forest Service Road 5106 to the campground.

Contact: Deerlodge National Forest, 8810A Business Loop, P.O. Box H, Philipsburg, MT 59858; 406/859-3211, fax 406/859-3689; website: www.fs.fed.us/r1/bdnf.

Trip notes: You can hike and fish in Deerlodge National Forest.

39 Lick Creek Campground

 5

Location: North of Darby; map MT8, grid d4.

Campsites, facilities: There are 54 RV or tent campsites, some with hookups. There are showers, laundry facilities, a store, and a sanitary disposal facility available.

Reservations, fees: No reservations are needed; the fee is $11 per night. Open April 1–October 1.

Directions: From Hamilton, go 10 miles south on U.S. 93 to the campground.

Contact: Lick Creek Campground; 406/821-3840.

Trip notes: This campground is near a fishing pond, and you may see the occasional moose. You can boat, fish, swim, and hike here.

40 Lake Como Lower

 7

Location: In Bitterroot National Forest; map MT8, grid d4.

Campsites, facilities: There are 12 RV or tent campsites, which can accommodate a maximum RV length of 50 feet. A wheelchair-accessible restroom and a trailer boat launch are available.

Reservations, fees: No reservations are needed; the fee is $7 per night. Open May 31–September 5. The stay limit is 14 days.

Directions: From Salmon, go 77 miles north on U.S. 93 to Darby. From Darby, go four miles north on U.S. 93, and five miles west on County Road 82 to the campground.

Contact: Bitterroot National Forest, 1801 N. 1st St., Hamilton, MT 59840; 406/363-7161.

Trip notes: This campground is near a fishing pond, and you may see the occasional moose. You can boat, fish, swim, and hike here.

41 Lake Como Upper

 7

Location: In Bitterroot National Forest; map MT8, grid e4.

Campsites, facilities: There are 10 RV or tent campsites, which can accommodate a maximum RV length of 16 feet.

Reservations, fees: No reservations are needed; the fee is $7 per night. Open May 31–September 5. The stay limit is 14 days.

Directions: From Salmon, go 77 miles north on U.S. 93 to Darby. From Darby, go four miles north on U.S. 93, and five miles west on County Road 82 to the campground.

Contact: Bitterroot National Forest, 1801 N. 1st St., Hamilton, MT 59840; 406/363-7161.

Trip notes: This campground is near a fishing pond, and you can see the occasional moose. You can boat, fish, swim, and hike here.

42 Martin Creek

 5

Location: In the Bitterroot National Forest; map MT8, grid e6.

Campsites, facilities: There are seven RV or tent campsites, which can accommodate a maximum RV length of 50 feet.

Reservations, fees: No reservations are needed; the fee is $7 per night. Open June 15–December 1. The stay limit is 14 days.

Directions: From Hamilton, go south on U.S. 93 35 miles to Sula. From Sula, go one mile west on U.S. 93, then four miles northeast on County Road 472 and 12 miles northeast on Forest Service Road 80 to the campground.

Contact: Bitterroot National Forest, Sula Ranger District, 7338 Hwy. 93 South, Sula, MT 59871; 406/821-3201, fax 406/821-3678.

Trip notes: You can hike and fish in Bitterroot National Forest.

43 Seymour

 5

Location: In Beaverhead National Forest; map MT8, grid e8.

Campsites, facilities: There are 17 RV or tent campsites, which can accommodate a maximum RV length of 16 feet. Pets are allowed on leashes.

Reservations, fees: No reservations are needed; there is no fee charged. Open May 25–September 15. The stay limit is 14 days.

Directions: From Butte, go south on I-15 19 miles to Highway 43 and then west to Wise River. From Wise River, go 11 miles west on Highway 43, then four miles north on Route 274, and eight miles northwest on Forest Service Road 934 to the campground.

Contact: Beaverhead National Forest, Hwy. 43, P.O. Box 100, Wise River, MT 59762; 406/832-3178, fax 406/832-3311; website: www.fs.fed.us /r1/bdnf.

Trip notes: You can fish and hike here.

44 Spring Gulch

 5

Location: In the Bitterroot National Forest; map MT8, grid e4.

Campsites, facilities: There are 10 RV or tent campsites, which can accommodate a maximum RV length of 50 feet.

Reservations, fees: No reservations are needed; the fee is $11 per night. Open June 1–September 15. The stay limit is 14 days.

Directions: From Hamilton, go south on U.S. 93 35 miles to Sula. From Sula, go five miles northwest on U.S. 93 to the campground.

Contact: Bitterroot National Forest, Sula Ranger District, 7338 Hwy. 93 South, Sula, MT 59871; 406/821-3201, fax 406/821-3678.

Trip notes: You can hike and fish in Bitterroot National Forest.

45 Jennings Camp

 6

Location: In the Bitterroot National Forest; map MT8, grid e5.

Campsites, facilities: There are four RV or tent campsites, which can accommodate a maximum RV length of 30 feet.

Reservations, fees: No reservations are needed; no fee is charged. Open June 15–December 1. The stay limit is 14 days.

Directions: From Hamilton, go south on U.S. 93 35 miles to Sula. From Sula, go one mile west on U.S. 93, then 10 miles northeast on County Road 472 to the campground.

Contact: Bitterroot National Forest, Sula

Ranger District, 7338 Hwy. 93 South, Sula, MT 59871; 406/821-3201, fax 406/821-3678.

Trip notes: You can fish and hike in Bitterroot National Forest.

46 Moosehead Campground, Store, & Rock Shop

 5

Location: Near Sula; map MT8, grid e4.

Campsites, facilities: There are 91 RV or tent campsites, some with hookups. Showers, a store, a sanitary disposal station, and museum and rock shop are available.

Reservations, fees: No reservations are needed; the fee is $17–21 per night. Open April 1–November 20.

Directions: From Hamilton, go south on U.S. 93 35 miles to Sula. From Sula, go three miles north on U.S. 93 at milepost 16 to the campground.

Contact: Moosehead Campground, Store, & Rock Shop, 6457 Hwy. 93 South, Conner, MT 59827; 406/821-3327.

Trip notes: You can hike and fish in Bitterroot National Forest and the Anaconda-Pintler Wilderness.

47 Sam Billings Memorial

 7

Location: In Lolo National Forest; map MT8, grid e3.

Campsites, facilities: There are 11 RV or tent campsites, which can accommodate a maximum RV length of 30 feet.

Reservations, fees: No reservations are needed; there is no fee. Open June 1–September 15. The stay limit is 14 days.

Directions: From Salmon, go 77 miles north on U.S. 93 to Darby. From Darby, go four miles south on U.S. 93, 13 miles southwest on Highway 473 and one mile northwest on Forest Service Road 5631 to the Sam Billings campground on the left.

Contact: Lolo National Forest, Building 24A,

Fort Missoula, Missoula, MT 59802; 406/329-3814.

Trip notes: This is a nice camping spot, and the trailhead for Boulder Creek is here. The Bitterroot River has good fishing.

48 Warm Springs

 5

Location: In the Bitterroot National Forest; map MT8, grid e4.

Campsites, facilities: There are 14 RV or tent campsites, which can accommodate a maximum RV length of 26 feet.

Reservations, fees: No reservations are needed; the fee is $8 per night. Open May 25–September 10. The stay limit is 14 days.

Directions: From Hamilton, go south on U.S. 93 35 miles to Sula. From Sula, go five miles northwest on U.S. 93, then one mile southwest on County Road 100; the campground is on the left.

Contact: Bitterroot National Forest, Sula Ranger District, 7338 Hwy. 93 South, Sula, MT 59871; 406/821-3201, fax 406/821-3678.

Trip notes: You can hike and fish in Bitterroot National Forest.

49 Sula Country Store, Campground, & RV Park

 5

Location: in Sula; map MT8, grid e5.

Campsites, facilities: There are 42 RV and tent campsites, some with hookups. Laundry facilities, showers, a store, a sanitary disposal facility, cabins and 24-hour gas and diesel are available.

Reservations, fees: No reservations are needed; the fee is $18–22 per night. Open year-round.

Directions: From U.S. 93 at the Idaho-Montana state line, go 13 miles north to Sula; the campground is on the right.

Contact: Sula Country Store, Campground, & RV Park, 7060 Hwy. 93 South, Sula, MT 59871;

406/821-3364.

Trip notes: You can fish on the east fork of the Bitterroot River and bike, hike, and view wildlife in the Anaconda-Pintler Wilderness.

50 East Bank

 6

Location: On the Big Hole River; map MT8, grid e8.

Campsites, facilities: There are five RV or tent campsites, which can accommodate a maximum RV length of 24 feet. A wheelchair-accessible restroom and trailer boat launch are available. Pets are allowed on leashes.

Reservations, fees: No reservations are needed; no fee is charged. Open year-round. The stay limit is 14 days.

Directions: From Butte, go south on I-15 19 miles to Highway 43 and then west to Wise River. From Wise River, go eight miles west on Highway 43 to the campground.

Contact: Bureau of Land Management, Butte Field Office, P.O. Box 3388, Butte, MT 59702; 406/494-5059.

Trip notes: This campground is on the Big Hole River, which is known for quality rafting and trout fishing. The rafting season is best from mid-May–mid-July, and guided trips are recommended.

51 Dickie Bridge

 5

Location: Near Butte; map MT8, grid e8.

Campsites, facilities: There are eight RV or tent campsites, which can accommodate a maximum RV length of 24 feet. Pets are allowed on leashes.

Reservations, fees: No reservations are needed; there is no fee. Open year-round. The stay limit is 14 days.

Directions: From Butte, go 19 miles south on I-15 to Divide. From Divide, go 18 miles west on Highway 43 to the campground.

Contact: Bureau of Land Management, Butte

Field Office, P.O. Box 3388, Butte, MT 59702; 406/494-5059.

Trip notes: You can fish and hike in the area.

52 Rombo

 6

Location: In Lolo National Forest; map MT8, grid e3.

Campsites, facilities: There are 15 RV or tent campsites; which can accommodate a maximum RV length of 40 feet.

Reservations, fees: No reservations are needed; the fee is $7 per night. Open June 25–September 6. The stay limit is 14 days.

Directions: From Salmon, go 77 miles north on U.S. 93 to Darby. From Darby, go four miles south on U.S. 93 to County Road 473, and take it 8.5 miles southwest to the Rombo campground on the right.

Contact: Lolo National Forest, Building 24A, Fort Missoula, Missoula, MT 59802; 406/329-3814.

Trip notes: The Bitterroot River has good fishing, and you can hike nearby.

53 Crazy Creek

 5

Location: In the Bitterroot National Forest; map MT8, grid e4.

Campsites, facilities: There are six RV or tent campsites, which can accommodate a maximum RV length of 26 feet.

Reservations, fees: No reservations are needed; the fee is $7 per night. Open May 25–September 15. The stay limit is 14 days.

Directions: From Hamilton, go south on U.S. 93 35 miles to Sula. From Sula, go five miles northwest on U.S. 93, then one mile southwest on County Road 100 and three miles southwest on Forest Service Road 370 to the campground.

Contact: Bitterroot National Forest, Sula Ranger District, 7338 Hwy. 93 South, Sula, MT 59871; 406/821-3201, fax 406/821-3678.

Trip notes: You can hike, bike, and fish in Bitterroot National Forest.

54 Indian Trees

     6

Location: In Bitterroot National Forest; map MT8, grid e4.

Campsites, facilities: There are 17 RV or tent campsites, which can accommodate a maximum RV length of 50 feet.

Reservations, fees: No reservations are needed; the fee is $9 per night. Open May 25–September 10. The stay limit is 14 days.

Directions: From Hamilton go south on U.S. 93 35 miles to Sula. From Sula, go six miles south on U.S. 93, then one mile southwest on Forest Service Road 729 to the campground.

Contact: Bitterroot National Forest, Sula Ranger District, 7338 Hwy. 93 South, Sula, MT 59871; 406/821-3201, fax 406/821-3678.

Trip notes: Lost Trail Hot Springs is a half mile away. You can fish and hike in Bitterroot National Forest.

55 Mussigbrod

    5

Location: In Beaverhead/Deerlodge National Forest; map MT8, grid e6.

Campsites, facilities: There are 10 RV campsites.

Reservations, fees: No reservations are needed; the fee is $7 per night. Open June 26–September 6. The stay limit is 16 days.

Directions: From Butte, go 19 miles south on I-15 to Highway 43, then go west to Wisdom. From Wisdom, go 1.5 miles west on Highway 43, nine miles on Lower North Fork Road, and 10 miles west on Mussigbrod Lake Road to the campground.

Contact: Beaverhead/Deerlodge National Forest, Wise River Ranger District, P.O. Box 100, Wise River, MT 59762; 406/832-3178.

Trip notes: You can boat, fish, and hike here.

56 Fourth of July

    6

Location: In the Beaverhead-Deerlodge National Forest; map MT8, grid f8.

Campsites, facilities: There are five RV or tent campsites, which can accommodate a maximum RV length of 24 feet.

Reservations, fees: No reservations are needed; the fee is $8 per night. Open June 15–September 15. The stay limit is 16 days.

Directions: From Butte, go south on I-15 19 miles to Divide, then go 12 miles west on Highway 43 to Wise River. From Wise River, go 11 miles southwest on Pioneer Mountains Scenic Byway (Forest Service Road 484) to the campground.

Contact: Beaverhead-Deerlodge National Forest, Hwy. 43, P.O. Box 100, Wise River, MT 59762; 406/832-3178; website: www.fs.fed.us/r1/bdnf.

Trip notes: The Pioneer Mountains Scenic Byway is a 40-mile drive through the Pioneer Mountains, between Highway 43 and County Road 278. You can hike and fish in the area, visit the ghost town of Coolidge, and see the remnants of the Elkhorn Mill and a narrow-gauge railroad that served the mill. You can dig in Crystal Park for amethyst, smoky quartz, and clear quartz crystals.

57 Boulder

    6

Location: In the Beaverhead-Deerlodge National Forest; map MT8, grid f8.

Campsites, facilities: There are 12 RV or tent campsites, which can accommodate a maximum RV length of 24 feet.

Reservations, fees: No reservations are needed; the fee is $8 per night. Open June 15–September 15. The stay limit is 16 days.

Directions: From Butte, go south on I-15 19 miles to Divide, then go 12 miles west on Highway 43 to Wise River. From Wise River, travel 12 miles southwest on Pioneer Mountains

Scenic Byway (Forest Service Road 484).

Contact: Beaverhead-Deerlodge National Forest, Hwy. 43, P.O. Box 100, Wise River, MT 59762; 406/832-3178; website: www.fs.fed.us/r1/bdnf.

Trip notes: The Pioneer Mountains Scenic Byway is a 40-mile drive through the Pioneer Mountains, between Highway 43 and County Road 278. You can hike and fish in the area, visit the ghost town of Coolidge, and see the remnants of the Elkhorn Mill and a narrow-gauge railroad that served the mill. You can dig in Crystal Park for amethyst, smoky quartz, and clear quartz crystals.

58 Lodgepole

 6

Location: In the Beaverhead-Deerlodge National Forest; map MT8, grid f8.

Campsites, facilities: There are 11 RV or tent campsites, which can accommodate a maximum RV length of 16 feet.

Reservations, fees: No reservations are needed; the fee is $8 per night. Open May 25–September 15. The stay limit is 16 days.

Directions: From Butte, go south on I-15 19 miles to Divide, then go 12 miles west on Highway 43 to Wise River. From Wise River, go 13 miles southwest on Pioneer Mountains Scenic Byway (Forest Service Road 484).

Contact: Beaverhead-Deerlodge National Forest, Hwy. 43, P.O. Box 100, Wise River, MT 59762; 406/832-3178; website: www.fs.fed.us/r1/bdnf.

Trip notes: The Pioneer Mountains Scenic Byway is a 40-mile drive through the Pioneer Mountains, between Highway 43 and County Road 278. You can hike and fish in the area, visit the ghost town of Coolidge, and see the remnants of the Elkhorn Mill and a narrow-gauge railroad that served the mill. You can dig in Crystal Park for amethyst, smoky quartz, and clear quartz crystals.

59 Beaverhead

 5

Location: At Clark Canyon Reservoir; map MT8, grid f8.

Campsites, facilities: There are five RV and tent campsites, a wheelchair-accessible restroom, and trailer boat launch.

Reservations, fees: No reservations are needed; there is no fee charged. Open year-round. The stay limit is 14 days.

Directions: From Dillon, go 20 miles south on I-15, and the campground is at Clark Canyon Reservoir.

Contact: U.S. Bureau of Reclamation, P.O. Box 30137, Billings, MT 59107-0137; 406/683-6472.

Trip notes: You can boat and fish here.

60 Painted Rock

 6

Location: In Bitterroot National Forest; map MT8, grid f3.

Campsites, facilities: There are 32 RV or tent campsites. A trailer boat launch is available.

Reservations, fees: No reservations are needed, and no fee is charged. Open year-round. The stay limit is 14 days.

Directions: From Hamilton, travel 20 miles south on U.S. 93, then 23 miles southwest on Route 473 to the campground.

Contact: Montana Fish, Wildlife & Parks, 1420 E. 6th Ave., Helena, Montana 59620; 406/444-2535.

Trip notes: You can hike and fish in Bitterroot National Forest.

61 Slate Creek

 6

Location: In Bitterroot National Forest; map MT8, grid f3.

Campsites, facilities: There are 13 RV or tent campsites, which can accommodate a maximum RV length of 30 feet.

Reservations, fees: No reservations are needed, and no fee is charged. Open June 25–September 6. The stay limit is 14 days.

Directions: From Missoula, go south on U.S. 93 65 miles to Darby. From Darby, go four miles south on U.S. 93, then 24 miles west on County Road 473 and two miles south on County Road 96 to the campground.

Contact: Bitterroot National Forest, West Fork Ranger District, 6735 W. Fork Rd., Darby, MT 59829; 406/821-3269, fax 406/821-3269.

Trip notes: You can hike and fish in Bitterroot National Forest.

62 Alta

 6

Location: In Bitterroot National Forest; map MT8, grid f3.

Campsites, facilities: There are 15 RV or tent campsites that can accommodate a maximum RV length of 30 feet.

Reservations, fees: No reservations are needed; the fee is $6 per night. Open June 25–September 6. The stay limit is 14 days.

Directions: From Missoula, go south on U.S. 93 65 miles to Darby. From Darby, drive four miles south on U.S. 93, then 22 miles southwest on West Fork Road (Route 473) to the campground.

Contact: Bitterroot National Forest, West Fork Ranger District, 6735 W. Fork Rd., Darby, MT 59829; 406/821-3269, fax 406/821-3269.

Trip notes: You can hike and fish in Bitterroot National Forest.

63 May Creek

 6

Location: West of Wisdom; map MT8, grid f6.

Campsites, facilities: There are 58 RV or tent campsites, which can accommodate a maximum RV length of 30 feet. Pets are allowed on leashes.

Reservations, fees: No reservations are needed; the fee is $4 per night. Open June

25–September 6. The stay limit is 16 days.

Directions: From Butte, go south on I-15 19 miles to Divide, then go 51 miles west on Highway 43 to Wisdom. From Wisdom, go 17 miles west on Highway 43 to the campground.

Contact: Beaverhead-Deerlodge National Forest, P.O. Box 238, Wisdom, MT 59761; 406/689-3243; website: www.fs.fed.us/r1/bdnf.

Trip notes: You can fish, swim, and boat here, and hiking trails are nearby. The Big Hole National Battlefield is just east of this campground.

64 Steel Creek

 5

Location: In Beaverhead-Deerlodge National Forest; map MT8, grid f7.

Campsites, facilities: There are seven RV or tent campsites.

Reservations, fees: No reservations are needed; the fee is $6 per night. Open June 26–September 6.

Directions: From Butte, go south on I-15 19 miles to Divide, then go 51 miles west on Highway 43 to Wisdom. From Wisdom, travel one mile north, then six miles east on Steel Creek Road to the campground.

Contact: Beaverhead-Deerlodge National Forest, P.O. Box 238, Wisdom, MT 59761; 406/689-3243; website: www.fs.fed.us/r1/bdnf.

Trip notes: Clark Canyon Reservoir has many fishing access sites and a park that has areas for boating, swimming, and fishing.

65 Mono Creek

 7

Location: In Beaverhead-Deerlodge National Forest; map MT8, grid f8.

Campsites, facilities: There are five RV or tent campsites, which can accommodate a maximum RV length of 16 feet.

Reservations, fees: No reservations are needed; the fee is $8 per night. Open June 15–September 30. The stay limit is 16 days.

Directions: From Butte, go south on I-15 19 miles to Divide, then go 12 miles west on Highway 43 to Wise River. From Wise River, go 23 miles southwest on Lower Elkhorn Road 2465 to the campground.

Contact: Beaverhead-Deerlodge National Forest, P.O. Box 238, Wisdom, MT 59761; 406/689-3243; website: www.fs.fed.us/r1/bdnf.

Trip notes: You can fish and hike in Beaverhead-Deerlodge National Forest.

66 Price Creek

   6

Location: In Beaverhead-Deerlodge National Forest; map MT8, grid f8.

Campsites, facilities: There are 28 RV or tent campsites.

Reservations, fees: No reservations are needed; the fee is $8 per night. Open May 22–September 15. The stay limit is 16 days.

Directions: From Dillon, drive three miles south on I-15, then 27 miles west on County Road 278 and 17 miles north on Pioneer Mountains Scenic Byway to the campground.

Contact: Beaverhead-Deerlodge National Forest, Dillon Ranger District, 420 Barrett St., Dillon, MT 59725-3572; 406/683-3900.

Trip notes: You can fish and hike in Beaverhead-Deerlodge National Forest. The Pioneer Mountains Scenic Byway is a 40-mile drive through the Pioneer Mountains, between Highway 43 and County Road 278. You can hike and fish in the area, visit the ghost town of Coolidge, and see the remnants of the Elkhorn Mill and a narrow-gauge railroad that served the mill. You can dig in Crystal Park for amethyst, smoky quartz, and clear quartz crystals.

67 Twin Lakes

   6

Location: Beaverhead-Deerlodge National Forest; map MT8, grid g6.

Campsites, facilities: There are 21 RV or tent campsites, which can accommodate a maxi-

mum RV length of 32 feet.

Reservations, fees: No reservations are needed; the fee is $8 per night. Open June 25–September 6. The stay limit is 16 days.

Directions: From Wisdom, go seven miles south on Route 278, then eight miles west on County Road 1290, five miles south on Forest Service Road 945 and six miles southwest on Forest Service Road 183 to the campground.

Contact: Beaverhead-Deerlodge National Forest, P.O. Box 238, Wisdom, MT 59761; 406/689-3243; website: www.fs.fed.us/r1/bdnf.

Trip notes: You can fish and hike in Beaverhead-Deerlodge National Forest.

68 Grasshopper

   6

Location: In Beaverhead-Deerlodge National Forest; map MT8, grid g8.

Campsites, facilities: There are 24 RV or tent campsites, which can accommodate a maximum RV length of 16 feet.

Reservations, fees: No reservations are needed; there is no fee. Open June 16–September 15. The stay limit is 16 days.

Directions: From Dillon, go three miles south on I-15, then 27 miles west on County Road 278 and 11.5 miles north on Pioneer Mountains Scenic Byway.

Contact: Beaverhead-Deerlodge National Forest, Dillon Ranger District, 420 Barrett St., Dillon, MT 59725-3572; 406/683-3900.

Trip notes: The Pioneer Mountains Scenic Byway is a 40-mile drive through the Pioneer Mountains, between Highway 43 and County Road 278. You can hike and fish in the area, visit the ghost town of Coolidge, and see the remnants of the Elkhorn Mill and a narrow-gauge railroad that served the mill. You can dig in Crystal Park for amethyst, smoky quartz, and clear quartz crystals.

69 Maverick Mountain RV Park

 5

Location: In Beaverhead-Deerlodge National Forest; map MT8, grid g8.

Campsites, facilities: There are 21 RV or tent campsites. Showers, a sanitary disposal facility, water, and electricity are available.

Reservations, fees: No reservations are needed; the fee is $9 and up per night. Open year-round.

Directions: From Dillon, go three miles south on I-15 to County Road 278, go 22 miles west on 278 to the junction of the Wise River/Polaris Road, then go north 11 miles to the RV park.

Contact: Maverick Mountain RV Park, Pioneer Mountains Scenic Byway, P.O. Box 460516, Polaris, MT 59746; 406/834-3452; email: polar @montana.com.

Trip notes: The Pioneer Mountains Scenic Byway is a 40-mile drive through the Pioneer Mountains, between Highway 43 and County Road 278. You can hike and fish in the area, visit the ghost town of Coolidge, and see the remnants of the Elkhorn Mill and a narrow-gauge railroad that served the mill. You can dig in Crystal Park for amethyst, smoky quartz, and clear quartz crystals.

70 Miner Lake

 6

Location: In Beaverhead-Deerlodge National Forest; map MT8, grid g6.

Campsites, facilities: There are 18 RV or tent campsites, which can accommodate a maximum RV length of 32 feet. There is a trailer boat launch.

Reservations, fees: No reservations are needed, and no fee is charged. Open June 1– September 15. The stay limit is 16 days.

Directions: From Butte, go south on I-15 19 miles to Divide, then go 51 miles west on Highway 43 to Wisdom. From Wisdom, go 19

miles south to Jackson on County Road 278, then seven miles west on County Road 182, then three miles west on Forest Service Road 182 to the campground.

Contact: Beaverhead-Deerlodge National Forest, P.O. Box 238, Wisdom, MT 59761; 406/689-3243; website: www.fs.fed.us/r1/bdnf.

Trip notes: You can fish and hike in Beaverhead-Deerlodge National Forest.

71 North Van Houten

 6

Location: In Beaverhead-Deerlodge National Forest; map MT8, grid h6.

Campsites, facilities: There are four tent sites.

Reservations, fees: No reservations are needed, and no fee is charged. Open June 25– September 6. The stay limit is 16 days.

Directions: From Dillon, go three miles south on I-15 to County Road 278, then 48 miles west on 278 to Jackson. From Jackson, go one mile south, then 10 miles on Skinner Meadows Road to the campground.

Contact: Beaverhead-Deerlodge National Forest, P.O. Box 238, Wisdom, MT 59761; 406/689-3243; website: www.fs.fed.us/r1/bdnf.

Trip notes: You can hike and fish in Beaverhead-Deerlodge National Forest.

72 South Van Houten

 6

Location: In Beaverhead-Deerlodge National Forest; map MT8, grid h6.

Campsites, facilities: There are three tent sites.

Reservations, fees: No reservations are needed, and no fee is charged. Open June 25– September 6. The stay limit is 16 days.

Directions: From Dillon, go three miles south on I-15 to County Road 278, then 48 miles west on 278 to Jackson. From Jackson, go one mile south, then 10 miles on Skinner Meadows Road to the campground.

Contact: Beaverhead-Deerlodge National Forest, P.O. Box 238, Wisdom, MT 59761; 406/689-3243; website: www.fs.fed.us/r1/bdnf.

Trip notes: You can hike and fish in Beaverhead-Deerlodge National Forest.

73 Bannack

    6

Location: Southwest of Dillon; map MT8, grid h8.

Campsites, facilities: There are 20 RV or tent campsites. There is a wheelchair-accessible restroom available.

Reservations, fees: No reservations are needed; the fee is $12 per night. Open year-round. The stay limit is 14 days.

Directions: From Dillon, drive south on I-15 to Exit 59 (County Road 278 exit). Head west on County Road 278 for 20 miles, turn south onto the paved Bannack road, and go four miles; then turn onto the gravel park-entrance road.

Contact: Department of Fish, Wildlife & Parks, 4200 Bannack Rd., Dillon, MT 59725; 406/834-3413, fax 406/834-3548.

Trip notes: The ghost town of Bannack was the site of Montana's first major gold discovery in 1862, at Grasshopper Creek. This strike set off a massive gold rush, and Bannack's population reached over 3000 by 1863. Bannack became Montana's first territorial capital in 1864. But when the gold ran out, the town died. Today there are over 50 historic log and frame structures on display on Main Street. You can fish in Grasshopper Creek and play golf in Dillon.

74 Reservoir Lake

    5

Location: In Beaverhead-Deerlodge National Forest; map MT8, grid h7.

Campsites, facilities: There are 16 RV or tent campsites, which can accommodate a maximum RV length of 16 feet. There is a trailer boat launch available.

Reservations, fees: No reservations are needed; there is no fee charged. Open June 16–September 15. The stay limit is 16 days.

Directions: From Dillon, go 19 miles south on I-15, then 17 miles west on County Road 324, and then Forest Service Road 181 for 18 miles to the campground.

Contact: Beaverhead-Deerlodge National Forest, Dillon Ranger District, 420 Barrett St., Dillon, MT 59725-3572; 406/683-3900.

Trip notes: You can boat and fish at Reservoir Lake and hike and fish in Beaverhead-Deerlodge National Forest.

WAYNE SCHERR

Madison Range, Lee Metcalf Wilderness

MAP MT9

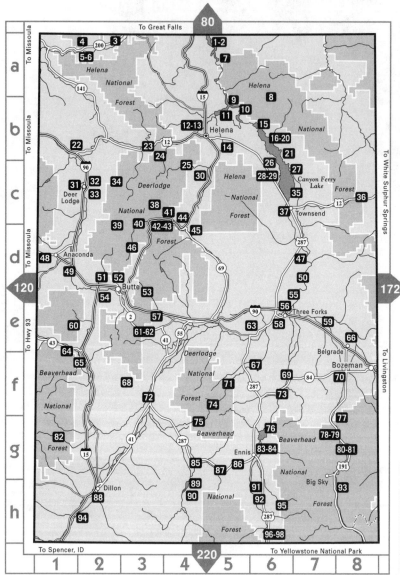

CHAPTER MT9

1	Departure Point	144	**36**	Skidway	154
2	Log Gulch	144	**37**	Roadrunner RV Park	154
3	Aspen Grove	144	**38**	Basin Canyon	154
4	Hooper Lake	145	**39**	Orofino	155
5	Spring Creek RV Park	145	**40**	Whitehouse	155
6	Sleepy Hollow Mobile Home & RV Park	145	**41**	Merry Widow RV Park	155
7	Holter Lake	146	**42**	Ladysmith	156
8	Vigilante	146	**43**	Mormon Creek	156
9	Black Sandy Beach	146	**44**	Free Enterprise Health Mine	156
10	Lakeside Resort	147	**45**	Sunset Trailer Court	156
11	H & C RV	147	**46**	Lowland	157
12	Helena Campground & RV Park	147	**47**	Toston Dam	157
13	Lincoln Road RV Park	148	**48**	Big Sky RV Park	157
14	Buzz In RV Park & Campground	148	**49**	Fairmont RV Park	157
15	Riverside	148	**50**	Fairweather	158
16	Kim's Marina & RV Resort	148	**51**	Butte KOA	158
17	Canyon Ferry RV Park & Storage	149	**52**	Mountain View RV Park	158
18	Chinaman's Gulch	149	**53**	Delmoe Lake	158
19	Jo Bonner	149	**54**	2 Bar Lazy H RV Park & Campground	159
20	Court Sheriff	150	**55**	Missouri Headwaters State Park	159
21	Hellgate	150	**56**	Fort Three Forks Motel & RV Park	159
22	JJ's Rough Country	150	**57**	Pipestone Campground	159
23	Cromwell Dixon	151	**58**	Three Forks KOA Campground	160
24	Moose Creek	151	**59**	Manhattan Camper Court	160
25	Park Lake	151	**60**	Beaver Dam	160
26	White Earth	151	**61**	Toll Mountain	160
27	Goose Bay Marina	152	**62**	Pigeon Creek	161
28	Silos	152	**63**	Lewis and Clark Caverns State Park	161
29	Silos RV & Fishing Camp	152	**64**	Divide Bridge	161
30	Alhambra RV Park	152	**65**	Maidenrock	161
31	Deer Lodge KOA	153	**66**	Lexley Acres	162
32	Indian Creek Campground	153	**67**	Harrison Lake	162
33	Squaw Rock	153	**68**	Humbug Spires	162
34	Kading	153			
35	Indian Road	154			(continues)

69 Greycliff	162	**85** Alder/Virginia City KOA	166
70 Bozeman KOA	163	**86** Camper Corner	167
71 Potosi	163	**87** Virginia City Campground	167
72 Skyline RV Park	163	**88** Dillon KOA	167
73 Red Mountain	163	**89** Ruby Reservoir	168
74 Branham Lakes	164	**90** Cottonwood	168
75 Mill Creek	164	**91** Varney Bridge	168
76 Lake Shore Lodge	164	**92** Cameron Store & Cabins	169
77 Spire Rock	164	**93** Red Cliff	169
78 Castle Rock Inn & RV Park	165	**94** Barretts Park	169
79 Greek Creek	165	**95** Bear Creek	169
80 Swan Creek	165	**96** West Madison	170
81 Moose Flat	165	**97** South Madison	170
82 Dinner Station	166	**98** Madison River Cabins & RV	170
83 Valley Garden	166		
84 Ennis	166		

1 Departure Point

 6

Location: At Holter Lake; map MT9, grid a5.

Campsites, facilities: There are 10 RV or tent campsites, which can accommodate a maximum RV length of 50 feet. A hand boat launch is available.

Reservations, fees: No reservations are needed; the fee is $12 per night. Open year-round. The stay limit is 14 days.

Directions: From Helena, go north on I-15 to Wolf Creek. From Wolf Creek, go three miles north on Recreation Road, then eight miles southeast on the county road to Holter Lake.

Contact: Bureau of Land Management, Butte Field Office, P.O. Box 3388, Butte, MT 59702; 406/494-5059.

Trip notes: You can boat, swim, and water-ski on Holter Lake, and fish for rainbow trout, kokanee salmon, walleyes, and perch. Lewis and Clark named the Gates of the Mountains when they traveled up the Missouri River. Boat tours are available at the Gates of the Mountains 16 miles north of Helena off I-15. You can hike in the area.

2 Log Gulch

 6

Location: At Holter Lake; map MT9, grid a5.

Campsites, facilities: There are 80 RV or tent campsites. Restrooms, water, and a trailer boat launch are available.

Reservations, fees: No reservations are needed; the fee is $12 per night. Open year-round. The stay limit is 14 days.

Directions: From Helena, go north on I-15 to Wolf Creek. From Wolf Creek, go three miles north on Recreation Road, cross bridge, then go seven miles southeast on the county road.

Contact: Bureau of Land Management, Butte Field Office, P.O. Box 3388, Butte, MT 59702; 406/494-5059.

Trip notes: You can fish, boat, swim, and water-ski at Holter Lake and hike in the area.

3 Aspen Grove

 5

Location: In Lolo National Forest; map MT9, grid a2.

Campsites, facilities: There are 20 RV or tent

campsites.

Reservations, fees: No reservations are needed for individuals, but group reservations are required. The fee is $5 per night. Open May 29–October 15. The stay limit is 14 days.

Directions: From Missoula, go east six miles on I-90 to Highway 200, then go east 73 miles to Lincoln. From Lincoln, go seven miles east on Highway 200 to the campground.

Contact: Lolo National Forest, Lincoln Ranger District, 7269 Hwy. 200, Lincoln, MT 59639; 406/362-4265.

Trip notes: You can fish and hike in Lolo National Forest.

◪ Hooper Lake

 7

Location: Near Lincoln; map MT9, grid a2.

Campsites, facilities: There are 15 RV or tent campsites, which can accommodate a maximum RV length of 25 feet. A wheelchair-accessible restroom is available. Pets are allowed on leashes.

Reservations, fees: No reservations are needed; the fee is $9 per night. Open April 1– October 31.

Directions: From Missoula, go east six miles on I-90 to Highway 200, then go east 73 miles to Lincoln. From Lincoln, Hooper Park Recreation Area is off Highway 200.

Contact: The City of Lincoln, 3201 Spurgin Rd., Lincoln, MT 59639; 406/362-4949.

Trip notes: Rogers Pass, east of Lincoln, is a migration route for eagles in October and November. The Bob Marshall Wilderness Area has trails from the upper Sun River area and from the Blackfoot Valley on the other side of the Continental Divide (you should contact a local guide before tackling this or any other wilderness area). The Scapegoat Wilderness is a rugged wilderness area north of Lincoln and adjacent to the Bob Marshall. The Sun River Canyon, northwest of Augusta, has a ruggedly beautiful landscape. The Blackfoot is popular with white-water enthusiasts, and

both the Blackfoot and the Little Blackfoot Rivers offer good fishing.

◯ Spring Creek RV Park

 6

Location: In Lincoln; map MT9, grid a2.

Campsites, facilities: There are 12 RV or tent campsites, some with hookups. Showers and a sanitary disposal facility are available.

Reservations, fees: No reservations are needed; the fee is $10 per night. Open May 1– December 1.

Directions: From Missoula, go east six miles on I-90 to Highway 200, then go east 73 miles to Lincoln. Get off at Lincoln; the campground is at the west end of town.

Contact: Spring Creek RV Park, P.O. Box 788, Lincoln, MT 59639; 406/362-4140.

Trip notes: This campground is on Spring Creek. Rogers Pass east of Lincoln is a migration route for eagles in October and November. The Bob Marshall Wilderness Area has trails from the upper Sun River area and from the Blackfoot Valley on the other side of the Continental Divide. You should contact a local guide before tackling this or any other wilderness area. The Scapegoat Wilderness is a spectacular wilderness area north of Lincoln and adjacent to the Bob Marshall. The Sun River Canyon, northwest of Augusta, has a ruggedly beautiful landscape. The Blackfoot is popular with white-water enthusiasts, and both the Blackfoot and the Little Blackfoot Rivers offer good fishing.

◯ Sleepy Hollow Mobile Home & RV Park

 5

Location: In Lincoln; map MT9, grid a2.

Campsites, facilities: There are 12 RV or tent campsites, some with hookups.

Reservations, fees: No reservations are needed; the fee is $9–21 per night. Open April 1–November 30, but there are some year-round.

Directions: From Missoula, go east six miles on I-90 to Highway 200, east 73 miles to Lincoln, then three blocks south on Stemple Pass Road to the RV park; the campground is right before the Blackfoot River.

Contact: Sleepy Hollow Mobile Home & RV Park, 402 Stemple Pass Rd., Lincoln, MT 59639; 406/362-4429.

Trip notes: Rogers Pass, east of Lincoln, is a migration route for eagles in October and November. The Bob Marshall Wilderness Area has trails from the upper Sun River area and from the Blackfoot Valley on the other side of the Continental Divide. Contact a local guide before tackling this or any other wilderness area. The Scapegoat Wilderness is spectacular wilderness area north of Lincoln and adjacent to the Bob Marshall. The Sun River Canyon, northwest of Augusta, has a ruggedly beautiful landscape. The Blackfoot is popular with white-water enthusiasts, and both the Blackfoot and the Little Blackfoot Rivers offer good fishing.

7 Holter Lake

 6

Location: Near Helena; map MT9, grid a5.

Campsites, facilities: There are 50 RV or tent campsites, which can accommodate a maximum RV length of 35 feet. A trailer boat launch is available.

Reservations, fees: No reservations are needed; the fee is $12 per night. Open year-round. The stay limit is 14 days.

Directions: From Helena, go north on I-15 to Exit 226 (Wolf Creek), then go three miles along the Missouri River to the lake.

Contact: Bureau of Land Management; 106 N. Parkmont, P.O. Box 3388, Butte, MT 59702; 406/ 494-5059, 406/235-4314.

Trip notes: You can boat, swim, and water-ski on Holter Lake, and fish for rainbow trout, kokanee salmon, walleyes, and perch. Lewis and Clark named the Gates of the Mountains when they traveled up the Missouri River. Boat tours

are available at the Gates of the Mountains, 16 miles north of Helena off I-15.

8 Vigilante

 6

Location: In Helena National Forest; map MT9, grid a6.

Campsites, facilities: There are 22 RV or tent campsites, which can accommodate a maximum RV length of 16 feet. Pets are allowed on leashes.

Reservations, fees: No reservations are needed; the fee is $10 per night. Open May 15–November 30. The stay limit is 14 days.

Directions: From Helena, go 20 miles northeast on County Road 280, then 12 miles northeast on the county road to the campground.

Contact: Helena National Forest, Helena Ranger District, 2001 Poplar, Helena, MT 59601; 406/449-5490, fax 406/449-5740; website: www.fs .fed.us/r1/helena.

Trip notes: The Vigilante Trail begins nine miles northeast up Magpie Gulch, joins Trail 247 (Hanging Valley Trail), and accesses the vista point at the end of Trail 247.

9 Black Sandy Beach

 6

Location: At Hauser Lake; map MT9, grid b5.

Campsites, facilities: There are 29 RV and four tent campsites, some with grills, picnic tables, and water. Wheelchair-accessible restrooms and a trailer boat launch are available.

Reservations, fees: No reservations are needed; the fee is $10 per night. Open year-round. The stay limit is 14 days.

Directions: From Helena, go seven miles north on I-15 to Lincoln Road (Exit 200), go five miles east on County Road 453, turn left at the stop sign, and then three miles on the county road north to the beach. This road is dirt and bumpy, so take it slow.

Contact: Fish, Wildlife & Parks, 930 Custer Ave., Helena, MT 59601; 406/444-4720.

Trip notes: This campground is on the shores of Hauser Lake, where you can fish for Kokanee salmon, rainbow and brown trout, walleye, and perch. You can boat, water-ski, and swim on the lake. There are three golf courses in Helena. The Helena area is known for sapphires as well as gold, and the Spokane Bar Mine is one of half a dozen digging sites.

10 Lakeside Resort

 5

Location: At Hauser Lake; map MT9, grid b5.

Campsites, facilities: There are 70 RV or tent campsites, some with hookups. A restaurant, store, gas, picnic area, and marina are available. And there are an RV park, bar, restaurant, casino, marina, tackle shop, playground, picnic area, and swimming beach at the resort.

Reservations, fees: No reservations are needed; the fee is $14–25 per night. Open April 1–October 1.

Directions: From U.S. 12 in Helena, take Montana Avenue north to Custer Avenue East, and at the Y, take a left onto York Road, and the resort is on the right.

Contact: Lakeside Resort, 5295 York Rd., P.O. Box 223, Helena, MT 59601; 406/227-6413, 406/227-6076, fax 406/443-3932; email: cdaily@aol.com.

Trip notes: This resort is on Hauser Lake, where you can fish for Kokanee salmon, rainbow and brown trout, walleye, and perch. You can boat, water-ski, and swim on the lake. There are three golf courses in Helena. The Helena area is known for sapphires, as well as gold, and the Spokane Bar Mine is one of half a dozen digging sites.

11 H & C RV

 4

Location: Near Hauser Lake; map MT9, grid b5.

Campsites, facilities: There are 19 RV or tent campsites, some with hookups. Showers,

laundry facilities, and a store are available.

Reservations, fees: No reservations are needed; the fee is $14 per night. Open May 1–October 1.

Directions: From Helena, go seven miles north on I-15 to Lincoln Road (Exit 200), and take Lincoln Road to the campground.

Contact: H & C RV, 7568 Hauser Dam Rd., Helena, MT 59601; 406/458-6390.

Trip notes: This campground is near Hauser Lake, where you can fish for Kokanee salmon, rainbow and brown trout, walleye, and perch. You can boat, water-ski, and swim on the lake. There are three golf courses in Helena. The Helena area is known for sapphires as well as gold, and the Spokane Bar Mine is one of half a dozen digging sites.

12 Helena Campground & RV Park

 4

Location: Near Helena; map MT9, grid b4.

Campsites, facilities: There are 100 RV or tent campsites, which can accommodate a maximum RV length of 50 feet; the campground also has three cabins. Hookups, showers, laundry facilities, and wheelchair-accessible restrooms are available. There is a swimming pool, hot tub, playground, volleyball court, basketball court, and game room.

Reservations, fees: Reservations are recommended; the fee is $20–27 per night. Open year-round.

Directions: From Helena on U.S. 12, take Montana Avenue north to Custer Avenue, go three miles past Custer Avenue and the campground is on the left.

Contact: Helena Campground & RV Park, 5820 N. Montana Ave., Helena, MT 59601; 406/458-4714, fax 406/458-6001; email: info@helenacampgroundrvpark.com; website: www.helenacampgroundrvpark.com.

Trip notes: This campground also offers proximity to the state capitol, Russell Art

Gallery, and city services. You can fish, boat, swim, and water-ski on Canyon Ferry, Hauser, and Holter Lakes, and hike in Helena National Forest.

13 Lincoln Road RV Park

      4

Location: In Helena; map MT9, grid b4.

Campsites, facilities: There are 65 RV or tent campsites, some with hookups. Showers, laundry facilities, large pull-through spaces, a store, and a gift shop are available.

Reservations, fees: No reservations are needed; the fee is $17 and up per night (discount with Good Sam card). Open year-round.

Directions: From I-15 at Helena, take Exit 200 and go west .5 mile; the campground is on the right.

Contact: Lincoln Road RV Park, P.O. Box 9708, Helena, MT 59601; 406/458-3725, 800/797-3725.

Trip notes: This campground also offers proximity to the state capitol, Russell Art Gallery, and city services. You can fish, boat, swim, and water-ski on Canyon Ferry, Hauser, and Holter Lakes, and hike in Helena National Forest.

14 Buzz In RV Park & Campground

      3

Location: In East Helena; map MT9, grid b5.

Campsites, facilities: There are 41 RV or tent campsites, some with hookups and pull-through sites. Showers and laundry facilities are available.

Reservations, fees: No reservations are needed; the fee is $10-15 per night for two people; additional people are $2 each per night. Open year-round.

Directions: From Helena, go three miles east on U.S. 12/287; the campground is on the left.

Contact: Buzz In RV Park & Campground, 3699 Old U.S. Hwy. 12 E., Helena, MT 59635; 406/449-1291, 888/227-8086, 406/227-9002.

Trip notes: This campground is along the Missouri River at the tip of Canyon Ferry Reservoir. You can boat, fish for trout and salmon, hike, water-ski, and swim at Canyon Ferry Reservoir. In the fall, Canyon Ferry is on the bald eagle migration route along the Rocky Mountain corridor from Canada to winter nesting sites. A visitor center has hands-on displays and interpretive information.

15 Riverside

      5

Location: At Canyon Ferry; map MT9, grid b6.

Campsites, facilities: There are 34 RV or tent campsites. A wheelchair-accessible restroom and a trailer boat launch are available.

Reservations, fees: No reservations are needed; the fee is $12 per night. The stay limit is 14 days.

Directions: From Helena, go nine miles east on U.S. 287, then nine miles northeast on County Road 284 and one mile northwest on Forest Service Road 224, toward the power plant.

Contact: Bureau of Reclamation/Bureau of Land Management, 7661 Canyon Ferry Rd., Helena, MT 59601; 406/475-3128 (summer/fall), 406/475-3319, fax 406/475-9147.

Trip notes: You can boat, fish for trout and salmon, hike, water-ski, and swim at Canyon Ferry Reservoir. In the fall Canyon Ferry is on the bald eagle migration route south along the Rocky Mountain corridor from Canada to the winter nesting sites. A visitor center has hands-on displays and interpretive information.

16 Kim's Marina & RV Resort

     4

Location: At Canyon Ferry Lake; map MT9, grid b6.

Campsites, facilities: There are 100 RV sites and 10 tent campsites. Hookups, showers, laundry facilities, a store, and a sanitary disposal station are available. Horseshoes, volleyball, tennis, boat rentals, and docks are on-site.

Reservations, fees: Reservations are accepted; the fee is $11–21 per night. Open April 1–October 1.

Directions: From Helena, take U.S. 287 south to Canyon Ferry Road, go east on Canyon Ferry Road to the Canyon Ferry Dam, cross the dam and Kim's Marina is 2.5 miles past the dam.

Contact: Kim's Marina and RV Resort, 8015 Canyon Ferry Rd., Helena, MT 59602; 406/475-3723, fax 406/475-9593.

Trip notes: You can boat, fish for trout and salmon, hike, water-ski, and swim at Canyon Ferry Reservoir. In the fall, Canyon Ferry is on the bald eagle migration route south along the Rocky Mountain corridor from Canada to winter nesting sites. A visitor center has hands-on displays and interpretive information.

17 Canyon Ferry RV Park & Storage

 4

Location: At Canyon Ferry Lake; map MT9, grid b6.

Campsites, facilities: There are seven RV or tent campsites, some with hookups. Showers, laundry facilities, and inside and outside storage are available.

Reservations, fees: No reservations are needed; the fee is $23.50 per night. Open May 1–October 1.

Directions: From Helena, take U.S. 12 south for 10 miles, turn east on Highway 287, and drive approximately eight miles; the RV park is on the left side of road .25 mile past the Canyon Ferry Visitor Center.

Contact: Canyon Ferry RV Park & Storage, 7950 Canyon Ferry Rd., Helena, MT 59601; tel./fax 406/475-3811.

Trip notes: You can boat, fish for trout and salmon, hike, water-ski, and swim at Canyon Ferry Reservoir. In the fall, Canyon Ferry is on the bald eagle migration route south along the Rocky Mountain corridor from Canada to winter nesting sites. A visitor center has hands-on displays and interpretive information. This campground is near the sapphire mines.

18 Chinaman's Gulch

 5

Location: At Canyon Ferry; map MT9, grid b6.

Campsites, facilities: There are 65 RV campsites. A wheelchair-accessible restroom and a trailer boat launch are available.

Reservations, fees: No reservations are needed; the fee is $12 per night. Open year-round. The stay limit is 14 days.

Directions: From Helena go nine miles east on U.S. 287, then 10 miles northeast on County Road 284 to the campground.

Contact: Bureau of Reclamation/Bureau of Land Management, 7661 Canyon Ferry Rd., Helena, MT 59601; 406/475-3128 (summer/fall), 406/475-3319, fax 406/475-9147.

Trip notes: The trailer boat launch requires four-wheel drive. You can boat, fish for trout and salmon, hike, water-ski, and swim at Canyon Ferry Reservoir. In the fall, Canyon Ferry is on the bald eagle migration route south, along the Rocky Mountain corridor from Canada, to their winter nesting sites. A visitor center has hands-on displays and interpretive information.

19 Jo Bonner

 5

Location: At Canyon Ferry Lake; map MT9, grid b6.

Campsites, facilities: There are 12 RV or tent campsites. Wheelchair-accessible restrooms and a trailer boat launch are available.

Reservations, fees: No reservations are needed; the fee is $12 per night. Open year-round. The stay limit is 14 days.

Directions: From Helena, go nine miles east on U.S. 287, then 12 miles northeast on County Road 284 to the campground.

Contact: Bureau of Reclamation/Bureau of Land Management, 7661 Canyon Ferry Rd., Helena, MT 59601; 406/475-3128 (summer/fall), 406/475-3319, fax 406/475-9147.

Trip notes: You can boat, fish for trout and salmon, hike, water-ski, and swim at Canyon Ferry Reservoir. In the fall, Canyon Ferry is on the bald eagle migration route south along the Rocky Mountain corridor from Canada to winter nesting sites. A visitor center has hands-on displays and interpretive information.

20 Court Sheriff

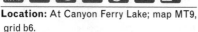 5

Location: At Canyon Ferry Lake; map MT9, grid b6.

Campsites, facilities: There are 65 RV campsites. A wheelchair-accessible restroom and trailer boat launch are available.

Reservations, fees: No reservations are needed; the fee is $12 per night. Open year-round. The stay limit is 14 days.

Directions: From Helena, go nine miles east on U.S. 287, then nine miles northeast on County Road 284 to the campground.

Contact: Bureau of Reclamation/Bureau of Land Management, 7661 Canyon Ferry Rd., Helena, MT 59601; 406/475-3128 (summer/fall), 406/475-3319, fax 406/475-9147.

Trip notes: You can boat, fish for trout and salmon, hike, water-ski, and swim at Canyon Ferry Reservoir. In the fall, Canyon Ferry is on the bald eagle migration route south along the Rocky Mountain corridor from Canada to winter nesting sites. A visitor center has hands-on displays and interpretive information.

21 Hellgate

 3

Location: At Canyon Ferry Reservoir; map MT9, grid b6.

Campsites, facilities: There are 130 RV or tent campsites. Wheelchair-accessible restrooms and a trailer boat launch are available.

Reservations, fees: No reservations are needed; the fee is $12 per night. Open year-round. The stay limit is 14 days.

Directions: From Helena, go nine miles east on U.S. 287, then 18 miles northeast on County Road 284 to the campground.

Contact: Bureau of Reclamation/Bureau of Land Management, 7661 Canyon Ferry Rd., Helena, MT 59601; 406/475-3128 (summer/fall), 406/475-3319, fax. 406/475-9147.

Trip notes: You can boat, fish for trout and salmon, hike, water-ski, and swim at Canyon Ferry Reservoir. In the fall, Canyon Ferry is on the bald eagle migration route south along the Rocky Mountain corridor from Canada to winter nesting sites. A visitor center has hands-on displays and interpretive information.

22 JJ's Rough Country

 4

Location: On the Clark Fork River; map MT9, grid b1.

Campsites, facilities: There are 17 RV or tent campsites. Water, electricity, a sanitary disposal station, restaurant, lounge, and a casino are available.

Reservations, fees: No reservations are needed; the fee is $12 per night. Open year-round.

Directions: From Missoula, go east on I-90 71 miles to Garrison. From Garrison, go 1.5 miles on Frontage Road; the campground is on the left.

Contact: JJ's Rough Country, 180 N. Frontage Rd., Garrison, MT 59731; 406/846-3267.

Trip notes: This campground is on the Clark Fork River.

23 Cromwell Dixon

 5

Location: In Helena National Forest; map MT9, grid b3.

Campsites, facilities: There are nine RV campsites, which can accommodate a maximum RV length of 22 feet, and five tent sites.

Reservations, fees: No reservations are needed; the fee is $10 per night. Open June 1–September 15. The stay limit is 16 days. Pets are allowed on leashes.

Directions: From Helena, go 15 miles west on U.S. 12 to the campground.

Contact: Helena National Forest, Helena Ranger District, 2100 Poplar, Helena, MT 59601; 406/449-5490, fax 406/449-5740; website: www.fs.fed.us/r1/helena.

Trip notes: This campground has roomy campsites and is surrounded by forest and grasslands. You can boat, fish for trout and salmon, hike, water-ski, and swim at nearby Canyon Ferry Reservoir. In the fall, Canyon Ferry is on the bald eagle migration route south, along the Rocky Mountain corridor from Canada, to winter nesting sites. A visitor center has hands-on displays and interpretive information.

24 Moose Creek

 5

Location: In Helena National Forest; map MT9, grid b3.

Campsites, facilities: There are nine tent campsites.

Reservations, fees: No reservations are needed; the fee is $5 per night. Open June 15–September 15. The stay limit is 14 days.

Directions: From Helena, go 10 miles west on U.S. 12, then four miles southwest on Rimini Road.

Contact: Helena National Forest, Helena, MT 59601; 406/449-5201; website: www.fs.fed.us/r1/helena.

Trip notes: You can fish and hike here.

25 Park Lake

 7

Location: In Helena National Forest; map MT9, grid c4.

Campsites, facilities: There are 22 RV or tent campsites. A hand boat launch is available for non-motorized boats only.

Reservations, fees: No reservations are needed; the fee is $8 per night. Open June 15–September 15. The stay limit is 14 days.

Directions: From Helena, go south on I-15 10 miles to the Clancy exit, then take Lump Gulch Road 11 miles west to the lake.

Contact: Helena National Forest, Helena Ranger District, 2001 Poplar St., Helena, MT 59601; 406/449-5490, fax 406/449-5740; website: www.fs.fed.us/r1/helena.

Trip notes: You can boat, fish, and hike in the area.

26 White Earth

 4

Location: At Canyon Ferry Lake; map MT9, grid c6.

Campsites, facilities: There are 40 RV or tent campsites. A wheelchair-accessible restroom and a trailer boat launch are available.

Reservations, fees: No reservations are needed; the fee is $12 per night. Open year-round. The stay limit is 14 days.

Directions: From Townsend, go 13 miles north on U.S. 287 to Winston, and then go five miles east on the county road to the campground.

Contact: Bureau of Reclamation/Bureau of Land Management, 7661 Canyon Ferry Rd., Helena, MT 59601; 406/475-3128 (summer/fall), 406/475-3319, fax. 406/475-9147.

Trip notes: You can boat, fish for trout and salmon, hike, water-ski, and swim at Canyon Ferry Reservoir. In the fall, Canyon Ferry is on the bald eagle migration route south along the Rocky Mountain corridor from Canada to winter nesting sites. A visitor center has hands-on displays and interpretive information.

27 Goose Bay Marina

 3

Location: On Canyon Ferry Lake; map MT9, grid c6.

Campsites, facilities: There are 68 RV and 30 tent campsites, some with hookups. Showers, a sanitary disposal facility, boat docks, propane gas, and a store are available.

Reservations, fees: No reservations are needed; the fee is $15 and up per night. Open April 1–November 1.

Directions: From Townsend, go east on U.S. 12 for two miles, turn north on Highway 284, turn west on the access road between mile markers 21 and 22 and drive three miles to the marina on the lake.

Contact: Goose Bay Marina, 300 Goose Bay Lane, Townsend, MT 59644; 406/266-3645.

Trip notes: You can boat, fish for trout and salmon, hike, water-ski, and swim at Canyon Ferry Reservoir. In the fall, Canyon Ferry is on the bald eagle migration route south along the Rocky Mountain corridor from Canada to winter nesting sites. A visitor center has hands-on displays and interpretive information.

28 Silos

 4

Location: At Canyon Ferry Lake; map MT9, grid c6.

Campsites, facilities: There are 40 RV or tent campsites. A wheelchair-accessible restroom and trailer boat launch are available.

Reservations, fees: No reservations are needed; the fee is $12 per night. Open year-round. The stay limit is 14 days.

Directions: From Townsend go eight miles north on U.S. 287, then go east on the county

road for one mile east to the campground on the lake's shore.

Contact: Bureau of Reclamation/Bureau of Land Management, 7661 Canyon Ferry Rd., Helena, MT 59601; 406/475-3128 (summer/fall), 406/475-3319, fax. 406/475-9147.

Trip notes: You can boat, fish for trout and salmon, hike, water-ski, and swim at Canyon Ferry Reservoir. In the fall, Canyon Ferry is on the bald eagle migration route along the Rocky Mountain corridor from Canada to winter nesting sites. A visitor center has hands-on displays and interpretive information.

29 Silos RV & Fishing Camp

 4

Location: At Canyon Ferry Lake; map MT9, grid c6.

Campsites, facilities: There are 42 RV campsites, some with hookups. A store, gas, boat rentals, storage, laundry facilities, a game room, and a sanitary disposal facility are available.

Reservations, fees: No reservations are needed; the fee is $4.50–13.50 per night. Open year-round.

Directions: From Townsend, go eight miles north on U.S. 287, and take a right at the sign.

Contact: Silos RV & Fishing Camp, 81 Silos Rd., Townsend, MT 59644; 406/266-3100, fax 406/266-4550.

Trip notes: You can boat, fish for trout and salmon, hike, water-ski, and swim at Canyon Ferry Reservoir. In the fall, Canyon Ferry is on the bald eagle migration route along the Rocky Mountain corridor from Canada to winter nesting sites. A visitor center has hands-on displays and interpretive information.

30 Alhambra RV Park

 5

Location: Near Helena; map MT9, grid c4.

Campsites, facilities: There are 27 RV and six tent campsites, some with hookups.

Showers, laundry facilities, and a store are available.

Reservations, fees: No reservations are needed; the fee is $16 per night.

Directions: From Helena, go 10 miles south on I-15 to Exit 182, take a left, then a right on Frontage Road, and watch for signs. The RV park is one mile down on right.

Contact: Alhambra RV Park, Hwy. 282 South #515, Clancy, MT 59634; 406/933-8020, 406/933-8020.

Trip notes: This campground is along Prickly Pear Creek, close to Helena, hiking and fishing.

31 Deer Lodge KOA

 5

Location: In Deer Lodge; map MT9, grid c1.

Campsites, facilities: There are 94 RV or tent campsites. Showers, laundry facilities, a store, water, electricity, and a sanitary disposal facility are available.

Reservations, fees: No reservations are needed; the fee is $14.50–19 per night. Open May 1–September 30.

Directions: From I-90 at Deer Lodge, take the exit at either end of town and go to the city center; the campground is at the stoplight on Main Street and Milwaukee Avenue.

Contact: Deer Lodge KOA, Park St., Deer Lodge, MT 59772; 800/562-1629.

Trip notes: This campground is in a shaded, grassy area at the river's edge. You can fish here. Be sure to visit the historic Grant-Kohrs Ranch, which was the home of one of Montana's largest cattle barons. The original furnishings are in the house, and there is horse-drawn equipment that was used in the 1800s.

32 Indian Creek Campground

 5

Location: In Deer Lodge; map MT9, grid c2.

Campsites, facilities: There are 54 RV and 20 tent campsites, some with hookups. Showers, laundry facilities, a store, and a sanitary disposal facility are available. There are wide pad campsites for tip-outs and awnings.

Reservations, fees: Reservations are suggested; the fee is $13.52–18.72 per night. Open April 1–October 1.

Directions: From I-90 at Deer Lodge, take Exit 184, go two blocks west and turn south on Maverick Lane to the campground.

Contact: Indian Creek Campground, 745 Maverick Lane, Deer Lodge, MT 59722; 406/846-3848, 800/294-0726, fax 406/846-3818.

Trip notes: You can hike and fish in Deerlodge National Forest. Be sure to visit the historic Grant-Kohrs Ranch, which was the home of one of Montana's largest cattle barons. The original furnishings are in the house and there is horse-drawn equipment used in the 1800s.

33 Squaw Rock

 5

Location: In Deerlodge National Forest; map MT9, grid c2.

Campsites, facilities: There are seven RV or tent campsites, which can accommodate a maximum RV length of 32 feet. A wheelchair-accessible restroom is available.

Reservations, fees: No reservations are needed; there is no fee. Open April 1–October 30. The stay limit is 16 days.

Directions: From Philipsburg on Highway 1, go 19 miles west off Rock Creek Road (Forest Service Road 102) to the campground.

Contact: Deerlodge National Forest, 8810A Business Loop, P.O. Box H, Philipsburg, MT 59858; 406/859-3211, fax 406/859-3689; website: www.fs.fed.us/r1/bdnf.

Trip notes: You can fish here.

34 Kading

 6

Location: In Helena National Forest; map MT9, grid c2.

Campsites, facilities: There are 14 RV or tent campsites.

Reservations, fees: No reservations are needed; there is no fee. Open June 1–September 15. The stay limit is 14 days.

Directions: From Helena, go east on U.S. 12 for 23 miles to Elliston. From Elliston, go one mile east on U.S. 12, four miles south on the county road and nine miles southwest on Forest Service Road 227 to the campground.

Contact: Helena National Forest, Helena Ranger District, 2001 Poplar St., Helena, MT 59601; 406/449-5490, fax 406/449-5740; website: www.fs.fed.us/r1/helena.

Trip notes: You can fish and hike here.

35 Indian Road

 4

Location: At Canyon Ferry Lake; map MT9, grid c6.

Campsites, facilities: There are 25 RV campsites and a trailer boat launch.

Reservations, fees: No reservations are needed; the fee is $12 per night. Open year-round. The stay limit is 14 days.

Directions: From Townsend, go one mile north on U.S. 287; the campground is at milepost 75.

Contact: Bureau of Reclamation/Bureau of Land Management, 7661 Canyon Ferry Rd., Helena, MT 59601; 406/475-3128 (summer/fall), 406/475-3319, fax. 406/475-9147.

Trip notes: This campground is along the Missouri River at the tip of Canyon Ferry Reservoir. You can boat, fish for trout and salmon, hike, water-ski, and swim at Canyon Ferry Reservoir. In the fall, Canyon Ferry is on the bald eagle migration route along the Rocky Mountain corridor from Canada to the winter nesting sites. A visitor center has hands-on displays and interpretive information.

36 Skidway

 6

Location: In Helena National Forest; map MT9, grid c8.

Campsites, facilities: There are 11 RV or tent

campsites, which can accommodate a maximum RV length of 16 feet. Pets are allowed on leashes.

Reservations, fees: No reservations are needed; there is no fee. Open June 1–October 1. The stay limit is 14 days.

Directions: From Townsend, go 23 miles east on U.S. 12 to the Skidway campground access sign, then two miles south on Forest Service Road 4042 to the campground.

Contact: Helena National Forest, 415 S. Front, Townsend, MT 59644; 406/266-3425.

Trip notes: You can hike and fish in Helena National Forest.

37 Roadrunner RV Park

 4

Location: Near Canyon Ferry Lake; map MT9, grid c6.

Campsites, facilities: There are 30 RV or tent campsites, some with hookups. Showers and laundry facilities are available.

Reservations, fees: No reservations are needed; the fee is $10 and up per night. Open year-round.

Directions: From U.S. 287, go to the north side of Townsend and the RV park.

Contact: Roadrunner RV Park, 704 N. Front St., 192 Hwy. 12 East #12, Townsend, MT 59644; 406/266-3278, 406/266-9900.

Trip notes: This campground is along the Missouri River at the tip of Canyon Ferry Reservoir. You can boat, fish for trout and salmon, hike, water-ski, and swim at Canyon Ferry Reservoir. In the fall, Canyon Ferry is on the bald eagle migration route along the Rocky Mountain corridor from Canada to winter nesting sites. A visitor center has hands-on displays and interpretive information.

38 Basin Canyon

 7

Location: In Beaverhead-Deerlodge National Forest; map MT9, grid c3.

Campsites, facilities: There are two RV or tent campsites, which can accommodate a maximum RV length of 16 feet.

Reservations, fees: No reservations are needed; no fee is charged. The stay limit is 16 days.

Directions: From Butte, go east on I-90 eight miles to I-15, then go north 27 miles on I-15 to Exit 156 to Basin. From Basin, go five miles north from I-15, then three miles on Forest Service Road 172 to the campground.

Contact: Beaverhead-Deerlodge National Forest, 3 Whitetail Rd., Whitehall, MT 59759; 406/287-3223; website: www.fs.fed.us/r1/bdnf.

Trip notes: You can hike and fish in Beaverhead-Deerlodge National Forest.

39 Orofino

   5

Location: In Beaverhead-Deerlodge National Forest; map MT9, grid d2.

Campsites, facilities: There are 10 RV or tent campsites, which can accommodate a maximum RV length of 22 feet.

Reservations, fees: No reservations are needed; there is no fee. Open May 25–September 15. The stay limit is 16 days.

Directions: From Deer Lodge, take Milwaukee Avenue east to Forest Service Road 82 (Boulder River Road), then go 13 miles southeast on Forest Service Road 82 to the campground.

Contact: Beaverhead-Deerlodge National Forest, Pintler Ranger District, 1 Hollenback Rd., Deer Lodge, MT 59722; 406/846-1770, fax 406/846-2127; website: www.fs.fed.us/r1/bdnf.

Trip notes: Be sure to visit the historic Grant-Kohrs Ranch, once the home of one of Montana's largest cattle barons. The original furnishings are in the house, and there is horse-drawn equipment that was used in the 1800s. Garnet State Park, west of Drummond, is a ghost town that is being restored to its original mining camp condition. There's a visitor center in Garnet with information, so be sure to stop in Deer Lodge to get directions to

Garnet. You can hike and fish in the forest.

40 Whitehouse

   5

Location: In Deerlodge National Forest; map MT9, grid d3.

Campsites, facilities: There are five RV or tent campsites, which can accommodate a maximum RV length of 22 feet. Wheelchair-accessible restrooms and water are available. Pets are allowed on leashes.

Reservations, fees: No reservations are needed, but the dispersed area can be reserved by calling the Jefferson Ranger District, 406/225-3391; the fee is $6 per night. Open June 1–September 15. The stay limit is 16 days.

Directions: From Butte, go 20 miles north on I-15, take the Bernice exit, and drive west for eight miles on Forest Service Road 82 to the campground.

Contact: Beaverhead-Deerlodge National Forest, 3 Whitetail Rd., Whitehall, MT 59759; 406/287-3223, 800/433-9206; website: www.fs.fed.us/r1/bdnf.

Trip notes: You can hike and fish here.

41 Merry Widow RV Park

    5

Location: Northeast of Butte; map MT9, grid c4.

Campsites, facilities: There are 57 RV or tent campsites, some with hookups. Showers, laundry facilities, a store, and a sanitary disposal station are available.

Reservations, fees: No reservations are needed; the fee is $6–10 per night. Open March 1–November 30.

Directions: From Butte, go 26 miles northeast on I-15 to Exit 156. Turn east, go on Frontage Road; the park is on the right.

Contact: Merry Widow RV Park, P.O. Box 129, Basin, MT 59631; 406/225-3220, 877/225-3220.

Trip notes: This campground is near the Boulder River, where you can fish, and you can play golf or hike nearby.

42 Ladysmith

    6

Location: In Beaverhead-Deerlodge National; map MT9, grid d3.

Campsites, facilities: There are six RV or tent campsites, which can accommodate a maximum RV length of 16 feet.

Reservations, fees: No reservations are needed; there is no fee. Open May 25–December 1. The stay limit is 16 days.

Directions: From Butte, go 20 miles north on I-15, take the Bernice exit, and then take Forest Service Road 82 west four miles to the campground.

Contact: Beaverhead-Deerlodge National Forest, 3 Whitetail Rd., Whitehall, MT 59759; 406/287-3223; website: www.fs.fed.us/r1/bdnf.

Trip notes: You can hike and fish in Beaverhead-Deerlodge National Forest.

43 Mormon Creek

  6

Location: Beaverhead-Deerlodge National Forest; map MT9, grid d3.

Campsites, facilities: There are 16 RV or tent campsites, which can accommodate a maximum RV length of 16 feet.

Reservations, fees: No reservations are needed; there is no fee.

Directions: From Butte, go 20 miles north on I-15, take the Bernice exit, and then take Forest Service Road 82 west about a mile to the campground. From Basin, go four miles west on I-15, then two miles west on Forest Service Road 82 to the campground.

Contact: Beaverhead-Deerlodge National Forest, 3 Whitetail Rd., Whitehall, MT 59759; 406/287-3223; website: www.fs.fed.us/r1/bdnf.

Trip notes: You can hike and fish in Beaverhead-Deerlodge National Forest.

44 Free Enterprise Health Mine

 3

Location: In Boulder; map MT9, grid c4.

Campsites, facilities: There are 20 RV campsites, some with hookups. There is a coin laundry, free showers, and a sanitary disposal station available.

Reservations, fees: No reservations are needed; the fee is based on a 10-day stay. Full hookups are $13 per night for two people, $2 per night for each additional person (three spots; reservations are suggested for these). Electric hookups only are $10 per night for two people, $2 for each additional person. Open April 1–October 31.

Directions: From Helena, take I-15 27 miles south and get off at Boulder, Exit 164. In Boulder, turn right at 2nd Street (hardware store) and go two miles to the top of the hill. Follow logo signs (posted in town and along the way).

Contact: Free Enterprise Health Mine, 149 Depot Hill Rd., P.O. Box 67, Boulder, MT 59632; 406/225-3383, fax 406/225-4259; email: info@radonmine.com; website: www.radonmine.com.

Trip notes: The Health Mine location offers a scenic view of the valley. There are claims of health benefits, with visitors from all over the United States and Canada coming to experience radon therapy.

45 Sunset Trailer Court

    5

Location: In Boulder; map MT9, grid d4.

Campsites, facilities: There are 24 RV or tent campsites, some with hookups. Showers and laundry facilities are available.

Reservations, fees: No reservations are needed; the fee is $12 per night. Open year-round.

Directions: From I-15 at Boulder, take Exit 164 to the high school, then turn right and go three blocks to the campground.

Contact: Sunset Trailer Court, 407 S. Adam, Boulder, MT 59632; 406/225-3387.

Trip notes: You can hike and fish in Beaverhead-Deerlodge National Forest. Nearby Elkhorn State Park is a ghost town where you can hike and picnic. It has excellent examples of frontier architecture from Montana's silver boom of the 1880s.

46 Lowland

 6

Location: In Beaverhead-Deerlodge National Forest; map MT9, grid d3.

Campsites, facilities: There are 11 RV or tent campsites, which can accommodate a maximum RV length of 22 feet. A wheelchair-accessible restroom is available.

Reservations, fees: No reservations are needed; there is no fee. Open May 25–September 15. The stay limit is 16 days.

Directions: From Butte, go eight miles northeast on I-15, then eight miles west on Forest Service Road 442 and two miles south on Forest Service Road 9485 to the campground.

Contact: Beaverhead-Deerlodge National Forest, 1820 Meadowlark, Butte, MT 59701; 406/494-2147, fax 406/434-7025; website: www.fs.fed.us/r1/bdnf.

Trip notes: You can hike and fish in Beaverhead-Deerlodge National Forest.

47 Toston Dam

 5

Location: Southeast of Helena; map MT9, grid d7.

Campsites, facilities: There are seven RV or tent campsites, which can accommodate a maximum RV length of 24 feet. A trailer boat launch is available. Pets are allowed on leashes.

Reservations, fees: No reservations are needed; there is no fee. Open year-round. The stay limit is 14 days.

Directions: From Townsend, go 13 miles south on U.S. 287 and go east on the road to Toston Dam.

Contact: Bureau of Land Management, Butte Field Office, P.O. Box 3388, Butte, MT 59702; 406/494-5059.

Trip notes: You can boat and fish here.

48 Big Sky RV Park

 5

Location: In Anaconda; map MT9, grid d1.

Campsites, facilities: There are 28 RV or tent campsites, some with full hookups. Showers, laundry facilities, water, electricity, and a sanitary disposal station are available. Pets are allowed on leashes.

Reservations, fees: No reservations are needed; the fee is $17 per night. Open May–September.

Directions: From Butte, go west on I-90 11 miles to Exit 208 and take Highway 1 west 8.5 miles to Cedar Street for .2 mile to Locust Street and the campground.

Contact: Big Sky RV Park, 200 N. Locust, Anaconda, MT 59711; 406/563-2967.

Trip notes: You can fish and take hiking trails here. This campground is near historic Washoe Park and a Jack Nicklaus signature golf course (Old Works Golf Course).

49 Fairmont RV Park

 4

Location: Near Anaconda; map MT9, grid d1.

Campsites, facilities: There are 136 RV or tent campsites, some with hookups and pull-through sites. Showers, laundry facilities, a store, water, electricity, and a sanitary disposal facility are available. Pets are allowed on leashes.

Reservations, fees: No reservations are needed; the fee is $18–22 per night. Open year-round.

Directions: From Butte, go west for 15 miles on I-90 to Exit 211 and then go three miles west to Fairmont Hot Springs Resort.

Contact: Fairmont RV Park, 1700 Fairmont Rd., Anaconda, MT 59711; 406/797-3505, 406/797-3282.

Trip notes: This RV Park is at Fairmont Hot Springs, where you can golf, swim, bike, and hike. Six tepees are for rent next to the hot springs.

50 Fairweather

   5

Location: Near Logan; map MT9, grid d7.

Campsites, facilities: There are 10 RV or tent campsites.

Reservations, fees: No reservations are needed; the fee is $6 per night. Open year-round. The stay limit is 14 days.

Directions: From Bozeman, go east on I-90 23 miles to Logan. From Logan, go one mile west on Route 205, then three miles north on Logan-Trident Road and seven miles northeast on Clarkston Road to the campground.

Contact: Fish, Wildlife & Parks, 1420 E. 6th Ave., P.O. Box 200701, Helena, MT 59620; 406/444-2449.

Trip notes: You can fish here.

51 Butte KOA

     4

Location: In Butte; map MT9, grid d2.

Campsites, facilities: There are 120 RV or tent campsites, some with hookups. Showers, laundry facilities, a store, and a sanitary disposal facility are available. A playground and deli are on-site.

Reservations, fees: No reservations are needed; the fee is $18–23 per night. Open April 15–October 31.

Directions: From I-90 in Butte, get off at Montana Street (Exit 126), go one block north to George Street, then one block east to the campground.

Contact: Butte KOA, 1601 Kaw Ave., Butte, MT 59701; 406/782-0663, 800/562-8089.

Trip notes: You can fish, swim, hike, and golf here.

52 Mountain View RV Park

   4

Location: In Butte; map MT9, grid d2.

Campsites, facilities: There are 10 RV or tent campsites, some with hookups. There is a sanitary disposal facility available.

Reservations, fees: No reservations are needed; the fee is $4.50 and up per night. Open year-round.

Directions: From Butte, go 2.1 miles south on Harrison Avenue to Warren Avenue and the RV park. Harrison Avenue is the second Butte exit westbound on I-90 (right after Continental Drive).

Contact: Mountain View RV Park, 5103 S. Warren Ave, Butte, MT 59701; 406/494-3211.

Trip notes: Humbug Spires, just south of Butte, are impressive 70 million-year-old white granite stones that rise to 600 feet. Sheepshead Mountain Recreation Area, about 15 miles north of Butte, has grassy meadows and sagebrush, with several streams and a small lake, surrounded by forest. The recreation area includes pavilions, picnic tables, barbecue grills, horseshoes, fishing pier, nature trail, volleyball court, ball fields, and paved trails. The entire recreation area is wheelchair accessible. Maney Lake is an easy-to-reach park with five miles of paved trail and a wheelchair-accessible fishing dock.

53 Delmoe Lake

      5

Location: In Beaverhead-Deerlodge National Forest; map MT9, grid e3.

Campsites, facilities: There are 25 RV or tent campsites, which can accommodate a maximum RV length of 35 feet.

Reservations, fees: No reservations are needed; the fee is $6 per night. Open May 26–September 17. The stay limit is 16 days.

Directions: From Butte, go east on I-90 17 miles to the Homestake exit off I-90, go 10 miles north on Forest Service Road 222 to Delmoe Lake.

Contact: Beaverhead-Deerlodge National Forest, 3 Whitetail Rd., Whitehall, MT 59759; 406/287-3223; website: www.fs.fed.us/r1/bdnf.

Trip notes: You can boat, fish, and swim at Delmoe Lake and hike in the forest.

54 2 Bar Lazy H RV Park & Campground

   4

Location: Near Butte; map MT9, grid e2.

Campsites, facilities: There are 24 RV campsites, some with hookups. Showers, laundry facilities, a store, and a sanitary disposal facility are available.

Reservations, fees: No reservations are needed; the fee is $12–19.50 per night. Open year-round.

Directions: From I-90 at Butte, go west and take Exit 122; go four miles west on the frontage road to the campground in the town of Rocker.

Contact: 2 Bar Lazy H RV Park & Campground, 122015 W. Brown Gulch Rd., Butte, MT 59701; 406/782-5464.

Trip notes: This campground is close to restaurants, gas, propane, and a motel. You can hike and fish in the national forest.

55 Missouri Headwaters State Park

   5

Location: Near Three Forks; map MT9, grid e6.

Campsites, facilities: There are 23 RV or tent campsites with picnic tables and grills. Wheelchair-accessible restrooms, water, and a trailer boat camp are available.

Reservations, fees: No reservations are needed; the fee is $11 per night. Open year-round. The stay limit is 14 days.

Directions: From Bozeman, go 27 miles west on I-90 to Exit 278, then go three miles east on County Road 205 and three miles north on County Road 286 to the Missouri Headwaters State Park.

Contact: Missouri Headwaters State Park, Montana Fish, Wildlife & Parks, 1400 S. 19th, Bozeman, MT 59718; 406/994-4042.

Trip notes: You can fish and hike here. Three Forks has a golf course and museums. The Headwaters State Park has foot trails, points of interest, and interpretive displays of the area's cultural and natural history. River floating and fishing are popular activities. This location is along the Lewis & Clark Trail.

56 Fort Three Forks Motel & RV Park

   3

Location: Near Three Forks; map MT9, grid e6.

Campsites, facilities: There are 13 RV campsites, some with hookups. Laundry facilities and a sanitary disposal facility are available.

Reservations, fees: No reservations are needed; the fee is $10 and up per night. Open year-round.

Directions: From Bozeman, go 30 miles west to Exit 274, which is the junction of U.S. 287, go north and the RV park is right there.

Contact: Fort Three Forks Motel & RV Park, 10776 U.S. 287, P.O. Box 970, Three Forks, MT 59752; 406/285-3233, 406/285-3234, 800/477-5690, fax 406/285-4362; email: fort3forks@aol.com.

Trip notes: This motel/campground is right off the interstate, near Three Forks, close to Lewis and Clark Caverns and Headwaters State Park.

57 Pipestone Campground

   5

Location: Near Butte; map MT9, grid e3.

Campsites, facilities: There are 55 RV campsites and 20 tent sites. Grills, picnic tables, restrooms, water, electricity, laundry, and showers are provided. A pool, playground, game room, and RV/car wash are available.

Reservations, fees: Reservations are accepted; the fee is $10 and up per night. Open April 1–October 15.

Directions: From Butte, go 25 miles east on I-90 to the Pipestone exit (Exit 241); the campground is on south frontage road adjacent to the interstate.

Contact: Pipestone Campground, 41 Bluebird Lane, Whitehall, MT 59759; 406/287-5224, fax 406/287-5224.

Trip notes: You can hike and fish in Beaverhead-Deerlodge National Forest.

58 Three Forks KOA Campground

     4

Location: In Three Forks; map MT9, grid e6.

Campsites, facilities: there are 70 RV or tent campsites, some with hookups. Showers, a store, a sanitary disposal facility, sauna, playground, swimming pool, and game room are available.

Reservations, fees: No reservations are needed; the fee is $18–24 per night. Open May 1–September 30.

Directions: From Bozeman, go 30 miles west to Exit 274, which is the junction of U.S. 287, go one mile south on U.S. 287 and the campground is on the right.

Contact: Three Forks KOA Campground, 15 KOA Rd., Three Forks, MT 59752; 406/285-3611.

Trip notes: Three Forks has a golf course and museums. The Headwaters State Park has foot trails, points of interest, and interpretive displays of the area's cultural and natural history. River floating and fishing are popular activities.

59 Manhattan Camper Court

   4

Location: In Manhattan; map MT9, grid e7.

Campsites, facilities: There are 32 RV campsites, 23 with pull-throughs, and some hookups. Showers and laundry facilities are available.

Reservations, fees: No reservations are needed; the fee is $16 per night. Open year-round.

Directions: From Bozeman, drive 18 miles west on I-90 to Manhattan, Exit 288, go north 500 feet to Wooden Shoe Lane, then west one block to the campground.

Contact: Manhattan Camper Court, 9110 Wooden Shoe Lane, Manhattan, MT 59741; 406/284-6930.

Trip notes: You can fish and hike nearby.

60 Beaver Dam

    7

Location: In the Deerlodge National Forest; map MT9, grid e1.

Campsites, facilities: There are 15 RV or tent campsites, which can accommodate a maximum RV length of 50 feet.

Reservations, fees: No reservations are needed; there is no fee. Open May 25–September 15. The stay limit is 16 days.

Directions: From Butte, go five miles west on I-90, then 12 miles south on I-15 and six miles west on Forest Service Road 96 to the campground.

Contact: Deerlodge National Forest, 1820 Meadow Lark, Butte, MT 59701; 406/494-2147, fax 406/434-7025; website: www.fs.fed.us/r1/bdnf.

Trip notes: You can hike and fish in Deerlodge National Forest.

61 Toll Mountain

    5

Location: In Beaverhead-Deerlodge National Forest; map MT9, grid e3.

Campsites, facilities: There are five RV or tent campsites, which can accommodate a maximum RV length of 22 feet. A wheelchair-accessible restroom is available.

Reservations, fees: No reservations are needed; there is no fee. Open May 25–September 15. The stay limit is 14 days.

Directions: From Bozeman, go west 57 miles on I-90 to Whitehall. From Whitehall, go 15 miles west on Highway 2, then three miles north on Forest Service Road 240 to the campground.

Contact: Beaverhead-Deerlodge National Forest, 3 Whitetail Rd., Whitehall, MT 59759; 406/287-3223; website: www.fs.fed.us/r1/bdnf.

Trip notes: You can fish and hike in Beaverhead-Deerlodge National Forest.

62 Pigeon Creek

 5

Location: In Beaverhead-Deerlodge National Forest; map MT9, grid e3.

Campsites, facilities: There are six tent campsites; trailers are not recommended.

Reservations, fees: No reservations are needed; there is no fee. Open May 25–September 15. The stay limit is 16 days.

Directions: From Whitehall, go 15 miles west of Whitehall on Highway 2, then five miles south on Forest Service Road 668 to the campground.

Contact: Beaverhead-Deerlodge National Forest, 3 Whitetail Rd., Whitehall, MT 59759; 406/287-3223; website: www.fs.fed.us/r1/bdnf.

Trip notes: You can fish and hike in Beaverhead-Deerlodge National Forest.

63 Lewis and Clark Caverns State Park

 5

Location: Near Three Forks; map MT9, grid e6.

Campsites, facilities: There are 20 RV and 20 tent campsites, some with grills and fire rings. There are handicap-accessible toilets and showers. A group use area, picnic tables, and a sanitary disposal station are available.

Reservations, fees: No reservations are needed; the fee is $10 per night. Open year-round. The stay limit is 14 days.

Directions: From Bozeman, go 36 miles west on I-90 to milepost 274, then take Highway 2 19 miles to Lewis and Clark Caverns State Park.

Contact: Fish, Wildlife & Parks, P.O. Box 949, Three Forks, MT 59752; 406/287-3541.

Trip notes: Lewis and Clark Caverns is one of the largest limestone caverns in the northwest. It is open from May 1–September 30, and guided tours are available for a fee. Three Forks has a golf course and museums.

64 Divide Bridge

 5

Location: On the Big Hole River; map MT9, grid f1.

Campsites, facilities: There are 15 RV and 10 tent campsites, which can accommodate a maximum RV length of 24 feet. Pets are allowed on leashes.

Reservations, fees: No reservations are needed, and no fee is charged. Open year-round. The stay limit is 14 days.

Directions: From Butte, go south on I-15 19 miles to Divide. From Divide, go 2.5 miles west on Highway 43 to the campground.

Contact: Bureau of Land Management, P.O. Box 3388, Butte, MT 59702; 406/494-5059.

Trip notes: This campground is along the Big Hole River, a popular spot for trout fishing and rafting.

65 Maidenrock

 6

Location: West of Melrose; map MT9, grid f1.

Campsites, facilities: There are 30 RV or tent campsites. A trailer boat launch is available.

Reservations, fees: No reservations are needed, and no fee is charged. Open year-round. The stay limit is seven days.

Directions: From I-15, take the Melrose exit at milepost 93 about 28 miles south of Butte; then drive six miles west and north on the county road to the campground.

Contact: Montana Department of Fish, Wildlife & Parks, 1400 S. 19th, Bozeman, MT 59718; 406/994-4042.

Trip notes: You can fish for trout and raft in the Big Hole River.

66 Lexley Acres

 3

Location: In Belgrade; map MT9, grid e8.

Campsites, facilities: There are 29 RV or tent campsites, some with hookups. There are showers, laundry facilities, water, electricity, sewer, and a sanitary disposal station. Pets are allowed on leashes.

Reservations, fees: Reservations are accepted; the fee is $10 and up per night. Open year-round.

Directions: please From Bozeman, go west on I-90 nine miles to Belgrade. In Belgrade, take Exit 298 off I-90 and go .5 mile south to the campground on the right.

Contact: Lexley Acres Mobile Home Park & Campground, 6071 Jackrabbit Lane, Belgrade, MT 59714; 406/388-6095.

Trip notes: There is a playground, store, and mall within a mile. You can hike and fish in nearby Gallatin National Forest.

67 Harrison Lake

 6

Location: East of Harrison Lake; map MT9, grid f6.

Campsites, facilities: There are 25 RV or tent campsites and a trailer boat launch.

Reservations, fees: No reservations are needed; the fee is $5 per night. Open year-round. The stay limit is 14 days.

Directions: From Bozeman, go west on Highway 84 about 30 miles to U.S. 287, then north 10 miles to Harrison. From Harrison, go five miles east on the county road to the lake, and follow signs.

Contact: Fish, Wildlife & Parks, Region 3, 1400 S. 19th, Bozeman, MT 59718; 406/994-0442.

Trip notes: You can fish, boat, water-ski, and swim here.

68 Humbug Spires

 6

Location: South of Divide; map MT9, grid f3.

Campsites, facilities: There are tent campsites, but camping is primitive, with no designated campsites. This is a non-motorized area. Camping for RVs is available five miles away at the Divide Bridge Campground on the Big Hole River.

Reservations, fees: No reservations are needed; there is no fee. Open year-round. The stay limit is 14 days.

Directions: From Butte, take I-90 west from Butte to I-15; go south on I-15 22 miles to the Moose Creek Exit (Exit 99), then go three miles northeast on Moose Creek Road to the campground. The To reach the Humbug Spires Primitive Area, look for the Moose Creek Trailhead across from the camp parking lot.

Contact: Humbug Spires, 106 N. Parkmont, P.O. Box 3388, Butte, MT 59702; 406/494-5059.

Trip notes: The Humbug Spires Primitive Area is popular with rock climbers. Impressive outcroppings of quartz monzonite, part of the Boulder Batholith, rise 300–600 feet into the air. There are climbing opportunities to challenge all levels of ability. The main trail extends up Moose Creek into the rock spires. When hiking in Humbug Spires, be sure to carry water, a compass, and a copy of the site map (primitive hiking experience suggested). The two-mile trail at the parking area winds along the creek through old-growth forest.

69 Greycliff

 5

Location: On Madison River; map MT9, grid f6.

Campsites, facilities: There are 30 RV or tent campsites and a trailer boat launch.

Reservations, fees: No reservations are needed; the fee is $5 per night. Open year-round. The stay limit is 14 days.

Directions: From Bozeman, drive 23 miles west on Highway 84, then six miles south on

Madison River Road to the campground.
Contact: Fish, Wildlife & Parks, Region 3, 1400 S. 19th, Bozeman, MT 59718; 406/994-0442.
Trip notes: You can boat and fish on the Madison River.

70 Bozeman KOA

 3

Location: West of Bozeman; map MT9, grid f8.
Campsites, facilities: There are 100 RV and 50 tent campsites. A game room, laundry facilities, miniature golf, and a playground are available.
Reservations, fees: Reservations are accepted; the fee is $23.95–33.95 per night. Open year-round.
Directions: From Bozeman, go eight miles west on U.S. 191; watch for signs.
Contact: Bozeman KOA, 81123 Gallatin Rd., U.S. 191, Bozeman, MT 59718; 800/562-3036.
Trip notes: This campground is next door to natural hot springs, where you can swim. You can fish and float in the Gallatin, Madison, and Yellowstone Rivers.

71 Potosi

 5

Location: In Beaverhead-Deerlodge National Forest; map MT9, grid f5.
Campsites, facilities: There are 15 RV or tent campsites, which can accommodate a maximum RV length of 22 feet. Pets are allowed on leashes.
Reservations, fees: No reservations are needed; there is no fee. Open June 1–September 30. The stay limit is 14 days.
Directions: From Bozeman, go west on Highway 84 about 30 miles to U.S. 287, then north 10 miles to Harrison. From Harrison, go seven miles west on Pony Road to Pony. At Pony take Willow Creek Road south for 10 miles to the campground.
Contact: Beaverhead-Deerlodge National Forest, 5 Forest Service Rd., Ennis, MT 59729;

406/682-4253; website: www.fs.fed.us/r1/bdnf.
Trip notes: You can fish on the Madison River and boat, swim, water-ski, canoe, and fish in Harrison Lake.

72 Skyline RV Park

 4

Location: North of Dillon; map MT9, grid f3.
Campsites, facilities: There are 38 RV and five tent sites. Showers, laundry facilities, water, and a sanitary disposal facility are available.
Reservations, fees: No reservations are needed; the fee is $10 and up per night. Open year-round.
Directions: From I-15 at Dillon, take Exit 63 east, then turn at the Exxon gas station to the RV park.
Contact: Skyline RV Park, 3525 Hwy. 91 North, Dillon, MT 59725: 406/683-4692.
Trip notes: You can fish, boat, and swim here, and a golf course is three miles away.

73 Red Mountain

 5

Location: Northeast of Norris; map MT9, grid f6.
Campsites, facilities: There are eight RV or tent campsites, which can accommodate a maximum RV length of 35 feet. There is hand-launch boat access.
Reservations, fees: No reservations are needed; the fee is $5 per night. Open May 15–September 30. The stay limit is 14 days.
Directions: From Bozeman, go west on Highway 84 to a sign that says "Bear Trap Recreation Area" (the sign was to be updated to include "Red Mountain" in 2001). Turn into the campground as directed on the sign, and you will see a sign that says "Red Mountain Campground." The road to Red Mountain Campground is almost directly across from the road that leads to Bear Trap Trailhead.
Contact: Bureau of Land Management, 1005 Selway Drive, Dillon, MT 59725; 406/683-2337;

website: www.mt.blm.gov/dfo; email: bzweb master@mt.blm.gov.

Trip notes: You can hike, boat, and fish here.

74 Branham Lakes

     6

Location: In Beaverhead-Deerlodge National Forest; map MT9, grid f5.

Campsites, facilities: There are six RV or tent campsites. This campground is not accessible by large RVs. A trailer boat launch is available. Pets are allowed on leashes.

Reservations, fees: No reservations are needed; there is no fee. Open July 1–September 15. The stay limit is 14 days.

Directions: From Dillon, go 26 miles north on Highway 41 to Twin Bridges, and then go east on Highway 287 nine miles to Sheridan. From Sheridan, go six miles east on Mill Creek Road to the campground. This road is not recommended for trailers.

Contact: Beaverhead-Deerlodge National Forest, P.O. Box 428, Sheridan, MT 59749; 406/842-5432; website: www.fs.fed.us/r1/bdnf.

Trip notes: You can boat, fish, and hike here.

75 Mill Creek

     5

Location: In Beaverhead-Deerlodge National Forest; map MT9, grid g4.

Campsites, facilities: There are 13 RV or tent campsites, which can accommodate a maximum RV length of 22 feet.

Reservations, fees: No reservations are needed; there is no fee. Open June 1–October 31. The stay limit is 16 days.

Directions: From Dillon, go 26 miles north on Highway 41 to Twin Bridges, and then go east on Highway 287 nine miles to Sheridan. From Sheridan, go seven miles east on Mill Creek Road to the campground.

Contact: Beaverhead-Deerlodge National Forest, P.O. Box 428, Sheridan, MT 59749; 406/ 842-5432; website: www.fs.fed.us/r1/bdnf.

Trip notes: You can boat, fish, and hike here.

76 Lake Shore Lodge

 5

Location: Northeast of Ennis; map MT9, grid g6.

Campsites, facilities: There are 22 RV or tent campsites. There are showers, laundry facilities, a store, hookups, water a playground, marina, and boat rentals.

Reservations, fees: Reservations are required; the fee is $13–20 per night. Open May 1–October 1.

Directions: From Ennis, drive eight miles north on U.S. 287 to McAllister, then 2.5 miles east on Ennis Lake Road to the campground.

Contact: Lake Shore Lodge, P.O. Box 160, McAllister, MT 59740; 406/682-4424, fax 406/682-4551.

Trip notes: Ennis is famous for its fly-fishing on the Madison River. The historic western towns of Virginia City and Nevada City are just west of Ennis. You can hike and fish in Beaverhead-Deerlodge National Forest, which surrounds Ennis.

77 Spire Rock

  6

Location: South of Bozeman; map MT9, grid g8.

Campsites, facilities: There are 10 RV or tent campsites, which can accommodate a maximum RV length of 16 feet.

Reservations, fees: No reservations are needed; the fee is $7 per night. Open June 15–September 15. The stay limit is 15 days.

Directions: From Bozeman, go 26 miles south on U.S. 191, then two miles east on Forest Service Road 1321 to the campground. U.S. 191 is a narrow, winding road filled with semi-trucks and tourists, so use caution when driving here.

Contact: Gallatin National Forest, Bozeman Ranger District, 3710 Fallon St., Suite C, Bozeman, MT 59718; 406/522-2520.

Trip notes: You can fish and hike here.

78 Castle Rock Inn & RV Park

 4

Location: South of Gallatin Gateway; map MT9, grid g7.

Campsites, facilities: There are 12 RV or tent campsites. Showers, laundry facilities, hookups, water, and a store are available. Pets are welcome.

Reservations, fees: No reservations are needed; the fee is $15–20 per night. Open year-round.

Directions: From Bozeman, go west on U.S. 191 to Jackrabbit Lane (north) and Gallatin Road (south), go south on Gallatin Road/U.S. 191 to Gallatin Gateway and then 25 miles south to Castle Rock Inn & RV Park, on the left. Be *very cautious* of traffic and conditions.

Contact: Castle Rock Inn & RV Park, 65840 Gallatin Rd., Gallatin Gateway, MT 59730; 406/763-4243; website: www.castlerockinn.com.

Trip notes: This campground is on the banks of the Gallatin River. You can fish at nearby Madison, Yellowstone, and Beaverhead Rivers. You can boat, swim, water-ski, canoe, and fish in Hebgen Lake, near West Yellowstone. In Yellowstone National Park, you can fish (with permit), hike, boat, canoe, and see wildlife in their spectacular habitat.

79 Greek Creek

 6

Location: In Gallatin National Forest; map MT9, grid g7.

Campsites, facilities: There are 14 RV or tent campsites, which can accommodate a maximum RV length of 25 feet. There is a hand-launch-only boat area.

Reservations, fees: No reservations are needed; the fee is $9 per night. Open June 15–September 15. The stay limit is 15 days.

Directions: From Bozeman, go 31 miles south on U.S. 191 to the campground. This is a narrow, winding road filled with semi-trucks and tourists, so use caution when driving here.

Contact: Gallatin National Forest, Bozeman Ranger District, 3710 Fallon St., Suite C, Bozeman, MT 59718; 406/522-2520.

Trip notes: You can fish at nearby Madison, Yellowstone, and Beaverhead Rivers. You can boat, swim, water-ski, canoe, and fish in Hebgen Lake, near West Yellowstone. In Yellowstone National Park, you can fish (with permit), hike, boat, canoe, and see wildlife in their spectacular habitat.

80 Swan Creek

 6

Location: In Gallatin National Forest; map MT9, grid g8.

Campsites, facilities: There are 11 RV or tent campsites, which can accommodate a maximum RV length of 16 feet.

Reservations, fees: No reservations are needed; the fee is $9 per night. Open June 15–September 15. The stay limit is 15 days.

Directions: From Bozeman, go 32 miles south on U.S. 191, then one mile east on Forest Service Road 481 to the campground. U.S. 191 is a narrow, winding road filled with semi-trucks and tourists, so use caution when driving here.

Contact: Gallatin National Forest, Bozeman Ranger District, 3710 Fallon St., Suite C, Bozeman, MT 59718; 406/522-2520.

Trip notes: You can fish here.

81 Moose Flat

 6

Location: In Gallatin National Forest; map MT9, grid g8.

Campsites, facilities: There are 14 RV or tent campsites, which can accommodate a maximum RV length of 30 feet. There is hand-launch boat access.

Reservations, fees: No reservations are needed; the fee is $9 per night. Open June 1–September 15. The stay limit is 15 days.

Directions: From Bozeman, go 32 miles south on U.S. 191 to the campground. This is a narrow, winding road filled with semi-trucks and tourists, so use caution when driving here. **Contact:** Gallatin National Forest, Bozeman Ranger District, 3710 Fallon St., Suite C, Bozeman, MT 59718; 406/522-2520.

Trip notes: You can boat, swim, water-ski, canoe, and fish in Hebgen Lake. In Yellowstone National Park, you can fish (with permit), hike, boat, canoe, and see wildlife in their spectacular habitat.

82 Dinner Station

    7

Location: In Beaverhead-Deerlodge National Forest; map MT9, grid g1.

Campsites, facilities: There are seven RV or tent campsites, which can accommodate a maximum RV length of 16 feet. A wheelchair-accessible restroom is available.

Reservations, fees: No reservations are needed, and no fee is charged. Open May 15–September 15. The stay limit is 16 days.

Directions: From Dillon, go 12 miles north on I-15, take Apex exit, and drive 12 miles northwest on Birch Creek Road to the campground.

Contact: Beaverhead-Deerlodge National Forest, Dillon Ranger District, 420 Barrett St., Dillon, MT 59725-3572; 406/683-3900.

Trip notes: This campground is along Birch Creek. A hiking trail nearby leads to Deerhead Lake.

83 Valley Garden

    5

Location: South of Ennis; map MT9, grid g6.

Campsites, facilities: There are four tent campsites. There is a trailer boat launch.

Reservations, fees: No reservations are needed; the fee is $5 per night. Open April 1–November 30. The stay limit is 14 days.

Directions: From Ennis on U.S. 287, go .25 mile south on U.S. 287 to milepost 48, then two miles north on the county road to the campground.

Contact: Fish, Wildlife & Parks, Region 3, 1400 S. 19th, Bozeman, MT 59718; 406/994-0442.

Trip notes: Ennis is famous for its fly-fishing on the Madison River. The historic western towns of Virginia City and Nevada City are just west of Ennis. You can hike and fish in Beaverhead-Deerlodge National Forest, which surrounds Ennis.

84 Ennis

    5

Location: Near Ennis; map MT9, grid g6.

Campsites, facilities: There are 15 RV campsites (which can accommodate a maximum RV length of 20 feet) and 15 tent campsites. A trailer boat launch is available. Pets are allowed on leashes.

Reservations, fees: No reservations are needed; the fee is $5 per night. Open April 1–November 30. The stay limit is 14 days.

Directions: From Ennis on U.S. 287, go .25 mile south on U.S. 287 to milepost 48 to the fishing access and campground.

Contact: Fish, Wildlife & Parks, Region 3, 1400 S. 19th, Bozeman, MT 59718; 406/994-0442.

Trip notes: Ennis is famous for its fly-fishing on the Madison River. The historic western towns of Virginia City and Nevada City are just west of Ennis. You can hike and fish in Beaverhead-Deerlodge National Forest, which surrounds Ennis.

85 Alder/Virginia City KOA

  5

Location: West of Virginia City; map MT9, grid g4.

Campsites, facilities: There are 59 RV or tent campsites. Laundry facilities, a sanitary disposal facility, and a store are available.

Reservations, fees: No reservations are needed; the fee is $16–23 per night. Open January 15–December 15. The stay limit is seven days.

Directions: From Virginia City, go nine miles

west on Highway 287 to the campground on the right.

Contact: Alder/Virginia City KOA, P.O. Box 103, Alder, MT 59710; 800/562-1898 or 406/842-5677.

Trip notes: This grassy camping area has pond fishing on location and is close to six major fishing rivers: Ruby, Yellowstone, Gallatin, Beaverhead, Jefferson and Madison Rivers, as well as their tributaries. There are numerous alpine lakes for additional fishing in or near Beaverhead-Deerlodge National Forest.

In 1997 the Montana Legislature voted to buy and restore the old mining towns of Virginia City and Nevada City. Many original buildings still stand where they were built. Old buildings from other parts of the state were brought in to create an outdoor museum, and a collection of music machines, such as an automatic violin player, was added. Today the two towns offer entertainment and a bit of real western history for all visitors.

86 Camper Corner
 4

Location: In Ennis; map MT9, grid g5.

Campsites, facilities: There are 30 RV and trailer campsites. There are showers, laundry facilities, hookups, water, and a sanitary disposal facility available.

Reservations, fees: No reservations are needed; the fee is $15 per night. Open May 1–October 31.

Directions: From the junction of U.S. 287 and Highway 287 in Ennis, go one block west on Highway 287 to the campground, which is on the right.

Contact: Camper Corner, P.O. Box 351, Ennis, MT 59729; 406/682-4514, 800/755-3474; website: www.campercorner.com.

Trip notes: You can fish at nearby Madison, Yellowstone, and Beaverhead Rivers. You can boat, swim, water-ski, canoe, and fish in Hebgen Lake, near West Yellowstone. In Yellow-

stone National Park, you can fish (with permit), hike, boat, canoe, and see wildlife in their spectacular habitat.

87 Virginia City Campground
 5

Location: map MT9, grid g5.

Campsites, facilities: There are 17 RV campsites, which can accommodate a maximum RV length of 50 feet, and 24 tent sites. Hookups, pull-through sites, showers, a sanitary disposal station, and water are available. Group sites can be arranged.

Reservations, fees: Reservations are strongly suggested; the fee is $15–21 per night. Open May 1–September 30.

Directions: From Ennis, go 14 miles west on U.S. 287 toward Virginia City, and the campground is on the left, right before you enter Virginia City.

Contact: Virginia City Campground, P.O. Box 188, 1302 E. Wallace (Hwy. 287), Virginia City, MT 59755; 888/833-5493 or 406/843-5493, fax 406/843-5283; email: vccamp@3rivers.net.

Trip notes: There are six major fishing rivers in the area: Ruby, Yellowstone, Gallatin, Beaverhead, Jefferson and Madison Rivers, as well as their tributaries. You can hike in Beaverhead-Deerlodge National Forest. In 1997 the Montana Legislature voted to buy and restore the old mining towns of Virginia and Nevada City. Many original buildings still stand where they were built. Old buildings from other parts of the state were brought in to create an outdoor museum, and a collection of music machines, such as an automatic violin player, was added. Today the two towns offer entertainment and a bit of real western history for all visitors.

88 Dillon KOA
 5

Location: In Dillon; map MT9, grid h2.

Campsites, facilities: There are 98 RV or

tent campsites. Showers, laundry facilities, a playground, swimming pool, and cabins are available.

Reservations, fees: Reservations are accepted; the fee is $17–24 per night. Open April 1–October 31.

Directions: From the junction of I-90 and I-15, go south on I-15 to Dillon, take Exit 63 to Montana Street, turn right, go two miles to Reeder Street, turn right and follow signs to the campground.

Contact: Dillon KOA, 735 W. Park St., Dillon, MT 59725; 406/683-2749, 800/562-2751.

Trip notes: You can fish in the Beaverhead River, and there is golfing nearby. Beaverhead Rock, approximately 15 miles north of Dillon on Highway 41, was so named in Lewis and Clark's journals because it resembled the head of a swimming beaver. It's now a national landmark. You can hike in Beaverhead-Deerlodge National Forest.

89 Ruby Reservoir

 5

Location: South of Twin Bridges; map MT9, grid h4.

Campsites, facilities: There are 10 RV or tent campsites, which can accommodate a maximum RV length of 35 feet. There is a trailer boat launch.

Reservations, fees: No reservations are needed; the fee is $5 per night. Open year-round. The stay limit is 14 days.

Directions: From Dillon, go north on Highway 41 26 miles to Twin Bridges. From Twin Bridges, go south on Highway 287 to Alder, then south to the east shore of Ruby Reservoir to the campground.

Contact: Bureau of Land Management, 1005 Selway Drive, Dillon, MT 59725; 406/683-2337; website: www.mt.blm.gov/dfo; email: bzwebmaster@mt.blm.gov.

Trip notes: You can boat, fish, and swim here.

90 Cottonwood

 5

Location: In Beaverhead-Deerlodge National Forest; map MT9, grid h4.

Campsites, facilities: There are 10 RV or tent sites.

Reservations, fees: No reservations are needed; there is no fee. Open May 26–November 30. The stay limit is 16 days.

Directions: From Alder, go nine miles on Ruby Road (a paved county road) to the Ruby Reservoir and the campground.

Contact: Beaverhead-Deerlodge National Forest, 5 Forest Service Rd., Ennis, MT 59729; 406/682-4253.

Trip notes: There are six major fishing rivers in the area: Ruby, Yellowstone, Gallatin, Beaverhead, Jefferson and Madison Rivers, as well as their tributaries. You can hike in Beaverhead-Deerlodge National Forest. In 1997 the Montana Legislature voted to buy and restore the old mining towns of Virginia City and Nevada City. Many original buildings still stand where they were built. Old buildings from other parts of the state were brought in to create an outdoor museum, and a collection of music machines, such as an automatic violin player, was added. Today the two towns offer entertainment and a bit of real western history for all visitors.

91 Varney Bridge

 5

Location: Southwest of Ennis; map MT9, grid h6.

Campsites, facilities: There are five tent campsites and a trailer boat launch.

Reservations, fees: No reservations are needed; the fee is $5 per night. Open year-round. The stay limit is 14 days.

Directions: From Ennis, go two miles west on Highway 287, then 10 miles south on the county road to the campground.

Contact: Fish, Wildlife & Parks, Region 3, 1400 S. 19th, Bozeman, MT 59718; 406/994-0442.

Trip notes: Ennis is famous for its fly-fishing on the Madison River. The historic western towns of Virginia City and Nevada City are just west of Ennis. You can hike and fish in Beaverhead-Deerlodge National Forest, which surrounds Ennis.

92 Cameron Store & Cabins

 5

Location: South of Ennis; map MT9, grid h6.

Campsites, facilities: There are 12 RV and six tent campsites. Cabins, a café, store, and propane gas are available.

Reservations, fees: No reservations are needed; the fee is $17 per night. Open year-round.

Directions: From Ennis, go 11 miles south on U.S. 287. The campground is on the right.

Contact: Cameron Store & Cabins, 3801 Hwy. 287 North, P.O. Box 268, Cameron, MT 59720; 406/682-7744; website: www.come-see-cameron.com.

Trip notes: This campground is a mile from the Madison River. You can boat, swim, water-ski, canoe, and fish in Hebgen Lake. In Yellowstone National Park, you can fish (with permit), hike, boat, canoe, and see wildlife in their spectacular habitat.

93 Red Cliff

 6

Location: In Gallatin National Forest; map MT9, grid h8.

Campsites, facilities: There are 68 RV or tent campsites and a hand-launch boat access. Pets are allowed on leashes.

Reservations, fees: No reservations are needed; the fee is $9 per night. Open May 15–September 15. The stay limit is 14 days.

Directions: From Bozeman, drive 48 miles south on U.S. 191, then .1 mile east on Forest Service Road 634 to the campground. U.S. 191 is a narrow, winding road filled with semi-trucks and tourists, so use caution when driving here.

Contact: Gallatin National Forest, Bozeman Ranger District, 3710 Fallon St., Suite C, Bozeman, MT 59718; 406/522-2520.

Trip notes: At this campground, there is access to the Gallatin River. You can also fish at the Madison and Yellowstone Rivers. You can boat, swim, water-ski, canoe, and fish in Hebgen Lake, near West Yellowstone. In Yellowstone National Park, you can fish (with permit), hike, boat, canoe, and see wildlife in their spectacular habitat.

94 Barretts Park

 5

Location: At Clark Canyon Reservoir; map MT9, grid h2.

Campsites, facilities: There are five RV or tent campsites, a wheelchair-accessible restroom, and a trailer boat launch.

Reservations, fees: No reservations are needed, and no fee is charged. Open year-round. The stay limit is 14 days.

Directions: From Dillon, go 20 miles south on I-15 to Clark Canyon Reservoir and the campground.

Contact: U.S. Bureau of Reclamation, P.O. Box 30137, Billings, MT 59107-0137; 406/247-7314.

Trip notes: You can boat and fish here.

95 Bear Creek

 5

Location: Near Ennis; map MT9, grid h6.

Campsites, facilities: There are 12 RV or tent campsites.

Reservations, fees: No reservations are needed; there is no fee. Open June 1–November 30. The stay limit is 16 days.

Directions: From Ennis, go 11 miles south on U.S. 28 to Cameron, then nine miles east of Cameron Community Center on Bear Creek Road to the campground, which is on the right side.

Contact: Beaverhead-Deerlodge National Forest, Madison Ranger District, 5 Service Forest Rd., Ennis, MT 59729; 406/682-4253.

Trip notes: Ennis is famous for its fly-fishing on the Madison River. The historic western towns of Virginia City and Nevada City are just west of Ennis. You can hike and fish in Beaverhead-Deerlodge National Forest, which surrounds Ennis.

96 West Madison

   6

Location: South of Ennis; map MT9, grid h6.

Campsites, facilities: There are 22 RV or tent campsites, which can accommodate a maximum RV length of 35 feet.

Reservations, fees: No reservations are needed; the fee is $4 per night. Open May 15–September 30. The stay limit is 14 days.

Directions: From Ennis, go 18 miles south on U.S. 287, then three miles south on the county road to the campground.

Contact: Bureau of Land Management, 1005 Selway Drive, Dillon, MT 59725; 406/683-2337; website: www.mt.blm.gov/dfo; email: bzwebmaster@mt.blm.gov.

Trip notes: You can fish in the Madison River.

97 South Madison

    5

Location: South of Ennis; map MT9, grid h6.

Campsites, facilities: There are 11 RV or tent campsites, which can accommodate a maximum RV length of 35 feet. A trailer boat launch is available.

Reservations, fees: No reservations are needed; the fee is $5 per night. Open year-round. The stay limit is 14 days.

Directions: From Ennis, go 26 miles south on U.S. 287, then one mile west to the campground.

Contact: Bureau of Land Management, 1005 Selway Drive, Dillon, MT 59725; 406/683-2337; email: bzwebmaster@mt.blm.gov; website: www.mt.blm.gov/dfo.

Trip notes: You can boat and fish here.

98 Madison River Cabins & RV

    5

Location: North of West Yellowstone; map MT9, grid h6.

Campsites, facilities: There are nine RV or tent campsites. Pull-through sites, water, electricity, laundry, and showers are available.

Reservations, fees: No reservations are needed; the fee is $6–20 per night. Cabins and weekly rates are available. Open May 1–September 30.

Directions: From Ennis, take U.S. 287 south toward Yellowstone for 35 miles to the campground on the right side, next to the Grizzly Bar.

Contact: Madison River Cabins & RV, 1403 Hwy. 287 N, Cameron, MT 59720; 406/682-4890; email: cabins@madison-river.com/ website: www.madison-river.com.

Trip notes: This campground is on the Madison River and 35 miles from West Yellowstone, the entrance to Yellowstone National Park.

MONTANA
CHAPTER MT10

WAYNE SCHERR

Hiking in Beartooth Mountains,
Absaroka-Beartooth Wilderness

MAP MT10

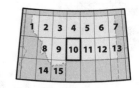

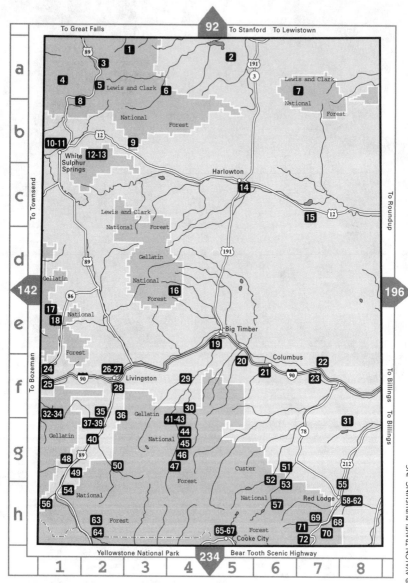

CHAPTER MT10

1	Dry Wolf	174
2	Ackley Lake State Park	174
3	Many Pines	174
4	Moose Creek	174
5	Kings Hill	174
6	Indian Hill	175
7	Crystal Lake	175
8	Jumping Creek	175
9	Spring Creek	175
10	Conestoga Campground	176
11	Springs Campground	176
12	Grasshopper Creek	176
13	Richardson Creek	177
14	Chief Joseph Park	177
15	Deadman's Basin	177
16	Half Moon	178
17	Fairy Lake	178
18	Battle Ridge	178
19	Spring Creek Campground & Trout Ranch	178
20	Big Timber KOA Campground	179
21	Cedar Hills Campground	179
22	Mountain Range RV Park	179
23	Itch-Kep-Pe Park	179
24	Sunrise Campground	180
25	Bear Canyon Campground	180
26	Osen's Campground	180
27	Paradise Livingston Campground	180
28	Windmill Park	181
29	McLeod Resort	181
30	East Boulder	181
31	Cooney	181
32	Langhor	181
33	Hood Creek	182
34	Chisholm	182
35	Rock Canyon RV Park	182
36	Pine Creek	183
37	Paradise Valley/ Livingston KOA	183
38	Mallard's Rest	183
39	Loch Leven	183
40	Yellowstone's Edge RV Park	184
41	West Boulder	184
42	Falls Creek	184
43	Big Beaver	184
44	Aspen	185
45	Chippy Park	185
46	Hells Canyon	185
47	Hicks Park	185
48	Canyon	186
49	Dailey Lake	186
50	Snow Bank	186
51	Pine Grove	186
52	Emerald Lake	187
53	Jimmy Joe	187
54	Carbella	187
55	Red Lodge KOA	187
56	Tom Miner	188
57	East Rosebud Lake	188
58	Palisades	188
59	Perry's RV Park & Campground	189
60	Cascade	189
61	Basin	189
62	Sheridan	190
63	Eagle Creek	190
64	Rocky Mountain Campground	190
65	Colter	191
66	Chief Joseph	191
67	Soda Butte	191
68	Ratine	191
69	Parkside	192
70	Limber Pine	192
71	Greenough Lake	192
72	M-K	193

1 Dry Wolf

 5

Location: In Lewis and Clark National Forest; map MT10, grid a2.

Campsites, facilities: There are 26 RV or tent campsites, which can accommodate a maximum RV length of 32 feet. A toilet and water are available.

Reservations, fees: No reservations are needed; the fee is $6 per night. Open May 1–September 1. The stay limit is 14 days.

Directions: From Stanford, follow U.S. 87 north for a mile to the Forest Service access sign, take a left and drive four miles to the Y intersection, where you go right for 15 miles. There will be a campground sign here; turn right to the campground.

Contact: Lewis and Clark National Forest, Judith Ranger District, P.O. Box 484, Stanford, MT 59479; 406/566-2292.

Trip notes: You can fish and hike here.

2 Ackley Lake State Park

 5

Location: West of Lewistown; map MT10, grid a5.

Campsites, facilities: There are 23 RV or tent primitive campsites, some with grills and picnic tables. Toilets, water (available seasonally), and a trailer boat ramp are provided. Pets are allowed on leashes.

Reservations, fees: No reservations are needed; there is no fee. Open year-round. The stay limit is 14 days.

Directions: From Lewistown, go 17 miles west on U.S. 87 to Hobson, milepost 58, then five miles south on Route 400 and two miles southwest on a county road to Ackley Lake.

Contact: Fish, Wildlife & Parks, P.O. Box 6609, Great Falls, MT 59406; 406/454-3441.

Trip notes: You can fish here for stocked rainbow trout. The park is designated as primitive and is pack-in, pack-out. A golf course is in Lewistown.

3 Many Pines

 5

Location: In Lewis and Clark National Forest; map MT10, grid a2.

Campsites, facilities: There are 23 RV and tent campsites, which can accommodate a maximum RV length of 22 feet. A wheelchair-accessible restroom and water are available.

Reservations, fees: No reservations are needed; the fee is $6 per night. Open May 1–November 1. The stay limit is 14 days.

Directions: From Great Falls, go 55 miles southeast on U.S. 89 to Neihart. From Neihart, go four miles on U.S. 89 to the campground.

Contact: Lewis and Clark National Forest, Belt Creek Station, 4234 Hwy. 89 N., Neihart, MT 49465; 406/236-5511.

Trip notes: You can hike and fish here.

4 Moose Creek

   5

Location: In Lewis and Clark National Forest; map MT10, grid a1.

Campsites, facilities: There are six RV or tent campsites, which can accommodate a maximum RV length of 22 feet. A toilet and water are available.

Reservations, fees: No reservations are needed; the fee is $6 per night. Open May 1–November 1. The stay limit is 14 days.

Directions: From White Sulphur Springs, go 18 miles north on U.S. 89, four miles west on Forest Service Road 119, then three miles north on Forest Service Road 204 to the campground.

Contact: Lewis and Clark National Forest, Belt Creek Station, 4234 Hwy. 89 N., Neihart, MT 49465; 406/236-5511.

Trip notes: You can fish here.

5 Kings Hill

     5

Location: In Lewis and Clark National Forest; map MT10, grid a2.

Campsites, facilities: There are 18 RV or tent campsites, which can accommodate a maximum RV length of 16 feet. A wheelchair-accessible restroom and water are available.

Reservations, fees: No reservations are needed; the fee is $6 per night. Open May 1–November 1. The stay limit is 14 days.

Directions: From White Sulphur Springs go 33 miles north on U.S. 89; the campground is on top of Kings Hill.

Contact: Lewis and Clark National Forest, King Hill Ranger District, P.O. Box A, White Sulphur Springs, MT 59645; 406/547-3361.

Trip notes: You can fish and hike here.

6 Indian Hill
 5

Location: In Lewis and Clark National Forest; map MT10, grid a3.

Campsites, facilities: There are seven RV or tent campsites, which can accommodate a maximum RV length of 22 feet. A toilet is available.

Reservations, fees: No reservations are needed; the fee is $6 per night. Open May 1–September 1. The stay limit is 14 days.

Directions: From Great Falls, go east on Highway 87 about 90 miles to Hobson. From Hobson, go 12 miles west on Route 239 to Utica, turn left on the county road, and go 15 miles southwest to the campground.

Contact: Lewis and Clark National Forest, Judith Ranger District, P.O. Box 484, Stanford, MT 59479; 406/566-2292.

Trip notes: You can fish and hike here.

7 Crystal Lake
 5

Location: In Lewis and Clark National Forest; map MT10, grid a7.

Campsites, facilities: There are 28 RV or tent campsites, which can accommodate a maximum RV length of 22 feet. Wheelchair-accessible restrooms and water are available.

Reservations, fees: No reservations are needed; the fee is $5–8 per night. Open May 1–October 1. The stay limit is 14 days.

Directions: From Lewistown, go nine miles west on U.S. 87, 16 miles south on the county road, then 8.5 miles south on Forest Service Road 275 to the campground.

Contact: Lewis and Clark National Forest, 1111 15th St. North, Great Falls, MT 59401; 406/791-7700.

Trip notes: This campground is in the Big Snowy Mountains, and you can fish, swim, and hike here.

8 Jumping Creek
 5

Location: In Lewis and Clark National Forest; map MT10, grid b1.

Campsites, facilities: There are 15 RV or tent campsites, which can accommodate a maximum RV length of 22 feet. A wheelchair-accessible restroom and water are available.

Reservations, fees: No reservations are needed; the fee is $6 per night. Open May 1–November 1. The stay limit is 14 days.

Directions: From White Sulphur Springs, go 22 miles northeast on U.S. 89 to the campground.

Contact: Lewis and Clark National Forest, King Hill Ranger District, P.O. Box A, White Sulphur Springs, MT 59645; 406/547-3361.

Trip notes: This campground was closed the summer of 2000, so check with the ranger district for the latest information. You can fish and hike here.

9 Spring Creek
 5

Location: In Lewis and Clark National Forest; map MT10, grid b3.

Campsites, facilities: there are 10 RV or tent campsites, which can accommodate a maximum RV length of 22 feet. A toilet and water are available.

Reservations, fees: Reservations are recommended; there is no fee. Open May 1–November 1. The stay limit is 14 days.

Directions: From White Sulphur Springs, take U.S. 12 east six miles to the Spring Creek Camp sign, turn left on Spring Creek Road, go four miles to a second Spring Creek Camp sign, and turn right; the campground is three miles ahead.

Contact: Lewis and Clark National Forest, Musselshell Ranger District, P.O. Box 1906, Harlowton, MT 59036; 406/632-4391.

Trip notes: You can fish and hike in Lewis and Clark National Forest.

10 Conestoga Campground

     4

Location: In White Sulphur Springs; map MT10, grid b1.

Campsites, facilities: There are 77 RV or tent campsites. Showers, laundry facilities, a store, a sanitary disposal station, electricity, water, and wheelchair-accessible restrooms are available.

Reservations, fees: No reservations are needed; the fee is $10.40–17.68 per night. Open year-round.

Directions: From White Sulphur Springs on U.S. 89, take South Street four blocks west to the campground.

Contact: Conestoga Campground, 815 8th Ave. West, P.O. Box 508, White Sulphur Springs, MT 59645; 406/547-3890, fax 406/547-3824.

Trip notes: There is a trout pond on-site. White Sulphur Springs was named for the white deposits around the hot sulfur springs in the area. A nine-hole golf course is on the south side of town, and mineral baths and swimming facilities maintained and operated by the Spa Motel. You can fly-fish on the Smith River and boat, swim, and water-ski on Newlan Creek Reservoir and Canyon Ferry Lake (40 minutes away). You can hike in the Big Belt Mountains and the Castle Mountains.

11 Springs Campground

    4

Location: In White Sulphur Springs; map MT10, grid b1.

Campsites, facilities: There are eight RV or tent campsites. Water and electricity are available.

Reservations, fees: No reservations are needed; the fee is $10 per night. Open May 1–December 1.

Directions: From U.S. 89/12/Main Street in White Sulphur Springs, continue west on Main Street three blocks to the west end of White Sulphur Springs (do not cross bridge), and the campground is on the right, on the North Fork of the Smith River.

Contact: Springs Campground, P.O. Box 350, White Sulphur Springs, MT 59645; 406/547-3921.

Trip notes: White Sulphur Springs was named for the white deposits around the hot Sulphur springs in the area. There is a nine-hole golf course on the south side of town; and mineral baths and swimming facilities maintained and operated by the Spa Motel. You can go fly-fishing on the Smith River and boat, swim, and water-ski on Newlan Creek Reservoir and Canyon Ferry Lake (40 minutes away). You can hike in the Big Belt Mountains and the Castle Mountains.

12 Grasshopper Creek

    5

Location: In Lewis and Clark National Forest; map MT10, grid b2.

Campsites, facilities: There are 12 RV or tent campsites, which can accommodate a maximum RV length of 16 feet. A toilet and water are available.

Reservations, fees: No reservations are needed; the fee is $6 per night. Open May 1–November 1. The stay limit is 14 days.

Directions: From White Sulphur Springs, go seven miles east on U.S. 12 to Forest Service

Road 211 (a dirt road); turn right and drive four miles to the T intersection, take a right and the campground is .2 mile ahead.

Contact: Lewis and Clark National Forest, Belt Creek Station, 4234 Hwy. 89 N., Neihart, MT 49465; 406/236-5511.

Trip notes: White Sulphur Springs was named for the white deposits around the hot sulfur springs in the area. A nine-hole golf course is on the south side of town, and mineral baths and swimming facilities are maintained and operated by the Spa Motel. You can go fly-fishing on the Smith River, and boat, swim, and water-ski on Newlan Creek Reservoir and Canyon Ferry Lake (40 minutes away). You can hike in the Big Belt Mountains and the Castle Mountains.

13 Richardson Creek
 5

Location: Near White Sulphur Springs; map MT10, grid b2.

Campsites, facilities: There are three RV or tent campsites, which can accommodate a maximum RV length of 16 feet. A toilet is available.

Reservations, fees: No reservations are needed; the fee is $6 per night. Open May 1–November 1. The stay limit is 14 days.

Directions: From White Sulphur Springs, go seven miles east on U.S. 12 to Forest Service Road 211 (a dirt road); turn right and drive five miles to the campground.

Contact: Lewis and Clark National Forest, Belt Creek Station, 4234 Hwy. 89 N., Neihart, MT 49465; 406/236-5511.

Trip notes: White Sulphur Springs was named for the white deposits around the hot sulfur springs in the area. There is a nine-hole golf course on the south side of town, and mineral baths and swimming facilities are maintained and operated by the Spa Motel. You can go fly-fishing on the Smith River, and boat, swim, and water-ski on Newlan Creek Reservoir and Canyon Ferry Lake (40 minutes away). You can

hike in the Big Belt Mountains and the Castle Mountains.

14 Chief Joseph Park
 4

Location: Near Lewis and Clark National Forest; map MT10, grid c5.

Campsites, facilities: There are 15 RV and unlimited tent campsites. Wheelchair-accessible restrooms, electricity, a playground, barbecues, a picnic area, and fishing pond are available. Pets are allowed on leashes.

Reservations, fees: No reservations are needed; the fee is $3–8.35 per night. Open April 1–October 31.

Directions: Chief Joseph's Park turnoff is on Highway 12, six blocks from Highway 191 if entering town from the south or west, and two blocks from the Electric Train Engine if entering town from the north or east.

Contact: Chief Joseph Park, P.O. Box 292, Harlowton, MT 59036; Harlowton, MT 59036; 406/632-5532.

Trip notes: The E-57B Electric Train Park commemorates the longest stretch of electric railway in North America. The E-57B electric engine was donated to the community by the Milwaukee Railroad upon its closing in 1980. Fischer Park contains a history of the engine and has benches.

15 Deadman's Basin
 4

Location: East of Harlowton; map MT10, grid c7.

Campsites, facilities: There are 80 RV and tent campsites. Restrooms, water, and a hand launch boat ramp are available.

Reservations, fees: No reservations are needed; there is no fee. Open year-round. The stay limit is seven days.

Directions: From Harlowton on U.S. 12, go 20 miles east to the campground.

Contact: Montana Fish, Wildlife & Parks, Region 5, 2300 Lake Elmo Drive, Billings, MT 59107; 406/247-2940.

Trip notes: You can swim, boat, water-ski, and fish at Deadman's Basin Reservoir. There's a golf course in Harlowton.

16 Half Moon

 6

Location: In Gallatin National Forest; map MT10, grid e4.

Campsites, facilities: There are eight RV or tent campsites, which can accommodate a maximum RV length of 22 feet. A toilet and water are available.

Reservations, fees: No reservations are needed; there is no fee. Open year-round. The stay limit is 15 days.

Directions: From U.S. 191 at Big Timber, go 11 miles north, then west on Big Timber Canyon Road for 12 miles to campground.

Contact: Gallatin National Forest, P.O. Box 196, Big Timber, MT 59011-0196; 406/932-5155.

Trip notes: You can swim, fish, and hike in Gallatin National Forest.

17 Fairy Lake

 6

Location: In Gallatin National Forest; map MT10, grid e1.

Campsites, facilities: There are nine campsites. Wheelchair-accessible restrooms and water are available.

Reservations, fees: No reservations are needed; there is no fee. Open July 1–September 1. The stay limit is 15 days.

Directions: From Bozeman, go 22 miles north on Highway 86, then five miles west on Fairy Lake Road to Fairy Lake.

Contact: Gallatin National Forest, 3710 Fallon St., Suite C, Bozeman, MT 59715; 406/522-2520.

Trip notes: You can fish and hike in Gallatin National Forest.

18 Battle Ridge

 6

Location: In Gallatin National Forest; map MT10, grid e1.

Campsites, facilities: There are 13 RV or tent campsites, which can accommodate a maximum RV length of 16 feet. Toilets and water are available.

Reservations, fees: No reservations are needed; there is no fee. Open June 10–September 30. The stay limit is 15 days.

Directions: From Bozeman, go 22 miles northeast on Highway 86 to the campground.

Contact: Gallatin National Forest, 3710 Fallon St., Suite C, Bozeman, MT 59715; 406/522-2520.

Trip notes: You can fish and hike in Gallatin National Forest.

19 Spring Creek Campground & Trout Ranch

 6

Location: South of Big Timber; map MT10, grid e5.

Campsites, facilities: There are 65 RV and eight tent campsites. Showers, laundry facilities, water, electricity, sewer, a store, and a sanitary disposal station are available. Pets are allowed on leashes.

Reservations, fees: Reservations are strongly suggested; the fee is $15–25 per night. Open April 1–October 1.

Directions: From Big Timber, go two miles south on Route 298 to the campground.

Contact: Spring Creek Campground & Trout Ranch, P.O. Box 1435, Big Timber, MT 59011; 406/932-4387; email:info@springcreekcampground.com.

Trip notes: This campground is along the Boulder River, in the Boulder Valley where *The Horse Whisperer* was filmed. The Yellowstone River is three miles away. Horseback riding, white-water rafting, and river float trips can be arranged. There is a golf course in Big Timber.

20 Big Timber KOA Campground

     5

Location: Big Timber; map MT10, grid f5.

Campsites, facilities: There are 75 RV or tent campsites, some with hookups. Showers, laundry facilities, water, electricity, sewer, store, and a sanitary disposal station are available, as well as hot tubs, a swimming pool, water slide, and mini-golf. Pets are allowed on leashes.

Reservations, fees: Reservations are accepted; the fee is $18–23 per night. Open May 15–September 4.

Directions: From Big Timber, take I-90 nine miles east to Exit 377; go south to the campground.

Contact: Big Timber KOA Campground, KOA, HC 88, Box 3634, Big Timber, MT 59011; 406/932-6569, fax 406/932-6569.

Trip notes: You can fish in nearby Boulder or Yellowstone Rivers.

21 Cedar Hills Campground

   6

Location: In Reedpoint; map MT10, grid f6.

Campsites, facilities: There are 24 RV or tent campsites. Showers, laundry facilities, hookups, propane gas, a store, and a sanitary disposal facility are available.

Reservations, fees: No reservations are needed; the fee is $5–8 per night. Open year-round.

Directions: From Billings, go west on I-90 to Exit 392 at Reedpoint, and the campground is right next to the interstate.

Contact: Cedar Hills Campground, Reedpoint, MT 59069; 406/326-2266.

Trip notes: This campground is less than a mile from the Yellowstone River where you can fish for rainbow and brown trout.

22 Mountain Range RV Park

   4

Location: Near Columbus; map MT10, grid f7.

Campsites, facilities: There are 50 RV or tent campsites. Showers, hookups, laundry facilities, a store, water, and a sanitary disposal facility are available.

Reservations, fees: No reservations are needed; the fee is $8–15 per night. Open March 1–November 30.

Directions: From Billings, go west on I-90 to exit 408 at Columbus, then go northwest on Lehmann Road to Sheep Dip Road. The RV park can be seen from I-90, which borders the south side of the park.

Contact: Mountain Range RV Park, 30 Mountain Range Rd., P.O. Box 116, Columbus, MT 59019; 406/322-1140, fax 406/322-6171; email: mountainrange@twoalpha.net.

Trip notes: This campground is convenient, with a family atmosphere. It is at the confluence of the Stillwater and Yellowstone Rivers, where you can fish.

23 Itch-Kep-Pe Park

   4

Location: Near Columbus; map MT10, grid f7.

Campsites, facilities: There are 30 RV or tent campsites. Restrooms, water, and a boat launch are available.

Reservations, fees: No reservations are needed; the fee is $8–12 per night. Open April 1–October 31. The stay limit is 14 days.

Directions: From Columbus, go south on Highway 78; before crossing the Yellowstone River (about 28 miles), turn right to Itch-Kep-Pe Park.

Contact: Itch-Kep-Pe Park, P.O. Box 783, Columbus, MT 59019; 406/322-4505.

Trip notes: You can fish in the Yellowstone River for rainbow and brown trout.

24 Sunrise Campground

 3

Location: Near Bozeman; map MT10, grid f1.

Campsites, facilities: There are 65 RV or tent campsites. There are showers, laundry facilities, water, electricity, sewer, and a sanitary disposal station. Pets are allowed on leashes.

Reservations, fees: Reservations are accepted; the fee is $10–15 per night. Open April 15–November 15.

Directions: From Bozeman, go two miles east on I-90, take Exit 309, and turn left at signs.

Contact: Sunrise Campground, 31842 Frontage Rd., Bozeman, MT 59715; 406/587-4797 or 877/437-2095.

Trip notes: This campground is close to downtown Bozeman, where there are restaurants and groceries. It is also near a railroad track. You can fish and hike in nearby Gallatin National Forest.

25 Bear Canyon Campground

 4

Location: Near Bozeman; map MT10, grid f1.

Campsites, facilities: There are 130 RV or tent campsites, some with full hookups and pull-throughs. Laundry facilities, water, electricity, sewer, showers, and a sanitary disposal station are available. Restrooms, a heated swimming pool, and store are on-site.

Reservations, fees: No reservations are needed; the fee is $10–13 per night. Open May–October.

Directions: From Bozeman, go three miles east on I-90 to Exit 313 and the campground.

Contact: Bear Canyon Campground; 4000 Bozeman Trail Rd., Bozeman, MT 59715; 406/587-1575 or 800/438-1575; email: Bearcc @gomontana .com.

Trip notes: You can hike and fish in Gallatin National Forest.

26 Osen's Campground

 4

Location: In Livingston; map MT10, grid f2.

Campsites, facilities: There are 55 RV or tent campsites, some with hookups. There are showers, laundry facilities, cable TV, water, electricity, sewer, a store, and a sanitary disposal station.

Reservations, fees: No reservations are needed; the fee is $14 per night. Open year-round.

Directions: In Livingston, go three blocks south on U.S. 89 at Exit 333, turn right on Merrill Lane, and drive to the campground.

Contact: Osen's Campground, 20 Merrill Lane, Livingston, MT 59047; 406/222-0591.

Trip notes: This campground has big RV sites and grassy tent sites. It is near the Yellowstone River, often called the longest free-flowing river in the lower 48 states (despite several tributary and irrigation dams) and known for its large rainbow, brown, and cutthroat trout.

27 Paradise Livingston Campground

 4

Location: In Livingston; map MT10, grid f2.

Campsites, facilities: There are 45 RV or tent campsites. Showers, laundry facilities, a store, water, electricity, sewer, and a sanitary disposal station are available. Families will enjoy the heated pool, cable TV, greenhouse, and gift shop.

Reservations, fees: No reservations are needed; the fee is $14 per night. Open May 1–October 31.

Directions: In Livingston at Exit 333, go one block north on U.S. 89, then west off Rogers Lane.

Contact: Paradise Livingston Campground, Rogers Lane, Livingston, MT; 406/222-1122.

Trip notes: This campground is near the Yellowstone River, often called the longest free-flowing river in the lower 48 states, known for its large rainbow, brown, and cutthroat trout.

28 Windmill Park

   4

Location: In Livingston; map MT10, grid f2.
Campsites, facilities: There are 25 RV or tent campsites. There are showers, laundry facilities, cable TV, water, electricity, sewer, and a sanitary disposal station.
Reservations, fees: Reservations are accepted; the fee is $15 and up per night. Open year-round.
Directions: In Livingston, go one mile south on U.S. 89, then turn at the railroad crossing at Billman Lane and go to the campground.
Contact: Windmill Park, Livingston, MT 59047; 406/222-2784 or fax 406/222-2784.
Trip notes: You can fish in the Yellowstone River. Yellowstone National Park is less than an hour away.

29 McLeod Resort

   6

Location: South of Big Timber; map MT10, grid f4.
Campsites, facilities: There are 15 RV or tent campsites. Showers, laundry facilities, cabins, water, and electricity are available.
Reservations, fees: No reservations needed; the fee is $15–25 per night. Open May 1–the end of October.
Directions: From Big Timber, go 16 miles south on Highway 298; the campground is on the right.
Contact: McLeod Resort, Hwy. 298 S, McLeod, MT 59052; 406/932-6167.
Trip notes: This campground is on the West Boulder River, where you can fish.

30 East Boulder

     7

Location: In Gallatin National Forest; map MT10, grid f4.

Campsites, facilities: There are two campsites, which can accommodate a maximum RV length of 16 feet. Water and toilets are available.
Reservations, fees: No reservations are needed; no fee is charged. The stay limit is 15 days. Open year-round.
Directions: From Big Timber, go 19 miles south on Highway 298, then six miles east on East Boulder Road to the campground.
Contact: Big Timber Ranger District, P.O. Box 196, Big Timber, MT 59011; 406/932-5155.
Trip notes: You can fish in the nearby river, and hike and fish in Gallatin National Forest.

31 Cooney

   5

Location: South of Columbus; map MT10, grid g8.
Campsites, facilities: There are 70 RV or tent campsites. Wheelchair-accessible restrooms, water, and a trailer boat ramp are available.
Reservations, fees: No reservations are needed; the fee is $10 per night. Open year-round. The stay limit is 14 days.
Directions: From Billings, go west 12 miles on I-90 to Laurel, go south 22 miles on U.S. 212 to Boyd, and then go five miles west on the county road to Cooney Reservoir State Park.
Contact: Montana Fish, Wildlife & Parks, Region 5, 2300 Lake Elmo Drive, Billings, MT 59107; 406/247-2940.
Trip notes: You can fish at Cooney Reservoir for brown, rainbow trout, crappie, and walleye.

32 Langhor

    6

Location: In Gallatin National Forest; map MT10, grid f1.
Campsites, facilities: There are 12 campsites, with tables and grills, which can accommodate a maximum RV length of 32 feet. Wheelchair-accessible restrooms, and water are available.

Reservations, fees: No reservations are needed; the fee is $9 per night. The stay limit is 15 days. Open mid-June–mid-September.

Directions: From Bozeman, go seven miles south on South 19th Avenue to Hyalite Canyon Road (Forest Road 62); then go six miles south on Hyalite Canyon Road to the campground.

Contact: Bozeman Ranger District, 3710 Fallon St., Suite C, Bozeman, MT 59718; 406/522-2520.

Trip notes: This campground has great views and good hiking opportunities. Nearby Palisades Falls (wheelchair-accessible) and Langhor Nature Trail are popular hikes. You can fish Hyalite Creek for rainbow, brook, brown, and cutthroat trout.

33 Hood Creek

     6

Location: In Gallatin National Forest; map MT10, grid f1.

Campsites, facilities: There are 13 RV sites, which can accommodate a maximum RV length of 16 feet, and five tent campsites. Vault toilets and water are available. The boat ramp requires only two-wheel drive with trailers.

Reservations, fees: No reservations are needed; the fee is $9 per night. The stay limit is 14 days. Open June 1–mid-September.

Directions: From Bozeman take South 19th Avenue south seven miles to Hyalite Canyon Road (Forest Road 62) and then go south 10 miles on Forest Road 62 to the campground.

Contact: Bozeman Ranger District, 3710 Fallon St., Suite C, Bozeman, MT 59718; 406/522-2520.

Trip notes: This campground is near Hyalite Reservoir, a no-wake area for boating, where you can fish for cutthroat and grayling. This scenic location has hiking nearby on Wild Horse Creek Trail.

34 Chisholm

    6

Location: In Gallatin National Forest; map MT10, grid f1.

Campsites, facilities: There are 10 RV or tent campsites, which can accommodate a maximum RV length of 55 feet, with picnic tables and grills. Wheelchair-accessible restrooms and water are available.

Reservations, fees: No reservations are needed; the fee is $9 per night. The stay limit is 14 days. Open June 1–mid-September.

Directions: From Bozeman, go seven miles south to Hyalite Canyon Road (Forest Road 62) and then go south on Forest Road 62 for 11 miles to the campground.

Contact: Bozeman Ranger District, 3710 Fallon St., Suite C, Bozeman, MT 59718; 406/522-2520.

Trip notes: This campground is near Hyalite Reservoir, among trees with a creek nearby. Hyalite Reservoir is a 300-acre no-wake lake where you can fish for grayling and cutthroat. Wild Horse Creek Trail is three miles away.

35 Rock Canyon RV Park

   6

Location: South of Livingston; map MT10, grid f2.

Campsites, facilities: There are 41 RV or tent campsites. Showers, laundry facilities, TV, water, electricity, and sewer are available.

Reservations, fees: No reservations are needed; the fee is $9 per night. Open May 1–the end of October.

Directions: From Livingston, go three miles south on U.S. 89 to the campground.

Contact: Rock Canyon RV Park, Livingston, MT 59047; 406/222-1096.

Trip notes: This campground is on the banks of the Yellowstone River, where you can fish.

36 Pine Creek

 5

Location: In Gallatin National Forest; map MT10, grid f2.

Campsites, facilities: There are 24 RV or tent campsites, which can accommodate a maximum RV length of 22 feet. Wheelchair-accessible restrooms and water are available.

Reservations, fees: No reservations are needed; the fee is $9 per night. The stay limit is 15 days. Open late May–mid-September.

Directions: From Livingston, go three miles south on U.S. 89 to East River Road (County Road 540), then go eight miles east on East River Road to Luccock Park Road. The campground is three miles along this narrow paved road.

Contact: Livingston District Office, 5242 Hwy. 89, South Livingston, MT 59047; 406/222-1892 (voice and TDD); fax 406/222-2546; website: www.fs.fed.us/rl/gallatin.

Trip notes: The trailhead for Pine Creek Trail begins about a quarter of a mile past the campground, and Jewell and Pine Creek Lakes are three miles up the trail. Creekside Trail is wheelchair accessible. This area was closed in 1999 for renovation. Check with the U.S. Forest Service for current status.

37 Paradise Valley/Livingston KOA

 6

Location: South of Livingston; map MT10, grid g2.

Campsites, facilities: There are 79 RV or tent campsites some with full hookups and pull-through sites. Showers, laundry facilities, a store, water, electricity, sewer, and a sanitary disposal station are available. A heated indoor pool and playground are provided. Pets are allowed on leashes.

Reservations, fees: Reservations are accepted; the fee is $14 and up per night. Open May 1–November 1.

Directions: From Livingston, drive nine miles south on U.S. 89, then one mile east to the campground.

Contact: Paradise Valley/Livingston KOA, 163 Pine Creek Rd., Livingston, MT; 406/222-0992 or 800/562-2805.

Trip notes: This campground is right on the Yellowstone River, the last free-flowing river in the lower 48 states, known for its large rainbow, brown, and cutthroat trout.

38 Mallard's Rest

 7

Location: South of Livingston; map MT10, grid g2.

Campsites, facilities: There are 13 RV or tent campsites. Restrooms, and water are available. The boat ramp requires four-wheel drive with trailers.

Reservations, fees: No reservations are needed; the fee is $5 per night. The stay limit is seven days. Open year-round.

Directions: From Livingston, go 13 miles south on U.S. 89 to milepost 42 and the campground.

Contact: Montana Department of Fish, Wildlife & Parks, 1400 S. 19th, Bozeman, MT 59718; 406/994-3552.

Trip notes: You can fish here. This scenic campground has an outstanding view of the Yellowstone River and the Absarokee Mountains.

39 Loch Leven

 5

Location: South of Livingston; map MT10, grid g2.

Campsites, facilities: There are 30 RV or tent campsites. Restrooms and water are provided. The boat ramp requires only a two-wheel drive with trailers.

Reservations, fees: No reservations are needed; the fee is $5 per night. The stay limit is 14 days. Open year-round.

Directions: From Livingston, go nine miles south on U.S. 89 to milepost 44, then two miles east on Pine Creek Road, and then four miles south on East River Road to the campground.

Contact: Montana Department of Fish, Wildlife & Parks, 1400 S. 19th, Bozeman, MT 59718; 406/994-4042.

Trip notes: You can fish here.

40 Yellowstone's Edge RV Park

   5

Location: South of Livingston; map MT10, grid g2.

Campsites, facilities: There are 81 RV sites that can accommodate large RVs, some with full hookups and phone hookups. Group facilities and some wheelchair-accessible facilities are available. Showers, laundry facilities, water, electricity, sewer, a store, and a sanitary disposal station are provided.

Reservations, fees: Reservations are accepted; the fee is $27.50 per night. Open early April–November 1.

Directions: From Livingston, go 18 miles south on U.S. 89 to the campground.

Contact: Yellowstone's Edge RV Park, 3502 Hwy. 89 S, Livingston, MT 59047-0678; 406/333-4036 or 800/865-7322 or fax 406/333-4052; email: edge@mtrv.com

Trip notes: This is a newer RV park with 3,000 feet of Yellowstone River frontage. You can fish and float on the Yellowstone River.

41 West Boulder

   6

Location: In Gallatin National Forest; map MT10, grid g4.

Campsites, facilities: There are 10 RV or tent campsites, which can accommodate a maximum RV length of 20 feet, with picnic tables and grills. There are restrooms and water (available only Memorial Day–Labor Day).

Reservations, fees: No reservations are needed; no fee is charged. Open year-round.

The stay limit is 15 days.

Directions: From Big Timber, go 16 miles west on Highway 298 to West Boulder Road (rough dirt road). Turn right and go seven miles to West Boulder campground sign; campground is six miles ahead.

Contact: Big Timber Ranger District, P.O. Box 196, Big Timber, MT 59011; 406/932-5155.

Trip notes: You can hike nearby Great Falls Creek Trail and Mill Creek Pass, or fish for rainbow, brown, brook, and cutthroat trout in West Boulder River.

42 Falls Creek

   6

Location: In Gallatin National Forest; map MT10, grid g4.

Campsites, facilities: There are eight campsites for tents only. There is a toilet available (no water).

Reservations, fees: No reservations are needed; no fees are charged. The stay limit is 15 days. Open year-round.

Directions: From Big Timber, go 34 miles southwest on Highway 298, then five miles south on County Road 212 to the campground.

Contact: Gallatin National Forest, Big Timber Ranger District, P.O. Box 196, Big Timber, MT 59011; 406/932-5155.

Trip notes: You can hike and fish in Gallatin National Forest.

43 Big Beaver

    6

Location: In Gallatin National Forest; map MT10, grid g4.

Campsites, facilities: There are five RV or tent campsites, which can accommodate a maximum RV length of 32 feet. Restrooms are available.

Reservations, fees: No reservations are needed, no fees are charged. The stay limit is 15 days. Open year-round.

Directions: From Big Timber, go 36 miles

south on Highway 298 to the campground.

Contact: Gallatin National Forest, Big Timber Ranger District, Hwy. 10 East, P.O. Box 196, Big Timber, MT 59011; 406/932-5155.

Trip notes: You can hike and fish in Gallatin National Forest.

44 Aspen

Location: In Gallatin National Forest; map MT10, grid g4.

Campsites, facilities: There are eight RV or tent campsites, which can accommodate a maximum RV length of 32 feet. Wheelchair-accessible restrooms and water are available.

Reservations, fees: No reservations are needed; no fee is charged. The stay limit is 15 days. Open year-round.

Directions: From Big Timber, go 37 miles southwest on Highway 298 to the campground.

Contact: Gallatin National Forest, Big Timber Ranger District, Hwy. 10 East, P.O. Box 196, Big Timber, MT 59011; 406/932-5155.

Trip notes: You can hike and fish in Gallatin National Forest.

45 Chippy Park

Location: In Gallatin National Forest; map MT10, grid g4.

Campsites, facilities: There are seven RV or tent campsites, which can accommodate a maximum RV length of 32 feet. Toilets are available, but water is not.

Reservations, fees: No reservations are needed; no fees are charged. The stay limit is 15 days. Open year-round, but access can be limited in the fall, winter, and spring.

Directions: From Big Timber, go 25 miles south on Highway 298, then 9.5 miles south on County Road 212 to the campground.

Contact: Big Timber Ranger District; Hwy. 10 East, P.O. Box 196, Big Timber, MT 59011; 406/932-5155.

Trip notes: Big Timber is the gateway to the Absaroka-Beartooth Wilderness and has some of the best blue-ribbon trout fishing anywhere on the Yellowstone and Boulder Rivers.

46 Hells Canyon

Location: In Gallatin National Forest; map MT10, grid g4.

Campsites, facilities: There are 11 RV or tent campsites, which can accommodate a maximum RV length of 16 feet. Vault toilets are available.

Reservations, fees: No reservations are needed; no fees are charged. The stay limit is 15 days. Open year-round.

Directions: From Big Timber, go 45 miles southwest on Route 298 (paved and rough gravel road) to the campground.

Contact: Gallatin National Forest, Big Timber Ranger District, P.O. Box 196, Big Timber, MT 59011; 406/932-5155.

Trip notes: This campground sits in the trees on a ridge. You can hike and fish in Gallatin National Forest.

47 Hicks Park

Location: In Gallatin National Forest; map MT10, grid g4.

Campsites, facilities: There are 16 RV or tent campsites, which can accommodate a maximum RV length of 32 feet. Wheelchair-accessible restrooms and water are available.

Reservations, fees: No reservations are needed; no fees are charged. The stay limit is 15 days. Open year-round.

Directions: From Big Timber go 48 miles southwest on Route 298 (25 miles are paved, and 20.7 miles are rough gravel) to the campground.

Contact: Gallatin National Forest, Big Timber Ranger District, P.O. Box 196, Big Timber, MT 59011; 406/932-5155.

Trip notes: This campground is along Boulder Creek, between the Absaroka and Beartooth Mountain ranges, a very scenic location. Hiking trails in the area include Upside Down and Lake Plateau, suitable for hiking, mountain biking, or horseback riding. You can fish for rainbow, cutthroat, brook, and brown trout in Boulder Creek.

48 Canyon

 6

Location: In Gallatin National Forest; map MT10, grid g1.

Campsites, facilities: There are 12 RV or tent campsites, which can accommodate a maximum RV length of 48 feet. There are toilets at the campground.

Reservations, fees: No reservations are needed; no fees are charged. The stay limit is 15 days. Open year-round.

Directions: From Livingston, go south about 20 miles on U.S. 89 to the campground.

Contact: Gallatin National Forest, Gardiner Ranger District; Hwy. 89, P.O. Box 5, Gardiner, MT 59030; 406/848-7375.

Trip notes: You can hike and fish in Gallatin National Forest.

49 Dailey Lake

 4

Location: South of Livingston; map MT10, grid g1.

Campsites, facilities: There are 35 RV or tent campsites. Wheelchair-accessible restrooms and water are available. The boat ramp requires only two-wheel drive with trailers.

Reservations, fees: No reservations are needed; no fees are charged. The stay limit is seven days. Open year-round.

Directions: From Livingston, go 22 miles south on U.S. 89 to Emigrant, then four miles south on County Road 540, and then six miles south west on the county road to the lake.

Contact: Montana Department of Fish, Wildlife & Parks, 1400 S. 19th, Bozeman, MT 59718; 406/994-4042.

Trip notes: This is a popular lake for wind surfing, since there is usually a good wind blowing, and you can swim and fish.

50 Snow Bank

 6

Location: In Gallatin National Forest; map MT10, grid g2.

Campsites, facilities: The campground has 11 RV or tent campsites, which can accommodate a maximum RV length of 22 feet. Vault restrooms and water are available.

Reservations, fees: No reservations are needed; the fee is $9 per night. Open late May–mid September. The stay limit is 14 days.

Directions: From Livingston, go three miles south on U.S. 89 to East River Road (County Road 540) and then go south on East River Road for 15 miles to Mill Creek (Forest Service Road 486). Take Mill Creek Road 11 miles (it becomes a dirt road), turn right at the campground sign, cross a bridge, and go to the campground on the right.

Contact: Livingston Ranger District, 5442 Hwy. 89 South, Livingston, MT 59047; 406/222-1892.

Trip notes: Campsites are along Mill Creek and on the hillside. Hiking trails are nearby, and you can fish for rainbow, cutthroat, and brown trout in the creek. Rehabilitation work took place in 1999, so check with the U.S. Forest Service for current conditions.

51 Pine Grove

 4

Location: In Custer National Forest; map MT10, grid g6.

Campsites, facilities: There are 46 RV or tent campsites, which can accommodate a maximum RV length of 30 feet. Wheelchair-accessible restrooms and water are available.

Reservations, fees: No reservations are needed; the fee is $6 per night. Open May

27–September 15. The stay limit is 10 days.

Directions: From Columbus, go south on Highway 78 to Route 419, and then west on Route 419 to Fishtail. From Fishtail, go one mile west on Route 419, six miles southwest on County Road 425, then eight miles south on Forest Service Road 72 to the campground.

Contact: Custer National Forest, P.O. Box 50760, 1310 Main St., Billings, MT 59105; 406/657-6361.

Trip notes: This campground is near Emerald Lake and West Rosebud Creek, where you can fish.

52 Emerald Lake

     6

Location: In Custer National Forest; map MT10, grid g6.

Campsites, facilities: There are 32 RV or tent campsites, which can accommodate a maximum RV length of 30 feet. Wheelchair-accessible restrooms and water are available.

Reservations, fees: No reservations are needed; the fee is $6 per night. Open May 27–September 5. The stay limit is 10 days.

Directions: From Columbus, go south on Highway 78 to Route 419, and west on Route 419 to Fishtail. From Fishtail, go one mile west on Route 419, six miles southwest on County Road 452, and 12 miles south on Forest Service Road 72 to the campground.

Contact: Custer National Forest, P.O. Box 50760, 1310 Main St., Billings, MT 59105; 406/657-6361.

Trip notes: You can fish here.

53 Jimmy Joe

   6

Location: In Custer National Forest; map MT10, grid h6.

Campsites, facilities: There are 10 RV or tent campsites, which can accommodate a maximum RV length of 16 feet. Restrooms are available.

Reservations, fees: No reservations are needed; the fee is $6 per night. Open May 27–September 5. The stay limit is 10 days.

Directions: From Columbus, go south 27 miles on Highway 78 to Roscoe. From Roscoe, go nine miles south on Forest Service Road 177 to the campground.

Contact: Custer National Forest, P.O. Box 50760, 1310 Main St., Billings, MT 59105; 406/657-6361.

Trip notes: You can fish here.

54 Carbella

    6

Location: South of Livingston; map MT10, grid h1.

Campsites, facilities: There are five RV or tent campsites, which can accommodate a maximum RV length of 35 feet. The boat ramp requires four-wheel drive with trailers. Pets are allowed on leashes.

Reservations, fees: No reservations are needed; no fees are charged. The stay limit is 14 days. Open May 1–October 30.

Directions: From Livingston, go south 46 miles on U.S. 89, then one mile west at Miner to the campground.

Contact: Bureau of Land Management, 106 N. Parkmont, P.O. Box 3388, Butte, MT 59702; 406/494-5059.

Trip notes: This is a primitive campground on the Yellowstone River, known for excellent trout fishing.

55 Red Lodge KOA

      6

Location: In Custer National Forest; map MT10, grid g8.

Campsites, facilities: There are 78 RV or tent campsites. Showers, laundry facilities, hookups, water, and a sanitary disposal facility are available. A swimming pool, playground, and store are on-site.

Reservations, fees: No reservations are

needed; the fee is $10–20 per night. Open May 21–September 7.

Directions: From the intersection of I-90 and U.S. 212 in Billings, go 38 miles south on U.S. 212 to the campground (on the east side of 212, four miles north of Red Lodge).

Contact: Red Lodge KOA, Red Lodge; 406/446-2364, 800/562-7540.

Trip notes: You can fish and hike in the Custer National Forest. The 69-mile Beartooth Scenic Drive has dramatic switchbacks overlooking snow-capped peaks, glaciers, alpine lakes, and plateaus. This road was described as the most scenic drive in America by CBS news correspondent Charles Kuralt.

56 Tom Miner
 7

Location: In the Absaroka Mountains; map MT10, grid h1.

Campsites, facilities: There are 12 RV or tent campsites, which can accommodate a maximum RV length of 22 feet, with picnic tables and grills. There are restrooms, and water is available.

Reservations, fees: No reservations are needed; the fee is $7 per night. Open Memorial Day–Labor Day. The stay limit is 14 days.

Directions: From Livingston, go south 46 miles on U.S. 89 to Tom Miner Road, then west to the intersection and sign for Tom Miner Basin. Go left eight miles to the next intersection with a Tom Miner campground sign. Continue left along Tom Miner Creek Road for three miles to the final intersection. Tom Miner Campground is mile on the right.

Contact: U.S. Forest Service, Gallatin National Forest, Gardiner District, Livingston, MT; 406/848-7375.

Trip notes: This campground is in a forested area along a creek. The hiking trailheads here include a three-mile loop through the Gallatin Petrified Forest, the Buffalo Horn Trail, and Rams Horn Peak.

57 East Rosebud Lake
 6

Location: In Custer National Forest; map MT10, grid h6.

Campsites, facilities: There are 14 RV or tent campsites, which can accommodate a maximum RV length of 16 feet. Restrooms, water, and a boat launch are available.

Reservations, fees: No reservations are needed; the fee is $6 per night. Open May 27–September 5. The stay limit is 10 days.

Directions: From Columbus, go south 27 miles on Highway 78 to Roscoe. From Roscoe, go 12 miles south on Forest Service Road 177 to the campground.

Contact: Custer National Forest, P.O. Box 50760, 1310 Main St., Billings, MT 59105; 406/657-6361.

Trip notes: You can fish and hike in the Custer National Forest.

58 Palisades
 6

Location: In Custer National Forest; map MT10, grid h8.

Campsites, facilities: There are six RV or tent campsites, which can accommodate a maximum RV length of 16 feet. There is a toilet, but no drinking water is available.

Reservations, fees: No reservations are needed; the fee is $6 per night. Open June 15–September 15. The stay limit is 10 days.

Directions: From Red Lodge, go one mile west on Forest Service Road 71, then two miles west on Forest Service Road 3010 to the campground.

Contact: Custer National Forest, P.O. Box 50760, 1310 Main St., Billings, MT 59105; 406/657-6361.

Trip notes: Nearby Rock Creek has brook, brown, and rainbow trout. The 69-mile Beartooth Scenic Drive has dramatic switchbacks overlooking snow-capped peaks, glaciers, alpine lakes, and plateaus. This road has been described as the most scenic drive in America by CBS news correspondent Charles Kuralt. The Beartooth Nature Center has native wild and domestic animals. The wild animals live at the Center because they cannot be returned to the wild. There are elk, deer, pronghorn, bears, mountain lions, wolves, bobcats, and foxes. You can fish and hike in the Custer National Forest.

59 Perry's RV Park & Campground

     4

Location: Near Red Lodge; map MT10, grid h8.

Campsites, facilities: There are 30 RV and 20 tent campsites. Hookups, showers, laundry facilities, a store, and a sanitary disposal facility are available.

Reservations, fees: No reservations are needed; the fee is $7–12 per night. Open May 25–October 1.

Directions: From Red Lodge go two miles south on U.S. 212 to the campground.

Contact: Perry's RV Park & Campground, HC 49, Box 3586, Red Lodge, MT 59068; 406/446-2722.

Trip notes: This is a shaded campground along Rock Creek, where you can fish for brook, brown, and rainbow trout. The 69-mile Beartooth Scenic Drive has dramatic switchbacks overlooking snow-capped peaks, glaciers, alpine lakes, and plateaus. This road has been described as the most scenic drive in America by CBS news correspondent Charles Kuralt. The Beartooth Nature Center has native wild and domestic animals. The wild animals live at the Center because they cannot be returned to the wild. There are elk, deer, pronghorn, bears, mountain lions, wolves, bobcats, and foxes. You can fish and hike in the Custer National Forest.

60 Cascade

   5

Location: In Custer National Forest; map MT10, grid h8.

Campsites, facilities: There are 31 RV or tent campsites, which can accommodate a maximum RV length of 30 feet. Restrooms and water are available.

Reservations, fees: Reservations are accepted; the fee is $6 per night. Open May 27–September 5.

Directions: From Red Lodge, go two miles south on U.S. 212, then 10 miles west on Forest Service Road 71 to the campground.

Contact: Custer National Forest, P.O. Box 50760, 1310 Main St., Billings, MT 59105; 406/657-6361.

Trip notes: The 69-mile Beartooth Scenic Drive has dramatic switchbacks overlooking snow-capped peaks, glaciers, alpine lakes, and plateaus. This road has been described as the most scenic drive in America by CBS news correspondent Charles Kuralt. The Beartooth Nature Center has native wild and domestic animals. The wild animals live at the Center because they cannot be returned to the wild. There are elk, deer, pronghorn, bears, mountain lions, wolves, bobcats, and foxes. You can fish and hike in the Custer National Forest.

61 Basin

   5

Location: In Custer National Forest; map MT10, grid h8.

Campsites, facilities: There are 30 RV or tent campsites, which can accommodate a maximum RV length of 30 feet. Wheelchair-accessible restrooms and water are available.

Reservations, fees: Reservations are accepted; the fee is $8 per night. Open May 27–September 5. The stay limit is 10 days.

Directions: From Red Lodge, go one mile south on U.S. 212, then seven miles west on

Forest Service Road 71 to the campground.

Contact: Custer National Forest, P.O. Box 50760, 1310 Main St., Billings, MT 59105; 406/657-6361.

Trip notes: The 69-mile Beartooth Scenic Drive has dramatic switchbacks overlooking snow-capped peaks, glaciers, alpine lakes, and plateaus. This road has been described as the most scenic drive in America by CBS news correspondent Charles Kuralt. The Beartooth Nature Center has native wild and domestic animals. The wild animals live at the Center because they cannot be returned to the wild. There are elk, deer, pronghorn, bears, mountain lions, wolves, bobcats, and foxes. You can fish and hike in the Custer National Forest.

62 Sheridan

   5

Location: In Custer National Forest; map MT10, grid h8.

Campsites, facilities: There are eight RV or tent campsites, which can accommodate a maximum RV length of 22 feet. Toilets and water are available.

Reservations, fees: Reservations are accepted; the fee is $6 per night. Open May 27–September 5. The stay limit is 10 days.

Directions: From Red Lodge, go five miles southwest on U.S. 212, then two miles southwest on Forest Service Road 379 to the campground.

Contact: Custer National Forest, P.O. Box 50760, 1310 Main St., Billings, MT 59105; 406/657-6361.

Trip notes: The 69-mile Beartooth Scenic Drive has dramatic switchbacks overlooking snow-capped peaks, glaciers, alpine lakes, and plateaus. This road has been described as the most scenic drive in America by CBS news correspondent Charles Kuralt. The Beartooth Nature Center has native wild and domestic animals. The wild animals live at the Center because they cannot be returned to

the wild. There are elk, deer, pronghorn, bears, mountain lions, wolves, bobcats, and foxes. You can fish and hike in the Custer National Forest.

63 Eagle Creek

    6

Location: In Gallatin National Forest; map MT10, grid h2.

Campsites, facilities: There are 10 campsites, which can accommodate a maximum RV length of 30 feet, and picnic tables and grills. Vault toilets and water are available.

Reservations, fees: No reservations are needed; the fee is $6 per night. The stay limit is 14 days. Open year-round.

Directions: From Livingston, go 57 miles south on U.S. 89 to Gardiner. From Gardiner (the north entrance of Yellowstone National Park), go two miles northeast on Jardine Road (unpaved) to the campground.

Contact: Gallatin National Forest, Gardiner Ranger District, Hwy. 89, P.O. Box 5, Gardiner, MT 59030; 406/848-7375.

Trip notes: This campground is near Eagle Creek, and the northeast entrance to Yellowstone National Park is three miles away. You can kayak and raft on nearby Yellowstone River. You can hike and fish in Gallatin National Forest.

64 Rocky Mountain Campground

     6

Location: In Gardiner; map MT10, grid h2.

Campsites, facilities: There are 70 RV or tent campsites, some with hookups and pull-through sites. Picnic tables, showers, laundry facilities, propane, water, electricity, sewer, and a sanitary disposal station are available. A store and playground are nearby. Pets are allowed on leashes.

Reservations, fees: No reservations are necessary; the fee is $16–22 per night. Open May

1–November 1.

Directions: From Livingston, go 57 miles south on U.S. 89 to Gardiner. From Gardiner (the north entrance of Yellowstone National Park), go one block east of U.S. 89 on Jardine Road.

Contact: Rocky Mountain Campground, 14 Jardine Rd., Gardiner, MT 59030; 406/848-7251.

Trip notes: This campground offers good views and proximity to Yellowstone National Park, where you can hike and fish.

65 Colter

Location: In Gallatin National Forest; map MT10, grid h5.

Campsites, facilities: There are 23 RV or tent campsites, which can accommodate a maximum RV length of 48 feet. Vault toilets and water are available.

Reservations, fees: No reservations are needed; the fee is $8 per night. The stay limit is 14 days. Open July 1–mid-September.

Directions: From Red Lodge go west 65 miles on U.S. 212 to Cooke City. The campground is two miles east of Cooke City on U.S. 212.

Contact: Gardiner Ranger District; Hwy. 89, P.O. Box 5, Gardiner, MT 59030; 406/848-7375.

Trip notes: This campground is five miles from the northeast entrance of Yellowstone National Park, where you can hike and fish.

66 Chief Joseph

Location: In Gallatin National Forest; map MT10, grid h5.

Campsites, facilities: There are six RV or tent campsites, which can accommodate a maximum RV length of 20 feet. There is a toilet, and water is available.

Reservations, fees: No reservations are needed; the fee is $8 per night. The stay limit is 14 days. Open early July–mid-September.

Directions: From Red Lodge, go west 65 miles on U.S. 212 to Cooke City. The campground is

four miles east of Cooke City on U.S. 212.

Contact: Gallatin National Forest, Gardiner Ranger District; Hwy. 89, P.O. Box 5, Gardiner, MT 59030; 406/848-7375.

Trip notes: You can hike and fish in Gallatin National Forest.

67 Soda Butte

Location: In Gallatin National Forest; map MT10, grid h5.

Campsites, facilities: There are 21 RV or tent campsites, which can accommodate a maximum RV length of 22 feet, with picnic tables and grills. Vault toilets and water are available.

Reservations, fees: No reservations are needed; the fee is $8 per night. Open July 1–mid-September. The stay limit is 15 days.

Directions: From Red Lodge, go west 65 miles on U.S. 212 to Cooke City. The campground is one mile east of Cooke City on U.S. 212.

Contact: Gardiner Ranger District, P.O. Box 5, Gardiner, MT 59030; 406/848-7375.

Trip notes: The campground is along Soda Butte Creek. The northeast entrance of Yellowstone National Park is five miles away, and the Beartooth Scenic Highway is a spectacular drive.

68 Ratine

Location: In Custer National Forest; map MT10, grid h7.

Campsites, facilities: There are seven campsites, toilets, and water. Trailers and RVs not recommended.

Reservations, fees: Reservations are accepted; the fee is $6 per night. Open May 27–September 5.

Directions: From Red Lodge, go five miles southwest on U.S. 212, then three miles southwest on Forest Service Road 379 to the campground.

Contact: Custer National Forest, P.O. Box 50760, 1310 Main St., Billings, MT 59105; 406/657-6361.

Trip notes: The 69-mile Beartooth Scenic Drive has dramatic switchbacks overlooking snow-capped peaks, glaciers, alpine lakes, and plateaus. This road has been described as the most scenic drive in America by CBS news correspondent Charles Kuralt. The Beartooth Nature Center has native wild and domestic animals. The wild animals live at the Center because they cannot be returned to the wild. There are elk, deer, pronghorn, bears, mountain lions, wolves, bobcats, and foxes. You can fish and hike in the Custer National Forest.

69 Parkside

 5

Location: In Custer National Forest; map MT10, grid h7.

Campsites, facilities: There are 28 RV or tent campsites, which can accommodate a maximum RV length of 30 feet. Wheelchair-accessible restrooms and water are available.

Reservations, fees: Reservations are accepted; the fee is $6 per night. Open May 27–September 5. The stay limit is 10 days.

Directions: From Red Lodge, drive 12 miles southwest on U.S. 212, then one mile southwest on Forest Service Road 421 to the campground.

Contact: Custer National Forest, P.O. Box 50760, 1310 Main St., Billings, MT 59105; 406/657-6361.

Trip notes: The 69-mile Beartooth Scenic Drive has dramatic switchbacks overlooking snow-capped peaks, glaciers, alpine lakes, and plateaus. This road has been described as the most scenic drive in America by CBS news correspondent Charles Kuralt. The Beartooth Nature Center has native wild and domestic animals. The wild animals live at the Center because they cannot be returned to the wild. There are elk, deer, pronghorn, bears, mountain lions, wolves, bobcats, and foxes. You can fish and hike in the Custer National Forest.

70 Limber Pine

 6

Location: In Custer National Forest; map MT10, grid h7.

Campsites, facilities: There are 13 RV or tent campsites, which can accommodate a maximum RV length of 35 feet. Restrooms and water are available.

Reservations, fees: Reservations are accepted; the fee is $6 per night. Open May 27–September 5. The stay limit is 10 days.

Directions: From Red Lodge, go 12 miles southwest on U.S. 212, then one mile southwest on Forest Service Road 421 to the campground.

Contact: Custer National Forest, P.O. Box 50760, 1310 Main St., Billings, MT 59105; 406/657-6361.

Trip notes: Nearby Rock Creek has brook, brown, and rainbow trout. The 69-mile Beartooth Scenic Drive has dramatic switchbacks overlooking snow-capped peaks, glaciers, alpine lakes, and plateaus. This road has been described as the most scenic drive in America by CBS news correspondent Charles Kuralt. The Beartooth Nature Center has native wild and domestic animals. The wild animals live at the Center because they cannot be returned to the wild. There are elk, deer, pronghorn, bears, mountain lions, wolves, bobcats, and foxes. You can fish and hike in the Custer National Forest.

71 Greenough Lake

 6

Location: In Custer National Forest; map MT10, grid h7.

Campsites, facilities: There are 18 RV or tent campsites, which can accommodate a maximum RV length of 30 feet. Wheelchair-accessible restrooms and water are available.

Reservations, fees: Reservations are accepted; the fee is $6 per night. Open May 27–September 5. The stay limit is 10 days.

Directions: From Red Lodge, travel 12 miles southwest on U.S. 212, then one mile southwest on Forest Service Road 421 to the campground.

Contact: Custer National Forest, P.O. Box 50760, 1310 Main St., Billings, MT 59105; 406/657-6361.

Trip notes: The 69-mile Beartooth Scenic Drive has dramatic switchbacks overlooking snow-capped peaks, glaciers, alpine lakes, and plateaus. This road has been described as the most scenic drive in America by CBS news correspondent Charles Kuralt. The Beartooth Nature Center has native wild and domestic animals. The wild animals live at the Center because they cannot be returned to the wild. There are elk, deer, pronghorn, bears, mountain lions, wolves, bobcats, and foxes. You can fish and hike in the Custer National Forest, and fish in Greenough Lake for rainbow trout.

72 M-K

 6

Location: In Custer National Forest; map MT10, grid h7.

Campsites, facilities: There are 10 RV or tent campsites, which can accommodate a maximum RV length of 16 feet. No drinking water, but a toilet is available.

Reservations, fees: No reservations are needed; the fee is $6 per night. Open May 30–September 5. The stay limit is 10 days.

Directions: From Red Lodge, go 12 miles southwest on U.S. 212, then four miles southwest on Forest Service Road 421 to the campground.

Contact: Custer National Forest, P.O. Box 50760, 1310 Main St., Billings, MT 59105; 406/657-6361.

Trip notes: The 69-mile Beartooth Scenic Drive has dramatic switchbacks overlooking snow-capped peaks, glaciers, alpine lakes, and plateaus. This road has been described as the most scenic drive in America by CBS news correspondent Charles Kuralt. The Beartooth Nature Center has native wild and domestic animals. The wild animals live at the Center because they cannot be returned to the wild. There are elk, deer, pronghorn, bears, mountain lions, wolves, bobcats, and foxes. You can fish and hike in the Custer National Forest.

Tepee tents

MAP MT11

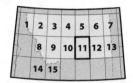

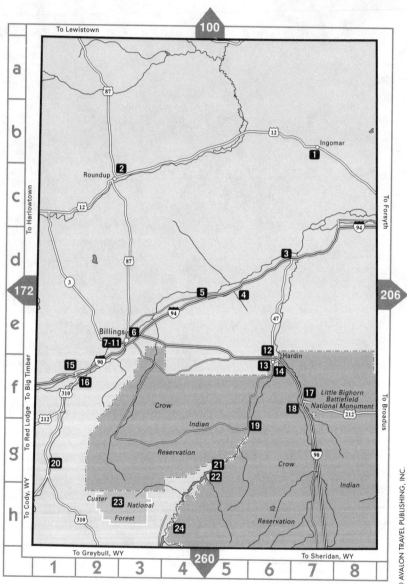

100

a

b

To Harlowtown

87

12

Ingomar

1

2 Roundup

c

12

94

To Forsyth

87

d

3

3

172

5

5 **4**

206

94

47

e

Billings

6

7-11

To Big Timber

15

90

12

12 Hardin

16

310

13

13 **14**

To Red Lodge

212

Crow

17

17 Little Bighorn
Battlefield
National Monument

18

18

212

To Broadus

f

Indian

19

19

g

To Cody, WY

20

20

Reservation

21

21

22

22

90

Crow

Indian

h

Custer

23

23 National

Reservation

Forest

310

24

24

260

© AVALON TRAVEL PUBLISHING, INC.

1 2 3 4 5 6 7 8

CHAPTER MT11

1 Historic Jersey
Lily Campground............197
2 Ideal Motel & RV Park......197
3 Little Bighorn Camp........198
4 Anita Reservoir 198
5 Huntley Diversion Dam....198
6 Eastwood Estates............198
7 Big Sky Campground 199
8 Trailer Village................199
9 Yellowstone River RV
Park and Campground 199
10 Billings Metro KOA 199
11 Casa Village..................199
12 Hardin KOA 200

13 Grandview
Campgrounds 200
14 Sunset Village RV 200
15 Pelican Truck Plaza Motel .200
16 Riverside Park 201
17 Battlefield Country
Market.......................201
18 Little Bighorn Camp.......201
19 Big Horn RV Park...........201
20 City Park Campground 202
21 Cottonwood Camp 202
22 Afterbay 202
23 Sage Creek..................202
24 Barry's Landing.............203

1 Historic Jersey Lily Campground

  4

Location: In Ingomar; map MT11, grid b7.

Campsites, facilities: There are 14 RV or tent campsites. Water, electricity, and a sanitary disposal facility are available.

Reservations, fees: No reservations are needed; the fee is $5 per night. Open year-round.

Directions: From Forsyth, go east 41 miles on U.S. 12 to Ingomar. From Ingomar, go .75 mile off U.S. 12 to the campground. The Jersey Lily Campground is on the corner of the first block when you come into town.

Contact: Historic Jersey Lily Campground, P.O. Box 85, Ingomar, MT 59039; 406/358-2278.

Trip notes: This campground is listed on the National Historic Register. In 1914, the Jersey Lily began as a bank, and, after the bank closed, it was reopened as a bar in 1948. It was later renamed the Jersey Lily in honor of Lillie Langtry, an actress in the late 1800s whose beauty was said to have entranced princes, kings, and Judge Roy Bean. Bean was so enamored of Langtry that he named a town and a bar in Texas after the actress. The cherrywood back bar of the Jersey Lily was brought from St. Louis by boat up the Missouri and Yellowstone Rivers and installed at Forsyth in the early 1900s. Ingomar's original frame school building, the Jersey Lily, and Bookman Store were all placed on the National Register of Historic places in September 1994.

2 Ideal Motel & RV Park

   4

Location: In Roundup; map MT11, grid c2.

Campsites, facilities: There are nine RV or tent campsites. Full hookups, showers, laundry facilities, and water are available.

Reservations, fees: No reservations are needed; the fee is $15 per night. Open year-round.

Directions: From Roundup at U.S. 87, go five blocks north to the campground.

Contact: Ideal Motel & RV Park, 926 Main St., Roundup, MT 59072; 406/323-3371, 888/323-3371.

Trip notes: This campground is in a central location and near a free swimming pool.

🔟 Little Bighorn Camp

  3

Location: Near Little Bighorn Battlefield; map MT11, grid d6.

Campsites, facilities: There are 20 RV and 15 tent campsites. Water, electricity, laundry facilities, and a store are available.

Reservations, fees: No reservations are needed; the fee is $10.92–13 per night. Open year-round.

Directions: From Hardin, go 18 miles south on I-90 to Exit 510, turn left, and drive over the pass to the campground.

Contact: Little Bighorn Campground, Junction I-90 & U.S. Hwy. 212, Little Bighorn Battlefield Exit, P.O. Box 266, Crow Agency, MT 59022; 406/638-2232, 406/638-2237, fax 406/638-2231.

Trip notes: This campground is on the Crow Indian Reservation. Crow Agency becomes the "tepee capital of the world" in mid-August during the annual Crow Fair celebration. Cultural tours are offered through Little Bighorn College; 406/638-7211.

🔟 Anita Reservoir

    6

Location: South of Pompeys Pillar; map MT11, grid e5.

Campsites, facilities: There are six RV and tent campsites. A hand launch boat ramp is available.

Reservations, fees: No reservations are needed; the fee is $6 per night. Open year-round. The stay limit is 14 days.

Directions: From Billings, go east on I-94 about 30 miles to Pompeys Pillar exit, then go four miles south to the campground.

Contact: Anita Reservoir, P.O. Box 30137, Billings, MT 59107-0137; 406/247-7314.

Trip notes: You can fish and boat at the Anita Reservoir. Pompeys Pillar is the only visible remains of the Lewis and Clark Expedition, which came through here in 1806. Captain

William Clark carved his name and the date on the rock outcropping now known as Pompeys Pillar. The Pillar rises 200 feet above the Yellowstone River, and, in addition to the Clark signature, there are numerous animal drawings made by past visitors.

🔟 Huntley Diversion Dam

     4

Location: East of Billings; map MT11, grid d4.

Campsites, facilities: There are RV and tent campsites. A trailer boat ramp is available, but no toilet and no water.

Reservations, fees: No reservations are needed; the fee is $5 per night. Open year-round. The stay limit is 14 days.

Directions: From Billings, go east on I-94 about 13 miles to the Huntley exit and then go one mile west on a gravel road to the campground.

Contact: U.S. Bureau of Reclamation, P.O. Box 30137, Billings, MT 59107-0137; 406/247-7314.

Trip notes: You can swim, boat, and fish here.

🔟 Eastwood Estates

   3

Location: In Billings; map MT11, grid e3.

Campsites, facilities: There are 20 RV or tent campsites. Hookups, laundry facilities, showers, and water are available.

Reservations, fees: No reservations are needed; the fee is $7–15 per night. Open year-round.

Directions: From I-90 at Billings, take Exit 452, drive a half mile east on U.S. 87, then nearly half a mile east to the campground.

Contact: Eastwood Estates, Billings, MT 59101; 406/245-7733.

Trip notes: Billings has golf and hiking areas. You can fish in the Yellowstone River.

7 Big Sky Campground

 3

Location: In Billings; map MT11, grid e2.

Campsites, facilities: There are 84 RV or tent campsites. Showers, laundry facilities, hookups, water, a convenience store, and a sanitary disposal facility are available.

Reservations, fees: No reservations are needed; the fee is $12–24 per night. Open year-round.

Directions: From I-90 at Billings, take Exit 446 (City Center Exit) north to the campground.

Contact: Big Sky Campground, Billings, MT 59101; 406/259-4110.

Trip notes: Billings has golf and hiking areas. You can fish in the Yellowstone River.

8 Trailer Village

 3

Location: In Billings; map MT11, grid e2.

Campsites, facilities: There are 45 RV or tent campsites. Showers, laundry facilities, hookups, water, and a playground are available. No large dogs are allowed.

Reservations, fees: No reservations are needed; the fee is $10–15 per night. Open year-round.

Directions: From I-90, take Exit 447, then go six blocks north on South Billings Boulevard to the campground.

Contact: Trailer Village, Billings, MT 59101; 406/248-8685.

Trip notes: These campsites are shady, grassy, and paved. Billings has golf and hiking areas. You can fish in the Yellowstone River.

9 Yellowstone River RV Park and Campground

 3

Location: In Billings; map MT11, grid e2.

Campsites, facilities: There are 105 RV or tent campsites. Showers, water, a store, and a sanitary disposal facility are available.

Reservations, fees: No reservations are needed; the fee is $12–25 per night. Open April 1–September 30.

Directions: From I-90 at Billings, take Exit 450 and go south a quarter mile on Garden Avenue; follow the green and yellow signs to the campground.

Contact: Yellowstone River RV Park and Campground, Billings, MT 59101; 406/259-0878.

Trip notes: Billings has golf and hiking areas. You can fish in the Yellowstone River.

10 Billings Metro KOA

 2

Location: In Billings; map MT11, grid e2.

Campsites, facilities: There are 175 RV or tent campsites. Hookups, a store, laundry facilities, showers, a sanitary disposal facility, and water are available. A playground, mini-golf, swimming pool, barbecue, and spa are on-site.

Reservations, fees: No reservations are needed; the fee is $12–18 per night. Open April 15–October 15.

Directions: From I-90 at Billings, take Exit 450, go south to Garden Avenue, then right .75 mile to the campground.

Contact: Billings Metro KOA, Billings, MT 59101; 406/252-3104, 800/562-8546.

Trip notes: Billings has golf and hiking areas. You can fish in the Yellowstone River.

11 Casa Village

 3

Location: In Billings; map MT11, grid e2.

Campsites, facilities: There are five RV or tent campsites. Showers, hookups, water, and a sanitary disposal facility are available.

Reservations, fees: No reservations are needed; the fee is $8–15 per night. Open April 1–November 1.

Directions: From I-90 in Billings, take Exit 446 to King Avenue, go west on King Avenue to 24th Street West, and then go one mile north on 24th Street West to campground.

Contact: Casa Village, 24th Street and Monad, Billings, MT 59101; 406/656-3910, 406/656-8564, fax 406/651-8840.

Trip notes: Billings has golf and hiking areas. You can fish in the Yellowstone River.

12 Hardin KOA

    3

Location: In Hardin; map MT11, grid e6.

Campsites, facilities: There are 68 RV or tent campsites. Showers, laundry facilities, a store, hookups, a sanitary disposal station, and water are available. Kamping Kabins, a playground, hot tub, and swimming pool are on-site.

Reservations, fees: No reservations are needed; the fee is $14.50–20.50 per night. Open April 1–September 30.

Directions: From Hardin, go one mile north on Highway 47 to the campground.

Contact: Hardin KOA, Hardin, MT 59034; 406/665-1635, 800/562-1635.

Trip notes: This campground is fifteen miles from Little Bighorn Battlefield National Monument. The Battlefield Visitor Center has an interpretive museum and bookstore. From Memorial Day to Labor Day ranger programs and talks are given throughout the day. You can fish in the Bighorn River for brown trout, rainbow trout, and smallmouth bass.

13 Grandview Campgrounds

   3

Location: In Hardin; map MT11, grid f6.

Campsites, facilities: There are 100 RV or tent campsites. Showers, laundry facilities, a store, hookups, water, and a sanitary disposal station are available.

Reservations, fees: No reservations are needed; the fee is $15.60–21 per night. Open year-round.

Directions: From I-90 at Hardin, take Exit 495, go four blocks south; the campground is on the right on County Road 313.

Contact: Grandview Campgrounds, 1002 N. Mitchell Ave., Hardin, MT 59034; 406/665-2489, or 800/622-9890.

Trip notes: There are a gift shop, swimming pool, tennis courts, and a playground nearby. You can fish in the Bighorn River for brown trout, rainbow trout, and smallmouth bass.

14 Sunset Village RV

   3

Location: In Hardin; map MT11, grid f6.

Campsites, facilities: There are 27 RV or tent campsites. Showers, laundry facilities, a playground, hookups, and a sanitary disposal facility are available.

Reservations, fees: No reservations are needed; the fee is $10 per night. Open May 1–October 31.

Directions: From I-90 near Hardin, take Exit 497, go two miles south on County Road 313 to the campground.

Contact: Sunset Village RV, 920 3rd St. S, Hardin, MT 59034; 406/738-4532.

Trip notes: There are a swimming pool and tennis courts nearby. The Little Bighorn Battlefield National Monument is nearby. The Battlefield Visitor Center has an interpretive museum and bookstore. From Memorial Day to Labor Day ranger programs and talks are given throughout the day. You can fish in the Bighorn River for brown trout, rainbow trout, and smallmouth bass.

15 Pelican Truck Plaza Motel

  3

Location: In Laurel; map MT11, grid f1.

Campsites, facilities: There are 55 RV or tent campsites, some with hookups. Showers, laundry facilities, a store, water, propane gas, and a sanitary disposal facility are available. A 24-hour restaurant, cabins, tepees, and gift shop are on-site.

Reservations, fees: No reservations are needed; the fee is $8–15 per night. Open year-round.

Directions: From Billings, go 10 miles west on I-90 to Exit 437 and take Exit 437 to the truck plaza.

Contact: Pelican Truck Plaza Motel, Laurel, MT 59101; 406/628-4324, fax 406/628-8442.

Trip notes: You can fish in the Yellowstone River for rainbow and brown trout.

16 Riverside Park

   4

Location: Near Laurel; map MT11, grid f2.

Campsites, facilities: There are 14 RV or tent campsites. Water, showers, and electricity are available.

Reservations, fees: No reservations are needed; the fee is $5–12 per night. Open May 19–September 30.

Directions: From Billings, go west on I-90 to exit 434, and then take U.S. 212 south for three-quarters of a mile to campground.

Contact: Riverside Park; 406/628-4796.

Trip notes: This campground is on the banks of the Yellowstone River, where you can fish for rainbow and brown trout.

17 Battlefield Country Market

   3

Location: On Crow Agency; map MT11, grid f7.

Campsites, facilities: There are 21 RV or tent campsites. Electricity, a store, and water are available.

Reservations, fees: No reservations are needed; the fee is $10 per night. Open May 1–September 30.

Directions: From Hardin, go south on I-90 to the junction of I-90 and U.S. 212 and follow the signs.

Contact: Battlefield Country Market, Hwy. 212 and I-90, Crow Agency, MT 59022; 406/638-4452.

Trip notes: This campground is a half mile from Little Bighorn Battlefield. You can fish in the nearby river.

18 Little Bighorn Camp

   4

Location: At Little Bighorn Battlefield; map MT11, grid f7.

Campsites, facilities: There are 20 RV campsites and 15 tent campsites. Showers, laundry facilities, a store, hookups, and a sanitary disposal facility are available.

Reservations, fees: No reservations are needed; the fee is $10.92–13 per night. Open year-round.

Directions: From Hardin, go south on I-90 to the junction of I-90 and U.S. 212 and follow the signs.

Contact: Little Bighorn Camp, Junction I-90 & U.S. Hwy. 212, Little Bighorn Battlefield Exit, P.O. Box 266, Crow Agency, MT 59022; 406/638-2232, 406/683-2237, fax 406/638-2231.

Trip notes: The Little Bighorn Battlefield is one mile from this campground. The Battlefield Visitor Center has an interpretive museum and bookstore. From Memorial Day to Labor Day ranger programs and talks are given throughout the day. You can fish in the Bighorn River for brown trout, rainbow trout, and smallmouth bass.

19 Big Horn RV Park

   3

Location: South of Hardin; map MT11, grid g6.

Campsites, facilities: There are 26 RV or tent campsites. Showers, a store, hookups, and a café are available.

Reservations, fees: Reservations are suggested; the fee is $15–22.50 per night. Open April 1–December 1.

Directions: From Hardin, go 30 miles south on County Road 313 and the campground is on the right.

Contact: Big Horn RV Park, P.O. Box 305, St. Xavier, MT 59074; 406/666-2460.

Trip notes: You can fish in the Bighorn River for brown trout, rainbow trout, and smallmouth bass.

20 City Park Campground

 4

Location: In Bridger; map MT11, grid g1.

Campsites, facilities: There are six RV campsites. A sanitary disposal facility, water, and electricity are available.

Reservations, fees: No reservations are needed; the fee is $10 per night. Open April 1 –October 31.

Directions: From Billings, go west 12 miles on I-90 to Laurel, south 27 miles on U.S. 310 to Bridger, and then go two blocks east to East Broadway (Main Street) to the campground.

Contact: City Park, P.O. Box 368, Bridger, MT 59014; 406/662-3677, fax 406/662-3116.

Trip notes: The city playground and swimming pool is next to the campground.

21 Cottonwood Camp

 4

Location: North of Fort Smith; map MT11, grid g5.

Campsites, facilities: There are 39 RV or tent campsites. Showers, laundry facilities, a store, hookups, and water are available. Cabin and boat rentals, guide and shuttle service, and kitchenette are on-site.

Reservations, fees: Reservations are suggested; the fee is $10–20 per night. Open year-round.

Directions: From Fort Smith, go three miles north on County Road 313, turn left, go 200 yards past the irrigation ditch and take the next left. (There's a sign at mile marker 37.)

Contact: Cottonwood Camp, P.O. Box 7667, Fort Smith, MT 59035; 406/666-2391, fax 406/666-2306.

Trip notes: You can fish in the Bighorn River for brown trout, rainbow trout, and smallmouth bass.

22 Afterbay

 5

Location: In Bighorn Canyon National Recreation Area; map MT11, grid g5.

Campsites, facilities: There are 48 RV or tent campsites. Wheelchair-accessible restrooms, water, and a trailer boat ramp are available.

Reservations, fees: No reservations are needed; the fee is $12 per night. Open year-round. The stay limit is 14 days.

Directions: From the Yellowtail Dam at Fort Smith (about 40 miles southwest of Hardin on County Road 313), go one mile northeast to Bighorn Canyon National Recreation Area.

Contact: Superintendent, Bighorn Canyon National Recreation Area, P.O. Box 458, Fort Smith, MT 59035; 406/666-2412.

Trip notes: The Yellowtail Dam is one of the largest reservoirs on the Missouri River, where you can fish, boat, swim, and water-ski. There are nature trails to hike and explore in the area.

23 Sage Creek

 6

Location: In Custer National Forest; map MT11, grid h2.

Campsites, facilities: There are 12 RV or tent campsites, which can accommodate a maximum RV length of 20 feet. A toilet is available.

Reservations, fees: No reservations are needed; the fee is $6 per night. Open June 15–September 15. The stay limit is 10 days.

Directions: From Billings, go west 12 miles on I-90 to Laurel, and then south 27 miles on U.S. 310 to Bridger. From Bridger, go three miles south on U.S. 310, then 22 miles southeast on the county road and one mile east on Forest Service Road 50 to the campground.

Contact: Custer National Forest, P.O. Box 50760, 1310 Main St., Billings, MT 59105; 406/657-6361.

Trip notes: The campground is known for its hummingbirds and green-tailed towhees. You can fish here. Twelve miles southeast of the campground is the Big Ice Cave. There is a trail leading to where you can see the ice floor of the cave, and a picnic area nearby.

24 Barry's Landing

 5

Location: In Bighorn Canyon Recreational Area; map MT11, grid h4.

Campsites, facilities: There are nine RV or tent campsites. Wheelchair-accessible restrooms and a trailer boat ramp are available.

Reservations, fees: No reservations are needed; the fee is $12 per night. Open year-round. The stay limit is 14 days.

Directions: From Lovell, Wyoming, go 27 miles north on Highway 37 to the campground.

Contact: Superintendent, Bighorn Canyon National Recreation Area, P.O. Box 458, Fort Smith, MT 59035; 406/666-2412.

Trip notes: The Yellowtail Dam is one of the largest reservoirs on the Missouri River, where you can fish, boat, swim, and water-ski. There are nature trails in the area to hike and explore.

Custer National Forest

MAP MT12

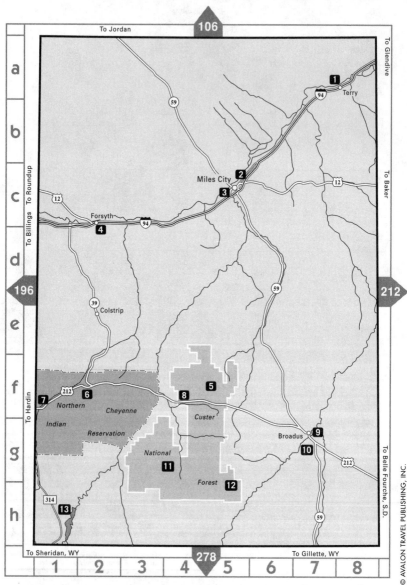

© AVALON TRAVEL PUBLISHING, INC.

CHAPTER MT12

1 Terry RV Oasis 207
2 Big Sky Camp and
RV Park 207
3 Miles City KOA 207
4 Rosebud Battlefield 208
5 Holiday Springs 208
6 Northern Cheyenne 208
7 Green Oasis
Campground 208
8 Red Shale 209
9 White Buffalo
Campground 209
10 La Rue's Wayside
Mobile/RV Park 209
11 Cow Creek 209
12 Doyle 210
13 Tongue River Reservoir ... 210

1 Terry RV Oasis

   3

Location: Northeast of Billings; map MT12, grid a7.

Campsites, facilities: There are 16 RV or tent campsites. Showers, laundry facilities, a sanitary disposal station, and water are available.

Reservations, fees: No reservations are needed; the fee is $12–16 per night. Open April 1–November 15.

Directions: From Miles City go 38 miles east on I-94 to Exit 176 at Terry, then go left on Yellowstone Avenue for 10 blocks to the campground.

Contact: Terry RV Oasis, 5 Pen Lane, Terry, MT 59349; 406/635-5520.

Trip notes: This is a clean, quiet campground with shady, grassy sites. The Yellowstone River, to the north, has good fishing and boating opportunities. The Terry Badlands, northwest of Terry on Highway 253, has excellent wildlife viewing.

2 Big Sky Camp and RV Park

   3

Location: In Miles City; map MT12, grid c5.

Campsites, facilities: There are 50 RV or tent campsites. Showers, laundry facilities, a store, a sanitary disposal facility, playground, swim-

ming pool, and water are available.

Reservations, fees: No reservations are needed; the fee is $11.45–12.45 per night. Open April 15–November 1.

Directions: From the junction of I-94 and U.S. 12 east of Miles City, take Exit 141, turn left, and you will see the campground about 50 yards ahead on the left.

Contact: Big Sky Camp and RV Park, RR Hwy. 12, P.O. Box 2366b, Miles City, MT 59301; 406/232-1511.

Trip notes: There is a golf course in Miles City, and you can boat and fish on the Yellowstone and Tongue Rivers.

3 Miles City KOA

   3

Location: In Miles City; map MT12, grid c5.

Campsites, facilities: There are 90 RV or tent campsites. Showers, laundry facilities, a store, a sanitary disposal facility, heated swimming pool, playground, and water are available. Pets are allowed on leashes.

Reservations, fees: No reservations are needed; the fee is $17–24 per night for two people. There is a discount with a KOA card. Open April 1–October 31.

Directions: From I-94 at Miles City, take Exit 135, go 2.4 miles, turn left at 4th Street and left at Palmer Street to the campground.

Contact: Miles City KOA, 1 Palmer St., Miles City, MT 59301; 406/232-3991.

Trip notes: From this campground you can walk to town and the museum. A golf course is in Miles City, and you can boat and fish on the Yellowstone and Tongue Rivers.

4 Rosebud Battlefield

 4

Location: Southeast of Billings; map MT12, grid d2.

Campsites, facilities: There are 10 RV or tent campsites. A trailer boat ramp, water, and toilets are available. Pets are allowed on leashes.

Reservations, fees: No reservations are needed; the fee is $5–10 per night. Open March 15–November 30. The stay limit is seven days.

Directions: From Billings, go east on I-90 to Exit 510, then east on Highway 212 25 miles to County Road 314; take County Road 314 south for 20 miles, then go three miles west on the county road to the battlefield.

Contact: Montana Fish, Wildlife & Parks, P.O. Box 1630, Miles City, MT 59301; 406/232-4365, 406/232-0900.

Trip notes: The Rosebud Battlefield State Park was the site of the 1876 battle between Sioux and Cheyenne Indians and General George Crook. The area is undeveloped, and removal of artifacts is prohibited. You can boat and fish on the Yellowstone River. Forsyth has a golf course.

5 Holiday Springs

   5

Location: In Custer National Forest; map MT12, grid f5.

Campsites, facilities: There are five RV campsites.

Reservations, fees: No reservations are needed; the fee is $5 per night. Open year-round. The stay limit is 14 days.

Directions: Ashland is 44 miles west of Broadus on U.S. 212. From Ashland, go five

miles east on U.S. 212, then 9.5 miles northeast on Forest Service Road 423, and east on Forest Service Road 777 to the campground.

Contact: Custer National Forest, P.O. Box 50760, 1310 Main St., Billings, MT 59105; 406/657-6361.

Trip notes: You can hike and fish in the Custer National Forest.

6 Northern Cheyenne

     3

Location: On the Northern Cheyenne Indian Reservation; map MT12, grid f2.

Campsites, facilities: There are several grassy RV or tent campsites. Water and electricity are available.

Reservations, fees: No reservations are needed; the fee is $6 per night. Open May 1–October 31.

Directions: From Miles City, go 67 miles south on Highway 59 to Broadus, then 66 miles west on U.S. 212 to Lame Deer. This campground is in Lame Deer on the Northern Cheyenne Indian Reservation.

Contact: Northern Cheyenne Campground, P.O. Box 991, Lame Deer, MT 59043; 406/477-8844 or 406/477-6284.

Trip notes: You can boat, swim, and fish for bass, crappie, perch, northern pike, and walleye in the Tongue River Reservoir to the south.

7 Green Oasis Campground

   4

Location: In Greybull; map MT12, grid f1.

Campsites, facilities: There are 21 RV or tent campsites. There are hookups, pull-through sites, a sanitary disposal facility, restrooms, showers, laundry facilities, picnic tables, grills, and water available.

Reservations, fees: Reservations are accepted; the fee is $15–22 per night. Open May 1–October 1.

Directions: From U.S. 14/16/20/Highway 789, take 12th Avenue North to the end of Greybull, and the campground is on the right.

Contact: Green Oasis Campground, 540 12th Ave. North, Greybull, WY 82426; 307/765-2856.

Trip notes: You can fish in the Greybull River.

8 Red Shale

 4

Location: In Custer National Forest; map MT12, grid f4.

Campsites, facilities: There are 14 RV or tent campsites, which can accommodate a maximum RV length of 30 feet. Wheelchair-accessible restrooms and water are available.

Reservations, fees: No reservations are needed; the fee is $6 per night. Open May 11–November 15. The stay limit is 14 days.

Directions: Ashland is 44 miles west of Broadus on U.S. 212. From Ashland, go six miles southeast on U.S. 212 to the campground.

Contact: Custer National Forest, P.O. Box 50760, 1310 Main St., Billings, MT 59105; 406/657-6361.

Trip notes: You can hike and fish in Custer National Forest.

9 White Buffalo Campground

 3

Location: In Broadus; map MT12, grid g7.

Campsites, facilities: There are 45 RV or tent campsites. Hookups, a sanitary disposal facility, showers, laundry facilities, and a playground are available.

Reservations, fees: No reservations are needed; the fee is $8–15 per night. Open May 1– November 30.

Directions: From Miles City, go 67 miles south on Highway 59 to Broadus; from U.S. 212, go one block east on Holt Street. The campground is at the east end of town.

Contact: White Buffalo Campground, Broadus, MT 59317; 406/436-2626.

Trip notes: Broadus has a nine-hole golf course and swimming pool.

10 La Rue's Wayside Mobile/RV Park

   3

Location: Southeast of Broadus; map MT12, grid g7.

Campsites, facilities: There are 27 RV or tent campsites. Showers, laundry facilities, a store, hookups, and a sanitary disposal facility are available.

Reservations, fees: No reservations are needed; the fee is $7–12 per night. Open year-round.

Directions: From Miles City, go 67 miles south on Highway 59 to Broadus, then three miles to the junction of U.S. 212 and Highway 59; the campground is just south of the junction.

Contact: La Rue's Wayside Mobile/RV Park, Broadus, MT 59317; 406/436-2510.

Trip notes: This campground is near a golf course, in a peaceful setting. Broadus has a swimming pool.

11 Cow Creek

 5

Location: In Custer National Forest; map MT12, grid g4.

Campsites, facilities: There are eight RV or tent campsites, which can accommodate a maximum RV length of 32 feet. A restroom is available.

Reservations, fees: No reservations are needed; the fee is $5 per night. Open May 15–November 1. The stay limit is 14 days.

Directions: Ashland is 44 miles west of Broadus on U.S. 212. From Ashland, go four miles east on U.S. 212, then 20 miles south on County Road 485 and five miles west on Forest Service Road 95 to the campground.

Contact: Custer National Forest, P.O. Box 50760, 1310 Main St., Billings, MT 59105; 406/657-6361.

Trip notes: You can hike and fish in the national forest. You can boat, swim, and fish for bass, crappie, perch, northern pike, and walleye in the Tongue River Reservoir to the southwest.

12 Doyle

 4

Location: In Custer National Forest; map MT12, grid h5.

Campsites, facilities: There are 19 RV campsites, plus tent sites. Restrooms, picnic tables, and grills are available.

Reservations, fees: No reservations are needed; the fee is $6 per night. Open May 15–October 31.

Directions: From Buffalo, travel 31 miles west on U.S. Highway 16 to the campground.

Contact: Custer National Forest, P.O. Box 50760, 1310 Main St., Billings, MT 59105; 406/657-6361.

Trip notes: You can hike and fish in the Custer National Forest.

13 Tongue River Reservoir

 5

Location: North of Sheridan, Wyoming, on the Montana side; map MT12, grid h1.

Campsites, facilities: There are 100 RV or tent campsites, some with grills. There are restrooms, water (seasonally), and a trailer boat ramp available at the dam end.

Reservations, fees: No reservations are needed; the fee is $12 per night. Open year-round. The stay limit is 14 days.

Directions: From Sheridan, Wyoming, take I-90 north to Highway 338, and then take 338 14 miles northeast to Decker. From Decker, go six miles north on County Road 314, then one mile east on the county road to the Tongue River Reservoir.

Contact: Fish, Wildlife & Parks, P.O. Box 1630, Miles City, MT 59301; 406/232-4365.

Trip notes: The north end, where the dam is, has red rock and dramatic landscape. The other end is near a mining area and has a bleak landscape. This lake offers good fishing for crappie, rock bass, largemouth bass, smallmouth bass, north pike, walleye, and perch. It's popular with water recreationists from nearby Sheridan. Sheridan, 26 miles to the south, has a golf course.

WAYNE SCHERR

Bison

MAP MT13

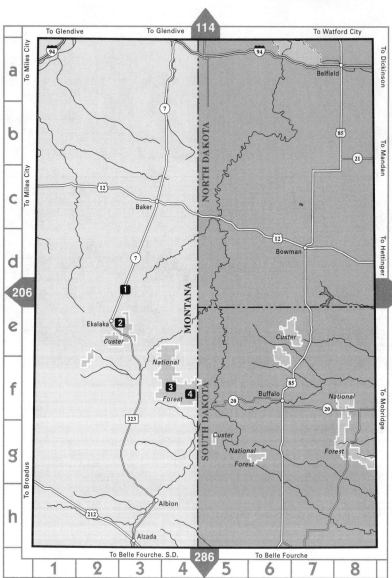

To Miles City

94

Belfield

To Dickinson

7

NORTH DAKOTA

85

To Miles City

12

21

To Mandan

Baker

12

Bowman

To Hettinger

206

MONTANA

1

Ekalaka **2**

Custer

Custer

National

3

4

Forest

323

SOUTH DAKOTA

85

20

Buffalo

National

To Mobridge

Custer

20

National

Forest

Forest

To Broadus

Albion

212

Alzada

1   2   3   4   5   6   7   8

© AVALON TRAVEL PUBLISHING, INC.

CHAPTER MT13

1 Medicine Rocks
State Park 213
2 Mrnak RV Park...............213
3 Lantis Spring 213
4 Wickham Gulch.............213

1 Medicine Rocks State Park

  3

Location: Between Baker and Ekalaka; map MT13, grid d3.

Campsites, facilities: There are 12 RV and tent campsites, which can accommodate a maximum RV length of 20 feet, some with grills and picnic tables. A toilet and water are available.

Reservations, fees: No reservations are needed; the fee is $12 per night. Open year round. The stay limit is 14 days.

Directions: From Baker, go 25 miles south on Highway 7; the park is 14 miles north of Ekalaka.

Contact: Montana Fish, Wildlife & Parks, Region 5, 2300 Lake Elmo Drive, Billings, Montana 406/247-2940.

Trip notes: This is a primitive, pack-in, pack-out campground. These sandstone rock formations were a special place to Native Americans, and today you will find antelope, mule deer, and sharp-tailed grouse here. The town of Baker has two golf courses.

2 Mrnak RV Park

  3

Location: In Ekalaka; map MT13, grid e3.

Campsites, facilities: There are 13 RV or tent campsites. Showers, electricity, and water are available.

Reservations, fees: No reservations are needed; the fee is $15 per night for two people.

Open April 1–December 1.

Directions: From Glendive, go 27 miles east on I-94 to Wibaux, then 80 miles south on Highway 7 to Ekalaka. This campground is in Ekalaka, west of the fairgrounds.

Contact: Mrnak RV Park, P.O. Box 497, Ekalaka, MT 59324; 406/775-6233.

Trip notes: A public swimming pool is nearby. Medicine Rocks State Park, 11 miles north, has sandstone rock formations that were a special place to Native Americans. Today you will find antelope, mule deer, and sharp-tailed grouse here.

3 Lantis Spring

 5

Location: In Custer National Forest; map MT13, grid f4.

Campsites, facilities: There are 10 RV or tent campsites, which can accommodate a maximum RV length of 30 feet. Restrooms and water are available.

Reservations, fees: No reservations are needed; there is no fee charged. Open May 1–November 15. The stay limit is 14 days.

Directions: From Ekalaka, take County Road 323 17 miles south to Forest Service Road 818; take it to the Long Pine Hills and the campground.

Contact: Custer National Forest, 2602 1st Ave. North, P.O. Box 2556, Billings, MT 59103; 605/797-4432, fax 605/797-4404; website: www.fs.fed .us/r1/custer.

Trip notes: You can fish, swim, boat, and hike in the Bighorn Canyon National Recreation Area.

4 Wickham Gulch

     6

Location: In Custer National Forest; map MT13, grid f4.

Campsites, facilities: There are four campsites, which can accommodate a maximum RV length of 14 feet. There is a restroom, and water is available.

Reservations, fees: No reservations are needed; there is no fee charged. Open May 1–November 15. The stay limit is 14 days.

Directions: From Ekalaka, drive 40 miles east; the campground is in Lone Pine Hills.

Contact: Custer National Forest, 2602 1st Ave. North, P.O. Box 2556, Billings, MT 59103; 605/797-4432, fax 605/797-4404; website: www.fs.fed.us/r1/custer.

Trip notes: A spring runs through this campground. You can fish, swim, boat, and hike in Bighorn Canyon National Recreation Area.

WAYNE SCHERR

Red Rock Lakes National Wildlife Refuge

MAP MT14

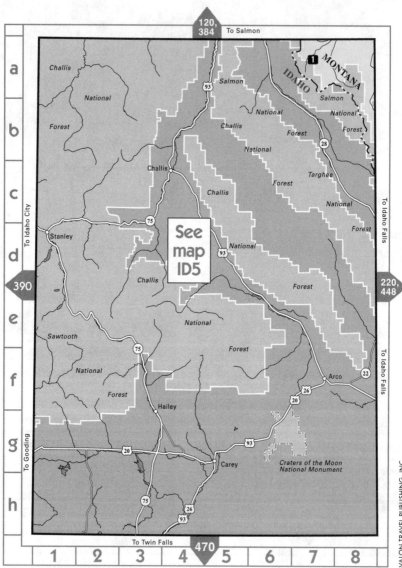

© AVALON TRAVEL PUBLISHING, INC.

CHAPTER MT14

1 Sacajawea Memorial........217

1 Sacajawea Memorial

     5

Location: In the Beaverhead-Deerlodge National Forest; map MT14, grid a7.

Campsites, facilities: There are two RV or tent campsites.

Reservations, fees: No reservations are needed, and no fee is charged. Open June 16– September 15, though campers compete with cows.

Directions: From Lemhi Pass, go 10 miles off County Road 324, west of Grant, to the campground.

Contact: Beaverhead-Deerlodge National Forest, Dillon Ranger District, 420 Barrett St., Dillon, MT 59725-3572; 406/683-3900.

Trip notes: You can hike and fish in Beaverhead-Deerlodge National Forest. Although camping is possible, the free-range cattle make the area undesirable.

MONTANA
CHAPTER MT15

Drift boat recreation, Madison River

MAP MT15

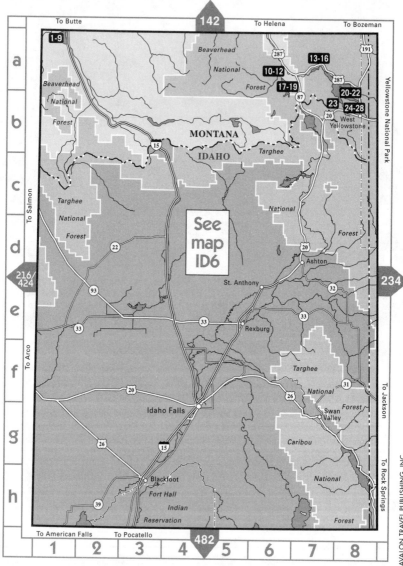

To Butte   **142**   To Helena   To Bozeman

1-9

Beaverhead

National

13-16

10-12

Forest

17-19

287

Beaverhead

87

20-22

National

23

24-28

Forest

West
Yellowstone

20

MONTANA

Yellowstone National Park

IDAHO

Targhee

15

Targhee

National

National

Forest

Forest

22

20

216/424

Ashton

234

93

32

St. Anthony

33

33

Rexburg

To Salmon

To Arco

33

Targhee

31

20

National

Forest

26

Idaho Falls

Swan
Valley

To Jackson

26

15

Caribou

National

To Rock Springs

Blackfoot

Fort Hall

39

Indian

Forest

Reservation

To American Falls   To Pocatello   **482**

1   2   3   4   5   6   7   8

a b c d e f g h

See map ID6

CHAPTER MT15

1 Cameahwait 221
2 Clark Canyon Reservoir ... 221
3 Hap Hawkins 222
4 Horse Prairie 222
5 Hunter's Beaverhead
 Marina & Park 222
6 Lewis and Clark 222
7 Little Joe 222
8 Lonetree 223
9 West Cameahwait 223
10 West Fork Cabins
 & RV Park 223
11 West Fork 223
12 Madison River 224
13 Beaver Creek 224
14 Campfire Lodge
 Resort 224
15 Cabin Creek 224
16 Yellowstone Holiday
 Resort 225
17 Wade Lake 225
18 Hilltop 225
19 Cliff Point 225
20 Rainbow Point 226
21 Lonesomehurst 226
22 Madison Arm Resort
 & Marina 226
23 Yellowstone Park KOA 227
24 Bakers Hole 227
25 Rustic Wagon RV
 Campground & Cabins 227
26 Hideaway RV Campground .. 227
27 Wagon Wheel
 Campground & Cabins 228
28 Yellowstone Grizzly
 RV Park 228

1 Cameahwait

      5

Location: At Clark Canyon Reservoir; map MT15, grid a1.

Campsites, facilities: There are 10 RV and tent campsites, and a wheelchair-accessible restroom.

Reservations, fees: No reservations are needed; there is no fee. Open year-round. The stay limit is 14 days.

Directions: From Dillon, go 20 miles south on I-15 to Clark Canyon Reservoir.

Contact: U.S. Bureau of Reclamation, P.O. Box 30137, Billings, MT 59107-0137; 406/683-6472.

Trip notes: The Clark Canyon Reservoir has good fishing for rainbow and brown trout, and you can boat, swim, and water-ski here.

2 Clark Canyon Reservoir

 5

Location: South of Dillon; map MT15, grid a1.

Campsites, facilities: There are 12 RV and tent campsites, a wheelchair-accessible restroom, and a trailer boat launch.

Reservations, fees: No reservations are needed; there is no fee. Open year-round. The stay limit is 14 days.

Directions: From Dillon, go 20 miles south on I-15 to Clark Canyon Reservoir.

Contact: U.S. Bureau of Reclamation, P.O. Box 30137, Billings, MT 59107-0137; 406/683-6472.

Trip notes: The Clark Canyon Reservoir has good fishing for rainbow and brown trout, and you can boat, swim, and water-ski here.

3 Hap Hawkins

    5

Location: At Clark Canyon Reservoir; map MT15, grid a1.

Campsites, facilities: There are nine RV and tent campsites, and a wheelchair-accessible restroom is available.

Reservations, fees: No reservations are needed; there is no fee. Open year-round. The stay limit is 14 days.

Directions: From Dillon, go 20 miles south on I-15 to Clark Canyon Reservoir.

Contact: U.S. Bureau of Reclamation, P.O. Box 30137, Billings, MT 59107-0137; 406/683-6472.

Trip notes: The Clark Canyon Reservoir has good fishing for rainbow and brown trout, and you can boat, swim, and water-ski here.

4 Horse Prairie

      5

Location: At Clark Canyon Reservoir; map MT15, grid a1.

Campsites, facilities: There are 12 RV and tent campsites, a wheelchair-accessible restroom, and a trailer boat launch.

Reservations, fees: No reservations are needed; there is no fee. Open year-round. The stay limit is 14 days.

Directions: From Dillon, go 20 miles south on I-15 to Clark Canyon Reservoir.

Contact: U.S. Bureau of Reclamation, P.O. Box 30137, Billings, MT 59107-0137; 406/683-6472.

Trip notes: The Clark Canyon Reservoir has good fishing for rainbow and brown trout, and you can boat, swim, and water-ski here.

5 Hunter's Beaverhead Marina & Park

   5

Location: South of Dillon; map MT15, grid a1.

Campsites, facilities: There are 57 RV or tent campsites. Showers, laundry facilities, docks, fuel, and a boat ramp are available.

Reservations, fees: No reservations are needed; the fee is $25 per night. Open year-round.

Directions: From Dillon, go 20 miles south on I-15 to Exit 44, go across the dam and turn left at the entrance to the marina.

Contact: Hunter's Beaverhead Marina and Park, 1225 Hwy. 324, Dillon, MT 59725; 406/683-5556.

Trip notes: You can fish in Beaverhead River, and golfing is nearby.

6 Lewis and Clark

     5

Location: At Clark Canyon Reservoir; map MT15, grid a1.

Campsites, facilities: There are 10 RV and tent campsites and a wheelchair-accessible restroom.

Reservations, fees: No reservations are needed; there is no fee charged. Open year-round. The stay limit is 14 days.

Directions: From Dillon, go 20 miles south on I-15 to Clark Canyon Reservoir.

Contact: U.S. Bureau of Reclamation, P.O. Box 30137, Billings, MT 59107-0137; 406/683-6472.

Trip notes: The Clark Canyon Reservoir has good fishing for rainbow and brown trout, and you can boat, swim, and water-ski here.

7 Little Joe

   6

Location: In the Beaverhead-Deerlodge National Forest; map MT15, grid a1.

Campsites, facilities: There are four RV or tent campsites, which can accommodate a maximum RV length of 16 feet.

Reservations, fees: No reservations are needed; the fee is $8 per night. Open May 25–September 15. The stay limit is 16 days.

Directions: From Butte, go south on I-15 19

miles to Divide, then go 12 miles west on Highway 43 to Wise River. From Wise River, go 20 miles southwest on Pioneer Mountains Scenic Byway (Forest Service Road 484) to the campground.

Contact: Beaverhead-Deerlodge National Forest, P.O. Box 238, Wisdom, MT 59761; 406/689-3243; website: www.fs.fed.us/r1/bdnf.

Trip notes: You can fish and hike in Beaverhead-Deerlodge National Forest.

8 Lonetree

 5

Location: At Clark Canyon Reservoir; map MT15, grid a1.

Campsites, facilities: There are RV and tent campsites. A wheelchair-accessible restroom and trailer boat launch are available.

Reservations, fees: No reservations are needed; there is no fee charged. Open year-round. The stay limit is 14 days.

Directions: From Dillon, drive 20 miles south on I-15 to Clark Canyon Reservoir.

Contact: U.S. Bureau of Reclamation, P.O. Box 30137, Billings, MT 59107-0137; 406/683-6472.

Trip notes: The Clark Canyon Reservoir has good fishing for rainbow and brown trout, and you can boat, swim, and water-ski here.

9 West Cameahwait

 5

Location: At Clark Canyon Reservoir; map MT15, grid a1.

Campsites, facilities: There are RV and tent campsites. A wheelchair-accessible restroom is available.

Reservations, fees: No reservations are needed; there is no fee. Open year-round. The stay limit is 14 days.

Directions: From Dillon, go 20 miles south on I-15 to Clark Canyon Reservoir.

Contact: U.S. Bureau of Reclamation, P.O. Box 30137, Billings, MT 59107-0137; 406/683-6472.

Trip notes: The Clark Canyon Reservoir has good fishing for rainbow and brown trout, and you can boat, swim, and water-ski here.

10 West Fork Cabins & RV Park

 5

Location: South of Ennis; map MT15, grid a6.

Campsites, facilities: There are 24 RV and 20 tent campsites. Showers, laundry facilities, raft rentals, and a fly shop are available.

Reservations, fees: No reservations are needed; the fee is $25 and up per night. Open May 1–November 30.

Directions: From Ennis, drive 35 miles south on U.S. 287 to the campground on the banks of the Madison River.

Contact: West Fork Cabins & RV Park, 1475 Hwy. 287 N., Cameron, MT 59720; 406/682-4802; email: garyjill@3rivers.net; website: www.garyevansmadisonguides.com.

Trip notes: This park is affiliated with a fly-fishing guide service. You can fish and float on the Madison River.

11 West Fork

 5

Location: In Beaverhead-Deerlodge National Forest; map MT15, grid a6.

Campsites, facilities: There are seven RV or tent campsites.

Reservations, fees: No reservations are needed; the fee is $12–18 per night. Open June 1–September 15. The stay limit is 16 days.

Directions: From Ennis, go 34 miles south on U.S. 287 to the campground. Be advised that there is a narrow bridge you must cross and it has a load limit, so make sure you are within the specifications.

Contact: Beaverhead-Deerlodge National Forest, 420 Barrett St., Dillon, MT 59725; 406/683-3900; website: www.fs.fed.us/r1/bdnf.

Trip notes: You can fish and float on the Madison River.

12 Madison River

  6

Location: In Beaverhead-Deerlodge National Forest; map MT15, grid a6.

Campsites, facilities: There are 10 RV campsites, which can accommodate a maximum RV length of 22 feet.

Reservations, fees: No reservations are needed; the fee is $8 per night. Open June 1–September 30. The stay limit is 14 days.

Directions: From Ennis, go 11 miles south on U.S. 28 to Cameron, and from Cameron, go 24 miles south on U.S. 287, then one mile southwest on County Road 8381 to the campground.

Contact: Beaverhead-Deerlodge National Forest, 5 Forest Service Rd., Ennis, MT 59729; 406/682-4253, fax 406/682-4233; website: www.fs.fed.us/r1/bdnf.

Trip notes: You can fish in the Madison River and hike in Beaverhead-Deerlodge National Forest.

13 Beaver Creek

    6

Location: Northwest of West Yellowstone; map MT15, grid a7.

Campsites, facilities: There are 64 RV or tent campsites, which can accommodate a maximum RV length of 32 feet. A trailer boat launch is available.

Reservations, fees: No reservations are needed; the fee is $10 and up per night. Open June 2–September 15. The stay limit is 14 days.

Directions: From West Yellowstone, go eight miles north on U.S. 191, then 15 miles west on U.S. 287 to the campground, which is on the left.

Contact: Gallatin National Forest, Hebgen Lake District, P.O. Box 520, Hwy. 287, West Yellowstone, MT 59758; 406/823-6961, fax 406/823-6990; website: www.fs.fed.us/r1/gallatin.

Trip notes: You can boat, swim, water-ski, canoe, and fish in Hebgen Lake. In Yellowstone National Park, you can fish (with per-

mit), hike, boat, canoe, and see wildlife in their spectacular habitat.

14 Campfire Lodge Resort

   5

Location: Near Yellowstone National Park; map MT15, grid a7.

Campsites, facilities: There are 21 RV or tent campsites. There are showers, a store, laundry facilities, hookups, water, cabins, and a café available.

Reservations, fees: No reservations are needed; the fee is $14–20 per night. Open May 20–September 10.

Directions: From West Yellowstone, go eight miles north on U.S. 191, then 14 miles west on U.S. 287 to the resort, which is on the river side.

Contact: Campfire Lodge Resort, Inc., 8500 Hebgen Lake, West Yellowstone, MT 59758; 406/646-7258.

Trip notes: This campground is close to Yellowstone National Park, where you can fish (with permit), hike, boat, canoe, and see wildlife in their spectacular habitat.

15 Cabin Creek

    6

Location: In Beaverhead-Deerlodge National Forest; map MT15, grid a7.

Campsites, facilities: There are 15 RV or tent campsites, which can accommodate a maximum RV length of 32 feet.

Reservations, fees: No reservations are needed; the fee is $10.50 per night. Open May 22–September 15. The stay limit is 15 days.

Directions: From West Yellowstone, go eight miles north on U.S. 191, then 14 miles west on U.S. 287 to the campground.

Contact: Beaverhead-Deerlodge National Forest, Madison Ranger District, 5 Service Forest Rd., Ennis, MT 59729; 406/682-4253.

Trip notes: You can boat, swim, water-ski, canoe, and fish in Hebgen Lake. In Yellowstone National Park, you can fish (with permit), hike, boat, canoe, and see wildlife in their spectacular habitat.

16 Yellowstone Holiday Resort

 5

Location: North of West Yellowstone; map MT15, grid a7.

Campsites, facilities: There are 42 RV or tent campsites, which can accommodate a maximum RV length of 70 feet. Showers, a store, hookups, a sanitary disposal station, docks, marinas, and cabins are available.

Reservations, fees: No reservations are needed; the fee is $20–32 per night. Open seasonally; call for specific dates.

Directions: From West Yellowstone, go eight miles north on U.S. 191, then five miles west on U.S. 287; the campground is on the left.

Contact: Yellowstone Holiday Resort, P.O. Box 759, West Yellowstone, MT 59758; 877/646-4242, fax (in season) 406/646-7117; email: yhr @wyellowstone.com; website: yellowstone-holiday.com.

Trip notes: This campground is on the shoreline of Hebgen Lake, eight miles from the entrance to Yellowstone Park. You can boat, swim, water-ski, canoe, and fish in Hebgen Lake. In Yellowstone National Park, you can fish (with permit), hike, boat, canoe, and see wildlife in their spectacular habitat.

17 Wade Lake

 6

Location: In Beaverhead-Deerlodge National Forest; map MT15, grid a6.

Campsites, facilities: There are 30 RV or tent campsites, which can accommodate a maximum RV length of 24 feet.

Reservations, fees: No reservations are needed; the fee is $8 per night. Open June 1–September 30. The stay limit is 14 days.

Directions: From West Yellowstone, go eight miles north on U.S. 191, then travel 27 miles

southwest on Forest Service Road 5721 to the campground.

Contact: Beaverhead-Deerlodge National Forest, Madison Ranger District, 5 Service Forest Rd., Ennis, MT 59729; 406/682-4253.

Trip notes: You can fish and swim at Wade Lake.

18 Hilltop

 6

Location: In Beaverhead-Deerlodge National Forest; map MT15, grid a6.

Campsites, facilities: There are 18 RV or tent campsites, which can accommodate a maximum RV length of 22 feet.

Reservations, fees: No reservations are needed; the fee is $7–10 per night. Open June 1–September 30. The stay limit is 14 days.

Directions: From West Yellowstone, go eight miles north on U.S. 191, 27 miles west on U.S. 287, and six miles southwest on Forest Service Road 5721.

Contact: Beaverhead-Deerlodge National Forest, 5 Forest Service Rd., Ennis, MT 59729; 406/682-4253; website: www.fs.fed.us/r1/bdnf.

Trip notes: You can fish and swim at Wade Lake. You can boat, swim, water-ski, canoe, and fish in Hebgen Lake, near West Yellowstone. In Yellowstone National Park, you can fish (with permit), hike, boat, canoe, and see wildlife in spectacular habitat.

19 Cliff Point

 7

Location: West of Yellowstone Park; map MT15, grid a6.

Campsites, facilities: There are six RV or tent campsites, which can accommodate a maximum RV length of 16 feet. A trailer boat launch is available. Pets are allowed on leashes.

Reservations, fees: No reservations are needed; the fee is $8 per night. Open June 1–September 15. The stay limit is 14 days.

Directions: From West Yellowstone, go eight miles north on U.S. 191, then 27 miles west on U.S. 287 and six miles southwest on Forest Service Road 5721 to the campground.

Contact: Beaverhead-Deerlodge National Forest, 5 Forest Service Rd., Ennis, MT 59729; 406/682-4253.

Trip notes: You can fish at nearby Madison, Yellowstone, and Beaverhead Rivers. You can boat, swim, water-ski, canoe, and fish in Hebgen Lake, near West Yellowstone. In Yellowstone National Park, you can fish (with permit), hike, boat, canoe, and see wildlife in their spectacular habitat.

20 Rainbow Point

 5

Location: At Hebgen Lake; map MT15, grid a8.

Campsites, facilities: There are 85 RV campsites *for hard-sided RVs only,* which can accommodate a maximum RV length of 32 feet. No tents are allowed.

Reservations, fees: No reservations are needed; the fee is $10.50 per night. Open May 22–September 15. The stay limit is 14 days.

Directions: From West Yellowstone, go five miles north on U.S. 191, three miles west on Forest Service Road 610, and two miles north on Forest Service Road 6954 to the campground.

Contact: Gallatin National Forest, Hebgen Lake District, P.O. Box 520, Hwy. 287, West Yellowstone, MT 59758; 406/823-6961, fax 406/823-6990; website: www.fs.fed.us/r1/gallatin.

Trip notes: You *must* have a hard-sided RV here, and no tents are allowed. This is bear country, so use appropriate precautions. You can fish, swim, and water-ski at Hebgen Lake.

21 Lonesomehurst

 6

Location: In Gallatin National Forest; map MT15, grid a8.

Campsites, facilities: There are 26 RV or tent campsites, which can accommodate a maximum RV length of 32 feet. A trailer boat launch is available.

Reservations, fees: No reservations are needed; the fee is $10.50 per night. Open May 22–September 15. The stay limit is 14 days.

Directions: From West Yellowstone, go seven miles west on U.S. 20, then four miles north on Hebgen Lake Road to the campground.

Contact: Gallatin National Forest, Hebgen Lake District, P.O. Box 520, Hwy. 287, West Yellowstone, MT 59758; 406/823-6961, fax 406/823-6990; website: www.fs.fed.us/r1/gallatin.

Trip notes: The Grizzly Discovery Center is an educational facility. This bear and wolf preserve offers the public rare insight into the animals' habits and behaviors, with live animals and exhibits. A portion of the proceeds goes to the International Grizzly Fund. There is a National Geographic IMAX Theater in the Grizzly Center. You can swim, fish, boat, water-ski, and canoe in Hebgen Lake, and hike in the surrounding forest.

22 Madison Arm Resort & Marina

 5

Location: Near West Yellowstone; map MT15, grid a8.

Campsites, facilities: There are 53 RV sites, which can accommodate a maximum RV length of 36 feet, and 22 tent campsites. There are laundry facilities, showers, a store, a sanitary disposal facility, hookups, water, a marina, and cabin rentals.

Reservations, fees: No reservations are needed; the fee is $20–26 per night. Open May 15–October 1.

Directions: From West Yellowstone, go three miles north on U.S. 191, then five miles west on Forest Service Road 291 to the campground.

Contact: Madison Arm Resort & Marina, South Shore Hebgen Lake, P.O. Box 1410, West Yellowstone, MT 59758; 406/646-9328, fax 406/

646-4367; email: jclarkson@wyellowstone.com; website: www.wyellowstone.com/clients /madisonarm.

Trip notes: This campground is in the Gallatin National Forest on the south shore of Hebgen Lake, where you can fish, boat, water-ski, and swim.

23 Yellowstone Park KOA

    5

Location: West of Yellowstone Park; map MT15, grid b7.

Campsites, facilities: There are 304 RV or tent campsites. Showers, laundry facilities, a store, hookups, water, barbecue, swimming pool, hot tub, and game room are available.

Reservations, fees: No reservations are needed; the fee is $30–40 per night. Open May 22–September 22.

Directions: From West Yellowstone, go six miles west on U.S. 20; the campground is on the right, two miles from the border.

Contact: Yellowstone KOA, 3305 Targhee Path, West Yellowstone, MT 59758; 406/646-7606, 800/562-7591.

Trip notes: This campground is close to Yellowstone National Park, where you can fish (with permit), hike, boat, canoe, and see wildlife in their spectacular habitat.

24 Bakers Hole

   6

Location: Near West Yellowstone National Park; map MT15, grid b8.

Campsites, facilities: There are 72 RV campsites, which can accommodate a maximum RV length of 32 feet. No tents are allowed. Wheelchair-accessible restrooms and water are available.

Reservations, fees: No reservations are needed; the fee is $12.50 per night. The stay limit is 15 days. Open late May–mid-September.

Directions: From Bozeman, go south to West Yellowstone; the campground sign is three miles north of West Yellowstone on U.S. 191.

Contact: Hebgen Lake Ranger District, Hwy. 287, P.O. Box 520, West Yellowstone, MT 59758; 406/823-6961.

Trip notes: Hard-sided vehicles only; no tents are allowed. This campground is near the Madison River and the west entrance of Yellowstone National Park.

25 Rustic Wagon RV Campground & Cabins

    5

Location: In West Yellowstone; map MT15, grid b8.

Campsites, facilities: There are 52 RV or tent campsites, with large pull-throughs for RVs. Showers, laundry facilities, modern restrooms, water, electricity, sewer, and a sanitary disposal station are available. A playground, cable TV, camp cabins, and store are provided.

Reservations, fees: Reservations are accepted; the fee is $15–25 per night. Open mid-April–mid-October.

Directions: From Bozeman, go to West Yellowstone to U.S. 20, go west on U.S. 20 (Firehole Avenue) to Electric Avenue, turn right, go three blocks to Gibbon Avenue and the campground.

Contact: Rustic Wagon RV Campground & Cabins, 624 U.S. 20, West Yellowstone, MT; 406/646-7387.

Trip notes: Just outside Yellowstone National Park, there are good fishing streams and plenty of places to hike here.

26 Hideaway RV Campground

     3

Location: In West Yellowstone; map MT15, grid b8.

Campsites, facilities: There are 17 RV or tent campsites. There are showers, water, electricity, cable TV, sewer, and a sanitary disposal station.

Reservations, fees: No reservations are needed; the fee is $15–25 per night. Open May 1–mid-October.

Directions: From Bozeman, go south to West Yellowstone, go two blocks west on U.S. 20 (Firehole Avenue) to Electric Avenue, turn right and go one block to the campground at the corner of Gibbon and Electric.

Contact: Hideaway RV Campground, Gibbon & Electric, West Yellowstone, MT 59758; 406/646-9049.

Trip notes: This is a quiet location with trees in the town of West Yellowstone, which is just outside Yellowstone National Park; there are good fishing streams and plenty of places to hike here.

27 Wagon Wheel Campground & Cabins

     4

Location: In West Yellowstone; map MT15, grid b8.

Campsites, facilities: There are 50 RV or tent campsites. Showers, laundry facilities, restrooms, water, electricity, sewer, and a sanitary disposal station are provided. A game room, cable TV, cottages, and log camp cabins are available. No pets are allowed.

Reservations, fees: Reservations are accepted; the fee is $22–32 per night. Open late May–mid-September.

Directions: From Bozeman, go south to West Yellowstone, drive three blocks west on U.S. 20 (Firehole Avenue), turn right on Faithful Street, and go one block north to the campground.

Contact: Wagon Wheel Campground & Cabins, 408 Gibbon Ave., West Yellowstone, MT 59758; 406/646-7872; website: www.yellowstone.com/wagonwheel.

Trip notes: Just outside Yellowstone National Park, there are good fishing streams and plenty of places to hike here.

28 Yellowstone Grizzly RV Park

     4

Location: In West Yellowstone; map MT15, grid b8.

Campsites, facilities: There are 152 RV sites, which can accommodate a maximum RV length of 70 feet, some with hookups. Group facilities and wheelchair-accessible facilities are available. Showers, laundry facilities, water, electricity, sewer, and a sanitary disposal station are provided. A store, cable TV, playground, and game room are on-site.

Reservations, fees: Open early May–late October.

Directions: From Bozeman, go south to West Yellowstone, then go left on Grey Wolf Avenue for two blocks to Electric Avenue and the RV park.

Contact: Yellowstone Grizzly RV Park, 210 S. Electric St., or P.O. Box 150, West Yellowstone, 59758; 406/646-4466 or fax 406/646-4335.

Trip notes: This is a full-service RV park within walking distance of town and four blocks from west entrance of Yellowstone National Park.

WYOMING

Chapter WY1 233
Chapter WY2 259
Chapter WY3 277
Chapter WY4 285
Chapter WY5 291
Chapter WY6 301
Chapter WY7 311
Chapter WY8 325

WYOMING STATE   231

Map WY1 234   Map WY5 292
Map WY2 260   Map WY6 302
Map WY3 278   Map WY7 312
Map WY4 286   Map WY8 326

WYOMING STATE MAP

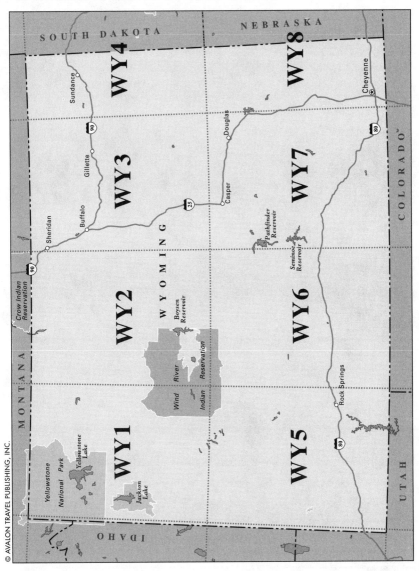

Becker Lake, Absaroka-Beartooth Mountains

MAP WY1

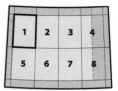

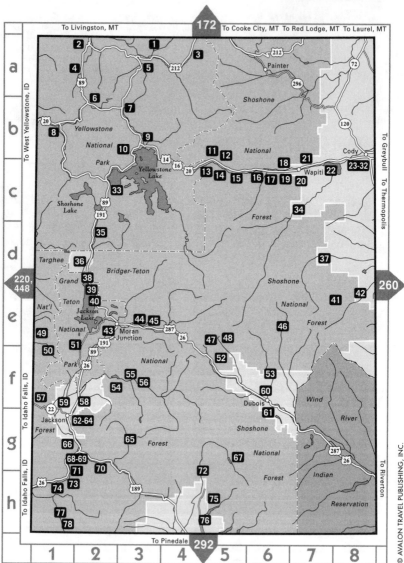

CHAPTER WY1

1	Slough Creek	236
2	Mammoth Campground	236
3	Pebble Creek	236
4	Indian Creek	237
5	Tower Falls	237
6	Norris	237
7	Canyon Campground	238
8	Madison	238
9	Fishing Bridge RV Park	238
10	Bridge Bay	239
11	Pahaska	239
12	Sleeping Giant	239
13	Three Mile	239
14	Newton Creek	239
15	Eagle Creek	240
16	Rex Hale	240
17	Clearwater	240
18	Wapiti	240
19	Elk Fork	241
20	Big Game	241
21	Hitching Post Campground	241
22	Buffalo Bill State Park	241
23	7K Motel and RV Park	242
24	Absaroka Bay RV Park	242
25	Buffalo Bill Village	242
26	Camp Cody RV Park	243
27	Mountain View Lodge	243
28	Cody KOA	243
29	Gateway Campground	243
30	Ponderosa Campground	244
31	River's View RV Park	244
32	Yellowstone Valley RV Park	244
33	Grant Village	245
34	Deer Creek	245
35	Lewis Lake	245
36	Flagg Ranch Village	246
37	Jack Creek	246
38	Lizard Creek	246
39	Colter Bay RV Park	247
40	Colter Bay	247
41	Brown Mountain	247
42	Wood River	248
43	Signal Mountain	248
44	Grand Teton Park RV Resort	248
45	Hatchet	248
46	Double Cabin	249
47	Brooks Lake	249
48	Pinnacles	249
49	Reunion Flat Group Area	250
50	Teton Canyon	250
51	Jenny Lake	250
52	Falls	250
53	Horse Creek	251
54	Gros Ventre	251
55	Atherton Creek	251
56	Crystal Creek	252
57	Trail Creek	252
58	Curtis Canyon	252
59	Teton Village KOA	252
60	Circle-Up Camper Court	253
61	Riverside Campground	253
62	Elk Country Inn & RV Park	253
63	Virginian Lodge RV Park	254
64	Wagon Wheel Campground	254
65	Granite Creek	254
66	Snake River Park KOA	254
67	Green River Lake	255
68	Lazy J Corral RV Park	255
69	Astoria Hot Springs	255
70	Hoback	256
71	Cabin Creek	256
72	Whiskey Grove	256
73	Elbow	256

(continues)

74 Station Creek 257   **77** Lynx Creek....................257
75 Narrows.......................257   **78** Murphy Creek...............258
76 New Fork Lake...............257

1 Slough Creek

 6

Location: In Yellowstone National Park; map WY1, grid a3.

Campsites, facilities: There are 29 RV or tent campsites, with picnic tables and grills. Pets must be on a leash, crated, or caged.

Reservations, fees: No reservations are needed; the fee is $10 per night. The stay limit is 14 days. Open late May–late October.

Directions: From Tower Junction in Yellowstone National Park, go 16 miles northeast on the northeast entrance road to the turnoff.

Contact: National Park Service, P.O. Box 168, Yellowstone National Park, WY 82190; 307/344-7381; website: www.nps.gov/yell.

Trip notes: Slough Creek Campground is 2.2 miles north of the main road along Slough Creek. The trailhead of Slough Creek Trail is here.

2 Mammoth Campground

 4

Location: In Yellowstone National Park; map WY1, grid a2.

Campsites, facilities: There are 85 RV or tent campsites with picnic tables and grills. Restrooms, propane gas, a store, visitor center, and post office are available. The park headquarters are here. Pets must be on a leash, crated, or caged.

Reservations, fees: No reservations are needed; the fee is $12 per night. The stay limit is 14 days. This is the only park campground that is open year-round.

Directions: From Livingston, go 57 miles south on U.S. 89 to Gardiner. From Gardiner (the north entrance of Yellowstone National Park), go five miles south on Grand Loop Road to Mammoth.

Contact: National Park Service, P.O. Box 168, Yellowstone National Park, WY 82190; 307/344-7381; website: www.nps.gov/yell.

Trip notes: This popular campground is near Mammoth Hot Springs, and is on a first-come, first-served basis. It has the lowest elevation of all the available campgrounds, making it a little warmer, but suffers from a lack of trees and scenery. Park naturalists hold educational programs nightly in the amphitheater. The nearby Albright Visitor Center has a historical display and bookstore.

3 Pebble Creek

 5

Location: In Yellowstone National Park; map WY1, grid a4.

Campsites, facilities: There are 36 RV or tent campsites, which can accommodate a maximum RV length of 25 feet. Wheelchair-accessible restrooms and water are available. Pets must be on a leash, crated, or caged.

Reservations, fees: No reservations are needed; the fee is $10 per night. The stay limit is 14 days. Open early June–end of September.

Directions: From U.S. 212 at Silver Gate, Montana (northeast entrance to Yellowstone National Park), go eight miles south to Pebble Creek Campground.

Contact: National Park Service, P.O. Box 168, Yellowstone National Park, WY 82190; 307/344-7381; website: www.nps.gov/yell.

Trip notes: One of the smallest campgrounds in the park, Pebble Creek is framed on three sides by the rugged Absaroka Mountains. Along Pebble Creek, this campground offers excellent opportunities for wildlife viewing. Pebble Creek trailhead is here.

4 Indian Creek

 5

Location: In Yellowstone National Park; map WY1, grid a1.

Campsites, facilities: There are 75 RV or tent campsites, which can accommodate a maximum RV length of 45 feet. Wheelchair-accessible restrooms and water are available. Pets must be on a leash, crated, or caged.

Reservations, fees: No reservations are needed; the fee is $10 per night. The stay limit is 14 days. Open early June–mid-September.

Directions: From Mammoth Junction in Yellowstone National Park, go seven miles south; the campground is on the west side.

Contact: National Park Service, P.O. Box 168, Yellowstone National Park, WY 82190; 307/344-7381; website: www.nps.gov/yell/

Trip notes: This campground is on a first-come, first-served basis and can fill up early in the day. It sits along Indian Creek, adjacent to a large meadow. Sheepeater Cliff, within walking distance, was home to the Shoshone, the only Native Americans to live year-round in what is now known as Yellowstone National Park.

5 Tower Falls

 5

Location: In Yellowstone National Park; map WY1, grid a3.

Campsites, facilities: There are 32 RV or tent campsites, which can accommodate a maximum RV length of 25 feet. Wheelchair-accessible restrooms, and water are available. The campground is near Tower Lodge, which has a gas station, store, and restaurant. Pets must be on a leash, crated, or caged.

Reservations, fees: No reservations are needed; the fee is $10 per night. The stay limit is 14 days. Open mid-May–end of September.

Directions: From Tower Junction in Yellowstone National Park, go three miles southeast to Tower Falls.

Contact: National Park Service, P.O. Box 168, Yellowstone National Park, WY 82190; 307/344-7381; website: www.nps.gov/yell/

Trip notes: The trailhead to Tower Falls is across the road, and the waterfall is a spectacular 100-foot drop, well worth seeing. There are many hiking trails in the area, and the park office has maps and information on the backcountry.

6 Norris

 5

Location: In Yellowstone National Park; map WY1, grid b2.

Campsites, facilities: There are 114 RV or tent campsites, which can accommodate a maximum RV length of 35 feet. Restrooms, water, and a ranger station are available. Pets must be on a leash, crated, or caged.

Reservations, fees: No reservations are needed; the fee is $12 per night. The stay limit is 14 days. Open mid-May–late September.

Directions: From U.S. 89 at Gardiner, Montana (the north entrance of Yellowstone National Park), go south 25 miles to Norris Junction.

Contact: National Park Service, P.O. Box 168, Yellowstone National Park, WY 82190; 307/344-7381; website: www.nps.gov/yell.

Trip notes: As with all Yellowstone National Park campgrounds, this one fills quickly. This campground is in a wooded area bordering a meadow where you can often find elk. The Norris Geyser Basin is to the west, within hiking or biking distance. The two hiking trails here are worth exploring: one leads to Whiterock Spring, and the other follows Solfatara Creek through a large meadow, then goes uphill to

Ice Lake. The nearby Gibbon River offers good fishing. A fishing permit is required; you can get one at the visitor centers, ranger stations, and general stores. The Museum of the National Park Ranger, just below the campground, has former park rangers willing to share anecdotes and historical facts that add immeasurably to your park experience.

7 Canyon Campground

   5

Location: In Yellowstone National Park; map WY1, grid b3.

Campsites, facilities: There are 280 RV or tent campsites, with picnic tables and grills. Hot showers, laundry facilities, restrooms, a store, and a sanitary disposal station are available. Pets must be on a leash, crated, or caged.

Reservations, fees: Reservations are accepted; the fee is $15 per night. The stay limit is 14 days. Wheelchair-accessible campsites can be reserved ahead. Open June-September.

Directions: From Canyon Junction in Yellowstone National Park, go .25 mile east to the campground.

Contact: AMFAC Parks & Resorts, P.O. Box 165, Yellowstone National Park, WY 82190; 307/344-7311.

Trip notes: This forested campground is one of the most popular in the park, and it fills up early.

8 Madison

     5

Location: In Yellowstone National Park; map WY1, grid b1.

Campsites, facilities: There are 280 RV or tent campsites with picnic tables and grills. Restrooms, water, and a sanitary disposal station are provided. Pets must be on a leash, crated, or caged.

Reservations, fees: Reservations are accepted; the fee is $15 per night. The stay limit is 14 days. Open May–October.

Directions: From Bozeman, go south to West Yellowstone; then go 14 miles east to Madison Junction in Yellowstone National Park.

Contact: AMFAC Parks & Resorts, P.O. Box 165, Yellowstone National Park, WY 82190; 307/344-7311.

Trip notes: The Madison River, below this campground, offers excellent fly-fishing. Fishing permits are required for anyone 16 years or older, and you can get them at visitors centers, ranger stations, and general stores. Elk and bison can often be seen to the west. You can hike or bike to the two-mile Firehole Canyon Drive for a view of scenic waterfalls. There are numerous trails in the area. This campground is less hectic than Grant Village or Canyon, but is still popular and usually filled. Park naturalists give nightly programs in the amphitheater, and the Information Station sells books on the area.

9 Fishing Bridge RV Park

      4

Location: In Yellowstone National Park; map WY1, grid b3.

Campsites, facilities: There are 340 campsites for hard-sided RVs only, some with full hookups. Hot showers, laundry facilities, water, electricity, sewers, a store, and a sanitary disposal station are available. Pets must be on a leash, crated, or caged.

Reservations, fees: Reservations are accepted; the fee is $27 per night. The stay limit is 14 days. Open May–September (possibly later depending on local bear activity; check with local agencies).

Directions: From the east gate of Yellowstone National Park, go 26 miles west, then one mile east of Lake Junction.

Contact: AMFAC Parks & Resorts, P.O. Box 165, Yellowstone National Park, WY 82190; 307/344-7311.

Trip notes: No tents are allowed here, only hard-sided RVs.

10 Bridge Bay

 4

Location: In Yellowstone National Park; map WY1, grid b3.

Campsites, facilities: There are 420 RV or tent campsites, with picnic tables and grills. Restrooms, water, and a sanitary disposal station are available. Pets must be on a leash, crated, or caged.

Reservations, fees: Reservations are accepted; the fee is $15 per night. Open May–September.

Directions: From Lake Junction in Yellowstone National Park, go three miles southwest to Bridge Bay.

Contact: AMFAC Parks and Resorts, P.O. Box 165, Yellowstone National Park, WY 82190; 307/344-7311

Trip notes: This campground is near the shores of Yellowstone Lake, close to the boat ramps and marina. It's popular with those interested in fishing and boating.

11 Pahaska

 6

Location: In Shoshone National Forest; map WY1, grid b5.

Campsites, facilities: There are 24 RV and additional tent campsites with picnic tables, grills, and water available.

Reservations, fees: Open mid-May–the end of September.

Directions: From Cody, drive 49 miles west on U.S. 14/16/20 to the campground.

Contact: Shoshone National Forest, P.O. Box 2140, Cody, WY 82414; 307/527-6241; website: www.fs.fed.us.

Trip notes: You can fish and hike in Shoshone National Forest.

12 Sleeping Giant

 6

Location: In Shoshone National Forest; map WY1, grid b5.

Campsites, facilities: There are six RV campsites for hard-sided camping only; tents are not allowed. Picnic tables, grills, water, and vault toilets are available.

Reservations, fees: No reservations are needed; the fee is $9 per night. The stay limit is 14 days. Open mid-May–the end of October.

Directions: From Cody, go 49 miles west on U.S. 16 to the campground.

Contact: Shoshone National Forest, P.O. Box 2140, Cody, WY 82414; 307/527-6241; website: www.fs.fed.us.

Trip notes: You can fish and hike in Shoshone National Forest.

13 Three Mile

 6

Location: In Shoshone National Forest; map WY1, grid c5.

Campsites, facilities: Hard-sided camping only, no tents allowed. Picnic tables and grills, water, and vault toilets are available.

Reservations, fees: No reservations are needed; the fee is $9 per night. The stay limit is 14 days. Open mid-May–the end of October.

Directions: From Cody, go 50 miles west on U.S. 16 to Three Mile Camp.

Contact: Shoshone National Forest, P.O. Box 2140, Cody, WY 82414; 307/527-6241; website: www.fs.fed.us.

Trip notes: You can fish and hike in Shoshone National Forest.

14 Newton Creek

 5

Location: In Shoshone National Forest; map WY1, grid c5.

Campsites, facilities: There are 31 RV campsites for hard-sided camping only; no tents allowed. There are picnic tables, grills, water, and vault toilets are available.

Reservations, fees: No reservations are needed; the fee is $9 per night. The stay limit is 14 days. Open mid-May–end of September.

Directions: From Cody, go 39 miles west on U.S. 14/16/20. Newton Creek is to the south.

Contact: Shoshone National Forest, P.O. Box 2140, Cody, WY 82414; 307/527-6241; website: www.fs.fed.us.

Trip notes: No tents or pop-up campers—this is bear country, so use appropriate precautions. You can fish and hike in Shoshone National Forest.

15 Eagle Creek

   6

Location: In Shoshone National Forest; map WY1, grid c5.

Campsites, facilities: There are 20 RV or tent campsites with picnic tables and grills. Vault toilets and water are available.

Reservations, fees: No reservations are needed; the fee is $9 per night. The stay limit is 14 days. Open mid-May–the end of October.

Directions: From Cody, go 46 miles west on U.S. 16 to the campground.

Contact: Shoshone National Forest, P.O. Box 2140, Cody, WY 82414; 307/527-6241; website: www.fs.fed.us

Trip notes: This campground is in a well-forested area near the river. You can fish and hike in Shoshone National Forest.

16 Rex Hale

    6

Location: In Shoshone National Forest; map WY1, grid c6.

Campsites, facilities: There are five RV or tent campsites with picnic tables and grills. Water and vault toilets are available.

Reservations, fees: No reservations are needed; the fee is $9 per night. The stay limit is 14 days. Open mid-May–the end of September.

Directions: From Cody, go 37 miles west on U.S. 14. Rex Hale is on the south side of the highway.

Contact: Shoshone National Forest, P.O. Box 2140, Cody, WY 82414; 307/527-6241; website: www.fs.fed.us

Trip notes: You can fish and hike in Shoshone National Forest.

17 Clearwater

   6

Location: West of Cody; map WY1, grid c6.

Campsites, facilities: There are 32 RV campsites and several tent sites. Restrooms, picnic tables, grills, and water are available.

Reservations, fees: No reservations are needed; the fee is $6 per night. Open May 15–September 30.

Directions: From Cody, drive 31 miles west on U.S. 14/16/20 to the campground.

Contact: Shoshone National Forest, Wapiti Ranger District, 203 A Yellowstone Ave., P.O. Box 1840, Cody, WY 82414; 307/527-6921; website: www.fs.fed.us.

Trip notes: Yellowstone National Park is to the west, and you can fish and hike in Shoshone National Forest.

18 Wapiti

   6

Location: West of Cody; map WY1, grid c6.

Campsites, facilities: There are numerous RV campsites, picnic tables, grills, restrooms, and water. No tents.

Reservations, fees: No reservations are needed; the fee is $6 per night. Open May 15–October 30.

Directions: From Cody, go 29 miles west on U.S. 14/16/20 to the campground.

Contact: Shoshone National Forest, Wapiti Ranger District, 203 A Yellowstone Ave., P.O. Box 1840, Cody, WY 82414; 307/527-6921; website: www.fs.fed.us.

Trip notes: Yellowstone National Park is to

the west, and you can fish and hike in Shoshone National Forest.

19 Elk Fork

 6

Location: West of Yellowstone; map WY1, grid c6.

Campsites, facilities: There are 13 RV campsites, and several tent sites. Picnic tables, grills, restrooms, and water are available.

Reservations, fees: No reservations are needed; the fee is $6 per night. Open May 15–October 30.

Directions: From Cody, go 29 miles west on U.S. 14/16/20 to the campground.

Contact: Shoshone National Forest, Wapiti Ranger District, 203 A Yellowstone Ave., P.O. Box 1840, Cody, WY 82414; 307/527-6921; website: www.fs.fed.us.

Trip notes: Yellowstone National Park is to the west, and you can fish and hike in Shoshone National Forest.

20 Big Game

 6

Location: West of Yellowstone; map WY1, grid c7.

Campsites, facilities: There are 16 RV and several tent campsites, some with picnic tables and grills. Restrooms and water are available.

Reservations, fees: No reservations are needed; the fee is $6 per night. Open May 15–September 30.

Directions: From Cody, go 28 miles west on U.S. 14/16/20 to the campground.

Contact: Shoshone National Forest, Wapiti Ranger District, 203 A Yellowstone Ave., P.O. Box 1840, Cody, WY 82414; 307/527-6921; website: www.fs.fed.us.

Trip notes: Yellowstone National Park is to the west, and you can fish and hike in Shoshone National Forest.

21 Hitching Post Campground

 6

Location: West of Yellowstone; map WY1, grid b7.

Campsites, facilities: There are 100 RV campsites and several tent sites. Hookups, restrooms, showers, picnic tables, grills, water, and a sanitary disposal facility are available.

Reservations, fees: No reservations are needed; the fee is $7–13 per night. Open April 1–October 30.

Directions: From Cody, go 20 miles west on U.S. 14/16/20 to North Fork Road and the campground.

Contact: Hitching Post Campground; 307/587-4149.

Trip notes: By Wapiti, west of Yellowstone National Park. You can fish and hike in Shoshone National Forest.

22 Buffalo Bill State Park

 6

Location: West of Yellowstone; map WY1, grid c7.

Campsites, facilities: There are 35 RV or tent campsites, some with picnic tables and grills. Pull-through sites, restrooms, water, and a sanitary disposal facility are available.

Reservations, fees: No reservations are needed; the fee is $6–9 per night. Open May 1–October 1.

Directions: From Cody, go nine miles west on U.S. 14/16/20 to the campground.

Contact: Buffalo Bill State Park, North Fork Campground, 47 Lakeside Rd.; 307/587-9227, fax 307/587-4990; email: rlives@missc.state .wy.us.

Trip notes: Cody was named for Buffalo Bill Cody over a hundred years ago. There are a golf course, two swimming pools, shopping, movies, and restaurants here. Yellowstone National Park is to the west. There are five museums in the area: Buffalo Bill Historical

Center, Whitney Gallery of Art, Plains Indian Museum, Cody Firearms Museum, and Old Trail Town Museum. You can float the Shoshone River Canyon. This area is popular with windsurfers.

23 7K Motel and RV Park

 5

Location: In Cody; map WY1, grid c8.

Campsites, facilities: There are 49 RV and tent campsites, some with picnic tables and grills. Hookups, pull-through sites, restrooms, showers, laundry facilities, water, swimming pool, and a sanitary disposal facility are available. Pets are allowed on leashes.

Reservations, fees: No reservations are needed; the fee is $12 and up per night. Open May 1–September 1.

Directions: From Powell, go south on U.S. 14A to Cody; take U.S. 14/16/20 to the west end of town; the campground is on the left.

Contact: 7K Motel & RV Park, 232 W. Yellowstone Ave., Cody, WY 82414; 307/587-5890 or 800/223-9204.

Trip notes: Cody was named for Buffalo Bill Cody over a hundred years ago. There are a golf course, two swimming pools, shopping, movies, and restaurants here. Yellowstone National Park is to the west. There are five museums in the area: Buffalo Bill Historical Center, Whitney Gallery of Art, Plains Indian Museum, Cody Firearms Museum, and Old Trail Town Museum. You can float the Shoshone River Canyon.

24 Absaroka Bay RV Park

 5

Location: In Cody; map WY1, grid c8.

Campsites, facilities: There are 114 RV or tent campsites, some with picnic tables and grills. Hookups, pull-through sites, restrooms, showers, laundry facilities, water, and a sanitary disposal facility are available.

Reservations, fees: No reservations are needed; the fee is $10 and up per night. Open May 15–September 15.

Directions: On U.S. 14/16/20 westbound at Cody, the campground is on the right as you enter town.

Contact: Absaroka Bay RV Park, 2001 Hwy. 14-16-20, Cody, WY 82414; 307/527-7440 or 800/557-7440.

Trip notes: Cody was named for Buffalo Bill Cody over a hundred years ago. A golf course, two swimming pools, shopping, movies, and restaurants are here. Yellowstone National Park is to the west. There are five museums in the area: Buffalo Bill Historical Center, Whitney Gallery of Art, Plains Indian Museum, Cody Firearms Museum, and Old Trail Town Museum. You can float the Shoshone River Canyon.

25 Buffalo Bill Village

 5

Location: In Cody; map WY1, grid c8.

Campsites, facilities: There are numerous RV or tent campsites, some with picnic tables and grills. Hookups and water are available.

Reservations, fees: No reservations are needed; the fee is $15 per night. Open May 1–September 30.

Directions: In Cody westbound on U.S. 14/16/20 toward the west side of Cody, look for the campground where the road takes a 90-degree left.

Contact: Buffalo Bill Village, 1701 Sheridan Ave., Cody, WY 82414-3821; 307/587-5544.

Trip notes: Cody was named for Buffalo Bill Cody over 100 years ago. There are a golf course, two swimming pools, shopping, movies, and restaurants here. Yellowstone National Park is to the west. There are five museums in the area: Buffalo Bill Historical Center, Whitney Gallery of Art, Plains Indian Museum, Cody Firearms Museum, and Old Trail Town Museum. You can float the Shoshone River Canyon.

26 Camp Cody RV Park

 5

Location: In Cody; map WY1, grid c8.

Campsites, facilities: There are 63 RV or tent campsites, some with picnic tables and grills. Pull-through sites, restrooms, showers, laundry facilities, swimming pool, water, and a sanitary disposal facility are available.

Reservations, fees: No reservations are needed; the fee is $18 and up per night. Open year-round.

Directions: Drive west on U.S. 14/16/20 to Cody; the campground is to the right after you pass the Buffalo Bill Historical Center.

Contact: Camp Cody RV Park, 415 Yellowstone Ave., Cody, WY 82414; 307/587-9730.

Trip notes: Cody was named for Buffalo Bill Cody over a hundred years ago. There are a golf course, two swimming pools, shopping, movies, and restaurants here. Yellowstone National Park is to the west. There are five museums in the area: Buffalo Bill Historical Center, Whitney Gallery of Art, Plains Indian Museum, Cody Firearms Museum, and Old Trail Town Museum. You can float the Shoshone River Canyon.

27 Mountain View Lodge

 5

Location: In Cody; map WY1, grid c8.

Campsites, facilities: There are 14 RV campsites and several tent sites. Hookups, pull-through sites, restrooms, showers, laundry facilities, picnic tables, grills, water, and a sanitary disposal station are here.

Reservations, fees: No reservations are needed; the fee is $10–16 per night. Open May 1–September 30.

Directions: From Greybull, go west on U.S. 14/16/20 to Cody; the campground is on North Fork Highway (U.S. 14).

Contact: Mountain View Lodge, 2776 N. Fork Hwy., Cody, WY 82414; 9307) 587-2081.

Trip notes: Cody was named for Buffalo Bill

Cody over a hundred years ago. There are a golf course, two swimming pools, shopping, movies, and restaurants here. Yellowstone National Park is to the west. There are five museums in the area: Buffalo Bill Historical Center, Whitney Gallery of Art, Plains Indian Museum, Cody Firearms Museum, and Old Trail Town Museum. You can float the Shoshone River Canyon.

28 Cody KOA

 5

Location: In Cody; map WY1, grid c8.

Campsites, facilities: There are 190 RV or tent campsites, some with hookups, pull-throughs, picnic tables, and grills. Restrooms, showers, a swimming pool, water, game room, hot tub, playground, and a sanitary disposal facility are available. There are on-site trail rides.

Reservations, fees: No reservations are needed; the fee is $18 and up per night. Open May 1–October 1.

Directions: In Cody on U.S. 14/16/20 westbound, the campground is on the right as you enter town.

Contact: Cody KOA, 5561 Greybull Hwy., Cody, WY 82414; 587-2369, 800/932-5267, fax 307/587-8013; email: codykoa@gocampingamerica .com.

Trip notes: Cody was named for Buffalo Bill Cody over a hundred years ago. There are a golf course, two swimming pools, shopping, movies, and restaurants here. Yellowstone National Park is to the west. There are five museums in the area: Buffalo Bill Historical Center, Whitney Gallery of Art, Plains Indian Museum, Cody Firearms Museum, and Old Trail Town Museum. You can float the Shoshone River Canyon.

29 Gateway Campground

 5

Location: In Cody; map WY1, grid c8.

Campsites, facilities: There are 74 RV

campsites, and several tent sites. Hookups, restrooms, showers, picnic tables, grills, and water are available.

Reservations, fees: No reservations are needed; the fee is $12 per night. Open April 1–October 1.

Directions: From Powell, go south on U.S. 14A to Cody; take U.S. 14/16/20 toward the west end of town; the campground is on the right.

Contact: Gateway Campground, 203 Yellowstone Ave., P.O. Box 2348, Cody, WY 82414; 307/587-2561; email: gateway@wyoming.com.

Trip notes: Cody was named for Buffalo Bill Cody over a hundred years ago. There are a golf course, two swimming pools, shopping, movies, and restaurants here. Yellowstone National Park is to the west. There are five museums in the area: Buffalo Bill Historical Center, Whitney Gallery of Art, Plains Indian Museum, Cody Firearms Museum, and Old Trail Town Museum. You can float the Shoshone River Canyon.

Ponderosa Campground
 5

Location: In Cody; map WY1, grid c8.

Campsites, facilities: There are 185 RV or tent campsites, some with hookups and pull-throughs. Restrooms, showers, laundry facilities, picnic tables, grills, game room, water, and a sanitary disposal station are available. Pets are allowed on leashes.

Reservations, fees: No reservations are needed; the fee is $15 and up per night. Open May 1–October 15.

Directions: From Powell, go south on U.S. 14A to Cody, take U.S. 14/16/20 and the campground is on the right after you pass the Buffalo Bill Historical Center.

Contact: Ponderosa Campground, 1815 8th St., Yellowstone Hwy., Cody, WY 82414; 307/587-9203.

Trip notes: Cody was named for Buffalo Bill Cody over a hundred years ago. There are a

golf course, two swimming pools, shopping, movies, and restaurants here. Yellowstone National Park is to the west. There are five museums in the area: Buffalo Bill Historical Center, Whitney Gallery of Art, Plains Indian Museum, Cody Firearms Museum, and Old Trail Town Museum. You can float the Shoshone River Canyon.

River's View RV Park
 5

Location: In Cody; map WY1, grid c8.

Campsites, facilities: There are five RV or tent campsites. Hookups, picnic tables, grills, water, and a sanitary disposal facility are available. Pets are allowed on leashes.

Reservations, fees: No reservations are needed; the fee is $10 and up per night. Open year-round.

Directions: This campground is in the town of Cody. From Powell, go south on U.S. 14A to Cody; take U.S. 14/16/20 toward the west end of town and the campground.

Contact: River's View RV Park, 109 W. Yellowstone Ave., Cody, WY 82414; 307/587-6074, 800/377-7255, fax 307/587-8644; email: cBaldwin @wyoming.com.

Trip notes: Cody was named for Buffalo Bill Cody over a hundred years ago. There are a golf course, two swimming pools, shopping, movies, and restaurants here. Yellowstone National Park is to the west. There are five museums in the area: Buffalo Bill Historical Center, Whitney Gallery of Art, Plains Indian Museum, Cody Firearms Museum, and Old Trail Town Museum. You can float the Shoshone River Canyon.

Yellowstone Valley RV Park
 5

Location: In Cody; map WY1, grid c8.

Campsites, facilities: There are 55 RV or tent campsites. Hookups, showers, laundry facilities, picnic tables, grills, water, restrooms, and a sanitary disposal station are available.

Reservations, fees: No reservations are needed; the fee is $10 and up per night. Open May 1–September 30.

Directions: From Powell, go south on U.S. 14A to Cody, take U.S. 14/16/20 toward the west end of town and the campground.

Contact: Yellowstone Valley RV Park, 3324 Yellowstone Park Hwy., Cody, WY 82414; 307/587-3961, 888/705-7703, fax 307/587-4656.

Trip notes: Cody was named for Buffalo Bill Cody over a hundred years ago. There are a golf course, two swimming pools, shopping, movies, and restaurants here. Yellowstone National Park is to the west. There are five museums in the area: Buffalo Bill Historical Center, Whitney Gallery of Art, Plains Indian Museum, Cody Firearms Museum, and Old Trail Town Museum. You can float the Shoshone River Canyon.

33 Grant Village

 4

Location: In Yellowstone National Park; map WY1, grid c2.

Campsites, facilities: There are 425 RV or tent campsites, with picnic tables and grills. Restrooms, hot showers, laundry facilities, water, and sanitary disposal station are available. A restaurant, visitor center, store, and post office are nearby. Pets must be on a leash, crated, or caged.

Reservations, fees: Reservations are accepted; the fee is $15 per night. Wheelchair-accessible campsites should be reserved. The stay limit is 14 days. Open June–October.

Directions: From West Thumb Junction in Yellowstone National Park, go two miles south.

Contact: AMFAC Parks & Resorts, P.O. Box 165, Yellowstone National Park, WY 82190; 307/344-7311.

Trip notes: This campground is the only one on Yellowstone Lake and is close to the boat ramp, one of only three ramps in the park. A

boating permit is required.

34 Deer Creek

 6

Location: South of Cody; map WY1, grid c7.

Campsites, facilities: There are seven RV campsites and several tent sites with picnic tables and grills.

Reservations, fees: No reservations are needed; the fee is $7 per night. Open year-round.

Directions: From Cody, go 47 miles southwest on Highway 291 to the campground.

Contact: Shoshone National Forest, Wapiti Ranger District, 203 A Yellowstone Ave., P.O. Box 1840, Cody, WY 82414; 307/527-6921; website: www.fs.fed.us.

Trip notes: You can fish and hike in Shoshone National Forest.

35 Lewis Lake

 5

Location: In Yellowstone National Park; map WY1, grid d2.

Campsites, facilities: There are 85 RV or tent campsites, which can accommodate a maximum RV length of 45 feet. Wheelchair-accessible restrooms, water, and a ranger station are available. The boat ramp requires only two-wheel drive with trailers. Pets must be on a leash, crated, or caged.

Reservations, fees: No reservations are needed; the fee is $10 per night. The stay limit is 14 days. Open early June–October.

Directions: From West Thumb Junction in Yellowstone National Park, go 10 miles south to Lewis Lake. The campground is on the west side.

Contact: National Park Service, P.O. Box 168, Yellowstone National Park, WY 82190; 307/344-7381; website: www.nps.gov/yell.

Trip notes: This campground is close to the boat ramp, one of only three areas in the park for boat launching. Due to the lake's high altitude, snow may linger into the season. A boating permit is required.

36 Flagg Ranch Village

 6

Location: South entrance to Yellowstone National Park; map WY1, grid d2.

Campsites, facilities: There are 170 RV or tent campsites, some with hookups, all with picnic tables and grills. There are pull-throughs, a sanitary disposal station, restrooms, hot showers, laundry facilities, and water. A restaurant, gas station, and store are in the area.

Reservations, fees: Reservations are accepted; the fee is $9–19 per night (Yellowstone National Park entrance fees apply). Open mid-May–mid-October.

Directions: From the south entrance of Yellowstone National Park, go two miles south on U.S. 89/287 to the campground.

Contact: Flagg Ranch Village, P.O. Box 187, Moran Junction, WY 83013; 800/443-2311 or 307/543-2861 for reservations; fax 307/543-2356; email:info@flaggranch.com.

Trip notes: This campground is on the northern end of John D. Rockefeller, Jr. Memorial Parkway, land that joins Yellowstone and Grand Teton National Parks. Float trips and fly-fishing trips can be arranged through local contacts.

37 Jack Creek

 9

Location: In Shoshone National Forest; map WY1, grid d7.

Campsites, facilities: There are seven RV or tent campsites, and a vault toilet is available.

Reservations, fees: No reservations are needed; no fee is required. Open year-round, depending on weather. The stay limit is 14 days.

Directions: From Cody, go south 31 miles on Highway 120 to Meeteetse. From Meeteetse, go 11 miles west on Highway 290, then 15.3 miles west on Forest Service Road 208 to the campground.

Contact: Shoshone National Forest, Wapiti Ranger District, 203 A Yellowstone Ave., P.O. Box 1840, Cody, WY 82414; 307/527-6921; website: www.fs.fed.us.

Trip notes: This remote campground is along Jack Creek and the Greybull River and near hiking trails in a beautiful location.

38 Lizard Creek

 7

Location: In Grand Teton National Park; map WY1, grid d2.

Campsites, facilities: There are 60 RV or tent campsites with picnic tables and grills. Restrooms, water, and a sanitary disposal station are available.

Reservations, fees: No reservations are accepted, but you can call 307/739-3603 for a recorded message about campsite status; the fee is $12 per night. Open May–mid-October. The stay limit is 14 days.

Directions: From Jackson, go north on U.S. 26/89/191 to Moran Junction. From Moran Junction, go 18 miles north on U.S. 89 to Jackson Lake.

Contact: Chief Ranger's Office, Grand Teton National Park, P.O. Box 170, Moose, WY 83012; 307/739-3300.

Trip notes: This campground is at the north end of the park in a forested area. Being a little off the well-traveled path, this campground sometimes has sites available when others have filled. Some of the sites are walk-in only. You can fish, boat, water-ski, swim, and canoe on Jackson Lake and hike in the area around the lake. The campgrounds in Grand Teton National Park fill early, so plan accordingly.

39 Colter Bay RV Park

 6

Location: In Grand Teton National Park; map WY1, grid e2.

Campsites, facilities: There are 112 RV sites and some tent sites with picnic tables and grills. Restrooms, hot showers, laundry facilities, water, and a sanitary disposal station available. There are also a restaurant, store, rental service, and visitor center nearby.

Reservations, fees: Reservations are accepted, but have to be made well in advance; the fee is $19–25 per night. Open mid-May–late September.

Directions: From Jackson, go north on U.S. 26/89/191 to Moran Junction. From Moran Junction, go 10 miles northwest on U.S. 89/287; the campground is on the east side of Jackson Lake.

Contact: Colter Bay RV Park, P.O. Box 240, Moran, WY 83013; 800/628-9988, 307/543-3100, or fax 307/543-3143.

Trip notes: White-water enthusiasts enjoy the nearby Snake River, and the best way for a beginner to get their feet wet is by contacting one of the numerous white-water rafting guides to arrange a trip. You can fish, boat, water-ski, swim, and canoe on Jackson Lake and hike in the area around the lake. The campgrounds in Grand Teton National Park fill early, so plan accordingly.

40 Colter Bay

 6

Location: In Grand Teton National Park; map WY1, grid e2.

Campsites, facilities: There are 310 RV or tent campsites, some with hookups, picnic tables, and grills. Restrooms, hot showers, laundry facilities, water, a sanitary disposal station, and a marina are available. Some campsites are walk-in only, some are tent only (though you can drive to them).

Reservations, fees: No reservations are needed (but telephone 307/739-3603 for a recorded message on the campground's current status); the fee is $12 per night. Open mid-May–September. The stay limit is 14 days.

Directions: From Jackson go 12 miles north to Moran, then eight miles northwest of Moran to the campground.

Contact: Chief Ranger's Office, Grand Teton National Park, P.O. Box 170, Moose, WY 83012; 307/739-3300.

Trip notes: This campground is on Jackson Lake where you can fish, boat, water-ski, or swim. The campgrounds in Grand Teton National Park fill up early, so plan accordingly. Nearby Hermitage Point trailhead offers several hiking options from one to nine miles long: Swan Lake and Heron Pond lead to good mountain views, and Lakeshore Trail is a moderate two-mile loop.

41 Brown Mountain

 7

Location: In Shoshone National Forest; map WY1, grid e8.

Campsites, facilities: There are six RV or tent campsites with picnic tables and grills. Vault toilets are available.

Reservations, fees: No reservations are needed; no fee is required. Open June–September 15. The stay limit is 14 days.

Directions: From Cody, go south 31 miles on Highway 120 to Meeteetse. From Meeteetse, go six miles southwest on Highway 290, then 19 miles south on Wood River Road (County Road 4DT) to the campground.

Contact: Shoshone National Forest, Wapiti Ranger District, 203 A Yellowstone Ave., P.O. Box 1840, Cody, WY 82414; 307/527-6921; website: www.fs.fed.us.

Trip notes: The campground is on the banks of Wood River not far from Kirwin Trailhead.

42 Wood River

 8

Location: In Shoshone National Forest; map WY1, grid e8.

Campsites, facilities: There are five RV or tent campsites with picnic tables and grills. Vault toilets are available.

Reservations, fees: No reservations are needed; no fee is required. Open June 1–November 15. The stay limit is 14 days.

Directions: From Cody, go south 31 miles on Highway 120 to Meeteetse. From Meeteetse, go six miles southwest on Highway 290, then 15.8 miles southwest on Wood River Road (County Road 4DT), then three miles west on Forest Service Road 200 to the campground.

Contact: Shoshone National Forest, Wapiti Ranger District, 203 A Yellowstone Ave., P.O. Box 1840, Cody, WY 82414; 307/527-6921; website: www.fs.fed.us.

Trip notes: This campground is on the banks of the Wood River, where you can fish for brook and cutthroat trout.

43 Signal Mountain

 6

Location: In Grand Teton National Park; map WY1, grid e2.

Campsites, facilities: There are 80 RV or tent campsites with picnic tables and grills. Restrooms, water, and a sanitary disposal station available. A boat launch is provided.

Reservations, fees: No reservations are needed, but call 307/739-3603 for a recorded message on campground status; the fee is $12 per night. Open mid-May–September. The stay limit is 14 days.

Directions: From Jackson, go north on U.S. 26/89/191 to Moran Junction, then west five miles to Moran. From Moran, go five miles northwest on U.S. 89/287, then two miles southwest on Teton Park Road to the campground.

Contact: Chief Ranger's Office, Grand Teton National Park, P.O. Box 170, Moose, Wyoming, 83012; 307/739-3300.

Trip notes: This campground overlooks Mount Moran and Jackson Lake, and fills up early, so plan accordingly. The road two miles south of Jackson Lake Junction is narrow and steep, but you can see some outstanding views. You can fish, boat, water-ski, swim, and canoe on Jackson Lake and hike in the area around the lake.

44 Grand Teton Park RV Resort

 6

Location: One mile east of Grand Teton National Park; map WY1, grid e3.

Campsites, facilities: There are 120 RV or tent campsites, some with hookups, picnic tables, and grills. Restrooms, hot showers, laundry facilities, water, propane, and a sanitary disposal station available. Pets are allowed on leashes.

Reservations, fees: Reservations are accepted; the fee is $20–30 per night. Open all year.

Directions: From Jackson, go north on U.S. 26/89/191 to Moran Junction. From Moran Junction, go six miles east on U.S. 287/26 to the campground.

Contact: Grand Teton Park RV Resort, P.O. Box 92, Moran, WY 83013; 307/733-1980 or 800/563-6469, fax 307/543-0927; website: www.yellowstonerv.com.

Trip notes: This campground is adjacent to the Willow Wildlife Habitat Area, near the entrance to Grand Teton and Yellowstone National Parks.

45 Hatchet

 6

Location: Bridger-Teton National Forest; map WY1, grid e3.

Campsites, facilities: There are nine RV or tent sites with picnic tables and grills. Vault toilets and water are available.

Reservations, fees: No reservations are needed; the fee is $10 per night. Open June 1–early September. The stay limit is 16 days.

Directions: From Jackson, go north on U.S. 26/89/191 to Moran Junction. From Moran Junction, go eight miles east on U.S. 26/287 to the campground.

Contact: Jackson Ranger District, 340 N. Cache, P.O. Box 1888, Jackson, WY 83001; 307/739-5570.

Trip notes: This campground is adjacent to the Willow Wildlife Habitat Area near the entrance to Grand Teton and Yellowstone National Parks.

46 Double Cabin
 7

Location: In Shoshone National Forest; map WY1, grid e6.

Campsites, facilities: There are 15 RV campsites, plus tent sites, with picnic tables and grills. Vault toilets and water are available.

Reservations, fees: No reservations are needed; the fee is $6 per night. Open June 1–September 30. The stay limit is 14 days.

Directions: From Lander, go north 76 miles on U.S. 287 to Dubois. From Dubois, go 29 miles north on Horse Creek Road-Wiggins Fork Road (paved and gravel) and the campground.

Contact: Shoshone National Forest, Wind River District, 203A Yellowstone Ave., P.O. Box 1840, Cody, WY 82414; 307/527-6921 or 307/455-2466 (Dubois).

Trip notes: Near the boundary of the Washakie Wilderness. Trailheads for Cougar Pass, Indian Point, Wiggins Fork, and Frontier Creek. You can fish in the Wiggins Fork River. There is petrified wood in the area. You can look, but it is illegal to remove it.

47 Brooks Lake
 7

Location: In Shoshone National Forest; map WY1, grid e5.

Campsites, facilities: There are 13 RV or tent sites with picnic tables and grills. Vault toilets, water, and a boat ramp are available.

Reservations, fees: No reservations are needed; the fee is $9 per night. Open June 20–September 30.

Directions: From Lander, go north 76 miles on U.S. 287 to Dubois. From Dubois, go 23 miles west on U.S. 287/26 to Brooks Lake Road (Forest Road 515), then five miles north to the campground.

Contact: Wind River District, 1403 W. Ramshorn, P.O. Box 186, Dubois, WY 82513; 307/455-2466.

Trip notes: This campground is close to Brooks Lake, where you can boat, and fish for rainbow and brook trout.

48 Pinnacles
 8

Location: In Shoshone National Forest; map WY1, grid e5.

Campsites, facilities: There are 21 RV or tent campsites with picnic tables and grills. Vault toilets and water are available.

Reservations, fees: No reservations are needed; the fee is $9 per night. Open June 20–September 3. The stay limit is 14 days.

Directions: From Lander, go north 76 miles on U.S. 287 to Dubois. From Dubois, go 23 miles west on U.S. 26/287, then five miles on Forest Service Road 515 (Brooks Lake Road) to the campground.

Contact: Forest Service, Wind River District, 1403 W. Ramshorn, P.O. Box 186, Dubois, WY 82513; 307/455-2466.

Trip notes: This campground is near Brooks Lake and offers excellent views of the Pinnacles and some of the most beautiful wilderness and mountain scenery in Wyoming. Be aware that this is bear country, so be sure to take all necessary precautions.

49 Reunion Flat Group Area

   7

Location: In Targhee National Forest; map WY1, grid e1.

Campsites, facilities: There are two RV or tent campsites. Drinking water and vault toilets are available. Pets are allowed on leashes.

Reservations, fees: Reservations are accepted; contact National Recreation Reservation Service at 877/444-6777 (a reservation fee applies), or check its website: www.reserveusa.com; the fee is $6 per night. Open June–September.

Directions: From Driggs, go six miles northeast on County Road 009, then three miles east on Forest Road 009 to the campground.

Contact: Teton Basin Ranger District, P.O. Box 777, Driggs, ID 83422; 208/354-3421, 208/354-2312, or 208/354-2313, fax 208/354-8505.

Trip notes: You can fish and hike nearby.

50 Teton Canyon

    8

Location: In Targhee National Forest; map WY1, grid f1.

Campsites, facilities: There are 20 RV or tent campsites, which can accommodate RVs up to 24 feet in length. Pull-through sites, wheelchair-accessible restrooms, drinking water, and a sanitary disposal station are available. Pets are allowed on leashes.

Reservations, fees: No reservations are needed; the fee is $8 per night. Open May 15–September 15. The stay limit is 14 days.

Directions: From Driggs, Idaho, go six miles northeast on County Road 009, then 4.5 miles east on Forest Road 009 to the campground.

Contact: Teton Basin Ranger District, P.O. Box 777, Driggs, ID 83422; 208/354-2312.

Trip notes: This campground is near Teton Creek and Jedidiah Smith Wilderness. Fishing

and hiking opportunities abound.

51 Jenny Lake

  7

Location: Grand Teton National Forest; map WY1, grid f1.

Campsites, facilities: There are 48 campsites with picnic tables and grills for tents only. No RVs are allowed. Restrooms, water, and a visitor center are available.

Reservations, fees: No reservations are needed; telephone 307/739-3603 for a recorded message on campground status; the fee is $12 per night. Open mid-May–September. The stay limit is seven days.

Directions: From Moose Junction, go eight miles north on Teton Park Road to the campground.

Contact: Chief Ranger's Office, Grand Teton National Park, P.O. Drawer 170, Moose, WY 83012-0170; 307/739-3600.

Trip notes: This campground usually fills by 8 A.M. in the summer because it's the smallest and closet to the Tetons. If you have more than one day in the park, you can secure a prized campsite here using a little strategy. Stay the first night in a private campground, then leave bright and early to arrive at Jenny Lake by 7 A.M. and claim a soon-to-be-vacated site. You can fish in Jenny Lake for lake and cutthroat trout. Lupine Meadows Trailhead is south of Jenny Lake. Hidden Falls and Inspiration Point Trails can be reached in the summer by a boat ride across the lake. This can be an area of bear activity; check with the Ranger's Office for the latest information.

52 Falls

  7

Location: In Shoshone National Forest; map WY1, grid f5.

Campsites, facilities: There are 44 RV or tent campsites with picnic tables and grills. Vault toilets and water are available.

Reservations, fees: No reservations are needed; the fee is $9 per night. Open from June 1–October 30. The stay limit is 14 days.

Directions: From Lander, go north 76 miles on U.S. 287 to Dubois. From Dubois, go 25 miles west on U.S. 287 to the campground.

Contact: Forest Service, Wind River District, 1403 W. Ramshorn, P.O. Box 186, Dubois, WY 82513; 307/455-2466.

Trip notes: There is a trailhead nearby for a hike to Brooks Lake Creek Falls. Be aware that this is bear country; be sure to take all necessary precautions.

53 Horse Creek

     7

Location: In Shoshone National Forest; map WY1, grid f6.

Campsites, facilities: There are nine RV campsites, plus tent sites, with picnic tables and grills. Vault toilets and water are available.

Reservations, fees: No reservations are needed; the fee is $6 per night. Open June 1–October 30. The stay limit is 14 days.

Directions: From Lander, go north 76 miles on U.S. 287 to Dubois. From Dubois, go north on Horse Creek Road (County Road 285, which is paved or graveled) 12 miles to the campground.

Contact: Shoshone National Forest, Wind River District, 1403 W. Ramshorn, P.O. Box 186, Dubois, WY 82513; 307/455-2466; website: www.fs.fed.us.

Trip notes: This campground is along Horse Creek, which offers good stream fishing.

54 Gros Ventre

 6

Location: Grand Teton National Forest; map WY1, grid f2.

Campsites, facilities: There are 360 RV and tent campsites with picnic tables and grills.

Restrooms, vault toilets, water, and a sanitary disposal station are available.

Reservations, fees: No reservations are needed, but call 307/739-3603 for a recorded message on campground status; the fee is $12 per night. Open May–early October. The stay limit is 17 days.

Directions: From Jackson, go north on U.S. 26/89/191 to Gros Ventre Junction and turn east toward Kelly. The campground is two miles southwest of Kelly on Gros Ventre Road.

Contact: Chief Ranger's Office, Grand Teton National Park, P.O. Drawer 170, Moose, WY 83012-0170; 307/739-3600.

Trip notes: Slide Lake was formed by a major landslide in 1925 in the Gros Ventre Canyon. You can fish in the Gros Ventre River for cutthroat, rainbow, and whitefish. There are hiking trails in the area.

55 Atherton Creek

 7

Location: Bridger-Teton National Forest; map WY1, grid f3.

Campsites, facilities: There are 14 RV or tent sites with picnic tables and grills. Vault toilets, water, and a boat ramp are provided.

Reservations, fees: No reservations are needed; the fee is $10 per night. Open June–early September. The stay limit is 16 days.

Directions: From Jackson, go seven miles north on U.S. 26/89 to Gros Ventre Junction, then southeast eight miles, through Kelly, to Gros Ventre Road. Take this road east for six miles to the campground.

Contact: Jackson Ranger District, 340 N. Cache, P.O. Box 1888, Jackson, WY 83001; 307/739-5570.

Trip notes: This campground is on Lower Slide Lake, which was created by a massive landslide in 1925, in the Gros Ventre Slide geological area.

56 Crystal Creek

   7

Location: Bridger-Teton National Forest; map WY1, grid f3.

Campsites, facilities: There are six RV or tent campsites with picnic tables and grills. Vault toilets and water are available.

Reservations, fees: No reservations are needed; the fee is $10 per night. Open June–early September. The stay limit is 16 days.

Directions: From Jackson, go seven miles north on U.S. 26/89 to Gros Ventre Junction, then northeast eight miles, through the town of Kelly, to Gros Ventre Road. Take this road east for 12 miles to the campground.

Contact: Jackson Ranger District, 340 N. Cache, P.O. Box 1888, Jackson, WY 83001; 307/739-5570.

Trip notes: This campground is on the Gros Ventre River, above Slide Lake. Slide Lake was formed by a major landslide in 1925 in the Gros Ventre Canyon. You can fish in the Gros Ventre River for cutthroat, rainbow, and whitefish. There are hiking trails in the area.

57 Trail Creek

    5

Location: In Targhee National Forest; map WY1, grid f1.

Campsites, facilities: There are 11 RV or tent campsites, which can accommodate RVs up to 20 feet in length, and pull-through sites. Vault toilets and drinking water are available. Pets are allowed on leashes.

Reservations, fees: No reservations are needed; the fee is $6 per night. Open June 15–September 15. The stay limit is 14 days.

Directions: From Jackson, go west on Highway 22, over Teton Pass to the camp (nearly to Idaho/Wyoming state line).

Contact: Teton Basin Ranger District, P.O. Box 777, Driggs, ID 83422; 208/354-2312.

Trip notes: This campground is near Trail Creek, where you can fish and hike.

58 Curtis Canyon

  5

Location: Bridger-Teton National Forest; map WY1, grid f2.

Campsites, facilities: There are 12 RV and tent campsites with picnic tables and grills. Vault toilets are available.

Reservations, fees: No reservations are needed; the fee is $10 per night. Open June 5–September 10. The stay limit is 16 days.

Directions: From Jackson, go six miles east from the National Elk Refuge Entrance (on Broadway Street one mile east of the town square) to Curtis Canyon (follow the signs). The campground is three miles east of Curtis Canyon.

Contact: Jackson Ranger District, 340 N. Cache, P.O. Box 1888, Jackson, WY 83001; 307/739-5570, 307/739-5400.

Trip notes: This campground is near the National Elk Refuge, a 25,000-acre elk winter feeding ground. Flat Creek is a popular spot for waterfowl, including trumpeter swans, and offers excellent viewing opportunities.

59 Teton Village KOA

     4

Location: South of Grand Teton National Park; map WY1, grid f1.

Campsites, facilities: There are 150 RV or tent campsites, some with hookups and pull-throughs. Picnic tables, grills, restrooms, hot showers, laundry facilities, water, and a sanitary disposal station are available, and a game room and playground are on-site.

Reservations, fees: Reservations are accepted; the fee is $26–34 per night. Open May–mid-October.

Directions: From Jackson, go five miles west on Highway 22/390 to the campground.

Contact: Teton Village KOA, P.O. Box 38, 2780 N. Moose-Wilson Rd., Teton Village, WY 83025; 307/733-5254 or (800) KOA-9043, fax 307/739-1298.

Trip notes: Jackson has excellent shopping, museums, and art galleries. The nearby Snake River has challenging white-water rafting and float trips. The many outfitters offer daily and overnight trips. You can fish the Snake River for cutthroat, brook, and lake trout. Mountain biking is popular here, and guided tours are available. You can go horseback riding nearby.

60 Circle-Up Camper Court

 4

Location: Center of Dubois, map WY1, grid f6.

Campsites, facilities: There are 100 RV or tent campsites, with picnic tables and grills, some with pull-throughs and hookups. Showers, restrooms, laundry facilities, water, and a sanitary disposal station are available. A pool and game room are provided.

Reservations, fees: Reservations are accepted; the fee is $18.50–22.50 per night. Open year-round.

Directions: From Lander, go north 76 miles on U.S. 287 to Dubois, go through town, turn right before the Conoco service station (the only one in town); the campground is one block off Main Street.

Contact: Circle-Up Camper Court, P.O. Box 1520, Dubois, WY 82513; 307/455-2238.

Trip notes: Variegated red rocks, called the badlands, are found all around Dubois. The National Bighorn Sheep Interpretive Center offers informative facts about bighorn sheep, hands-on exhibits, and interpretive scenes. You can golf at nine-hole Antelope Golf Course. On Trail Lake Road you can see ancient petroglyphs on the rocks near Trail Lake. You can mountain bike through Whiskey Basin, around Table Mountain, and along other roads and trails.

61 Riverside Campground

 5

Location: East of Dubois; map WY1, grid g6.

Campsites, facilities: There are 40 RV or tent campsites, some with hookups, and pull-throughs. Showers, picnic tables, grills, water, restrooms, and a sanitary disposal station are available.

Reservations, fees: Reservations are accepted; the fee is $15–20 per night. Open May 1–October 1.

Directions: From Lander, go north 76 miles on U.S. 26/287 to Dubois. The campground is two miles east of Dubois.

Contact: Riverside Campground, P.O. Box 642, 5810 U.S. 26, Dubois, WY 82513; 307/455-2337.

Trip notes: This is a quiet, shady campground with private riverbank fishing access on Wind River. You can golf at the nine-hole Antelope Golf Course.

62 Elk Country Inn & RV Park

 5

Location: In downtown Jackson; map WY1, grid g2.

Campsites, facilities: There are 10 RV campsites, some with hookups, picnic tables, and grills. No tents are allowed. Restrooms, hot showers, laundry facilities, water, and a sanitary disposal station are available.

Reservations, fees: Reservations are accepted; the fee is $30 per night. Open all year.

Directions: In Jackson, go one mile east on Broadway Street, then right on Pearl Street to the campground.

Contact: Elk Country Inn & RV Park, P.O. Box 1255, 480 W. Pearl St., Jackson, WY 83001; 307/733-2364 or 800/4-TETONS (800/483-8667), fax 307/733-4465; email: townsquareinns@wyoming.com.

Trip notes: Jackson is a good location from which to raft or float the Snake River, fish the nearby lakes and rivers, hike, bike or arrange trail rides on horseback in the forest. The shopping and dining aren't bad, either.

63 Virginian Lodge RV Park

    4

Location: In Jackson; map WY1, grid g2.

Campsites, facilities: There are 105 RV campsites, some with hookups and pull-throughs. No tents are allowed. Picnic tables and grills, restrooms, hot showers, laundry facilities, water, and a sanitary disposal station are available. A game room, swimming pool, and hot tub are on-site.

Reservations, fees: Reservations are accepted; the fee is $35–43 per night. Open mid-May–mid-October.

Directions: From the center of the town of Jackson, go one mile west on Broadway Street to the campground.

Contact: Virginian Lodge RV Park, P.O. Box 1052, 750 W. Broadway, Jackson, WY 83001; 307/733-7189 or 800/321-6982.

Trip notes: Jackson is a good location from which to raft or float the Snake River, fish the nearby lakes and rivers, hike, bike or arrange trail rides on horseback in the forest. The shopping and dining aren't bad, either.

64 Wagon Wheel Campground

     4

Location: In Jackson; map WY1, grid g2.

Campsites, facilities: There are 35 RV or tent campsites. Hot showers, laundry facilities, water, and a sanitary disposal station are available.

Reservations, fees: Reservations are accepted; the fee is $18–27 per night. Open May–September.

Directions: From Jackson Town Square, go five blocks north to the campground.

Contact: Wagon Wheel Campground, P.O. Box 1463, 505 N. Cache, Jackson, WY 83001; 307/733-4588.

Trip notes: Jackson is a good location from which to raft or float the Snake River, fish the nearby lakes and rivers, hike, bike or arrange trail rides on horseback in the forest. The shopping and dining aren't bad, either.

65 Granite Creek

   6

Location: Bridger-Teton National Forest; map WY1, grid g3.

Campsites, facilities: There are 52 RV sites, plus tent sites, with picnic tables and grills. Vault toilets and drinking water are available.

Reservations, fees: Reservations are accepted (a service fee is charged); the camping fee is $12 per night. Open June–early September. The stay limit is 10 days.

Directions: From Hoback Junction (U.S. 189/191 and U.S. 26/89) go 12 miles south on U.S. 189/191, then left eight miles to the campground.

Contact: Bridger-Teton National Forest, Jackson Ranger District, 25 Rosencrans Lane, Jackson, WY 83001; 307/739-5400; website: www.fs.fed.us/btnf/welcome.htm. For reservations, contact the National Recreation Reservation Service, 877/444-6777 or check the website: www.reserveusa.com (a service fee applies).

Trip notes: This is a forested campground on Granite Creek, near Granite Hot Springs. Granite Canyon Road is rough gravel, and a bumpy ride, but the mountain view and 50 foot waterfall are worth the drive.

66 Snake River Park KOA

     5

Location: South of Jackson; map WY1, grid g1.

Campsites, facilities: There are 30 RV campsites, plus tent sites, picnic tables and grills. Restrooms, laundry facilities, hot showers, water, and a sanitary disposal station are available. There is also a game room and playground on-site.

Reservations, fees: Reservations are accepted; the fee is $26–36 per night. Open April 1–mid-October.

Directions: From Hoback Junction (U.S.

189/191 and U.S. 26/89), go one mile north to the campground.

Contact: Snake River Park KOA, 9705 S. Hwy. 89, Jackson, WY 83001; 307/733-7078 or 800/ KOA-1878 (800/562-1878), fax 360/733-0412.

Trip notes: Jackson has excellent shopping, museums, and art galleries. The nearby Snake River has challenging white-water rafting, and float trips. The many outfitters offer daily and overnight trips. You can fish the Snake River for cutthroat, brook, and lake trout. Mountain biking is popular here, and guided tours are available.

67 Green River Lake

 6

Location: Bridger-Teton National Forest; map WY1, grid g5.

Campsites, facilities: There are 36 RV or tent campsites with picnic tables and grills, and group sites are available. Water is provided.

Reservations, fees: Reservations are accepted through the National Recreation Reservation Service, 877/444-6777, or check the website: www.reserveusa.com (a service fee applies); the camping fee is $7 per night. Open June 15–September 1. The stay limit is 10 days.

Directions: From Pinedale, go six miles west to Highway 352, go 25 miles north on Highway 352, then 31 miles north on the forest service road to the campground.

Contact: Pinedale Ranger District, 210 W. Pine St., P.O. Box 220, Pinedale, WY 82941; 307/ 367-4326.

Trip notes: This campground is on Green River Lakes, where you can fish. The trailheads for several trails that go into the Bridger Wilderness are nearby.

68 Lazy J Corral RV Park

 5

Location: Near Hoback Junction; map WY1, grid g1.

Campsites, facilities: There are 24 RV campsites, some with hookups, picnic tables, and grills. No tents are allowed. There are pull-throughs, restrooms, hot showers, laundry facilities, water, and a sanitary disposal station.

Reservations, fees: Reservations are accepted; the fee is $20 per night. Open May 1– November 1.

Directions: From Jackson go south 12 miles on U.S. 189/191 to Hoback Junction. From Hoback Junction (U.S. 26/89 and U.S. 189/191) go north to the camp on the left side of the road.

Contact: Lazy J Corral, 10755 S. Hwy. 89, Jackson, WY 83001; 307/733-1554.

Trip notes: Jackson has excellent shopping, museums, and art galleries. The nearby Snake River has challenging white-water rafting and float trips. The many outfitters offer daily and overnight trips. You can fish the Snake River for cutthroat, brook, and lake trout. Mountain biking is popular here, and guided tours are available.

69 Astoria Hot Springs

 5

Location: South of Jackson; map WY1, grid g2.

Campsites, facilities: There are 82 RV sites, some with hookups, and 28 tent sites with tables and grills. Restrooms, hot showers, laundry facilities, a sanitary disposal station, and water are available. A hot springs pool and playground are here also.

Reservations, fees: Reservations are accepted; the fee is $18–22 per night. Open mid-May–September 1.

Directions: From Jackson, go 17 miles south on U.S. 191/189.

Contact: Astoria Hot Springs, 12500 S. U.S. Hwy. 89, Jackson, WY 83001; 307/733-2659.

Trip notes: This campground may not be open, so check first to avoid being disappointed. It's near the confluence of the Snake and Hoback Rivers. The Snake River has challenging white-water rafting, and float trips. The many outfitters offer daily and overnight trips. You can fish the Snake River for cutthroat, brook, and lake trout. Mountain biking is popular here, and guided tours are available. Jackson has excellent shopping, museums, and art galleries.

70 Hoback

 5

Location: Bridger-Teton National Forest; map WY1, grid g2.

Campsites, facilities: There are 14 RV or tent sites with picnic tables and grills. Vault toilets and water are available.

Reservations, fees: No reservations are needed; the fee is $12 per night. Open June 5–September 10. The stay limit is 10 days.

Directions: From Jackson go south 12 miles on U.S. 189/191 to Hoback Junction. From Hoback Junction (U.S. 189/191 and U.S. 26/89) go south eight miles on U.S. 189/191 to the campground.

Contact: Bridger-Teton National Forest, Jackson Ranger District, 340 N. Cache, P.O. Box 1888, Jackson, WY 83001; 307/739-5570.

Trip notes: This campground is along the banks of the Hoback River.

71 Cabin Creek

 6

Location: Bridger-Teton National Forest; map WY1, grid h2.

Campsites, facilities: There are 10 RV or tent sites with picnic tables and grills. Vault toilets are available.

Reservations, fees: No reservations are needed; the fee is $10 per night. Open late May–early September. The stay limit is 16 days.

Directions: From Jackson go south on U.S. 189 to Hoback Junction, then go west on U.S. 26/89 toward Alpine for seven miles to the campground.

Contact: Greys River Ranger District, 145 Washington St., P.O. Box 338, Afton, WY 83110; 307/886-3166.

Trip notes: The nearby Snake River is popular with white-water enthusiasts. If you are new to the sport, the best way to get your feet wet is by contacting one of the numerous white-water rafting guides in the area.

72 Whiskey Grove

 5

Location: In Bridger-Teton National Forest; map WY1, grid h4.

Campsites, facilities: There are nine RV or tent campsites with picnic tables and grills. Vault toilets and water are available.

Reservations, fees: No reservations are needed; the fee is $4 per night. Open June 15–September. The stay limit is 10 days.

Directions: From Pinedale, go six miles west on U.S. 191 to Highway 352, then north 29 miles to the campground.

Contact: Pinedale Ranger District, 210 W. Pine St., P.O. Box 220, Pinedale, WY 82941; 307/367-4326.

Trip notes: This campground is on the Green River, with Kendall Warm Springs to the north.

73 Elbow

 4

Location: Bridger-Teton National Forest; map WY1, grid h1.

Campsites, facilities: There are 17 RV or tent campsites with picnic tables and grills. Restrooms and water are available.

Reservations, fees: Reservations are accepted (required for group camping); the fee is $8 per night. Open June–early September. The stay limit is 16 days.

Directions: From Jackson, go south on U.S. 189 to Hoback Junction, then go west on U.S. 26/89 toward Alpine 10 miles to the campground.

Contact: Jackson Ranger District, 25 Rosencrans Lane, Jackson, WY 83001; 307/739-5400.

Trip notes: This campground is along the Snake River, where you can float and fish for brook and cutthroat trout. For hikers, the Wyoming Range National Recreation Trail is nearby.

74 Station Creek

 5

Location: In Bridger-Teton National Forest; map WY1, grid h1.

Campsites, facilities: There are 15 RV or tent campsites with picnic tables and grills, and water is available.

Reservations, fees: Reservations are accepted; the fee is $10 per night. Open early June–early September. The stay limit is 16 days.

Directions: From Jackson go south on U.S. 189 to Hoback Junction, then go west on U.S. 26/89 toward Alpine 12 miles to the campground.

Contact: Jackson Ranger District, 25 Rosencrans Lane, Jackson, WY 83001; 307/739-5400.

Trip notes: This campground is along the Snake River, where you can fish for cutthroat, brook, and lake trout. Rafting and floating is also a popular activity on the Snake River. You can hike in the Bridger-Teton National Forest.

75 Narrows

 5

Location: In Bridger-Teton National Forest; map WY1, grid h5.

Campsites, facilities: There are nine RV or tent campsites with picnic tables and grills. Water and vault toilets are available.

Reservations, fees: Reservations are accepted, contact the National Recreation Reservation Service at 877/444-6777 (a reservation fee applies) or check the website: www.reserveusa.com; the fee is $5 per night. Open June–September 10. The stay limit is 10 days.

Directions: From Pinedale, go west on U.S. 191 to Highway 352, then north 15 miles to New Fork Lake Road. Go six miles to New Fork

Lake and the campground.

Contact: Pinedale Ranger District, 210 W. Pine St., P.O. Box 220, Pinedale, WY 82941; 307/367-4326.

Trip notes: This campground is near New Fork Trailhead and New Fork Lakes where you can fish for brook, rainbow, and lake trout.

76 New Fork Lake

 6

Location: In Bridger-Teton National Forest; map WY1, grid h5.

Campsites, facilities: There are 15 RV or tent campsites with picnic tables and grills. Vault toilets and water are available.

Reservations, fees: No reservations are needed; the fee is $4 per night. Open June 1–September 10. The stay limit is 10 days.

Directions: From Pinedale, go west on U.S. 191 to Highway 352, then north 15 miles to New Fork Lake Road and three miles on New Fork Lake Road to the campground.

Contact: Pinedale Ranger District, 210 W. Pine St., P.O. Box 220, Pinedale, WY 82941; 307/367-4326.

Trip notes: This campground is on New Fork Lakes where you can fish for brook, rainbow, and lake trout.

77 Lynx Creek

 6

Location: In Bridger-Teton National Forest; map WY1, grid h1.

Campsites, facilities: There are 14 RV or tent campsites with picnic tables and grills. Vault toilets are available.

Reservations, fees: No reservations are needed; the fee is $3 per night. Open June–September. The stay limit is 16 days.

Directions: From Jackson, go south on U.S. 189 to Hoback Junction, then go west on U.S. 26/89 23 miles to Alpine. From Alpine, go 13 miles southeast on Forest Service Road 10138 (Greys River Road) to the campground.

Contact: Greys River Ranger District, 145 Washington St., P.O. Box 338, Afton, WY 83110; 307/886-3166.

Trip notes: This campground is along Greys River, where you can fish for cutthroat.

78 Murphy Creek

 6

Location: In Bridger-Teton National Forest; map WY1, grid h1.

Campsites, facilities: There are 10 RV or tent campsites with picnic tables and grills. Water and vault toilets are available.

Reservations, fees: No reservations are needed; the fee is $5 per night. Open June–September. The stay limit is 16 days.

Directions: From Jackson, go south on U.S. 189 to Hoback Junction, then go west on U.S. 26/89 23 miles to Alpine. From Alpine, go 15 miles southeast on Forest Road 10138 (Greys River Road) to the campground.

Contact: Greys River Ranger District, 145 Washington St., P.O. Box 338, Afton, WY 83110; 307/886-3166.

Trip notes: This campground is along Greys River, where you can fish for cutthroat.

WAYNE SCHERR

Pinnacles, Wapiti Valley

MAP WY2

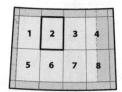

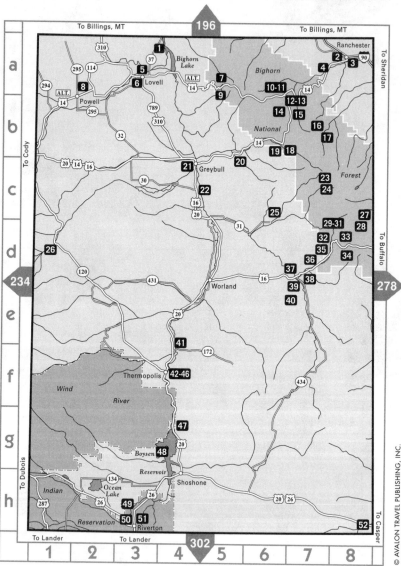

To Billings, MT

To Billings, MT

196

310

37

1

Bighorn Lake

Ranchester

2

3

90

a

295

114

5

7

Bighorn

4

To Sheridan

294

ALT.

8

6

Lovell

ALT.

14

10-11

14

b

14

Powell

295

789

9

12-13

14

15

32

310

16

17

To Cody

14

National

b

20

14

16

14

19

18

20

Greybull

Forest

c

30

22

23

24

16

25

27

d

20

26

31

29-31

28

120

32

33

234

431

Worland

16

35

34

278

36

To Buffalo

37

38

20

39

d

40

e

41

172

42-46

Thermopolis

434

f

Wind

River

47

g

48

Boysen

Reservoir

To Dubois

134

Shoshone

Ocean Lake

Indian

49

20

26

h

287

26

50

26

51

52

To Casper

Reservation

Riverton

To Lander

To Lander

302

1 2 3 4 5 6 7 8

CHAPTER WY2

1 Horseshoe Bend 261
2 Lazy R 262
3 Conner Battlefield State Historic Site 262
4 Foothills Motel & Campground 262
5 Camp Big Horn RV Park 262
6 Lovell Camper Park 263
7 Porcupine 263
8 Park County Fairgrounds 263
9 Bald Mountain 263
10 North Tongue 264
11 Prune Creek 264
12 Sibley Lake 264
13 Tie Flume 264
14 Owen Creek 265
15 Dead Swede 265
16 Ranger Creek 265
17 East Fork 265
18 Cabin Creek Trailer Park 266
19 Shell Creek 266
20 Shell Campground 266
21 Greybull KOA 266
22 Rose Garden RV Park 266
23 Paintrock Lakes 267
24 Medicine Lodge Lake 267
25 Medicine Lodge State Archeological Site 267
26 Oasis Campground 268
27 Hunter Corrals 268
28 Circle Park 268
29 West Tensleep Lake 268
30 Deer Park 269
31 Sitting Bull Creek 269
32 Island Park 269
33 Lakeview 269
34 Bull Creek 270
35 Boulder Park 270
36 Leigh Creek 270
37 Ten Broek RV Park & Cabins 271
38 Meadowlark Resort 271
39 Worland Cowboy Campground 271
40 Castle Gardens 271
41 Country Camping RV and Tent Park 272
42 Eagle RV Park 272
43 Fountain of Youth RV Park 272
44 Grandview RV Park 273
45 M/K RV Park 273
46 New RV Park 274
47 Boysen Marina 274
48 Boysen State Park 274
49 Owl Creek Kampground ... 275
50 Rudy's Camper Court 275
51 Riverton RV Park 275
52 Hells Half Acre Campground 276

1 Horseshoe Bend

 4

Location: At Bighorn Lake; map WY2, grid a3.

Campsites, facilities: There are 128 RV campsites and several tent sites. Restrooms, picnic tables, grills, water, and a sanitary disposal facility are available.

Reservations, fees: No reservations are needed; the fee is $5 per night. Open year-round.

Directions: From Cody, go east 47 miles on Highway 14 to U.S. 310 and then east three miles to Lovell. From Lovell, go two miles east on U.S. 14A to Junction 37, then 14 miles north on Highway 37 to the campground.

Contact: National Park Service, P.O. Box 487, Lovell, WY 82431; 307/548-2251.

Trip notes: The Pryor Mountain Wild Horse Range is to the northwest, and the horses are considered unique because of their primitive colors and markings. The Bighorn Canyon National Recreation Area is nearby, where you can boat, and fish for walleye, trout, sauger, ling, perch, and rainbow trout in the 71 mile-long Bighorn Lake. There are several short hiking trails in the area.

2 Lazy R

    4

Location: In Ranchester; map WY2, grid a8.

Campsites, facilities: There are 32 RV campsites (no tents). Pull-through sites, hookups, restrooms, showers, water, and a sanitary disposal facility are available.

Reservations, fees: No reservations are needed; the fee is $14–16 per night. Open April 1–November 1.

Directions: From Sheridan, take I-90 north 13 miles to Exit 9 at Ranchester; go west on U.S. 14 to the campground. This campground is on the Ranchester's main street.

Contact: Lazy R, P.O. Box 286, Ranchester, WY 82839; 307/655-9284.

Trip notes: You can fish in the Bighorn River and hike in Bighorn National Forest.

3 Conner Battlefield State Historic Site

    4

Location: Near the Tongue River; map WY2, grid a8.

Campsites, facilities: There are numerous RV and tent campsites. Pull-through sites, restrooms, picnic tables, grills, and water are available.

Reservations, fees: No reservations are needed; the fee is $9 per night. Open May 1–October 1.

Directions: From Sheridan, take I-90 north 13

miles to Exit 9 at Ranchester; go south at the Catholic church to the campground.

Contact: State Park, P.O. Box 520, Story, WY 82842; 307/684-7629.

Trip notes: You can fish in the Tongue River for brown trout.

4 Foothills Motel & Campground

   4

Location: In Dayton; map WY2, grid a7.

Campsites, facilities: There are 50 RV campsites and some tent sites. Hookups, pull-through sites, a sanitary disposal facility, restrooms, showers, laundry facilities, picnic tables, grills, and water are available.

Reservations, fees: No reservations are needed; the fee is $11.75–17 per night. Open April 15–November 15.

Directions: From Sheridan, take I-90 north 13 miles to Exit 9 at Ranchester; stay on U.S. 14 to Dayton, turn left to the campground.

Contact: Foothills Motel & Campground, 101 N. Main, P.O. Box 174, Dayton, WY 82836; 307/655-2547.

Trip notes: This campground is by the river, where you can fish.

5 Camp Big Horn RV Park

     5

Location: In Lovell; map WY2, grid a3.

Campsites, facilities: There are 27 RV or tent campsites, some with picnic tables and grills. Hookups, restrooms, showers, laundry facilities, water, and a sanitary disposal facility are available.

Reservations, fees: No reservations are needed; the fee is $7–12 per night. Open year-round.

Directions: From Cody, go east 47 miles on Highway 14 to U.S. 310 and east three miles to Lovell; the campground is on Main Street (U.S. 310) on the east end of town.

Contact: Camp Big Horn RV Park, 595 E Main

St., Lovell, WY 82431; 307/548-2725, fax 307/548-7479.

Trip notes: Near Bighorn Canyon National Recreation Area, where you can boat, and fish for walleye, trout, sauger, ling, perch, and rainbow trout in the 71 mile-long Bighorn Lake. There are several short hiking trails in the area.

6 Lovell Camper Park

 5

Location: In Lovell; map WY2, grid a3.

Campsites, facilities: There are 13 RV or tent campsites, restrooms, showers, water, and a sanitary disposal facility.

Reservations, fees: No reservations are needed; no fee is charged. Open May 1–September 30.

Directions: From Cody, go east 47 miles on Highway 14 to U.S. 310 and east three miles to Lovell; go north on Pennsylvania Avenue and then east on 2nd Street to Quebec Avenue and the campground.

Contact: Lovell Camper Park, 40 Quebec Ave., Lovell, WY 82421; 307/548-6551, fax 307/548-7614.

Trip notes: Near Bighorn Canyon National Recreation Area, where you can boat and fish for walleye, trout, sauger, ling, perch, and rainbow trout in the 71 mile-long Bighorn Lake. There are several short hiking trails in the area.

7 Porcupine

 4

Location: In Bighorn National Forest; map WY2, grid a5.

Campsites, facilities: There are 16 RV campsites, plus tent sites. Restrooms, picnic tables, grills, and water are available.

Reservations, fees: No reservations are needed; the fee is $10 per night. Open June 15–October 31.

Directions: From Lovell, go 33 miles east on

U.S. 14A, then 1.6 miles north on Forest Service Road 13 to the campground.

Contact: Bighorn National Forest, Lovell District Office, P.O. Box 367, Lovell, WY 82431; 307/765-4435.

Trip notes: The Medicine Wheel archaeological site lies west of this campground, and it was designated a National Historic Landmark in 1970. Measuring approximately 80 feet in diameter, this rock landmark is estimated to have been constructed A.D.1200–1700. You can hike in Bighorn National Forest and fish in the Bighorn River.

8 Park County Fairgrounds

 4

Location: In Powell; map WY2, grid a2.

Campsites, facilities: There are 130 RV campsites and several tent sites, picnic tables, and grills. Hookups, pull-through sites, restrooms, showers, laundry facilities, water, and a sanitary disposal station are available.

Reservations, fees: No reservations are needed; the fee is $5 per night. Open May 1–September 1.

Directions: From Cody, go east 15 miles on Highway 14 to Powell. Turn north to the fairgrounds.

Contact: Park County Fairgrounds, 655 E. 5th St., Powell, WY 82435; 307/754-5421, fax 307/754-5947.

Trip notes: Near Bighorn Canyon National Recreation Area, where you can boat, and fish for walleye, trout, sauger, ling, perch, and rainbow trout in the 71 mile-long Bighorn Lake. There are several short hiking trails in the area.

9 Bald Mountain

 4

Location: Bighorn National Forest; map WY2, grid a5.

Campsites, facilities: There are 15 RV campsites, plus tent sites. Restrooms, picnic tables, grills, and water are available.

Reservations, fees: No reservations are needed; the fee is $10 per night. Open June 15–October 31.

Directions: From Lovell, travel 33 miles east on U.S. 14A to the campground.

Contact: Bighorn National Forest, Lovell District Office, P.O. Box 367, Lovell, WY 82431; 307/765-4435.

Trip notes: You can fish in the Bighorn River and hike in Bighorn National Forest.

10 North Tongue

 5

Location: Bighorn National Forest; map WY2, grid a6.

Campsites, facilities: There are 12 RV campsites, plus tent sites. Restrooms, picnic tables, grills, and water are available.

Reservations, fees: No reservations are needed; the fee is $9 per night. Open June 15–October 31.

Directions: From Sheridan, take I-90 north 13 miles to Exit 9 at Ranchester; stay on U.S. 14 to Dayton. From Dayton, go 29 miles southwest on U.S. 14, then one mile north on the Forest Service Road to the campground.

Contact: Bighorn National Forest, Lovell District Office, P.O. Box 367, Lovell, WY 82431; 307/765-4435.

Trip notes: You can fish in the Bighorn River and hike in Bighorn National Forest.

11 Prune Creek

 4

Location: In Bighorn National Forest; map WY2, grid a6.

Campsites, facilities: There are 21 RV campsites, plus tent sites. Restrooms, picnic tables, grills, and water are available.

Reservations, fees: No reservations are needed; the fee is $10 per night. Open June 15–October 31.

Directions: From Sheridan, take I-90 north 13

miles to Exit 9 at Ranchester; stay on U.S. 14 to Dayton. From Dayton, go 26 miles south on U.S. 14 to the campground.

Contact: Bighorn National Forest, Lovell District Office, P.O. Box 367, Lovell, WY 82431; 307/765-4435.

Trip notes: You can fish in the Bighorn River and hike in Bighorn National Forest.

12 Sibley Lake

 5

Location: Southwest of Dayton; map WY2, grid b7.

Campsites, facilities: There are 10 RV campsites, plus tent sites. Restrooms, picnic tables, grills, and water are available.

Reservations, fees: No reservations are needed; the fee is $10–13 per night. Open June 15–October 31.

Directions: From Sheridan, take I-90 north 13 miles to Exit 9 at Ranchester; stay on U.S. 14 to Dayton. From Dayton, go 25 miles southwest on U.S. 14 to the campground.

Contact: Bighorn National Forest, Lovell District Office, P.O. Box 367, Lovell, WY 82431; 307/765-4435.

Trip notes: You can fish in the Bighorn River and hike in Bighorn National Forest.

13 Tie Flume

 5

Location: Southwest of Dayton; map WY2, grid b7.

Campsites, facilities: There are 25 RV campsites, plus tent sites. Restrooms, picnic tables, grills, and water are available.

Reservations, fees: No reservations are needed; the fee is $9 per night. Open June 15 –October 31.

Directions: From Sheridan, take I-90 north 13 miles to Exit 9 at Ranchester; stay on U.S. 14 to Dayton. From Dayton, go 34 miles southwest on U.S. 14, then two miles east on Forest Service Road 26 to the campground.

Contact: Bighorn National Forest, Lovell District Office, P.O. Box 367, Lovell, WY 82431; 307/765-4435.

Trip notes: You can fish in the Bighorn River and hike in Bighorn National Forest.

14 Owen Creek

   5

Location: In Bighorn National Forest; map WY2, grid b6.

Campsites, facilities: There are seven RV campsites, plus tent sites. Restrooms, picnic tables, grills, and water are available.

Reservations, fees: No reservations are needed; the fee is $9 per night. Open June 1–October 31.

Directions: From Sheridan, take I-90 north 13 miles to Exit 9 at Ranchester; stay on U.S. 14 to Dayton. From Dayton, go 34 miles southwest on U.S. 14 to the campground.

Contact: Bighorn National Forest, Lovell District Office, P.O. Box 367, Lovell, WY 82431; 307/765-4435.

Trip notes: You can fish in the Bighorn River and hike in Bighorn National Forest.

15 Dead Swede

  5

Location: In Bighorn National Forest; map WY2, grid b7.

Campsites, facilities: There are 22 RV or tent campsites. Restrooms, picnic tables, grills, and water are available.

Reservations, fees: No reservations are needed; the fee is $9 per night. Open June 15–October 31.

Directions: From Sheridan, take I-90 north 13 miles to Exit 9 at Ranchester; stay on U.S. 14 to Dayton. From Dayton, go 34 miles southwest on U.S. 14, then four miles southeast on Forest Service Road 26 to the campground.

Contact: Bighorn National Forest, Bighorn National Forest, 1969 S. Sheridan Ave., Sheridan, WY 82801; 307/672-0751, 307/655-2356; web-

site: www.fs.fed.us.

Trip notes: You can hike and fish in Bighorn National Forest.

16 Ranger Creek

 4

Location: In Bighorn National Forest; map WY2, grid b7.

Campsites, facilities: There are 11 RV campsites, plus tent sites. Restrooms, picnic tables, grills, and water are available.

Reservations, fees: No reservations are needed; the fee is $9 per night. Open June 1–October 31.

Directions: From Cody, take U.S. 14/16/20 54 miles east to Greybull. From Greybull, take U.S. 14 16 miles to Shell. From Shell, go 15 miles northeast on U.S. 14, then two miles on the forest service road to the campground.

Contact: Bighorn National Forest, Lovell District Office, P.O. Box 367, Lovell, WY 82431; 307/765-4435.

Trip notes: You can fish in the Bighorn River and hike in Bighorn National Forest.

17 East Fork

  5

Location: In Bighorn National Forest; map WY2, grid b7.

Campsites, facilities: There are 12 RV campsites, plus tent sites. Restrooms, picnic tables, grills, and water are available.

Reservations, fees: No reservations are needed; the fee is $8 per night. Open June 1–October 31.

Directions: From Sheridan, go south on I-90 and take Exit 33, go west one mile to the stop sign, and take Highway 335 to Big Horn. From Big Horn, go 17 miles southwest to the campground.

Contact: Bighorn National Forest, Bighorn National Forest, 1969 S. Sheridan Ave., Sheridan, WY 82801; 307/672-0751, 307/655-2356; website: www.fs.fed.us.

Trip notes: You can hike and fish in Bighorn National Forest.

18 Cabin Creek Trailer Park

  5

Location: In Bighorn National Forest; map WY2, grid b6.

Campsites, facilities: There are 26 RV or tent campsites. Restrooms, picnic tables, grills, and water are available.

Reservations, fees: Reservations are needed; the fee is $105 per month. Open June 1–October 31.

Directions: From Cody, take U.S. 14/16/20 54 miles east to Greybull. From Greybull, take U.S. 14 16 miles to Shell. From Shell, go 15 miles northeast on U.S. 14, turn right on Road 17 and you are there.

Contact: Bighorn National Forest, Lovell District Office, P.O. Box 367, Lovell, WY 82431; 307/765-4435.

Trip notes: You can hike and fish in Bighorn National Forest.

19 Shell Creek

   4

Location: In the Bighorn National Forest; map WY2, grid b6.

Campsites, facilities: There are 11 RV campsites, plus tent sites. Restrooms, picnic tables, grills, and water are available.

Reservations, fees: No reservations are needed; the fee is $8 per night. Open May 30–October 31.

Directions: From Cody, take U.S. 14/16/20 54 miles east to Greybull. From Greybull, take U.S. 14 16 miles to Shell. From Shell, go 15 miles northeast on U.S. 14, then one mile south on the forest service road to the campground.

Contact: Bighorn National Forest, Lovell District Office, P.O. Box 367, Lovell, WY 82431; 307/765-4435.

Trip notes: You can fish in the Bighorn River

and hike in Bighorn National Forest.

20 Shell Campground

    4

Location: East of Greybull; map WY2, grid c5.

Campsites, facilities: There are 34 RV or tent campsites. There are hookups, pull-through sites, a sanitary disposal facility, restrooms, showers, laundry facilities, picnic tables, grills, and water available.

Reservations, fees: No reservations are needed; the fee is $10–15 per night. Open April 1–November 15.

Directions: From Greybull, go 15 miles east on U.S. 14 to the campground.

Contact: Shell Campground, P.O. Box 16, Shell, WY 82441; 307/765-2342.

Trip notes: You can fish in the Bighorn River and hike in Bighorn National Forest.

21 Greybull KOA

   4

Location: In Greybull; map WY2, grid c4.

Campsites, facilities: There are 62 RV and tent campsites. Restrooms, showers, a swimming pool, laundry facilities, picnic tables, grills, a game room, water, and a sanitary disposal facility are available.

Reservations, fees: No reservations are needed; the fee is $18–25 per night. Open April 15–October 31.

Directions: From Cody, go 52 miles east on U.S. 16/20 and turn left on North 4th Avenue; the campground is four blocks down, where the street ends.

Contact: Greybull KOA, 333 N. 2nd, P.O. Box 387, Greybull, WY 82426; 307/765-2555.

Trip notes: You can fish in the Greybull River.

22 Rose Garden RV Park

   4

Location: In Basin; map WY2, grid c5.

Campsites, facilities: There are eight RV

campsites, but no tents are allowed. Hookups, pull-through sites, picnic tables, and grills are available.

Reservations, fees: No reservations are needed; the fee is $10 per night. Open May 15–September 15.

Directions: From Greybull, go eight miles south on U.S. 20, through Basin. The campground is on the south side of town, on the east side of U.S. 20.

Contact: Rose Garden RV Park, P.O. Box 849, S. 4th St., Hwy. 20, Basin, WY, 82410; 307/568-2943.

Trip notes: You can fish in the Bighorn River and hike in Bighorn National Forest.

23 Paintrock Lakes

     4

Location: In Bighorn National Forest; map WY2, grid c7.

Campsites, facilities: There are eight RV campsites, plus tent sites. Restrooms, picnic tables, grills, and water are available.

Reservations, fees: No reservations are needed; the fee is $8 per night. Open May 30–October 30.

Directions: From Cody, take U.S. 14/16/20 54 miles east to Greybull. From Greybull, take U.S. 14 16 miles to Shell. From Shell, go 15 miles northeast on U.S. 14, then 25 miles southeast on Forest Service Road 17 to the campground.

Contact: Bighorn National Forest, Lovell District Office, P.O. Box 367, Lovell, WY 82431; 307/765-4435.

Trip notes: You can fish and hike in Bighorn National Forest.

24 Medicine Lodge Lake

    5

Location: In Bighorn National Forest; map WY2, grid c7.

Campsites, facilities: There are eight RV campsites, plus tent sites. Restrooms, picnic tables, grills, and water are available.

Reservations, fees: No reservations are needed; the fee is $8 per night. Open May 30–October 31.

Directions: From Cody, take U.S. 14/16/20 54 miles east to Greybull. From Greybull, take U.S. 14 16 miles to Shell. From Shell, go 15 miles northeast on U.S. 14, then 25 miles southeast on Forest Service Road 17 to the campground.

Contact: Bighorn National Forest, Lovell District Office, P.O. Box 367, Lovell, WY 82431; 307/765-4435.

Trip notes: You can fish in the Bighorn River and hike in Bighorn National Forest.

25 Medicine Lodge State Archeological Site

   5

Location: Near Hyattville; map WY2, grid c6.

Campsites, facilities: There are 25 RV and tent campsites, some with picnic tables and grills. Pull-through sites, restrooms, and water are available. Pets are allowed on leashes.

Reservations, fees: No reservations are needed; the fee is $9 per night. The stay limit is 14 days.

Directions: From Worland, go 22 miles north to Manderson, and then take Highway 31 22 miles to Hyattville. Just before going down the hill into the town, turn north onto Cold Springs Road. Follow this asphalt county road for about 4.5 miles until you come to a large yellow and brown sign that reads "Medicine Lodge Wildlife Habitat Mgt. and Archeological Site." Turn left onto a gravel road at that sign and drive 1.5 miles to the site.

Contact: Medicine Lodge State Archeological Site, P.O. Box 62, Hyattville, WY 82428; 307/469-2234, fax 307/469-2264.

Trip notes: The Medicine Lodge site has long been known for its Indian petroglyphs and pictographs, over 60 cultural levels spanning some 10,000 years of human occupation. There is a self-guided nature trail and visitor center.

26 Oasis Campground

 4

Location: In Meeteetse; map WY2, grid d1.

Campsites, facilities: There are numerous RV or tent campsites, picnic tables, grills, and restrooms.

Reservations, fees: No reservations are needed; the fee is $5–12 per night. Open year-round.

Directions: From Cody, go south 31 miles on Highway 120 to Meeteetse. This campground is on the north side of the bridge.

Contact: Oasis Campground, P.O. Box 86, Meeteese, WY 82433; 307/868-2551.

Trip notes: The Wood and Greybull Rivers are nearby, where you can fish for cutthroat trout.

27 Hunter Corrals

 5

Location: On the southeast face of the Bighorn Mountains; map WY2, grid c8.

Campsites, facilities: There are nine horse-camping units available, and restrooms, picnic tables, grills, and water.

Reservations, fees: Two sites can be reserved through the U.S. Forest Service Reservation Center, 800/280-2267, but the rest of the sites are first-come, first-served. The fee is $10 per night. Open May 15–October 31. The stay limit is seven days.

Directions: From Buffalo, go 13 miles west on U.S. 16; then take the forest service road three miles to the campground.

Contact: Bureau of Land Management, 1425 Fort St., Buffalo, WY 82834; 307/684-1100.

Trip notes: This campground gets very busy, as it is the jumping-off point for the Cloud Peak Wilderness, where you can hike and fish.

28 Circle Park

 5

Location: In the Cloud Peak Wilderness; map WY2, grid d8.

Campsites, facilities: There are 10 RV camp-sites, which can accommodate a maximum RV length of 16, plus tent sites. Restrooms, grills, picnic tables, and water are available.

Reservations, fees: No reservations are needed; the fee is $9 per night. Open May 15 –October 31. The stay limit is 14 days.

Directions: From Buffalo, go 15 miles west on U.S. 16, then west 2.5 miles on Forest Service Road 30 to the campground.

Contact: Bureau of Land Management, 1425 Fort St., Buffalo, WY 82834; 307/684-1100.

Trip notes: The Circle Trailhead begins near here, leading into the Cloud Peak Wilderness area, and accesses the South Fork Ponds vicinity. There are several lakes within walking distance.

29 West Tensleep Lake

 5

Location: In Bighorn National Forest; map WY2, grid d7.

Campsites, facilities: There are 10 RV or tent campsites, which can accommodate a maximum RV length of 22 feet. Restrooms, picnic tables, grills, and water are available.

Reservations, fees: Sites 3–10 can be reserved through the U.S. Forest Service Reservation Center, 800/280-2267, but the rest of the sites are first-come, first-served. The fee is $9 per night. Open June 15–September 30. The stay limit is 14 days.

Directions: From Worland, go 27 miles east on U.S. 16 to Ten Sleep. From Ten Sleep, go 20 miles northeast on U.S. 16 then seven miles on Forest Service Road 27 to the campground.

Contact: Bighorn National Forest, Tensleep Ranger District, 2009 Big Horn Ave., Worland, WY 82401; 307/347-8291.

Trip notes: You can hike the popular West Tensleep Lake Trail in the Cloud Peak Wilderness. Six miles east of the town of Ten Sleep, the 10,000-acre Tensleep Preserve, owned by the Nature Conservancy, has trails and wildlife, along with tours and activities. You can fish in Bighorn National Forest.

30 Deer Park

    5

Location: In Bighorn National Forest; map WY2, grid d7.

Campsites, facilities: There are seven RV campsites, which can accommodate a maximum RV length of 22 feet, plus tent sites. Restrooms, picnic tables, grills, and water are available.

Reservations, fees: No reservations are needed; the fee is $8 per night. Open June 15–September 30. The stay limit is 14 days.

Directions: From Worland, go 27 miles east on U.S. 16 to Ten Sleep. From Ten Sleep, go 20 miles northeast on U.S. 16 then 5.25 miles north on Forest Service Road 27 to the campground.

Contact: Bighorn National Forest, Tensleep Ranger District, 2009 Big Horn Ave., Worland, WY 82401; 307/347-8291.

Trip notes: Six miles east of the town of Ten Sleep, the 10,000-acre Tensleep Preserve, owned by the Nature Conservancy, has trails and wildlife, along with tours and activities. You can fish in Bighorn National Forest.

31 Sitting Bull Creek

    4

Location: In Bighorn National Forest; map WY2, grid d8.

Campsites, facilities: There are 43 RV campsites, which can accommodate a maximum RV length of 50 feet, plus tent sites. Vault toilets, picnic tables, grills, and water are available.

Reservations, fees: No reservations are needed; the fee is $10 per night. Open June 15–September 30. The stay limit is 14 days.

Directions: From Worland, go 27 miles east on U.S. 16 to Ten Sleep. From Ten Sleep, go 23 miles northeast on U.S. 16, then one mile north on Forest Service Road 432 to the campground.

Contact: Bighorn National Forest, Tensleep

Ranger District, 2009 Big Horn Ave., Worland, WY 82401; 307/347-8291.

Trip notes: There is a primitive nature trail nearby. Six miles east of the town of Ten Sleep, the 10,000-acre Tensleep Preserve, owned by the Nature Conservancy, has trails and wildlife, along with tours and activities. You can fish in Bighorn National Forest.

32 Island Park

  4

Location: In Bighorn National Forest; map WY2, grid d7.

Campsites, facilities: There are 10 RV campsites, which can accommodate a maximum RV length of 35 feet, plus tent sites. Restrooms, picnic tables, grills, and water are available.

Reservations, fees: No reservations are needed; the fee is $8 per night. Open June 15–September 30. The stay limit is 14 days.

Directions: From Worland, go 27 miles east on U.S. 16 to Ten Sleep. From Ten Sleep, go 23 miles northeast on U.S. 16, then three miles north on Forest Service Road 27 to the campground.

Contact: Bighorn National Forest, Tensleep Ranger District, 2009 Big Horn Ave., Worland, WY 82401; 307/347-8291.

Trip notes: There are hiking trails nearby. Six miles east of the town of Ten Sleep, the 10,000-acre Tensleep Preserve, owned by the Nature Conservancy, has trails and wildlife, along with tours and activities. You can fish in Bighorn National Forest.

33 Lakeview

  4

Location: In Bighorn National Forest; map WY2, grid d8.

Campsites, facilities: There are 10 RV campsites, which can accommodate a maximum RV length of 22 feet, and tent campsites. Restrooms, picnic tables, grills, and water are available.

Reservations, fees: Five sites can be reserved through U.S. Forest Service Reservation Center, 800/280-2267, but the rest of the sites are first-come, first-served. The fee is $10 per night. Open June 15–September 30. The stay limit is 14 days.

Directions: From Worland, go 27 miles east on U.S. 16 to Ten Sleep. From Ten Sleep, go 15 miles northeast on U.S. 16 to the campground.

Contact: Bighorn National Forest, Tensleep Ranger District, 2009 Big Horn Ave., Worland, WY 82401; 307/347-8291.

Trip notes: Six miles east of the town of Ten Sleep, the 10,000-acre Tensleep Preserve, owned by the Nature Conservancy, has trails and wildlife, along with tours and activities. You can fish in Bighorn National Forest.

34 Bull Creek
   4

Location: Northeast of Ten Sleep; map WY2, grid d8.

Campsites, facilities: There are 10 RV or tent campsites, which can accommodate a maximum RV length of 16 feet. Vault toilets, picnic tables, and grills are available.

Reservations, fees: No reservations are needed; the fee is $7 per night. Open June 15–September 30. The stay limit is 14 days.

Directions: From Worland, go 27 miles east on U.S. 16 to Ten Sleep. From Ten Sleep, go 25 miles northeast on U.S. 16, then less than .1 mile east on Forest Service Road 433 to the campground.

Contact: Bighorn National Forest, Tensleep Ranger District, 2009 Big Horn Ave., Worland, WY 82401; 307/347-8291.

Trip notes: The 10,000-acre Tensleep Preserve, owned by the Nature Conservancy, is six miles east of the town of Ten Sleep, and has trails and wildlife, along with tours and activities.

35 Boulder Park
   4

Location: North of Ten Sleep; map WY2, grid d7.

Campsites, facilities: There are six RV or tent campsites and 28 30-day campsites. Restrooms, picnic tables, grills, and water available.

Reservations, fees: This is a concession-operated campground. The six campsites are $9 per night; the 30-day sites are $170 for 30 days. Open June 1–September 30.

Directions: From Worland, go 27 miles east on U.S. 16 to Ten Sleep. From Ten Sleep, go 13 miles northeast on U.S. 16 to the campground.

Contact: Gallatin Canyon Campgrounds, Perry and Esther Fishbaugh, 8628 Huffine Lane, Bozeman, MT 59715; 406/587-0455.

Trip notes: The 10,000-acre Tensleep Preserve, owned by the Nature Conservancy, is six miles east of the town of Ten Sleep, and has trails and wildlife, along with tours and activities.

36 Leigh Creek
   6

Location: In Bighorn National Forest; map WY2, grid d7.

Campsites, facilities: There are 11 RV or tent campsites with picnic tables and grills. Vault toilets and water are available.

Reservations, fees: No reservations are needed, $9 per night. Open May 15–October 31.

Directions: From Worland, go east 28 miles on U.S. 16 to Ten Sleep. From Ten Sleep, go nine miles northeast on U.S. 16 to the campground.

Contact: Bighorn National Forest, 1425 Fort St., Buffalo, WY 82834; 307/684-1100.

Trip notes: The Tensleep Preserve is 10,000 acres managed by the Nature Conservancy, where you can see wildlife and hike area trails. Cloud Peak Wilderness is 189,000 acres with excellent hiking trails.

Ten Broek RV Park & Cabins

 5

Location: In Ten Sleep; map WY2, grid d7.

Campsites, facilities: There are 70 RV and tent campsites, some with hookups, picnic tables, and grills. Restrooms, showers, laundry facilities, water, a sanitary disposal station, and a game room are available.

Reservations, fees: Reservations are accepted; the fee is $11–12 per night. Open April 15–November 1.

Directions: From Worland, go east 28 miles on U.S. 16 to Ten Sleep. The campground is on the west end of town.

Contact: Ten Broek RV Park & Cabins, P.O. Box 10, Ten Sleep, WY 82442; 307/366-2250.

Trip notes: You can fish in nearby mountain creeks for rainbow, brown, and brook trout.

Meadowlark Resort

  5

Location: East of Worland; map WY2, grid d7.

Campsites, facilities: There are 12 RV or tent campsites, some with full hookups. Restrooms, showers, and a rental shop are available.

Reservations, fees: Reservations are accepted; the fee is $15 per night. Open June–September.

Directions: From Worland, go east 28 miles on U.S. 16 to Ten Sleep. From Ten Sleep, go 21 miles east on U.S. 16 to the campground.

Contact: Dean and Karen Cox, Meadowlark Resort, Box 86, Ten Sleep, WY 82442; 307/366-2424 or 800/858-5672; fax 307/366-2477.

Trip notes: You can fish in the Bighorn River at Meadowlark Lake. Three scenic byways are nearby: The Cloud Peak Highway (U.S. 16), Bighorn Byway (U.S. 14), or the Medicine Wheel Passage (U.S. 14A). The Gooseberry Painted Desert is 3,000 acres 30 miles west of Worland.

Worland Cowboy Campground

  5

Location: Near Worland; map WY2, grid e7.

Campsites, facilities: There are 44 RV and tent campsites, some with hookups, pull-throughs, picnic tables, and grills. Restrooms, showers, laundry facilities, a game room, water, and a sanitary disposal station are available.

Reservations, fees: Reservations are accepted; the fee is $16–20 per night. Open year-round.

Directions: From Worland, go east one mile on U.S. 16 to the campground.

Contact: Berry and Ruth Reed, Worland Cowboy Campground, 2401 Big Horn #3, Worland, WY 82401; 307/347-2329 or 307/347-8804.

Trip notes: The 18-hole Green Hills Municipal Golf Course is two miles south of Worland. You can fish in the Bighorn River at Meadowlark Lake. Three scenic byways are nearby: The Cloud Peak Highway (U.S. 16), Bighorn Byway (U.S. 14), or the Medicine Wheel Passage (U.S. 14A). The Gooseberry Painted Desert is 3,000 acres, 30 miles west of Worland.

 Castle Gardens

   7

Location: East of Worland; map WY2, grid e7.

Campsites, facilities: Two RV or tent campsites with picnic tables and grills. Vault toilets are available.

Reservations, fees: No reservations are needed, and no fees are charged. Open June 1–October 31. The stay limit is 14 days.

Directions: From Worland, go east 28 miles on U.S. 16 to Ten Sleep. One mile west of Ten Sleep, take the Castle Gardens turnoff and follow the unpaved road to the campground.

Contact: Worland Field Office, 101 S. 23rd St., P.O. Box 119, Worland, WY 82401-0119; 307/347-5100, fax 307/347-6195; website: www.wy.blm.gov.

Trip notes: You can hike, fish, or climb in the Bighorn Mountains. The sandstone rock formations make this an unusually scenic area. The Bighorn River offers good fishing for sauger, bass, walleye, and catfish.

41 Country Camping RV and Tent Park

 5

Location: Near Thermopolis; map WY2, grid e4.

Campsites, facilities: There are 42 RV sites with hookups and some pull-throughs, and 25 shaded, grassy tent sites. Wheelchair-accessible restrooms, showers, laundry facilities, picnic tables, grills, water, a sanitary disposal station, and a boat ramp are available. Pets are allowed on leashes.

Reservations, fees: Reservations are accepted; the fee is $13.50–18 per night. Open April–October.

Directions: From Thermopolis, go five miles north on U.S. 20 to the campground.

Contact: Country Camping RV & Tent Park, 710 E. Sunnyside Lane, Thermopolis, WY 82443; 307/864-2416 or 800/609-2244; email: camp@trib .com.

Trip notes: This campground is just outside Thermopolis, and offers a quiet rural location. Anglers will appreciate the nearby blue-ribbon trout fishing in the Bighorn River.

42 Eagle RV Park

 5

Location: In Thermopolis; map WY2, grid f4.

Campsites, facilities: There are 33 RV sites, some with hookups and pull-throughs, and 20 tent sites with picnic tables. Restrooms, showers, laundry facilities, water, a sanitary disposal station, and a pool are available. Pets are allowed on leashes.

Reservations, fees: Reservations are accepted; the fee is $12.50–20 per night. Open April–November.

Directions: The RV park is at the south end of town, 1.9 miles from the stoplight (the town's only one) on U.S. 20.

Contact: Randy and Brenda Evans, Eagle RV Park, 204 Hwy. 20 South, Thermopolis, WY 82443; 307/864-5262; email: eaglerv@wyoming.com or website: www.interbasin.com/eagle.

Trip notes: Hot Springs State Park is one of the world's largest mineral hot springs and is the source of the town's name. The word *thermopolis* translates into "hot city." You can play golf at the Legion nine-hole golf course in Thermopolis and soak in the Big Spring at Hot Springs State Park. There are guided riverboat trips available, and good fishing in the Bighorn River. The Hot Springs Historical Museum displays artifacts of frontier days.

The Wyoming Dinosaur Museum features bones and skeletons from a site nearby, and you can watch workers clean and prepare excavated bones for assembly and study.

Legend Rock State Petroglyph Site, 30 miles northwest of Thermopolis, offers a chance to view the historical writing on the cliff's face. Petroglyphs at the Legend Rock State site represent at least three styles of Native American art, one of which is related to early Hopi. Charcoal layers at the site have been estimated at over 2,000 years old. Visiting arrangements must be made through Hot Springs State Park, 220 Park St., Thermopolis, WY 82443; 307/864-2176. The site has a public restroom and picnic tables.

43 Fountain of Youth RV Park

 5

Location: Near Thermopolis; map WY2, grid f4.

Campsites, facilities: There are 64 RV sites, some with hookups and pull-throughs, and four tent sites. This is a wheelchair-accessible campground. Picnic tables, restrooms, showers, laundry facilities, water, grills, a sanitary disposal station, and a hot mineral pool are available.

Reservations, fees: Reservations are accepted; the fee is $18.50 per night. Open March 1–October 31.

Directions: From Thermopolis, go 1.5 miles north on U.S. 20 to the campground.

Contact: Mary and Tom Berry, Fountain of Youth RV Park, 250 N. Hwy. 20, P.O. Box 711, Thermopolis, WY 82443; 307/864-3265 or fax 307/864-3388.

Trip notes: You can play golf at the Legion nine-hole golf course in Thermopolis and soak in the Big Spring at Hot Springs State Park. There are guided riverboat trips available, and good fishing in the Bighorn River. The Hot Springs Historical Museum displays artifacts of frontier days.

The Wyoming Dinosaur Museum features bones and skeletons from a site nearby, and you can watch workers clean and prepare excavated bones for assembly and study.

Legend Rock State Petroglyph Site, 30 miles northwest of Thermopolis, offers a chance to view the historical writing on the cliff's face. Petroglyphs at the Legend Rock State site represent at least three styles of Native American art, one of which is related to early Hopi. Charcoal layers at the site have been estimated at over 2,000 years old. Visiting arrangements must be made through Hot Springs State Park, 220 Park St., Thermopolis, WY 82443; 307/864-2176. The site has a public restroom and picnic tables.

44 Grandview RV Park

      5

Location: In Thermopolis; map WY2, grid f4.

Campsites, facilities: There are 25 RV or tent campsites, some with hookups and pull-throughs. Restrooms, showers, laundry facilities, picnic tables, grills, water, and a sanitary disposal station are on-site. Pets are allowed on leashes.

Reservations, fees: Reservations are accepted; the fee is $13–16 per night. Open April–October.

Directions: The RV park is at the south end of town, one mile south of the Hot Spring State Park.

Contact: Grandview RV Park, 122 Hwy. 20 South, Thermopolis, WY 82443; tel./fax 307/864-3463.

Trip notes: You can play golf at the Legion nine-hole golf course in Thermopolis and soak in the Big Spring at Hot Springs State Park. There are guided riverboat trips available, and good fishing in the Bighorn River. The Hot Springs Historical Museum displays artifacts of frontier days.

The Wyoming Dinosaur Museum features bones and skeletons from a site nearby, and you can watch workers clean and prepare excavated bones for assembly and study.

Legend Rock State Petroglyph Site, 30 miles northwest of Thermopolis, offers a chance to view the historical writing on the cliff's face. Petroglyphs at the Legend Rock State site represent at least three styles of Native American art, one of which is related to early Hopi. Charcoal layers at the site have been estimated at over 2,000 years old. Visiting arrangements must be made through Hot Springs State Park, 220 Park St., Thermopolis, WY 82443; 307/864-2176. The site has a public restroom and picnic tables.

45 M/K RV Park

     5

Location: Near Thermopolis; map WY2, grid f4.

Campsites, facilities: There are 13 RV or tent campsites, some with hookups, picnic tables, and grills. Restrooms, showers, laundry facilities, store, water, and a sanitary disposal station are available.

Reservations, fees: Reservations are accepted; the fee is $10–12.50 per night. Open May–September 10.

Directions: From U.S. 20/Highway 789, continue on Shoshoni Street to the RV park.

Contact: M/K RV Park, 720 Shoshoni St., Thermopolis, WY 82443; 307/864-2778.

Trip notes: You can play golf at the Legion nine-hole golf course in Thermopolis, and soak in the Big Spring at Hot Springs State Park.

There are guided riverboat trips available, and good fishing in the Bighorn River. The Hot Springs Historical Museum displays artifacts of frontier days.

The Wyoming Dinosaur Museum features bones and skeletons from a site nearby, and you can watch workers clean and prepare excavated bones for assembly and study.

Legend Rock State Petroglyph Site, 30 miles northwest of Thermopolis, offers a chance to view the historical writing on the cliff's face. Petroglyphs at the Legend Rock State site represent at least three styles of Native American art, one of which is related to early Hopi. Charcoal layers at the site have been estimated at over 2,000 years old. Visiting arrangements must be made through Hot Springs State Park, 220 Park St., Thermopolis, WY 82443; 307/864-2176. The site has a public restroom and picnic tables.

46 New RV Park

 5

Location: In Thermopolis; map WY2, grid f4.
Campsites, facilities: There are 10 RV campsites, some with hookups, picnic tables, grills, and water. No tents are allowed.
Reservations, fees: Reservations are accepted; the fee is $9.50 per night. Open April 1–November 1.
Directions: From the intersection of U.S. 20 and Highway 120 in Thermopolis, go east to 2nd Street and the RV park.
Contact: New RV Park, 113 N. 2nd, Thermopolis, WY 82443; 307/864-3926.
Trip notes: You can play golf at the Legion nine-hole golf course in Thermopolis, and soak in the Big Spring at Hot Springs State Park. There are guided riverboat trips and good fishing in the Bighorn River. The Hot Springs Historical Museum displays artifacts of frontier days.

The Wyoming Dinosaur Museum features bones and skeletons from a site nearby, and you can watch workers clean and prepare excavated bones for assembly and study.

Legend Rock State Petroglyph Site, 30 miles northwest of Thermopolis, offers a chance to view the historical writing on the cliff's face. Petroglyphs at the Legend Rock State site represent at least three styles of Native American art, one of which is related to early Hopi. Charcoal layers at the site have been estimated at over 2,000 years old. Visiting arrangements must be made through Hot Springs State Park, 220 Park St., Thermopolis, WY 82443; 307/864-2176. The site has a public restroom and picnic tables.

47 Boysen Marina

 5

Location: At Boysen Reservoir; map WY2, grid g4.
Campsites, facilities: There are numerous RV and tent sites, some with hookups, and restrooms, showers, water, and a restaurant. Pets are allowed on leashes.
Reservations, fees: Reservations are accepted; the fee is $12.50 per night. Open December 1–October 1.
Directions: From Thermopolis, go 20 miles south on U.S. 20 toward Shoshoni to Boysen Reservoir.
Contact: Boysen Marina, 827 Brannon Rd., Shoshoni, WY 82649; 307/876-2772.
Trip notes: This campground is on Boysen Reservoir near Boysen State Park. This 35,000-acre park includes the reservoir where you can fish for walleye, perch, sauger, crappie, ling, rainbow, cutthroat, and brown trout. Fishing licenses are required and are available at the Boysen Lake Marina. You can also swim, boat, and water-ski on the reservoir.

48 Boysen State Park

 5

Location: Near Shoshoni; map WY2, grid g4.
Campsites, facilities: There are numerous RV and tent sites, some with pull-throughs, picnic tables and grills. Vault toilets, water,

and a sanitary disposal station are available. Pets are allowed on leashes.

Reservations, fees: No reservations are needed; the fee is $4–9 per night. Open all year, but services are only available in season. The stay limit is 14 days.

Directions: From Thermopolis, go 20 miles south on U.S. 20 toward Shoshoni to park headquarters, 13 miles north of Shoshoni.

Contact: Boysen State Park, 15 Ash, Shoshoni, WY 82649; 307/876-2796; or contact the Division of State Parks & Historical Sites, Cheyenne, WY 82009; 307/777-6323.

Trip notes: This 35,000-acre park includes the reservoir where you can fish for walleye, perch, sauger, crappie, ling, rainbow, cutthroat and brown trout. Fishing licenses are required and are available at the Boysen Lake Marina. You can also swim, boat, and water-ski on the reservoir.

49 Owl Creek Kampground

 5

Location: Near Riverton, on the Wind River Reservation; map WY2, grid h3.

Campsites, facilities: There are 20 RV sites with partial to full hookups, pull-throughs, and numerous tent sites with picnic table and grills. Showers, laundry facilities, water, restrooms, propane, and a sanitary disposal station are available. Pets are allowed on leashes. A playground, store, and a group tenting area are on-site.

Reservations, fees: Reservations are accepted; the fee is $16.50 per night. Open May 15–September 15.

Directions: From Riverton, go five miles east on U.S. 26 to the campground.

Contact: Frank & Pat Petek, Owl Creek Kampground, 11124 U.S. 26 East-789, Riverton, WY 82501; 307/856-2869.

Trip notes: You can golf at the 18-hole Riverton Country Club and hike or mountain bike on the nearby 25-mile gravel trail developed from a former railroad.

50 Rudy's Camper Court

 5

Location: In Riverton; map WY2, grid h3.

Campsites, facilities: There are 24 RV or tent campsites, some with hookups, picnic tables, and grills. Showers, restrooms, water, and a sanitary disposal station are available.

Reservations, fees: Reservations are accepted; the fee is $10.50–16.50 per night. Open year-round.

Directions: From Shoshoni, take U.S. 26 to Riverton; after the third light (there's a Norwest Bank), turn right on Rosefield and go a half block to the campground.

Contact: Rudy's Camper Court, 622 E. Lincoln, Riverton, WY 82501; 307/856-9764.

Trip notes: You can golf at the 18-hole Riverton Country Club and hike or mountain bike on the nearby 25-mile gravel trail developed from a former railroad.

51 Riverton RV Park

 5

Location: In Riverton; map WY2, grid h3.

Campsites, facilities: There are 66 RV or tent campsites with picnic tables and grills, some hookups, and pull-throughs. Showers, laundry facilities, water, restrooms, and a sanitary disposal station are available.

Reservations, fees: Reservations are accepted; the fee is $10–20 per night. Open year-round.

Directions: From Shoshoni, take U.S. 26 to Riverton; this campground is on Park Street.

Contact: Riverton RV Park, 1618 E. Park, Riverton, WY 82501; 307/856-3913 or 800/528-3913; fax 307/856-9559.

Trip notes: You can golf at the 18-hole Riverton Country Club and hike or mountain bike on the nearby 25-mile gravel trail developed from a former railroad.

52 Hells Half Acre Campground

   4

Location: West of Casper; map WY2, grid h8.

Campsites, facilities: There are 40 RV or tent campsites, some with hookups, picnic tables, and grills. Restrooms, showers, water, and a sanitary disposal station are available.

Reservations, fees: Reservations are accepted; the fee is $3–15 per night. Open May 1–November 1.

Directions: From Casper, go 40 miles west on U.S. 20/26 to the campground.

Contact: Hells Half Acre, P.O. Box 80, Powder River, WY 82648; 307/472-0018.

Trip notes: The campground is in 320 acres of colorful badlands. The Indians used this area as a buffalo jump, driving the animals over a cliff to their deaths. The movie *Starship Troopers* was filmed here.

WAYNE SCHERR

Tent camping, Wyoming

MAP WY3

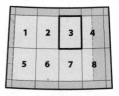

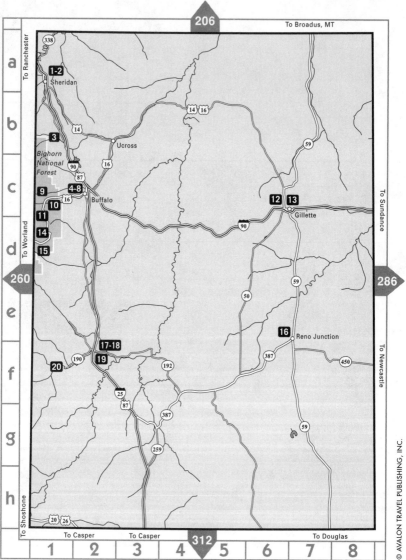

To Broadus, MT

338
1-2
Sheridan
14 16
59
14
3
Ucross
Bighorn
National
Forest
16
90
87
9
4-8
Buffalo
12 13
10
Gillette
16
11
90
14
15

50
59

16
Reno Junction
17-18
387
450
20
190
19
192

25
87
387

259
59

To Casper   To Casper   To Douglas

To Ranchester
To Worland
To Shoshone
To Sundance
To Newcastle

206
260
286
312

20 26

© AVALON TRAVEL PUBLISHING, INC.

a b c d e f g h

1 2 3 4 5 6 7 8

CHAPTER WY3

1 Big Horn Mountain KOA
  Campground 279
2 Sheridan RV Park 279
3 Wagon Box Campground ..279
4 Mountain View Motel and
  Campground 280
5 Buffalo KOA
  Campground 280
6 Deer Park Campground ...280
7 Indian Campground 281
8 Big Horn Mountain
  Campground 281
9 Middle Fork 281

10 Tie Hack 281
11 South Fork.....................281
12 High Plains Campground ..282
13 Greentrees Crazy Woman
   Campground 282
14 Crazy Woman 282
15 Lost Cabin.....................282
16 Sagebluff RV Park...........283
17 Kaycee RV Park #1.........283
18 Kaycee RV Park #2.........283
19 Kaycee Town Park...........283
20 Hole in the Wall
   Campground 284

1 Big Horn Mountain KOA Campground

   5

Location: In Sheridan; map WY3, grid a1.

Campsites, facilities: There are 80 RV campsites and several tent sites, with picnic tables and grills. Hookups, a sanitary disposal facility, restrooms, showers, laundry facilities, water, a swimming pool, and game room are available.

Reservations, fees: No reservations are needed; the fee is $15–22 per night. Open May 1–October 5.

Directions: From I-90 at Sheridan, take Exit 20, turn right, and follow the signs.

Contact: Big Horn Mountain KOA Campground, 63 Decker Rd., P.O. Box 35A, Sheridan, WY 82801; 307/674-8766.

Trip notes: There are several streams in this area where you can fish. Sheridan has a golf course.

2 Sheridan RV Park

    4

Location: In Sheridan; map WY3, grid a1.

Campsites, facilities: There are 38 RV or tent campsites. There are hookups, pull-through sites, a sanitary disposal facility, restrooms, showers, laundry facilities, and water available.

Reservations, fees: No reservations are needed; the fee is $15–17 per night. Open April 1–November 1.

Directions: From I-90 at Sheridan, Exit 25, go west; at the first light turn left; the RV Park is across from ACE Hardware.

Contact: Sheridan RV Park, 807 Avoca Ave., Sheridan, WY 82801; 307/674-0722.

Trip notes: You can fish and hike in Bighorn National Forest.

3 Wagon Box Campground

   4

Location: South of Sheridan; map WY3, grid b1.

Campsites, facilities: There are 36 RV or tent campsites. Hookups, a sanitary disposal facility, restrooms, showers, laundry facilities, picnic tables, grills, and water are available.

Reservations, fees: No reservations are needed; the fee is $12–18 per night. Open year-round.

Directions: From Sheridan, go south on I-90 and take Exit 33, go west one mile to the stop sign, turn south on U.S. 87 and go five miles to Highway 194, and then turn right on Highway 340. Drive through the town of Story; the campground is behind the Wagon Box Inn on the right.

Contact: Wagon Box Campground, 103 N. Piney, Story, WY 82842; 307/683-2445, 800/308-2444.

Trip notes: You can fish in the Bighorn River and hike in Bighorn National Forest.

4 Mountain View Motel and Campground

 4

Location: In Buffalo; map WY3, grid c2.

Campsites, facilities: There are 21 RV or tent campsites. Hookups, pull-through sites, a sanitary disposal facility, restrooms, showers, laundry facilities, picnic tables, grills, and water are available.

Reservations, fees: No reservations are needed; the fee is $10–15 per night. Open year-round.

Directions: From Gillette, go 67 miles west on I-90 to Buffalo. Turn left onto North Main Street/U.S. 16 to Fort Street, and turn right to the campground.

Contact: Mountain View Motel and Campground, 585 Fort St., Buffalo, WY 82834; 307/684-2881.

Trip notes: Buffalo has a swimming pool, the Clear Creek Trail System for hiking or biking, and a golf course.

5 Buffalo KOA Campground

 5

Location: In Buffalo; map WY3, grid c2.

Campsites, facilities: There are 87 RV or tent campsites. Hookups, a sanitary disposal facility, restrooms, showers, laundry facilities, a swimming pool, picnic tables, grills, game room, and water are available.

Reservations, fees: No reservations are needed; the fee is $14–27 per night. Open April 15–October 15.

Directions: From I-25 at Buffalo, take Exit 299; the campground is east on U.S. 16.

Contact: Buffalo KOA Campground, 87 Hwy. 16, Buffalo, WY 82834; 307/684-5423, 800/562-5403.

Trip notes: Buffalo has a swimming pool, the Clear Creek Trail System for hiking or biking, and a golf course.

6 Deer Park Campground

 4

Location: In Buffalo; map WY3, grid c2.

Campsites, facilities: There are 76 RV campsites, which can accommodate a maximum RV length of 85 feet. Hookups, pull-through sites, a sanitary disposal facility, restroom, showers, swimming pool, laundry facilities, picnic tables, grill, game room, and water are available.

Reservations, fees: No reservations are needed; the fee is $14–21 per night. Open May 1–October 10. Group facilities can be arranged.

Directions: From I-25 at Buffalo take Exit 299; the campground is almost a mile east on U.S. 16.

Contact: Deer Park Campground, 146 U.S. 16 E, P.O. Box 568, Buffalo, WY 82834; 307/684-5722, 800/222-9960; email: information@deerparkrv.com; website: www.deerparkrv.com.

Trip notes: Buffalo has a swimming pool, the Clear Creek Trail System for hiking or biking, and a golf course.

7 Indian Campground

 4

Location: In Buffalo; map WY3, grid c2.

Campsites, facilities: There are 120 RV or tent campsites. Hookups, a sanitary disposal facility, restrooms, showers, swimming pool, laundry facilities, picnic tables, grills, and water are available.

Reservations, fees: No reservations are needed; the fee is $15–21 per night. Open April 1–October 31.

Directions: From I-25 at Buffalo, take Exit 299; the campground is to the left off U.S. 16 east of town.

Contact: Indian Campground, 660 E. Hart St., Buffalo, WY 82834; 307/684-9601.

Trip notes: Buffalo has a swimming pool, the Clear Creek Trail System for hiking or biking, and a golf course.

8 Big Horn Mountain Campground

 4

Location: West of Buffalo; map WY3, grid c2.

Campsites, facilities: There are 73 RV or tent campsites, some with hookups and pull-through sites. A sanitary disposal facility, restrooms, showers, swimming pool, laundry facilities, picnic tables, grills, and water are available.

Reservations, fees: No reservations are needed; the fee is $14–18 per night. Open year-round.

Directions: From Buffalo, go two miles west on U.S. 16 to the campground.

Contact: Big Horn Mountain Campground, 8935 Hwy. 16 West, Buffalo, WY 82834; 307/684-2307.

Trip notes: Buffalo has a swimming pool, the Clear Creek Trail System for hiking or biking, and a golf course.

9 Middle Fork

 5

Location: West of Buffalo; map WY3, grid c1.

Campsites, facilities: There are nine RV campsites, which can accommodate a maximum RV length of 16 feet, plus tent sites. Restrooms, picnic tables, grills, and water are available.

Reservations, fees: No reservations are needed; the fee is $10 per night. Open May 15–October 31. The stay limit is 14 days.

Directions: From Buffalo, go 14 miles west on U.S. 16, then less than one-half mile west off the highway to the campground.

Contact: Bureau of Land Management, 1425 Fort St., Buffalo, WY 82834; 307/684-1100.

Trip notes: You can fish for small trout in the Middle Fork of Clear Creek.

10 Tie Hack

 5

Location: West of Buffalo; map WY3, grid c1.

Campsites, facilities: There are nine RV campsites, plus tent sites. Restrooms, picnic tables, grills, and water are available.

Reservations, fees: No reservations are needed; the fee is $10 per night. Open May 15–October 31.

Directions: From Buffalo, go 15 miles west on U.S. 16 to the campground.

Contact: Bureau of Land Management, 1425 Fort St., Buffalo, WY 82834; 307/684-1100.

Trip notes: You can fish in Crazy Woman Creek.

11 South Fork

   6

Location: West of Buffalo; map WY3, grid c1.

Campsites, facilities: There are 10 RV campsites, which can accommodate a maximum RV length of 16 feet, and five walk-in units for tents. Restrooms, picnic tables, grills, and water are available.

Reservations, fees: No reservations are needed; the fee is $10 per night. Open May 15–October 31. The stay limit is 14 days.

Directions: From Buffalo, go 15 miles west on U.S. 16, then less than one-half mile east off the highway to the campground.

Contact: Bureau of Land Management, 1425 Fort St., Buffalo, WY 82834; 307/684-1100.

Trip notes: You can fish in the South Fork of Clear Creek.

12 High Plains Campground

   4

Location: In Gillette; map WY3, grid c6.

Campsites, facilities: There are 65 RV campsites, plus tent sites. Hookups, pull-through sites, a sanitary disposal station, restrooms, showers, laundry facilities, picnic tables, grills, and water are available.

Reservations, fees: Reservations are accepted; the fee is $11–15 per night. Open year-round.

Directions: From I-90 take Exit 129 at Gillette and go one mile south to the campground.

Contact: High Plains Campground, 1600 Garner Lake Rd. S., Gillette, WY 82818; 307/687-7339.

Trip notes: Gillette has two golf courses and a swimming pool.

13 Greentrees Crazy Woman Campground

   4

Location: In Gillette; map WY3, grid c7.

Campsites, facilities: There are 85 RV campsites and 16 tent sites. Hookups, pull-through sites, a sanitary disposal facility, restrooms, showers, a swimming pool, laundry facilities, game room, picnic tables, grills, and water are available.

Reservations, fees: Reservations are accepted; the fee is $16–30 per night. Open year-round.

Directions: From I-90 at Gillette, take Exit 124

for one mile to the campground.

Contact: Greentrees Crazy Woman Campground, 1001 W. 2nd, Gillette, WY 82818; 307/682-3665.

Trip notes: Gillette has two golf courses and a swimming pool.

14 Crazy Woman

   4

Location: West of Buffalo; map WY3, grid d1.

Campsites, facilities: There are six RV campsites, which can accommodate a maximum RV length of 14 feet, plus tent sites. Restrooms, picnic tables, grills, and water are available.

Reservations, fees: No reservations are needed; the fee is $9 per night. Open May 15–September 30. The stay limit is 14 days.

Directions: From Buffalo, go 26 miles west on U.S. 16, then less than a half mile west on a dirt road to the campground.

Contact: Bureau of Land Management, 1425 Fort St., Buffalo, WY 82834; 307/684-1100.

Trip notes: This campground is near a meadow and you can fish in Crazy Woman Creek.

15 Lost Cabin

   5

Location: West of Buffalo; map WY3, grid d1.

Campsites, facilities: There are 19 RV campsites, which can accommodate a maximum RV length of 45 feet, plus tent sites. Restrooms, picnic tables, grills, and water are available.

Reservations, fees: No reservations are needed; the fee is $9 per night. Open May 15–October 31. The stay limit is 14 days.

Directions: From Buffalo, travel 27 miles west on U.S. 16 to the campground.

Contact: Bureau of Land Management, 1425 Fort St., Buffalo, WY 82834; 307/684-1100.

Trip notes: You can fish in Crazy Woman Creek.

16 Sagebluff RV Park

   3

Location: Southwest of Gillette; map WY3, grid e6.

Campsites, facilities: There are 65 RV or tent campsites, some with hookups. Restrooms, showers, laundry facilities, and water are available.

Reservations, fees: No reservations are needed; the fee is $9–15 per night. Open year-round.

Directions: From Gillette, go south 38 miles on Highway 59 to Wright. From Wright, go west on Highway 387 for three miles to the campground on the left.

Contact: Sagebluff RV Park, P.O. Box 286, Wright, WY 82732; 307/464-1305.

Trip notes: Wright was born of necessity; the Atlantic Richfield Company needed housing for its coal-mining employees. This town is virtually in the middle of nowhere. There is a recreation center with a pool and a museum.

17 Kaycee RV Park #1

   3

Location: In Kaycee; map WY3, grid f2.

Campsites, facilities: There are 17 RV or tent campsites, some with hookups, picnic tables, and grills. Restrooms, water, and a sanitary disposal station are available.

Reservations, fees: Reservations are accepted; the fee is $5–15 per night. Open year-round.

Directions: From Buffalo, go south on I-25 for 46 miles to Exit 254. Turn left at the stop sign and go through Kaycee to the campground on the right.

Contact: Kaycee RV Park, 42 Mayoworth Rd.; P.O. Box 11, Kaycee, WY 82639; 307/738-2233.

Trip notes: This campground is next to Middle Fork Powder River, where you can fish for brown trout.

18 Kaycee RV Park #2

   3

Location: In Kaycee; map WY3, grid f2.

Campsites, facilities: There are 10 RV or tent campsites, some with hookups, picnic tables, and grills. Restrooms, showers, water, and a sanitary disposal station are available.

Reservations, fees: Reservations are accepted; the fee is $5–15 per night. Open year-round.

Directions: From Buffalo, go south on I-25 for 46 miles to Exit 254. Turn right; the campground is on the right.

Contact: Kaycee RV Park #2, 101 Old Barnum Rd.; P.O. Box 11, Kaycee, WY 82639; 307/738-2233.

Trip notes: This campground is next to Middle Fork Powder River, where you can fish for brown trout.

19 Kaycee Town Park

   3

Location: In downtown Kaycee; map WY3, grid f2.

Campsites, facilities: There are numerous RV and tent sites, with picnic tables and grills. Restrooms, water, and a sanitary disposal station are here.

Reservations, fees: No reservations are needed; no fees are charged. Open year-round. The stay limit is five days.

Directions: From Buffalo, go south on I-25 for 46 miles to Exit 254; turn left at the stop sign, then right into Kaycee; the campground is on the right.

Contact: Town of Kaycee, P.O. Box 265, Kaycee, WY 82639.

Trip notes: This campground is next to Middle Fork Powder River, where you can fish for brown trout.

20 Hole in the Wall Campground

     5

Location: West of Kaycee; map WY3, grid f1.

Campsites, facilities: There are 11 RV or tent campsites, some with hookups. Water is available.

Reservations, fees: Reservations are accepted; the fee is $5–10 per night. Open May–October.

Directions: From Casper go north 64 miles on I-25 to Kaycee. At Kaycee, go north on Highway 191 to the Barnum Road exit, and take Barnum Road west for 17 miles to the campground.

Contact: Hole in the Wall Campground, 1773 Barnum Rd., Kaycee, WY 82639; 307/738-2340.

Trip notes: You can play golf at the Legion nine-hole golf course in Thermopolis and soak in the Big Spring at Hot Springs State Park.

There are guided riverboat trips and good fishing at the Bighorn River. The Hot Springs Historical Museum displays artifacts of frontier days.

The Wyoming Dinosaur Museum features bones from a site nearby, and you can watch workers clean and prepare excavated bones for assembly and study.

Legend Rock State Petroglyph Site, 30 miles northwest of Thermopolis, offers a chance to view the historical writing on the cliff's face. Petroglyphs at the Legend Rock State site represent at least three styles of Native American art, one of which is related to early Hopi. Charcoal layers at the site have been estimated at over 2,000 years old. Visiting arrangements must be made through Hot Springs State Park, 220 Park St., Thermopolis, WY 82443; 307/864-2176. The site has a public restroom and picnic tables.

Horses at ranger station,
Shoshone National Forest

WAYNE SCHERR

MAP WY4

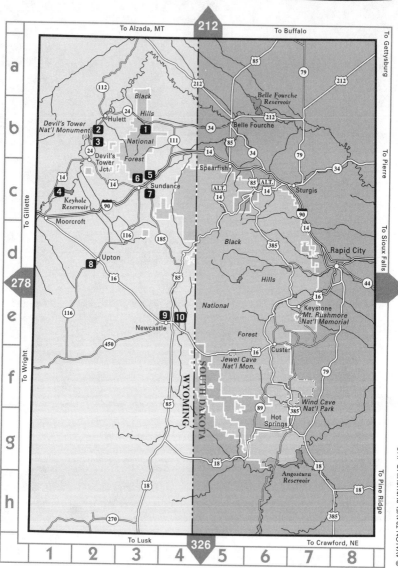

To Alzada, MT   **212**   To Buffalo

To Gettysburg

112

Black

Hills

Hulett

Devil's Tower
Nat'l Monument

National

Devil's
Tower
Jct.

Forest

Sundance

Keyhole
Reservoir

Moorcroft

Upton

116

90

185

116

450

Newcastle

WYOMING

SOUTH DAKOTA

To Wright

To Gillette

To Lusk   **326**

85

79

212

Belle Fourche
Reservoir

Belle Fourche

Spearfish

ALT.

ALT.

Sturgis

Rapid City

Black

Hills

National

Forest

Keystone
Mt. Rushmore
Nat'l Memorial

Custer

Jewel Cave
Nat'l Mon.

Wind Cave
Nat'l Park

Hot
Springs

Angostura
Reservoir

To Crawford, NE

To Pierre

To Sioux Falls

To Pine Ridge

© AVALON TRAVEL PUBLISHING, INC.

CHAPTER WY4

1 Bearlodge 287
2 Belle Fourche River 287
3 Devils Tower KOA 287
4 Keyhole State Park 287
5 Reuter 288
6 Cook Lake Campground ... 288
7 Mountain View
  Campground 288
8 County Market Conoco 288
9 Rimrock RV 289
10 Crystal Park
  Campground 289

1 Bearlodge

 6

Location: At the edge of Black Hills National Forest; map WY4, grid b3.

Campsites, facilities: There are eight RV campsites, plus tent sites. There are restrooms, picnic tables, and grills available.

Reservations, fees: No reservations are needed; the fee is $10 per night. Open year-round.

Directions: From Sundance, go 10 miles east to Exit 199 and then nine miles north on Highway 111 to Aladdin. From Aladdin, go seven miles west on Highway 24 to the campground.

Contact: Black Hills National Forest, Bearlodge Ranger District, P.O. Box 680, Sundance, WY 82729; 307/783-1361; website: www.fs.fed.us.

Trip notes: You can hike and fish in the national forest.

2 Belle Fourche River

 4

Location: At Devils Tower National Monument; map WY4, grid b2.

Campsites, facilities: There are 51 RV campsites, which can accommodate a maximum RV length of 35 feet. There are no hookups, but there are tent sites. Restrooms, picnic tables, grills, and water are available.

Reservations, fees: No reservations are needed; the fee is $12 per night (there's an $8 vehicle fee). Open year-round.

Directions: From Sundance, go north on U.S. 14 for 28 miles to Highway 24; take Highway 24 six miles to Devils Tower, on the left.

Contact: Belle Fourche River, P.O. Box 10, Devils Tower, WY 82714; 307/467-5283.

Trip notes: You can hike and rock-climb here.

3 Devils Tower KOA

 4

Location: At Devils Tower National Monument; map WY4, grid b2.

Campsites, facilities: There are 145 RV or tent campsites. Hookups, a sanitary disposal facility, restrooms, showers, laundry facilities, picnic tables, grills, and water are available.

Reservations, fees: No reservations are needed; the fee is $20–26 per night. Open May 1–September 25.

Directions: From Sundance, go north on U.S. 14 for 28 miles to Highway 24; take Highway 24 six miles to Devils Tower, on the left.

Contact: Devils Tower KOA, P.O. Box 100, Devils Tower, WY 82714; 307/467-5395, 800/562-5785.

Trip notes: You can hike and rock-climb here.

4 Keyhole State Park

 5

Location: East of Moorcroft; map WY4, grid c1.

Campsites, facilities: There are numerous RV and tent sites. Pull-through sites, a sanitary disposal facility, restrooms, picnic tables, grills, and water are available.

Reservations, fees: No reservations are needed; the fee is $14 per night. Open May 1–October 1.

Directions: From Moorcroft, go 12 miles east on I-90, take Exit 165, and then go six miles north on the paved road to the state park.

Contact: Keyhole State Park, 353 McKean Rd., Moorcroft, WY 82721; 307/756-3596.

Trip notes: You can hike here.

5 Reuter

 6

Location: In Black Hills National Forest; map WY4, grid c3.

Campsites, facilities: There are 24 RV campsites, plus tent sites. Restrooms, picnic tables, grills, and water are available.

Reservations, fees: No reservations are needed; the fee is $8 per night. Open year-round.

Directions: From Sundance, go two miles west on U.S. 14, then turn right onto the road (it has no name) and continue three or four miles to the campground on the left.

Contact: Black Hills National Forest, Hwy. 14 East, P.O. Box 680, Sundance, WY 82729; 307/283-1361; website: www.fs.fed.us.

Trip notes: You can hike and fish in Black Hills National Forest.

6 Cook Lake Campground

    5

Location: In the Black Hills National Forest; map WY4, grid c3.

Campsites, facilities: There are 34 RV campsites, plus tent sites. Restrooms, a game room, and water available.

Reservations, fees: No reservations are needed; the fee is $9–13 per night. Open year-round.

Directions: From Sundance, go west on U.S. 14 for two miles; turn right to the campground.

Contact: Black Hills National Forest, Hwy. 14 East, P.O. Box 680, Sundance, WY 82729; 307/283-1361; website: www.fs.fed.us.

Trip notes: You can hike in the area.

7 Mountain View Campground

    5

Location: Near Black Hills National Forest; map WY4, grid c3.

Campsites, facilities: There are 63 RV or tent campsites. Hookups, a sanitary disposal facility, restrooms, showers, swimming pool, laundry facilities, picnic tables, grills, game room, and water are available.

Reservations, fees: No reservations are needed; the fee is $15–22 per night. Open April–November.

Directions: From Sundance, go one mile east on U.S. 14, and you will see a big yellow sign for the campground.

Contact: Mountain View Campground, N. Gov. Valley Rd., Sundance, WY 82729; 307/283-2270, 800/792-8439.

Trip notes: You can hike in Black Hills National Forest.

8 County Market Conoco

  3

Location: Near Moorcroft; map WY4, grid d2.

Campsites, facilities: There are six RV campsites, some with hookups, picnic tables, and grills.

Reservations, fees: No reservations are needed; the fee is $10 per night. Open year-round.

Directions: From Sheridan, take I-90 136 miles east to Moorcroft, then take U.S. 16 19 miles southeast to Upton, and the campground is right there.

Contact: County Market Conoco, 909 2nd St., Upton, WY 82730; 307/468-2551.

Trip notes: You can hike in the area.

Rimrock RV

 5

Location: In Newcastle; map WY4, grid e4.

Campsites, facilities: There are 55 RV or tent campsites, some with hookups, picnic tables, and grills. Showers, restrooms, laundry facilities, water, a sanitary disposal station, and swimming pool are available.

Reservations, fees: Reservations are accepted; the fee is $5–15 per night. Open April 1–October 31.

Directions: From Gillette, take I-90 26 miles to Moorcroft, then take U.S. 16 east 48 miles to Newcastle. The RV park is on the right.

Contact: Rimrock RV, 2206 W. Main, Newcastle, WY 82701; 307/746-2007, 307/746-2207; fax 307/746-4273; email: lhsuccess@yahoo.com.

Trip notes: Newcastle is a gateway community to the Black Hills of South Dakota.

Crystal Park Campground

 5

Location: In Newcastle; map WY4, grid e4.

Campsites, facilities: There are 100 RV or tent campsites, some with hookups, picnic tables, and grills. Showers, restrooms, laundry facilities, water, and a swimming pool are available.

Reservations, fees: No reservations are needed; the fee is $9–13 per night. Open April–November.

Directions: From Gillette, take I-90 26 miles to Moorcroft, then take U.S. 16 east 48 miles to Newcastle. At the junction of U.S. 16 and U.S. 85, go through the stoplight on the northeast corner of the junction and go straight to the campground.

Contact: Crystal Park Campground, 2 Fountain Plaza, Newcastle, WY 82701; 307/746-4426 or 800/882-8858; fax 307/746-3206.

Trip notes: Newcastle is a gateway community to the Black Hills of South Dakota.

Flaming Gorge National Recreation Area

MAP WY5

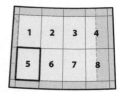

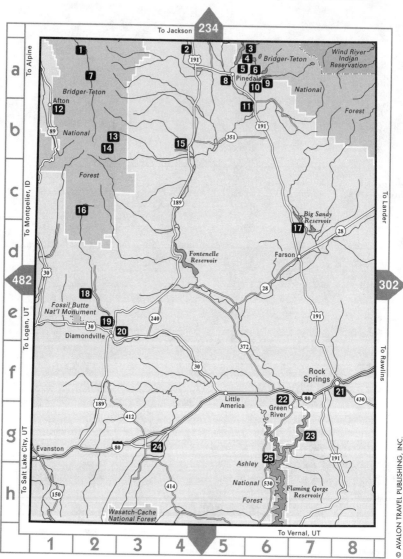

© AVALON TRAVEL PUBLISHING, INC.

CHAPTER WY5

1 Moose Flat 293
2 Warren Bridge 293
3 Trails End 294
4 Fremont Lake 294
5 Lakeside Lodge Resort
    & Marina 294
6 Half Moon 294
7 Forest Park 295
8 Pinedale Campground 295
9 Scab Creek..................... 295
10 Boulder Lake 295
11 Wind River View
    Campground 296
12 Swift Creek................... 296
13 Sacajawea 296

14 Middle Piney Lake 296
15 Harper's Park & RV 297
16 Hams Fork 297
17 Big Sandy Recreation
    Area 297
18 Lake Viva Naughton 297
19 Foothills Mobile Home
    & RV Park 298
20 Riverside RV Park........... 298
21 Rock Springs KOA........... 298
22 Tex's Travel Camp 299
23 Firehole Canyon 299
24 Lyman/Fort Bridger
    KOA............................. 299
25 Buckboard Crossing........ 300

1 Moose Flat

     5

Location: In Bridger-Teton National Forest; map WY5, grid a2.

Campsites, facilities: There are 10 RV or tent campsites with picnic tables and grills. Water and vault toilets are available.

Reservations, fees: No reservations are needed; the fee is $5 per night. Open June–September. The stay limit is 16 days.

Directions: From Jackson, go south on U.S. 189 to Hoback Junction, then go west on U.S. 26/89 23 miles to Alpine. From Alpine, go 23 miles southeast on Forest Road 10138 (Greys River Road) to the campground.

Contact: Greys River Ranger District, 145 Washington St., P.O. Box 338, Afton, WY 83110; 307/886-3166.

Trip notes: This campground is along Greys River, where you can fish for cutthroat.

2 Warren Bridge

   5

Location: West of Pinedale; map WY5, grid a4.

Campsites, facilities: There are 16 or more RV and tent sites with picnic tables, grills, and restrooms are available.

Reservations, fees: No reservations are needed; the fee is $6 per night. Open June 1–October 31. The stay limit is 16 days.

Directions: From Pinedale, go west on U.S. 191 to U.S. 189, then north 24 miles. The campground is on left before you cross the bridge.

Contact: Pinedale Field Office, Bureau of Land Management, 432 E. Mill St., P.O. Box 768, Pinedale, WY 82941-0768; 307/367-5300 or fax 307/367-5329.

Trip notes: You can fish for trout in the Green River. There are several camping sites along the west side of the Green River, but they are not recommended for trailers or RVs because the road is precipitous. These sites have no fee and a 14-day stay limit.

3 Trails End

 7

Location: In Bridger-Teton National Forest; map WY5, grid a5.

Campsites, facilities: There are eight RV or tent campsites with picnic tables and grills. Water and vault toilets are provided.

Reservations, fees: No reservations are needed; the fee is $7 per night. Open June 25–September. The stay limit is 10 days.

Directions: From Pinedale, go north on Fremont Lake Road to Forest Service Road 134 and follow it 11 miles to the campground at the northeast end of Fremont Lake.

Contact: Pinedale Ranger District, 210 W. Pine St., P.O. Box 220, Pinedale, WY 82941; 307/367-4326.

Trip notes: This campground is in a very scenic area at the north end of Fremont Lake. Trails into the Bridger-Teton Wilderness begin nearby.

4 Fremont Lake

 6

Location: Bridger-Teton National Forest; map WY5, grid a5.

Campsites, facilities: There are 53 RV or tent sites with picnic tables and grills. Vault toilets, water, and a boat ramp are available.

Reservations, fees: Reservations are accepted; the fee is $6 per night. Open May 25–September 10. The stay limit is 10 days.

Directions: From Pinedale, go three miles northeast on Fremont Lake Road, then four miles northeast on Forest Service Road 134 to the campground.

Contact: Pinedale Ranger District, 210 W. Pine St., P.O. Box 220, Pinedale, WY 82941; 307/367-4326.

Trip notes: This campground is on the east side of Fremont Lake, where you can fish for cutthroat and lake trout.

5 Lakeside Lodge Resort & Marina

 4

Location: North of Pinedale on Fremont Lake; map WY5, grid a5.

Campsites, facilities: There are 26 RV or tent campsites, some with hookups, picnic tables, and grills. Restrooms, hot showers, water, and a sanitary disposal station are available. A restaurant and marina are at the site.

Reservations, fees: Reservations are accepted; the fee is $10–20 per night. Open mid-May–mid-October.

Directions: From Pinedale, go four miles north of town on Fremont Lake Road (Forest Road 134) to the east end of Fremont Lake to the campground.

Contact: Lakeside Lodge Resort & Marina, P.O. Box 1819, Pinedale, WY 82941; Reservations 307/367-2221, fax 307/367-6673; email: lakesidelodge@wyoming.com; website: www.lakesidelodge.com.

Trip notes: You can fish for cutthroat and lake trout in Fremont Lake.

6 Half Moon

 6

Location: Bridger-Teton National Forest; map WY5, grid a6.

Campsites, facilities: There are 18 RV or tent campsites with picnic tables and grills. Vault toilets are provided, and a boat ramp is nearby.

Reservations, fees: No reservations are needed; the fee is $4 per night. Open June 1–early September. The stay limit is 10 days.

Directions: From Pinedale, go north on Fremont Lake Road and then bear east to the campground on the northwest shore of Half Moon Lake.

Contact: Pinedale Ranger District, 210 W. Pine St., P.O. Box 220, Pinedale, WY 82941; 307/367-4326.

Trip notes: This campground is at Half Moon Lake, near Fremont Lake, where you can fish for cutthroat and lake trout.

7 Forest Park

 6

Location: Bridger-Teton National Forest; map WY5, grid a2.

Campsites, facilities: There are 13 RV and tent campsites with picnic tables and grill. Vault toilets and water are available.

Reservations, fees: No reservations are needed; the fee is $5 per night. Open June–September. The stay limit is 16 days.

Directions: From Jackson, go south on U.S. 189 to Hoback Junction, then go west on U.S. 26/89 23 miles to Alpine. From Alpine, go 36 miles southeast on Forest Road 10138 (Greys River Road) to the campground.

Contact: Greys River Ranger District, 145 Washington St., P.O. Box 338, Afton, WY 83110; 307/886-3166.

Trip notes: The Greys River Loop Road is a good one for mountain biking but narrow for RV traffic. The campground is near Greys River in elk wintering feeding ground. You can fish for cutthroat in Greys River.

8 Pinedale Campground

 5

Location: In Bridger-Teton National Forest; map WY5, grid a5.

Campsites, facilities: There are 60 RV or tent campsites, some with hookups, picnic tables, and grills. Restrooms, hot showers, laundry facilities, water, and a sanitary disposal station are available. A playground is on-site.

Reservations, fees: Reservations are accepted; the fee is $11–18 per night. Open May–October. The stay limit is 10 days.

Directions: Pinedale Campground is at the west end of Pinedale.

Contact: Pinedale Campground, P.O. Box 246, 204 S. Jackson, Pinedale, WY 82941; 307/367-4555; fax 307/367-2397.

Trip notes: This campground is along the Greys River, where you can fish for cutthroat.

9 Scab Creek

 6

Location: Northeast of Boulder; map WY5, grid a6.

Campsites, facilities: There are 10 RV or tent campsites with picnic tables and grills. Vault toilets and water are available.

Reservations, fees: No reservations are needed; no fee is required. Open June 1–October 31. The stay limit is 14 days.

Directions: From U.S. 191 at Pinedale, go 12 miles southeast to Boulder, then seven miles east on Highway 353 to Scab Creek Road (County Road 122), then left on BLM 5423 to the campground.

Contact: Pinedale Field Office, 432 E. Mill St., P.O. Box 768, Pinedale, WY 82941-0768; 307/367-5300, fax 307/367-5329; website: www.wy.blm.gov.

Trip notes: Scab Creek Trailhead is close by this campground for hiking, biking, and horseback riding.

10 Boulder Lake

 6

Location: In Bridger-Teton National Forest; map WY5, grid a6.

Campsites, facilities: There are 20 tent campsites, with picnic tables and grills. Vault toilets are available. No trailers.

Reservations, fees: No reservations are needed; the fee is $4 per night. Open June–mid-October. The stay limit is 10 days.

Directions: From Pinedale go 12 miles south on U.S. 191 to Boulder. From Boulder, go 2.5 miles east on Highway 353 to Boulder Lake Road (County Road 125); turn north and follow it for 10 miles. The campground is on the east side of Boulder Lake.

Contact: Bridger-Teton National Forest, Pinedale Ranger District, 210 W. Pine St., P.O. Box 220, Pinedale, WY 82941; 307/367-4326; website: www.fs.fed.us.

Trip notes: This campground is on Boulder Lake, where you can fish for rainbow and

Mackinaw trout, and there are trailheads for North Fork and Boulder Canyon Trails.

11 Wind River View Campground

    4

Location: Southwest of Bridger Wilderness; map WY5, grid b5.

Campsites, facilities: There are 22 RV or tent campsites, some with hookups and pull-throughs. Picnic tables, grills, restrooms, hot showers, laundry facilities, water, and a sanitary disposal station are available. A game room is on the premises.

Reservations, fees: Reservations are accepted; the fee is $4 per night for members. Open May 15–September 15.

Directions: From Jackson, go south 100 miles on U.S. 191 to Boulder. The campground is two miles north of Boulder on U.S. 191.

Contact: Wind River View Campground, 8889 Hwy. 191, Boulder WY 82923; 307/537-5453

Trip notes: You can fish, boat, and hike in the area.

12 Swift Creek

   5

Location: In Bridger-Teton National Forest; map WY5, grid b1.

Campsites, facilities: There are 13 RV or tent campsites with picnic tables and grills. Water and vault toilets are available.

Reservations, fees: No reservations are needed; the fee is $5 per night. Open June–early September. The stay limit is 16 days.

Directions: From Jackson, go south on U.S. 189 to Hoback Junction, then go west on U.S. 26/89 23 miles to Alpine, then 33 miles south on U.S. 89 to Afton. From Afton, go east on Swift Creek Canyon Road for two miles to the campground.

Contact: Greys River Ranger District, 145 Washington, P.O. Box 338, Afton, WY 83110; 307/886-3166.

Trip notes: East of the campground is Periodic Springs, a rare cold-water geyser, and Shawnee Falls, which tumbles into Swift Creek.

13 Sacajawea

     5

Location: In Bridger-Teton National Forest; map WY5, grid b2.

Campsites, facilities: There are 26 RV or tent campsites with picnic tables and grills. Water and vault toilets are available.

Reservations, fees: No reservations are needed; the fee is $4 per night. Open June 15–September 30. The stay limit is 16 days.

Directions: From Jackson, go south 88 miles on U.S. 189 to Big Piney. From Big Piney, go west on Middle Piney Road (Highway 350) 25 miles to Forest Road 10024, then ahead to Middle Piney Lake.

Contact: Big Piney Ranger District, Hwy. 189, P.O. Box 218, Big Piney, WY 83113; 307/276-3375.

Trip notes: This campground is along Middle Piney Creek.

14 Middle Piney Lake

   5

Location: In Bridger-Teton National Forest; map WY5, grid b2.

Campsites, facilities: There are six RV or tent campsites with picnic tables and grills. Water and vault toilets are available.

Reservations, fees: No reservations are needed; the fee is $4 per night. Open early June–September. The stay limit is 16 days.

Directions: From Jackson go south 88 miles on U.S. 189 to Big Piney. From Big Piney, go west on Middle Piney Road (Highway 350) 25 to Forest Road 10024, then west to Middle Piney Lake.

Contact: Big Pinedale Ranger District, 210 W. Pine St., P.O. Box 220, Pinedale, WY 82941; 307/367-4326.

Trip notes: The road to Middle Piney Lake is narrow, so RVs are not allowed. The campground is on Middle Piney Lake, where you can fish for brown, brook, rainbow, cutthroat, and lake trout. No powerboats are permitted on lake.

15 Harper's Park & RV

 4

Location: In Marbleton; map WY5, grid b4.

Campsites, facilities: There are 25 RV or tent campsites, some with hookups, picnic tables, and grills. Pull-throughs, restrooms, hot showers, laundry facilities, a game room, water, and a sanitary disposal station are available.

Reservations, fees: Reservations are accepted; the fee is $10–17 per night. Open all year.

Directions: From Jackson, go 90 miles south on U.S. 189 to Marbleton. The campground is on 3rd Street, directly behind Town Hall.

Contact: Harper's Park & RV, 23 E. 2nd St., P.O. Box 4478, Marbleton, WY 83113; 307/276-3611 for reservations.

Trip notes: You can hike in the Bridger-Teton National Forest, and fish in one of the many creeks and streams nearby.

16 Hams Fork

 6

Location: In the Bridge-Teton National Forest; map WY5, grid c2.

Campsites, facilities: There are 10 RV or tent sites with picnic tables and grills. Vault toilets and water are available.

Reservations, fees: No reservations are needed; the fee is $5 per night. Open June–September, depending on the weather. The stay limit is 16 days.

Directions: From Kemmerer, take U.S. 189 two miles north to Frontier and the junction of Highway 233; go north on Highway 233 (which turns to a gravel road) for almost 40 miles to the campground on the right.

Contact: Bridge-Teton National Forest, Kem-

merer Ranger District, Hwy. 189, P.O. Box 31, Kemmerer, WY 83101; 307/877-4515.

Trip notes: The Hams Fork Wildlife Trail is along the Hams Fork River and offers an excellent opportunity to observe wildlife. Moose are frequently seen along the river's edge, and cow moose with calves are out in June and July. Word of caution: moose are very protective of their young and not afraid of challenging people. Stay far away to ensure your own safety and that of the animals. The Ham's Fork River offers good trout fishing.

17 Big Sandy Recreation Area

 5

Location: North of Rock Springs; map WY5, grid d7.

Campsites, facilities: There are 11 RV or tent sites with picnic tables and grills. Vault toilets are available.

Reservations, fees: No reservations are needed; no fee is charged. Open year-round. There is a stay limit of 14 days.

Directions: From Rock Springs, go north on U.S. 191 to Big Sandy Recreation Area, then east to the fork in the road, where you can see the shore areas of Big Sandy Reservoir.

Contact: Bureau of Reclamation, Wyoming Game & Fish, 5400 Bishop Blvd., Cheyenne, WY 82006; 307/777-4600.

Trip notes: You can swim, boat or fish for brook, rainbow, cutthroat, or catfish at Big Sandy Reservoir. This reservoir is popular with windsurfers.

18 Lake Viva Naughton

 5

Location: North of Kemmerer; map WY5, grid e2.

Campsites, facilities: There are 15 RV sites, with no maximum RV length. Hookups, pull-throughs, a sanitary disposal station, restrooms, and showers are available. A restaurant, store, cocktail lounge, and game room are on the property. Along the lakeshore are several acres for tent camping.

Reservations, fees: Reservations are accepted; the fee is $5–15 per night. Open year-round.

Directions: From Kemmerer, take U.S. 189 two miles north to Frontier and the junction of Highway 233; go north on Highway 233 for 16 miles to the campground on the left.

Contact: Lake Viva Naughton, P.O. Box 111, Kemmerer, WY 83101; 307/877-9669 or 307/877-6363.

Trip notes: This campground is on Lake Viva Naughton at the Fossil Butte National Monument. Several abandoned mine sites are in the area, so be very cautious. Sandhill Cranes and Canada geese can be seen in the meadows near the river and reservoir. You can boat and fish on Viva Naughton Reservoir.

19 Foothills Mobile Home & RV Park

   4

Location: In Kemmerer, map WY5, grid e2.
Campsites, facilities: There are 40 RV sites with hookups and no size limit on RVs, but no tent sites. Pull-throughs, picnic tables, grills, cable TV, and a sanitary disposal station are available. Only self-contained RVs are allowed. Pets are permitted on a leash.

Reservations, fees: Reservations are accepted; the fee is $8–14 per night. Open year-round.

Directions: In Kemmerer, take Highway 189 north one mile. Just beyond the Texaco station take a right into the RV park.

Contact: Foothills Mobile Home & RV Park, P.O. Box 408, Kemmerer, Wyoming, 83101; tel./fax 307/877-6634.

Trip notes: This is a spacious 20-acre park with an area for walking dogs. The park is backed up to BLM land, where an antelope herd often grazes in early morning and evening. The Hams Fork Wildlife Trail is at the north end of Kemmerer, where you can learn more about local wildlife. The Fossil Country Frontier Museum is open Monday–Friday in the summer and has free admission. Twelve miles to the west is the Fossil Butte National Monument, where there are rock formations dating back 50 million years and excellent examples of fossilized fish, insects, plants, and birds. The visitor center is open daily throughout the summer.

20 Riverside RV Park

  4

Location: In Kemmerer; map WY5, grid e2.
Campsites, facilities: There are 30 RV sites, with no size limit, but no tent sites. Hookups, picnic tables, grills, a sanitary disposal station, cable TV, and phone service are available.

Reservations, fees: Reservations are accepted; the fee is $13 per night. Open May 1–October 15.

Directions: In Kemmerer on Highway 189 North, turn at the Riverside RV Park sign, go south four blocks, and follow the river to the park.

Contact: Riverside RV Park, 216 Spinel St., Kemmerer, WY 83101; 307/877-3416.

Trip notes: This RV park is on the Hams Fork River, close to golfing and a children's fishing pond. The Hams Fork Wildlife Trail is at the north end of Kemmerer, where you can learn more about local wildlife. The Fossil Country Frontier Museum is open Monday–Friday in the summer and has free admission. Twelve miles to the west is the Fossil Butte National Monument, where there are rock formations dating back 50 million years and excellent examples of fossilized fish, insects, plants, and birds. The visitor center is open daily throughout the summer.

21 Rock Springs KOA

  3

Location: In Rock Springs; map WY5, grid f8.

Campsites, facilities: There are 58 RV sites and 10 tent sites. Restrooms, showers, laundry, a pool, and a game room are available, along with a store and a sanitary disposal station.

Reservations, fees: Reservations are accepted; $17–22 per night. Open April–mid-October.

Directions: From I-80 at Rock Springs, take Exit 99 and then go northeast to the campground, which is on the left at the west end of town.

Contact: Rock Springs KOA, 86 Foothill Blvd., P.O. Box 2910, Rock Springs, WY 82902; 307/362-3063 or 800/KOA-8699 (800/562-8699).

Trip notes: The Rock Springs Historical Museum is in the old city hall. Admission is free, and the building has old jail cells and local artifacts.

22 Tex's Travel Camp

  4

Location: Near Green River; map WY5, grid f6.

Campsites, facilities: There are 52 RV sites, some with hookups, and 20 tent sites with picnic tables and grills. Restrooms, showers, a store, laundry facilities, and a sanitary disposal station are available.

Reservations, fees: Reservations are accepted; $16–26 per night. Open May–September.

Directions: From Green River, go west on I-80 to Exit 85. The campground is on the south side of the interstate.

Contact: Tex's Travel Camp, Star Route 2, Box 101, Green River, WY 82935; 307/875-2630.

Trip notes: This campground is along the Green River with trees and some grassy areas.

23 Firehole Canyon

     6

Location: Near Flaming Gorge National Recreation Area; map WY5, grid g7.

Campsites, facilities: There are 40 RV or tent sites. Restrooms, showers, and water are available.

Reservations, fees: Reservations are accepted for an additional fee of $8.65; the camping fee is $10–12 per night. Open May–September. The stay limit is 14 days.

Directions: From Rock Springs, go south on I-80 to Highway 191, then about 13 miles to the Firehole Canyon turnoff, and then west on Forest Service Road 106 for eight miles to campground on the right.

Contact: Firehole Canyon, Flaming Gorge National Recreation Area, 800/280-2267.

Trip notes: Flaming Gorge Reservoir is a popular spot for boating, boat tours, rafting, swimming, water-skiing, and fishing. The Red Canyon Visitor Center, off Highway 44 in Utah, is a good place to begin. You'll find plenty of information and a good view of the gorge. Flaming Gorge Lake is known for large lake trout, smallmouth bass, kokanee salmon, and other cold-water fish. The Green River, below the dam, has active rainbow, brook, cutthroat, and brown trout fishing in a beautiful setting. There are hiking trails in the southern portion of Flaming Gorge and the Uinta Mountains to the southeast.

24 Lyman/Fort Bridger KOA

  4

Location: In Lyman; map WY5, grid g3.

Campsites, facilities: There are 35 RV sites with pull-throughs, some with full hookups, and 16 tent sites. The campground has picnic tables, grills, restrooms, showers, an outdoor pool, and a sanitary disposal station.

Reservations, fees: Reservations are accepted; the fee is $16–20 per night.

Directions: From Evanston, go 36 miles east on I-80 to Exit 41 (Highway 413) and take the road south for about a mile. The campground is on the right.

Contact: Lyman/Fort Bridger KOA, Star Route P.O. Box 55, Lyman, WY, 82927; 307/786-2762 or 800/526-2762.

Trip notes: This area is rich with wildlife and has few tourists. Early morning is the best time to see moose, but mule deer, beaver, antelope, grouse, and hawks are abundant. Mormons settled the Fort Bridger/Lyman area in the mid-1800s. Fort Bridger was founded by Jim Bridger, a famous mountain man, and is open for tours daily throughout the summer.

25 Buckboard Crossing

      7

Location: In the Flaming Gorge National Recreation Area; map WY5, grid g6.

Campsites, facilities: There are 35 RV or tent sites with picnic tables and grills. Restrooms, water, showers, and a sanitary disposal station are on-site, and a boat ramp, marina, and store are nearby.

Reservations, fees: Reservations are accepted though the National Recreation Reservation Service at 877/444-6777 (a reservation fee applies) or check the website: www.reserveusa.com. Fees are $12 per night. Open May–September. The stay limit is 14 days.

Directions: From Green River, go 23 miles southwest on Highway 530, then two miles east on Forest Service Road 009 to the marina.

Contact: Flaming Gorge National Recreation Area, P.O. Box 278, Manila, UT 84046; 801/784-3445. The phone number for Buckboard Marina is 307/875-6927.

Trip notes: Flaming Gorge Reservoir is a popular spot for boating, boat tours, rafting, swimming, water-skiing, and fishing. The Red Canyon Visitor Center, off Highway 44 in Utah, is a good place to begin. You'll find plenty of information and a good view of the gorge. Flaming Gorge Lake is known for large lake trout, smallmouth bass, kokanee salmon, and other cold-water fish. The Green River, below the dam, has active rainbow, brook, cutthroat, and brown trout fishing in a beautiful setting. There are hiking trails in the southern portion of Flaming Gorge and the Uinta Mountains to the southeast.

WAYNE SCHERR

South Pass City
Ghost Town

MAP WY6

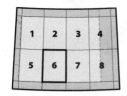

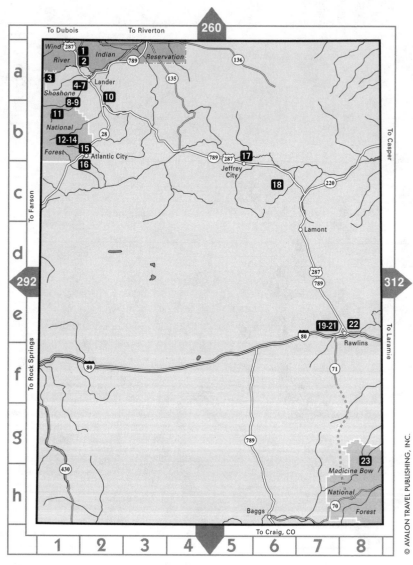

CHAPTER WY6

1 Rocky Acres
   Campground 303
2 Sleeping Bear RV Park
   & Campground 303
3 Dickinson Creek............ 304
4 Holiday Lodge
   Campground 304
5 Lander City Park 304
6 Maverick Mobile
   Home Park.................... 304
7 Ray Lake Campground
   & Café......................... 305
8 Sinks Canyon State Park .. 305
9 Sinks Canyon
   Campground 305
10 Hart Ranch Hideout
   RV Park & Campground ... 306

11 Worthen Meadows 306
12 Fiddlers Campground 306
13 Popo Agie 307
14 Louis Lake.................... 307
15 Big Atlantic Gulch 307
16 Atlantic City 308
17 River Campground 308
18 Cottonwood 308
19 RV World Campground 308
20 Western Hills
   Campground 309
21 American Presidents
   Campground 309
22 Rawlins KOA
   Kampground 310
23 Jack Creek 310

1 Rocky Acres Campground

    5

Location: On the Wind River Indian Reservation; map WY6, grid a2.

Campsites, facilities: There are 12 full RV hookups, and 40–50 grassy tent sites with picnic tables and grills. Showers, laundry facilities, restrooms, water, and a sanitary disposal station are available. Horseshoes and a store are on-site.

Reservations, fees: Reservations are accepted; the fee is $10–13.50 per night. Open May 1–October 1.

Directions: From the junction of U.S. 287 and Highway 789 at Lander, go five miles northwest on U.S. 287; the campground is on the right.

Contact: Rocky Acres Campground, 5700 U.S. Hwy. 287, P.O. Box 1565, Lander, WY 82520; 307/332-6953; fax 307/332-8505; email: rockyacres @rmisp.com; website: www.rmisp.com.

Trip notes: You can golf at the 18-hole Riverton Country Club, and hike or mountain bike on the nearby 25-mile gravel trail developed from a former railroad.

2 Sleeping Bear RV Park & Campground

     5

Location: In Lander; map WY6, grid a2.

Campsites, facilities: There are 36 RV or tent campsites with picnic tables and grills. Hookups and large pull-through sites are available. A restaurant and game room are nearby. Pets are allowed on leashes. Showers, laundry facilities, water, and a sanitary disposal station are provided, and wheelchair-accessible restrooms and camping sites are available.

Reservations, fees: Reservations are accepted; the fee is $13.50–25 per night. Open year-round.

Directions: From the junction of U.S. 287 and Highway 789 at Lander, go to the east edge of the city, off Highway 789, and enter the park at the Hitching Rack sign.

Contact: Chris & Dave McIlrath, Sleeping Bear RV Park and Campground, 715 E. Main, Lander, WY 82520; 307/332-5159 or 888/SLP-BEAR (888/757-2327); email: slpbear@yahoo.com; website: www.SLEEPING-RV-PARK.com.

Trip notes: You can golf at the 18-hole Riverton Country Club and hike or mountain bike on the nearby 25-mile gravel trail developed from a former railroad.

3 Dickinson Creek

 6

Location: In Shoshone National Forest; map WY6, grid a1.

Campsites, facilities: There are 15 RV or tent sites, which can accommodate a maximum RV length of 20 feet, with picnic tables and grills. There are vault toilets, but no hookups.

Reservations, fees: No reservations are needed; no fee is charged. Open July–September 15. The stay limit is 16 days.

Directions: From the junction of U.S. 287 and Highway 789 at Lander, go 15 miles northwest on U.S. 287 to Fort Washakie, then southwest on Trout Creek Road (County Road 294) to Moccasin Lake.

Contact: Shoshone National Forest, Washakie District, 333 E. Main St., Lander, WY 82520; 307/332-5460; website: www.fs.fed.us.

Trip notes: This campground is on Moccasin Lake, where you can fish for cutthroat and Mackinaw trout.

4 Holiday Lodge Campground

 5

Location: In Lander; map WY6, grid a1.

Campsites, facilities: There are two RV sites, which can accommodate a maximum RV length of 16 feet, and eight tent sites with picnic tables and grills. Showers, laundry fa-

cilities, water, electricity, and restrooms are available.

Reservations, fees: Reservations are accepted; the fee is $5–15 per night. Open Memorial Day–Labor Day.

Directions: From Lander, go to the east end of town to the junction of U.S. 287 and Highway 789, and turn on MacFarlane Drive along the Popo Agie River to reach the campground.

Contact: Holiday Lodge Campground; 210 MacFarlane Dr., Lander, WY 82520; 307/332-2511 or 800/624-1974; fax 307/332-2256.

Trip notes: You can fish in the Popo Agie River for rainbow, brook, brown, and cutthroat trout, sauger and whitefish.

5 Lander City Park

 5

Location: In Lander; map WY6, grid a1.

Campsites, facilities: There are seven RV sites with no hookups, and unlimited tent sites. The park has scattered picnic tables and grills. Vault toilets, water, and a playground are available.

Reservations, fees: No reservations are needed; no fee is charged. Open May 1–September 30. The stay limit is three days.

Directions: From the junction of U.S. 287 and Highway 789 in Lander, go north on U.S. 287 to 3rd Street, go south on 3rd Street to Fremont Street and the city park.

Contact: City of Lander, 405 Fremont St., Lander, WY 82520; 307/332-4647.

Trip notes: You can fish in the Popo Agie River for rainbow, brook, brown, and cutthroat trout, sauger, and whitefish.

6 Maverick Mobile Home Park

 4

Location: In Lander, map WY6, grid a1.

Campsites, facilities: There are 60 RV or tent campsites with picnic tables and grills, some with hookups and pull-throughs. There are showers, laundry facilities, water, restrooms, and a sanitary disposal station.

Reservations, fees: Reservations accepted; the fee is $8–15 per night. Open April 1– September 30.

Directions: From the junction of U.S. 287 and Highway 789 in Lander, go north on U.S. 287 (Main Street) to 2nd Street and the campground.

Contact: Maverick Mobile Home Park, 1104 N. 2nd St., Lander, WY 82520; 307/332-3142 or 800/ 337-3142.

Trip notes: There is a six-acre lake here where you can fish. You can fish in the Popo Agie River for rainbow, brook, brown, and cutthroat trout, sauger and whitefish.

7 Ray Lake Campground & Café

   5

Location: Near Lander; map WY6, grid a1.

Campsites, facilities: There are 20 RV sites with full or partial hookups; 20 RV sites with no hookups, and 15 tent sites. Showers, picnic tables, grills, water, restrooms, a sanitary disposal station, and a café are available.

Reservations, fees: Reservations are accepted; the fee is $7–15 per night. Open May 1– September 30.

Directions: From the junction of U.S. 287 and Highway 789 at Lander, go eight miles north on U.S. 287; the campground is on left.

Contact: Joe & LuAnn Malek, Ray Lake Campground and Café, 39 Ray Lake Rd., Lander, WY 82520; 307/322-9333.

Trip notes: You can fish and hike in the area; the Popo Agie Wilderness is to the west.

8 Sinks Canyon State Park

     6

Location: Southwest of Lander; map WY6, grid b1.

Campsites, facilities: There are 30 RV sites with pull-throughs but no hookups, and 10 tent sites with picnic tables and grills. Vault toi-

lets, water, a visitor center, and a playground are available. Pets are allowed on leashes. There are two campgrounds: Sawmill (north end) and Popo Agie (south end).

Reservations, fees: No reservations are needed; the fee is $6 per night. Open June– October. The stay limit is 14 days.

Directions: From the junction of U.S. 287 and Highway 789 in Lander, go north on U.S. 287 (Main Street) to 3rd Street, go south on 3rd Street to Fremont Street, take Fremont Street west and go seven miles southwest on Sinks Canyon Road (County Road 131) to the campground.

Contact: Wyoming State Parks and Historic Sites, Cheyenne, WY 82003; 307/777-6323; or 307/332-6333.

Trip notes: You can hike and fish, and there are excellent wildlife viewing opportunities. The name "Sinks" is used to describe mysterious disappearing/reappearing Popo Agie River at the Sinks Canyon Visitor Center. This is a popular area for traditional and sport climbing, offering three different types of rocks: sandstone, granite, and dolomite.

9 Sinks Canyon Campground

   6

Location: Southwest of Lander; map WY6, grid b1.

Campsites, facilities: There are nine RV or tent campsites, which can accommodate RVs up to 20 feet in length. Picnic tables, fire grates, restrooms, and water are available.

Reservations, fees: No reservations are needed; the fee is $6 per night.

Directions: From the junction of U.S. 287 and Highway 789 in Lander, go north on U.S. 287 (Main Street) to 3rd Street, go south on 3rd Street to Fremont Street, take Fremont Street west and go seven miles southwest on Sinks Canyon Road (County Road 131) past the park to the campground.

Contact: Sinks Canyon State Park, 3079 Sinks Canyon Rd., Lander, WY 82520; 307/332-6333.

Trip notes: You can hike and fish, and there are excellent wildlife viewing opportunities. The name "Sinks" is used to describe mysterious disappearing/reappearing Popo Agie River at the Sinks Canyon Visitor Center. This is a popular area for traditional and sport climbing, offering three different types of rocks: sand stone, granite, and dolomite.

🔟 Hart Ranch Hideout RV Park & Campground

 5

Location: Southeast of Lander; map WY6, grid a2.

Campsites, facilities: There are 83 RV or tent campsites, some with hookups and pull-throughs, and picnic tables and grills. Laundry facilities, showers, water, restrooms, and a game room are available. Pets are allowed on leashes.

Reservations, fees: Reservations are accepted; the fee is $13.50–18 per night with membership. Open year-round.

Directions: From the junction of U.S. 287 and Highway 769 at Lander, go eight miles southeast on U.S. 287 to the junction with Highway 28; the campground is one mile east on U.S. 287.

Contact: Hart Ranch Hideout RV Park & Campground, 7192 Hwy. 789-287, Lander, WY 82520; 307/332-3836; email: hartranch@campwyoming.com.

Trip notes: The campground is on the Little Popo Agie River, where you can fish for brown and rainbow trout. There is a small frontier town with turn-of-the-century buildings and displays.

🔟🔟 Worthen Meadows

 6

Location: In Shoshone National Forest; map WY6, grid b1.

Campsites, facilities: There are 28 RV or tent sites, which can accommodate a maximum

RV length of 24 feet, but no hookups. Picnic tables, grills, water, vault toilets, and a boat ramp are available.

Reservations, fees: No reservations are needed; the fee is $6 per night. Open July–mid-September. The stay limit is 16 days.

Directions: From the junction of U.S. 287 and Highway 789 in Lander, go north on U.S. 287 (Main Street) to 3rd Street, go south on 3rd Street to Fremont Street, take Fremont Street west and go 11 miles southwest on Sinks Canyon Road (County Road 131), then south on Louis Lake Road (Forest Service Road 300) for seven miles, then west on Forest Service Road 302 to the campground.

Contact: Shoshone National Forest, Washakie District, 333 E. Main St., Lander, WY 82520; 307/332-5460; website: www.fs.fed.us.

Trip notes: This campground is near Sinks Canyon and several lakes where you can boat, fish, and swim. Sheep Bridge Trail, Stough Creek Lakes Trail, and Worthington Meadows Trail begin here.

🔟🔟 Fiddlers Campground

 6

Location: In Shoshone National Forest; map WY6, grid b1.

Campsites, facilities: There are 13 RV or tent sites, which can accommodate a maximum RV length of 24 feet. Wheelchair-accessible toilets, picnic tables, grills, water, and a boat ramp are available, but there are no hookups.

Reservations, fees: No reservations are needed; the fee is $6 per night. Open July–September 15. The stay limit is 14 days.

Directions: From the junction of U.S. 287 and Highway 789 in Lander, go north on U.S. 287 (Main Street) to 3rd Street, go south on 3rd Street to Fremont Street, take Fremont Street west and go 11 miles southwest on Sinks Canyon Road (County Road 131), then south on Louis Lake Road (Forest Service Road 300) for 13 miles to Fiddler's Lake and campground.

Contact: Shoshone National Forest, Washakie

District, 333 E. Main St., Lander, WY 82520; 307/332-5460; website: www.fs.fed.us.

Trip notes: This campground is on Fiddler's Lake, where you can boat, and fish. Sheep Bridge Trail, Stough Creek Lakes Trail, and Worthington Meadows Trail begin here.

13 Popo Agie

       6

Location: In Shoshone National Forest; map WY6, grid b1.

Campsites, facilities: There are four RV or tent campsites with picnic tables, grills, and a pit toilet.

Reservations, fees: No reservations are needed; no fee is charged. Open July 1–September 30. The stay limit is 14 days.

Directions: From the junction of U.S. 287 and Highway 789 in Lander, go north on U.S. 287 (Main Street) to 3rd Street, go south on 3rd Street to Fremont Street, take Fremont Street west and go 11 miles southwest on Sinks Canyon Road (County Road 131), then south on Louis Lake Road (Forest Service Road 300) for 16 miles to the campground.

Contact: Shoshone National Forest, Washakie District, 333 E. Main St., Lander, WY 82520; 307/332-5460; website: www.fs.fed.us.

Trip notes: This campground is near several lakes where you can boat, fish, and swim. Sheep Bridge Trail, Stough Creek Lakes Trail, and Worthington Meadows Trail begin here.

14 Louis Lake

     6

Location: In Shoshone National Forest; map WY6, grid b1.

Campsites, facilities: There are nine RV or tent campsites, which can accommodate a maximum RV length of 24 feet, with picnic tables and grills but no hookups. Vault toilets, water, and a boat access are available.

Reservations, fees: No reservations are needed; the fee is $6 per night. Open July–

September. The stay limit is 16 days.

Directions: From the junction of U.S. 287 and Highway 789 in Lander, go north on U.S. 287 (Main Street) to 3rd Street, go south on 3rd Street to Fremont Street, take Fremont Street west and go 11 miles southwest on Sinks Canyon Road (County Road 131), then south on Louis Lake Road (Forest Service Road 300) for 20 miles to Louis Lake. The campground is on the east side of the lake.

Contact: Shoshone National Forest, Washakie District, 333 E. Main St., Lander, WY 82520; 307/332-5460; website: www.fs.fed.us.

Trip notes: This campground is on Louis Lake, and fishing and hiking popular in the area. This campground is near several lakes where you can boat, fish, and swim. Sheep Bridge Trail, Stough Creek Lakes Trail, and Worthington Meadows Trail begin here.

15 Big Atlantic Gulch

   6

Location: In South Pass City, a historical gold-mining area; map WY6, grid b2.

Campsites, facilities: There are eight RV or tent sites with picnic tables and grills. There are vault toilets and water, but no hookups.

Reservations, fees: No reservations are needed; the fee is $6 per night. Open June–October. The stay limit is 14 days.

Directions: From Lander, go 25 miles south on Highway 28 to Atlantic City Road, then half a mile to Fort Stambaugh Loop Road; the campground is on the left. These are remote mountain roads, so prepare accordingly.

Contact: Lander Field Office, 1335 Main St., P.O. Box 589, Lander, WY 82520-0589; 307/332-8400, fax 307/332-8447; website: www.wy.blm.gov.

Trip notes: This campground is in the historic South Pass City mining district. South Pass City, south of Atlantic City, is a state historical site. The former mining town is being restored and has a saloon, hotel, visitor center, and history programs. A historic nature trail offers a short hike. Fishing opportunities are nearby.

16 Atlantic City

   6

Location: In South Pass City historical gold-mining area; map WY6, grid c2.

Campsites, facilities: There are 18 RV or tent campsites with picnic tables and grills, but no hookups. Vault toilets and water are available.

Reservations, fees: No reservations are needed; the fee is $6 per night. Open June–October. The stay limit is 14 days.

Directions: From Lander, go 25 miles south on Highway 28 to Atlantic City Road; the campground is one mile on the right.

Contact: Lander Field Office, 1335 Main St., P.O. Box 589, Lander, WY 82520-0589; 307/332-8400; website: www.wy.blm.gov.

Trip notes: This campground is in the historic South Pass City mining district. These are remote mountain roads, so prepare accordingly. South Pass City, south of Atlantic City, is a state historical site. The former mining town is being restored and has a saloon, hotel, visitor center, and history programs. A historic nature trail offers a short hike. Fishing opportunities are nearby.

17 River Campground

   4

Location: West of Jeffrey City; map WY6, grid b5.

Campsites, facilities: There are 25 RV or tent campsites, some with hookups, picnic tables, and grills. Restrooms, showers, water, and a sanitary disposal station are available.

Reservations, fees: Reservations are accepted; the fee is $9–$11.50 per night. Open May 1–September 30.

Directions: From Casper, go west 74 miles on Highway 220 to U.S. 287. Go north 21 miles on U.S. 287/Highway 798 to Jeffrey City. From Jeffrey City, go west on U.S. 287 for 19 miles to the campground.

Contact: River Campground, 4181 Highway 789, Jeffrey City, WY 82310; 307/544-9319.

Trip notes: This campground is in a sparse area, but it's near Carmody Lake, where you can fish for rainbow trout.

18 Cottonwood

     6

Location: On Green Mountain; map WY6, grid c6.

Campsites, facilities: There are 18 RV and tent sites with picnic tables and fire rings. A vault toilet and water are available.

Reservations, fees: No reservations are necessary; the fee is $6 per night. Open June–October. The stay limit is 14 days.

Directions: From Jeffrey City, go east on U.S. 287 for six miles, then south on Green Mountain turnoff (BLM 2411) for 9.5 miles to the campground. Jeffrey City is 67 miles northwest of Rawlins on U.S. 287.

Contact: Rawlins Field Office, Bureau of Land Management, 1300 N. 3rd St., P.O. Box 2407, Rawlins, WY 82301-2407; 307/328-4200, or fax 307/328-4224.

Trip notes: Pathfinder Reservoir is to the east, and you can swim, boat, and fish for walleye, brown, cutthroat, and rainbow trout. The Pathfinder National Wildlife Refuge is home to many birds and animals.

19 RV World Campground

      4

Location: In Rawlins; map WY6, grid e7.

Campsites, facilities: There are 100 RV sites, some with full hookups, and five tent sites with tables and grills. Restrooms, showers, laundry facilities, and a store are available. A playground, game room, heated pool, and miniature golf course are provided.

Reservations, fees: Reservations are accepted; the fee is $14–20 per night. Open April–September.

Directions: From I-80 at Rawlins, take Exit 211 and follow Business Loop (Spruce Street) for a little over a quarter of a mile to 23rd and turn left; go to Wagon Circle and turn left. The campground is a half mile on the right.

Contact: RV World Campground, 3101 Wagon Circle Rd., P.O. Box 1282, Rawlins, WY 82301; 307/328-1091: email: rvwrld@coffey.com.

Trip notes: For history buffs, the Wyoming Frontier Prison and the Carbon County Museum offer a glimpse into this area's rough western past. The historic district includes some interesting old buildings and artifacts. Seminoe State Park, to the northeast on the northwest shores of Seminoe Reservoir, is home to pronghorn antelope, sage grouse, and a wide variety of wildlife. You can fish for brown, rainbow, and cutthroat trout and walleye in the reservoir; and the "miracle mile" between Fort Fred Steele State Historical Site and Gray Reef Area is known for excellent fishing. Fishing licenses are required. You can swim, water-ski, and boat in the reservoir. The Seminoe Mountains and surrounding area offer hiking opportunities and wildlife viewing.

20 Western Hills Campground

 4

Location: In Rawlins; map WY6, grid e7.

Campsites, facilities: There are 165 RV sites, some with full hookups, cable TV, and pull-throughs, and 12 tent sites. Restrooms, showers, laundry facilities, a game room, and playground are provided. A sanitary disposal station and store are available.

Reservations, fees: Reservations are accepted; the fee is $12–17 per night. Open year-round.

Directions: From I-80 west at Rawlins, take U.S. 287N/I-80 Business Loop exit; stay to the left where the off-ramp forks, go left on I-80 Business Loop keep straight to West Spruce Street, and turn right on South Wagon Circle Road.

Contact: Western Hills Campground, 2500 Wagon Circle Rd., P.O. Box 760, Rawlins, WY

82301: 307/324-2596, 208/324-3598; email: whctrib.com.

Trip notes: For history buffs, the Wyoming Frontier Prison and the Carbon County Museum offer a glimpse into this area's rough western past. The historic district includes some interesting old buildings and artifacts. Seminoe State Park, to the northeast on the northwest shores of Seminoe Reservoir, is home to pronghorn antelope, sage grouse, and a wide variety of wildlife. You can fish for brown, rainbow, and cutthroat trout and walleye in the reservoir; and the "miracle mile" between Fort Fred Steele State Historical Site and Gray Reef Area is known for excellent fishing. Fishing licenses are required. You can swim, water-ski and boat in the reservoir. The Seminoe Mountains and surrounding area offer hiking opportunities and wildlife viewing.

21 American Presidents Campground

 4

Location: In Rawlins; map WY6, grid e7.

Campsites, facilities: There are 72 RV or tent sites with picnic tables and grills. Restrooms, laundry facilities, showers, and a sanitary disposal station are available. A playground is nearby.

Reservations, fees: Reservations are accepted; the fee is $9–16 per night. Open mid-June–October.

Directions: From I-80 at Rawlins, take Exit 211, follow Business Loop (Spruce Street) for a little less than .25 mile to the campground on the right.

Contact: American Presidents Campground, 2346 W. Spruce St., Rawlins, WY 82301; 307/324-3218, 800/294-3218 or fax 307/324-3509.

Trip notes: For history buffs, the Wyoming Frontier Prison and the Carbon County Museum offer a glimpse into this area's rough western past. The historic district includes some interesting old buildings and artifacts. Seminoe State Park, to the northeast on the northwest shores of Seminoe Reservoir, is home to pronghorn antelope, sage grouse, and a wide variety of wildlife. You can fish for brown, rainbow, and cutthroat trout and walleye in the reservoir; and the "miracle mile" between Fort Fred Steele State Historical Site and Gray Reef Area is known for excellent fishing. Fishing licenses are required. You can swim, water-ski, and boat in the reservoir. The Seminoe Mountains and surrounding area offer hiking opportunities and wildlife viewing.

west shores of Seminoe Reservoir, is home to pronghorn antelope, sage grouse, and a wide variety of wildlife. You can fish for brown, rainbow, and cutthroat trout and walleye in the reservoir; and the "miracle mile" between Fort Fred Steele State Historical Site and Gray Reef Area is known for excellent fishing. Fishing licenses are required. You can swim, water-ski and boat in the reservoir. The Seminoe Mountains and surrounding area offer hiking opportunities and wildlife viewing.

22 Rawlins KOA Kampground

       4

Location: In Rawlins; map WY6, grid e8.

Campsites, facilities: There are 50 RV sites, some with full hookups, and eight tent sites with picnic tables and some grills. A covered picnic area is provided. Restrooms, showers, laundry facilities, a game room, playground, store, and a sanitary disposal station are available. Kamper Kabins are available to rent.

Reservations, fees: Reservations are accepted; the fee is $17.95–26.95. Open April–October.

Directions: From I-80 at Rawlins, take Exit 214 north to the I-80 frontage road, turn left and go a quarter of a mile to the campground.

Contact: Rawlins KOA, 205 E. Hwy. 71, Rawlins, WY 82301; 307/328-2021 or 800/562-7559.

Trip notes: For history buffs, the Wyoming Frontier Prison and the Carbon County Museum offer a glimpse into this area's rough western past. The historic district includes some interesting old buildings and artifacts. Seminoe State Park, to the northeast on the north-

23 Jack Creek

    6

Location: In Medicine Bow National Forest; map WY6, grid g8.

Campsites, facilities: This campground has 20 RV or tent sites, some pull-throughs, with picnic tables and grills. Vault toilets and water are provided.

Reservations, fees: No reservations are offered; the fee is $7 per night. Open June–October. The stay limit is 14 days.

Directions: From Rawlins go east on I-80 to Highway 130, then south 21 miles to Saratoga. From Saratoga, go 19 miles south on Highway 130 to Encampment, then seven miles west on Highway 70 to Forest Service Road 443; take that road north to Forest Service Road 452 and turn west to the campground.

Contact: Medicine Bow National Forest, S. Hwy. 130, P.O. Box 249, Saratoga, WY 82331; 307/326-5258.

Trip notes: You can fish and hike in the Medicine Bow National Forest.

WAYNE SCHERR

Elk

MAP WY7

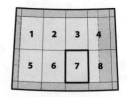

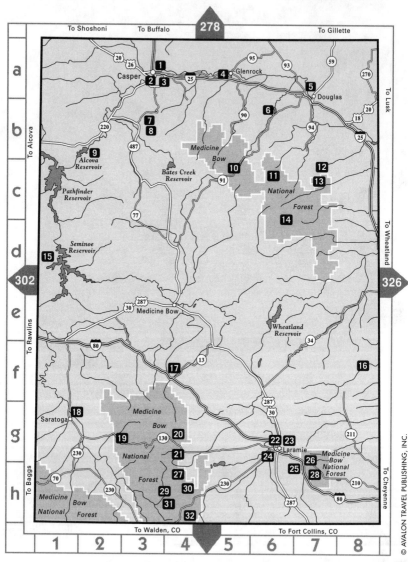

To Shoshoni   To Buffalo   **278**   To Gillette

a

20 26 **1**
Casper **2 3** 25 **4** Glenrock 93 95 59 270
To Alcova **5** Douglas To Lusk

b
220 **7** 90 **6** 94 18
8 487 Medicine 25
9 Bow
Alcova Bates Creek **10** **11** **12** 20
Reservoir Reservoir 91 **13**

c
Pathfinder National Forest
Reservoir 77 **14**

d
15 Seminoe
Reservoir

302 326

e
30 287 Medicine Bow Wheatland 34
To Rawlins Reservoir

f
80 13 **16**
17 287
30

g
18 Medicine
Saratoga Bow **22 23** 211
19 **20** Laramie
230 130 **21** **24** Medicine
National **27** **26** Bow
To Baggs 70 **25** National
230 Forest **29** **30** **28** Forest
Medicine **31** 230 210
Bow **32** 287 80
National Forest To Cheyenne

h

1 2 3 4 5 6 7 8
To Walden, CO   To Fort Collins, CO

© AVALON TRAVEL PUBLISHING, INC.

312 Wyoming

CHAPTER WY7

1 Antelope Run
   Campground 313
2 Casper KOA 313
3 Fort Caspar
   Campground 314
4 Deer Creek RV
   Campground 314
5 Douglas Jackalope KOA 314
6 Ayers Natural Bridge 315
7 Lodgepole 315
8 Rim Campground 315
9 Alcova Lake
   Campground 316
10 Campbell Creek 316
11 Curtis Gulch 316
12 Esterbrook Lodge 317
13 Esterbrook 317
14 Friend Park 317
15 Seminoe State Park 318

16 Diamond Guest Ranch 318
17 Arlington Outpost 318
18 Saratoga Lake 318
19 South Brush Creek 319
20 Brooklyn Lake 319
21 Libby Creek/Willow
   Campground 319
22 Riverside Campground 320
23 Snowy Range Trailer
   Park 320
24 Laramie KOA 320
25 Tie City 320
26 Yellow Pine 321
27 Rob Roy Campground 321
28 Vedauwoo 321
29 Bobbie Thompson 322
30 Lake Owen 322
31 Pelton Creek 322
32 Boswell Creek 322

1 Antelope Run Campground

 5

Location: North of Casper; map WY7, grid a3.

Campsites, facilities: There are 65 RV or tent campsites, some with hookups, picnic tables, and grills. Restrooms, showers, a pool, laundry facilities, water, and a sanitary disposal station are available.

Reservations, fees: Reservations are accepted; the fee is $12–18 per night. Open April –October.

Directions: From Casper, go three miles north on I-25 to Bar Nunn; take Exit 191 to the campground.

Contact: Antelope Run Campground, 1101 Prairie Lane, Bar Nunn, WY 82601; 307/577-1664 or 800/992-1460.

Trip notes: This campground is next to City Park. You can fish for brown, rainbow, cut-throat, and walleye on the North Platte River, at the northeast end of town, and the Parkway Trail is a pleasant four-mile walk. Historic Fort Caspar is nearby. Casper has three golf courses.

2 Casper KOA

 4

Location: In Casper, map WY7, grid a3.

Campsites, facilities: There are 87 RV or tent campsites, some with hookups, picnic tables, and grills. Restrooms, showers, laundry facilities, water, and a sanitary disposal station are available. A swimming pool and miniature golf course are on-site.

Reservations, fees: Reservations are accepted; the fee is $14–19 per night. Open year-round.

Directions: From I-25 at Casper, take Exit 185

to East Yellowstone and the campground.

Contact: Casper KOA, 2800 E. Yellowstone, Casper, WY 82609; 307/237-5155 or 800/KOA-3259 (800/562-3259), fax 307/266-4886.

Trip notes: You can fish for brown, rainbow, cutthroat, and walleye on the North Platte River at the northeast end of town, and the Parkway Trail is a pleasant four-mile walk. The town of Casper has three golf courses. Historic Fort Caspar has restored fort buildings and summer reenactments of scenes from the history of the American West. Fort Caspar Museum is on the Oregon, California, Mormon Pioneer, and Pony Express Trails and the transcontinental telegraph line.

❸ Fort Caspar Campground

   4

Location: Near Historic Fort Caspar; map WY7, grid a3.

Campsites, facilities: There are 92 RV sites with full hookups and 15 tent sites with picnic tables, and grills. Restrooms, showers, laundry facilities, water, and a playground are available.

Reservations, fees: Reservations are accepted; the fee is $11–16 per night. Open year-round.

Directions: In Casper, take I-25 Exit 188B and turn south on Poplar (toward Casper Mountain), then turn right at Collins Street and follow it to the museum entrance at the intersection of Collins and Wyoming Boulevard. This campground is behind the historic Fort Caspar Museum.

Contact: Fort Caspar Campground, 4205 Fort Caspar Rd., Casper, WY 82604; 307/234-3260; 888/243-7709, or fax 307/423-2955.

Trip notes: You can fish for brown, rainbow, cutthroat, and walleye on the North Platte River, at the northeast end of town, and the Parkway Trail is a pleasant four-mile walk. Casper has three golf courses. Historic Fort Caspar has restored fort buildings and summer reenactments of scenes from the history of the American West. Fort Caspar Museum is on the Oregon, California, Mormon Pioneer, and Pony Express Trails and the transcontinental telegraph line.

❹ Deer Creek RV Campground

   4

Location: In Glenrock, map WY7, grid a5.

Campsites, facilities: There are 65 RV or tent campsites, some with hookups and pull-throughs. Restrooms, showers, laundry facilities, water, and a sanitary disposal station are available.

Reservations, fees: Reservations are accepted; the fee is $12–14 per night. Open April 1–November 15.

Directions: From Casper, go south 21 miles on I-25 to Glenrock; take Exit 165, turn left at the four-way stop, then right to the campground.

Contact: Deer Creek RV Campground, 302 Millar Lane, P.O. Box 1003, Glenrock, WY 82637; 307/436-8121 or fax 307/436-5779; email: ldcreek@aol.com.

Trip notes: Glenrock has a nine-hole golf course. The nearby North Platte River has fair to good fishing for catfish.

❺ Douglas Jackalope KOA

     5

Location: Northwest of Douglas; map WY7, grid a7.

Campsites, facilities: There are 60 RV sites, most with full hookups, and grassy tent sites with picnic tables and grills. Restrooms, showers, laundry facilities, water, and a sanitary disposal station are available. Cable TV, a store, game room, swimming pool, horseshoes, and a playground are on-site. Pets are allowed on leashes.

Reservations, fees: Reservations are accepted; the fee is $16–21 per night. Open April–October.

Directions: From Casper, go east on I-25 to

Exit 140 at Douglas, turn right on Highway 91, and the campground is on the right.

Contact: Douglas Jackalope KOA, P.O. Box 1190, 168 Cold Springs Rd., Douglas, WY 82633; 307/358-2164.

Trip notes: Douglas has an 18-hole golf course, the Douglas Community Club, which also has a putting green and a 250-yard driving range. The Wyoming Pioneer Memorial Museum has displays of Native American, pioneer, and military artifacts and an actual one-room schoolhouse from LaPrele. The nearby North Platte River has fair to good fishing for catfish. Glendo State Park is to the southeast.

6 Ayers Natural Bridge

   5

Location: Southwest of Douglas; map WY7, grid b6.

Campsites, facilities: There are nine RV sites and five tent sites with picnic tables and grills. Restrooms are provided. No pets are allowed. Overnight camping requires permission from the caretaker.

Reservations, fees: No reservations are needed; no fee is charged, although donations are accepted. Open May–October, from 8 A.M.–8 P.M. The stay limit is three days.

Directions: From Douglas, go 12 miles west on I-25 to Exit 151, then south on Natural Bridge Road (County Road 13) five miles to the campground.

Contact: Ayers National Bridge, Converse County, Route 1, 208 Natural Bridge Rd., Douglas, WY 82633; 307/358-3532.

Trip notes: Ayers Natural Bridge is one of the few natural bridges in existence that has water flowing under it. The surrounding red sandstone walls are part of the Casper sandstone formation, which is more than 280 million years old. There are hiking trails in the Medicine Bow National Forest south of here.

7 Lodgepole

 5

Location: Southwest of Casper; map WY7, grid b3.

Campsites, facilities: There are 15 RV or tent campsites with picnic tables and grills. Vault toilets and water are available.

Reservations, fees: No reservations are needed; the fee is $5 per night. Open June 15–October 31. The stay limit is 14 days.

Directions: From U.S. 20/26 in Casper, take the Casper Mountain Road exit (Casper College and UW Casper), go nine miles south on Casper Mountain Road past the college, then eight miles on County Road 505 to Muddy Mountain and the campground.

Contact: Casper Field Office, 2987 Prospector Dr., Casper, WY 82604; 307/261-7600; fax 307/234-1525.

Trip notes: This campground is on Muddy Mountain, near hiking and a mountain biking trail. The Mountain Nature Trail is a Bureau of Land Management trail and has been designed to accommodate the physically challenged. Casper has three golf courses.

8 Rim Campground

    5

Location: On Muddy Mountain; map WY7, grid b3.

Campsites, facilities: There are eight RV or tent campsites with picnic tables and grills. Vault toilets are available.

Reservations, fees: No reservations are needed; the fee is $5 per night. Open June 15–October 31. The stay limit is 14 days.

Directions: From U.S. 20/26 in Casper, take the Casper Mountain Road exit (Casper College and UW Casper), go nine miles south on Casper Mountain Road past the college, then eight miles on County Road 505 to Muddy Mountain and the campground.

Contact: Casper Field Office, 2987 Prospector Dr., Casper, WY 82604; 307/261-7600, fax 307/

234-1525; website: www.wy.blm.gov.

Trip notes: This campground is on Muddy Mountain near hiking and a mountain biking trail. The Mountain Nature Trail is a Bureau of Land Management trail and has been designed to accommodate the physically challenged. Casper has three golf courses.

9 Alcova Lake Campground

     5

Location: West of Casper; map WY7, grid b2.

Campsites, facilities: There are six RV campsites, plus tent sites, with picnic tables and grills. Restrooms, water, and a sanitary disposal station are available. A restaurant and marina are on the north side.

Reservations, fees: Reservations are not needed; the fee is $5–12. Open April 1–October 15.

Directions: From Casper, go 28 miles west on County Road 407 to the campground.

Contact: Natrona County Parks, 538 S.E. Wyoming Blvd., Casper, WY 82609-04204; 307/235-9311.

Trip notes: You can fish, sail, boat, and waterski on Alcova Reservoir. The Cottonwood Creek Dinosaur Trail, on the south side of the lake, is an interesting climb taking you through 240 million years of geological history. Fremont Canyon, south of Alcova Reservoir, has numerous rock-climbing routes.

10 Campbell Creek

 5

Location: In Medicine Bow National Forest; map WY7, grid c5.

Campsites, facilities: There are eight RV or tent sites, which can accommodate a maximum RV length of 22 feet, with picnic tables and fire grates. Vault toilets and water are available.

Reservations, fees: No reservations are needed; the fee is $5 per night. Open May 15–October 15. The stay limit is 14 days.

Directions: From Douglas, go two miles on Esterbrook Road (Highway 94), turn right and go three miles on Chalk Buttes Road; turn left on Highway 91, which becomes County Road 24 where the pavement ends. Continue 14 miles to the campground.

Contact: Medicine Bow National Forest, 2468 Jackson St., Laramie, WY 82070; 307/745-2300.

Trip notes: This campground is at the western end of the Laramie Mountains in a remote area. La Prele Guard Station, 2.5 miles past Twin Peaks Trailhead, can be reserved for public use. Contact the District Office (2250 E. Richards, Douglas, WY 82633; 307/358-4690 or 307/358-1604). Twin Peaks Trail begins three miles from the campground. This area has private and public land side-by-side, so make sure you are on public land when camping or hiking.

11 Curtis Gulch

 7

Location: In Medicine Bow National Forest; map WY7, grid c6.

Campsites, facilities: There are six RV or tent sites, which can accommodate a maximum RV length of 22 feet, with picnic tables and fire grates. Restrooms and water are available.

Reservations, fees: No reservations are needed; the fee is $5 per night. Open May 15–October 15. The stay limit is 14 days.

Directions: From Douglas, go six miles north on I-25 to Exit 146, go west and then south about 20 miles on Highway 91 (which turns into a gravel road, County Road 224) to County Road 16, go 14 miles, then turn northeast on Forest Service Road 658 to Curtis Gulch.

Contact: Medicine Bow National Forest, 2468 Jackson St., Laramie, WY 82070; 307/745-2300.

Trip notes: This is a very scenic campsite, surrounded by granite rock formations, and is popular with climbers. The La Bonte Creek Trail is a two-mile hike through meadows, forests, and a canyon. Curtis Gulch Trailhead is 50 yards west. Fishing opportunities are nearby.

12 Esterbrook Lodge

 6

Location: In Medicine Bow National Forest; map WY7, grid c7.

Campsites, facilities: There are four RV sites and a number of grassy tent sites. Hookups, restrooms, showers, picnic tables, grills, water, and a game room are available.

Reservations, fees: Reservations are accepted; the fee is $5–15 per night. Open all year.

Directions: From Douglas, go south 17 miles on Highway 94 to Esterbrook Road (County Road 5), then go 11 miles south to Forest Service Road 633 to the campground.

Contact: Esterbrook Lodge, 32 Pine-Esterbrook, Douglas, Wyoming, 82633; 307/358-6103.

Trip notes: Several hiking trails are nearby. Sunset Ridge Trail is a 1.6-mile uphill hike terminating with a spectacular scenic view. Black Mountain Lookout, 6.5 miles southeast, is one of the few manned fire lookouts remaining in the United States. Be warned; the road to the lookout is only for 4WD vehicles.

13 Esterbrook

 6

Location: In Medicine Bow National Forest; map WY7, grid c7.

Campsites, facilities: There are 12 RV or tent sites, which can accommodate a maximum RV length of 22 feet. Picnic tables, fire grates, vault toilets, and water are available.

Reservations, fees: No reservations are needed; the fee is $5 per night. Open May 15–October 15. The stay limit is 14 days.

Directions: From Douglas, go south 17 miles on Highway 94 to Esterbrook Road (County Road 5), then go 11 miles south to Forest Road 633, and three miles east to the campground.

Contact: Medicine Bow National Forest, 2468

Jackson St., Laramie, WY 82070; 307/745-2300 or 307/358-4690.

Trip notes: This campground is in a forested area along a ridge north of Laramie Peak.

14 Friend Park

 8

Location: In Medicine Bow National Forest; map W7, grid c6.

Campsites, facilities: There are three RV sites and eight tent sites, with tables and grills. Travel trailers are not recommended because there is no place to turn around. There are vault toilets and a hand pump for water.

Reservations, fees: No reservations needed; the fee is $5 per night. Open June 1–October 31. The maximum stay is 14 days.

Directions: From Douglas, take Highway 94 (Exit 140) off I-25, follow it for 16 miles to County Route 5/Esterbrook Road. Go left on County Route 5/Esterbrook Road (a rough dirt road) and go 11 miles to the Esterbrook Work Center. Note that this road divides and then comes back together, so either right or left will work. Once you reach the Esterbrook Work Center, go to the right for 15 miles to Forest Service Route 671/Bear Creek Road, and then take a left. This is a steep, narrow road, so use caution. In about three miles you will come to the Friend Park campground sign. Take a left and the campground is ahead one mile.

Contact: Medicine Bow National Forest, Douglas Ranger District, 2250 E. Richards St., Douglas, WY 82633, tel. 307/358-4690, fax 307/358-3072.

Trip notes: This forested campground, near Friend Creek, has good sites for tents and small RVs. There are wild turkey and bighorn sheep in the area. Laramie Peak is 10,200 feet high and there are good rock climbing opportunities nearby. You can hike the five-mile Laramie Peak Trail or the four-mile Friend Peak Trail from the spur trail or at the trailheads, a third of a mile from the campground entrance. You can fish Friend Creek for brook trout.

15 Seminoe State Park

 6

Location: Northeast of Rawlins at the Seminoe Reservoir; map WY7, grid d1.

Campsites, facilities: There are 94 RV and tent sites, most with tables and grills, at North and South Red Hills. Vault toilets and water are available, and there are boat ramps. Pets are allowed on leashes.

Reservations, fees: No reservations; the fee is $4–9 per night. Open May–mid-October. The stay limit is 14 days.

Directions: From Rawlins, go east on I-80 to Exit 219, then north on Seminoe Road (County Road 351) for 34 miles to the campground.

Contact: Seminoe State Park, Seminoe Dam Route, Sinclair, WY 82334; 307/320-3013.

Trip notes: Seminoe State Park, situated on the northwest shores of Seminoe Reservoir, is home to pronghorn antelope, sage grouse, and a wide variety of wildlife. You can fish for brown, rainbow, and cutthroat trout and walleye in the reservoir; and the "miracle mile" between Fort Fred Steele State Historical Site and Gray Reef Area is known for excellent fishing. Fishing licenses are required. You can swim, boat, and water-ski in the reservoir. The Seminoe Mountains and surrounding area offer hiking opportunities and wildlife viewing.

16 Diamond Guest Ranch

 5

Location: West of Chugwater; map WY7, grid f8.

Campsites, facilities: There are 136 RV or tent sites with picnic tables and grills, some with hookups. Showers, restrooms, laundry facilities, and a sanitary disposal station are available. A swimming pool is on-site.

Reservations, fees: Reservations are suggested; the fee is $14–70 per night. Open May 27–September 2.

Directions: From Cheyenne, take I-25 north to Chugwater, take Exit 54 onto Diamond

Road, and drive 12 miles to the ranch.

Contact: Diamond Guest Ranch, P.O. Box 236, Chugwater, WY 82210; 307/422-3564, 800/932-4222, or fax 307/422-3310; website: www.diamondgr.com.

Trip notes: This ranch has 75,000 acres and plenty of activities for all, including horseback riding.

17 Arlington Outpost

 5

Location: In Arlington; map WY7, grid f4.

Campsites, facilities: There are 50 RV sites, some with hookups, and 20 tent sites with picnic tables and grills. Restrooms, showers, water, laundry facilities, a game room, and a sanitary disposal station are available.

Reservations, fees: Reservations are accepted; the fee is $10–16.75 per night. Open May–October.

Directions: From Laramie, go west on I-80 40 miles to Arlington. In Arlington get off I-80 at Exit 272. The campground is at the intersection of I-80 and U.S. 13, on the north side of I-80.

Contact: Arlington Outpost, P.O. Box 95, Rock River, WY 82083; tel./fax 307/378-2350.

Trip notes: Medicine Bow National Forest, less than two miles to the south, has hiking trails and fishing opportunities.

18 Saratoga Lake

 5

Location: In Saratoga, at Saratoga Lake; map WY7, grid g1.

Campsites, facilities: There are 50 RV or tent sites, some with picnic tables, fire pits, and some with hookups. Vault toilets, water, a playground, and a sanitary disposal station are available.

Reservations, fees: No reservations are needed; the fee is $7.50–10 per night. Open year-round.

Directions: From Rawlins go east on I-80 to

Highway 130, then south 21 miles to Saratoga. From Saratoga, go 1.5 miles north on Highway 130 to Saratoga Lake.

Contact: Saratoga Lake Campground, Saratoga, WY 82331.

Trip notes: You can fish, boat, water-ski, and windsurf at Saratoga Lake and the North Platte River; and the town of Saratoga has free mineral hot springs. The Saratoga Lake Wetlands, adjacent to the campground, has a wide variety of animals and birds that frequent the area.

19 South Brush Creek

 6

Location: In Medicine Bow National Forest; map WY7, grid g3.

Campsites, facilities: There are 21 RV or tent sites with picnic tables and fire pits. Vault toilets and water are available.

Reservations, fees: No reservations are needed; the fee is $10 per night. Open May 15–October 1. The stay limit is 14 days.

Directions: From Rawlins go east on I-80 to Highway 130, then south 21 miles to Saratoga. From Saratoga, go 21 miles south on Highway 130 to Brush Creek Road (Forest Service Road 100), then 1.5 miles to the campground.

Contact: Medicine Bow National Forest, 2468 Jackson St., Laramie, WY 82070; 307/745-2300.

Trip notes: This campground is along Brush Creek, where you can fish for brown, brook, and rainbow trout. Hiking trails are nearby.

20 Brooklyn Lake

 6

Location: In Medicine Bow Mountains; map WY7, grid g4.

Campsites, facilities: There are 19 RV or tent sites, some with pull-throughs, picnic tables, and fire pits. Vault toilets and water are available.

Reservations, fees: No reservations are need-

ed; the fee is $10 per night. Open July 15–September 10. The stay limit is 14 days.

Directions: From Laramie, go 40 miles west on Highway 130 to Centennial. From Centennial, go eight miles west on Highway 130 to Brooklyn Lake Road (Forest Service Road 317), then two miles north to the campground.

Contact: Medicine Bow National Forest, 2468 Jackson St., Laramie, WY 82070; 307/745-2300.

Trip notes: Centennial is a turn-of-the-century gold mining town. Hiking trails include the popular North Gap Lake Trail, a steep four-mile mountain trail, and Sheep Lake Trail, 8.2 miles of up-and-downhill sections rated difficult.

21 Libby Creek/Willow Campground

 7

Location: In Medicine Bow National Forest; map WY7, grid g4.

Campsites, facilities: There are 16 RV or tent sites, with picnic tables and fire pits. Vault toilets and water are available.

Reservations, fees: Reservations are accepted. Contact the National Recreation Reservation Service, 877/444-6777, or check the website: www.reserveusa.com. The fee is $10 per night. Open May 26–September 30. The stay limit is 14 days.

Directions: From Laramie, go 40 miles west on Highway 130 to Centennial. From Centennial, go west on Highway 130 for two miles, then south on Barber Lake Road to the campground.

Contact: Medicine Bow National Forest, 2468 Jackson St., Laramie, WY 82070; 307/745-2300.

Trip notes: This campground is along Libby Creek and near the Snowy Range Scenic Byway, which runs between Saratoga and Laramie across the summit of the Snowy Range and offers spectacular views. You can hike and fish in the Medicine Bow National Forest.

22 Riverside Campground

   2

Location: In Laramie; map WY7, grid g6.

Campsites, facilities: There are 30 RV or tent sites, some with hookups, and pull-throughs. Showers, restrooms, laundry facilities, water, and a sanitary disposal station are available.

Reservations, fees: No reservations are needed; the fee is $7–13 per night. Open year-round.

Directions: From I-80 at Laramie, take Exit 310; go east on Curtis Street to McCue Street. Turn right on McCue; the camp area is behind the truck stop.

Contact: Riverside Campground, 1559 McCue St., Laramie, WY 82212; 307/721-7405.

Trip notes: There is a swimming pool and golf course in Laramie, as well as many museums and historical displays. Laramie Peak is the highest point in the Laramie Mountains and is accessible from the trailhead at Friend Park Campground. It's a steep 5.5-mile climb, but the panoramic view from the top is spectacular. The Laramie Plains Lake is nearby, and the Pole Mountain area and Vedauwoo to the southeast has fishing, hiking, and climbing opportunities.

23 Snowy Range Trailer Park

     4

Location: In Laramie; map WY7, grid g6.

Campsites, facilities: There are 20 RV or tent campsites, some with hookups. Showers, restrooms, laundry facilities, water, and a sanitary disposal station are available.

Reservations, fees: No reservations are needed; the fee is $10–17 per night. Open year-round.

Directions: From I-80 at Laramie, take the Snowy Range exit, Exit 311, and go west on Taylor Street to the trailer park.

Contact: Snowy Range Trailer Park, 404 S. Taylor, Laramie, WY 82212; 307/745-0297 or 800/742-7289.

Trip notes: Laramie has a swimming pool and golf course and many museums and historical displays. Laramie Peak is the highest point in the Laramie Mountains and is accessible from the trailhead at Friend Park Campground. It's a steep 5.5-mile climb, but the panoramic view from the top is spectacular. Laramie Plains Lake is nearby, and the Pole Mountain area and Vedauwoo, to the southeast, has fishing, hiking, and climbing opportunities.

24 Laramie KOA

     4

Location: In Laramie; map WY7, grid g6.

Campsites, facilities: There are 105 RV and tent campsites with picnic tables and grills, some with hookups and pull-throughs. Restrooms, showers, laundry facilities, water, a sanitary disposal station, and game room are available.

Reservations, fees: Reservations are accepted; the fee is $15–21 per night. Open March 1–November 30.

Directions: From I-80 at Laramie, take Exit 310; go east on Curtis Street to McCue Street. Turn right on McCue, then right on Baker Street to the campground.

Contact: Laramie KOA, 1271 Baker St., Laramie, WY 82070; 307/742-6553.

Trip notes: Laramie has a swimming pool and golf course and many museums and historical displays. Laramie Peak is the highest point in the Laramie Mountains and is accessible from the trailhead at Friend Park Campground. It's a steep 5.5-mile climb, but the panoramic view from the top is spectacular. Laramie Plains Lake is nearby, and the Pole Mountain area and Vedauwoo to the southeast has fishing, hiking, and climbing opportunities.

25 Tie City

    4

Location: Near Laramie; map WY7, grid h7.

Campsites, facilities: There are 18 RV sites,

which can accommodate a maximum RV length of 32 feet, and tent sites with picnic tables and grills. Restrooms are available.

Reservations, fees: No reservations are needed; the fee is $0 per night. Open May 25–October 31. The stay limit is 14 days.

Directions: From Laramie, go 10 miles southeast on I-80 to Exit 323, then east on Highway 210 to the campground on the right.

Contact: Medicine Bow National Forest, 2468 Jackson St., Laramie, WY 82070; 307/745-2300; website: www.fs.fed.us.

Trip notes: There is a swimming pool and golf course in Laramie. There are many museums and historical displays. Laramie Peak is the highest point in the Laramie Mountains and is accessible from the trailhead at Friend Park Campground. It's a steep 5.5-mile climb, but the panoramic view from the top is spectacular. The Laramie Plains Lake is nearby, and the Pole Mountain area and Vedauwoo to the southeast has fishing, hiking, and climbing opportunities.

26 Yellow Pine

 4

Location: Near Laramie; map WY7, grid g7.

Campsites, facilities: There are 19 RV sites, which can accommodate a maximum RV length of 32 feet, plus tent sites, picnic tables, grills and restrooms.

Reservations, fees: No reservations are needed; the fee is $7 per night. Open May 24–September 30. The stay limit is 14 days.

Directions: From Laramie, go 10 miles southeast on I-80 to Exit 323, then .7 mile east on Highway 210 to Forest Service Road 712 (Telephone Road) to the campground.

Contact: Medicine Bow National Forest, 2468 Jackson St., Laramie, WY 82070; 307/745-2300; website: www.fs.fed.us.

Trip notes: A swimming pool, golf course and many museums and historical displays are in Laramie. Laramie Peak is the highest point in the Laramie Mountains and is accessible from

the trailhead at Friend Park Campground. It's a steep 5.5-mile climb, but the panoramic view from the top is spectacular. The Laramie Plains Lake is nearby, and the Pole Mountain area and Vedauwoo to the southeast have fishing, hiking, and climbing opportunities.

27 Rob Roy Campground

 6

Location: In the Medicine Bow National Forest; map WY7, grid h4.

Campsites, facilities: There are 65 RV or tent sites with picnic tables and fire pits. Vault toilets, water, and a boat ramp are available.

Reservations, fees: No reservations are needed; the fee is $10 per night. Open June 15–October 1. The stay limit is 14 days.

Directions: From Laramie go west on Highway 130 (the Centennial Road) for 17 miles to Highway 11; go south on Highway 11 for 11 miles to to Albany. In Albany, go nearly three miles west on Forest Service Road 500; stay right and go nearly six miles more to the turnoff to the campground.

Contact: Medicine Bow National Forest, 2468 Jackson St., Laramie, WY 82070; 307/745-2300.

Trip notes: This campground is at Rob Roy Reservoir, where you can fish for brown, brook, and rainbow trout.

28 Vedauwoo

 4

Location: Near Laramie; map WY7, grid h7.

Campsites, facilities: There are 28 RV or tent sites, 11 of which can accommodate a maximum RV length of 32 feet. Picnic tables and grills are provided.

Reservations, fees: No reservations are needed; the fee is $7 per night. Open May 1–October 31. The stay limit is 14 days.

Directions: From Laramie, take I-80 east 15 miles to Vedauwoo Rd. (Exit 329), and then take Exit 329 to the stop sign at Vedauwoo Road. Turn left on Vedauwoo Rd. and drive 1.2

miles to the campground sign for Vedauwoo. Turn left at the sign and the campground is about a third of a mile ahead on the right.

Contact: Medicine Bow National Forest, 2468 Jackson St., Laramie, WY 82070; 307/745-2300; website: www.fs.fed.us.

Trip notes: Vedauwoo is a popular area for rock climbing and hiking; the unique granite formations were sacred to the Arapahoe.

29 Bobbie Thompson

    7

Location: In Medicine Bow National Forest; map WY7, grid h4.

Campsites, facilities: There are 18 RV or tent sites, some with pull-throughs, and tables and grills. Vault toilets and water are available.

Reservations, fees: No reservations are needed; the fee is $10 per night. Open June–mid-October. The stay limit is 14 days.

Directions: From Laramie go west on Highway 130 (the Centennial Road) for 17 miles to Highway 11; go south on Highway 11 for 11 miles to to Albany. In Albany, go three miles west on Forest Service Road 500, then southwest on Forest Service Road 542 to Forest Service Road 543. The campground is just south of the junction.

Contact: Medicine Bow National Forest, 2468 Jackson St., Laramie, WY 82070; 307/745-2300.

Trip notes: This campground, which is forested and spacious, has Douglas Creek along the east side, which offers good fishing for brook, brown, and rainbow trout.

30 Lake Owen

     7

Location: In Medicine Bow National Forest; map WY7, grid h4.

Campsites, facilities: There are 35 RV or tent sites with picnic tables, fire pits, and grills. Vault toilets, water, and a boat ramp are available.

Reservations, fees: No reservations are needed; the fee is $10 per night. Open June–mid-October. The stay limit is 14 days.

Directions: From Laramie go west on Highway 130 (the Centennial Road) for 17 miles to Highway 11; go south on Highway 11 for 11 miles to to Albany. In Albany, go three miles west on Forest Service Road 500, then south on Forest Service Road 513 for 2.5 miles to Forest Service Road 517, and then nearly three miles east on Forest Service Road 540 to Lake Owen.

Contact: Medicine Bow National Forest, 2468 Jackson St., Laramie, WY 82070; 307/745-2300.

Trip notes: You can fish and boat on Lake Owen.

31 Pelton Creek

   7

Location: In the Medicine Bow National Forest; map WY7, grid h4.

Campsites, facilities: There are 15 RV or tent sites, with picnic tables, fire pits, and grills. Vault toilets and water are available.

Reservations, fees: No reservations are needed; the fee is $10 per night. Open June 15–September 15. The stay limit is 14 days.

Directions: From Laramie, go 43 miles southwest on Highway 230 to Forest Service Road 898 (you will cross the state line and return). Drive nine miles northwest to the campground.

Contact: Medicine Bow National Forest, 2468 Jackson St., Laramie, WY 82070; 307/745-2300.

Trip notes: Trailheads for the Platte Ridge and Douglas Creek Trails are here. Douglas Creek Trail is 9.5 miles long and is considered an easy hike.

32 Boswell Creek

    6

Location: In Medicine Bow National Forest; map WY7, grid h4.

Campsites, facilities: There are nine RV or tent sites, with picnic tables and grills. Vault toilets and water are available.

Reservations, fees: No reservations are needed; the fee is $10 per night. Open June–mid-September. The stay limit is 14 days.

Directions: From Laramie, go 42 miles southwest on Highway 230, then three miles east on Forest Service Road to the campground.

Contact: Medicine Bow National Forest, 2468 Jackson St., Laramie, WY 82070; 307/745-2300.

Trip notes: Boswell Creek runs through this campground, which is at the southernmost edge of the state.

Camping creekside

MAP WY8

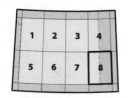

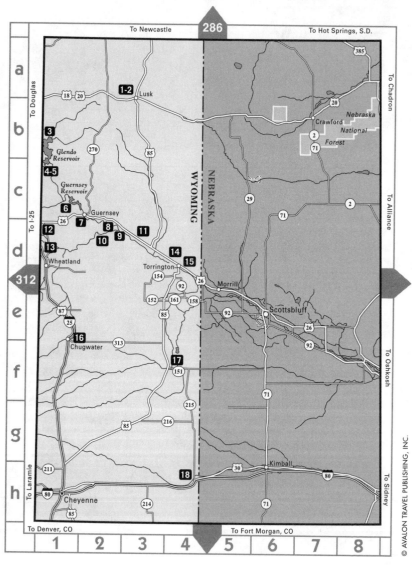

CHAPTER WY8

1 B Q Corral 327
2 Prairie View
   Campground 327
3 Glendo State Park 327
4 Lakeview Motel &
   Campground 328
5 Glendo Marina 328
6 Guernsey State Park.......328
7 Larson Park
   Campground 329
8 Chuckwagon RV & Gifts ...329
9 Bennett Court 329
10 Carnahan Ranch 330
11 Pony Soldier RV Park.......330
12 Wheatland City Park
   (Lewis Park) 330
13 Arrowhead RV Camp.......330
14 Goshen County
   Fairgrounds 331
15 Pioneer Municipal Park....331
16 Pitzer's RV Park.............331
17 Hawk Springs State
   Recreation Area............331
18 Pine Bluffs RV Park........332

1 B Q Corral

  4

Location: Near Lusk; map WY8, grid a3.

Campsites, facilities: There are 12 RV or tent campsites, some with hookups, picnic tables, and grills. Restrooms, showers, a sanitary disposal station, and a restaurant are available.

Reservations, fees: Reservations are accepted; the fee is $10–15 per night. Open April 1–October 15.

Directions: From U.S. 85 and U.S. 18/20 at Lusk, go south two miles on U.S. 85 to the campground.

Contact: B Q Corral, 702 S. Main, P.O. Box 1279, Lusk, WY 82225; 307/334-0128.

Trip notes: Lusk has a nine-hole golf course, and the Stagecoach Museum has exhibits of pioneer rooms, a post office, and old-time vehicles.

2 Prairie View Campground

  4

Location: West of Lusk; map WY8, grid a3.

Campsites, facilities: There are 29 RV sites, some with hookups, and 20 tent sites with picnic tables and grills. Restrooms, showers, laundry facilities, water, a sanitary disposal station, and a store are available.

Reservations, fees: Reservations are accepted; the fee is $14 per night. Open April 15–October 15.

Directions: From U.S. 85 and U.S. 18/20 at Lusk, go two miles west on U.S. Highway 18/20 to the campground.

Contact: Prairie View Campground, 3925 Hwy. 20, P.O. Box 1168, Lusk, WY 82225; 307/334-9904 or 307/334-2827; email: luprview@coffey.com.

Trip notes: Lusk has a nine-hole golf course, and the Stagecoach Museum has exhibits of pioneer rooms, a post office, and old-time vehicles.

3 Glendo State Park

     5

Location: North of Douglas; map WY8, grid b1.

Campsites, facilities: There are numerous RV or tent sites, some with pull-throughs, picnic tables and grills. Vault toilets, water, a sanitary disposal station, and a marina are available.

Reservations, fees: No reservations are needed; the fee is $4–9 per night. Open May 1–October 1. The stay limit is 14 days.

Directions: From Douglas, go south 24 miles on I-25 to Glendo. Go .5 mile east to the park entrance.

Contact: Glendo State Park, P.O. Box 398, Glendo, WY 82213; 307/735-4433.

Trip notes: You can swim, boat, water ski, and fish for walleye and catfish in Glendo Reservoir. Hiking trails offer informative displays. The reservoir level fluctuates, as this is a prime irrigation source. Many boaters cruise up the North Platte River canal to see the sheer rock canyon that provides a home to bald eagles.

4 Lakeview Motel & Campground

 5

Location: In Glendo; map WY8, grid c1.

Campsites, facilities: There are 20 RV or tent campsites. Restrooms, laundry facilities, water, a game room, and a sanitary disposal station are available.

Reservations, fees: Reservations are accepted; the fee is $10–12 per night. Open all year.

Directions: From Douglas, go south 24 miles on I-25 to Glendo. This campground is at the north end of town.

Contact: Lakeview Motel & Campground, P.O. Box 231, 422 6th St., Glendo, WY 82213; 307/735-4461.

Trip notes: You can swim, boat, water ski, and fish for walleye and catfish in Glendo Reservoir. Hiking trails offer informative displays. The reservoir level fluctuates, as this is a prime irrigation source. Many boaters cruise up the North Platte River canal in order to see the sheer rock canyon that provides a home to bald eagles.

5 Glendo Marina

 5

Location: At Glendo State Park; map WY8, grid c1.

Campsites, facilities: There are seven RV campsites; no tents are allowed. Hookups, a marina, restaurant, groceries, and fishing supplies and licenses are available.

Reservations, fees: Reservations are accepted; the fee is $15 per night. Open May 1–October 1.

Directions: From Douglas, go south 24 miles on I-25 to Glendo. Go 3.5 miles east of Glendo State Park to the marina.

Contact: Glendo Marina, P.O. Box 187, 383 Glendo Park Rd., Glendo, WY 82213; 307/735-4216 or fax 307/735-4203.

Trip notes: You can swim, boat, water ski, and fish for walleye and catfish in Glendo Reservoir. Hiking trails offer informative displays. The reservoir level fluctuates, as this is a prime irrigation source. Many boaters cruise up the North Platte River canal in order to see the sheer rock canyon that provides a home to bald eagles.

6 Guernsey State Park

 6

Location: Near Guernsey; map WY8, grid c1.

Campsites, facilities: There are 140 total RV or tent sites with picnic tables and grills, some with pull-throughs, but no hookups. Restrooms, water, and a sanitary disposal station are available. There are four boat ramps. Pets are allowed on leashes.

Reservations, fees: Reservations are not needed; the fee is $4 per vehicle per night, and there is an entrance fee of $2 per resident, $4 per nonresident. Open year-round. The stay limit is 14 days.

Directions: From Wheatland, go north on I-25 to U.S. 26. Take U.S. 26 east 15 miles to Highway 317, and then take a left for 1.5 miles to the entrance to the state park.

Contact: Guernsey State Park, P.O. Box 429, Guernsey, WY 82214; 307/836-2334.

Trip notes: Guernsey State Park includes 6,227 acres of land and the Guernsey Reservoir. You can boat, water-ski, and swim at the reservoir, but be aware that water levels can vary dramatically, so check with the state park office in the park for updated conditions. The town of Guernsey has stores, restaurants, service station, and a post office. The Volksmarch Trail has two loops, with several major climbs, and is considered a difficult trail.

7 Larson Park Campground

     4

Location: In Guernsey; map WY8, grid d2.

Campsites, facilities: There are 16 RV or tent sites, some with partial hookups, picnic tables and grills. Showers, restrooms, and water are available.

Reservations, fees: Reservations are accepted; the fee is $5–8 per night. Open year-round.

Directions: From Wheatland, go north on I-25 to U.S. 26. Take U.S. 26 east 15 miles to Highway 317, and then take a left for 1.5 miles to the entrance to the state park.

Contact: Larson Park Campground, Guernsey, WY 82214; 307/836-2255.

Trip notes: There is a nine-hole golf course right by the campground. Guernsey State Park and the Guernsey Reservoir is three miles west on U.S. 26, right on Highway 317. You can boat, water-ski and swim at the reservoir, but be aware that water levels can vary dramatically, so check with the state park office in Guernsey State Park (307/836-2334) for updated conditions. The town of Guernsey has stores, restaurants, service station, and a post office. The Volksmarch Trail has two loops, with several major climbs, and is considered a difficult trail.

8 Chuckwagon RV & Gifts

    5

Location: At Fort Laramie; map WY8, grid d2.

Campsites, facilities: There are 18 RV sites or tent sites, with picnic tables and grills, some with hookups. Restrooms, showers, water, and a sanitary disposal station are available.

Reservations, fees: No reservations are needed; the fee is $10–13 per night. Open April 15–October 15.

Directions: From Torrington, go west on U.S. 26/85 21 miles to Fort Laramie. From Fort Laramie, go to the west end of town, turn south from U.S. 26 to Highway 160 to camp.

Contact: Chuckwagon RV & Gifts, 314 Pioneer Court, Fort Laramie, WY 82212; 307/837-2304.

Trip notes: Fort Laramie National Historic Site, three miles southwest of town, sits on 832 acres near the confluence of the North Platte and Laramie Rivers. Founded as Fort Williams in 1834, the site has a visitor center museum with displays of historical artifacts, and many of the original buildings have been restored.

9 Bennett Court

   4

Location: In Fort Laramie; map WY8, grid d2.

Campsites, facilities: There are seven RV sites with full hookups and three tent sites.

Reservations, Fees: Reservations are accepted; the fee is $9–12 per night. Open year-round.

Directions: From Torrington, go west on U.S. 26/85 21 miles to Fort Laramie. In Fort Laramie, off U.S. 26, 3.5 blocks north on Laramie Avenue.

Contact: Bennett Court, P.O. Box 54, Fort Laramie, WY 82212; 307/837-2270.

Trip notes: Fort Laramie National Historic Site, three miles southwest of town, sits on 832-acres near the confluence of the North Platte and Laramie Rivers. Founded as Fort Williams in 1834, many of the original buildings have been restored, and the visitor center museum has displays of historical artifacts.

10 Carnahan Ranch

 5

Location: Near Fort Laramie National Historic Site; map WY8, grid d2.

Campsites, facilities: Camping is allowed in a large meadow, with an unspecified number of sites. Campers will find potable water, electricity available for two RVs, a community building with showers, 2,400 acres available for hiking, and longhorn cattle.

Reservations, fees: Reservations are accepted; the fee is $15–20 per night per camping unit, with a $5 surcharge for electricity. A camping unit includes up to six people in one tent. Open May–October 1. Reservations are recommended.

Directions: From Torrington, go west on U.S. 26/85 21 miles to Fort Laramie. From Fort Laramie, go southwest three miles on Highway 160. The campground is on left.

Contact: Carnahan Ranch, HC 72, Box 440, Fort Laramie, WY 82212; 800/837-6730, fax 307/837-2917.

Trip notes: This campground is adjacent to the Carnahan Ranch, a working cattle ranch, and near the Fort Laramie Historical Site.

11 Pony Soldier RV Park

 4

Location: East of Fort Laramie; map WY8, grid d3.

Campsites, facilities: There are 65 RV or tent campsites, some with hookups, picnic tables, and grills. Showers, restrooms, laundry facilities, water, a sanitary disposal station, and a game room are available.

Reservations, fees: No reservations are needed; the fee is $7–12 per night. Open April 15–October 15.

Directions: From Fort Laramie, go five miles east on U.S. 26 or from Lingle, five miles west on U.S. 26. Lingle is 11 miles west of Torrington on U.S. 26/85; Fort Laramie is 21 miles west of Torrington.

Contact: Pony Soldier RV Park, P.O. Box 575, Lingle, WY 82223; 307/837-3078.

Trip notes: You can fish on the Laramie and North Platte Rivers, along U.S. 26, for rainbow and brown trout.

12 Wheatland City Park (Lewis Park)

 4

Location: In Wheatland; map WY8, grid d1.

Campsites, facilities: There are 33 RV or tent campsites, some with hookups, picnic tables, and grills. Showers, restrooms, water, and a sanitary disposal station are available.

Reservations, fees: No reservations are needed, and no fee is charged. Open year-round. The stay limit is three days.

Directions: This campground is in the town of Wheatland. From Cheyenne, go 70 miles north on I-25, get off at Exit 78 to stop sign; turn left on 16th Street and right on South Street (which turns into 9th Street). Turn right on High Street to 8th, then right to the campsites at the park.

Contact: City of Wheatland, 600 9th St., Wheatland, WY 82201; 307/322-2822.

Trip notes: Wheatland has a nine-hole golf course and swimming pool. Wyoming Game & Fish Sybille Wildlife Research and Education Center is southwest of town on Highway 34. This center has a nature trail, big game, and information on the black-footed ferret recovery effort.

13 Arrowhead RV Camp

 4

Location: In Wheatland; map WY8, grid d1.

Campsites, facilities: There are 24 RV sites, some with full hookups, and eight tent sites with picnic tables. Restrooms, laundry facilities, and a sanitary disposal station are available.

Reservations, Fees: No reservations are taken; the fee is $5–10 per night. Open year-round.

Directions: From Cheyenne, go 70 miles north on I-25, take Exit 80 at Wheatland, and turn right on 16th Street; the campground is on the right.

Contact: Arrowhead RV Camp, 2005 N. 16th St., Wheatland, WY 82201; 307/322-5607 or 307/322-3467.

Trip notes: Wheatland has a nine-hole golf course and a swimming pool. The Wyoming Game & Fish Sybille Wildlife Research and Education Center is southwest of Wheatland on Highway 34. This center has a nature trail, big game, and information on the black-footed ferret recovery effort.

14 Goshen County Fairgrounds

 4

Location: In Torrington; map WY8, grid d4.

Campsites, facilities: There are 20 RV sites, some with hookups, and tent sites with picnic tables and grills. Restrooms, showers, water, and a sanitary disposal station are available.

Reservations, fees: No reservations are needed; the fee is $5–8 per night. Open year-round.

Directions: From Torrington, go west on U.S. 26 to the Goshen County Shop Road, and turn right; then almost immediately turn left to the fairgrounds.

Contact: Goshen County Fairgrounds, Drawer F, Hwy. 85-26 West, Torrington, WY 82340; 307/532-2525.

Trip notes: There is an 18-hole golf course and municipal swimming pool in the town of Torrington.

15 Pioneer Municipal Park

 4

Location: In Torrington, map WY8, grid d4.

Campsites, facilities: There are 10 RV sites and tent sites, some with hookups, picnic tables, and grills. Showers, restrooms, and a

sanitary disposal station are available.

Reservations, fees: No reservations are needed; no fee is charged. Open May 1–September 30. The stay limit is 10 days.

Directions: This campground is in Torrington on West 15th Avenue and Avenue "E" Street.

Contact: Pioneer Municipal Park, Torrington Chamber of Commerce, 350 W. 21st St., Torrington, WY 82340; 307/532-3879.

Trip notes: There is an 18-hole golf course and municipal swimming pool in town.

16 Pitzer's RV Park

 4

Location: In Chugwater; E9, grid e2.

Campsites, facilities: There are eight RV campsites, some with hookups, but the hookups are seasonal.

Reservations, fees: No reservations are needed; the fee is $10 per night. Open year-round.

Directions: From Cheyenne, take I-25 north to Chugwater; the campground is in the town of Chugwater, at 3rd Street and Clay Street.

Contact: Pitzer's RV Park, 207 Clay Ave., Chugwater, WY 82210; 307/422-3421.

Trip notes: Chugwater is known for its chili, and there are signs everywhere advertising the fact.

17 Hawk Springs State Recreation Area

 5

Location: At Hawk Springs; map WY8, grid f4.

Campsites, facilities: There are 26 RV or tent sites with picnic tables and fire pits, some with pull-throughs. Vault toilets, water, a boat ramp, and a playground are available.

Reservations, fees: No reservations are needed; the fee is $4–9 per night. Open year-round. The stay limit is 14 days.

Directions: From Torrington go south on U.S. 85 to five miles south of Hawk Springs, and then east three miles on the dirt road to camp.

Contact: Wyoming State Parks, 122 W. 25th, Herschler Bldg. 1-E, Cheyenne, WY 82002; 307/777-6323

Trip notes: This is an important stopover for waterfowl migration. You can fish, boat, and swim at the reservoir.

18 Pine Bluffs RV Park

   3

Location: In Pine Bluffs; map WY8, grid h4.

Campsites, facilities: There are 130 RV or tent campsites, some with hookups, picnic tables, and grills. Showers, laundry facilities, restrooms, water, and a sanitary disposal station are available.

Reservations, fees: No reservations are needed; the fee is $10–20 per night. Open year-round.

Directions: From Cheyenne, take I-80 east 40 miles to Pine Bluffs; take Exit 401 and go 1.5 miles on the business loop to Butler Street; then turn on Paint Brush Street to the campground.

Contact: Pine Bluffs RV Park, 10 Paint Brush, Pine Bluffs, WY 82082; 307/245-3665 or 800/294-4968.

Trip notes: There is an archeology dig site nearby; for information contact the University of Wyoming Archeology Lab at 307/245-9372. There are nature trails nearby.

IDAHO

Chapter ID1.............................337
Chapter ID2.............................367
Chapter ID3.............................383
Chapter ID4.............................389
Chapter ID5.............................423
Chapter ID6.............................447
Chapter ID7.............................465
Chapter ID8.............................469
Chapter ID9.............................481

IDAHO STATE 335

Map ID1 338   Map ID6 448
Map ID2 368   Map ID7 466
Map ID3 384   Map ID8 470
Map ID4 390   Map ID9 482
Map ID5 424

IDAHO STATE MAP

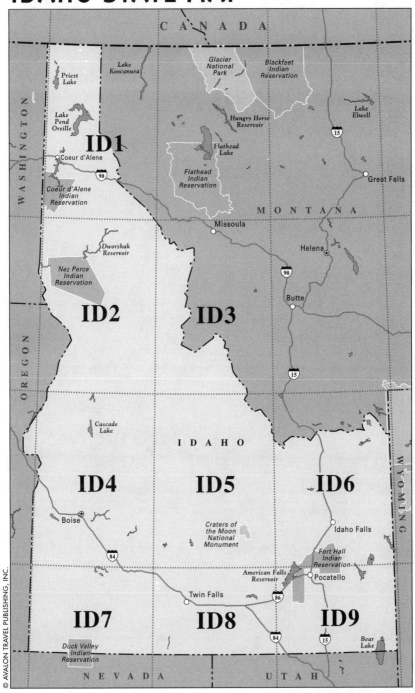

Tent camping

MAP ID1

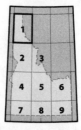

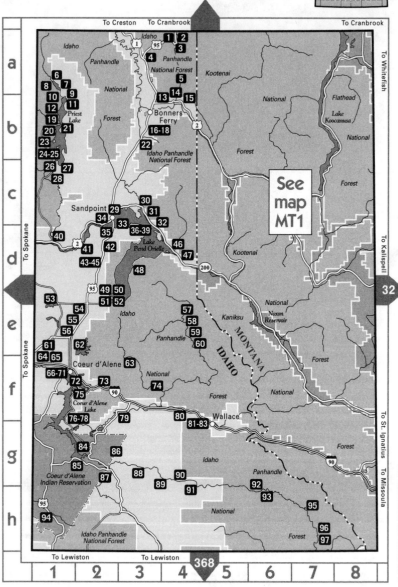

CHAPTER ID1

1 Robinson Lake.................340
2 Cooper Creek 340
3 Idyl Acres RV Park..........341
4 Brush Lake Campground..341
5 Meadow Creek 341
6 Navigation 341
7 Trapper Creek 342
8 Plowboy 342
9 Geisingers 342
10 Osprey..........................343
11 Lionhead 343
12 Beaver Creek.................344
13 Smith Lake....................344
14 Hemlock's Country Inn 344
15 Twin Rivers Canyon
Resort 344
16 Town & Country Motel
& RV Park 345
17 Bonners Ferry Resort......345
18 Deep Creek Resort 345
19 Kaniksu Resort RV
& Marina 346
20 Reeder Bay....................346
21 Indian Creek..................346
22 Blue Lake Campground 346
23 Upper Luby Bay 347
24 Lower Luby Bay..............347
25 Priest Lake RV Resort
& Marina 347
26 Outlet..........................348
27 Sundance Village RV
Park 348
28 Dickensheet 348
29 Springy Point
Recreation Area............349
30 Trestle Creek RV Park 349
31 R-Place RV Park..............349
32 Idaho Country Resort......349
33 Alpine Trailer Park 349
34 Edgewater Resort...........350

35 Albeni Cove
Recreation Area............350
36 Fox Farm RV Resort 350
37 Bottle Bay Resort 351
38 Sam Owen.....................351
39 Island View Resort..........351
40 Priest River
Recreation Area............352
41 Riley Creek
Recreation Area............352
42 Garfield Bay Resort 352
43 Round Lake State Park.....352
44 Travel America Plaza.......352
45 Sandy Beach Resort 353
46 River Lake RV Park 353
47 River Delta Resort..........353
48 Whiskey Rock 353
49 Scenic Bay Marina..........354
50 MacDonald's
Hudson Bay Resort 354
51 Farragut State Park........354
52 Bayview Scenic Motel
& RV Park 354
53 Silver Beach Resort 355
54 Kelso Lake Resort...........355
55 Silverwood RV Park 355
56 Alpine Country Store
& RV Park 356
57 Big Hank.......................356
58 Berlin Flats 356
59 Devil's Elbow 356
60 Kit Price.......................356
61 Westside Resort 357
62 Mokins Bay....................357
63 Honeysuckle..................357
64 Suntree RV Park 357
65 Coeur d'Alene RV Resort..358
66 Boulevard Motel
& RV Park 358

(continues)

67 Cedar Motel & RV Park 358	82 Blue Anchor Trailer
68 Coeur d'Alene KOA 358	& RV Park 362
69 Monte Vista Motel	83 Silver Leaf Motel
& RV Park 359	& RV Park 362
70 Shady Acres	84 Harrison City RV Park 362
Campground 359	85 Heyburn State Park 362
71 Beyond Hope Resort........359	86 Misty Meadows RV Park
72 Robin Hood RV Park &	& Camping 363
Campground 359	87 Ed's R & R Shady River
73 Wolf Lodge Campground..360	RV Park.......................363
74 Bumblebee...................360	88 Shadowy St. Joe.............363
75 Squaw Bay	89 St. Joe Lodge & Resort.....364
Camping Resort 360	90 Big Creek.....................364
76 Rockford Bay Resort 360	91 Huckleberry..................364
77 Bell Bay 361	92 Turner Flat 364
78 Albertini's Carlin	93 Tin Can Flat...................365
Bay Resort....................361	94 RV Park Milepost 382......365
79 Killarney Lake...............361	95 Conrad Crossing 365
80 Kellogg/Silver	96 Fly Flat.........................365
Valley KOA....................361	97 Spruce Tree 366
81 Crystal Gold Mine	
& RV Park 362	

1 Robinson Lake

        6

Location: In Idaho Panhandle National Forest; map ID1, grid a4.

Campsites, facilities: There are 10 RV or tent campsites, which can accommodate a maximum RV length of 32 feet. Wheelchair-accessible restrooms, vault toilets, water, and a boat ramp are available.

Reservations, fees: No reservations are needed; the fee is $6 per night. Open May 15–October 1.

Directions: From Eastport, go seven miles south on U.S. 95, then one mile north on Forest Service Road 448; the campground is on right side.

Contact: Idaho Panhandle National Forest, Bonners Ferry Ranger District, Route 4, Box 4860, Bonners Ferry, ID 83805; 208/267-5561.

Trip notes: You can hike, boat, fish, and swim here.

2 Cooper Creek

   6

Location: In Idaho Panhandle National Forest; map ID1, grid a4.

Campsites, facilities: There are 16 RV or tent campsites, which can accommodate a maximum RV length of 32 feet. Wheelchair-accessible restrooms and water are available.

Reservations, fees: No reservations are needed; the fee is $6 per night. Open May 15–October 1.

Directions: From the Canadian border, go two miles south on U.S. 95, then one mile east on Forest Service Road 2517 to the campground.

Contact: Idaho Panhandle National Forest, Bonners Ferry Ranger District, Route 4, Box

4860, Bonners Ferry, ID 83805; 208/267-5561.

Trip notes: This campground is on the banks of the Moyie River. The Upper Moyie offers recreational rafting, but it's experts only on the Lower Moyie. From here it's a short and relatively easy hike to Copper Falls, a spectacular 80-foot waterfall.

3 Idyl Acres RV Park

 6

Location: In Idaho Panhandle National Forest; map ID1, grid a4.

Campsites, facilities: There are 10 RV or tent campsites, some with pull-throughs and hookups. Showers are available. Pets are allowed on leashes.

Reservations, fees: Reservations are accepted; the fee is $15 per night. Open May–September.

Directions: From the Canadian border, go four miles south on U.S. 95 to the campground.

Contact: Idyl Acres RV Park, HCR 61, P.O. Box 170, Bonners Ferry, ID 83805; 208/267-3629.

Trip notes: This is a nicely landscaped campground. You can fish in the Moyie River for brook, cutthroat, rainbow trout, and whitefish. Round Prairie Creek has brook trout. You can hike in the Idaho Panhandle National Forest. You can boat and swim at Robinson Lake.

4 Brush Lake Campground

 5

Location: In Kaniksu National Forest; map ID1, grid a3.

Campsites, facilities: There are four RV or tent campsites. A boat ramp is nearby.

Reservations, fees: No reservations are needed, and no fee is charged.

Directions: From Bonners Ferry go 19 miles north on Highway 95, then southeast three miles on Forest Service Road 1004 to the campground.

Contact: Idaho Panhandle National Forest, Bonners Ferry Ranger District, Route 4, Box

4860, Bonners Ferry, ID 83805; 208/267-5561.

Trip notes: This campground is in the Kaniksu National Forest, where you can fish and hike. There are excellent wildlife viewing opportunities.

5 Meadow Creek

 6

Location: In the Idaho Panhandle Forest; map ID1, grid a4.

Campsites, facilities: There are 22 RV or tent campsites, which can accommodate a maximum RV length of 22 feet. Vault toilets and water available.

Reservations, fees: No reservations are needed; the fee is $5 per night. Open May 15 to October 1.

Directions: From Bonners Ferry, go north three miles on U.S. 95 to the junction of U.S. 92 and U.S. 2, turn right on U.S. 2, go 2.5 miles, and then take a left on Meadow Creek Road. The campground is 10 miles ahead.

Contact: Idaho Panhandle National Forest, Bonners Ferry Ranger District, Route 4, Box 4860, Bonners Ferry, ID 83805; 208/267-5561.

Trip notes: There are fishing and recreational rafting on the Upper Moyie River and whitewater and expert rafting on the Lower Moyie River.

6 Navigation

 6

Location: Near Priest Lake; map ID1, grid a1.

Campsites, facilities: There are five tent campsites; this campground is accessible by boat or hiking only.

Reservations, fees: No reservations are needed; the fee is $0–10 per night.

Directions: From Sandpoint, take U.S. 2 22 miles west to Priest River; turn north onto Highway 57 at the stoplight and drive to Beaver Creek and the campground.

Contact: Priest Lake Ranger District, 32203 Hwy. 57, Priest River,

ID 83856; 208/443-2512.

Trip notes: This is a pack-in, pack-out campground. You can fish, boat, or swim on Upper Priest Lake. You can fish for Mackinaw, the predominant species in Priest Lake. Trophy-size fish have been caught here. You can boat and swim in Priest Lake. You can hike and bike in the area, either gut-wrenching climbs to the peaks on the east side of the lake or leisurely rides on the Lakeshore Trail on the west side. The Priest Lake Trails pamphlet, available at the Priest Lake Ranger District, has more information. The Priest Lake Golf Course has a nine-hole course (soon to be 18) along with a driving range and putting green.

⁊ Trapper Creek

 6

Location: Near Priest River; map ID1, grid a1.
Campsites, facilities: There are five tent campsites, accessible only by boat or hiking in.
Reservations, fees: No reservations are needed; no fee is charged.
Directions: From Sandpoint, go 22 miles on U.S. 2 to Priest River, and then take Highway 57 north 19 miles to Priest Lake. From Priest Lake, go to Kalispell boat launch; the campground is on the east side of Upper Creek Lake.
Contact: Idaho Panhandle National Forest, Priest Lake Ranger District, 32203 Hwy. 57, HCR 5, Box 207, Priest River, ID 83856; 208/443-2512, 800/280-2267.
Trip notes: This is a boat-in, boat-out campground. You can fish for Mackinaw, the predominant species in Priest Lake. Trophy-size fish have been caught here. You can boat and swim in Priest Lake. You can hike and bike in the area, either gut-wrenching climbs to the peaks on the east side of the lake or leisurely rides on the Lakeshore Trail on the west side. The Priest Lake Trails pamphlet, available at the Priest Lake Ranger District, has more information. The Priest Lake Golf Course has

nine holes of golf (soon to be 18) along with a driving range and putting green.

⅛ Plowboy

 6

Location: At Upper Priest Lake; map ID1, grid a1.
Campsites, facilities: There are four tent campsites, and this campground is accessible by boat or hiking only.
Reservations, fees: No reservations are needed, and no fee is charged.
Directions: From Sandpoint, take U.S. 2 to Priest River; at the stoplight, turn on Highway 57 and drive to Beaver Creek. The campground is on the southwest shore of Upper Priest Lake.
Contact: Priest Lake Ranger District, 32203 Hwy. 57, Priest River, ID 83856; 208/443-2512.
Trip notes: This is a pack-in and pack-out campground. You can fish, boat, or swim on Upper Priest Lake. You can fish for Mackinaw, the predominant species in Priest Lake. Trophy-size fish have been caught here. You can boat and swim in Priest Lake. You can hike and bike in the area, either gut-wrenching climbs to the peaks on the east side of the lake or leisurely rides on the Lakeshore Trail on the west side. The Priest Lake Trails pamphlet, available at the Priest Lake Ranger District, has more information. The Priest Lake Golf Course has nine holes of golf (soon to be 18) along with a driving range and putting green.

⑨ Geisingers

 6

Location: In the Idaho Panhandle National Forest; map ID1, grid b1.
Campsites, facilities: There are two campsites, which are accessible by boat or hiking in only.
Reservations, fees: No reservations are needed, and no fee is charged.
Directions: From Sandpoint, go 22 miles on

U.S. 2 to Priest River, and take Highway 57 north 19 miles to Priest Lake. From Priest Lake, go to Kalispell boat launch.

Contact: Priest Lake Ranger District, 32203 Hwy. 57, Priest River, ID 83856; 208/443-2512.

Trip notes: This campground is pack-in, pack-out, accessible by boat or hiking in only. It is on Upper Priest Lake on the southeast side. You can fish for Mackinaw, the predominant species in Priest Lake. Trophy-size fish have been caught here. You can boat and swim in Priest Lake and hike and bike in the area, either gut-wrenching climbs to the peaks on the east side of the lake or leisurely rides on the Lakeshore Trail on the west side. The Priest Lake Trails pamphlet, available at the Priest Lake Ranger District, has more information. The Priest Lake Golf Course has a nine-hole course (soon to be 18) along with a driving range and putting green.

10 Osprey

 6

Location: At Priest Lake; map ID1, grid b1.

Campsites, facilities: There are 16 RV and tent campsites, which can accommodate a maximum RV length of 20 feet. Vault toilets and water are available.

Reservations, fees: No reservations are needed; the fee is $8 per night. Open June 15–September 10.

Directions: From Sandpoint, go 22 miles on U.S. 2 to Priest River, take Highway 57 north 19 miles to Priest Lake, then two miles northeast on Forest Service Road 237 to the campground, which is on the west side of Priest Lake.

Contact: Idaho Panhandle National Forest, Priest Lake Ranger District, 32203 Hwy. 57, HCR 5, Box 207, Priest River, ID 83856; 208/443-2512, 800/280-2267.

Trip notes: You can hike, fish, and swim here. You can fish for Mackinaw, the predominant species in Priest Lake. Trophy-size fish have been caught here. You can boat and swim in Priest Lake and hike and bike in the area, either gut-wrenching climbs to the peaks on the east side of the lake or leisurely rides on the Lakeshore Trail on the west side. The Priest Lake Trails pamphlet, available at the Priest Lake Ranger District, has more information. The Priest Lake Golf Course has nine holes of golf (soon to be 18) along with a driving range and putting green.

11 Lionhead

 6

Location: Northeast end of Priest Lake; map ID1, grid b1.

Campsites, facilities: There are 47 RV or tent campsites with picnic tables and grills.

Reservations, fees: No reservations are needed; the fee is $9 per night. Group camping is available by reservation.

Directions: From Sandpoint, take U.S. 2 22 miles west to Priest River, turn north at the stoplight onto Highway 57, drive 22 miles, and then turn right at Coolin Road to Coolin; the campground is approximately 23 miles north of Coolin, on the East Lakeshore Road on the right.

Contact: Priest Lake State Park, Indian Creek Bay #423, Coolin, ID 83821; 208/443-2200.

Trip notes: You can fish for Mackinaw, the predominant species in Priest Lake. Trophy-size fish have been caught here. You can boat and swim in Priest Lake and hike and bike in the area, either gut-wrenching climbs to the peaks on the east side of the lake or leisurely rides on the Lakeshore Trail on the west side. The Priest Lake Trails pamphlet, available at the Priest Lake Ranger District, has more information. The Priest Lake Golf Course is a nine-hole course (soon to be 18) and has a driving range and putting green.

12 Beaver Creek

 6

Location: Near Priest Lake; map ID1, grid b1.

Campsites, facilities: There are 40 RV or tent campsites, which can accommodate a maximum RV length of 35 feet.

Reservations, fees: Reservations are accepted; the fee is $9 per night. Open Memorial Day–Labor Day. The stay limit is 14 days.

Directions: From Sandpoint, go 22 miles on U.S. 2 to Priest River, take Highway 57 north 34 miles to Nordman, and then go 12 miles north on paved Reeder Bay Road to the campground.

Contact: Idaho Panhandle National Forest, Priest Lake Ranger District, HCR 5, Box 207, Priest River, ID 83856; 208/443-2512, 800/280-2267.

Trip notes: You can fish for Mackinaw, the predominant species in Priest Lake. Trophy-size fish have been caught here. You can boat and swim in Priest Lake and hike and bike in the area, either gut-wrenching climbs to the peaks on the east side of the lake or leisurely rides on the Lakeshore Trail on the west side. The Priest Lake Trails pamphlet, available at the Priest Lake Ranger District, has more information. The Priest Lake Golf Course is a nine-hole course (soon to be 18) and has a driving range and putting green.

13 Smith Lake

 6

Location: In the Idaho Panhandle Forest; map ID1, grid b4.

Campsites, facilities: There are seven RV or tent campsites. Water and a boat ramp are available.

Reservations, fees: No reservations are needed, and no fee is charged. Open May 15–October 31.

Directions: From Bonners Ferry, go five miles north on U.S. 95, then east two miles on Forest Service Road 1005 to the campground.

Contact: Idaho Panhandle National Forest, Bonners Ferry Ranger District, Route 4, Box 4860, Bonners Ferry, ID 83805; 208/267-5561.

Trip notes: You can swim and boat in the lake. This is an excellent area for wildlife viewing.

14 Hemlock's Country Inn

 5

Location: Near the Kootenai River; map ID1, grid a4.

Campsites, facilities: There are 12 RV or tent campsites, some with hookups and pull-throughs. Laundry facilities, showers, propane gas, a restaurant, and an RV service/repair shop are available.

Reservations, fees: No reservations are needed; the fee is $8–15 per night. Open year-round.

Directions: From Kalispell, go west 107 miles on U.S. 2, through Libby to Troy. Go 14 miles west of Troy; the campground is on the left of the highway.

Contact: Hemlock's Country Inn, HCR 62, P.O. Box 79, Hwy. 2, Moyie Springs, ID 83845; 208/267-6048 or 888/267-6048.

Trip notes: You can hike in the area and fish in the Kootenai River.

15 Twin Rivers Canyon Resort

 6

Location: Near Moyie Springs; map ID1, grid b4.

Campsites, facilities: There are 68 RV or tent campsites, which can accommodate a maximum RV length of 65 feet. Hookups, wheelchair-accessible restrooms, showers, and a sanitary disposal station are available. Pets are allowed on leashes.

Reservations, fees: No reservations are needed; the fee is $13–19 per night. Open April 1–October 31.

Directions: From Bonners Ferry, go three miles north on U.S. 95, then east on U.S. 2, then one mile east of Moyie Springs. The campground is two miles after the first right after the bridge.

Contact: Twin Rivers Canyon Resort, HCR 62, P.O. Box 25, Moyie Springs, ID 83845; 208/267-5932.

Trip notes: This is a family-oriented campground, with forested scenery and canyon rivers. Moyie River Outlook and Bridge is a half mile to the west on U.S. 2. This bridge is one of the highest in the state and has terrific views of the river and dam. You can boat, swim, fish, raft, and hike in this area.

16 Town & Country Motel & RV Park

 4

Location: In Bonners Ferry; map ID1, grid b3.
Campsites, facilities: There are thirteen RV or tent campsites, which can accommodate a maximum RV length of 35 feet. Hookups, showers, a sanitary disposal station, hot tub, swimming pool, and coffee shop are available. Pets are allowed on leashes.

Reservations, fees: Reservations are accepted; the fee is $15 per night. Open year-round.

Directions: From Sandpoint, take U.S. 95 to South 3rd Street. The campground is on the left.

Contact: Town & Country Motel & RV Park, Route 4, Box 4664, Bonners Ferry, ID 83805; 208/267-7915.

Trip notes: You can fish and swim here.

17 Bonners Ferry Resort

 5

Location: In Bonners Ferry; map ID1, grid b3.
Campsites, facilities: There are 61 RV or tent campsites, some with hookups. Wheelchair-accessible restrooms, laundry facilities, showers, a swimming pool, restaurant, and a sanitary disposal station are available. Pets are allowed on leashes.

Reservations, fees: No reservations are needed; the fee is $14 per night.
Directions: From Sandpoint, take U.S. 95 north to Bonners Ferry. The campground is at the south end of town.

Contact: Bonners Ferry Resort, Route 4, Box 4700, 6438 S. Main, Bonners Ferry, ID 83805; 208/267-2422.

Trip notes: You can golf nearby. Bonners Ferry was established in 1864 by Edwin Bonner, an entrepreneur from Washington state. The Boundary County Free Museum on Main Street has a collection of over 10,000 items relating to local history. Kootenai National Wildlife Refuge, just west of Bonners Ferry, is home to waterfowl and wild animals and has two waterfalls, Snow Falls and Myrtle Creek.

18 Deep Creek Resort

 6

Location: In Kaniksu National Forest; map ID1, grid b4.
Campsites, facilities: There are 12 RV and 40 tent sites, some with hookups. Showers, laundry facilities, barrier-free access, and a restaurant are available. Pets are allowed on leashes.

Reservations, fees: No reservations are needed; the fee is $8.50–12.50 per night.
Directions: From Sandpoint, go 24 miles north on U.S. 95 to Bonners Ferry, then seven miles south of Bonners Ferry on Old Highway 95 to the campground.

Contact: Deep Creek Resort, Route 4, Box 628, Bonners Ferry, ID 83805; 208/267-2729 or 800/689-2729.

Trip notes: This campground is near McArthur Reservoir, where you can fish for perch and bullheads. McArthur Wildlife Management Area is on U.S. 95, home to waterfowl, moose, elk, Canada geese, and bald eagles.

19 Kaniksu Resort RV & Marina

 6

Location: On Priest Lake, map ID1, grid b1.

Campsites, facilities: There are 77 RV or tent campsites, some with pull-throughs. Showers, laundry facilities, store, water, full-service marina, and a restaurant are available.

Reservations, fees: Reservations are accepted; the fee is $16–84 per night. Open year-round.

Directions: From Post Falls take the Highway 41 exit north to Oldtown, turn east (right) on U.S. Highway 2 and continue east to Priest River. Go north on Highway 57 to the intersection, the only stoplight in Priest River. Go north (the only direction you can go) for 36.5 miles. Right after you pass the 36-mile marker, look for the Nordman Store, Bar, and Post Office (a big log building) on the left side of the road. A paved road, Reeder Bay Road, runs in front of the store and turns to the right. (If you stay on Highway 57, it becomes a gravel road, and you'll know you missed the turn.) Follow Reeder Bay Road for 3.6 miles, past the Grandview Resort, turn right at the turnoff (there is a sign for Kaniksu Resort).

Contact: Kaniksu Resort RV & Marina, HC 1, P.O. Box 152, Nordman, ID 83848; 208/443-2609 or 208/443-3864; website: www.imbris.net /~kaniksu

Trip notes: This campground is on Priest Lake, facing the Selkirk Mountains. You can fish for Mackinaw, the predominant species in Priest Lake. Trophy-size fish have been caught here. You can boat and swim in Priest Lake. You can hike and bike in the area, either gut-wrenching climbs to the peaks on the east side of the lake or leisurely rides on the Lakeshore Trail on the west side. The Priest Lake Trails pamphlet, available at the Priest Lake Ranger District, has more information. The Priest Lake Golf Course has nine holes, soon to be 18, along with a driving range and putting green.

20 Reeder Bay

 6

Location: In Idaho Panhandle National Forest; map ID1, grid b1.

Campsites, facilities: There are 24 RV or tent campsites, which can accommodate a maximum RV length of 50 feet. Wheelchair-accessible restrooms and water are available.

Reservations, fees: Reservations are accepted; the fee $10 per night. Open May 25–October 5.

Directions: From Sandpoint, go 22 miles west on U.S. 2 to Priest River. From Priest River on Highway 57, go 39 miles north, then three miles east on Forest Service Road 1339.

Contact: Idaho Panhandle National Forest, Priest Lake Ranger District, HCR 5, Box 207, Priest River, ID 83856; 208/443-2512, 800/280-2267.

Trip notes: You can hike, fish, swim, and boat here.

21 Indian Creek

 6

Location: Near Priest Lake, map ID1, grid b1.

Campsites, facilities: There are 93 RV or tent campsites, some with hookups. A sanitary disposal station is available.

Reservations, fees: Reservations are accepted; the fee is $12–18 per night.

Directions: From Sandpoint, take U.S. 2 22 miles west to Priest River; at the stoplight, turn north on Highway 57 and drive 22 miles to the road to Coolin; at Coolin, take East Lakeshore Road north for 12 miles to campground.

Contact: Priest Lake State Park, Indian Creek Bay #423, Coolin, ID 83821; 208/443-2200.

Trip notes: You can fish and hike in the area.

22 Blue Lake Campground

5

Location: North of Sandpoint; map ID1, grid b3.

Campsites, facilities: There are 50 RV or tent campsites, some with hookups, which can accommodate a maximum RV length of 60 feet. Laundry facilities, showers, wheelchair-accessible restrooms, and a sanitary disposal station are available. Pets are allowed on leashes.

Reservations, fees: No reservations are needed; the fee is $9.99–14.99. Open April 1–October 31.

Directions: From Sandpoint, go north on U.S. 95 22 miles to mile marker 498. Turn left on the road across the railroad.

Contact: Blue Lake Campground & RV Park, HRC 01, P.O. Box 277, Naples, ID 83847; 208/267-2029.

Trip notes: This campground is in a forested, lakeside area. Blue Lake is a tiny, private, spring-fed lake with rainbow trout, catfish, and brown bluegill.

23 Upper Luby Bay

     6

Location: In Idaho Panhandle National Forest; map ID1, grid b1.

Campsites, facilities: There are 27 RV or tent campsites, which can accommodate a maximum RV length of 55 feet. Water and a sanitary disposal station are available.

Reservations, fees: Reservations are accepted; the fee is $10 per night. Open May 20–October 5.

Directions: From Sandpoint, take U.S. 2 22 miles west to Priest River, then go 28 miles north on Highway 57 to the Luby Bay sign. Turn right, go almost two miles northeast on Forest Service Road 1337 to the stop sign, and turn left almost one mile north on Forest Service Road 237, a dirt road, to the campground sign. Lower Luby Bay campground is to the right and Upper Luby Bay campground is to the left.

Contact: Idaho Panhandle National Forest, Priest Lake Ranger District, HCR 5, Box 207, Priest River, ID 83856; 208/443-2512 or 800/280-2267.

Trip notes: You can fish, swim, boat, and hike in the area.

24 Lower Luby Bay

   6

Location: In Idaho Panhandle National Forest; map ID1, grid b1.

Campsites, facilities: There are 25 RV or tent campsites, which can accommodate a maximum RV length of 55 feet. Water and a sanitary disposal station are available.

Reservations, fees: Reservations are accepted; the fee is $10 per night. Open May 20–October 5.

Directions: From Sandpoint, take U.S. 2 22 miles west to Priest River, then go 28 miles north on Highway 57 to the Luby Bay sign. Turn right, go almost two miles northeast on Forest Service Road 1337 to the stop sign, and turn left almost one mile north on Forest Service Road 237, a dirt road, to the campground sign. Lower Luby Bay campground is to the right and Upper Luby Bay campground is to the left.

Contact: Idaho Panhandle National Forest, Priest Lake Ranger District, HCR 5, Box 207, Priest River, ID 83856; 208/443-2512, 800/280-2267.

Trip notes: You can fish, swim, boat, and hike in the area. A historical museum, marina, and public boat launch are close by.

25 Priest Lake RV Resort & Marina

     5

Location: At Priest Lake; map ID1, grid b1.

Campsites, facilities: There are 16 RV or tent campsites, some with hookups. Wheelchair-accessible restrooms, showers, and propane gas are available. Pets are allowed on leashes.

Reservations, fees: No reservations are needed; the fee is $10–12.50 per night.

Directions: From Sandpoint, take U.S. 2 22 miles west to Priest

River. From Priest River, take Highway 57 north to mile marker 31, and then follow signs. This campground is on the water in Kalispell Bay at Priest Lake.

Contact: Priest Lake RV Resort & Marina, HCR 5, P.O. Box 172, Priest Lake, ID 83856; 208/443-2405 or fax 208/446-2299.

Trip notes: You can fish for Mackinaw, the predominant species in Priest Lake. Trophy-size fish have been caught here. You can boat and swim in Priest Lake. You can hike and bike in the area, either gut-wrenching climbs to the peaks on the east side of the lake or leisurely rides on the Lakeshore Trail on the west side. The Priest Lake Trails pamphlet, available at the Priest Lake Ranger District, has more information. The Priest Lake Golf Course has nine holes (soon to be 18) and a driving range and putting green.

26 Outlet

  6

Location: At Priest River; map ID1, grid c1.

Campsites, facilities: There are 27 RV or tent campsites, which can accommodate a maximum RV length of 22 feet. Water is available.

Reservations, fees: No reservations are needed; the fee is $8 per night. Open May 25–September 10.

Directions: From Sandpoint, take U.S. 2 22 miles west to Priest River. From Priest River, go 26 miles north on Highway 57, then one mile northeast on Forest Service Road 237. This campground is on the west side of Priest Lake.

Contact: Idaho Panhandle National Forest, Priest Lake Ranger District, HCR 5, Box 207, Priest River, ID 83856; 208/443-2512, 800/280-2267.

Trip notes: You can fish for Mackinaw, the predominant species in Priest Lake. Trophy-size fish have been caught here. You can boat and swim in Priest Lake. You can hike and bike in the area, either gut-wrenching climbs to the peaks on the east side of the lake or leisurely

rides on the Lakeshore Trail on the west side. The Priest Lake Trails pamphlet, available at the Priest Lake Ranger District, has more information. The Priest Lake Golf Course has nine holes of golf (soon to be 18) along with a driving range and putting green.

27 Sundance Village RV Park

     5

Location: In Coolin; map ID1, grid c1.

Campsites, facilities: There are 12 RV or tent campsites, some with hookups. There are showers, laundry facilities, and a restaurant available. Pets are allowed on leashes.

Reservations, fees: No reservations are needed; the fee is $18 and up per night.

Directions: From Sandpoint, go west on U.S. 2 to Priest River, turn right on Highway 57 and go 22 miles. Look for the Coolin exit, turn right, and drive five miles to the RV park.

Contact: Sundance Village RV Park, P.O. Box 189, Coolin, ID 83821; 208/443-4066 or fax 208/443-2754.

Trip notes: You can boat, bike, hike, and fish in the area.

28 Dickensheet

     6

Location: At Priest Lake; map ID1, grid c1.

Campsites, facilities: There are 11 RV or tent campsites, with picnic tables and grills. Restrooms are available.

Reservations, fees: No reservations are needed; the fee is $7 per night.

Directions: From Sandpoint, take U.S. 2 22 miles west to Priest River, turn north at the stoplight onto Highway 57, drive 22 miles and then turn right at Coolin Road to Coolin; the campground is four miles south of Coolin, nestled along the banks of Priest River.

Contact: Priest Lake State Park, Indian Creek Bay #423, Coolin, ID 83821; 208/443-2200

Trip notes: This campground is along the Priest River. You can fish for Mackinaw, the predominant species in Priest Lake. Trophy-size fish have been caught here. You can boat and swim in Priest Lake. You can hike and bike in the area, either gut-wrenching climbs to the peaks on the east side of the lake or leisurely rides on the Lakeshore Trail on the west side. The Priest Lake Trails pamphlet, available at the Priest Lake Ranger District, has more information. The Priest Lake Golf Course has nine holes (soon to be 18) and a driving range and putting green.

29 Springy Point Recreation Area

 5

Location: Near Sandpoint; map ID1, grid c2.
Campsites, facilities: There are 40 RV or tent campsites. Showers, water, and a sanitary disposal station are available.
Reservations, fees: No reservations are needed; the fee is $14 per night. Open May 15–October 9.
Directions: From Sandpoint, go 1.5 miles south on U.S. 95, then three miles west on Lakeshore Drive.
Contact: Army Corps of Engineers, 2376 E. Hwy. 2, Oldtown, ID 83882-9243; 208/437-3133.
Trip notes: You can boat, fish, and swim here.

30 Trestle Creek RV Park

 5

Location: East of Sandpoint; map ID1, grid c3.
Campsites, facilities: There are 11 RV or tent campsites, some with hookups. A sanitary disposal station is available.
Reservations, fees: No reservations are needed; the fee is $15 per night.
Directions: From Sandpoint, go north to Highway 200, and then 12 miles east on Highway 200 to the campground, which is on the left side.
Contact: Trestle Creek RV Park, 560 Hwy. 200, Hope, ID 83836; 208/264-5894.
Trip notes: You can boat and fish on Lake Pend Oreille and hike in the area.

31 R-Place RV Park

 5

Location: East of Sandpoint; map ID1, grid c3.
Campsites, facilities: There are 18 RV or tent campsites, some with hookups. Showers, a sanitary disposal station, and a restaurant are available.
Reservations, fees: No reservations are needed; the fee is $15 per night.
Directions: From Sandpoint, go 12 miles east on Highway 200 to Trestle Creek. The campground is on the left.
Contact: R-Place RV Park, 700 Hwy. 200, Hope, ID 83836; 208/264-5558.
Trip notes: You can hike, fish, and boat at Lake Pend Oreille.

32 Idaho Country Resort

 4

Location: East of Sandpoint; map ID1, grid c4.
Campsites, facilities: There are 187 RV or tent campsites, some with hookups. Wheelchair-accessible restrooms, showers, laundry facilities, store, propane gas, and a sanitary disposal station are available. Pets are allowed on leashes.
Reservations, fees: No reservations are needed; the fee is $25 and up per night.
Directions: From Sandpoint, go 12 miles east on Highway 200 to the campground, on the right.
Contact: Idaho Country Resort, 141 Idaho Country Rd., Hope, ID 83836; 208/264-5505 or 800/307-3050, fax 208/264-5521.
Trip notes: You can fish, boat, swim, and water-ski on Lake Pend Oreille.

33 Alpine Trailer Park

 4

Location: In Sagle; map ID1, grid c3.
Campsites, facilities: There are 15 RV campsites with hookups.
Reservations, fees: No reservations are needed; the fee is $15

per night. Open year-round.

Directions: From Sandpoint, go south on U.S. 95 to Sagle Road, and then go east on Sagle Road to the trailer park.

Contact: Alpine Trailer Park, 91 Sagle Rd. #19, P.O. Box 585, Sagle, ID 83860; 208/265-0179.

Trip notes: You can fish at Lake Pend Oreille for kamloop, whitefish, kokanee, cutthroat trout, brown trout, bull trout, Mackinaw, largemouth and smallmouth bass, crappie, perch, and bullhead (catfish). There is an abundance of wildlife at Lake Pend Oreille, from mountain goats to eagles. Ospreys, a large fish-eating hawk, nest in the tops of snags and power poles. A handful of eagle's nests can be found around the lake, and eagles can be seen at Denton Slough and the Clark Fork River delta. You can also see tundra swans, Canada geese, many species of ducks, and two species of loons. Mountain goats inhabit Bernard Peak (near Bayview) at the south end of the lake, where they make their home on the rocky cliffs at Bernard Point near Echo Bay. You can boat, swim, and water-ski at Lake Pend Oreille.

34 Edgewater Resort

 6

Location: In Sandpoint; map ID1, grid c2.

Campsites, facilities: There are 20 RV campsites, which can accommodate a maximum RV length of 40 feet. A restaurant is available. Pets are allowed on leashes.

Reservations, fees: Reservations are accepted; the fee is $25 per night. Open year-round.

Directions: From Trestle Creek go east on Highway 200 to Sandpoint. Highway 200 does a loop; follow it until it turns into U.S. 95; then it changes to a one-way street. Turn left, then turn right at Bridge Street.

Contact: Edgewater Resort, 56 Bridge St., Sandpoint, ID 83809; 800/635-2534 or 208/263-3194.

Trip notes: This resort is adjacent to the city beach and hotel facilities. You can boat, fish, and swim here.

35 Albeni Cove Recreation Area

 6

Location: At Priest Lake; map ID1, grid d2.

Campsites, facilities: There are 14 RV or tent campsites, which can accommodate a maximum RV length of 30 feet. Water is available. Pets are allowed on leashes.

Reservations, fees: No reservations are needed; the fee is $12 per night. Open May 13–September 10.

Directions: From Sandpoint, take U.S. 2 22 miles west to Priest River. From Priest River, go another six miles west, and then two miles east of Oldtown. The recreation area is east of 4th Street.

Contact: Army Corps of Engineers, 208/437-3133. Army Corps of Engineers, 2376 E. Hwy. 2, Oldtown, ID 83882-9243; 208/437-3133.

Trip notes: You can fish, boat, swim, and water-ski at Lake Pend Oreille and Priest River Lake. You can hike in the Kanisku National Forest and state lands. You can fish for Mackinaw, the predominant species in Priest Lake. Trophy-size fish have been caught here. You can boat and swim in Priest Lake. You can hike and bike in the area, either gut-wrenching climbs to the peaks on the east side of the lake or leisurely rides on the Lakeshore Trail on the west side. The Priest Lake Trails pamphlet, available at the Priest Lake Ranger District, has more information. The Priest Lake Golf Course is a nine-hole course (soon to be 18) and has a driving range and putting green.

36 Fox Farm RV Resort

 5

Location: West of Sandpoint; map ID1, grid d3.

Campsites, facilities: There are 12 RV or tent campsites, some with hookups. Laundry facilities and showers are available. Pets are allowed on leashes.

Reservations, fees: No reservations are needed; the fee is $15 per night.

Directions: From Sandpoint, go eight miles

west on Highway 2 to the resort on the Pend Oreille River.

Contact: Fox Farm RV Resort, 3160 Dufort Rd., Sagle, ID 83860; 208/263-8896.

Trip notes: You can fish in the Pend Oreille River for spiny rays, whitefish, bass, rainbow, and cutthroat trout. You can hike and raft in the area.

37 Bottle Bay Resort

     5

Location: Near Lake Pend Oreille; map ID1, grid d3.

Campsites, facilities: There are seven RV or tent campsites, some with hookups. Wheelchair-accessible restrooms, showers, laundry facilities, and a restaurant are available. Pets are allowed on leashes.

Reservations, fees: No reservations are needed; the fee is $16–20 per night.

Directions: From Sandpoint, go south on Highway 95 for a half mile to Bottle Bay Road, then turn east. Cross the railroad tracks, keep left, go seven miles, turn left at the Bottle Bay Resort sign.

Contact: Bottle Bay Resort, 1360 Bottle Bay Rd., Sandpoint, ID 83864; 208/263-5916; website: www.keokee.com/bottlebay.

Trip notes: You can swim, boat, fish, and water-ski on Lake Pend Oreille. Hidden Lakes Golf Resort is seven miles east of Sandy.

38 Sam Owen

    6

Location: On Lake Pend Oreille; map ID1, grid d3.

Campsites, facilities: There are 80 RV or tent campsites, which can accommodate a maximum RV length of 30 feet. Hookups, wheelchair-accessible restrooms, water, and a sanitary disposal station are available.

Reservations, fees: Reservations are accepted, call 877/444-6777; the fee is $12 per night. Open May 1–October 31.

Directions: From Sandpoint, go 15 miles east on Highway 200 to Hope. From Hope, go three miles southeast on Highway 200, then two miles west on County Road 1002. From Clark Fork the campground is eight miles west. Look for the sign on Highway 200.

Contact: Idaho Panhandle National Forest, Priest Lake Ranger District, HCR 5, Box 207, Priest River, ID 83856; 208/443-2512, 800/280-2267.

Trip notes: You can swim, boat, fish, and water-ski on Lake Pend Oreille. You can fish for Mackinaw, the predominant species in Priest Lake. Trophy-size fish have been caught here. You can boat and swim in Priest Lake. You can hike and bike in the area, either gut-wrenching climbs to the peaks on the east side of the lake or leisurely rides on the Lakeshore Trail on the west side. The Priest Lake Trails pamphlet, available at the Priest Lake Ranger District, has more information. The Priest Lake Golf Course has nine holes of golf (soon to be 18), along with a driving range and putting green.

39 Island View Resort

     5

Location: Near Lake Pend Oreille; map ID1, grid d3.

Campsites, facilities: There are 65 RV or tent campsites, some with hookups. Laundry facilities, showers, a store, and propane gas are available. Pets are allowed on leashes.

Reservations, fees: No reservations are needed; the fee is $22 per night. Open May 1–October 1.

Directions: From Sandpoint, go 15 miles east on Highway 200 to Hope. From Hope, go two miles east, turn right on Peninsula Road, and go two miles to the resort.

Contact: Island View Resort, 1767 Peninsula Rd., Hope, ID 83836; 208/264-5509.

Trip notes: This campground is within a game refuge. You can swim, boat, fish, and water-ski on Lake Pend Oreille.

40 Priest River Recreation Area

    6

Location: At Priest River; map ID1, grid d1.

Campsites, facilities: There are 20 RV or tent campsites. Showers, water, and a sanitary disposal station are available.

Reservations, fees: No reservations are needed; the fee is $14 per night. Open May 13–September 24.

Directions: From Priest River, drive one mile east on U.S. 2 to the recreation area.

Contact: Army Corps of Engineers, U.S. Hwy. 2, Oldtown, ID 83822; 208/437-3133.

Trip notes: There is boating, fishing, and swimming at this location.

41 Riley Creek Recreation Area

     5

Location: Near Priest River; map ID1, grid d2.

Campsites, facilities: There are 68 RV or tent sites. Water and a sanitary disposal station are available.

Reservations, fees: No reservations are needed; the fee is $14 per night. Open May 13–September 10.

Directions: From Priest River, go eight miles east on U.S. 2, then right on Riley Creek. The campground is three miles ahead at the end of the road.

Contact: Army Corps of Engineers, U.S. Hwy. 2, Oldtown, ID 83822; 208/437-3133.

Trip notes: You can boat, fish, and swim here.

42 Garfield Bay Resort

      5

Location: On Lake Pend Oreille; map ID1, grid d2.

Campsites, facilities: There are 24 full RV hookups and several tent sites. A boat moorage and guest docks are available.

Reservations, fees: No reservations are needed; the fee is $18.50 per night.

Directions: From Sandpoint, go south on U.S. 95 to Sagle Road and turn left. Follow this road, which becomes Garfield Bay Road, for 7.5 miles to the resort.

Contact: Garfield Bay Resort, 60 W. Garfield Bay, Sagle, ID 83860; 208/263-1078.

Trip notes: You can swim, boat, fish, and water-ski on Lake Pend Oreille.

43 Round Lake State Park

     5

Location: At Round Lake; map ID1, grid d2.

Campsites, facilities: There are 53 RV or tent campsites, which can accommodate a maximum RV length of 24 feet. Showers and a sanitary disposal station are available.

Reservations, fees: No reservations are needed; the fee is $7–12. Open year-round.

Directions: From Sandpoint, go 10 miles south on U.S. 95, then two miles west on Dufort Road to the campground.

Contact: Round Lake State Park, 1880 W. Dufort Rd., Sagle, ID 83860; 208/263-3489.

Trip notes: You can hike, boat, fish, and swim at Round Lake.

44 Travel America Plaza

    4

Location: Near Lake Pend Oreille; map ID1, grid d2.

Campsites, facilities: There are 82 RV or tent campsites, some with pull-through sites. Wheelchair-accessible restrooms, showers, laundry facilities, a sanitary disposal station, convenience store, and golf driving range are available.

Reservations, fees: No reservations are needed; the fee is $12–15 per night. Open year-round.

Directions: From Sandpoint, go six miles

south on U.S. 95. The campground is on the west side.

Contact: Travel America Plaza, P.O. Box 199, Sagle, ID 83860; 208/263-6522, or 208/263-7511.

Trip notes: You can swim, boat, fish, and water-ski on Lake Pend Oreille. A golf driving range is nearby.

45 Sandy Beach Resort

        5

Location: On Cocolalla Lake; map ID1, grid d2.

Campsites, facilities: There are 90 RV and tent sites. Wheelchair-accessible restrooms, showers, groceries, laundry facilities, a sanitary disposal station, and boat docks are available. Pets are allowed on leashes.

Reservations, fees: No reservations are needed; the fee is $16–21 per night.

Directions: From Sandpoint, go 10 miles south on U.S. 95, turn right on Loop Road, and go two miles to the campground. Watch for the small sign.

Contact: Sandy Beach Resort, 4405 Loop Rd., Cocolalla, ID 83813; 208/263-4328, fax 208/263-3253.

Trip notes: You can swim, boat, and fish for brook and brown trout on Cocolalla Lake.

46 River Lake RV Park

      5

Location: East of Lake Pend Oreille; map ID1, grid d4.

Campsites, facilities: There are 31 RV or tent campsites with full hookups. Showers, laundry facilities, restrooms, propane gas, a sanitary disposal station, boat ramps, and docks are available. Pets are allowed on leashes.

Reservations, fees: No reservations are needed; the fee is $16 per night. Open May 1–October 1.

Directions: From Sandpoint, go 27 miles east on Highway 200 to Clark Fork. From Clark Fork, go 2.5 miles southeast to the campground.

Contact: River Lake RV Park, 145 N. River

Lake Rd., Clark Fork, ID 83811; 208/266-1115.

Trip notes: This campground is on the Clark Fork River where you can fish for brown, bull, cutthroat, and rainbow trout. You can swim, boat, fish, and water-ski on Lake Pend Oreille.

47 River Delta Resort

Location: On Clark Fork River; map ID1, grid d4.

Campsites, facilities: There are 56 RV and tent campsites, some with hookups. Showers, laundry facilities, propane gas, a game room, and a boat ramp are available. Pets are allowed on leashes.

Reservations, fees: No reservations are needed; the fee is $15 per night. Open April 1–September 30.

Directions: From Sandpoint, go 27 miles east on Highway 200 to Clark Fork. From Clark Fork, go four miles east, two miles west of the Montana state line. The campground is on the north side of the river.

Contact: River Delta Resort, 60190 Hwy. 200, Clark Fork, ID 83811; 208/266-1335.

Trip notes: You can fish for brown, bull, cutthroat, and rainbow trout on the Clark Fork River. You can swim, boat, fish, and water-ski on Lake Pend Oreille.

48 Whiskey Rock

      5

Location: On Lake Pend Oreille; map ID1, grid d3.

Campsites, facilities: There are nine RV or tent campsites, which can accommodate a maximum RV length of 16 feet. Picnic tables and vault toilets are available. Pets are allowed on leashes.

Reservations, fees: No reservations are needed, and no fee is charged. Open May 15–October 1.

Directions: From Sandpoint, go 27 miles east on Highway 200 to Clark Fork. From Clark Fork, go 30 miles southwest on Forest Service Road 278. The campground is on the southeast shore of Lake Pend Oreille.

Contact: Idaho Panhandle National Forest, Sandpoint Ranger District, 1500 Hwy. 2, Sandpoint, ID 83864; 208/263-5111.

Trip notes: You can boat, fish, swim, and water-ski on Lake Pend Oreille.

49 Scenic Bay Marina

Location: On Lake Pend Oreille; map ID1, grid e2.

Campsites, facilities: There are 15 RV or tent campsites, some with hookups. Wheelchair-accessible restrooms and showers are available. Pets are allowed on leashes.

Reservations, fees: No reservations are needed; the fee is $10–16 per night.

Directions: From Sandpoint, go south on U.S. 95, through Careywood; take a left on Careywood/Bayview Road, go 6.5 miles to Bayview, and turn left on Scenic Bay Drive. The marina is at the end of this road.

Contact: Scenic Bay Marina, P.O. Box 36, Bayview, ID 83803; 208/683-2243, fax 208/683-3893.

Trip notes: You can boat, fish, swim, and water-ski on Lake Pend Oreille.

50 MacDonald's Hudson Bay Resort

Location: On Lake Pend Oreille; map ID1, grid e2.

Campsites, facilities: There are 10 RV or tent campsites, some with hookups. Wheelchair-accessible restrooms, laundry facilities, showers, propane gas, and a sanitary disposal station are available. Pets are allowed on leashes.

Reservations, fees: No reservations are needed; the fee is $12 and up per night.

Directions: From Sandpoint, go 26 miles south

on U.S. 95 to Highway 54 to Bayview. From Bayview, go .75 mile east on Hudson Bay Road, and the campground is on the left.

Contact: MacDonald's Hudson Bay Resort, P.O. Box 38, Bayview, ID 83803; 208/683-2211.

Trip notes: You can boat, fish, swim, and water-ski on Lake Pend Oreille.

51 Farragut State Park

Location: On Lake Pend Oreille; map ID1, grid e2.

Campsites, facilities: There are 183 RV or tent campsites, which can accommodate a maximum RV length of 33 feet. Hookups, pull-throughs, showers, water, wheelchair-accessible restrooms, a sanitary disposal station, and a playground are available.

Reservations, fees: Reservations are accepted; call 208/683-2425. The fee is $7–16 per night. Open year-round. The stay limit is 15 days.

Directions: From Coeur d'Alene, take U.S. 95 north to Athol; take Highway 54 four miles east to the park entrance.

Contact: Farragut State Park, E. 13400 Ranger Rd., Athol, ID 83801; 208/683-2425.

Trip notes: This park is at the base of the Coeur d'Alene Mountains at Lake Pend Oreille. You can hike, bike, fish, swim, boat, and water-ski here.

52 Bayview Scenic Motel & RV Park

Location: At Coeur d'Alene Lake; map ID1, grid e2.

Campsites, facilities: There are eight RV or tent campsites, some with hookups. Cable TV and movies and a sanitary disposal station are available. Pets are allowed on leashes.

Reservations, fees: No reservations are needed; the fee is $19–25 per night.

Directions: From Coeur d'Alene, take U.S. 95 north to Highway 54 to Athol. At the light, turn right; the RV park is on the left on the corner of 6th and Main Streets.

Contact: Bayview Scenic Motel & RV Park, P.O. Box 70, Bayview, ID 83083; 208/683-2215.

Trip notes: You can boat, fish, swim, and water-ski on Lake Pend Oreille.

53 Silver Beach Resort

     6

Location: On Spirit Lake; map ID1, grid e1.

Campsites, facilities: There are 40 RV or tent campsites, some with hookups. Wheelchair-accessible restrooms, laundry facilities, and showers are available. Pets are allowed on leashes.

Reservations, fees: No reservations are needed; the fee is $15–20 per night.

Directions: From Post Falls go east on I-90 to Exit 7, take Highway 41 north to Rathdrum, then go 10 miles north on Highway 41 to Spirit Lake, then southwest on Main Street 2.5 miles to the campground.

Contact: Silver Beach Resort, 8350 W. Spirit Lake Rd., Spirit Lake, ID 83869; 208/623-4842.

Trip notes: Spirit Lake has two small islands, a public boat ramp, and a dock. You can fish, boat, water-ski, and swim at the lake. Spirit Lake is next to Kanisku National Forest, which has hiking and biking trails. Two golf courses are nearby, one at Stoneridge Resort in Blanchard about five miles to the north; the other is Twin Lakes Golf Course, about four miles to the south.

54 Kelso Lake Resort

     5

Location: North of Coeur d'Alene; map ID1, grid e2.

Campsites, facilities: There are 18 RV or tent campsites, some with hookups. Showers and wheelchair-accessible restrooms are available. Pets are allowed on leashes.

Reservations, fees: No reservations are needed; the fee is $10–14 per night. Open April 1–October 1.

Directions: From Coeur d'Alene, go 25 miles north on U.S. 95 to Athol. Continue through Athol for five miles and turn left at the sign (which is on the right) on Granite Loop. Drive 2.3 miles to the T intersection, go left on Granite Hill, and you will see the resort.

Contact: Kelso Lake Resort, 1450 Kelso Lake Rd., Athol, ID 83801; 208/683-2297; website: www.kelsolakeresort.bigbass.com.

Trip notes: You can boat, fish, swim, and hike here.

55 Silverwood RV Park

    4

Location: Across from Silverwood Theme Park; map ID1, grid e1.

Campsites, facilities: There are 126 RV or tent campsites, some with hookups. Wheelchair-accessible restrooms, laundry facilities, showers, and propane gas are available. Pets are allowed on leashes.

Reservations, fees: No reservations are needed; the fee is $17–19 per night. Open May 1–October 31.

Directions: From Coeur d'Alene, go 15 miles north on U.S. 95 to the campground.

Contact: Silverwood RV Park, N. 26225 Hwy. 95, Athol, ID 93801; 208/683-3400.

Trip notes: The Silverwood RV Park is connected by a pedestrian tunnel to the Silverwood Theme Park on the other side of the highway. Silverwood Theme Park is a Victorian turn-of-the-century, seasonal theme park; website: www.silverwood4fun.com. It offers rides, shows, attractions, games of skill, food services, and retail shops.

56 Alpine Country Store & RV Park

 4

Location: At Hayden Lake; map ID1, grid e1.

Campsites, facilities: There are 25 RV or tent campsites, some with hookups. Laundry facilities, showers, and barrier-free access are available. Pets are allowed on leashes.

Reservations, fees: No reservations are needed; the fee is $16.65–18.50 per night. Open May–October.

Directions: From Coeur d'Alene, go 10 miles north on U.S. 95.

Contact: Alpine Country Store & RV Park, 17400 N. Hwy. 95, Hayden, ID 83835; 208/772-4305.

Trip notes: You can golf in Hayden and fish, boat, and swim at Hayden Lake.

57 Big Hank

 6

Location: Idaho Panhandle National Forest; map ID1, grid e4.

Campsites, facilities: There are 30 RV or tent campsites, which can accommodate a maximum RV length of 22 feet. Vault toilets, water, and barrier-free access are available.

Reservations, fees: No reservations are needed; the fee is $5–10 per night.

Directions: From Prichard, go 20 miles northwest on Forest Service Road 208 to a big meadow; the campground is in the northeast corner.

Contact: Idaho Panhandle National Forest, Wallace Ranger District, P.O. Box 14, Silverton, ID 83867; 208/752-1221.

Trip notes: There are hiking and biking trails in the forest.

58 Berlin Flats

 6

Location: In Idaho Panhandle National Forest; map ID1, grid e4.

Campsites, facilities: There are nine RV or tent campsites, which can accommodate a maximum RV length of 22 feet. Vault toilets and water are available.

Reservations, fees: No reservations are needed; the suggested donation is $5 per night. Open Memorial Day–Labor Day. The stay limit is 14 days.

Directions: From Prichard, go 13 miles north on Forest Service Road 208, then seven miles north on Forest Service Road 412. This road is paved until the last half mile, which is dirt. The campground is on the left.

Contact: Idaho Panhandle National Forest, Wallace Ranger District, P.O. Box 14, Silverton, ID 83867; 208/752-1221.

Trip notes: There are hiking and biking trails in the forest.

59 Devil's Elbow

 6

Location: In Idaho Panhandle National Forest; map ID1, grid e4.

Campsites, facilities: There are 20 RV or tent campsites, which can accommodate a maximum RV length of 22 feet. Vault toilets, water, and barrier-free access are available.

Reservations, fees: No reservations are needed; the fee is $5–10 per night. Open May 15–September 10.

Directions: From Prichard, go 14 miles northwest on Forest Service Road 208; the campground is on the left.

Contact: Idaho Panhandle National Forest, Wallace Ranger District, P.O. Box 14, Silverton, ID 83867; 208/752-1221.

Trip notes: You can boat, fish and hike in the area.

60 Kit Price

 6

Location: In Idaho Panhandle National Forest; map ID1, grid e4.

Campsites, facilities: There are 52 RV or

tent campsites, which can accommodate a maximum RV length of 22 feet. Wheelchair-accessible toilets and water are available.

Reservations, fees: No reservations are needed; the fee is $5–10 per night. Open May 15–October 1.

Directions: From Prichard, go 11 miles northwest on Forest Service Road 208 to the campground.

Contact: Idaho Panhandle National Forest, Wallace Ranger District, P.O. Box 14, Silverton, ID 83867; 208/752-1221.

Trip notes: There are hiking and biking trails in the national forest.

61 Westside Resort

 5

Location: At Hauser Lake; map ID1, grid e1.
Campsites, facilities: There are 10 RV or tent campsites. Laundry facilities are available.

Reservations, fees: No reservations are needed; the fee is $10–12 per night.

Directions: From Coeur d'Alene, go west on I-90 about eight miles to Post Falls. Go north to Highway 53, then to Hauser Lake Road, and the resort is on the left.

Contact: Westside Resort, W. 6905 Hauser Lake Rd., Post Falls, ID 83854-8514; 208/773-4968, fax 208/773-2423.

Trip notes: You can swim, fish, and boat on Hauser Lake.

62 Mokins Bay

 6

Location: Near Hayden Lake; map ID1, grid e2.
Campsites, facilities: There are 15 RV or tent campsites, which can accommodate a maximum RV length of 22 feet. Vault toilets and water are available.

Reservations, fees: No reservations are needed; the fee is $10 per night. Open May 15 –September 15.

Directions: In Coeur d'Alene, take U.S. 95 north 6.1 miles to Lancaster Road. Turn right onto Lancaster Road and go 6.3 miles to the Y intersection. Take a left and go 5.3 miles to the campground sign at Mokins Drive. Turn left on Mokins Drive (a gravel road) and go a tenth of a mile to the campground, where the entrance is on the left.

Contact: Idaho Panhandle National Forest, Fernan Ranger District, 2502 E. Sherman Ave., Coeur d'Alene, ID 83814; 208/769-3000.

Trip notes: You can boat and fish on Hayden Lake. This campground is near the eastern shore of Hayden Lake in heavily wooded pines.

63 Honeysuckle

 5

Location: In Idaho Panhandle National Forest; map ID1, grid f3.
Campsites, facilities: There are eight RV or tent campsites, which can accommodate a maximum RV length of 16 feet. Wheelchair-accessible restrooms and water are available.

Reservations, fees: No reservations are needed; the fee is $10 per night. Open May 20–September 15.

Directions: From Coeur d'Alene, go 11 miles northeast on Forest Service Road 268, and then 11 miles east on Forest Service Road 612; the campground is on the left.

Contact: Idaho Panhandle National Forest, Fernan Ranger District, 2502 E. Sherman Ave., Coeur d'Alene, ID 83814; 208/769-3000.

Trip notes: You can hike, bike, and fish in Idaho Panhandle National Forest.

64 Suntree RV Park

 4

Location: In Post Falls; map ID1, grid f1.
Campsites, facilities: There are 111 RV or tent campsites, some with hookups. Showers, laundry facilities, a sanitary disposal station, and a swimming pool are available. Pets are allowed on leashes.

Reservations, fees: No reservations are needed; the fee is

$18–20 per night. Open year-round.

Directions: From I-90, turn left onto Pleasant View Road; turn right on 5th Avenue to the end of the block. Take a right, then a left at the dead end; turn on the dirt road to the RV park.

Contact: Suntree RV Park, 401 Idahline, Post Falls, ID 83854; tel./fax 208/773-9982.

Trip notes: You can boat, fish, swim, and water-ski on Coeur d'Alene Lake.

65 Coeur d'Alene RV Resort

 5

Location: In Post Falls; map ID1, grid f1.

Campsites, facilities: There are 191 RV or tent campsites, some with hookups. Laundry facilities, showers, propane gas, barrier-free access, a swimming pool, and a sanitary disposal station are available. A clubhouse and putting green are on-site. Pets are allowed on leashes.

Reservations, fees: Reservations are accepted; the fee is $24–27 per night. Open year-round.

Directions: From I-90 go west to Exit 7, go north on Highway 41 to Mullan Avenue, then west one mile to the resort on the left.

Contact: Coeur d'Alene RV Resort, 2600 E. Mullan Ave., Post Falls, ID 83854; 208/773-3527, fax 208/773-9232.

Trip notes: You can boat, fish, swim, and water-ski on Coeur d'Alene Lake.

66 Boulevard Motel & RV Park

 4

Location: In Coeur d'Alene; map ID1, grid f1.

Campsites, facilities: There are 38 RV or tent campsites, some with hookups. A sanitary disposal station is available. Pets are allowed on leashes.

Reservations, fees: No reservations are needed; the fee is $12–18 per night. Open year-round.

Directions: From Sandpoint, go south to Coeur d'Alene on U.S. 95; take Exit 11 (where

Outback Steakhouse is), turn left, go over the overpass, and you can see the RV park to the west.

Contact: Boulevard Motel & RV Park, 2400 Seltice Way, Coeur d'Alene, ID 83814; 208/664-4978.

Trip notes: You can boat, fish, swim, and water-ski on Coeur d'Alene Lake.

67 Cedar Motel & RV Park

 4

Location: In Coeur d'Alene; map ID1, grid f1.

Campsites, facilities: There are 39 RV or tent campsites, some with hookups. Laundry facilities, showers, a swimming pool, and a sanitary disposal station are on-site. Pets are allowed on leashes.

Reservations, fees: No reservations are needed; the fee is $14–17 per night. Open April 15–October 15.

Directions: From Sandpoint, go south on U.S. 95 to I-90 and Coeur d'Alene; then take the Sherman exit, go straight, and you will see the RV park.

Contact: Cedar Motel & RV Park, 319 Coeur d'Alene Lake Drive, Coeur d'Alene, ID 83814; 208/664-2278.

Trip notes: You can boat, fish, swim, and water-ski on Coeur d'Alene Lake.

68 Coeur d'Alene KOA

 4

Location: In Coeur d'Alene; map ID1, grid f1.

Campsites, facilities: There are 112 RV or tent campsites, some with pull-through sites. Laundry facilities, propane gas, a swimming pool, store, playground, game room, mini-golf, and rentals of paddle boats, canoes, and kayaks are available. Pets are allowed on leashes.

Reservations, fees: Reservations are accepted; the fee is $17.50–28 per night. Open year-round.

Directions: From I-90 at Coeur d'Alene, take

Exit 22 and go .25 mile south to the campground, which is on the left side.

Contact: Coeur d'Alene KOA, E. 10700 Wolf Lodge Bay Rd., Coeur d'Alene, ID 83814; 208/664-4471, 800/562-2609, or fax 208/765-1409; website: www.koakampgrounds.com.

Trip notes: You can fish, swim, boat, and water-ski on Coeur d'Alene Lake.

69 Monte Vista Motel & RV Park

 4

Location: In Coeur d'Alene; map ID1, grid f1.

Campsites, facilities: There are 12 RV or tent campsites, some with hookups. Laundry facilities and showers are available. Pets are allowed on leashes.

Reservations, fees: No reservations are needed; the fee is $11 per night.

Directions: From Sandpoint, take U.S. 95 south to I-90 east; take the Sherman exit and go straight to the stoplight. At the light, go straight two blocks; the RV park is on the left.

Contact: Monte Vista Motel & RV Park, 320 S. Coeur d'Alene Lake Drive, Coeur d'Alene, ID 83814; 208/765-2369 or fax 208/664-8201.

Trip notes: You can fish, swim, boat, and water-ski on Coeur d'Alene Lake.

70 Shady Acres Campground

 3

Location: In Coeur d'Alene; map ID1, grid f1.

Campsites, facilities: There are 30 RV or tent campsites, some with pull-throughs and hookups. Laundry facilities, wheelchair-accessible restrooms, and showers are available. Pets are allowed on leashes.

Reservations, fees: No reservations are needed; the fee is $17 and up per night. Open year-round.

Directions: From I-90 at Coeur d'Alene, take Exit 12; turn left and at Neider turn right. Take a left on Government Way; look for Shady Acres (across from Safeway).

Contact: Shady Acres Campground, N. 3630 Government Way, Coeur d'Alene, ID 83815; 208/664-3087.

Trip notes: You can fish, swim, boat, and water-ski on Coeur d'Alene Lake.

71 Beyond Hope Resort

 5

Location: Near Lake Pend Oreille; map ID1, grid f1.

Campsites, facilities: There are 90 RV or tent campsites, some with hookups. Showers are available. Pets are allowed on leashes.

Reservations, fees: No reservations are needed; the fee is $16.50 and up per night.

Directions: From Sandpoint, take Highway 200 east through the town of Hope. At the yellow intersection sign, turn right onto Sam Owen Road, pass the Sam Owen campground, and look for the sign for Beyond Hope Resort.

Contact: Beyond Hope Resort, 248 Beyond Hope, Hwy. 200 East, ID 83856; 208/264-5251.

Trip notes: You can fish and boat on Lake Pend Oreille.

72 Robin Hood RV Park & Campground

 3

Location: In Coeur d'Alene; map ID1, grid f2.

Campsites, facilities: There are 80 RV or tent campsites, some with hookups. Showers, laundry facilities, wheelchair-accessible restrooms, and a playground are available. Pets are allowed on leashes.

Reservations, fees: Reservations are accepted; the fee is $15.50–19.50 per year. Open year-round.

Directions: From I-90 at Coeur d'Alene, take Sherman Road to the west end of town; the campground is on Lincoln Way.

Contact: Robin Hood RV Park & Campground, 703 Lincoln Way, Coeur d'Alene, ID 83814; 208/664-2306.

Trip notes: You can fish, swim, boat, and water-ski on Coeur d'Alene Lake.

73 Wolf Lodge Campground

    3

Location: In Coeur d'Alene; map ID1, grid f2.

Campsites, facilities: There are 100 RV or tent campsites, some with hookups. Laundry facilities and showers are available. Pets are allowed on leashes.

Reservations, fees: No reservations are needed; the fee is $13–23 per night. Open May 15–October 1.

Directions: From Coeur d'Alene, take Exit 22 off I-90, turn left, go east on Frontage Road to a stop sign, and turn right; the campground is a mile and a half down on the left.

Contact: Wolf Lodge Campground, 12425 E. I-90, Coeur d'Alene, ID 83814; 208/664-2812.

Trip notes: You can fish, swim, boat, and water-ski on Coeur d'Alene Lake.

74 Bumblebee

   6

Location: In the Idaho Panhandle National Forest; map ID1, grid f3.

Campsites, facilities: There are 25 RV or tent campsites, which can accommodate a maximum RV length of 16 feet. Barrier-free access and water are available.

Reservations, fees: No reservations are needed; the fee is $10 per night. Open May 15–October 1.

Directions: From Coeur d'Alene on I-90, go 28 miles east to Exit 43, then six miles north on Forest Service Road 9 and three miles west on Forest Service Road 209 to the campground.

Contact: Idaho Panhandle National Forest, Fernan Ranger District, 2502 E. Sherman Ave., Coeur d'Alene, ID 83814; 208/769-3000.

Trip notes: You can hike and fish in the Idaho Panhandle National Forest.

75 Squaw Bay Camping Resort

 3

Location: In Coeur d'Alene; map A1, grid f2.

Campsites, facilities: There are 50 RV or tent campsites, some with hookups. Laundry facilities, showers, a sanitary disposal station, boat slips, a water slide, lakefront RV sites, a store, and a restaurant are available. Pets are allowed on leashes.

Reservations, fees: No reservations are needed; the fee is $15–28 per night. Open April 1–October 1.

Directions: From Coeur d'Alene, take I-90 east to Exit 22 and go seven miles south on Highway 97; the campground is on the right.

Contact: Squaw Bay Camping Resort, P.O. Box 174, Coeur d'Alene, ID 83816; 208/664-6782.

Trip notes: You can fish, swim, boat, and water-ski on Coeur d'Alene Lake.

76 Rockford Bay Resort

    5

Location: On Coeur d'Alene Lake; map ID1, grid f2.

Campsites, facilities: There are RV campsites with full hookups. Laundry facilities and a restaurant are available.

Reservations, fees: No reservations are needed; the fee is $20 per night. Open April 15–October 15.

Directions: From Coeur d'Alene, go 14 miles south on U.S. 95. This campground is on Coeur d'Alene Lake.

Contact: Rockford Bay Resort, W. 8700 Rockford Bay Rd., Coeur d'Alene, ID 83814; 208/664-6931; email: rockford4@juno.com; website: www.preys.com/highway.

Trip notes: You can fish, swim, boat, and water-ski on Coeur d'Alene Lake.

77 Bell Bay

    6

Location: In the Idaho Panhandle National Forest; map ID1, grid f2.

Campsites, facilities: There are 26 RV or tent campsites, which can accommodate a maximum RV length of 22 feet. Vault toilets, water, and barrier-free access are available.

Reservations, fees: No reservations are needed; the fee is $10 per night. Open Memorial Day–Labor Day. The stay limit is 14 days.

Directions: From Coeur d'Alene, go 10 miles east on I-90 to exit 22, take Highway 97 south toward Harrison; three miles north of Harrison, take County Road 314 west for three miles to Bell Bay.

Contact: Idaho Panhandle National Forest, Fernan Ranger District, 2502 E. Sherman Ave., Coeur d'Alene, ID 83814; 208/769-3000.

Trip notes: You can hike and fish in the Idaho Panhandle National Forest.

78 Albertini's Carlin Bay Resort

    7

Location: On Coeur d'Alene Lake; map ID1, grid f2.

Campsites, facilities: There are 12 RV or tent campsites, some with hookups. Showers, propane gas facilities, barrier-free access, a restaurant, and a sanitary disposal station are available. Pets are allowed on leashes.

Reservations, fees: No reservations are needed; the fee is $8–15 per night. Open April 1–September 30.

Directions: From Coeur d'Alene, go 10 miles east on I-90 to exit 22; take Highway 97 south to Carlin Bay Resort on the right.

Contact: Albertini's Carlin Bay Resort, HCR 2, Box 45, Harrison, ID 83833; 208/689-3295.

Trip notes: You can fish, swim, boat, and water-ski on Coeur d'Alene Lake.

79 Killarney Lake

    6

Location: East of Coeur d'Alene; map ID1, grid f3.

Campsites, facilities: There are 11 RV or tent campsites, which can accommodate a maximum RV length of 24 feet. Wheelchair-accessible restrooms are available. Pets are allowed on leashes.

Reservations, fees: No reservations are needed; the fee is $5 and up per night. Open year-round.

Directions: From Coeur d'Alene, go about 21 miles east on I-90; take Exit 34 and then go five miles south to Killarney Lake Road and 3.5 miles to the lake and the campground.

Contact: Bureau of Land Management, Coeur d'Alene District Office, 1808 N. 3rd St., Coeur d'Alene, ID 83814; 208/769-5000.

Trip notes: You can hike, boat, and fish here.

80 Kellogg/Silver Valley KOA

     5

Location: West of Kellogg; map ID1, grid f4.

Campsites, facilities: There are 43 RV campsites, some with pull-throughs and hookups, which can accommodate a maximum RV length of 50 feet. There are numerous grassy sites for tents. Showers, laundry facilities, propane gas, a sanitary disposal station, a swimming pool, and playground are available. Group facilities can be arranged. Pets are allowed on leashes.

Reservations, fees: No reservations are needed; the fee is $20–27 per night. Open year-round.

Directions: From Coeur d'Alene, take I-90 33 miles east to Exit 45 and follow the signs 200 yards to the campground.

Contact: Kellogg/Silver Valley KOA, P.O. Box 949, Pinehurst, ID 83580; 208/682-3612, 208/682-9464; email: kellogggkoa@nidlink.com.

Trip notes: You can hike, golf, fish, and mountain bike the trails at Silver Mountain.

81 Crystal Gold Mine & RV Park

 6

Location: In Coeur d'Alene National Forest; map ID1, grid g4.

Campsites, facilities: There are 21 RV or tent campsites, which can accommodate a maximum RV length of 40 feet, and some hookups. Pets are allowed on leashes.

Reservations, fees: No reservations are needed; the fee is $7.50 per night. Open May 1–October 1.

Directions: From Coeur d'Alene, go 33 miles east on I-90. From Kellogg, go one mile east on Cameron Avenue to the campground.

Contact: Crystal Gold Mine & RV Park, P.O. Box 510, Kellogg, ID 83837; 208/783-4653.

Trip notes: You can hike and fish in the Coeur d'Alene National Forest.

82 Blue Anchor Trailer & RV Park

 4

Location: In Osburn; map ID1, grid g4.

Campsites, facilities: There are 30 RV or tent campsites, which can accommodate a maximum RV length of 40 feet. Laundry facilities, hookups, a sanitary disposal station, showers, and propane gas are available. Pets are allowed on leashes.

Reservations, fees: No reservations are needed; the fee is $13.50–19 per night. Open year-round.

Directions: From Coeur d'Alene, go east on I-90 to exit 57 at Osburn, go three blocks south to Mullan Street, then four blocks west on Mullan Street to the RV park.

Contact: Blue Anchor Trailer & RV Park, P.O. Box 645, Osburn, ID 83849; 208/752-3443.

Trip notes: You can golf nearby, and fish in the Coeur d'Alene River for whitefish, cutthroat, and rainbow trout.

83 Silver Leaf Motel & RV Park

 3

Location: Near Silverton; map ID1, grid g4.

Campsites, facilities: There are 15 RV or tent campsites, some with hookups. Wheelchair-accessible restrooms, laundry facilities, showers, and a sanitary disposal station are available. A swimming pool is on-site. Pets are allowed on leashes.

Reservations, fees: No reservations are needed; the fee is $5–10 per night.

Directions: From Silverton, take Exit 60 off I-90; the campground is between Silverton and Wallace.

Contact: Silver Leaf Motel & RV Park, P.O. Box 151, Silverton, ID 83867; 208/752-0222.

Trip notes: You can fish in the Coeur d'Alene River for whitefish, cutthroat, and rainbow trout.

84 Harrison City RV Park

 4

Location: On Coeur d'Alene Lake; map ID1, grid g2.

Campsites, facilities: There are 21 RV or tent campsites, some with hookups. Showers and a sanitary disposal station are available. Pets are allowed on leashes.

Reservations, fees: Reservations are accepted; the fee is $9–15 per night. Open April–October.

Directions: From Coeur d'Alene, go south 35 miles on Highway 97 to the campground.

Contact: Harrison City, P.O. Box 73, W. Harrison St., Harrison, ID 83833; 208/689-3212.

Trip notes: You can fish, swim, boat, and water-ski on Coeur d'Alene Lake.

85 Heyburn State Park

 6

Location: On Chatcolet Lake; map ID1, grid g2.

Campsites, facilities: There are 132 RV or

tent campsites, some with pull-through sites and hookups. Showers, flush toilets, water, a playground, and a sanitary disposal station are available.

Reservations, fees: No reservations are needed; the fee is $0–18 per night. Open year-round.

Directions: From Coeur d'Alene, go south on Highway 95 to Plummer; the park is at the junction of Highway 95 and Highway 5, between Plummer and St. Maries.

Contact: Heyburn State Park, 1291 Chatcolet Rd., Plummer, ID 83851; 208/686-1308, fax 208/686-3003; email: HEY@idpr.state.id.us.

Trip notes: You can hike, swim, boat and fish at Chatcolet Lake. There are 132 sites in three campgrounds: Chatcolet, Hawleys Landing, and Benewah. You can fish for pike or bass in the lakes. Osprey and blue heron are common here. You can boat, water-ski, sail, and canoe. Hiking and horse trails are shaded by 400-year-old ponderosa pines. The Rocky Point Marina offers a public boat ramp, store, fuel dock, restroom, and parking. The Chatq'ele' Interpretive Center is in the former Rocky Point Lodge and features displays and information from the Civilian Conservation Corps, the Coeur d'Alene Indian Tribe, other local history, and wildlife.

86 Misty Meadows RV Park & Camping

 5

Location: Along the St. Joe River; map ID1, grid g2.

Campsites, facilities: There are 20 RV or tent campsites, some with hookups. Pets are allowed on leashes.

Reservations, fees: Reservations are accepted; the fee is $8.50–15 per night. Open April 30–September 15.

Directions: From St. Maries, go east on Highway 5 to Forest Service Road 50, turn left, go three miles and Misty Meadows RV Park is on the right.

Contact: Misty Meadows RV Park & Camping, HC 03, P.O. Box 52, St. Maries, ID 83861; 208/245-2639 or 208/245-4679.

Trip notes: You can fish, boat, swim, and hike in the area.

87 Ed's R & R Shady River RV Park

 5

Location: In St. Maries; map ID1, grid g2.

Campsites, facilities: There are 14 RV or tent campsites. Hookups, propane gas, and a sanitary disposal facility are available. Pets are allowed on leashes.

Reservations, fees: No reservations are needed; the fee is $9–10 per night. Open year-round.

Directions: From Highway 3, this campground is at the junction of the St. Joe River and Highway 3.

Contact: Ed's R & R Shady River RV Park, 1211 Lincoln, St. Maries, ID 83861; 208/245-3549.

Trip notes: You can fish, float, and raft the St. Joe River. Heyburn State Park, to the west, has fishing, boating, hiking, and mountain biking.

88 Shadowy St. Joe

 7

Location: In Idaho Panhandle National Forest; map ID1, grid g3.

Campsites, facilities: There are 13 RV or tent campsites, which can accommodate a maximum RV length of 45 feet. Wheelchair-accessible restrooms and water are available.

Reservations, fees: No reservations are needed; the fee is $6 per night. Open May 1–October 31.

Directions: From St. Maries, go one mile east on Highway 3, then 10 miles east on Forest Service Road 50 to the campground.

Contact: Idaho Panhandle National Forest, St. Joe (St. Maries) Ranger District, P.O. Box 407, St. Maries, ID

83861; 208/245-2531.

Trip notes: You can fish, float, and raft the St. Joe River. Heyburn State Park, to the west, has fishing, boating, hiking, and mountain biking.

89 St. Joe Lodge & Resort

 5

Location: In Calder; map ID1, grid g3.

Campsites, facilities: There are 20 RV or tent campsites. Hookups, showers, propane gas, restaurant, and a sanitary disposal facility are available. Pets are allowed on leashes.

Reservations, fees: No reservations are needed; the fee is $12.50 per night.

Directions: From St. Maries, go 35 miles east on County Road 50 to the campground.

Contact: St. Joe Lodge & Resort, Route 3, Box 350, Calder, ID 83808; 208/546-3462.

Trip notes: You can fish, float, and raft the St. Joe River. Heyburn State Park to the west has fishing, boating, hiking, and mountain biking.

90 Big Creek

 5

Location: In Shoshone National Forest; map ID1, grid g4.

Campsites, facilities: There are eight RV or tent campsites, which can accommodate a maximum RV length of 30 feet. Hookups and wheelchair-accessible restrooms are available.

Reservations, fees: No reservations are needed; the fee is $6 per night. Open June 1–October 31.

Directions: From St. Maries, go 25 miles east on County Road 50 to Calder. From Calder, go five miles east on County Road 347, then three miles northwest on Forest Service Road 537 (Big Creek Road) to the campground.

Contact: Idaho Panhandle National Forest, St. Joe (St. Maries) Ranger District, P.O. Box 407, St. Maries, ID 83861; 208/245-2531.

Trip notes: You can fish, float, and raft the St.

Joe River. Heyburn State Park to the west has fishing, boating, hiking, and mountain biking.

91 Huckleberry

 5

Location: In Shoshone National Forest; map ID1, grid h4.

Campsites, facilities: There are 39 RV or tent campsites, which can accommodate a maximum RV length of 50 feet. Wheelchair-accessible restrooms, hookups, water, and a sanitary disposal station are available. Pets are allowed on leashes.

Reservations, fees: No reservations are needed; the fee is $7 and up per night. Open April 1–November 30.

Directions: From St. Maries, go 25 miles east on County Road 50 to Calder. From Calder, go five miles east on St. Joe River Road to the campground.

Contact: Bureau of Land Management, Coeur d'Alene District Office, 1808 N. 3rd St., Coeur d'Alene, ID 83814; 208/769-5000.

Trip notes: You can fish, float, and raft the St. Joe River. Heyburn State Park to the west has fishing, boating, hiking, and mountain biking.

92 Turner Flat

 6

Location: In the Idaho Panhandle National Forest; map ID1, grid g6.

Campsites, facilities: There are 11 RV or tent campsites, which can accommodate a maximum RV length of 35 feet. Vault toilets and water are available.

Reservations, fees: No reservations are needed; the fee is $6 per night. Open June 1–October 31.

Directions: From Wallace, go south 22 miles to Avery. From Avery, go eight miles east on Forest Service Road 218 to the campground.

Contact: Idaho Panhandle National Forest, St. Joe (Avery) Ranger District, HC Box 1,

Avery, ID 83802; 208/245-4517.

Trip notes: You can hike and fish here. The St. Joe River offers excellent fly-fishing and challenging white water.

93 Tin Can Flat

    6

Location: In the Idaho Panhandle National Forest; map ID1, grid h6.

Campsites, facilities: There are 11 RV or tent campsites, which can accommodate a maximum RV length of 32 feet. There are vault toilets and water available.

Reservations, fees: No reservations are needed; the fee is $6 per night. Open June 1–October 31.

Directions: From Wallace, go south 22 miles to Avery. From Avery, go 10 miles east on Forest Service Road 218 to the campground.

Contact: Idaho Panhandle National Forest, St. Joe (Avery) Ranger District, HC Box 1, Avery, ID 83802; 208/245-4517.

Trip notes: You can hike and fish. The St. Joe offers excellent fly-fishing and challenging white water.

94 RV Park Milepost 382

   4

Location: On Coeur d'Alene National Indian Reservation; map ID1, grid h1.

Campsites, facilities: There are six RV or tent campsites. Laundry facilities, showers, hookups, pull-through sites, and a restaurant are available.

Reservations, fees: No reservations are needed; the fee is $10–12 per night. Open year-round.

Directions: From Coeur d'Alene, go south on U.S. 95 about 46 miles to Tensed. This campground is at 2nd Street and D Street; register at Cross Keys.

Contact: RV Park Milepost 382, P.O. Box 128, Tensed, ID 83870; 208/274-5023.

Trip notes: McCroskey State Park nearby is popular with mountain bikers.

95 Conrad Crossing

    6

Location: In Idaho Panhandle National Forest; map ID1, grid h7.

Campsites, facilities: There are eight RV or tent sites, which can accommodate a maximum RV length of 16 feet.

Reservations, fees: No reservations are needed; the fee is $6 per night. Open July 1–October 31.

Directions: From Wallace, go south 22 miles from Avery. From Avery, go 28 miles east on Forest Service Road 218 to the campground.

Contact: Idaho Panhandle National Forest, St. Joe (Avery) Ranger District, HC Box 1, Avery, ID 83802; 208/245-4517.

Trip notes: You can hike and fish here and St. Joe River offers excellent fly-fishing and challenging white water.

96 Fly Flat

     6

Location: In Idaho Panhandle National Forest; map ID1, grid h7.

Campsites, facilities: There are 14 RV or tent sites, which can accommodate a maximum RV length of 32 feet. Restrooms and water are available.

Reservations, fees: No reservations are needed; the fee is $6 per night. Open July 1–October 31.

Directions: From Wallace, go south 22 miles to Avery. From Avery, go 33 miles east on Forest Service Road 218 to the campground.

Contact: Idaho Panhandle National Forest, St. Joe (Avery) Ranger District, HC Box 1, Avery, ID 83802; 208/245-4517.

Trip notes: You can hike, fish, and swim here.

97 Spruce Tree

 6

Location: In Idaho Panhandle National Forest; map ID1, grid h7.

Campsites, facilities: There are nine RV or tent campsites, which can accommodate a maximum RV length of 35 feet, some with pull-through sites. Vault toilets and water are available.

Reservations, fees: No reservations are needed; the fee is $6 per night. Open June 1–October 31.

Directions: From Wallace, go south 22 miles to Avery. From Avery, go 43 miles east on Forest Service Road 218 to the campground.

Contact: Idaho Panhandle National Forest, St. Joe (Avery) Ranger District, HC Box 1, Avery, ID 83802; 208/245-4517.

Trip notes: You can hike, fish, and swim here.

WAYNE SCHERR

Looking out from the inside

MAP ID2

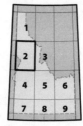

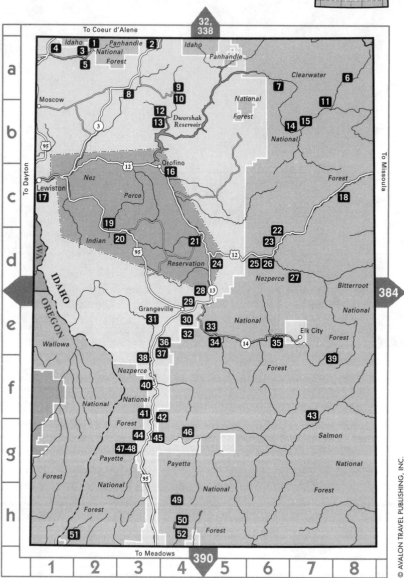

To Coeur d'Alene

32, 338

Idaho Panhandle National Forest

Idaho Panhandle

Clearwater

National Forest

Moscow

Dworshak Reservoir

National

Forest

Orofino

Nez Perce

Lewiston

To Dayton

WA

IDAHO

OREGON

Indian

Reservation

Nezperce

Grangeville

National Forest

Wallowa

National

Nezperce

National

Forest

Elk City

Bitterroot

National

Forest

Payette

National

Forest

Payette

National

Forest

Salmon

National

Forest

Forest

Forest

To Missoula

384

To Meadows

390

© AVALON TRAVEL PUBLISHING, INC.

368 Idaho

CHAPTER ID2

1 Giant White Pine 369
2 Emerald Creek 370
3 Laird Park 370
4 Scenic "6" Park 370
5 Pines RV Campground 370
6 Hidden Creek 371
7 Aquarius 371
8 Little Boulder Creek 371
9 Huckle Berry Heaven 371
10 Canyon Creek 372
11 Kelly Forks 372
12 Dent Acres 372
13 Dworshak State Park 372
14 Washington Creek 373
15 Noe Creek 373
16 Hidden Village 373
17 Hells Gate State Park 373
18 Wilderness Gateway 374
19 Winchester Lake
State Park 374
20 Miss Lily's Saloon
and Buggy Stop 374
21 Lewis Clark Resort 375
22 Apgar 375
23 Three Rivers Resort 375
24 River Junction RV Park 375
25 Wild Goose 376
26 Ryan's Wilderness Inn 376
27 O'Hara Bar 376

28 Harpster RV Park 376
29 Mountain View
Mobile Home & RV Park ...377
30 Sundown RV Park 377
31 Pine Bar 377
32 Fish Creek 377
33 Castle Creek 378
34 South Fork 378
35 Junction Lodge 378
36 Whitebird Motel
& RV Park 378
37 Swift Water RV Park 379
38 Hammer Creek 379
39 Red River 379
40 Slate Creek 379
41 River Front Gardens
RV Park 380
42 Prospector's Gold
RV & Campground 380
43 Lodgepole Pine Inn 380
44 Riverside RV Park 380
45 River Village RV Park 380
46 Spring Bar 381
47 Windy Saddle 381
48 Seven Devils 381
49 Hazard Lake 381
50 Grouse Campground 382
51 Hells Canyon Park 382
52 Last Chance 382

1 Giant White Pine

 7

Location: In Idaho Panhandle National Forest; map ID2, grid a2.

Campsites, facilities: There are 14 RV or tent campsites, which can accommodate a maximum RV length of 30 feet. A vault toilet and water are available. Pets are allowed on leashes.

Reservations, fees: No reservations are needed; the fee is $6 per night. Open May 20–September 8.

Directions: From Moscow go north on U.S. 95 for 17 miles to Highway 6, and then go east on Highway 6 the 10 miles to Harvard. From Harvard, go seven miles north on Highway 6 to the campground.

Contact: Idaho Panhandle National Forest, Fernan Ranger

District, 2502 E. Sherman Ave., Coeur d'Alene, ID 83814; 208/769-3000.

Trip notes: The White Pine Recreation Trail is five miles, combining Trails 228, 224B, and 224A to form a loop, and is considered easy to moderately difficult. There are scenic views along this trail, which runs through coniferous forests and riparian vegetation.

② Emerald Creek

 8

Location: In St. Joe National Forest; map ID2, grid a3.

Campsites, facilities: There are 18 RV and tent campsites, which can accommodate a maximum RV length of 22 feet. A vault toilet and water are available.

Reservations, fees: No reservations are needed; the fee is $6 per night. Open May 15–October 1.

Directions: From St. Maries, go south on Highway 3 approximately 31 miles to Clarkia. From Clarkia, go five miles northwest on U.S. 3, then six miles south on Forest Service Road 447 to the campground.

Contact: Idaho Panhandle National Forest, St. Joe (St. Maries) Ranger District, P.O. Box 407, St. Maries, ID 83861; 208/245-2531.

Trip notes: You can fish and hike in the forest or dig for garnets and fossils nearby.

③ Laird Park

 5

Location: East of Potlatch; map ID2, grid a2.

Campsites, facilities: There are 31 RV or tent campsites, which can accommodate a maximum RV length of 35 feet. Wheelchair-accessible restrooms, water, and a playground are available.

Reservations, fees: No reservations are needed; the fee is $6 per night. Open May 20–September 8.

Directions: From Moscow go north on U.S. 95 for 17 miles to Highway 6, and then go east

on Highway 6 for 10 miles to Harvard. From Harvard go three miles northeast on Highway 6, then one mile southeast on Forest Service Road 447 to the campground.

Contact: Forest Service, Palouse Ranger District, Route 2, Box 4, Potlatch, ID 83855; 208/875-1131.

Trip notes: You can fish and hike in the St. Joe National Forest; the White Pine National Scenic Byway is northeast of Potlatch.

④ Scenic "6" Park

 5

Location: In Potlatch; map ID2, grid a1.

Campsites, facilities: There are 24 RV or tent campsites. Hookups, pull-through sites, a playground, and a sanitary disposal station are available. Pets are allowed on leashes.

Reservations, fees: Reservations are accepted; the fee is $7–12 per night. Open year-round.

Directions: From Moscow, take U.S. 95 north 17 miles to Potlatch; exit at Highway 6 and head east to the campground.

Contact: Scenic "6" Park, 145 Hwy. 6, Potlatch, ID 83855; 208/875-0707.

Trip notes: The White Pine Recreation Trail is five miles, combining Trails 228, 224B, and 224A to form a loop, and is considered easy to moderately difficult. There are scenic views along this trail, which runs through coniferous forests and riparian vegetation.

⑤ Pines RV Campground

 5

Location: East of Potlatch; map ID2, grid a2.

Campsites, facilities: There are 20 RV or tent campsites. Hookups are available. Pets are allowed on leashes.

Reservations, fees: No reservations are needed; the fee is $12 per night. Open year-round.

Directions: From Moscow go north on U.S. 95 for 17 miles to Highway 6, and then go east on Highway 6 for 12 miles to the campground.

Contact: Pines RV Campground, 4510 Hwy. 6, Harvard, ID 83855; 208/875-0831.

Trip notes: The White Pine Recreation Trail is five miles, combining Trails 228, 224B, and 224A to form a loop, and is considered easy to moderately difficult. There are scenic views along this trail, which runs through coniferous forests and riparian vegetation.

6 Hidden Creek

    6

Location: In Clearwater National Forest; map ID2, grid a8.

Campsites, facilities: There are 13 RV or tent campsites, which can accommodate a maximum RV length of 22 feet. Restrooms and water are available. Pets are allowed on leashes.

Reservations, fees: No reservations are needed; the fee is $5 per night. Open June 15–October 31.

Directions: From Orofino, go south eight miles on U.S. 12 to Highway 11, then go 29 miles northeast to Pierce. From Pierce, go one mile south on Highway 11, then 55 miles northeast on Forest Service Road 250 to the campground.

Contact: Clearwater National Forest, Forest Supervisor, 12730 U.S. Hwy. 12, Orofino, ID 83544; 208/476-4541.

Trip notes: You can fish and hike here.

7 Aquarius

      6

Location: In Clearwater National Forest; map ID2, grid a6.

Campsites, facilities: There are seven RV or tent campsites, which can accommodate a maximum RV length of 22 feet. Restrooms and water are available. Pets are allowed on leashes.

Reservations, fees: No reservations are needed; the fee is $5 per night. Open June–September.

Directions: From Orofino, go south eight miles on U.S. 12 to Highway 11, then go 29 miles northeast to Pierce. From Pierce, go 11 miles north on Highway 11, then 25 miles northeast of the town of Headquarters on Forest Service Road 247 to the campground.

Contact: Clearwater National Forest, Forest Supervisor, 12730 U.S. Hwy. 12, Orofino, ID 83544; 208/476-4541.

Trip notes: You can fish in the Clearwater River or boat, swim, water-ski, or fish on the Dworshak Reservoir.

8 Little Boulder Creek

      6

Location: East of Moscow; map ID2, grid a2.

Campsites, facilities: There are 17 RV or tent campsites, which can accommodate a maximum RV length of 35 feet. A wheelchair-accessible restroom and water are available. Pets are allowed on leashes.

Reservations, fees: No reservations are needed; the fee is $6 per night. Open May 20–September 8.

Directions: From St. Maries, go south on Highway 3 for 46 miles to Deary. From Deary, go four miles east on Highway 8, then three miles southeast on County Road 1963 to the campground.

Contact: Forest Service, Palouse Ranger District, Route 2, Box 4, Potlatch, ID 83855; 208/875-1131.

Trip notes: You can fish at the Elk Creek Reservoir and fish, boat, water-ski, and swim at Dworshak Reservoir.

9 Huckle Berry Heaven

     4

Location: In Elk River; map ID2, grid a4.

Campsites, facilities: There are 20 RV or tent campsites. Wheelchair-accessible restrooms, hookups, propane gas, and a sanitary disposal station are available.

Reservations, fees: No reservations are needed; the fee is $20

per night. Open year-round.

Directions: From Moscow, take Highway 8 east until it ends near Elk River, and the campground is on the right.

Contact: Huckle Berry Heaven, P.O. Box 165, Elk River, ID 83827; 208/826-3405, fax 208/826-3284.

Trip notes: This campground is at Elk Creek Reservoir; Dworshak Reservoir is to the south.

10 Canyon Creek

     5

Location: In Clearwater Mountains; map ID2, grid a4.

Campsites, facilities: There are 12 RV or tent campsites, which can accommodate a maximum RV length of 22 feet.

Reservations, fees: No reservations are needed; the fee is $6 per night. Open April 30–September 30.

Directions: From Orofino, go 11 miles north on Orofino/Elk River Road to the campground.

Contact: Idaho Fish & Game Department, Bruneau, ID 83604; 208/845-2324.

Trip notes: Dworshak Reservoir is to the south, where you can fish, boat, water-ski, and swim.

11 Kelly Forks

      6

Location: in Clearwater National Forest; map ID2, grid a7.

Campsites, facilities: There are 14 RV or tent campsites. Restrooms and water are available. Pets are allowed on leashes.

Reservations, fees: No reservations are needed; the fee is $5 per night. Open May 31–October 31.

Directions: From Orofino, go south eight miles on U.S. 12 to Highway 11, then go 29 miles northeast to Pierce. From Pierce, go one mile south on Highway 11, then 47 miles northeast on Forest Service Road 250 to the campground.

Contact: Clearwater National Forest, Forest Supervisor, 12730 U.S. Hwy. 12, Orofino, ID 83544; 208/476-4541.

Trip notes: You can fish in the Clearwater River or boat, swim, water-ski, and fish on the Dworshak Reservoir.

12 Dent Acres

     6

Location: At Dworshak Reservoir; map ID2, grid b3.

Campsites, facilities: There are 50 RV or tent campsites, which can accommodate a maximum RV length of 35 feet. Showers and water are available.

Reservations, fees: No reservations are needed; the fee is $10–13 per night. Open May 1–September 30.

Directions: From Orofino, go 25 miles north on the country road to Dworshak Reservoir and campground.

Contact: Idaho Fish & Game Department, Bruneau, ID 83604; 208/845-2324.

Trip notes: You can boat, fish, swim, and hike at Dworshak Reservoir and surrounding areas.

13 Dworshak State Park

   6

Location: On the western shore of Dworshak Reservoir; map ID2, grid b3.

Campsites, facilities: There are 105 RV or tent campsites, which can accommodate a maximum RV length of 35 feet. Hookups, showers, wheelchair-accessible restrooms, a sanitary disposal facility, water, and a playground are available.

Reservations, fees: No reservations are needed; the fee is $9–15 per night. Open April–October 31. The stay limit is 15 days.

Directions: From Orofino, go three miles west on Highway 7, then 21 miles northwest on County Road P-1 to the park.

Contact: Dworshak State Park, P.O. Box 2028, Orofino, ID 83544; 208/476-5994.

Trip notes: You can boat, fish, swim, water-ski, and hike at Dworshak Reservoir. The Nez Perce National Historic Park is at Spaulding.

14 Washington Creek

    6

Location: In Clearwater National Forest; map ID2, grid b7.

Campsites, facilities: There are 23 RV or tent campsites; which can accommodate a maximum RV length of 35 feet. Vault toilets and water are available. Pets are allowed on leashes.

Reservations, fees: No reservations are needed; the fee is $5 per night. Open May 31–September 8.

Directions: From Orofino, go south eight miles on U.S. 12 to Highway 11, then go 29 miles northeast to Pierce. From Pierce, go one mile south on Highway 11, then 39 miles northeast on Forest Service Road 250, and six miles northeast on Forest Service Road 247 to the campground.

Contact: Clearwater National Forest, Forest Supervisor, 12730 U.S. Hwy. 12, Orofino, ID 83544; 208/476-4541.

Trip notes: You can fish on the North Fork River and Kelly Creek and raft or kayak the North Fork River. There are several hiking trails nearby.

15 Noe Creek

    7

Location: In Clearwater National Forest; map ID2, grid b7.

Campsites, facilities: There are six RV or tent campsites, which can accommodate a maximum RV length of 22 feet. Restrooms and water are available. Pets are allowed on leashes.

Reservations, fees: No reservations are needed; the fee is $5 per night. Open May 31–October 31.

Directions: From Orofino, go south eight

miles on U.S. 12 to Highway 11, then go 29 miles northeast to Pierce. From Pierce, go one mile south on Highway 11, then 40 miles northeast on Forest Service Road 250 to the campground.

Contact: Clearwater National Forest, Forest Supervisor, 12730 U.S. Hwy. 12, Orofino, ID 83544; 208/476-4541.

Trip notes: You can fish on North Fork River and Kelly Creek and raft or kayak on North Fork River. Several hiking trails are nearby.

16 Hidden Village

      5

Location: East of Lewiston; map ID2, grid c4.

Campsites, facilities: There are 26 RV or tent campsites. Wheelchair-accessible restrooms, laundry facilities, hookups, showers, and a sanitary disposal facility are available. Pets are allowed on leashes.

Reservations, fees: No reservations are needed; the fee is $12–25 per night. Open year-round.

Directions: From Lewiston, take U.S. 12 east for 25 miles toward Orofino. Hidden Village is six miles before you reach Orofino on the left side.

Contact: Hidden Village, 14615 Hwy. 12 #87, Orofino, ID 83544; 208/476-3416.

Trip notes: You can boat, fish, swim, water-ski, and hike at Dworshak Reservoir. The Nez Perce National Historic Park is at Spaulding.

17 Hells Gate State Park

     6

Location: South of Lewiston; map ID2, grid c1.

Campsites, facilities: There are 93 RV or tent campsites, which can accommodate a maximum RV length of 60 feet. Showers, wheelchair-accessible restrooms, hookups, pull-through sites, water, and a playground are available. Pets are allowed on leashes.

Reservations, fees: Reservations are accepted; the fee is $6–12 per night. Open year-round.

Directions: From Lewiston, go four miles south on Snake River Avenue to the state park.

Contact: Hells Gate State Park, 3620A Snake River Ave., Lewiston, ID 83501; 208/799-5051.

Trip notes: You can hike, mountain bike, boat, swim, raft, and fish in the Snake River. Hells Canyon, the deepest river gorge in North America, has some of the world's largest rapids for rafting and jet-boating.

18 Wilderness Gateway

 7

Location: In Clearwater National Forest; map ID2, grid c8.

Campsites, facilities: There are 91 RV or tent campsites, which can accommodate a maximum RV length of 40 feet, some with pull-through sites. Wheelchair-accessible restrooms, water, a sanitary disposal facility, and a playground are available. Pets are allowed on leashes.

Reservations, fees: Reservations are accepted; the fee is $8 per night. Open May 25–October 10.

Directions: From Orofino, go 31 miles south on U.S. 12 to Kooskia. From Kooskia, go 49 miles east on U.S. 12 to the campground.

Contact: Clearwater National Forest, Forest Supervisor, 12730 U.S. Hwy. 12, Orofino, ID 83544; 208/476-4541.

Trip notes: The Lochsa River runs along here. Designated a Wild and Scenic River, white-water enthusiasts are familiar with these waters. You can fish here, but there are several restrictions, so check with Idaho Fish & Game for current information.

19 Winchester Lake State Park

 6

Location: On Nez Perce Indian Reservation; map ID2, grid c2.

Campsites, facilities: There are 75 RV or tent campsites, which can accommodate a maximum RV length of 50 feet. Hookups, showers, wheelchair-accessible restrooms, water, and a sanitary disposal station are available. Pets are allowed on leashes.

Reservations, fees: No reservations are needed; the fee is $8 per night. Open year-round.

Directions: From Lewiston, take U.S. 95 south to Winchester. Take Business 95, then turn left at the stop sign and follow signs to the campground.

Contact: Winchester Lake State Park, P.O. Box 186, Winchester, ID 83555; 208/924-7563.

Trip notes: You can boat, fish, and hike here.

20 Miss Lily's Saloon and Buggy Stop

 4

Location: On Nez Perce Indian Reservation; map ID2, grid d3.

Campsites, facilities: There are 12 RV or tent campsites, which can accommodate a maximum RV length of 30 feet. Hookups are available.

Reservations, fees: Reservations are accepted; the fee is $14 per night. Open year-round.

Directions: From Lewiston, go south on U.S. 95 for 44 miles to Winchester. This campground is in Winchester, off the U.S. 95 business loop.

Contact: Miss Lily's Saloon and Buggy Stop, 301 Joseph Ave., Winchester, ID 83555; 208/924-5048.

Trip notes: You can boat, fish, and hike here.

21 Lewis Clark Resort

 6

Location: Near Kamiah; map ID2, grid d4.

Campsites, facilities: There are 227 RV or tent campsites. Wheelchair-accessible restrooms, laundry facilities, hookups, showers, propane gas, a restaurant, clubhouse, and a sanitary disposal facility are available. Pets are allowed on leashes.

Reservations, fees: No reservations are needed; the fee is $15–40 per night. Open year-round.

Directions: From Orofino, go east on U.S. 12 23 miles to Kamiah. From Kamiah, go 1.5 miles east. From the junction of Highway 162 and U.S. 12, go two miles south on U.S. 12 to the resort.

Contact: Lewis Clark Resort, Route 1, Box 17X, Kamiah, ID 83536; 208/935-2556.

Trip notes: You can fish in the Clearwater River and hike nearby.

22 Apgar

 7

Location: In Clearwater National Forest; map ID2, grid d6.

Campsites, facilities: There are seven RV or tent campsites, which can accommodate a maximum RV length of 22 feet. Wheelchair-accessible restrooms and water are available. Pets are allowed on leashes.

Reservations, fees: No reservations are needed; the fee is $6 per night. Open May–September.

Directions: From Orofino, go 31 miles south on U.S. 12 to Kooskia. From Kooskia, go 29 miles east on U.S. 12 to the campground.

Contact: Clearwater National Forest, Forest Supervisor, 12730 U.S. Hwy. 12, Orofino, ID 83544; 208/476-4541.

Trip notes: This campground is in a timbered setting. Designated a Wild and Scenic River, the Lochsa River runs near here. Whitewater enthusiasts are familiar with these waters,

and you can fish here, but there are several restrictions, so check with Idaho Fish & Game for current information. The DeVoto Memorial Cedar Grove is worth a visit.

23 Three Rivers Resort

 5

Location: In Clearwater National Forest; map ID2, grid d6.

Campsites, facilities: There are 50 RV or tent campsites, some with hookups. Showers, wheelchair-accessible restrooms, a swimming pool, and a restaurant are available. Pets are allowed on leashes.

Reservations, fees: No reservations are needed; the fee is $15–39 per night. Open May 1–October 30.

Directions: From Orofino, go 31 miles south on U.S. 12 to Kooskia. From Kooskia, go 25 miles east on U.S. 12 to the campground.

Contact: Three Rivers Resort, HC 75, P.O. Box 61, Kooskia, ID 83539; 208/926-4430.

Trip notes: Designated a Wild and Scenic River, the Lochsa River runs near here, and white-water enthusiasts are familiar with these waters. You can fish here, but there are several restrictions, so check with Idaho Fish & Game for current information. The DeVoto Memorial Cedar Grove is worth a visit.

24 River Junction RV Park

 5

Location: Near Kooskia; map ID2, grid d5.

Campsites, facilities: There are 29 RV or tent campsites. Wheelchair-accessible restrooms, laundry facilities, and a sanitary disposal station are available. Pets are allowed on leashes.

Reservations, fees: No reservations are needed; the fee is $6–14 per night. Open year-round.

Directions: From Orofino, go 31 miles south on U.S. 12 to Kooskia. From U.S. 12 at milepost 74, go .1 mile east of Highway 13 to the RV park.

Contact: River Junction RV Park, P.O. Box 413, Kooskia, ID 83539; 208/926-7865.

Trip notes: This campground is on the Clearwater River, outside Kooskia. You can fish in the Clearwater River and hike nearby.

25 Wild Goose

 6

Location: In Clearwater National Forest; map ID2, grid d6.

Campsites, facilities: There are six RV or tent campsites, which can accommodate a maximum RV length of 22 feet. Wheelchair-accessible restrooms and water are available. Pets are allowed on leashes.

Reservations, fees: No reservations are needed; the fee is $6 per night. Open May–September.

Directions: From Orofino, go 31 miles south on U.S. 12 to Kooskia. From Kooskia, go 20 miles east on U.S. 12 to the campground.

Contact: Clearwater National Forest, Forest Supervisor, 12730 U.S. Hwy. 12, Orofino, ID 83544; 208/476-4541.

Trip notes: The Lochsa River, designated a Wild and Scenic River, runs near here, and whitewater enthusiasts are familiar with these waters. You can fish here, but there are several restrictions, so check with Idaho Fish & Game for current information. The DeVoto Memorial Cedar Grove is worth a visit.

26 Ryan's Wilderness Inn

 5

Location: In Clearwater National Forest; map ID2, grid d6.

Campsites, facilities: There are six RV or tent campsites. Wheelchair-accessible restrooms and a restaurant are available. Pets are allowed on leashes.

Reservations, fees: No reservations are needed; the fee is $10–19 per night.

Directions: From Orofino, go 31 miles south

on U.S. 12 to Kooskia. From U.S. 12, take exit at milepost 97.5 to Inn.

Contact: Ryan's Wilderness Inn, HC 75, P.O. Box 60-A2, Lowell, ID 83539; 208/926-4706.

Trip notes: The Lochsa River runs near here. Designated a Wild and Scenic River, whitewater enthusiasts are familiar with these waters. You can fish here but there are several restrictions, so check with Idaho Fish & Game for current information. The DeVoto Memorial Cedar Grove is worth a visit.

27 O'Hara Bar

 6

Location: In Nez Perce National Forest; map ID2, grid d7.

Campsites, facilities: There are 34 RV or tent campsites, which can accommodate a maximum RV length of 20 feet. Wheelchair-accessible restrooms and water are available.

Reservations, fees: Reservations are accepted; the fee is $6 per night. Open May 24–October 1.

Directions: From Orofino, go 31 miles south on U.S. 12 to Kooskia. From Kooskia, go 24 miles east on U.S. 12, then seven miles southeast on County Road 223 and one mile south on Forest Service Road 651 to the campground.

Contact: Nez Perce National Forest, Elk City Ranger District, P.O. Box 416, Elk City, ID 83525; 208/842-2245.

Trip notes: You can boat, fish, and swim here.

28 Harpster RV Park

 4

Location: Near Grangeville; map ID2, grid d4.

Campsites, facilities: There are 26 RV or tent campsites, which can accommodate a maximum RV length of 55 feet. Wheelchair-accessible restrooms, laundry facilities, hookups, showers, propane gas, and a sanitary disposal facility are available. Pets are allowed on leashes.

Reservations, fees: No reservations are needed; the fee is $10–14 per night. Open year-round.

Directions: From Grangeville, go 12 miles northeast on Highway 13 to the campground.

Contact: Harpster RV Park, HC 66, P.O. Box 337, Kooskia, ID 83539; 208/983-2312.

Trip notes: You can explore Lewis and Clark Long Camp Country and fish, white-water raft, hike, and mountain bike nearby.

29 Mountain View Mobile Home & RV Park

 4

Location: Near Grangeville; map ID2, grid e4.

Campsites, facilities: There are 24 RV or tent campsites. Hookups, pull-through sites, showers, laundry facilities, and a sanitary disposal facility are available. Pets are allowed on leashes.

Reservations, fees: No reservations are needed; the fee is $5–14 per night. Open year-round.

Directions: From the junction of U.S. 95 and U.S. 13 (Main Street) in Grangeville, go east eight blocks on Main Street to Hall Street, then north six blocks to the RV Park.

Contact: Mountain View Mobile Home & RV Park, P.O. Box 25, 127 Cunningham St., Grangeville, ID 83530; 208/983-2328, 800/452-8227.

Trip notes: You can explore Lewis and Clark Long Camp Country, and fish, white-water raft, hike, and mountain bike nearby.

30 Sundown RV Park

 4

Location: In Grangeville; map ID2, grid e4.

Campsites, facilities: There are 28 RV or tent campsites. Hookups, laundry facilities, pull-through sites, and showers are available. Pets are allowed on leashes.

Reservations, fees: No reservations are needed; the fee is $14.50 per night.

Directions: From Orofino, go 57 miles south on U.S. 12 to Grangeville. This campground is at the junction of Highway 13 and U.S. 95.

Contact: Sundown RV Park, 102 N. C St., Grangeville, ID 83530; 208/983-9113.

Trip notes: You can explore Lewis and Clark Long Camp Country, and fish, white-water raft, hike, and mountain bike nearby.

31 Pine Bar

 5

Location: West of Grangeville; map ID2, grid e3.

Campsites, facilities: There are five RV or tent campsites. A vault toilet, water, and a boat ramp are available. Pets are allowed on leashes.

Reservations, fees: No reservations are needed; the fee is $7 per night. Open year-round.

Directions: From Grangeville, go west on U.S. 95 to Cottonwood. From Cottonwood, go 11 miles south on Graves Creek Road to the campground.

Contact: Bureau of Land Management, Coeur d'Alene District Office, 1808 N. 3rd St., Coeur d'Alene, ID 83814; 208/769-5000.

Trip notes: This campground is along the Salmon River, where you can hike, boat, swim, and fish.

32 Fish Creek

 6

Location: In Nez Perce National Forest; map ID2, grid e4.

Campsites, facilities: There are eight RV or tent campsites, which can accommodate a maximum RV length of 16 feet. Wheelchair-accessible restrooms are available.

Reservations, fees: No reservations are needed; the fee is $6 per night. Open June–September.

Directions: From Grangeville, go one mile east on Highway 13, then one mile south on County Road 17 and seven miles southeast on Forest Service Road 221.

Contact: Nez Perce National Forest, Route 2, Box 475, Grangeville, ID 83530; 208/983-1950.

Trip notes: You can fish here.

33 Castle Creek

 6

Location: In Nez Perce National Forest; map ID2, grid e5.

Campsites, facilities: There are eight RV or tent campsites, which can accommodate a maximum RV length of 22 feet. Wheelchair-accessible restrooms, a sanitary disposal station, and water are available.

Reservations, fees: No reservations are needed; the fee is $6 per night. Open June–October.

Directions: From Grangeville, go one mile east on Highway 13, then 10 miles southeast on County Road 17, and six miles southeast on Highway 14 to the campground.

Contact: Nez Perce National Forest, Route 2, Box 475, Grangeville, ID 83530; 208/983-1950.

Trip notes: This campground is on the Clearwater River, where you can fish and swim.

34 South Fork

 6

Location: In Nez Perce National Forest; map ID2, grid e5.

Campsites, facilities: There are eight RV or tent campsites, which can accommodate a maximum RV length of 22 feet. A sanitary disposal facility and water are available. Pets are allowed on leashes.

Reservations, fees: No reservations are needed; the fee is $6 per night. Open June 1–October 1.

Directions: From Grangeville, go one mile east on Highway 13, then 10 miles southeast on County Road 17, and six miles southeast on Highway 14 to the campground.

Contact: Nez Perce National Forest, Route 2, Box 475, Grangeville, ID 83530; 208/983-1950.

Trip notes: You can fish and swim on the Clearwater River.

35 Junction Lodge

 5

Location: In Nez Perce National Forest; map ID2, grid e6.

Campsites, facilities: There are 14 RV or tent campsites, some with hookups. There is a restaurant available. Pets are allowed on leashes.

Reservations, fees: No reservations are needed; the fee is $16 per night. Open year-round.

Directions: From Grangeville, go east on Highway 14 to Elk City. From Elk City, go six miles west on Highway 14 to the campground.

Contact: Junction Lodge, HC 67, P.O. Box 98, Grangeville, ID 83530; 208/842-2459.

Trip notes: Red River Hot Springs are nearby. You can fish and hike in the national forest.

36 Whitebird Motel & RV Park

 4

Location: South of Grangeville; map ID2, grid e4.

Campsites, facilities: There are 15 RV or tent campsites. Wheelchair-accessible restrooms, laundry facilities, hookups, and a sanitary disposal facility are available.

Reservations, fees: No reservations are needed; the fee is $14 per night. Open

Directions: From Grangeville, go 16 miles south on U.S. 95 to White Bird. This campground is two blocks off U.S. 95 in downtown White Bird.

Contact: Whitebird Motel & RV Park, P.O. Box 1, Hwy. 95, White Bird, ID 83554; 208/839-2308, 208/839-2434.

Trip notes: The Hammer Creek Recreation Area is nearby for rafting, and Hells Canyon Recreation Area is to the west, where you can hike, mountain bike, and fish.

37 Swift Water RV Park

 4

Location: South of Grangeville, map ID2, grid e3.

Campsites, facilities: There are 27 RV or tent campsites, which can accommodate a maximum RV length of 45 feet. There are laundry facilities, propane gas, and a sanitary disposal facility available.

Reservations, fees: No reservations are needed; the fee is $10–16 per night. Open year-round.

Directions: From Grangeville, go 16 miles south on U.S. 12 to White Bird and campground.

Contact: Swift Water RV Park, HC 01, P.O. Box 24, White Bird, ID 83554; 208/839-2700.

Trip notes: The Hammer Creek Recreation Area is nearby for rafting, and Hells Canyon Recreation Area, where you can hike, mountain bike, and fish, is to the west.

38 Hammer Creek

 4

Location: South of Grangeville; map ID2, grid f3.

Campsites, facilities: There are eight RV or tent campsites, which can accommodate a maximum RV length of 26 feet. Wheelchair-accessible restrooms and water are available. Pets are allowed on leashes.

Reservations, fees: No reservations are needed; the fee is $7 per night. Open year-round.

Directions: From Grangeville, go 16 miles south on U.S. 95 to White Bird, then 1.5 miles south on U.S. 95, and 1.5 miles north on the county road to the campground.

Contact: Bureau of Land Management, Coeur d'Alene District Office, 1808 N. 3rd St., Coeur d'Alene, ID 83814; 208/769-5000.

Trip notes: The Hammer Creek Recreation Area is nearby for rafting, Hells Canyon Recreation Area is to the west, where you can

hike, mountain bike, and fish.

39 Red River

 7

Location: In Nez Perce National Forest; map ID2, grid f7.

Campsites, facilities: There are 40 RV or tent campsites, which can accommodate a maximum RV length of 16 feet. Restrooms and water are available.

Reservations, fees: Reservations are accepted; the fee is $8 per night. Open June 1–October 31.

Directions: From Grangeville, go east on Highway 14 to Elk City. From Elk City, go three miles southwest on Highway 14, then 14 miles southeast on County Road 222 and six miles northeast on County Road 234 to the campground.

Contact: Nez Perce National Forest, Elk City Ranger District, P.O. Box 416, Elk City, ID 83525; 208/842-2245.

Trip notes: Red River Hot Springs are nearby. You can fish and hike in the national forest.

40 Slate Creek

 4

Location: South of White Bird; map ID2, grid f3.

Campsites, facilities: There are six RV or tent campsites, which can accommodate a maximum RV length of 21 feet. Wheelchair-accessible restrooms, water, and a sanitary disposal station. Pets are allowed on leashes.

Reservations, fees: No reservations are needed; the fee is $7 per night. Open year-round.

Directions: From White Bird, go 10 miles south on U.S. 95 to the campground.

Contact: Bureau of Land Management, Route 3, Box 1811, Cottonwood, ID 83522; 208/962-3245.

Trip notes: You can boat, fish, and swim here.

41 River Front Gardens RV Park

 4

Location: South of Grangeville; map ID2, grid f3.

Campsites, facilities: There are 32 RV or tent campsites, some with hookups and pull-through sites. Showers are available. Pets are allowed on leashes.

Reservations, fees: Reservations are accepted; the fee is $15–18 per night. Open year-round.

Directions: From Grangeville, go south on U.S. 95 about 35 miles; the RV park is between Slate Creek and Lucile.

Contact: River Front Gardens RV Park, HCO 1, P.O. 15, Lucile, ID 83542; 208/628-3777.

Trip notes: You can fish in the Snake River to the west.

42 Prospector's Gold RV & Campground

 4

Location: In Lucile; map ID2, grid f4.

Campsites, facilities: There are 50 RV or tent campsites, some with hookups and pull-through sites. Wheelchair-accessible restrooms are available. Pets are allowed on leashes.

Reservations, fees: No reservations are needed; the fee is $4–15 per night.

Directions: From Grangeville, go about 40 miles south on U.S. 95 to Lucile, and you are there.

Contact: Prospector's Gold RV & Campground, P.O. Box 313, Lucile, ID 83542; 208/628-3773.

Trip notes: You can fish in the Snake River to the west.

43 Lodgepole Pine Inn

 6

Location: In Nez Perce National Forest; map ID2, grid f7.

Campsites, facilities: There are seven RV or tent campsites, some with hookups. Wheelchair-accessible restrooms, showers, laundry facilities, a restaurant, and a sanitary disposal facility are available. Pets are allowed on leashes.

Reservations, fees: No reservations are needed; the fee is $5 per night. Open year-round.

Directions: From Grangeville, travel 80 miles southeast on Highway 14 to the campground.

Contact: Lodgepole Pine Inn, P.O. Box 58, Dixie, ID 83525; 208/842-2523.

Trip notes: You can hike and fish in Nez Perce National Forest.

44 Riverside RV Park

 5

Location: In Riggins; map ID2, grid g3.

Campsites, facilities: There are 15 RV and tent campsites, some with hookups and pull-through sites. A sanitary disposal station is available. Pets are allowed on leashes.

Reservations, fees: No reservations are needed; the fee is $15 per night.

Directions: From Sawmill Bridge, go north to the campground.

Contact: Riverside RV Park, P.O. Box 1270, Riggins, ID 83549; 208/628-3390 or 208/628-3698.

Trip notes: You can fish here.

45 River Village RV Park

 5

Location: In Riggins; map ID2, grid g3.

Campsites, facilities: There are 32 RV or tent campsites, which can accommodate a maximum RV length of 40 feet. Laundry facilities, showers, hookups, and a sanitary disposal station are available. Pets are allowed on leashes.

Reservations, fees: No reservations are needed; the fee is $14–15 per night. Open year-round.

Directions: From Grangeville, go south on U.S. 95 for about 40 miles to Riggins. This RV park is the second business at the north end of town.

Contact: River Village RV Park, P.O. Box 2, 1434 N. Hwy. 95, Riggins, ID 83549; 208/628-3441 or 208/628-3506.

Trip notes: You can fish and hike here.

46 Spring Bar

 4

Location: In Nez Perce National Forest; map ID2, grid g4.

Campsites, facilities: There are 18 RV or tent campsites, which can accommodate a maximum RV length of 20 feet. Vault toilets and water are available.

Reservations, fees: No reservations are needed; the fee is $10 per night. Open April 1– October 31.

Directions: From Grangeville, go south on U.S. 95 41 miles to Riggins; from Riggins, go one mile south on U.S. 95; the campground is on Forest Service Road 1614.

Contact: Nez Perce Forest, HC 10, P.O. Box 70, Whitebird, ID 83664; 208/839-2211 or 208/628-3916.

Trip notes: You can boat, fish, and swim here.

47 Windy Saddle

 5

Location: In Hells Canyon National Recreation Area; map ID2, grid g3.

Campsites, facilities: There are four tent campsites. Wheelchair-accessible restrooms are available. Pets are allowed on leashes. Trailers are not recommended on Forest Service Road 517.

Reservations, fees: No reservations are needed; there is no fee. Open July 1– October 1.

Directions: From Grangeville, go south on U.S. 95 about 40 miles to Riggins. From Riggins, go 17 miles southwest on U.S. 95; the campground is west on Forest Service Road 517. Trailers are not recommended on Forest

Service Road 517.

Contact: U.S. Reclamation Bureau, HC NRA, P.O. Box 832, Riggins, ID 83549; 208/628-3916.

Trip notes: You can fish and hike here.

48 Seven Devils

 5

Location: In Hells Canyon National Recreation Area; map ID2, grid g3.

Campsites, facilities: There are seven tent campsites, and vault toilets are available. Pets are allowed on leashes.

Reservations, fees: No reservations are needed; there is no fee charged. Open July 1– October 1.

Directions: From Grangeville, go south on U.S. 95 40 miles to Riggins. From Riggins, go 17 miles southwest on U.S. 95, turn west on Forest Service Road 517 and follow it to the campground. Trailers are not recommended on Forest Service Road 517.

Contact: U.S. Reclamation Bureau, HC NRA, P.O. Box 832, Riggins, ID 83549; 208/628-3916.

Trip notes: You can fish and hike here.

49 Hazard Lake

 5

Location: In Payette National Forest; map ID2, grid h4.

Campsites, facilities: There are 12 RV or tent campsites, which can accommodate a maximum RV length of 22 feet. Vault toilets and water are available.

Reservations, fees: No reservations are needed; the fee is $5–8 per night. Open July 1–September 30.

Directions: From Grangeville, go south on U.S. 95 78 miles to New Meadows. From New Meadows, go six miles east on Highway 55, then 19 miles north on Forest Service Road 50257, and one mile east on Forest Service Road 50259 to the campground.

Contact: Payette National Forest, New Meadows Ranger District,

P.O. Box J, New Meadows, ID 83654; 208/347-2141.

Trip notes: You can hike, boat, fish and swim here.

50 Grouse Campground

     5

Location: In Payette National Forest; map ID2, grid h4.

Campsites, facilities: There are seven RV or tent campsites, which can accommodate a maximum RV length of 16 feet. Vault toilets and water are available. Pets are allowed on leashes.

Reservations, fees: No reservations are needed; the fee is $5–8 per night. Open July 1–September 30.

Directions: From Grangeville, go south on U.S. 95 78 miles to New Meadows. From New Meadows, go six miles southeast on Highway 55, then nine miles north on Forest Service Road 257 to the campground.

Contact: Payette National Forest, New Meadows Ranger District, P.O. Box J, New Meadows, ID 83654; 208/347-2141.

Trip notes: This campground is on Goose Lake.

51 Hells Canyon Park

 5

Location: Northwest of Cambridge; map ID2, grid h1.

Campsites, facilities: There are 23 RV or tent campsites, which can accommodate a maximum RV length of 40 feet. Showers, restrooms, water, hookups, and a sanitary disposal station are available.

Reservations, fees: Reservations are strongly suggested; the fee is $10 and up per night.

Open March 1–October 31.

Directions: From Weiser, go 31 miles north on U.S. 95 to Cambridge. From Cambridge, take Highway 71 northwest for about 60 miles to the park.

Contact: Idaho Power, 1221 W. Idaho St., P.O. Box 70, Boise, ID 83707; 208/388-2231 or 800/422-3143; website: www.idahopower.com. Hells Canyon National Recreation Area, P.O. Box 832, Riggins, ID 83549; 208/628-3916.

Trip notes: Call the 24-hour recreation information number, 800/422-3143, for up-to-date messages about parks, reservoir levels, and water flows, as conditions do vary. You can hike, boat, and fish here for steelhead, rainbow trout, Chinook salmon, sturgeon, and smallmouth bass.

52 Last Chance

    5

Location: In Payette National Forest; map ID2, grid h4.

Campsites, facilities: There are 23 RV or tent campsites, which can accommodate a maximum RV length of 45 feet. Wheelchair-accessible restrooms and water are available. Pets are allowed on leashes.

Reservations, fees: No reservations are needed; the fee is $5–8 per night. Open June 1–October 31.

Directions: From Grangeville, go south on U.S. 95 78 miles to New Meadows. From New Meadows, go four miles east on Highway 55 and two miles north on Forest Service Road 453 to the campground.

Contact: Payette National Forest, New Meadows Ranger District, P.O. Box J, New Meadows, ID 83654; 208/347-2141.

Trip notes: You can fish and hike here.

CHAPTER ID3

Mountain goat

MAP ID3

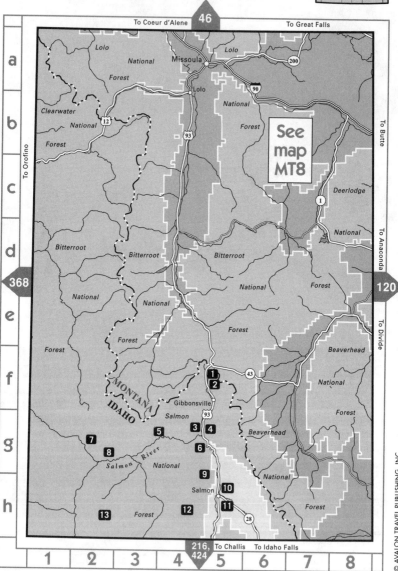

© AVALON TRAVEL PUBLISHING, INC.

CHAPTER ID3

1 Broken Arrow 385
2 Twin Creek....................385
3 Cummings Lake Lodge 385
4 Wagonhammer Springs
   Campground 386
5 Spring Creek
   Campground 386
6 North Fork Motel &
   Campground 386

7 Corn Creek 386
8 Ebenezer Bar
   Campground 387
9 Wallace Lake..................387
10 Century II Campground ...387
11 Salmon Meadows............387
12 Cougar Point 388
13 Crags...........................388

1 Broken Arrow

 5

Location: In Gibbonsville; map ID3, grid f5.
Campsites, facilities: There are 12 RV or tent campsites. Wheelchair-accessible restrooms, a restaurant, hookups, and showers available. Pets are allowed on leashes.
Reservations, fees: No reservations are needed; the fee is $5 per night.
Directions: From Salmon, go 33 miles north on U.S. 93 to the campground.
Contact: Broken Arrow, P.O. Box 26, Gibbonsville, Salmon, ID 83463; 208/856-2241.
Trip notes: Gibbonsville was established in 1877 after placer gold was discovered on Anderson and Dahlonega Creeks. By 1895 it had a thirty-stamp mill, employing nearly six hundred men. The ore bins and the A. D. & M. mine remain. You can hike and fish in Salmon-Challis National Forest.

2 Twin Creek

 6

Location: In Salmon-Challis National Forest; map ID3, grid f5.
Campsites, facilities: There are 46 RV or tent campsites, which can accommodate a maximum RV length of 32 feet. A vault toilet and water are available.

Reservations, fees: No reservations are needed; the fee is $5 per night. Open June 1–September 15.
Directions: From Salmon, go north 32 miles on U.S. 93 to Gibbonsville. From Gibbonsville, go five miles northwest on U.S. 93, then half a mile northwest on Forest Service Road 60449 to the campground.
Contact: Salmon-Challis National Forest, North Fork Ranger District, P.O. Box, 180, North Fork, ID 83466-0180; 208/865-2383.
Trip notes: Gibbonsville was established in 1877 after placer gold was discovered on Anderson and Dahlonega Creeks. By 1895 it had a thirty-stamp mill, employing nearly six hundred men. The ore bins and the A. D. & M. mine remain. You can hike and fish in Salmon-Challis National Forest.

3 Cummings Lake Lodge

 5

Location: North of North Fork; map ID3, grid g4.
Campsites, facilities: There are seven RV and tent campsites. Wheelchair-accessible restrooms, hookups, and pull-through sites are available. Pets are allowed on leashes.
Reservations, fees: No reservations are needed; the fee is $15 per night.
Directions: From Salmon, go 21

miles north on U.S. 93 to North Fork. From North Fork, go three miles north, then west up Hull Creek to the lodge.

Contact: Cummings Lake Lodge, P.O. Box 8, North Fork, ID 83466; 208/865-2424.

Trip notes: You can hike and fish in Salmon-Challis National Forest. The Salmon River Road starts at North Fork and winds west along the Wild and Scenic Salmon River. You can see Rocky Mountain bighorn sheep, mountain goats, bald eagles, river otter, and elk in this beautiful, rugged canyon.

4 Wagonhammer Springs Campground

 5

Location: North of Salmon; map ID3, grid g5.

Campsites, facilities: There are 16 RV or tent campsites. Hookups, laundry facilities, showers, and a sanitary disposal facility are available. Pets are allowed on leashes.

Reservations, fees: No reservations are needed; the fee is $10 and up per night. Open June 1–November 15.

Directions: From Salmon, go 18 miles north on U.S. 93.

Contact: Wagonhammer Springs Campground, U.S. 93, North Fork, ID 83466; 208/865-2477.

Trip notes: You can hike and fish in Salmon-Challis National Forest. The Salmon River Road starts at North Fork and winds west along the Wild and Scenic Salmon River. You can see Rocky Mountain bighorn sheep, mountain goats, bald eagles, river otter, and elk in this beautiful, rugged canyon.

5 Spring Creek Campground

 6

Location: In Salmon-Challis National Forest; map ID3, grid g5.

Campsites, facilities: There are five RV or tent campsites, which can accommodate a maximum RV length of 32 feet. Wheelchair-

accessible restrooms and water are available. Pets are allowed on leashes.

Reservations, fees: No reservations are needed; the fee is $5 per night. Open March–November.

Directions: From Salmon, go 21 miles north on U.S. 93 to North Fork. From North Fork, go 18 miles west on Salmon River Road 030 to the campground.

Contact: Salmon-Challis National Forest, North Fork Ranger District, P.O. Box 180, North Fork, ID 83466-0180; 208/865-2700.

Trip notes: You can boat, fish, swim, and hike here.

6 North Fork Motel & Campground

 5

Location: In North Fork; map ID3, grid g5.

Campsites, facilities: There are 30 RV or tent campsites. Wheelchair-accessible restrooms, a restaurant, laundry facilities, hookups, showers, and propane gas are available. Pets are allowed on leashes.

Reservations, fees: No reservations are needed; the fee is $8–13 per night. Open year-round.

Directions: From Salmon, go north on U.S. 93 to North Fork and the campground.

Contact: North Fork Motel and Campground, P.O. Box 100, North Fork, ID 83466; 208/865-2412.

Trip notes: You can hike and fish in Salmon-Challis National Forest. The Salmon River Road starts at North Fork and winds west along the Wild and Scenic Salmon River. You can see Rocky Mountain bighorn sheep, mountain goats, bald eagles, river otter, and elk in this beautiful, rugged canyon.

7 Corn Creek

 6

Location: In Salmon-Challis National Forest; map ID3, grid g2.

Campsites, facilities: There are 12 RV and

tent campsites, which can accommodate a maximum RV length of 22 feet. Vault toilets and water are available.

Reservations, fees: No reservations are needed; the fee is $5 per night. Open March 1–October 31.

Directions: From Salmon go 21 miles north on U.S. 93 to North Fork, then 19 miles west to Shoup. From Shoup, go 29 miles west on Forest Service Road 60030 to the campground.

Contact: Salmon-Challis National Forest, North Fork Ranger District, P.O. Box 180, North Fork, ID 83466-0180; 208/865-2700.

Trip notes: You can boat, fish, swim, and hike here.

8 Ebenezer Bar Campground
 6

Location: In Salmon-Challis National Forest; map ID3, grid g2.

Campsites, facilities: There are 11 RV or tent campsites, which can accommodate a maximum RV length of 32 feet. Wheelchair-accessible restrooms and water are available. Pets are allowed on leashes.

Reservations, fees: No reservations are needed; the fee is $5 per night. Open June 1–October 15.

Directions: From Salmon, go 21 miles north on U.S. 93 to North Fork. From North Fork, go 34.4 miles west on Salmon River Road 030 to the campground.

Contact: Salmon-Challis National Forest, North Fork Ranger District, P.O. Box 180, North Fork, ID 83466-0180; 208/865-2700.

Trip notes: You can fish and hike in the national forest. The Salmon Wild and Scenic River is popular for whitewater rafting; a guide service is recommended.

9 Wallace Lake
 6

Location: In Salmon-Challis National Forest; map ID3, grid g5.

Campsites, facilities: There are 12 RV or tent campsites, which can accommodate a maximum RV length of 20 feet. A vault toilet and water are available.

Reservations, fees: No reservations are needed; the fee is $4 per night. Open June 15–September 20.

Directions: From Salmon, go 3.2 miles north to U.S. 93, then 14 miles northwest on Forest Service Road 60023 and four miles south on Forest Service Road 60020 to the campground.

Contact: Salmon and Challis National Forests, Forest Supervisor, Hwy. 93 North, RR 2, Box 600, Salmon, ID 83467; 208/756-5100.

Trip notes: You can fish and hike in Salmon-Challis National Forest.

10 Century II Campground
 6

Location: In Salmon; map ID3, grid h5.

Campsites, facilities: There are 25 RV or tent campsites. Wheelchair-accessible restrooms and a sanitary disposal station. Pets are allowed on leashes.

Reservations, fees: No reservations are needed; the fee is $17 per night.

Directions: On U.S. 93 at Salmon, the campground is on the left, next to the Wagon West Hotel.

Contact: Century II Campground, 603 Hwy. 93 North, Salmon, ID 83467; 208/756-2063.

Trip notes: You can fish, raft, canoe, float, and kayak on the Salmon River, and a great blue heron rookery is nearby.

11 Salmon Meadows
 5

Location: In Salmon; map ID3, grid h5.

Campsites, facilities: There are 51 RV campsites, which can accommodate a maximum RV length of 65 feet. Laundry facilities, hookups, showers, pull-through sites, and a sanitary disposal station are available. Pets are allowed on leashes.

Group facilities can be arranged.

Reservations, fees: Reservations are accepted; the fee is $13–17 per night. Open April–November.

Directions: This campground is in Salmon, three blocks north of Main Street on St. Charles Street.

Contact: Salmon Meadows, P.O. Box 705, 400 N. St. Charles St., Salmon, ID 83467; 208/756-2640, 888/723-2640; fax 208/756-3771; email: smeadows@ida.net.

Trip notes: You can fish, raft, canoe, float, and kayak on the Salmon River, and there is a great blue heron rookery nearby.

12 Cougar Point

  6

Location: In the Salmon-Challis National Forest; map ID3, grid h4.

Campsites, facilities: There are 12 RV or tent campsites, which can accommodate a maximum RV length of 20 feet. There is a vault toilet and water available.

Reservations, fees: No reservations are needed; the fee is $4 per night. Open June 1–September 20.

Directions: From Salmon, go five miles south on U.S. 93 and 12 miles west on Forest Service Road 60021 to the campground.

Contact: Salmon-Challis National Forests, Forest Supervisor, Hwy. 93 North, RR 2, Box 600, Salmon, ID 83467; 208/756-5100.

Trip notes: You can canoe, kayak, float, and fish on the Salmon River. Be on the lookout for rattlesnakes.

13 Crags

 6

Location: In Salmon-Challis National Forest; map ID3, grid h2.

Campsites, facilities: There are 11 RV or tent campsites. Vault toilets and water are available.

Reservations, fees: No reservations are needed; the fee is $5 per night. Open July 1–October 15.

Directions: From Cobalt, go nine miles southwest on Forest Service Road 60055, then seven miles northwest on Forest Service Road 112 and 13 miles north on Forest Service Road 114 to the campground.

Contact: Salmon-Challis National Forest, Route 2, Box 600, Salmon ID 83467; 208/756-5100.

Trip notes: You can fish and hike in the national forest.

Alpine meadow

WAYNE SCHERR

MAP ID4

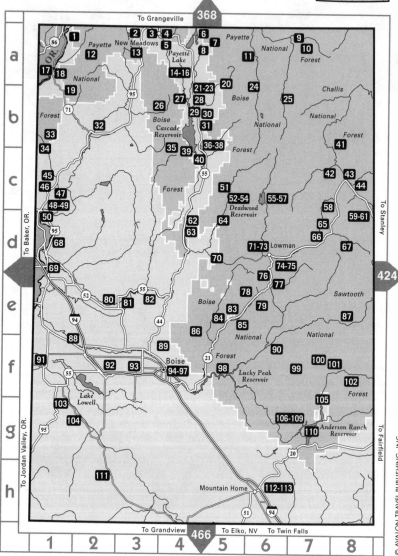

CHAPTER ID4

1	Copperfield Park	392
2	Cold Springs	392
3	Meadows RV Park	393
4	Zim's Hot Springs	393
5	Pinehurst Resort	393
6	Upper Payette Lake	393
7	Lake Fork	394
8	Ponderosa State Park	394
9	Yellow Pine	394
10	Golden Gate	394
11	Buckhorn Bar	395
12	Lafferty	395
13	Evergreen	395
14	Lakeview Village	395
15	McCall Campground	396
16	Murph's RV Park	396
17	McCormick Park	396
18	Woodhead Park	396
19	Brownlee	397
20	Kennally Creek	397
21	Mountain View RV Park	397
22	Southwestern Idaho Senior Citizens Recreation Association	398
23	Westside RV Park	398
24	Shoreline	398
25	Pen Basin	398
26	Cabin Creek	399
27	Canyon Creek	399
28	Amanita	399
29	Poison Creek	399
30	West Mountain	399
31	Rainbow Point	400
32	Frontier Motel & RV Park	400
33	Spring Creek	400
34	Paradise/Justrite	400
35	Big Flat	401
36	Water's Edge RV Resort	401
37	Pinewood Lodge-Motel-RV Park & Storage	401
38	Warm Lake Lodge	401
39	French Creek	402
40	Arrowhead RV Park on the River	402
41	Boundary Creek	402
42	Bear Valley	402
43	Lola Creek	403
44	Beaver Creek	403
45	Mann Creek Campground	403
46	Steck	403
47	Indian Hot Springs	404
48	Monroe Creek Campground	404
49	Indianhead Motel & RV Park	404
50	Gateway RV Park	404
51	Silver Creek Plunge	404
52	Silver Creek	405
53	Trail Creek	405
54	Rattlesnake	405
55	Riverside	405
56	Hower's	406
57	Cozy Cove	406
58	Bull Trout Lake	406
59	Stanley Lake	407
60	Lakeview	407
61	Salmon River	407
62	Big Eddy	407
63	Swinging Bridge	408
64	Tie Creek	408
65	Bonneville	408
66	Helende	408
67	Grandjean	409
68	Lazy River RV Park	409
69	Neat Retreat	409
70	Hot Springs	409
71	Park Creek	410
72	New Haven Lodge	410
73	Pine Flats	410
74	Mountain View	410

(continues)

(continues)

75 Kirkham Hot Springs.......411
76 Edna Creek...................411
77 Hayfork.........................411
78 Bad Bear.......................411
79 Ten Mile........................412
80 Holiday Motel & RV 412
81 Capital Mobile Park.........412
82 Montour Wildlife Area.....412
83 Warm Springs Resort......413
84 Grayback Gulch 413
85 Black Rock 413
86 Shafer Butte 413
87 Power Plant 414
88 Caldwell Campground
       & RV Park.....................414
89 Hi Valley RV Park............414
90 Ninemeyer.....................414
91 Snake River RV Resort.....415
92 Mason Creek RV Park 415
93 The Playground
       Sports & RV Park 415
94 On the River RV Park 416

95 Americana Kampground .416
96 Fiesta RV Park 416
97 Mountain View RV Park .417
98 Willow Creek...............417
99 Big Roaring River Lake
       and Big Trinity Lake 417
100 Chaparral...................417
101 Abbot 418
102 Baumgartner 418
103 River Haven RV Park 418
104 Given's Hot Springs 418
105 Dog Creek 419
106 Deer Creek Lodge.........419
107 Anderson Ranch Reservoir
        Campgrounds..............419
108 Nester's Riverside
        Campground 420
109 Pine Resort.................420
110 Fall Creek Resort
        and Marina 420
111 Silver City Lodgings......420
112 Mountain Home KOA.....421
113 The Wagon Wheel.........421

1 Copperfield Park

      6

Location: In Hells Canyon; map ID4, grid a1.
Campsites, facilities: There are 62 RV and 10 tent campsites, some with hookups and pull-through sites. Wheelchair-accessible restrooms, water, showers, and a sanitary disposal station are available.
Reservations, fees: Reservations are strongly suggested; the fee is $10 and up per night. Open March 1–October 31.
Directions: From Weiser, go 31 miles north on U.S. 95 to Cambridge. From Cambridge, take Highway 71 northwest for about 60 miles to the park.
Contact: Idaho Power, 1221 W. Idaho St., P.O. Box 70, Boise, ID 83707; 208/388-2231 or 800/422-3143; website: www.idahopower.com.

Trip notes: Call the 24-hour toll-free recreation information line, 800/422-3143, for up-to-date messages about parks, reservoir levels, and water flows, as conditions do vary. You can hike, boat, and fish here for steelhead, rainbow trout, Chinook salmon, sturgeon, and smallmouth bass.

2 Cold Springs

   5

Location: In New Meadows; map ID4, grid a3.
Campsites, facilities: There are five RV or tent campsites, which can accommodate a maximum RV length of 22 feet. Vault toilets and water are available. Pets are allowed on leashes.
Reservations, fees: No reservations are needed; the fee is $5–8 per night. Open May 1–October 31.

Directions: From Grangeville, go south on U.S. 95 78 miles to New Meadows. From New Meadows, go eight miles southwest on U.S. 95, then 2.5 miles west on Forest Service Road 089 and one mile west on Forest Service Road 50091. From Banks, go 9.5 miles north on Highway 55.

Contact: Payette National Forest, New Meadows Ranger District, P.O. Box J, New Meadows, ID 83654; 208/347-2141 or 208/365-7000.

Trip notes: You can boat and fish here.

3 Meadows RV Park

   6

Location: Near New Meadows; map ID4, grid a3.

Campsites, facilities: There are 37 RV or tent campsites, some with hookups. Pull-through sites, showers, laundry facilities, and a sanitary disposal station are available. Pets are allowed on leashes.

Reservations, fees: Reservations are accepted; the fee is $10–15 per night. Open April 15–October 31.

Directions: From Grangeville, go south on U.S. 95 78 miles to New Meadows. From New Meadows, go 2.5 miles east on Highway 55 to the RV park.

Contact: Meadows RV Park, P.O. Box 60, New Meadows, ID 83654; 208/347-2325.

Trip notes: The Payette National Forest, where you can fish, hike, view wildlife, and explore, surrounds the Meadows Valley.

4 Zim's Hot Springs

 5

Location: Near New Meadows; map ID4, grid a4.

Campsites, facilities: There are 12 RV or tent campsites, some with hookups. Wheelchair-accessible restrooms, showers, swimming pool, and a sanitary disposal facility are available. Pets are allowed on leashes.

Reservations, fees: No reservations are needed; the fee is $10 per night. Open May–October.

Directions: New Meadows is 78 miles south of Grangeville on U.S. 95. The hot springs is four miles north of New Meadows on U.S. 95.

Contact: Zim's Hot Springs, P.O. Box 314, New Meadows, ID 83654; 208/347-2686.

Trip notes: The Payette National Forest, where you can fish, hike, view wildlife, and explore, surrounds the Meadows Valley.

5 Pinehurst Resort

     4

Location: In New Meadows; map ID4, grid a4.

Campsites, facilities: There are 10 RV or tent campsites, some with hookups. Propane gas is available. Pets are allowed on leashes.

Reservations, fees: Reservations are accepted; the fee is $40–60 per night.

Directions: From Grangeville, go 60 miles south on U.S. 95 (13 miles south of Riggins) to the resort on the left side of the highway.

Contact: Pinehurst Resort, 9604 Hwy. 95, New Meadows, ID 83654; 208/628-3323.

Trip notes: The Payette National Forest, where you can fish, hike, view wildlife, and explore, surrounds the Meadows Valley.

6 Upper Payette Lake

      6

Location: In Payette National Forest; map ID4, grid a4.

Campsites, facilities: There are nine RV or tent campsites, which can accommodate a maximum RV length of 22 feet. Pull-through sites, vault toilets, and water are available. Pets are allowed on leashes.

Reservations, fees: No reservations are needed; the fee is $6–10 per night. Open June 20–October 1.

Directions: From Cascade, go 28 miles north on Highway 55 to McCall. From McCall, go 18.5 miles north on

Forest Service Road 21 to the lake.

Contact: Payette National Forest, McCall Ranger District, P.O. Box 1026, McCall, ID 83638; 208/634-0417.

Trip notes: You can boat, fish, swim, and hike here.

7 Lake Fork

 5

Location: In Payette National Forest; map ID4, grid a5.

Campsites, facilities: There are nine RV or tent campsites, which can accommodate a maximum RV length of 22 feet. Vault toilets and water are available. Pets are allowed on leashes.

Reservations, fees: No reservations are needed; the fee is $4 per night. Open June 15–October 15.

Directions: From Cascade, go 28 miles north on Highway 55 to McCall. From McCall, go 9.5 miles east on Forest Service Road 48 to the campground.

Contact: Payette National Forest, McCall Ranger District, P.O. Box 1026, McCall, ID 83638; 208/634-0417.

Trip notes: You can hike and fish here.

8 Ponderosa State Park

 6

Location: Northeast of McCall; map ID4, grid a4.

Campsites, facilities: There are 170 RV or tent campsites, which can accommodate a maximum RV length of 35 feet; some are pull-through sites. Showers, accessible restrooms, water, and a sanitary disposal facility are available.

Reservations, fees: No reservations are needed; the fee is $5–15 per night. Open May 20–October 15.

Directions: From Cascade, go 28 miles north on Highway 55 to McCall. From McCall, go 1.5 miles northeast to the campground.

Contact: Ponderosa State Park, Miles Standish Rd., McCall, ID 83638; 208/634-2164.

Trip notes: You can hike, boat, fish, and swim here.

9 Yellow Pine

 6

Location: In Boise National Forest; map ID4, grid a7.

Campsites, facilities: There are 14 RV or tent campsites, which can accommodate a maximum RV length of 22 feet. Vault toilets and water are available.

Reservations, fees: No reservations are needed; there is no fee. Open June 1–October 15.

Directions: From McCall, go east to Yellow Pine. From Yellow Pine, go one mile south on Forest Service Road 413 to the campground.

Contact: Boise National Forest, Cascade Ranger District, P.O. Box 696, Cascade, ID 83611; 208/382-7400.

Trip notes: You can fish and hike in Boise National Forest.

10 Golden Gate

 6

Location: In Boise National Forest; map ID4, grid a7.

Campsites, facilities: There are nine RV or tent campsites, which can accommodate a maximum RV length of 22 feet. A vault toilet is available.

Reservations, fees: No reservations are needed, and no fee is charged. Open June 1–October 15.

Directions: From McCall, go east to Yellow Pine. From Yellow Pine, go two miles south on Forest Service Road 413 to the campground.

Contact: Boise National Forest, Cascade Ranger District, P.O. Box 696, Cascade, ID 83611; 208/382-7400.

Trip notes: You can fish and hike in Boise National Forest.

11 Buckhorn Bar

 5

Location: In Payette National Forest; map ID4, grid a6.

Campsites, facilities: There are 15 RV or tent campsites, which can accommodate a maximum RV length of 45 feet. Wheelchair-accessible restrooms are available. Pets are allowed on leashes.

Reservations, fees: No reservations are needed; the fee is $4 per night. Open June 1– September 15.

Directions: From Cascade, go 28 miles north on Highway 55 to McCall. From McCall, go 39 miles northeast on Forest Service Road 48, then 7.5 miles south on Forest Service Road 674 to the campground.

Contact: Payette National Forest, McCall Ranger District, P.O. Box 1026, McCall, ID 83638; 208/634-0417.

Trip notes: You can fish and swim here.

12 Lafferty

 6

Location: In Payette National Forest; map ID4, grid a2.

Campsites, facilities: There are eight RV or tent campsites, which can accommodate a maximum RV length of 16 feet. Vault toilets, pull-through sites, and water are available. Pets are allowed on leashes.

Reservations, fees: No reservations are needed; the fee is $4 per night. Open May 25– October 31

Directions: From Council, go 24 miles northwest on Forest Service Road 002 to the campground.

Contact: Payette National Forest, P.O. Box 567, 500 E. Whitley, Council, Idaho 83612; 208/253-0100.

Trip notes: You can hike and fish in the Payette National Forest.

13 Evergreen

 6

Location: In Payette National Forest; map ID4, grid a3.

Campsites, facilities: There are 12 RV or tent campsites, which can accommodate a maximum RV length of 22 feet. Vault toilets and water are available. Pets are allowed on leashes.

Reservations, fees: No reservations are needed; the fee is $5 per night. Open June 1– September 10.

Directions: From Council, go 14 miles north on U.S. 95 to the campground.

Contact: Payette National Forest, P.O. Box 567, 500 E. Whitley, Council, Idaho 83612; 208/253-0100.

Trip notes: You can hike and fish in the Payette National Forest.

14 Lakeview Village

 5

Location: In McCall; map ID4, grid a4.

Campsites, facilities: There are 84 RV or tent campsites, some with hookups. Wheelchair-accessible restrooms, laundry facilities, showers, propane gas, and a sanitary disposal station are available. Pets are allowed on leashes.

Reservations, fees: No reservations are needed; the fee is $13.50–16 per night. Open May–November.

Directions: From Grangeville, go south on U.S. 95 78 miles to New Meadows. From New Meadows, go south on Highway 55 to the McCall exit, go east, turn on Railroad Avenue. Follow the winding road to the next stop sign, turn right, and continue to the next stop. Turn left on Davis, and follow Davis to the campground, at the Y in the road.

Contact: Lakeview Village, #1 Pearl St., P.O. Box 8, McCall, ID 83638; 208/634-5280.

Trip notes: You can boat, fish, swim, and hike in the Payette National Forest and Payette Lake.

15 McCall Campground

 5

Location: In McCall; map ID4, grid a4.

Campsites, facilities: There are 36 RV or tent campsites, some with hookups. Laundry facilities, showers, propane gas, and a sanitary disposal station are available. Pets are allowed on leashes.

Reservations, fees: No reservations are needed; the fee is $13.25–15.75 per night. Open year-round.

Directions: From Cascade, Payette Lake is 29 miles north on Highway. From Payette Lake, go 1.5 miles south on Highway 55 to the campground.

Contact: McCall Campground, 190 Krahn Lane, McCall, ID 83638; 208/634-5165.

Trip notes: You can boat, fish, swim, and hike in the Payette National Forest.

16 Murph's RV Park

 4

Location: South of McCall; map ID4, grid a4.

Campsites, facilities: There are 22 RV or tent campsites, some with hookups. Laundry facilities, showers, and a restaurant are available. Pets are allowed on leashes.

Reservations, fees: Reservations are accepted; the fee is $15 per night. Open summer only.

Directions: From Cascade go 23 miles north on Highway 55 to Lake Fork. From Lake Fork, go .25 mile northeast on Big Creek/Stignite Road to the RV park.

Contact: Murph's RV Park, P.O. Box 684, Lakefork, ID 83635; 208/634-5527.

Trip notes: You can boat, fish, swim, and hike in the Payette National Forest and at Payette Lake.

17 McCormick Park

 5

Location: In Hells Canyon Recreation Area; map ID4, grid a1.

Campsites, facilities: There are 34 RV or tent campsites, which can accommodate a maximum RV length of 30 feet. Wheelchair-accessible restrooms, showers, water, hookups and a sanitary disposal station are available.

Reservations, fees: Reservations are strongly suggested. Open March 1–October 31.

Directions: From Weiser, go 31 miles north on U.S. 95 to Cambridge. From Cambridge, take Highway 71 toward Brownlee Dam; take a right just before crossing the Snake River Bridge; the campground is a half mile north.

Contact: Idaho Power, 1221 W. Idaho St., P.O. Box 70, Boise, ID 83707; 208/388-2231 or 800/422-3143; website: www.idahopower.com. Hells Canyon National Recreation Area, P.O. Box 832, Riggins, ID 83549; 208/628-3916.

Trip notes: Call the 24-hour toll-free recreation information line (800/422-3143) for up-to-date messages about parks, reservoir levels, and water flows, as conditions do vary. You can hike, boat, and fish here for steelhead, rainbow trout, Chinook salmon, sturgeon, and smallmouth bass.

18 Woodhead Park

 6

Location: In Hells Canyon National Recreation Area; map ID4, grid a1.

Campsites, facilities: There are RV or tent campsites, some with hookups. Wheelchair-accessible restrooms, water, showers, and a sanitary disposal facility are available. Pets are allowed on leashes.

Reservations, fees: Reservations are strongly suggested; the fee is $10 and up per night. Open March 1–October 31. Call the 24-hour toll-free recreation information line, 800/422-3143, for up-to-date messages about parks, reservoir levels, and water flows, as conditions do vary.

Directions: From Weiser, go 31 miles north on U.S. 95 to Cambridge. From Cambridge, take Highway 71 toward Brownlee Dam; the campground is a half mile before you get to the dam.

Contact: Idaho Power, 1221 W. Idaho St., P.O. Box 70, Boise, ID 83707; 208/388-2231 or 800/422-3143; website: www.idahopower.com. Hells Canyon National Recreation Area, P.O. Box 832, Riggins, ID 83549; 208/628-3916.

Trip notes: Call the 24-hour toll-free recreation information line (800/422-3143) for up-to-date messages about parks, reservoir levels, and water flows, as conditions do vary. You can hike, boat, and fish here for steelhead, rainbow trout, Chinook salmon, sturgeon, and smallmouth bass.

19 Brownlee

 6

Location: In Hells Canyon National Recreation Area; map ID4, grid b1.

Campsites, facilities: There are 11 RV or tent campsites, which can accommodate a maximum RV length of 16 feet. Vault toilets and water are available. Pets are allowed on leashes.

Reservations, fees: No reservations are needed; the fee is $4 per night. Open May 15–October 31.

Directions: From Weiser, go 31 miles north on U.S. 95 to Cambridge. From Cambridge, go 16.6 miles northwest on Highway 71, then one mile east on Forest Service Road 044 to the campground.

Contact: Idaho Power, 1221 W. Idaho St., P.O. Box 70, Boise, ID 83707; 208/388-2231 or 800/422-3143; website: www.idahopower.com. Hells Canyon National Recreation Area, P.O. Box 832, Riggins, ID 83549; 208/628-3916.

Trip notes: Call the 24-hour toll-free recreation information line (800/422-3143) for up-to-date messages about parks, reservoir levels, and water flows, as conditions do vary. You can hike, boat, and fish here for steelhead, rainbow trout, Chinook salmon, sturgeon, and smallmouth bass.

20 Kennally Creek

 5

Location: In Boise National Forest; map ID4, grid a5.

Campsites, facilities: There are 10 RV or tent campsites, which can accommodate a maximum RV length of 22 feet. There are vault toilets and water available. Pets are allowed on leashes.

Reservations, fees: No reservations are needed; the fee is $4 per night. Open June 1–October 15.

Directions: From Cascade go 16 miles north on Highway 55 to Donnelly. From Donnelly, go three miles north on Highway 55, then 17 miles east on Forest Service Road 388 to the campground.

Contact: Boise National Forest, Cascade Ranger District, Hwy. 55, P.O. Box 696, Cascade, ID 83611; 208/382-7400 or 208/634-1453.

Trip notes: You can hike and fish here.

21 Mountain View RV Park

 5

Location: In Donnelly at the north end of Cascade Lake; map ID4, grid b4.

Campsites, facilities: There are 40 RV or tent campsites, some with hookups. Laundry facilities, showers, and a sanitary disposal station are available. Pets are allowed on leashes.

Reservations, fees: No reservations are needed; the fee is $15–55 per night.

Directions: From Cascade, go 14 miles north on Highway 55 to the campground.

Contact: Mountain View RV Park, P.O. Box 488, Donnelly, ID 83615; 208/325-8373.

Trip notes: There is a public boat dock and campground at the north end of Cascade Lake, and you can fish and boat there.

22 Southwestern Idaho Senior Citizens Recreation Association

 5

Location: In Donnelly; map ID4, grid b4.

Campsites, facilities: There are 175 RV or tent campsites, some with hookups. Showers, accessible restrooms, and a sanitary disposal station are available. Pets are allowed on leashes.

Reservations, fees: No reservations are needed; the fee is $3–5 per night.

Directions: From Highway 55 going north, turn left at Loomis Lane (the road after Gold Fork Road), then follow the signs to the campground.

Contact: Southwestern Idaho Senior Citizens Recreation Association, P.O. Box 625, Donnelly, ID 83615; 208/325-8130.

Trip notes: There is a public boat dock and campground at the north end of Cascade Lake, and you can fish and boat there.

23 Westside RV Park

 5

Location: In Donnelly; map ID4, grid b5.

Campsites, facilities: There are 43 RV or tent campsites, some with hookups. Wheelchair-accessible restrooms, laundry facilities, showers, propane gas, and a sanitary disposal station. Pets are allowed on leashes.

Reservations, fees: No reservations are needed; the fee is $15 per night. Open May 1–October 31.

Directions: From Highway 55, go a half mile west on Roseberry Road to the campground.

Contact: Westside RV Park, P.O. Box 648, Donnelly, ID 83615; 208/325-4100.

Trip notes: There is a public boat dock and campground at the north end of Cascade Lake, and you can fish and boat there.

24 Shoreline

 5

Location: In Boise National Forest; map ID4, grid a6.

Campsites, facilities: There are 25 RV or tent campsites, which can accommodate a maximum RV length of 40 feet. Pull-through sites, vault toilets, and water are available.

Reservations, fees: Reservations are accepted; the fee is $8 per night. Open May 15–September 15.

Directions: From Cascade, go one mile north on Highway 55, then 24 miles northeast on Forest Service Road FH 22 and one mile southwest on Forest Service Road 489 to the campground.

Contact: Boise National Forest, Cascade Ranger District, Hwy. 55, P.O. Box 696, Cascade, ID 83611; 208/382-4271 or 208/382-7400.

Trip notes: You can boat, fish, and swim here.

25 Pen Basin

 6

Location: In Boise National Forest; map ID4, grid b6.

Campsites, facilities: There are six RV or tent campsites, which can accommodate a maximum RV length of 22 feet. A vault toilet is available.

Reservations, fees: No reservations are needed, and no fee is charged. Open June 1–October 15.

Directions: From McCall, go east to Yellow Pine. From Yellow Pine, go 30 miles south on Forest Service Road 413, then three miles south on Forest Service Road 579 to the campground.

Contact: Boise National Forest, Cascade Ranger District, P.O. Box 696, Cascade, ID 83611; 208/382-7400.

Trip notes: You can fish and hike in Boise National Forest.

26 Cabin Creek

 5

Location: In Boise National Forest; map ID4, grid b3.

Campsites, facilities: There are 12 RV or tent campsites, which can accommodate a maximum RV length of 22 feet. Vault toilets and water are available. Pets are allowed on leashes.

Reservations, fees: No reservations are needed; the fee is $5 per night. Open May 25–October 31.

Directions: From Council, go four miles south on U.S. 95, then 10 miles east on Forest Service Road 186 to the campground.

Contact: Boise National Forest, Cascade Ranger District, Hwy. 55, P.O. Box 696, Cascade, ID 83611; 208/382-7400 or 208/634-1453.

Trip notes: You can fish and hike here.

27 Canyon Creek

 5

Location: In Boise National Forest; map ID4, grid b4.

Campsites, facilities: There are seven RV or tent campsites, which can accommodate a maximum RV length of 22 feet. Vault toilets and water are available. Pets are allowed on leashes.

Reservations, fees: No reservations are needed; the fee is $8 per night. Open May 15–November 1.

Directions: From Boise go 42 miles north on Highway 55 to Banks. From Banks, go nine miles north on Highway 55.

Contact: Boise National Forest, 1805 Hwy. 16, #5, Emmett, ID 83617; 208/365-7000.

Trip notes: You can hike and fish in Boise National Forest.

28 Amanita

 5

Location: Boise National Forest; map ID4, grid b4.

Campsites, facilities: There are 10 RV or tent campsites, which can accommodate a maximum RV length of 22 feet. Wheelchair-accessible restrooms, water, and a swimming pool are available.

Reservations, fees: Reservations are accepted; the fee is $8 per night. Open May 15–September 15.

Directions: From Cascade go 16 miles north on Highway 55 to Donnelly. From Donnelly, go 4.8 miles southwest on Forest Road 422 to the campground.

Contact: Boise National Forest, Cascade Ranger District, Hwy. 55, P.O. Box 696, Cascade, ID 83611; 208/382-7400.

Trip notes: You can hike and fish in Boise National Forest.

29 Poison Creek

 6

Location: At Cascade Reservoir; map ID4, grid b4.

Campsites, facilities: There are 44 RV or tent campsites, which can accommodate a maximum RV length of 32 feet. Pull-through sites, accessible restrooms, and water are available. Pets are allowed on leashes.

Reservations, fees: No reservations are needed; the fee is $9 per night. Open May 15–October 15.

Directions: From Cascade, go 23.5 miles north on Forest Service Road 422 to the campground on the west side of Cascade Reservoir.

Contact: Poison Creek State Park, P.O. Box 709, Cascade, ID 83611; 208/382-4258.

Trip notes: You can hike, boat, fish, and swim here.

30 West Mountain

 6

Location: At Cascade Reservoir; map ID4, grid b5.

Campsites, facilities: There are 36 RV or tent campsites, which can accommodate a maximum RV length of 32 feet. Wheelchair-accessible restrooms, water, pull-through sites, and a sanitary disposal facility are available. Pets are allowed on leashes.

Reservations, fees: No reservations are needed; the fee is $9 per night. Open May 15–September 10.

Directions: From Cascade, go 23 miles north and the campground is on the west side of Cascade Reservoir.

Contact: West Mountain State Park; P.O. Box 709, Cascade, ID 83611; 208/382-4258.

Trip notes: You can fish, boat, hike, and swim here.

31 Rainbow Point

 5

Location: In Boise National Forest; map ID4, grid b5.

Campsites, facilities: There are 12 RV or tent campsites, which can accommodate a maximum RV length of 35 feet. Wheelchair-accessible restrooms and water are available.

Reservations, fees: Reservations are accepted; the fee is $10 per night. Open May 15 though September 15.

Directions: From Cascade go 16 miles north on Highway 55 to Donnelly. From Donnelly, go 4.7 miles southwest on County Road 422 to the campground.

Contact: Boise National Forest, Cascade Ranger District, Hwy. 55, P.O. Box 696, Cascade, ID 83611; 208/382-4271 or 208/382-7400.

Trip notes: You can boat and fish here.

32 Frontier Motel & RV Park

 5

Location: In Cambridge; map ID4, grid b2.

Campsites, facilities: There are nine RV campsites, some with hookups. Laundry facilities, showers, and a sanitary disposal station are available. Pets are allowed on leashes.

Reservations, fees: Reservations are suggested; the fee is $5–15 per night.

Directions: From Weiser, go 30 miles north on U.S. 95 to Cambridge; it's on the left.

Contact: Frontier Motel & RV Park, 240 Superior St., P.O. Box 178, Cambridge, ID 83610; 208/257-3851.

Trip notes: You can hike and fish in the area.

33 Spring Creek

 5

Location: Payette National Forest; map ID4, grid b1.

Campsites, facilities: There are 14 RV or tent campsites, which can accommodate a maximum RV length of 45 feet. Vault toilets and water are available. Pets are allowed on leashes.

Reservations, fees: No reservations are needed; the fee is $5–10 per night. Open June 1–October 31.

Directions: From Weiser, go 12.5 miles north on U.S. 95, then 11.5 miles north on the county road and Forest Service Road 009 to the campground.

Contact: Payette National Forest, Weiser Ranger District, 275 E. 7th St., Weiser, ID 83672; 208/549-4200.

Trip notes: You can fish and hike here.

34 Paradise/Justrite

 5

Location: In Payette National Forest; map ID4, grid c1.

Campsites, facilities: There are eight RV or tent campsites, which can accommodate a maximum RV length of 20 feet. Vault toilets are provided. Pets are allowed on leashes.

Reservations, fees: No reservations are needed; the fee is $5–10 per night. Open June 1–October 31.

Directions: From Weiser, go 12.5 miles north on U.S. 95, then 13 miles northwest on the county road and Forest Road 009 to the campground.

Contact: Payette National Forest, Weiser Ranger District, 275 E. 7th St., Weiser, ID 83672; 208/549-4200.

Trip notes: You can hike and fish in Payette National Forest.

35 Big Flat

 5

Location: In Payette National Forest; map ID4, grid b4.

Campsites, facilities: There are 13 RV or tent campsites, which can accommodate a maximum RV length of 45 feet. Wheelchair-accessible restrooms and water are available.

Reservations, fees: No reservations are needed; the fee is $5 per night. Open May 30–October 31.

Directions: From Council, go 12 miles south on U.S. 95, then 14 miles southeast and east on Forest Service Road 50206.

Contact: Payette National Forest, P.O. Box 567, 500 E. Whitley, Council, ID 83612; 208/253-0100.

Trip notes: You can hike and fish here.

36 Water's Edge RV Resort

 5

Location: In Cascade; map ID4, grid b5.

Campsites, facilities: There are 91 RV or tent campsites, some with hookups. Pull-through sites, accessible restrooms, laundry facilities, showers, and propane gas are available. Pets are allowed on leashes.

Reservations, fees: No reservations are needed; the fee is $18 per night. Open May–October.

Directions: This campground is at the north end of Cascade, off Highway 55 at Payette River Bridge.

Contact: Water's Edge RV Resort, P.O. Box 1018, Cascade, ID 83611; 208/382-3120, 800/574-2038, fax 208/382-3035.

Trip notes: This campground is .25 mile from Cascade Lake. Kayaks and canoes are free for guests' use on the Payette River. You can fish, watch birds, golf, and play tennis here.

37 Pinewood Lodge-Motel-RV Park & Storage

 4

Location: In Cascade; map ID4, grid b5.

Campsites, facilities: There are 12 RV or tent campsites, some with hookups. Showers and a sanitary disposal station are available. Pets are allowed on leashes.

Reservations, fees: Reservations are suggested; the fee is $15–18.50 per night. Open May 15–October 30.

Directions: From Boise, travel north on Highway 55 for 74 miles to Cascade. The RV park is the first place on the right as you enter town.

Contact: Pinewood Lodge-Motel-RV Park & Storage, P.O. Box 745, Cascade, ID 83611; 208/382-4948.

Trip notes: You can fish and boat on Cascade Lake.

38 Warm Lake Lodge

 5

Location: In Cascade; map ID4, grid b5.

Campsites, facilities: There are seven RV or tent campsites. Wheelchair-accessible restrooms, laundry facilities, showers, propane gas, a restaurant, and sanitary disposal station are available.

Reservations, fees: No reservations are needed; the fee is $15 per night.

Directions: Cascade is 72 miles north of Boise on Highway 55. From Cascade, drive 26 miles east on Warm Lake Road to the campground.

Contact: Warm Lake Lodge, P.O. Box 450, Cascade, ID 83611; 800/632-3553.

Trip notes: You can fish and boat on Cascade Lake.

39 French Creek

 5

Location: In Boise National Forest; map ID4, grid c4.

Campsites, facilities: There are 21 RV or tent campsites, which can accommodate a maximum RV length of 30 feet. The campground has vault toilets and water.

Reservations, fees: Reservations are suggested; the fee is $10 per night. Open May 15–September 15.

Directions: From Cascade, drive four miles south on Forest Service Road 3898, then five miles west and north on Forest Service Road 422 to the campground.

Contact: Boise National Forest, Cascade Ranger District, Hwy. 55, P.O. Box 696, Cascade, ID 83611; 208/382-4271 or 208/382-7400.

Trip notes: You can boat and fish here.

40 Arrowhead RV Park on the River

 5

Location: In Cascade; map ID4, grid c4.

Campsites, facilities: There are 110 RV or tent campsites, some with hookups. Wheelchair-accessible restrooms, laundry facilities, showers, propane gas, a sanitary disposal station, and a fitness center are available. Pets are allowed on leashes.

Reservations, fees: No reservations are needed; the fee is $16.75–27 per night. Open April 1–November 1.

Directions: Cascade is 72 miles north of Boise on scenic Highway 55. The park is 1.5 miles south of Cascade.

Contact: Arrowhead RV Park on the River, P.O. Box 337, Cascade, ID 83611; 208/382-4534 or 208/375-2961.

Trip notes: This campground is one mile from the lake, and activities on site include archery, horseshoes, and woodcarving.

41 Boundary Creek

 7

Location: In Frank Church–River of No Return Wilderness Area; map ID4, grid b8.

Campsites, facilities: There are four RV or tent campsites, which can accommodate a maximum RV length of 22 feet. Vault toilets and water are available. Pets are allowed on leashes.

Reservations, fees: No reservations are needed; the fee is $5 per night. Open June 15–September 10.

Directions: From Challis, go south on Highway 75 52 miles to Stanley. From Stanley, drive 20 miles northwest on Highway 21, then 11 miles west on Fir Creek Road 198 and 13 miles north on Boundary Creek Road 668 to the campground.

Contact: Salmon-Challis National Forest, Middle Fork Ranger District, Hwy. 93 North, P.O. Box 750, Challis, ID 83226; 208/879-4101.

Trip notes: You can fish and hike here. Boundary Creek is popular with whitewater rafters.

42 Bear Valley

 6

Location: In Boise National Forest; map ID4, grid c7.

Campsites, facilities: There are 10 RV or tent campsites, which can accommodate a maximum RV length of 22 feet. A vault toilet is available. Pets are allowed on leashes.

Reservations, fees: No reservations are needed; there is no fee charged. Open July 1–September 30.

Directions: From Challis, go south on Highway 75 52 miles to Stanley, northwest on Highway 21 to the Cape Horn Turnoff, then 12 miles north on Cape Horn Turnoff to the campground. From Lowman, 33 miles east of Banks, go 36 miles northeast on Highway 21 to the Cape Horn Turnoff, and then north 12 miles to the campground.

Contact: Boise National Forest, Lowman

Ranger District, Hwy. 21, HC 77, P.O. Box 3020, Lowman, ID 83637; 208/259-3361.

Trip notes: You can fish and hike in Boise National Forest.

43 Lola Creek

 5

Location: In Salmon-Challis National Forest; map ID4, grid c8.

Campsites, facilities: There are 27 RV or tent campsites, which can accommodate a maximum RV length of 16 feet. Vault toilets and water are available.

Reservations, fees: No reservations are needed; the fee is $5 per night. Open June 15–September 15.

Directions: From Challis, go south on Highway 75 52 miles to Stanley. From Stanley, drive 17 miles northwest on Highway 21, then one mile northwest on Forest Service Road 083 to the campground.

Contact: Salmon-Challis National Forest, Yankee Fork Ranger District, Hwy. 75, HC 67, P.O. Box 650, Clayton, ID 83227; 208/838-2201.

Trip notes: You can fish and hike in Salmon-Challis National Forest.

44 Beaver Creek

 6

Location: In Salmon-Challis National Forest; map ID4, grid c8.

Campsites, facilities: There are 10 RV or tent campsites, which can accommodate a maximum RV length of 32 feet. Pets are allowed on leashes.

Reservations, fees: No reservations are needed; the fee is $5 per night. Open June 15–September 10.

Directions: From Challis, go south on Highway 75 52 miles to Stanley. From Stanley, go 17 miles northwest on Highway 21, then three miles north on Beaver Creek Road 008 to the campground.

Contact: Salmon-Challis National Forest, Yankee Fork Ranger District, Hwy. 75, HC 67, P.O. Box 650, Clayton, ID 83227; 208/838-2201.

Trip notes: You can fish and hike in Salmon-Challis National Forest.

45 Mann Creek Campground

 5

Location: North of Weiser; map ID4, grid c1.

Campsites, facilities: There are 14 RV or tent campsites, which can accommodate a maximum RV length of 32 feet. Wheelchair-accessible restrooms are available. Pets are allowed on leashes.

Reservations, fees: No reservations are needed, and no fee is charged. Open April 1–October 30.

Directions: From Weiser, go 18 miles north on U.S. 95 to the campground.

Contact: Bureau of Land Management, Route 3, P.O. Box 1811, Cottonwood, ID 83522; 208/962-3245.

Trip notes: You can hike, fish, boat, and swim here.

46 Steck

 5

Location: West of Weiser; map ID4, grid c1.

Campsites, facilities: There are 23 RV or tent campsites, which can accommodate a maximum RV length of 25 feet. Wheelchair-accessible restrooms, vault toilets and water are available.

Reservations, fees: No reservations are needed, and no fee is charged. Open April 15–October 31.

Directions: From Weiser, drive 22 miles west on Olds Ferry Road to the campground.

Contact: Bureau of Land Management, Boise District Office, 3948 Development Ave., Boise, ID 83705; 208/384-3300.

Trip notes: You can hike, boat, and fish here.

47 Indian Hot Springs

 5

Location: Northwest of Weiser; map ID4, grid c1.

Campsites, facilities: There are 11 RV or tent campsites, some with hookups. Laundry facilities, showers, a sanitary disposal station, and a swimming pool are available. Pets are allowed on leashes.

Reservations, fees: No reservations are needed; the fee is $8–12 per night.

Directions: From Weiser, go six miles northwest to the campground.

Contact: Indian Hot Springs, 914 Hot Springs Rd., Weiser, ID 83672; 208/549-0070.

Trip notes: You can hike, boat, and fish here.

48 Monroe Creek Campground

 5

Location: Near Weiser; map ID4, grid c1.

Campsites, facilities: There are 66 RV or tent campsites, some with hookups. Wheelchair-accessible restrooms, laundry facilities, showers, and a sanitary disposal station are available. Pets are allowed on leashes.

Reservations, fees: No reservations are needed; the fee is $13–17.50 per night. Open April 1–November 15.

Directions: From Weiser, go 1.5 miles north on U.S. 95 to the campground.

Contact: Monroe Creek Campground, 822 U.S. 95, Weiser, ID 83672; 208/549-2026.

Trip notes: You can hike, boat, and fish here.

49 Indianhead Motel & RV Park

 5

Location: In Weiser; map ID4, grid c1.

Campsites, facilities: There are 12 RV or tent campsites, some with hookups. Showers and laundry facilities are available. Pets are allowed on leashes.

Reservations, fees: No reservations are needed; the fee is $20 per night. Open year-round.

Directions: From U.S. 95 at Weiser, drive south to the RV park at the intersection of U.S. 95 and Indianhead Road.

Contact: Indianhead Motel & RV Park, 747 U.S. 95, Weiser, ID 83672; 208/549-0331.

Trip notes: You can hike, boat, and fish here.

50 Gateway RV Park

 4

Location: In Weiser; map ID4, grid d1.

Campsites, facilities: There are 20 RV or tent campsites, some with hookups and pull-through sites. Showers are available. Pets are allowed on leashes.

Reservations, fees: Reservations are accepted; the fee is $14 per night. Open year-round.

Directions: In Weiser, at the U.S. 95 spur, go east on U.S. 95/East 7th Street to the RV park.

Contact: Gateway RV Park, 229 E. 7th St., Weiser, ID 83672; 208/549-2539.

Trip notes: You can hike, boat, and fish here.

51 Silver Creek Plunge

 6

Location: On Silver Creek; map ID4, grid c5.

Campsites, facilities: There are 200 RV or tent campsites, some with hookups. Propane gas, a sanitary disposal station, and a swimming pool are available. Pets are allowed on leashes.

Reservations, fees: No reservations are needed; the fee is $10 per night. Open June 1–September 30.

Directions: From Boise, take Highway 55 north to Banks and turn right to Garden Valley, toward Lowman on the Banks-Lowman Road. Turn left onto the Middle Fork Road and go one mile to Crouch. Go through Crouch, and head north on the Middle Fork Road for approximately 22 miles to Silver Creek Plunge, follow signs.

Contact: Silver Creek Plunge, 2334 Silver Creek Rd., Garden Valley, ID 83622; 208/870-0586; website: www.silvercreekplunge.com.

Trip notes: Silver Creek runs through this campground, and you can fish for stocked rainbow trout.

52 Silver Creek

 6

Location: In Payette National Forest; map ID4, grid c5.

Campsites, facilities: There are five RV or tent campsites, which can accommodate a maximum RV length of 22 feet. Vault toilets and water are available. Pets are allowed on leashes.

Reservations, fees: No reservations are needed; the fee is $7–10 per night. Open June 1–September 30.

Directions: From Boise, take Highway 55 north 42 miles to Banks and turn right to Garden Valley on Banks-Lowman Road. From Garden Valley, go 10 miles east on Banks-Lowman Road, then 19 miles north on Forest Service Road 698 and seven miles northeast on Forest Service Road 671.

Contact: Payette National Forest, New Meadows Ranger District, P.O. Box J, New Meadows, ID 83654; 208/347-2141 or 208/365-7000.

Trip notes: You can fish and hike here.

53 Trail Creek

 5

Location: In Payette National Forest; map ID4, grid c5.

Campsites, facilities: There are 11 RV or tent campsites, which can accommodate a maximum RV length of 22 feet. Vault toilets are available. Pets are allowed on leashes.

Reservations, fees: No reservations are needed; the fee is $7–10 per night. Open May 15–September 30.

Directions: From Boise, take Highway 55 north 42 miles to Banks and turn right to Garden

Valley on Banks-Lowman Road. From Garden Valley, go 10 miles east on Banks-Lowman Road, then 19 miles north on Forest Service Road 698.

Contact: Payette National Forest, New Meadows Ranger District, P.O. Box J, New Meadows, ID 83654; 208/347-2141 or 208/365-7000.

Trip notes: You can hike and fish in Payette National Forest.

54 Rattlesnake

 5

Location: In Payette National Forest; map ID4, grid c5.

Campsites, facilities: There are seven RV or tent campsites, which can accommodate a maximum RV length of 22 feet. Vault toilets are available. Pets are allowed on leashes.

Reservations, fees: No reservations are needed; the fee is $7–10 per night. Open May 15–September 30

Directions: From Boise, take Highway 55 north 42 miles to Banks and turn right to Garden Valley on Banks-Lowman Road. From Garden Valley, go 10 miles east on Banks-Lowman Road, then 18 miles north on Forest Service Road 698.

Contact: Payette National Forest, New Meadows Ranger District, P.O. Box J, New Meadows, ID 83654; 208/347-2141 or 208/365-7000.

Trip notes: You can hike and fish in Payette National Forest.

55 Riverside

 6

Location: In Boise National Forest; map ID4, grid c6.

Campsites, facilities: There are 18 RV or tent campsites, which can accommodate a maximum RV length of 22 feet. Vault toilets and water are available. Pets are allowed on leashes.

Reservations, fees: No reservations are needed; the fee is $4 per night. Group sites can be reserved. Open June 15–September 15.

Directions: From Boise, take Highway 55 north 42 miles to Banks and turn right toward Garden Valley on Banks-Lowman Road. Lowman is 33 miles east of Banks on Banks-Lowman Road. From Lowman, go 36 miles northeast on Highway 21, then 28 miles west on Forest Service Road 579 and seven miles south on Forest Service Road 555 to the campground.

Contact: Boise National Forest; Lowman Ranger District, Hwy. 21, HC 77, P.O. Box 3020, Lowman, ID 83637; 208/259-3361.

Trip notes: This campground is at Deadwood Reservoir, where you can boat and fish. You can hike and fish in Boise National Forest.

56 Hower's

 6

Location: In Boise National Forest; map ID4, grid c6.

Campsites, facilities: There are six RV or tent campsites, which can accommodate a maximum RV length of 22 feet. Vault toilets are available. Pets are allowed on leashes.

Reservations, fees: No reservations are needed; the fee is $4 per night. Open July 1–September 30.

Directions: From Boise, take Highway 55 north 42 miles to Banks and turn right toward Garden Valley on Banks-Lowman Road. Lowman is 33 miles east of Banks on Banks-Lowman Road. From Lowman, drive 36 miles northeast on Highway 21, then 28 miles west on Forest Service Road 579 and 7.5 miles south on Forest Service Road 555 to the campground.

Contact: Boise National Forest, Lowman Ranger District, Hwy. 21, HC 77, P.O. Box 3020, Lowman, ID 83637; 208/259-3361.

Trip notes: This campground is near Deadwood Reservoir, where you can boat and fish. You can hike and fish in Boise National Forest.

57 Cozy Cove

 6

Location: In Boise National Forest; map ID4, grid c6.

Campsites, facilities: There are nine RV or tent campsites, which can accommodate a maximum RV length of 16 feet. Vault toilets are available. Pets are allowed on leashes.

Reservations, fees: No reservations are needed; the fee is $5 per night. Open July 1–September 30.

Directions: From Boise, take Highway 55 north 42 miles to Banks and turn right toward Garden Valley on Banks-Lowman Road. Lowman is 33 miles east of Banks on Banks-Lowman Road. From Lowman, go 36 miles northeast on Highway 21, 28 miles west on Forest Service Road 579, then 11 miles south on Forest Service Road 555.

Contact: Boise National Forest; Lowman Ranger District, Hwy. 21, HC 77, P.O. Box 3020, Lowman, ID 83637; 208/259-3361.

Trip notes: This campground is at the south end of Deadwood Reservoir, where you can boat and fish. You can hike and fish in Boise National Forest.

58 Bull Trout Lake

 6

Location: In Boise National Forest; map ID4, grid c7.

Campsites, facilities: There are 19 RV or tent campsites, which can accommodate a maximum RV length of 16 feet. Pets are allowed on leashes.

Reservations, fees: Reservations are accepted; the fee is $8–15 per night. Open July–September 30.

Directions: From Boise, go 42 miles north on Highway 55 to Banks, then 33 miles east of Banks to Lowman. From Lowman, go 34 miles northeast on Highway 21, then two miles southwest on Forest Service Road 520 to the campground.

Contact: Boise National Forest; Lowman Ranger District, Hwy. 21, HC 77, P.O. Box 3020, Lowman, ID 83637; 208/259-3361.

Trip notes: You can fish, boat, and hike in Boise National Forest.

59 Stanley Lake

     6

Location: In the Sawtooth National Recreation Area; map ID4, grid d8.

Campsites, facilities: There are 19 RV or tent campsites, which can accommodate a maximum RV length of 22 feet. Wheelchair-accessible restrooms and water are available.

Reservations, fees: No reservations are needed; the fee is $5–10 per night. Open June 15–September 15.

Directions: From Challis, go south on Highway 75 52 miles to Stanley. From Stanley, go five miles west on Highway 21, then 2.5 miles west on Forest Service Road 455 to the recreation area.

Contact: Sawtooth National Recreation Area, 2647 Kimberly Rd., Twin Falls, ID 83301; 208/737-3200, fax 208/737-3236.

Trip notes: Stanley Lake is one of Idaho's lesser-known lakes, but it is a great place to canoe, fish, hike, and camp.

60 Lakeview

     5

Location: In Sawtooth National Recreation Area; map ID4, grid d8.

Campsites, facilities: The six RV or tent campsites can accommodate a maximum RV length of 22 feet. Vault toilets and water are available.

Reservations, fees: No reservations are needed; the fee is $8–15 per night. Open June 15–September 15.

Directions: From Challis, go south on Highway 75 52 miles to Stanley. From Stanley, go two miles west on Highway 21, then 5.5 miles west on Forest Service Road 455 to the campground.

Contact: Sawtooth National Forest, Sawtooth National Recreation Area, Star Route, Ketchum, ID 83304; 208/727-5000 or 208/727-5013.

Trip notes: You can boat, swim, fish, and hike in the area. This campground is on the southwest side of Stanley Lake.

61 Salmon River

   5

Location: In the Sawtooth National Forest; map ID4, grid d8.

Campsites, facilities: There are 30 RV or tent campsites, which can accommodate a maximum RV length of 32 feet. There are vault toilets and water available.

Reservations, fees: No reservations are needed; the fee is $8–24 per night. Open May 20–September 15.

Directions: From Challis, go south on Highway 75 toward Stanley. The campground is five miles before Stanley on Highway 75.

Contact: Sawtooth National Forest, Sawtooth National Recreation Area, HC 64, P.O. Box 8291, Ketchum, ID 83304; 208/727-5000 or 208/727-5013.

Trip notes: You can fish on the Salmon River, and float or raft the Salmon River April–September. This river is rated Class II and Class III, and guided trips are suggested.

62 Big Eddy

    5

Location: In Payette National Forest; map ID4, grid d4.

Campsites, facilities: There are four RV or tent campsites. Vault toilets are available. Pets are allowed on leashes.

Reservations, fees: No reservations are needed; the fee is $7–10 per night. Open May 6–November 11.

Directions: Banks is 42 miles north of Boise on Highway 55. From Banks, go 15 miles north on Highway 55 to the campground.

Contact: Payette National Forest, New Meadows Ranger District, P.O. Box J, New Meadows, ID 83654; 208/347-2141 or 208/365-7000.

Trip notes: You can hike and fish in Payette National Forest.

63 Swinging Bridge

 5

Location: In Payette National Forest; map ID4, grid d4.

Campsites, facilities: There are 11 RV or tent campsites, which can accommodate a maximum RV length of 22 feet. Vault toilets and water are available. Pets are allowed on leashes.

Reservations, fees: No reservations are needed; the fee is $7–10 per night. Open May 15–October 1.

Directions: Banks is 42 miles north of Boise on Highway 55. From Banks, go eight miles north on Highway 55 to the campground.

Contact: Payette National Forest, New Meadows Ranger District, P.O. Box J, New Meadows, ID 83654; 208/347-2141 or 208/365-7000.

Trip notes: You can hike and fish in Payette National Forest.

64 Tie Creek

 5

Location: In Payette National Forest; map ID4, grid d5.

Campsites, facilities: There are seven RV or tent campsites, which can accommodate a maximum RV length of 30 feet. Wheelchair-accessible restrooms and water are available. Pets are allowed on leashes.

Reservations, fees: No reservations are needed; the fee is $7–10 per night. Open May 15–October 25.

Directions: From Boise, take Highway 55 north 42 miles to Banks and turn right to Garden Valley on Banks-Lowman Road. From Garden Valley, go 10 miles east on Banks-Lowman Road, then 11 miles north on Forest Service Road 698 to the campground.

Contact: Payette National Forest, New Meadows Ranger District, P.O. Box J, New Meadows, ID 83654; 208/347-2141 or 208/365-7000.

Trip notes: You can hike and fish in Payette National Forest.

65 Bonneville

 4

Location: In Boise National Forest; map ID4, grid d7.

Campsites, facilities: There are 12 RV or tent campsites, which can accommodate a maximum RV length of 30 feet. Wheelchair-accessible restrooms, water, and pull-through sites are available. Pets are allowed on leashes.

Reservations, fees: Reservations are accepted; the fee is $5–10 per night. Open May 5–September 30.

Directions: From Boise, go 42 miles north on Highway 55 to Banks, then 33 miles east of Banks to Lowman. From Lowman, go 19 miles northeast on Highway 21, then six miles north on Forest Service Road 025 to the campground.

Contact: Boise National Forest, Lowman Ranger District, Hwy. 21, HC 77, P.O. Box 3020, Lowman, ID 83637; 208/259-3361.

Trip notes: You can boat and fish here.

66 Helende

 5

Location: In Boise National Forest; map ID4, grid d7.

Campsites, facilities: There are 10 RV or tent campsites. Wheelchair-accessible restrooms and water are available. Pets are allowed on leashes.

Reservations, fees: No reservations are needed; the fee is $11–15 per night. Open May 20–September 30.

Directions: From Boise, go 42 miles north on Highway 55 to Banks, then 33 miles east of Banks to Lowman. From Lowman, go nine miles east on Highway 21 to the campground.

Contact: Boise National Forest, Lowman Ranger District, Hwy. 21, HC 77, P.O. Box 3020, Lowman, ID 83637; 208/259-3361.

Trip notes: You can hike and fish in Boise National Forest.

67 Grandjean

 5

Location: In Sawtooth National Forest; map ID4, grid d8.

Campsites, facilities: There are 31 RV or tent campsites, which can accommodate a maximum RV length of 22 feet. There are vault toilets, and water is available. Pets are allowed on leashes.

Reservations, fees: No reservations are needed; the fee is $11–15 per night. Open June 15–September 15.

Directions: From Challis, go south on Highway 75 52 miles to Stanley. From Stanley, go west on Highway 21, then north on Forest Service Road 524 to Grandjean.

Contact: Sawtooth National Forest, Sawtooth National Recreation Area, Star Route, Ketchum, ID 83304; 208/727-5000 or 208/727-5013.

Trip notes: This campground is on the South Fork of the Payette River, and you can hike and fish in Sawtooth National Forest.

68 Lazy River RV Park

 4

Location: In Payette National Forest; map ID4, grid d1.

Campsites, facilities: There are 12 RV or tent campsites, some with hookups. Showers, laundry facilities, and a sanitary disposal station are available. Pets are allowed on leashes.

Reservations, fees: No reservations are needed; the fee is $10 per night.

Directions: Payette is 15 miles south of Weiser on U.S. 95. From Payette, go four miles north on U.S. 95 to the campground.

Contact: Lazy River RV Park, 11575 N. River Rd., Payette, ID 83661; 208/642-9667.

Trip notes: You can hike and fish in the Payette National Forest.

69 Neat Retreat

 4

Location: Near Fruitland; map ID4, grid d1.

Campsites, facilities: There are 40 RV campsites, some with hookups. Wheelchair-accessible restrooms, laundry facilities, pull-through sites, showers, propane gas, and cable/TV movies. Pets are allowed on leashes. Group facilities can be reserved.

Reservations, fees: No reservations are needed; the fee is $19.25 per night. Open year-round.

Directions: From Boise, westbound, leave I-84 at Exit 376B. Turn east for one mile to the junction of U.S. 95; turn left (north) on U.S. 95 and drive a half mile to the campground; look for signs.

Contact: Neat Retreat, 2700 U.S. 95, Fruitland, ID 83619; 208/452-4324 or 800/433-7806.

Trip notes: This campground has beautiful mountain scenery, and three rivers converge here. Seven golf courses are nearby.

70 Hot Springs

 6

Location: In Payette National Forest; map ID4, grid d5.

Campsites, facilities: There are 10 RV or tent campsites, which can accommodate a maximum RV length of 35 feet. Wheelchair-accessible restrooms and water are available. Pets are allowed on leashes. Two group sites can be reserved. Natural mineral water hot springs are nearby.

Reservations, fees: No reservations are needed; the fee is $10 per night. Open April 1–October 30.

Directions: From Boise, take Highway 55 north 42 miles to Banks and turn right on Banks-Lowman Road, going 10 miles to Garden Valley. From Garden Valley, go two miles east on Banks-

Lowman Road to the campground, which is one mile after entering Forest Service land.

Contact: Payette National Forest, New Meadows Ranger District, P.O. Box J, New Meadows, ID 83654; 208/347-2141 or 208/365-7000.

Trip notes: Mineral water hot springs here reach a temperature of 105 degrees and flow into volunteer-built sand pools on the riverbank. You can hike and fish in Payette National Forest.

71 Park Creek

 5

Location: In Boise National Forest; map ID4, grid d6.

Campsites, facilities: There are 26 RV or tent campsites, which can accommodate a maximum RV length of 32 feet. Pull-through sites, vault toilets, water, and a restaurant are available. Pets are allowed on leashes.

Reservations, fees: No reservations are needed; the fee is $10 per night. Open May 20–September 30.

Directions: Lowman is 33 miles east of Banks. Banks is 42 miles north of Boise on Highway 55. From Lowman, go .3 mile east on Highway 21, then three miles northeast on Forest Service Road 582.

Contact: Boise National Forest, Lowman Ranger District, Hwy. 21, HC 77, P.O. Box 3020, Lowman, ID 83637; 208/259-3361.

Trip notes: You can hike and fish in Boise National Forest.

72 New Haven Lodge

 5

Location: In Boise National Forest; map ID4, grid d6.

Campsites, facilities: There are nine RV or tent sites, some with hookups. Wheelchair-accessible restrooms, a sanitary disposal station, a restaurant, and a swimming pool. Propane gas is available. Pets are allowed on leashes.

Reservations, fees: No reservations are needed; the fee is $7–10 per night.

Directions: Lowman is 33 miles east of Banks. Banks is 42 miles north of Boise on Highway 55. From Lowman, go to milepost 76 on Highway 21.

Contact: New Haven Lodge, 7655 Hwy. 21, Lowman, ID 83637; 208/259-3344.

Trip notes: You can hike and fish in Boise National Forest.

73 Pine Flats

 5

Location: In Boise National Forest; map ID4, grid d6.

Campsites, facilities: There are 27 RV or tent campsites, which can accommodate a maximum RV length of 32 feet. Pull-through sites, vault toilets, and water are available. Pets are allowed on leashes.

Reservations, fees: Reservations are accepted; the fee is $10 per night. Open May 20–September 30.

Directions: Lowman is 33 miles east of Banks. Banks is 42 miles north of Boise on Highway 55. The campground is five miles west of Lowman on Banks-Lowman Road.

Contact: Boise National Forest, Lowman Ranger District, Hwy. 21, HC 77, P.O. Box 3020, Lowman, ID 83637; 208/259-3361.

Trip notes: You can hike and fish in Boise National Forest.

74 Mountain View

 5

Location: In Boise National Forest; map ID4, grid d6.

Campsites, facilities: There are 14 RV or tent campsites, which can accommodate a maximum RV length of 32 feet. Wheelchair-accessible restrooms, pull-through sites, and water are available. Pets are allowed on leashes.

Reservations, fees: Reservations are accepted; the fee is $10 per night. Open May 20–September 30.

Directions: From Lowman, go a half mile east on Highway 21 to the campground.

Contact: Boise National Forest, Lowman Ranger District, Hwy. 21, HC 77, P.O. Box 3020, Lowman, ID 83637; 208/259-3361.

Trip notes: You can hike and fish in Boise National Forest.

75 Kirkham Hot Springs

 5

Location: In Boise National Forest; map ID4, grid d7.

Campsites, facilities: There are 16 RV or tent campsites, which can accommodate a maximum RV length of 32 feet. Wheelchair-accessible restrooms, pull-through sites, and water are available. Pets are allowed on leashes.

Reservations, fees: Reservations are accepted; the fee is $10 per night. Open May 20–September 30.

Directions: From Lowman, go 4.2 miles east on Highway 21 to the campground.

Contact: Boise National Forest, Lowman Ranger District, Hwy. 21, HC 77, P.O. Box 3020, Lowman, ID 83637; 208/259-3361.

Trip notes: You can hike and fish in Boise National Forest.

76 Edna Creek

 5

Location: In Boise National Forest; map ID4, grid e6.

Campsites, facilities: There are nine RV or tent campsites, which can accommodate a maximum RV length of 16 feet. A vault toilet and water are available.

Reservations, fees: No reservations are needed; the fee is $6 per night. Open June 1–October 15.

Directions: From Idaho City go 34 miles north on Highway 21 to Lowman. From Lowman, go 18 miles on Highway 21 to the campground.

Contact: Idaho City Ranger District, Hwy. 21, P.O. Box 129, Idaho City, ID 83631; 208/392-6681 or 208/364-4330.

Trip notes: You can fish and hike in Boise National Forest.

77 Hayfork

 4

Location: In Boise National Forest; map ID4, grid e6.

Campsites, facilities: There are six RV or tent campsites, which can accommodate a maximum RV length of 22 feet. A vault toilet and water are available.

Reservations, fees: No reservations are needed; the fee is $8 per night. Open June 1–October 15.

Directions: From Idaho City, go 10 miles northeast on Highway 21 to the campground.

Contact: Idaho City Ranger District, Hwy. 21, P.O. Box 129, Idaho City, ID 83631; 208/392-6681, 208/364-4330.

Trip notes: Boise Basin was once the richest gold field in the state. You can fish and mountain bike here.

78 Bad Bear

 4

Location: In Boise National Forest; map ID4, grid e6.

Campsites, facilities: There are eight RV or tent campsites, which can accommodate a maximum RV length of 22 feet. A vault toilet and water are available.

Reservations, fees: No reservations are needed; the fee is $6 per night. Open June–October.

Directions: From Idaho City, go 9.5 miles northeast on Highway 21 to the campground.

Contact: Idaho City Ranger District, Hwy. 21, P.O. Box 129, Idaho City, ID 83631; 208/392-6681, 208/364-4330.

Trip notes: Boise Basin was once the richest gold field in the state. You can fish, hike, and mountain bike here.

79 Ten Mile

 4

Location: In Boise National Forest; map ID4, grid e6.

Campsites, facilities: There are 14 RV or tent campsites, which can accommodate a maximum RV length of 22 feet. A vault toilet and water are available.

Reservations, fees: No reservations are needed; the fee is $6 per night. Open June 1–October 15.

Directions: From Idaho City, go 9.3 miles northeast on Highway 21 to the campground.

Contact: Idaho City Ranger District, Hwy. 21, P.O. Box 129, Idaho City, ID 83631; 208/392-6681, 208/364-4330.

Trip notes: Boise Basin was once the richest gold field in the state. You can fish and mountain bike here.

80 Holiday Motel & RV

 3

Location: In Emmett; map ID4, grid e2.

Campsites, facilities: There are 15 RV or tent campsites, some with hookups. Wheelchair-accessible restrooms and laundry facilities are available. Pets are allowed on leashes.

Reservations, fees: No reservations are needed; the fee is $24 per night.

Directions: From Highway 16 at Emmett, go north onto South Washington Avenue (Highway 52); the campground is just past the intersection with 12th Street.

Contact: Holiday Motel & RV, 1111 S. Washington Ave., Emmett, ID 83617; 208/365-4479.

Trip notes: Emmett has a nine-hole golf course.

81 Capital Mobile Park

 3

Location: In Emmett; map ID4, grid e3.

Campsites, facilities: There are 15 RV or tent campsites. Hookups, showers, and laundry facilities are available. Pets are allowed on leashes.

Reservations, fees: Reservations are accepted; the fee is $25 and up per night. Open year-round.

Directions: From Highway 16 at Emmett, turn right onto S. Washington Avenue. Go one mile and turn right to Main Street and the campground.

Contact: Capital Mobile Park, 1508 E. Main, Emmett, ID 83617; 208/356-3889.

Trip notes: Gem County Golf Course has nine holes, and Emmett has a sanitary disposal station. North and west is the Fort Boise Wildlife Management Area at the confluence of the Snake, Boise, and Owyhee Rivers, where you can see wild turkeys, waterfowl, hawks, and herons.

82 Montour Wildlife Area

 5

Location: North of Boise; map ID4, grid e3.

Campsites, facilities: There are 17 RV or tent campsites, which can accommodate a maximum RV length of 32 feet. Picnic tables, grills, a vault toilet, and water are available.

Reservations, fees: Reservations are accepted, call 208/398-8211; the fee is $5 per night. Open April 1–October 31.

Directions: From Emmett at Highway 16, go 13 miles east on Highway 52. Turn south at the Sweet-Ola junction and cross the Payette River to the wildlife area.

Contact: Montour Wildlife Area, Project Manager, Snake River Area Office, 214 Broadway Ave., Boise, ID 83702; 208/365-2682 or 208/334-9084.

Trip notes: This campground is above the Black Canyon Reservoir, where you can fish for smallmouth bass and rainbow trout. You can canoe and float the Payette River. This wildlife area has 1,055 acres of waterfowl habitat and is home to waterfowl, raptors, and mammals.

83 Warm Springs Resort

 4

Location: Near Idaho City; map ID4, grid e5.

Campsites, facilities: There are 22 RV or tent campsites, which can accommodate a maximum RV length of 40 feet. Hookups, showers, and a restaurant are available. Pets are allowed on leashes.

Reservations, fees: Reservations are accepted; the fee is $18 per night. Open year-round.

Directions: The resort is 1.25 miles southwest of town on Highway 21.

Contact: Warm Springs Resort, P.O. Box 28, Idaho City, ID 83831; 208/392-4437.

Trip notes: This campground has natural artesian springs in a swimming pool. Boise Basin was once the richest gold field in the state. You can fish, hike, and mountain bike in the national forest.

84 Grayback Gulch

 6

Location: In Boise National Forest; map ID4, grid e5.

Campsites, facilities: There are 14 RV or tent campsites, which can accommodate a maximum RV length of 22 feet. A vault toilet and water are available.

Reservations, fees: Reservations are accepted; the fee is $6 per night. Open May 1–October 31.

Directions: From Idaho City, go 2.4 miles south on Highway 21 to the campground.

Contact: Idaho City Ranger District, Hwy. 21, P.O. Box 129, Idaho City, ID 83631; 208/392-6681, 208/364-4330.

Trip notes: Boise Basin was once the richest gold field in the state. You can fish, hike, and mountain bike here.

85 Black Rock

 4

Location: In Boise National Forest; map ID4, grid e5.

Campsites, facilities: There are 11 RV or tent campsites, which can accommodate a maximum RV length of 22 feet. A vault toilet and water are available.

Reservations, fees: No reservations are needed; the fee is $6 per night. Open June 1–October 15.

Directions: From Idaho City, go two miles northeast on Highway 21, then 18 miles east on Forest Service Road 327 to the campground.

Contact: Idaho City Ranger District, Hwy. 21, P.O. Box 129, Idaho City, ID 83631; 208/392-6681, 208/364-4330.

Trip notes: This campground has natural artesian springs in a swimming pool. Boise Basin was once the richest gold field in the state. You can fish, hike, and mountain bike in the national forest.

86 Shafer Butte

 6

Location: In Boise National Forest; map ID4, grid e4.

Campsites, facilities: There are seven RV or tent campsites, which can accommodate a maximum RV length of 22 feet. Wheelchair-accessible restrooms and water are available. Pets are allowed on leashes.

Reservations, fees: Reservations are accepted; the fee is $6 per night. Open July 1–September 30.

Directions: From Boise, travel 16 miles northeast on Bogus Basin Road; then go three miles north on Forest Service Road 374 and 1.5 miles east on Shafer Butte Road to the campground.

Contact: Forest Supervisor, Boise National Forest, 1249 S. Vinnell Way, Boise, ID 83709; 208/373-4100.

Trip notes: You can mountain bike and hike on Corral Loop trail. The trail is a difficult 15 miles off Bogus Basin Road at the Corral Loop turnoff.

87 Power Plant

 4

Location: In the Sawtooth National Forest; map ID4, grid e8.

Campsites, facilities: There are 30 RV or tent campsites, which can accommodate a maximum RV length of 22 feet. A vault toilet and water are available.

Reservations, fees: No reservations are needed; there is no fee. Open June 1–October 1.

Directions: From Boise, go east on Forest Service Road 268 (Middle Fork Road) for 75 miles to Atlanta. From Atlanta, go 1.5 miles northeast on Forest Service Road 268 to the campground.

Contact: Idaho City Ranger District, Hwy. 21, P.O. Box 129, Idaho City, ID 83631; 208/392-6681, 208/364-4330.

Trip notes: Atlanta Hot Springs and Chattanooga Hot Springs are near Atlanta. You can fish and hike here.

88 Caldwell Campground & RV Park

 4

Location: In Caldwell; map ID4, grid f1.

Campsites, facilities: There are 85 RV or tent campsites, some with hookups and pull-through sites. Laundry facilities, showers, propane gas, and a sanitary disposal facility are available.

Reservations, fees: No reservations are needed; the fee is $12–18 per night.

Directions: From Boise, go west on I-84 21 miles to Caldwell. Take Exit 26 North, go 100 yards on Old Highway to the access road, and then south 100 yards to the campground.

Contact: Caldwell Campground & RV Park, P.O. Box 1101, Caldwell, ID 83606; 208/454-0279.

Trip notes: The Fort Boise Wildlife Management Area is at the confluence of the Boise, Snake, and Owyhee Rivers, and has 1,500 acres for wild turkeys, waterfowl, hawks, herons, and owls. Caldwell has two golf courses: Fairview Golf Course (nine holes) and Purple Sage (18 holes). There are also several museums in town.

89 Hi Valley RV Park

 3

Location: In Boise; map ID4, grid f4.

Campsites, facilities: There are 194 RV or tent campsites, some with hookups and pull-through sites. Showers, laundry facilities, and a recreation hall are available.

Reservations, fees: No reservations are needed; the fee is $18–25 per night.

Directions: From Highway 44, go one mile north on Horseshoe Bend Road to the RV park.

Contact: Hi Valley RV Park, 10555 Horseshoe Bend Rd., Boise, ID 83703; 208/939-8080, 888/457-5959; website: www.idahoheartland.net.

Trip notes: There are off-road mountain bike and hiking trails north of town.

90 Ninemeyer

 5

Location: In Boise National Forest; map ID4, grid f6.

Campsites, facilities: There are eight RV or tent campsites, which can accommodate a maximum RV length of 22 feet. A vault toilet is available.

Reservations, fees: No reservations are needed; the fee is $6 per night. Open May 25–October 1.

Directions: From Boise, go east on Forest Service Road 268 (Middle Fork Road) for 75 miles to Atlanta. From Atlanta, go 27 miles west on Forest Service Road 268, and you can see steam from the hot springs across from the campground.

Contact: Forest Supervisor, Boise National Forest, 1249 S. Vinnell Way, Boise, ID 83709; 208/373-4100.

Trip notes: There are natural hot springs here. You can fish on the Middle Fork Boise River and hike in the area. Atlanta is an old mining town on the edge of the Sawtooth Mountains, well off the beaten path.

91 Snake River RV Resort

     5

Location: Near Homedale; map ID4, grid f1.

Campsites, facilities: There are 35 RV or tent campsites, some with hookups and pull-through sites. Laundry facilities and showers are available. Pets are allowed on leashes.

Reservations, fees: No reservations are needed; the fee is $15.50 per night.

Directions: From Boise, go west on I-84 21 miles to Caldwell. From Caldwell, take Highway 55 to U.S. 95, and from U.S. 95, go east on Pioneer Road to river and campground, just to the southeast of Homedale.

Contact: Snake River RV Resort, Route 1, P.O. Box 1062-2000, Homedale, ID 83628; 208/337-3744.

Trip notes: You can fish for bass in the Snake River. Jump Creek Falls, northwest of Marsing, has a 60-foot waterfall, and hiking trails are nearby. Experienced rock climbers enjoy the challenge of the steep canyon.

92 Mason Creek RV Park

     4

Location: In Nampa; map ID4, grid f2.

Campsites, facilities: There are 78 RV or tent campsites, some with hookups and pull-through sites. Wheelchair-accessible restrooms, showers, and laundry facilities are available. Pets are allowed on leashes.

Reservations, fees: Reservations are accepted; the fee it $13.50–19 per night. Open year-round.

Directions: From Boise, go west on I-84 to Exit 36; go a half mile south to Franklin Boulevard and the campground.

Contact: Mason Creek RV Park, 807 Franklin Blvd., Nampa, ID 83687; 208/465-7199, 800/768-7199.

Trip notes: A 140-mile round trip through the Owyhee Mountains takes you to the home of a variety of wildlife, raptors, waterfowl, songbirds, bluebirds, pronghorn antelope, and deer, but viewing is allowed from vehicles only. The road can become impassable at times due to the weather, so check ahead of time on conditions. Four-wheel drive vehicles are highly recommended, and you might want to schedule two days to make the trip. Mountain biking and hiking trails wind through the Owyhee Mountains. Lake Lowell is a popular location for bird watching, but it is closed to boats October 1–April 14.

93 The Playground Sports & RV Park

     4

Location: Near Boise; map ID4, grid f3.

Campsites, facilities: There are 72 RV or tent campsites, some with hookups and pull-through sites. Wheelchair-accessible restrooms, laundry facilities, showers, a store, children's playground, and swimming pool are available. Pets are allowed on leashes.

Reservations, fees: No reservations are needed; the fee is $20 per night.

Directions: From U.S. 30 west, take Exit 44, to Meridian/Kuna. Turn left onto Meridian Road/Highway 69, then left on West Overland Road, which becomes East Overland Road and leads to the campground.

Contact: The Playground Sports & RV Park, 1780 E. Overland Rd., Meridian, ID 83642; 800/668-7529, 208/887-1022.

Trip notes: There are three golf courses nearby. Meridian is just outside Boise and north of the Snake River Birds of Prey National Conservation Area.

Indian Creek Winery, southwest of Meridian, produces pinot noir, cabernet sauvignon, chardonnay, and Riesling, and is open by appointment. Lake Lowell is closed to boating October 1–April 15.

94 On the River RV Park

 6

Location: In Boise; map ID4, grid f4.

Campsites, facilities: There are 182 RV or tent campsites, some with hookups and pull-through sites. Showers, laundry facilities, wheelchair-accessible facilities, propane gas, and a sanitary disposal facility are available.

Reservations, fees: Reservations are accepted; the fee is $18.50 per night. Open year-round.

Directions: From I-84 at Boise, take Exit 50, go north on Cole Road, west on Mountain View, north on Glenwood, then east on Marigold. This campground is on the Boise River, next to a greenbelt.

Contact: On the River RV Park, 6000 Glenwood, Boise ID 83714; 208/375-7432, 800/375-7432; website: www.internetoutlet.net.

Trip notes: Boise has several golf courses. There is a 25-mile greenbelt along the Boise River where you can walk, jog, or bike. Lucky Peak Reservoir is east of town, where you can boat, swim, water-ski, and fish. The Payette River offers good rafting opportunities.

95 Americana Kampground

 3

Location: In Boise; map ID4, grid f4.

Campsites, facilities: There are 90 RV or tent campsites, some with hookups. Showers, pull-through sites, laundry facilities, propane gas, and a sanitary disposal facility are available. Pets are allowed on leashes.

Reservations, fees: No reservations are needed; the fee is $16 and up per night. Open year-round.

Directions: From I-84 at Boise, take Exit 52, the Orchard Exit (City Center), turn right on Emerald Street, and continue to Americana Boulevard. Americana Terrace is across from Ann Morrison Park. The campground is in the heart of Boise.

Contact: Americana Kampground, 3600 Americana Terrace, Boise, ID 83706; 208/344-5733.

Trip notes: The Boise River Greenbelt is a 29-mile paved trail that parallels the Boise River. Floating the Boise River is a popular activity; from Barber Park, it's four miles to Municipal Park. The Black Cliffs, columnar basalt formations, are a favorite of rock climbers. Boise Nature Center has information about the river environments.

96 Fiesta RV Park

 4

Location: In Boise; map ID4, grid f4.

Campsites, facilities: There are 142 RV paved and grass campsites, which can accommodate a maximum RV length of 80 feet. Pull-through sites, hookups, showers, laundry facilities, game room, playground, swimming pool, and sanitary disposal station are available. There are some wheelchair-accessible facilities, and groups can be accommodated.

Reservations, fees: Reservations are recommended; the fee is $18–29 per night. Open year-round.

Directions: From I-84 at Boise, take Exit 46 north 1.75 miles to Fairview Avenue, turn right, and go 1.75 miles. The RV Park is on the right.

Contact: Fiesta RV Park, 11101 Fairview, Boise, ID 83713; 208/375-8207, 888/784-3246; website: www.fiestarv.com.

Trip notes: Boise has several golf courses. There is a 25-mile greenbelt along the Boise River where you can walk, jog, or bike. Lucky Peak Reservoir is east of town, where you can boat, swim, water-ski, and fish. The Payette River offers good rafting opportunities.

97 Mountain View RV Park

Location: In Boise; map ID4, grid f4.

Campsites, facilities: There are 63 RV or tent campsites, some with full hookups and pull-through sites. Laundry facilities, showers, wheelchair-accessible restrooms, and a sanitary disposal facility are available. Pets are allowed on leashes.

Reservations, fees: No reservations are needed; the fee is $20 per night.

Directions: From I-84 at Boise, take Exit 54 and go east on Airport Way to the campground.

Contact: Mountain View RV Park, 2040 Airport Way, Boise, ID 83714; 208/345-4141, fax 208/345-4170.

Trip notes: Boise has several golf courses. There is a 25-mile greenbelt along the Boise River that you can walk, jog, or bike. Lucky Peak Reservoir is east of town, where you can boat, swim, water-ski, and fish. The Payette River offers good rafting opportunities.

98 Willow Creek

 4

Location: In Boise National Forest; map ID4, grid f5.

Campsites, facilities: There are nine RV or tent campsites, which can accommodate a maximum RV length of 20 feet. Wheelchair-accessible restrooms, vault toilets, and water are available.

Reservations, fees: No reservations are needed; the fee is $6 per night. Open May 15–October 15.

Directions: From Boise, go 16 miles east on Highway 21, then 23 miles east on Forest Service Road 268 to the campground.

Contact: Forest Supervisor, Boise National Forest, 1249 S. Vinnell Way, Boise, ID 83709; 208/373-4100.

Trip notes: You can swim and fish in the Middle Fork Boise River and hike in the area.

99 Big Roaring River Lake and Big Trinity Lake

 7

Location: In Sawtooth National Forest; map ID4, grid f7.

Campsites, facilities: There are 29 RV or tent campsites, which can accommodate a maximum RV length of 22 feet. A vault toilet and water are available.

Reservations, fees: No reservations are needed; the fee is $7 per night. Open July 15–October 1.

Directions: From Mountain Home, go 34 miles northeast on Highway 20, then 29 miles northeast on Forest Service Road 61, then 15 miles on Forest Service Road 172, and three miles south on Forest Service Road 129 to the campground.

Contact: Mountain Home Ranger District, 2180 American Legion Blvd., Mountain Home, ID 83647; 208/587-7961

Trip notes: You can hike trails like the Rainbow Basin Trail, which has its trailhead in Big Trinity Lake campground and leads to several alpine lakes where you can fish for trout. There are good mountain biking trails in the area.

100 Chaparral

 6

Location: In Sawtooth National Forest; map ID4, grid f7.

Campsites, facilities: There are seven RV or tent campsites, which can accommodate a maximum RV length of 22 feet. There are a vault toilet, store, and restaurant are available.

Reservations, fees: No reservations are needed; there is no fee charged. Open May–September.

Directions: From Mountain Home go five miles east on U.S. 20 to Forest Service Road 61, then go north about 35 miles to Featherville. From Featherville, go three miles east on Forest

Service Road 70000 to the campground.

Contact: Sawtooth National Forest, Fairfield Ranger District, P.O. Box 189, Fairfield, ID 83327; 208/764-2202.

Trip notes: Anderson Ranch Reservoir Recreation Area has good fishing for kokanee salmon, rainbow trout, and bass. You can boat, swim, and water-ski here.

101 Abbot

 5

Location: In Sawtooth National Forest; map ID4, grid f8.

Campsites, facilities: There are seven RV or tent campsites, which can accommodate a maximum RV length of 16 feet. There is a vault toilet available.

Reservations, fees: No reservations are needed; No fee is charged. Open June 20–September 30.

Directions: From Mountain Home go five miles east on U.S. 20 to Forest Service Road 61, then go north about 35 miles to Featherville. From Featherville, go two miles east on Forest Service Road 70000 to the campground.

Contact: Sawtooth National Forest, Fairfield Ranger District, P.O. Box 189, Fairfield, ID 83327; 208/764-2202.

Trip notes: Anderson Ranch Reservoir Recreation Area has good fishing for kokanee salmon, rainbow trout, and bass. You can boat, swim, and water-ski here.

102 Baumgartner

 7

Location: Sawtooth National Forest; map ID4, grid f8.

Campsites, facilities: There are 31 RV or tent campsites. Vault toilets, hot tub, and water are available. Pets are allowed on leashes.

Reservations, fees: No reservations are needed; the fee is $6 per night. Open May–September.

Directions: From Mountain Home go five

miles east on U.S. 20 to Forest Service Road 61, then go north about 35 miles to Featherville. From Featherville, go 12 miles east on Forest Service Road 227 to the campground.

Contact: Sawtooth National Forest, Fairfield Ranger District, P.O. Box 189, Fairfield, ID 83327; 208/764-2202.

Trip notes: This is a popular destination for people seeking the South Fork Boise River. There is a nice natural mineral pool here maintained by the Forest Service. You can fish, float, raft, kayak, and swim here. A nature trail is nearby.

103 River Haven RV Park

 4

Location: In Marsing, west of Boise; map ID4, grid g1.

Campsites, facilities: There are 45 RV or tent campsites, some with hookups Wheelchair-accessible restrooms, laundry facilities, showers, propane gas, and a sanitary disposal station are available. Pets are allowed on leashes.

Reservations, fees: No reservations are needed; the fee is $7.50–12.50 per night.

Directions: From Boise, go 35 miles west on Highway 55 to Marsing. From Marsing, go 2.5 miles upriver on old Bruneau Highway to the campground.

Contact: River Haven RV Park, Route 1, Box 810, Marsing, ID; 208/896-4268.

Trip notes: You can fish for bass in the Snake River. Jump Creek Falls, northwest of Marsing, has a 60-foot waterfall, and hiking trails are nearby. Experienced rock climbers enjoy the challenge of the steep canyon.

104 Given's Hot Springs

 4

Location: Southwest of Nampa; map ID4, grid g2.

Campsites, facilities: There are 18 RV or tent campsites, some with hookups. Wheelchair-accessible restrooms, showers, a swimming pool, and restaurant are available. Pets are allowed on leashes.

Reservations, fees: No reservations are needed; the fee is $7.50–12.50 per night.

Directions: From Boise, go 35 miles west on Highway 55 to Marsing. From Marsing, go 11 miles south on Highway 78 to the hot springs.

Contact: Given's Hot Springs, HC 79, P.O. Box 103, Melba, ID 83641; 800/874-6046, 208/495-2000, fax 208/286-0925.

Trip notes: The Deer Flat National Wildlife Refuge is 115 miles along the Snake River and home to beavers, mink, red fox, waterfowl, raptors, and songbirds. Lake Lowell is closed to boating October 1–April, and the islands are closed certain times of year; check with the refuge for more information (13751 Upper Embankment, 208/467-9278). Indian rock writings are nearby.

105 Dog Creek

 6

Location: In Sawtooth National Forest; map ID4, grid g7.

Campsites, facilities: There are 12 RV or tent campsites, which can accommodate a maximum RV length of 22 feet. A vault toilet and water are available.

Reservations, fees: Reservations are accepted; the fee is $6 per night. Open May 15–October 1.

Directions: From Mountain Home, go 34 miles northeast on Highway 20, then 24 miles north on Forest Service Road 61 to the campground.

Contact: Mountain Home Ranger District, 2180 American Legion Blvd., Mountain Home, ID 83647; 208/587-7961.

Trip notes: Anderson Ranch Reservoir Recreation Area has good fishing for kokanee salmon, rainbow trout, and bass. You can boat, swim, and water-ski here.

106 Deer Creek Lodge

 4

Location: At Anderson Ranch Reservoir Recreation Area; map ID4, grid g6.

Campsites, facilities: There are 20 RV or tent campsites. Hookups, propane gas, and a restaurant are available. Pets are allowed on leashes.

Reservations, fees: No reservations are needed; the fee is $4.50–12 per night.

Directions: From Mountain Home, drive 30 miles northeast on Forest Service Road 61 to the reservoir.

Contact: Deer Creek Lodge, HC 87, P.O. Box 615, Pine, ID 83647; 208/653-2454.

Trip notes: Anderson Ranch Reservoir Recreation Area has good fishing for kokanee salmon, rainbow trout, and bass. You can boat, swim, and water-ski here.

107 Anderson Ranch Reservoir Campgrounds

 5

Location: At Anderson Ranch Reservoir Recreation Area; map ID4, grid g6.

Campsites, facilities: There are several RV or tent campsites, which can accommodate a maximum RV length of 32 feet. Pull-through sites and vault toilets are available. Pets are allowed on leashes.

Reservations, fees: No reservations are needed; the fee is $6 per night. Open May 1–October 30.

Directions: From Mountain Home, go 30 miles northeast on Forest Service Road 61 to the reservoir.

Contact: Mountain Home Ranger District, 2180 American Legion Blvd., Mountain Home, ID 83647; 208/587-7961.

Trip notes: Anderson Ranch Reservoir Recreation Area has good fishing for kokanee salmon, rainbow trout, and bass. You can boat, swim, and water-ski here.

108 Nester's Riverside Campground

 5

Location: At Anderson Ranch Reservoir Recreation Area; map ID4, grid g6.

Campsites, facilities: There are eight RV or tent campsites. Wheelchair-accessible restrooms, water, and propane gas are available. Pets are allowed on leashes.

Reservations, fees: No reservations are needed; the fee is $4–5 per night. Open year-round.

Directions: From Mountain Home go 30 miles northeast on Forest Service Road 61 to the reservoir.

Contact: Nester's Riverside Campground, HC 87, P.O. Box 210, Pine, ID 83647; 208/653-2222.

Trip notes: Anderson Ranch Reservoir Recreation Area has good fishing for kokanee salmon, rainbow trout, and bass. You can boat, swim, and water-ski here.

109 Pine Resort

 5

Location: At Anderson Ranch Reservoir Recreation Area; map ID4, grid g7.

Campsites, facilities: There are 10 RV or tent campsites. There are hookups, wheelchair-accessible restrooms, propane gas, laundry facilities, a restaurant, and a sanitary disposal facility here. Pets are allowed on leashes.

Reservations, fees: No reservations are needed; the fee is $9 and up per night.

Directions: From Mountain Home, go 30 miles northeast on Forest Service Road 61 to the reservoir.

Contact: Pine Resort, HC 87, P.O. Box 200, Pine, ID 83647; 208/653-2323.

Trip notes: Anderson Ranch Reservoir Recreation Area has good fishing for kokanee salmon, rainbow trout, and bass. You can boat, swim, and water-ski here.

110 Fall Creek Resort and Marina

 5

Location: Near Anderson Ranch Reservoir; map ID4, grid g7.

Campsites, facilities: There are 30 RV or tent campsites. Wheelchair-accessible restrooms, a restaurant, hot tub, hookups, showers, propane gas, and a sanitary disposal station are available.

Reservations, fees: No reservations are needed; the fee is $11 per night. Open year-round.

Directions: From Mountain Home, go north on Highway 20, then 11 miles west at milepost 116 to the marina.

Contact: Fall Creek Resort and Marina, HC 87, P.O. Box 85, Fall Creek, ID 83647; 208/653-2242.

Trip notes: Anderson Ranch Reservoir Recreation Area has good fishing for kokanee salmon, rainbow trout, and bass. You can boat, swim, and water-ski here.

111 Silver City Lodgings

 4

Location: In Murphy; map ID4, grid h2.

Campsites, facilities: There are six RV or tent campsites.

Reservations, fees: No reservations are needed; the fee is $10 and up per night.

Directions: From Murphy, this campground is on the main street.

Contact: Silver City Lodgings, P.O. Box 56, Murphy, ID 83650; 208/583-4111.

Trip notes: There are cabins and a group hostel available. Murphy is a very small town, but it has the Owyhee County Historical Museum, which illustrates local history. You can fish for bass in the Snake River. Jump Creek Falls, northwest of Marsing, has a 60-foot waterfall, and hiking trails are nearby. Experienced rock climbers enjoy the challenge of the steep canyon.

112 Mountain Home KOA

 4

Location: In Mountain Home; map ID4, grid h6.

Campsites, facilities: There are 43 RV or tent campsites, some with hookups. Wheelchair-accessible restrooms, laundry facilities, showers, propane gas, and a sanitary disposal facility are available. Pets are allowed on leashes.

Reservations, fees: No reservations are needed; the fee is $15–22 per night. Open March 1–November 1.

Directions: From Boise, go east on I-84 to Exit 90, follow Highway 30 for 3.5 miles to the Chevron station, take a left on East 10th North, go two blocks and the campground is on the left.

Contact: Mountain Home KOA, 220 E. 10 North, Mountain Home, ID 83647; 208/587-5111.

Trip notes: Three parks are nearby. The Snake River Birds of Prey National Area is 482 acres along 81 miles of the Snake River Canyon, home to the largest number of nesting raptors in the U.S. You can mountain bike or hike the Swans Fall Loop, a 17.5-mile trail that follows the Snake River. You can walk or bike in the C. J. Strike Wildlife Management Area and see deer, raptors, and waterfowl. Bruneau Dunes State Park is to the south. Mountain Home has two nine-hole golf courses.

113 The Wagon Wheel

 3

Location: In Mountain Home; map ID4, grid h6.

Campsites, facilities: There are 10 RV or tent campsites. Hookups, laundry facilities, and showers are available. Pets are allowed on leashes.

Reservations, fees: Reservations are accepted; the fee is $10–20 per night. Open year-round.

Directions: From Boise, go east on I-84 to Exit 95, go west on American Legion Boulevard to East 5th North and the campground.

Contact: The Wagon Wheel, 1880 E. 5th North, Mountain Home, ID 83647; 208/587-5994.

Trip notes: There are three parks nearby. The Snake River Birds of Prey National Area is 482 acres along 81 miles of the Snake River Canyon, home to the largest number of nesting raptors in the U.S. You can mountain bike or hike the Swans Fall Loop, a 17.5-mile trail that follows the Snake River. You can walk or bike in the C. J. Strike Wildlife Management Area and see deer, raptors, and waterfowl. Bruneau Dunes State Park is to the south. Mountain Home has two nine-hole golf courses.

WAYNE SCHERR

Mesa Falls

MAP ID5

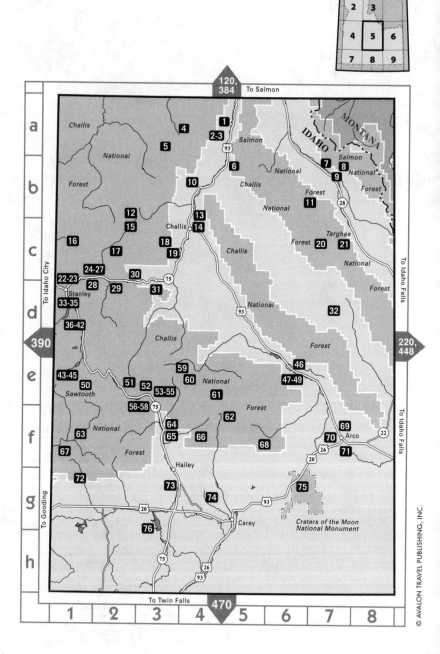

CHAPTER ID5

1	Heald's Haven	426
2	Williams Lake Resort	426
3	Williams Lake	426
4	Iron Lake	426
5	Morgan Bar	427
6	Salmon River Campground & RV Park	427
7	McFarland	427
8	Smokey Cubs	427
9	Lema's Store & RV Park	428
10	Cottonwood	428
11	Big Eight Mile	428
12	Mosquito Flat Reservoir	428
13	Challis Hot Springs	429
14	Challis All Valley RV Park	429
15	Mill Creek	429
16	Bonanza	429
17	Custer	429
18	Bayhorse	430
19	Bayhorse Lake	430
20	Timber Creek	430
21	Meadow Lake	430
22	Sheep Trail	431
23	Elk Creek	431
24	Mormon Bend	431
25	Pole Flat	431
26	Flat Rock	432
27	Blind Creek	432
28	Basin Creek	432
29	Upper and Lower O'Brien	432
30	Torreys Burnt Creek Inn	433
31	Holman Creek	433
32	Summit Creek	433
33	Elk Mountain RV Resort	433
34	Iron Creek	434
35	Sunny Gulch	434
36	Chinook Bay	434
37	Mountain View	434
38	Glacier View	435
39	Outlet	435
40	Point	436
41	Mount Heyburn	436
42	Sockeye	436
43	Smokey Bear (Alturas Lake)	437
44	North Shore Alturas Lake	437
45	Alturas Inlet	437
46	Mackay Reservoir	437
47	Wagon Wheel Motel & RV Park	438
48	River Park Golf Course and RV Campground	438
49	White Knob Motel & RV Park	438
50	Chemeketan	439
51	Prairie Creek	439
52	Caribou	439
53	Baker Creek	439
54	Murdock	440
55	North Fork	440
56	Easley	440
57	Boulder View	440
58	Wood River	440
59	Park Creek	441
60	Phi Kappa	441
61	Wildhorse	441
62	Star Hope	442
63	Canyon	442
64	Sun Valley Resort	442
65	The Meadows RV Park	442
66	Federal Gulch	443
67	Bounds	443
68	Iron Bog	443

(continues)

69 Mountain View RV Park....444
70 Carroll's Travel Plaza
& RV Park 444
71 Landing Zone RV Park......444
72 Soldier Creek RV Park 445
73 Riverside RV
& Campground 445

74 Littlewood Reservoir.......445
75 Craters of the Moon
National Monument 445
76 Burren West LLC
RV/Trailer Park..............446

1 Heald's Haven

    5

Location: South of Salmon; map ID5, grid a4.

Campsites, facilities: There are 20 RV or tent campsites. Hookups, showers, propane gas, pull-through sites, and a sanitary disposal facility are available.

Reservations, fees: No reservations are needed; the fee is $10–13 per night. Open April–November.

Directions: From Salmon, travel 12 miles south on U.S. 93 to the campground.

Contact: Heald's Haven, HC 61, P.O. Box 15, Salmon, ID 83467; 208/756-3929.

Trip notes: You can fish, raft, canoe, float, and kayak on the Salmon River.

2 Williams Lake Resort

      7

Location: Southwest of Salmon; map ID5, grid a4.

Campsites, facilities: There are 20 RV or tent campsites. Hookups, wheelchair-accessible restrooms, a restaurant, laundry facilities, and showers are available. Pets are allowed on leashes.

Reservations, fees: No reservations are needed; the fee is $18 per night.

Directions: From Salmon, go 15 miles southwest on U.S. 93 to Williams Lake.

Contact: Williams Lake Resort, P.O. Box 1150, Salmon, ID 83467; 208/756-2007.

Trip notes: You can fish and boat on Williams Lake and hike in the surrounding forest.

3 Williams Lake

    7

Location: South of Salmon; map ID5, grid a4.

Campsites, facilities: There are 11 RV or tent campsites, which can accommodate a maximum RV length of 28 feet. There are vault toilets, wheelchair-accessible restrooms, and water available.

Reservations, fees: No reservations are needed; the fee is $5 per night. Open May 1–October 31.

Directions: From Salmon, go four miles south on U.S. 93, cross Shoup Bridge, and continue seven miles on Forest Service Road to lake.

Contact: Bureau of Land Management, Salmon District Office, P.O. Box 430, Hwy. 93 South, Salmon, ID 83467; 208/756-5400.

Trip notes: You can fish and boat on Williams Lake and hike in the surrounding forest.

4 Iron Lake

    6

Location: Salmon-Challis National Forest; map ID5, grid a3.

Campsites, facilities: There are eight undeveloped RV or tent campsites, which can accommodate a maximum RV length of 20 feet. Vault toilets and water are available.

Reservations, fees: No reservations are needed; the fee is $4 per night. Open July 15–September 20.

Directions: From Salmon, drive five miles south on U.S. 93, then 20 miles west on Forest Service Road 60021 and 21 miles south on For-

est Service Road 60020 to the campground.
Contact: Salmon-Challis National Forest, Route 2, Box 600, Salmon ID 83467; 208/756-5100.

Trip notes: You can boat, fish, and hike in the area.

5 Morgan Bar

 5

Location: North of Challis; map ID5, grid a3.
Campsites, facilities: There are eight RV or tent campsites, which can accommodate a maximum RV length of 28 feet. A vault toilet is available.

Reservations, fees: No reservations are needed; the fee is $5 per night. Open April 1–October 31.

Directions: From Challis, go north eight miles on U.S. 93 to milepost 254, turn left on Forest Service Road 55 (a gravel road), and then drive 25 miles to the campground.

Contact: Bureau of Land Management, Route 2, Box 610, Salmon, ID 83467; 208/756-5400.

Trip notes: Morgan Creek is five miles from this camp, and you can swim, boat, fish, and hike nearby. Many varieties of songbirds inhabit the area.

6 Salmon River Campground & RV Park

 5

Location: South of Salmon; map ID5, grid b5.
Campsites, facilities: There are 16 RV or tent campsites. Laundry facilities and a sanitary disposal facility are available.

Reservations, fees: No reservations are needed; the fee is $6–14 per night. Open year-round.

Directions: From Salmon, go 22 miles south on U.S. 93 to the campground.

Contact: Salmon River Campground & RV Park, HC 61, P.O. Box 87, Salmon, ID 83467; 208/894-4549.

Trip notes: The Salmon River Mountains are to the west. You can fish, boat, and hike here.

7 McFarland

 4

Location: South of Lemhi; map ID5, grid b7.
Campsites, facilities: There are 10 RV or tent campsites, which can accommodate a maximum RV length of 28 feet. Vault toilets and water are available.

Reservations, fees: No reservations are needed; the fee is $5 per night. Open May 1–November 30.

Directions: From Salmon, go 30 miles south on Highway 28 to Lemhi. From Lemhi, go five miles south on Highway 28 to the campground.

Contact: Bureau of Land Management, Salmon District Office, P.O. Box 430, Hwy. 93 South, Salmon, ID 83467; 208/756-5400.

Trip notes: The Lemhi River runs near here, and mule deer, white-tailed deer, pronghorn antelope, and coyotes abound in the area, along with waterfowl and songbirds. You can fish the Lemhi River for whitefish, brook trout, bull trout, cutthroat trout, and rainbow trout.

8 Smokey Cubs

 4

Location: East of Leadore; map ID5, grid b7.
Campsites, facilities: There are eight RV or tent campsites. A vault toilet and water are available.

Reservations, fees: No reservations are needed; the fee is $5 per night. Open May 1–October 31.

Directions: From Salmon, go south on Highway 28 45 miles to Leadore. From Leadore, go three miles east on Highway 29 to the campground.

Contact: Bureau of Land Management, Salmon District Office, P.O. Box 430, Hwy. 93 South, Salmon, ID 83467; 208/756-5400.

Trip notes: You can fish the Lemhi River for whitefish, brook trout, bull trout, cutthroat trout, and rainbow trout.

9 Lema's Store & RV Park

  4

Location: In Leadore; map ID5, grid b7.

Campsites, facilities: There are 10 RV or tent campsites. There are hookups, propane gas, showers, and a sanitary disposal facility. Pets are allowed on leashes.

Reservations, fees: No reservations are needed; the fee is $8 per night. Open April–November.

Directions: From Salmon, go south on Highway 28 45 miles to Leadore. The campground is on the east side of the highway.

Contact: Lema's Store & RV Park, P.O. Box 204, Leadore, ID 83464; 208/768-2647.

Trip notes: You can fish the Lemhi River for whitefish, brook trout, bull trout, cutthroat trout, and rainbow trout.

10 Cottonwood

   5

Location: North of Challis; map ID5, grid b4.

Campsites, facilities: There are 14 RV and tent campsites, which can accommodate a maximum RV length of 30 feet. Wheelchair-accessible restrooms, water, a playground, and pull-through sites are provided. Pets are allowed on leashes.

Reservations, fees: No reservations are needed; the fee is $5–10 per night. Open year-round.

Directions: From Challis, drive 15 miles north on U.S. 93 to the campground.

Contact: Bureau of Land Management, Route 2, Box 610, Salmon, ID 83467; 208/756-5400.

Trip notes: You can fish or float in the Salmon River and hike the nearby trails. The Pahsimeroi fish hatchery has steelhead trout.

11 Big Eight Mile

 5

Location: In the Salmon National Forest, Lemhi Range; map ID5, grid b6.

Campsites, facilities: There are eight RV or tent campsites, which can accommodate a maximum RV length of 24 feet. Vault toilets, and drinking water are available.

Reservations, fees: No reservations are needed; there is no fee. Open June 15–September 30.

Directions: From Salmon, go south on Highway 28 45 miles to Leadore. From Leadore, go 6.7 miles west on the county highway, then 1.5 miles southwest on the county highway, and then five miles southwest on Forest Service Road 60096 to the campground.

Contact: Salmon National Forest, Leadore Ranger District, P.O. Box 180, Leadore, ID 83464; 208/768-2500.

Trip notes: Leadore is an old mining town, a ghost town now. You can hike and fish in Salmon National Forest.

12 Mosquito Flat Reservoir

     5

Location: In Salmon-Challis National Forest; map ID5, grid b2.

Campsites, facilities: There are nine RV or tent campsites, which can accommodate a maximum RV length of 32 feet. Wheelchair-accessible restrooms, pull-through sites, and vault toilets are available. Pets are allowed on leashes.

Reservations, fees: No reservations are needed; there is no fee. Open June–October.

Directions: From Challis, go 15 miles west on County Road 080 to Challis Creek Road and the campground.

Contact: Salmon-Challis National Forest, North Fork Ranger District, P.O. Box 180, North Fork, ID 83466-0180; 208/879-4100.

Trip notes: You can fish and swim here.

13 Challis Hot Springs

    5

Location: In Challis; map ID5, grid b4.

Campsites, facilities: There are 27 RV campsites with hookups, and a grassy area with trees for tents. Showers, a swimming pool, and a sanitary disposal station are available.

Reservations, fees: Reservations are suggested; the fee is $13.50–17.50 per night. Open year-round.

Directions: From U.S. 93 at Challis, drive 4.5 miles north on Hot Springs Road to the end of the road and the hot springs.

Contact: Challis Hot Springs, HC 63, P.O. Box 1779, Challis, ID 83226; 208/879-4442.

Trip notes: There are natural mineral pools, and this campground is close to the banks of Salmon River. You can golf in Challis, Salmon, and Sun Valley.

14 Challis All Valley RV Park

    4

Location: In Challis; map ID5, grid c4.

Campsites, facilities: There are 65 RV or tent campsites, some with hookups. Wheelchair-accessible restrooms, laundry facilities, showers, and propane gas. Pets are allowed on leashes.

Reservations, fees: No reservations are needed; the fee is $10–15 per night.

Directions: From Ramshorn, go one block off U.S. 93 to the campground.

Contact: Challis All Valley RV Park, P.O. Box 928, Challis, ID 83226; 208/879-2393.

Trip notes: You can fish in the Salmon River.

15 Mill Creek

   6

Location: In Salmon-Challis National Forest; map ID5, grid c2.

Campsites, facilities: There are eight RV or tent campsites, which can accommodate a maximum RV length of 35 feet. Vault toilets, pull-through sites, and drinking water are available.

Reservations, fees: No reservations are needed; the fee is $5 per night. Open June 15– September 30.

Directions: From Challis, travel 4.5 miles west on Garden Creek Road, then 11 miles west on Mill Creek Road 070 to the campground.

Contact: Salmon-Challis National Forest, Challis Ranger District, U.S. 93, HC 63, P.O. Box 1669, Challis, ID 83226; 208/879-4321.

Trip notes: You can hike and fish in Salmon-Challis National Forest.

16 Bonanza

   6

Location: In Salmon-Challis National Forest; map ID5, grid c1.

Campsites, facilities: There are 10 RV and tent campsites, which can accommodate a maximum RV length of 35 feet. Vault toilets and water are available. Pets are allowed on leashes.

Reservations, fees: Reservations are accepted; the fee is $5 per night. Open June 15– September 10.

Directions: From Challis, go south on Highway 75 toward Stanley. Fifteen miles before Stanley, go eight miles north on Forest Service Road 013 (Yankee Fork), then 25 miles west on Forest Service Road 074 to the campground.

Contact: Salmon-Challis National Forest, Yankee Fork Ranger District, Hwy. 75, HC 67, P.O. Box 650, Clayton, ID 83227; 208/838-2201.

Trip notes: You can fish and hike in Salmon-Challis National Forest.

17 Custer

    6

Location: In Challis National Forest; map ID5, grid c2.

Campsites, facilities: There are six RV or tent campsites, which can accommodate a maximum RV length of 32 feet. Vault toilets and pull-through sites are available. Pets are allowed on leashes.

Reservations, fees: No reservations are needed; the fee is $5 per night. Open June 15–September 10.

Directions: From Challis, go south on Highway 75 toward Stanley. Fifteen miles before Stanley, go eight miles north on Forest Service Road 013 (Yankee Fork Road) and three miles northeast on Forest Service Road 070 to the campground.

Contact: Salmon-Challis National Forest, Yankee Fork Ranger District, Hwy. 75, HC 67, P.O. Box 650, Clayton, ID 83227; 208/838-2201.

Trip notes: You can fish and hike in Salmon-Challis National Forest.

18 Bayhorse

 5

Location: South of Challis; map ID5, grid c3.

Campsites, facilities: There are 11 RV or tent campsites, which can accommodate a maximum RV length of 28 feet. Wheelchair-accessible restrooms and drinking water are available.

Reservations, fees: No reservations are needed; the fee is $5 per night. Open May 1–October 31.

Directions: From Challis, drive eight miles south on U.S. 93, and then take Highway 75 to Bayhorse.

Contact: Bureau of Land Management, Salmon District Office, P.O. Box 430, Hwy. 93 South, Salmon, ID 83467; 208/756-5400.

Trip notes: You can fish, hike, and boat here.

19 Bayhorse Lake

 5

Location: In the Salmon-Challis National Forest; map ID5, grid c3.

Campsites, facilities: There are six RV or tent campsites, which can accommodate a maximum RV length of 21 feet. Pets are allowed on leashes.

Reservations, fees: No reservations are needed; the fee is $5 per night. Open July 1–September 10.

Directions: From Challis, go two miles south on U.S. 93, then seven miles south on Highway 75 and eight miles west on Forest Service Road 051 to the campground.

Contact: Salmon-Challis National Forest, Yankee Fork Ranger District, Hwy. 75, HC 67, P.O. Box 650, Clayton, ID 83227; 208/838-2201.

Trip notes: You can boat, fish, and hike at Bayhorse Lake and in Salmon-Challis National Forest.

20 Timber Creek

 6

Location: In Salmon-Challis National Forest; map ID5, grid c7.

Campsites, facilities: There are 12 RV or tent campsites, which can accommodate a maximum RV length of 32 feet. Water is available, and pets are allowed on leashes.

Reservations, fees: No reservations are needed; the fee is $4 per night. Open June 15–September 15.

Directions: From Arco, go north 27 miles on U.S. 93 to Mackay. From Mackay, go seven miles south on U.S. 93, then 28 miles on Pass Creek Road 122, and 13 miles north on Sawmill Canyon Road 101 to the campground.

Contact: Salmon-Challis National Forests, Lost River Ranger District, Hwy. 93 North, P.O. Box 507, Mackay, ID 83251; 208/588-2224.

Trip notes: You can hike and fish in Salmon-Challis National Forest.

21 Meadow Lake

 6

Location: In the Salmon National Forest; map ID5, grid c7.

Campsites, facilities: There are 15 RV or tent campsites, which can accommodate a maximum RV length of 16 feet. There are vault toilets, and water available.

Reservations, fees: No reservations are needed; there is no fee charged. Open July 1–September 5.

Directions: From Salmon, go south on Highway 28 45 miles to Leadore. From Leadore, go 16.8 miles southeast on Highway 28, then two miles west on the county highway, and then four miles southwest on Forest Service Road 60002 to the campground.

Contact: Salmon National Forest, Leadore Ranger District, P.O. Box 180, Leadore, ID 83464; 208/768-2500.

Trip notes: You can boat and fish on Meadow Lake and hike in Salmon National Forest.

22 Sheep Trail

 6

Location: In the Sawtooth National Forest; map ID5, grid c1.

Campsites, facilities: There are four RV or tent campsites, which can accommodate a maximum RV length of 30 feet. Vault toilets and water are available. Group sites up to 40 can be arranged.

Reservations, fees: Reservations are accepted; the fee is $8–15 per night. Open June 15–September 15.

Directions: From Challis, go south on Highway 75 52 miles to Stanley. From Stanley, go 12 miles west on Highway 21 to the campground.

Contact: Sawtooth National Forest, Sawtooth National Recreation Area, Star Route, Ketchum, ID 83304; 208/727-5000 or 208/727-5013.

Trip notes: You can hike and fish in Sawtooth National Forest.

23 Elk Creek

 5

Location: In the Sawtooth National Forest; map ID5, grid c1.

Campsites, facilities: There are three RV or tent campsites, which can accommodate a maximum RV length of 30 feet. Vault toilets and water are available. Group sites up to 40

can be arranged.

Reservations, fees: Reservations are accepted; the fee is $8–15 per night. Open June 15–September 15.

Directions: From Challis, go south on Highway 75 52 miles to Stanley. From Stanley, go 10.5 miles west on Highway 21 to the campground.

Contact: Sawtooth National Forest, Sawtooth National Recreation Area, Star Route, Ketchum, ID 83304; 208/727-5000 or 208/727-5013.

Trip notes: You can hike and fish in Sawtooth National Forest.

24 Mormon Bend

 5

Location: In Sawtooth National Forest; map ID5, grid c1.

Campsites, facilities: There are 17 RV or tent campsites, which can accommodate a maximum RV length of 22 feet. Vault toilets and water are available.

Reservations, fees: No reservations are needed; the fee is $8–15 per night. Open May 20–September 15.

Directions: From Challis, go south on Highway 75 toward Stanley. The campground is seven miles east of Stanley on Highway.

Contact: Sawtooth National Forest, Sawtooth National Recreation Area, Star Route, Ketchum, ID 83304; 208/727-5000 or 208/727-5013.

Trip notes: You can fish here and visit the Land of Yankee Fork Interpretive Center, which has a visitor center, exhibits, and slide presentation on mining history.

25 Pole Flat

 5

Location: In Salmon-Challis National Forest; map ID5, grid c1.

Campsites, facilities: There are 10 RV or tent campsites, which can accommodate a maximum RV length of 32 feet. Vault toilets and water are available.

Reservations, fees: No reservations are needed; the fee is $4 per night. Open June 15–September 10.

Directions: From Challis, go south on Highway 75 toward Stanley. Fifteen miles before Stanley, go three miles north on Forest Service Road 013 to the campground.

Contact: Salmon-Challis National Forest, Yankee Fork Ranger District, Hwy. 75, HC 67, P.O. Box 650, Clayton, ID 83227; 208/838-2201.

Trip notes: You can fish and hike in Salmon-Challis National Forest.

26 Flat Rock

   5

Location: In the Salmon-Challis National Forest; map ID5, grid c1.

Campsites, facilities: There are nine RV or tent campsites, which can accommodate a maximum RV length of 32 feet. Vault toilets and water are available.

Reservations, fees: No reservations are needed; the fee is $5 per night. Open June 15–September 10.

Directions: From Challis, go south on Highway 75 toward Stanley. Fifteen miles before Stanley, go two miles north on Forest Service Road 013 (Yankee Fork Road) to the campground.

Contact: Salmon-Challis National Forest, Yankee Fork Ranger District, Hwy. 75, HC 67, P.O. Box 650, Clayton, ID 83227; 208/838-2201.

Trip notes: You can fish and hike in Salmon-Challis National Forest.

27 Blind Creek

     5

Location: In Sawtooth National Forest; map ID5, grid c2.

Campsites, facilities: There are four RV or tent campsites, which can accommodate a maximum RV length of 32 feet. Wheelchair-accessible restrooms are available. Pets are allowed on leashes.

Reservations, fees: No reservations are needed; the fee is $5 per night. Open June 15–September 10.

Directions: From Challis, go south on Highway 75 toward Stanley. Fifteen miles before Stanley, go one mile north on Yankee Fork Road 013 to the campground.

Contact: Sawtooth National Forest, Sawtooth National Recreation Area, HC 64, P.O. Box 8291, Ketchum, ID 83304; 208/727-5000 or 208/727-5013.

Trip notes: You can fish and hike in Sawtooth National Forest.

28 Basin Creek

    5

Location: In the Sawtooth National Forest; map ID5, grid d1.

Campsites, facilities: There are 15 RV or tent campsites, which can accommodate a maximum RV length of 22 feet. Vault toilets and water are available.

Reservations, fees: No reservations are needed; the fee is $8–15 per night. Open May 20–September 15.

Directions: From Challis, go south on Highway 75 toward Stanley. The campground is nine miles east of Stanley on Highway 75.

Contact: Sawtooth National Forest, Sawtooth National Recreation Area, Star Route, Ketchum, ID 83304; 208/727-5000 or 208/727-5013.

Trip notes: You can hike and fish in Sawtooth National Forest.

29 Upper and Lower O'Brien

    5

Location: In Sawtooth National Forest; map ID5, grid d2.

Campsites, facilities: There are 20 RV or tent campsites, which can accommodate a maximum RV length of 22 feet. Vault toilets, water, a store, and a restaurant are available.

Reservations, fees: No reservations are needed; the fee is $8–15 per night. Open June–September.

Directions: From Challis, go south on Highway 75 toward Stanley. Seventeen miles east of Stanley, go two miles on Forest Service Road 454 to the campground.

Contact: Sawtooth National Forest, Sawtooth National Recreation Area, Star Route, Ketchum, ID 83304; 208/727-5000 or 208/727-5013, ParkNet 877/444-6777.

Trip notes: You can hike and fish in Sawtooth National Forest.

30 Torreys Burnt Creek Inn

 5

Location: In Clayton; map ID5, grid c2.

Campsites, facilities: There are 15 RV or tent campsites, some with hookups. Laundry facilities, showers, propane gas, a restaurant, and a sanitary disposal station are available.

Reservations, fees: No reservations are needed; the fee is $12 per night.

Directions: From Stanley, go 21 miles east on Highway 75 to the campground.

Contact: Torreys Burnt Creek Inn, HC 67, P.O. Box 725, Clayton, ID 83227; 208/838-2313.

Trip notes: You can hike and fish in Sawtooth National Forest.

31 Holman Creek

 6

Location: In the Sawtooth National Forest; map ID5, grid d3.

Campsites, facilities: There are 10 RV or tent campsites, which can accommodate a maximum RV length of 22 feet. Vault toilets and water are available.

Reservations, fees: No reservations are needed; the fee is $8–15 per night. Open June 15–September 15.

Directions: From Challis, go south on Highway 75 toward Stanley. The campground is 26 miles northeast of Stanley on Highway 75.

Contact: Sawtooth National Forest, Sawtooth National Recreation Area, Star Route, Ketchum, ID 83304; 208/727-5000 or 208/727-5013.

Trip notes: You can fish here, and visit the Land of Yankee Fork Interpretive Center, which has a visitor center, exhibits, and slide presentation on mining history. You can hike in Sawtooth National Forest.

32 Summit Creek

 6

Location: Northwest of Howe; map ID5, grid d7.

Campsites, facilities: There are 12 RV or tent campsites, which can accommodate a maximum RV length of 30 feet. A vault toilet is available.

Reservations, fees: No reservations are needed; the fee is $5 per night. Open May 1–October 31.

Directions: From Arco go east seven miles on U.S. 26 to Highway 26/20, then 15 miles north to Howe. From Howe, go 40 miles northwest on the county road to the campground.

Contact: Bureau of Land Management, Salmon District Office, P.O. Box 430, Hwy. 93 South, Salmon, ID 83467; 208/756-5400.

Trip notes: You can fish in Summit Creek.

33 Elk Mountain RV Resort

 5

Location: In Sawtooth National Forest; map ID5, grid d1.

Campsites, facilities: There are 27 RV or tent campsites, some with hookups. Showers, laundry facilities, wheelchair-accessible restrooms, a restaurant, propane gas, and a sanitary disposal facility are available. Pets are allowed on leashes.

Reservations, fees: No reservations are needed; the fee is $18 per night. Open year-round.

Directions: From Challis, go south on Highway 75 52 miles to Stanley. From Stanley, go four miles west on Highway 21 to the campground.

Contact: Elk Mountain RV Resort, P.O. Box 115, Stanley, ID

83278; 208/774-2202 or 800/428-9023.

Trip notes: You can hike and fish in Sawtooth National Forest.

34 Iron Creek

 6

Location: In Sawtooth National Recreation Area; map ID5, grid d1.

Campsites, facilities: There are nine RV or tent campsites, which can accommodate a maximum RV length of 22 feet. Vault toilets and water are available.

Reservations, fees: No reservations are needed; the fee is $8–15 per night. Open June 15–September 15.

Directions: From Challis, go south on Highway 75 52 miles to Stanley. From Stanley, go two miles west on Highway 21, then four miles south on Forest Service Road 619 to the campground.

Contact: Sawtooth National Forest, Sawtooth National Recreation Area, Star Route, Ketchum, ID 83304; 208/727-5000 or 208/727-5013.

Trip notes: The Sawtooth Lake is the largest lake in the Sawtooth Wilderness Area. The Iron Creek Trail, which begins at the campground, is a popular if fairly difficult 10-mile roundtrip hike to the lake. It offers excellent views.

35 Sunny Gulch

 5

Location: In the Sawtooth National Forest; map ID5, grid d1.

Campsites, facilities: There are 19 RV or tent campsites, which can accommodate a maximum RV length of 22 feet. Vault toilets and water are available.

Reservations, fees: No reservations are needed; the fee is $9 per night. Open May 20–September 15.

Directions: From Challis, go south on Highway 75 52 miles to Stanley. From Stanley, go 3.2 miles south on Highway 75 to the campground.

Contact: Sawtooth National Forest, Sawtooth National Recreation Area, Star Route, Ketchum, ID 83304; 208/727-5000 or 208/727-5013.

Trip notes: You can hike and fish in Sawtooth National Forest.

36 Chinook Bay

 6

Location: In Sawtooth National Forest; map ID5, grid d1.

Campsites, facilities: There are 13 RV or tent campsites, which can accommodate a maximum RV length of 22 feet. There are accessible restrooms, laundry facilities, water, showers, and a sanitary disposal facility available.

Reservations, fees: No reservations are needed; the fee is $11–15 per night. Open June 15–September 15.

Directions: From Challis, go south on Highway 75 52 miles to Stanley. From Stanley, go five miles south on Highway 75, then a half a mile southwest on Forest Service Road 214 to campground.

Contact: Sawtooth National Forest, Sawtooth National Recreation Area, Star Route, Ketchum, ID 83304; 208/727-5000, 208/727-5013.

Trip notes: You can fish and boat on Redfish Lake and there are several hiking trails in the area. Fishhook Creek Trail is an easy four-plus mile hike. Bridal Veil Falls Trail takes you to the falls, which tumble hundreds of feet, but this trail can become inaccessible in the early spring, because of runoff. Flatrock Junction is an easy trail through Redfish Canyon.

37 Mountain View

 5

Location: In Sawtooth National Forest; map ID5, grid d1.

Campsites, facilities: The seven RV or tent campsites can accommodate a maximum RV length of 22 feet. Pull-through sites, showers, water, laundry facilities, wheelchair-accessible restrooms, and a sanitary disposal facility are provided.

Reservations, fees: No reservations are needed; the fee is $11–15 per night. Open May 20–September 15.

Directions: From Challis, go south on Highway 75 52 miles to Stanley. From Stanley, go five miles south on Highway 75, then .5 mile southwest on Forest Service Road 214 to the campground.

Contact: Sawtooth National Forest, Sawtooth National Recreation Area, Star Route, Ketchum, ID 83304; 208/727-5000, 208/727-5013, or 208/737-3200.

Trip notes: This campground is at Redfish Lake, named for the sockeye salmon that once were so abundant that the lake appeared red in spawning season. The fish are now on the endangered species list. You can boat, fish, swim, and hike in the area. The Redfish Lake Rock Shelter is a natural shelter that was used by Native Americans for thousands of years. This shelter is on the north side of Redfish Creek.

38 Glacier View

Location: In Sawtooth National Recreation Area; map ID5, grid d1.

Campsites, facilities: There are 65 RV or tent campsites, which can accommodate a maximum RV length of 32 feet. Wheelchair-accessible restrooms, showers, laundry facilities, water, a playground, and a sanitary disposal station.

Reservations, fees: Reservations are accepted; the fee is $11–15 per night. Open May–September.

Directions: From Challis, go south on Highway 75 52 miles to Stanley. From Stanley, go five miles south on Highway 75, then 2.4 miles southwest on Forest Service Road 214 to Redfish Lake.

Contact: Sawtooth National Forest, Sawtooth National Recreation Area, Star Route, Ketch-

um, ID 83304; 208/727-5000, 208/727-5013, or 208/737-3200.

Trip notes: Redfish Lake is named for the sockeye salmon that once were so abundant that the lake appeared red in spawning season. The fish are now on the endangered species list. You can boat, fish, swim, and hike in the area. The Redfish Lake Rock Shelter is a natural shelter that was used by Native Americans for thousands of years. This shelter is on the north side of Redfish Creek.

39 Outlet

 5

Location: In Sawtooth National Forest; map ID5, grid d1.

Campsites, facilities: There are 46 RV or tent campsites, which can accommodate a maximum RV length of 40 feet. Wheelchair-accessible restrooms, laundry facilities, showers, water, and a sanitary disposal station.

Reservations, fees: Reservations are accepted; the fee is $11–15 per night. Open June 15–September 30.

Directions: From Challis, go south on Highway 75 52 miles to Stanley. From Stanley go five miles south on Highway 75, then 2.4 miles southwest on Forest Service Road 214 to the campground.

Contact: Sawtooth National Forest, Sawtooth National Recreation Area, Star Route, Ketchum, ID 83304; 208/727-5000, 208/727-5013, or 208/737-3200.

Trip notes: Redfish Lake is named for the sockeye salmon that once were so abundant that the lake appeared red in spawning season. The fish are now on the endangered species list. You can boat, fish, swim, and hike in the area. The Redfish Lake Rock Shelter is a natural shelter that was used by Native Americans for thousands of years. This shelter is on the north side of Redfish Creek.

40 Point

 5

Location: In Sawtooth National Forest; map ID5, grid d1.

Campsites, facilities: There are 17 RV or tent campsites, which can accommodate a maximum RV length of 20 feet. Restrooms, showers, laundry facilities, and water are available.

Reservations, fees: Reservations area accepted; the fee is $11–15 per night. Open June 15–September 15.

Directions: From Challis, go south on Highway 75 52 miles to Stanley. From Stanley, go five miles south on Highway 75, then 2.6 miles southwest on Forest Service Road 214 to the campground.

Contact: Sawtooth National Forest, Sawtooth National Recreation Area, Star Route, Ketchum, ID 83304; 208/727-5000, 208/727-5013, or 208/737-3200.

Trip notes: Redfish Lake is named for the sockeye salmon that once were so abundant that the lake appeared red in spawning season. The fish are now on the endangered species list. You can boat, fish, swim, and hike in the area. The Redfish Lake Rock Shelter is a natural shelter that was used by Native Americans for thousands of years. This shelter is on the north side of Redfish Creek.

41 Mount Heyburn

 5

Location: In Sawtooth National Forest; map ID5, grid d1.

Campsites, facilities: There are 20 RV or tent campsites, which can accommodate a maximum RV length of 22 feet. Laundry facilities, wheelchair-accessible restrooms, pull-through sites, showers, and a sanitary disposal station are available.

Reservations, fees: No reservations are needed; the fee is $11–15 per night. Open May 20–September 15.

Directions: From Challis, go south on High-

way 75 52 miles to Stanley. From Stanley, go five miles south on Highway 75, then 3.1 miles south on Forest Service Road 214 to the campground.

Contact: Sawtooth National Forest, Sawtooth National Recreation Area, Star Route, Ketchum, ID 83304; 208/727-5000, 208/727-5013, or 208/737-3200.

Trip notes: Redfish Lake is named for the sockeye salmon that once were so abundant that the lake appeared red in spawning season. The fish are now on the endangered species list. You can boat, fish, swim, and hike in the area. The Redfish Lake Rock Shelter is a natural shelter that was used by Native Americans for thousands of years. This shelter is on the north side of Redfish Creek.

42 Sockeye

 5

Location: In the Sawtooth National Recreation Area; map ID5, grid d1.

Campsites, facilities: There are 23 RV or tent campsites, which can accommodate a maximum RV length of 22 feet. Wheelchair-accessible restrooms, pull-through sites, showers, laundry facilities, water, and a sanitary disposal station are available.

Reservations, fees: No reservations are needed; the fee is $11–15 per night. Open May 20–September 15.

Directions: From Challis, go south on Highway 75 52 miles to Stanley. From Stanley, go five miles south on Highway 75, then 2.6 miles southwest on Forest Service Road 214 to the campground.

Contact: Sawtooth National Forest, Sawtooth National Recreation Area, Star Route, Ketchum, ID 83304; 208/727-5000, 208/727-5013, or 208/737-3200.

Trip notes: Redfish Lake is named for the sockeye salmon that once were so abundant that the lake appeared red in spawning season. The fish are now on the endangered species list. You can boat, fish, swim, and hike in the area. The Redfish Lake Rock Shelter is a natural shelter that was used by Native Americans for thousands of years. This shelter is on the north side of Redfish Creek.

43 Smokey Bear (Alturas Lake)

 6

Location: In Sawtooth National Recreation Area; map ID5, grid e1.

Campsites, facilities: There are 12 RV or tent campsites, which can accommodate a maximum RV length of 25 feet. Wheelchair-accessible restrooms and water are available.

Reservations, fees: No reservations are needed; the fee is $9 per night. Open May 20–October 15.

Directions: From Challis go south on Highway 75 for about 54 miles (10 miles past Obsidian), then 3.4 miles southwest on Forest Service Road 205 to Alturas Lake.

Contact: Sawtooth National Forest, Sawtooth National Recreation Area, Star Route, Ketchum, ID 83304; 208/727-5000, 208/727-5013.

Trip notes: You can fish, swim, and boat at Alturas Lake and hike in the surrounding area.

44 North Shore Alturas Lake

 6

Location: In Sawtooth National Recreation Area; map ID5, grid e1.

Campsites, facilities: There are 15 RV or tent campsites, which can accommodate a maximum RV length of 32 feet. Wheelchair-accessible restrooms and water are available.

Reservations, fees: No reservations are needed; the fee is $9 per night. Open May 20–September 15.

Directions: From Obsidian, go 9.8 miles south on Highway 75, then 3.7 miles southwest on Forest Service Road 205 to the campground.

Contact: Sawtooth National Forest, Sawtooth National Recreation Area, Star Route, Ketchum, ID 83304; 208/727-5000, 208/727-5013.

Trip notes: You can fish, swim, and boat at Alturas Lake and hike in the surrounding area.

45 Alturas Inlet

 6

Location: In the Sawtooth National Recreation Area; map ID5, grid e1.

Campsites, facilities: There are 29 RV or tent campsites, which can accommodate a maximum RV length of 32 feet. Wheelchair-accessible restrooms and water are available.

Reservations, fees: No reservations are needed; the fee is $9 per night. Open May 20–September 15.

Directions: From Challis go south on Highway 75 for about 53 miles (9.8 miles past Obsidian), then 5.5 miles southwest on Forest Service Road 205 to the campground.

Contact: Sawtooth National Forest, Sawtooth National Recreation Area, Star Route, Ketchum, ID 83304; 208/727-5000, 208/727-5013.

Trip notes: This campground is on the north shore of Alturas Lake, where you can boat, swim, and fish. Cabin Creek Lakes Trail is an eight-mile roundtrip hike.

46 Mackay Reservoir

 5

Location: West of Idaho Falls; map ID5, grid e6.

Campsites, facilities: There are 57 RV or tent campsites, which can accommodate a maximum RV length of 28 feet. Wheelchair-accessible restrooms, water, and a sanitary disposal facility are available. Pets are allowed on leashes.

Reservations, fees: No reservations are needed; the fee is $4 per night.

Directions: From Mackay, go four miles northwest on U.S. 93 to the reservoir.

Contact: Bureau of Land Management, Salmon District Office, P.O. Box 430, Hwy. 93 South, Salmon, ID 83467; 208/756-5400.

Trip notes: You can boat and swim at Mackay Reservoir, which, along with nearby Big Lost River, is also a popular location for trout fishing. You can hike across the dam to Black Daisy Canyon or along the marsh for a half mile, or take a trip to Idaho's highest mountain, Borah Peak. Mackay has a nine-hole golf course. An annual mountain bike challenge is held in the White Knob Mountains in the summer.

47 Wagon Wheel Motel & RV Park

 5

Location: North of Arco; map ID5, grid e6.
Campsites, facilities: There are 18 RV or tent campsites. Wheelchair-accessible restrooms, laundry facilities, hookups, showers, and a playground are available. Pets are allowed on leashes.

Reservations, fees: No reservations are needed; the fee is $6 and up per night. Open May 1–October 15.

Directions: From Idaho Falls, go 96 miles northwest on U.S. 93 to Mackay, the highway goes right through town, watch for signs.

Contact: Wagon Wheel Motel and RV Park, P.O. Box 22, 809 Custer Ave., Mackay, ID 83251; 208/588-3331.

Trip notes: You can boat and swim at Mackay Reservoir, five miles north of Mackay, which is also a popular location for trout fishing, along with nearby Big Lost River. You can hike across the dam to Black Daisy Canyon, or along the marsh for half a mile, or take a trip to Idaho's highest mountain, Borah Peak. Mackay has a nine-hole golf course. The White Knob Mountains, to the west of Mackay, holds an annual mountain bike challenge in the summer.

48 River Park Golf Course and RV Campground

 5

Location: In Mackay; map ID5, grid e6.
Campsites, facilities: There are 18 RV or tent campsites. Wheelchair-accessible restrooms, laundry facilities, hookups, showers, and a sanitary disposal station are available. Pets are allowed on leashes.

Reservations, fees: No reservations are needed; the fee is $7–15 per night. Open April–October.

Directions: From Idaho Falls, go 96 miles northwest on U.S. 93 to Mackay, the highway goes right through town, watch for signs.

Contact: River Park Golf Course and RV Campground, 717 Capital Ave., P.O. Box 252, Mackay, ID 83521; 208/588-2296.

Trip notes: You can boat and swim at Mackay Reservoir, five miles north of Mackay, which is also a popular location for trout fishing, along with nearby Big Lost River. You can hike across the dam to Black Daisy Canyon, or along the marsh for half a mile, or take a trip to Idaho's highest mountain, Borah Peak. Mackay has a nine-hole golf course. The White Knob Mountains, to the west of Mackay, holds an annual mountain bike challenge in the summer.

49 White Knob Motel & RV Park

 5

Location: In Mackay; map ID5, grid e6.
Campsites, facilities: There are 21 RV or tent campsites. Laundry facilities, hookups, showers, a swimming pool, propane gas, and a sanitary disposal facility are available. Pets are allowed on leashes.

Reservations, fees: No reservations are needed; the fee is $10 per night. Open year-round.

Directions: From Mackay, go two miles south on U.S. 93 to the motel.

Contact: White Knob Motel & RV Park, P.O. Box 180, Mackay, ID 83521; 208/588-2622.

Trip notes: You can boat and swim at Mackay Reservoir, which is also a popular location for trout fishing, along with nearby Big Lost River. You can hike across the dam to Black Daisy Canyon or along the marsh for half a mile or take a trip to Idaho's highest mountain, Borah Peak. Mackay has a nine-hole golf course. The White Knob Mountains, to the west of Mackay, holds an annual mountain bike challenge in the summer.

50 Chemeketan

 6

Location: Sawtooth National Recreation Area; map ID5, grid e1.

Campsites, facilities: There are 10 RV or tent campsites, which can accommodate a maximum RV length of 16 feet. A vault toilet is available.

Reservations, fees: Reservations are accepted; the fee is $9 per night. Open June 1–September 30. Group sites to 150 are available.

Directions: From Challis go south on Highway 75 for about 44 miles to Obsidian). From Obsidian, go 19 miles south on Highway 75, then 4.5 miles south on Forest Service Road 215 to the campground.

Contact: Sawtooth National Forest, Sawtooth National Recreation Area, Star Route, Ketchum, ID 83304; 208/727-5000, 208/727-5013.

Trip notes: You can hike and fish in the Sawtooth National Forest.

51 Prairie Creek

 5

Location: In Sawtooth National Forest; map ID5, grid e2.

Campsites, facilities: There are 10 RV or tent campsites, which can accommodate a maxi-

mum RV length of 32 feet. A vault toilet is available.

Reservations, fees: No reservations are needed; the fee is $5 per night. Open June 15–September 15.

Directions: From Ketchum, go 18 miles north on Highway 75 to the campground.

Contact: Sawtooth National Forest, Sawtooth National Recreation Area, Star Route, Ketchum, ID 83304; 208/727-5000, 208/727-5013.

Trip notes: You can fish and swim here.

52 Caribou

 5

Location: In Sawtooth National Forest; map ID5, grid e3.

Campsites, facilities: There are seven RV or tent campsites, which can accommodate a maximum RV length of 22 feet. There is a vault toilet, and water is available.

Reservations, fees: No reservations are needed; the fee is $6 per night. Open June–September.

Directions: From Ketchum, go seven miles north on Highway 75, then three miles north on Forest Service Road 146 to the campground.

Contact: Sawtooth National Forest, Sawtooth National Recreation Area, Star Route, Ketchum, ID 83304; 208/727-5000, 208/727-5013.

Trip notes: You can fish and hike here.

53 Baker Creek

 5

Location: In Sawtooth National Forest; map ID5, grid e3.

Campsites, facilities: There are 10 RV or tent campsites, which can accommodate a maximum RV length of 32 feet. There is a vault toilet, and water is available.

Reservations, fees: No reservations are needed; the fee is $7 per night. Open May 1–September 15.

Directions: From Ketchum, go 15 miles north on Highway 75, then one mile south on Baker Creek Road to the campground.

Contact: Sawtooth National Forest, Sawtooth National Recreation Area, Star Route, Ketchum, ID 83304; 208/727-5000, 208/727-5013.

Trip notes: You can swim here.

54 Murdock

 5

Location: In Sawtooth National Forest; map ID5, grid e3.

Campsites, facilities: There are 11 RV or tent campsites, which can accommodate a maximum RV length of 22 feet. Wheelchair-accessible restrooms are available.

Reservations, fees: No reservations are needed; the fee is $6 per night. Open May 20–September 15.

Directions: From Ketchum, go seven miles north on Highway 75, then one miles north on Forest Service Road 146 to the campground.

Contact: Sawtooth National Forest, Sawtooth National Recreation Area, Star Route, Ketchum, ID 83304; 208/727-5000, 208/727-5013.

Trip notes: You can hike and fish here.

55 North Fork

 5

Location: In Sawtooth National Recreation Area; map ID5, grid e3.

Campsites, facilities: There are 30 RV or tent campsites, which can accommodate a maximum RV length of 22 feet. A vault toilet and water are available.

Reservations, fees: No reservations are needed; the fee is $6 per night. Open May 20–September 5.

Directions: From Ketchum, go eight miles north on Highway 75 to the campground.

Contact: Sawtooth National Forest, Sawtooth National Recreation Area, Star Route, Ketchum, ID 83304; 208/727-5000, 208/727-5013.

Trip notes: You can hike and fish here.

56 Easley

 5

Location: In Sawtooth National Forest; map ID5, grid f2.

Campsites, facilities: There are 10 RV or tent campsites, which can accommodate a maximum RV length of 22 feet. Wheelchair-accessible restrooms and water are available.

Reservations, fees: Reservations are accepted; the fee is $6 per night. Open June 15–September 15.

Directions: From Ketchum, go 14.5 miles north on Highway 75 to the campground.

Contact: Sawtooth National Forest, Sawtooth National Recreation Area, Star Route, Ketchum, ID 83304; 208/727-5000, 208/727-5013.

Trip notes: You can fish and swim here.

57 Boulder View

 5

Location: In Sawtooth National Forest; map ID5, grid f2.

Campsites, facilities: There are 20 RV or tent campsites, which can accommodate a maximum RV length of 22 feet. Wheelchair-accessible restrooms, water, and a store are available. Pets are allowed on leashes.

Reservations, fees: Reservations are accepted; the fee is $6 per night. Open June–September.

Directions: From Ketchum, go 15.5 miles north on Highway 75, then one mile on Forest Service Road 040 to the campground.

Contact: Sawtooth National Forest, Sawtooth National Recreation Area, Star Route, Ketchum, ID 83304; 208/727-5000, 208/727-5013.

Trip notes: You can swim and fish for trout in the Big Wood River.

58 Wood River

 5

Location: In Sawtooth National Forest; map ID5, grid f3.

Campsites, facilities: There are 32 RV or tent campsites, which can accommodate a maximum RV length of 22 feet. A vault toilet and water are available.

Reservations, fees: No reservations are needed; the fee is $9 per night. Open May 20–September 15.

Directions: From Ketchum, go 10 miles northwest on Highway 75 to the campground.

Contact: Sawtooth National Forest, Sawtooth National Recreation Area, Star Route, Ketchum, ID 83304; 208/727-5000, 208/727-5013.

Trip notes: You can fish in the Big Wood River, Warm Springs Creek, and Trail Creek. You can hike and mountain bike on Trail Creek Trail, Aspen Loop Trail, Proctor Mountain Trail, and others nearby.

59 Park Creek

 5

Location: In the Challis National Forest; map ID5, grid e4.

Campsites, facilities: There are 17 RV or tent campsites, which can accommodate a maximum RV length of 32 feet. A vault toilet and water are available. Pets are allowed on leashes.

Reservations, fees: No reservations are needed; the fee is $6 per night. Open June 30–September 15.

Directions: From Ketchum, go east two miles on Trail Creek Road to Sun Valley. From Sun Valley, go 12 miles northeast on Trail Creek Road to the campground.

Contact: Salmon-Challis National Forests, Lost River Ranger District, Hwy. 93 North, P.O. Box 507, Mackay, ID 83251; 208/588-2224.

Trip notes: There are several hiking, biking, and horseback riding trails in the area. Aspen Loop is an easy 1.75-mile trail, Corral Creek is a difficult seven-mile trail, and Proctor Mountain is a trail for the ambitious hiker. The trailheads are behind Trail Creek cabin.

60 Phi Kappa

 5

Location: In Challis National Forest; map ID5, grid e4.

Campsites, facilities: There are 21 RV or tent campsites, which can accommodate a maximum RV length of 32 feet. A vault toilet and water are available. Pets are allowed on leashes.

Reservations, fees: No reservations are needed; the fee is $4 per night. Open June 30–September 15.

Directions: From Ketchum, go 15 miles northeast on Trail Creek Road to the campground.

Contact: Salmon and Challis National Forests, Lost River Ranger District, Hwy. 93 North, P.O. Box 507, Mackay, ID 83251; 208/588-2224.

Trip notes: The Sun Valley Trail System is a 10-mile hike/bike trail that connects to the Wood River Trail System, a 20-mile trail that follows the old Union-Pacific railroad right-of-way. You can fish in the nearby river.

61 Wildhorse

 5

Location: In Challis National Forest; map ID5, grid e4.

Campsites, facilities: There are 15 RV or tent campsites, which can accommodate a maximum RV length of 32 feet. Vault toilets and water are available. Pets are allowed on leashes.

Reservations, fees: No reservations are needed; the fee is $4 per night. Open June 30–September 15.

Directions: From Ketchum, go east two miles on Trail Creek Road to Sun Valley. From Sun Valley, go 20 miles northeast on Trail Creek Road, then three miles on Forest Service Road 135, and six miles on Forest Service Road 136 to the campground.

Contact: Salmon-Challis National Forests, Lost River Ranger

District, Hwy. 93 North, P.O. Box 507, Mackay, ID 83251; 208/588-2224.

Trip notes: You can hike and fish here.

62 Star Hope

    4

Location: In Challis National Forest; map ID5, grid f5.

Campsites, facilities: There are 20 RV or tent campsites, which can accommodate a maximum RV length of 32 feet. Vault toilets and water are available. Pets are allowed on leashes.

Reservations, fees: No reservations are needed; the fee is $4 per night. Open June 30–September 15.

Directions: From Mackay go 16 miles northwest on U.S. 93, then 17 miles southwest on Trail Creek Road 208, 20 miles southeast on Forest Service Road 135, and nine miles southwest on Copper Basin Loop Road 138 to the campground.

Contact: Salmon-Challis National Forests, Lost River Ranger District, Hwy. 93 North, P.O. Box 507, Mackay, ID 83251; 208/588-2224.

Trip notes: Craters of the Moon National Monument is southeast. This monument was designated in 1924 to preserve unique volcanic features, including lava flows, cinder cones, spatter cones, and lava tubes (caves). The Craters of the Moon Lava Field is the largest basaltic lava field in the United States. A large number of plants and animals live in this harsh volcanic and high-desert environment.

63 Canyon

  5

Location: In Sawtooth National Forest; map ID5, grid f1.

Campsites, facilities: There are six RV or tent campsites. Wheelchair-accessible restrooms and water are available. Pets are allowed on leashes.

Reservations, fees: No reservations are needed; the fee is $6 per night. Open May–September.

Directions: From Fairfield, go 26 miles north on Forest Service Road 094 and 227, past Big Smokey Guard Station to the campground.

Contact: Sawtooth National Forest, Fairfield Ranger District, P.O. Box 189, Fairfield, ID 83327; 208/764-2202.

Trip notes: This campground is in an open setting, near good fishing and a three-mile hiking trail that leads to Skillern Hot Springs. The hot springs are on Big Smokey Creek and are undeveloped.

64 Sun Valley Resort

     5

Location: In Ketchum; map ID5, grid f3.

Campsites, facilities: There are 80 RV or tent campsites. There are laundry facilities, hookups, showers, propane gas, a swimming pool, and a sanitary disposal facility. Pets are allowed on leashes.

Reservations, fees: No reservations are needed; the fee is $18–27 per night. Open year-round.

Directions: From the junction of U.S. 75 and Elkhorn Road, go one block north on U.S. 75 to Ketchum/Sun Valley.

Contact: Sun Valley Resort, P.O. Box 548, Ketchum, ID 83340; 208/726-3429.

Trip notes: You can mountain bike and hike on the Adams Gulch Area Trail System 1.5 miles north of Ketchum on Highway 75. Shadyside Trail, south of Adams Gulch, is a 1.5-mile one-way hike. Adams Gulch Loop is a 5.5-mile moderately difficult hike.

65 The Meadows RV Park

     4

Location: Near Ketchum; map ID5, grid f3.

Campsites, facilities: There are 45 RV or tent campsites, which can accommodate a maximum RV length of 40 feet. Wheelchair-accessible restrooms, laundry facilities, hookups, showers, pull-through sites, and a sanitary disposal facility are available. Pets are allowed on leashes.

Reservations, fees: Reservations are accepted; the fee is $9–18 per night. Open year-round.

Directions: From Ketchum, go three miles south on Highway 75 and then take Broadway Run south to the campground.

Contact: The Meadows RV Park, Broadway Run, P.O. Box 1440, Sun Valley, ID 83353; 208/726-5445.

Trip notes: You can fish in the Big Wood River, Warm Springs Creek, and Trail Creek. You can hike and mountain bike on Trail Creek Trail, Aspen Loop Trail, Proctor Mountain Trail, and others nearby.

66 Federal Gulch

     5

Location: In Sawtooth National Forest; map ID5, grid f4.

Campsites, facilities: There are nine RV or tent campsites, which can accommodate a maximum RV length of 22 feet. A vault toilet and water are available.

Reservations, fees: No reservations are needed; the fee is $6 per night. Open May 15–October 15.

Directions: From Hailey, travel six miles north on Highway 75, then 11.5 miles east on East Fork River Road (Forest Service Road 118) to the campground.

Contact: Sawtooth National Forest, Ketchum Ranger District, P.O. Box 2356, Ketchum, ID 83340; 208/622-5371.

Trip notes: This campground is along the Wood River, where you can fish for trout. The Sun Valley Trail System is a 10-mile hike/bike trail that connects to the Wood River Trail System, a 20-mile trail that follows the old Union-Pacific railroad right-of-way.

67 Bounds

   5

Location: In Sawtooth National Forest; map ID5, grid f1.

Campsites, facilities: There are 12 RV or tent campsites, which can accommodate a maximum RV length of 16 feet. Vault toilets, water, and a sanitary disposal facility are available.

Reservations, fees: No reservations are needed; the fee is $5 per night. Open June 1–September 30.

Directions: From Mountain Home go five miles east on U.S. 20 to Forest Service Road 61, then go north about 35 miles to Featherville. From Featherville, go 23 miles east on Forest Service Road 227 to the campground.

Contact: Sawtooth National Forest, Fairfield Ranger District, P.O. Box 189, Fairfield, ID 83327; 208/764-2202.

Trip notes: You can fish here.

68 Iron Bog

   6

Location: In Challis National Forest; map ID5, grid f5.

Campsites, facilities: There are 21 RV or tent campsites, which can accommodate a maximum RV length of 32 feet. There is water available. Pets are allowed on leashes.

Reservations, fees: No reservations are needed; the fee is $4 per night. Open June 30–September 15.

Directions: From Mackay, go 10 miles southeast on U.S. 93, then 15 miles southwest on the county road, then 7.2 miles southwest on Forest Service Road 137 to the campground.

Contact: Salmon-Challis National Forests, Lost River Ranger District, Hwy. 93 North, P.O. Box 507, Mackay, ID 83251; 208/588-2224.

Trip notes: You can fish and hike in the Challis National Forest.

69 Mountain View RV Park

 4

Location: In Arco; map ID5, grid f7.

Campsites, facilities: There are 34 RV or tent campsites. Laundry facilities, hookups, showers, pull-through sites, and a sanitary disposal station are available. Pets are allowed on leashes.

Reservations, fees: No reservations are needed; the fee is $12–16 per night. Open May 1–October 31.

Directions: From Idaho Falls, go 74 miles west on U.S. 20 to Arco; the park is right on U.S. Highways 20, 26 and 93 (these major U.S. routes combine into one highway between Arco and Carey, Idaho).

Contact: Mountain View RV Park, 705 W. Grand Ave., Arco, ID 83213; 800/845-1460, 208/527-3707.

Trip notes: North of Arco is the towering Mount Borah, the highest peak in Idaho. There is a fault line at the base of the peak, a result of the 1983 quake. You can fish for brook, rainbow trout, and whitefish in Big Lost River, and rainbow, bull, and brook trout in Little Lost River. You can hike nearby.

Have you ever wanted to see a nuclear power plant? Then this is the place for you. The world's first nuclear power plant is just east of Arco, and the now-abandoned plant is open for visitors in late June and early July.

70 Carroll's Travel Plaza & RV Park

 4

Location: At Arco; map ID5, grid f7.

Campsites, facilities: There are 42 RV or tent campsites. Laundry facilities, hookups, restaurant, playground, and a sanitary disposal facility are available. Pets are allowed on leashes.

Reservations, fees: No reservations are needed; the fee is $10.50 per night. Open year-round.

Directions: From Arco, go east on U.S. 20-26 to the RV park.

Contact: Carroll's Travel Plaza & RV Park, Route 1, Box 20A, Arco, ID 83213; 208/527-3504.

Trip notes: North of Arco is the towering Mount Borah, the highest peak in Idaho. There is a fault line at the base of the peak, a result of the 1983 quake. You can fish for brook, rainbow trout, and whitefish in Big Lost River, and rainbow, bull, and brook trout in Little Lost River. You can hike nearby.

Have you ever wanted to see a nuclear power plant? Then this is the place for you. The world's first nuclear power plant is just east of Arco, and the now-abandoned plant is open for inspection in late June and early July.

71 Landing Zone RV Park

 4

Location: Near Arco; map ID5, grid f7.

Campsites, facilities: There are 63 RV or tent campsites. Hookups, laundry facilities, playground, and a sanitary disposal station are available.

Reservations, fees: No reservations are needed; the fee is $12–17 per night. Open April 15–November 1.

Directions: From Arco, go .25 mile south on the county road to the RV park.

Contact: Landing Zone RV Park, 2424 N. 3000 West, Arco, ID 83213; 208/527-8513.

Trip notes: North of Arco is the towering Mount Borah, the highest peak in Idaho. There is a fault line at the base of the peak, a result of the 1983 quake. You can fish for brook, rainbow trout, and whitefish in Big Lost River, and rainbow, bull, and brook trout in Little Lost River. You can hike nearby.

Have you ever wanted to see a nuclear power plant? Then this is the place for you. The world's first nuclear power plant is just east of Arco; the now-closed plant is open for your inspection in late June and early July.

72 Soldier Creek RV Park

 4

Location: North of Fairfield; map ID5, grid g1.

Campsites, facilities: There are 11 RV and tent campsites. Wheelchair-accessible restrooms, hookups, laundry facilities, showers, and a sanitary disposal facility are available. Pets are allowed on leashes.

Reservations, fees: No reservations are needed; the fee is $12–15 per night. Open year-round.

Directions: From Fairfield, go 10 miles north on Soldier Creek Road to the campground.

Contact: Soldier Creek RV Park, Route 1, Fairfield, ID 83327; 208/764-2684.

Trip notes: Fairfield has a museum in an old railroad depot. Sawtooth National Forest is to the north.

73 Riverside RV & Campground

 4

Location: In Bellevue; map ID5, grid g3.

Campsites, facilities: There are 38 RV or tent campsites. Hookups, pull-through sites, and showers are available. Pets are allowed on leashes.

Reservations, fees: Reservations are accepted; the fee is $5–30 per night. Open May–November.

Directions: From Hailey go south on Highway 75 four miles to Bellevue. From the center of town in Bellevue, turn west on Broadford Road to the campground.

Contact: Riverside RV & Campground, P.O. Box 432, 403 Broadford Road, Bellevue, ID 83313; 208/788-2020.

Trip notes: Silver Creek is a fly-fisher's delight. The Silver Creek Preserve is owned by the Nature Conservancy and has a visitor center. Magic Reservoir is to the south.

74 Littlewood Reservoir

 6

Location: In the Challis National Forest; map ID5, grid g4.

Campsites, facilities: There are 21 RV or tent campsites, which can accommodate a maximum RV length of 60 feet. Pull-through sites, wheelchair-accessible restrooms, and water are available. Pets are allowed on leashes.

Reservations, fees: No reservations are needed; the fee is $6 per night. Open May 15–September 30.

Directions: From Shoshone, go 39 miles northeast on U.S. 26 to Carey. From Carey, go 11 miles northwest to the reservoir.

Contact: Bureau of Reclamation, 1150 N. Curtis Rd., Boise, ID 83706; 208/436-4187, 208/378-5312.

Trip notes: You can boat, swim, and fish for brook and rainbow trout at Littlewood Reservoir. Silver Creek also has large trout.

75 Craters of the Moon National Monument

 6

Location: South of Arco; map ID5, grid g6.

Campsites, facilities: There are 52 RV or tent campsites. Pull-through sites, wheelchair-accessible restrooms, and water are available.

Reservations, fees: No reservations are needed; the fee is $10 per night. Open May 1–October 1.

Directions: From Arco, go 18 miles southwest on U.S. 93 to the monument.

Contact: Superintendent, Craters of the Moon National Monument, P.O. Box 29, Arco, ID 83213; 208/527-3267.

Trip notes: This 53,546 acre area has a unique and unusual geology, a result of 2,000-year-old lava flows and notable because of the variety of volcanic features concentrated into this one place. The Craters of the Moon National Monument was designated in 1924 to preserve unique volcanic features, including lava flows, cinder cones, spatter cones, and lava tubes (caves). The Craters of the Moon Lava Field is the largest basaltic lava field in the United States. There are a large number of plants and animals living in this harsh volcanic and high desert environment. There is a visitor's center, which offers interpretive displays, and exhibits, along with Park Service Rangers to answer questions. There are also several hiking trails.

76 Burren West LLC RV/Trailer Park

      4

Location: At West Magic Reservoir; map ID5, grid g3.

Campsites, facilities: There are 35 RV or tent campsites. Hookups are available. Pets are allowed on leashes.

Reservations, fees: No reservations are needed; the fee is $10–14 per night. Open year-round.

Directions: From Shoshone, go north on Highway 75 to a turnoff that leads to the west shore of the reservoir.

Contact: Burren West LLC RV/Trailer Park, P.O. Box 852, Shoshone, ID 83352; 208/487-2571, 208/736-0866.

Trip notes: This campground is at West Magic Reservoir, where you can fish for trout, boat, swim, and water-ski.

WAYNE SCHERR

Sand dunes

MAP ID6

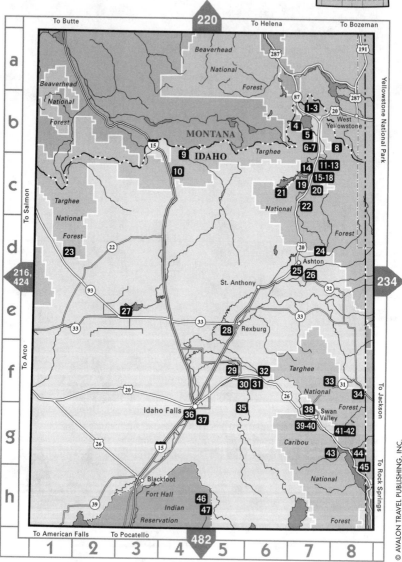

CHAPTER ID6

1 Redrock RV &
   Camping Park 449
2 Wild Rose Ranch 450
3 Staley Springs Lodge 450
4 Valley View General
   Store & RV Park 450
5 Henry's Lake State Park ... 451
6 Village Motel & RV 451
7 Macks Inn Resort 451
8 Big Springs 452
9 Steel Creek Group Area ... 452
10 Stoddard Creek 452
11 Upper Coffee Pot 452
12 Buffalo Loops A-G 453
13 Snowy River
    Campground 453
14 Flat Rock 453
15 Pond's Lodge 454
16 Robin's Roost 454
17 McCrea Bridge 454
18 Aspen Lodge 455
19 Box Canyon 455
20 Buttermilk 455
21 West End 456
22 Riverside 456
23 Birch Creek 456
24 Warm River 457
25 Jessen's RV &
    Bed & Breakfast 457
26 Aspen Acres Golf Club
    & RV Park 457
27 Haven Motel
    & Trailer Park 457
28 Rainbow Lake
    & Campground 458
29 Mountain River Ranch
    RV Park 458
30 7N Ranch 458
31 Heise Hot Springs 458
32 Kelly's Island 459
33 Pine Creek 459
34 Mike Harris 459
35 Juniper Park 459
36 Sunnyside Acres Park 460
37 Shady Rest Campground .. 460
38 South Fork Lodge 460
39 Falls 460
40 Falls Group Area 461
41 Palisades 461
42 Palisades RV Park
    & Cabins 461
43 Calamity 461
44 Big Elk Creek 462
45 Blowout 462
46 Graves Creek 462
47 Cutthroat Trout 462

1 Redrock RV & Camping Park

     5

Location: Above Henry's Lake; map ID6, grid b7.

Campsites, facilities: There are 44 RV and 10 tent campsites. Hookups, showers, a mini-mart, pull-through sites, and a sanitary disposal facility are available.

Reservations, fees: No reservations are needed; the fee is $14–16 per night. Open May 15–September 15.

Directions: From St. Anthony, Idaho, go 45 miles north on U.S. 20 to Henry's Lake State Park, go west at milepost 398 and drive five miles west on Red Rock Pass Road to the campground.

Contact: Redrock RV & Camping Park, HC 66, P.O. Box 256, Island Park, ID 83429; 800/RED-ROCK (800/

733-7635), 208/558-7442, or 800/473-3762.

Trip notes: This is in a mountain location, and you can boat, fish, swim, and hike in the area. Island Park was a collapsed volcano in prehistoric times. The former caldera is 18 miles long and 23 miles wide and marked by a 1,200-foot scarp on the south and west rims. You can golf at Island Park Village Golf Course.

❷ Wild Rose Ranch

 5

Location: Near Ashton; map ID6, grid b7.

Campsites, facilities: There are 45 RV or tent campsites, which can accommodate a maximum RV length of 30 feet. A sanitary disposal station and a restaurant are available.

Reservations, fees: No reservations are needed; the fee is $20 per night. Open year-round.

Directions: From St. Anthony, Idaho, go north on U.S. 20, turn left on Highway 87, and continue four miles. The campground is on the north shore of Henry's Lake.

Contact: Wild Rose Ranch, HC 66, P.O. Box 140, Island Park, ID 83429; 208/558-7201.

Trip notes: You can boat and fish on Henry's Lake, which opens right before Memorial Day, but be aware that the winds can be volatile. You can boat, water-ski, and fish for kokanee salmon, whitefish, brook, rainbow, and cutthroat trout in the 7,000-acre Island Park Reservoir. The Box Canyon Trail is a six-mile hike, with a trailhead at Box Canyon Campground. Island Park was a collapsed volcano in prehistoric times. The former caldera is 18 miles long and 23 miles wide and marked by a 1,200-foot scarp on the south and west rims. You can golf at Island Park Village Golf Course.

❸ Staley Springs Lodge

 5

Location: On Henry's Lake; map ID6, grid b7.

Campsites, facilities: There are 44 RV or tent campsites. Hookups, showers, a mini-mart, restaurant, and a sanitary disposal facility are available.

Reservations, fees: No reservations are needed; the fee is $17–23 per night.

Directions: From St. Anthony, go north on Highway 20, turn left on Highway 87, and continue four miles. This campground is on the northwest shore of Henry's Lake.

Contact: Staley Springs Lodge, HC 66, P.O. Box 26, Island Park, ID 83429; 208/558-7471 or fax 208/558-7300.

Trip notes: You can boat and fish in Henry's Lake. You can boat, water-ski, and fish for kokanee salmon, whitefish, brook, rainbow, and cutthroat trout in the 7,000-acre Island Park Reservoir. The Box Canyon Trail is a six-mile hike, with a trailhead at Box Canyon Campground. Island Park was a collapsed volcano in prehistoric times. The former caldera is 18 miles long and 23 miles wide and marked by a 1,200-foot scarp on the south and west rims. You can golf at Island Park Village Golf Course.

❹ Valley View General Store & RV Park

 5

Location: South of West Yellowstone; map ID6, grid b7.

Campsites, facilities: There are 53 RV or tent campsites, which can accommodate a maximum RV length of 75 feet. There are wheelchair-accessible restrooms, laundry facilities, hookups, showers, propane gas, and a mini-mart. Pets are allowed on leashes.

Reservations, fees: No reservations are needed; the fee is $16–22 per night. Open May 31–October 1.

Directions: From West Yellowstone, take U.S. 20 south for 13.5 miles; the RV Park is on the east side, across from the lake.

Contact: Valley View General Store & RV Park, HC 66, P.O. Box 26, Island Park, ID 83429; 208/558-7443.

Trip notes: Island Park was a collapsed volcano in prehistoric times. The former caldera is 18 miles long and 23 miles wide and marked by a 1,200-foot scarp on the south and west rims. You can boat, water-ski, and fish for kokanee salmon, whitefish, brook, rainbow, and cutthroat trout in the 7,000-acre Island Park Reservoir. The Box Canyon Trail is a six-mile hike, with a trailhead at Box Canyon Campground. You can golf at Island Park Village Golf Course.

5 Henry's Lake State Park

 6

Location: In Island Park; map ID6, grid b7.

Campsites, facilities: There are 50 RV or tent campsites, which can accommodate a maximum RV length of 40 feet. Wheelchair-accessible restrooms, showers, hookups, pull-through sites, and a sanitary disposal facility are provided.

Reservations, fees: No reservations are needed; the fee is $12–16 per night. Open May 30–September 30. The stay limit is 15 days.

Directions: From St. Anthony, Idaho, go north on Highway 20 to the county road, turn west on the county road, and drive for two miles to Henry's Lake State Park entrance.

Contact: Henry's Lake State Park, HC 66, P.O. Box 20, Island Park, ID 83429; 208/558-7532.

Trip notes: You can boat here, but be aware that the lake is unpredictable due to winds. You can boat, water-ski, and fish for kokanee salmon, whitefish, brook, rainbow, and cutthroat trout in the 7,000-acre Island Park Reservoir. The Box Canyon Trail is a six-mile hike, with a trailhead at Box Canyon Campground.

6 Village Motel & RV

 5

Location: Northwest of Macks Inn; map ID6, grid b7.

Campsites, facilities: There are 77 RV or tent campsites. There are 60 full hookups, a restau-

rant, laundry facilities, showers, mini-mart, pull-through sites, and a sanitary disposal station available.

Reservations, fees: No reservations are needed; the fee is $19.50 per night. Open March–December.

Directions: From St. Anthony, go north 45 miles on U.S. 20 to Macks Inn. From Macks Inn, go one mile north on U.S. 20; at milepost 395, go west on Sawtelle Peak Road, and turn right at the entrance to the RV park.

Contact: Village Motel & RV, HC 66, P.O. Box 15x, Island Park, ID 83429; 208/558-9366, 800/574-0404.

Trip notes: This is a wooded campground in a mountain setting where you can boat, fish, and hike. Island Park was a collapsed volcano in prehistoric times. The former caldera is 18 miles long and 23 miles wide and marked by a 1,200-foot scarp on the south and west rims. You can golf at Island Park Village Golf Course.

7 Macks Inn Resort

 5

Location: South of West Yellowstone; map ID6, grid b7.

Campsites, facilities: There are 73 RV or tent campsites. Laundry facilities, hookups, showers, propane gas, a mini-mart, and a sanitary disposal facility are available.

Reservations, fees: No reservations are needed; the fee is $17–25 per night.

Directions: From West Yellowstone, go 20 miles south on Highway 191 to the campground, which is on the left side. U.S. 191 is a narrow, winding road filled with semi-trucks and tourists, so use caution when driving here.

Contact: Macks Inn Resort, P.O. Box 10, Macks Inn, ID 83433; 208/558-7272.

Trip notes: This campground has trees and is near the Coffee Pot Rapids Trail, an easy 2.5-mile hike. You can boat, water-ski, and fish for kokanee salmon, whitefish, brook, rainbow, and cutthroat trout in the

7,000-acre Island Park Reservoir. The Box Canyon Trail is a six-mile hike, with a trailhead at Box Canyon Campground.

8 Big Springs

 6

Location: In Targhee National Forest; map ID6, grid b8.

Campsites, facilities: There are 17 RV or tent campsites, which can accommodate a maximum RV length of 32 feet. Wheelchair-accessible facilities and pull-through sites are provided.

Reservations, fees: No reservations are needed; the fee is $8 per night. Open June–September.

Directions: From St. Anthony, go north 45 miles on U.S. 20 to Macks Inn. From Macks Inn, go 4.5 miles east on Forest Service Road 059 to the campground.

Contact: Targhee National Forest, Island Park Ranger District, HC 65, P.O. Box 975, Island Park, ID 83429; 208/558-7301.

Trip notes: There are trailheads here and a one-mile interpretive trail to the boat-launch area. There are a historical cabin built in the 1930s and geological sites. You can boat, water-ski, and fish for kokanee salmon, whitefish, brook, rainbow, and cutthroat trout in the 7,000-acre Island Park Reservoir. The Box Canyon Trail is a six-mile hike, with a trailhead at Box Canyon Campground.

9 Steel Creek Group Area

 5

Location: In Targhee National Forest; map ID6, grid b4.

Campsites, facilities: There is one RV campsite, which can accommodate a maximum RV length of 22 feet. A wheelchair-accessible restroom and water are available.

Reservations, fees: Reservations are required for this group site; the fee is $40–100 per night, for 50–200 people, respectively. Open May 15–October 15.

Directions: From Dubois go north 16 miles on I-15 to Exit 184 (Stoddard Creek Area. Drive 17 miles southeast on Forest Service Road 006 and 1.2 miles west on Forest Service Road 478 to the campground.

Contact: Targhee National Forest, Dubois Ranger District, 225 W. Main, Dubois, ID 83423; 208/374-5422.

Trip notes: West Camas Creek and Steel Creek are nearby. You can hike and fish in Targhee National Forest.

10 Stoddard Creek

 5

Location: In Targhee National Forest; map ID6, grid c4.

Campsites, facilities: There are 24 RV or tent campsites, which can accommodate a maximum RV length of 32 feet. Wheelchair-accessible restrooms, pull-through sites, and water are available.

Reservations, fees: No reservations are needed; the fee is $6 per night. Open May 15–October 15.

Directions: From Dubois go north 16 miles on I-15 to Exit 184 (Stoddard Creek Area), turn left at the stop sign onto Forest Service Road 002. Drive one mile, turn left at the campground sign.

Contact: Targhee National Forest, Dubois Ranger District, 225 W. Main, Dubois, ID 83423; 208/374-5422.

Trip notes: You can hike and fish in Targhee National Forest.

11 Upper Coffee Pot

 5

Location: In Targhee National Forest; map ID6, grid c7.

Campsites, facilities: There are 15 RV or tent campsites, which can accommodate a maximum RV length of 32 feet.

Reservations, fees: No reservations are needed; the fee is $9–10 per night. Open May 25–September 15. The stay limit is 16 days.

Directions: Macks Inn is 45 miles of St. Anthony on U.S. 20. From Macks Inn, go two miles south on U.S. 20, then two miles southwest on Forest Service Road 130.

Contact: Targhee National Forest, Island Park Ranger District, HC 65, P.O. Box 975, Island Park, ID 83429; 208/558-7301.

Trip notes: You can fish and hike here. Island Park was a collapsed volcano in prehistoric times. You can boat, water-ski, and fish for kokanee salmon, whitefish, brook, rainbow, and cutthroat trout in the 7,000-acre Island Park Reservoir. The Box Canyon Trail is a six-mile hike, with a trailhead at Box Canyon Campground. The former caldera is 18 miles long and 23 miles wide and marked by a 1,200-foot scarp on the south and west rims. You can golf at Island Park Village Golf Course.

12 Buffalo Loops A-G

 6

Location: In the Targhee National Forest; map ID6, grid c7.

Campsites, facilities: There are 127 RV or tent campsites, which can accommodate a maximum RV length of 32 feet. Wheelchair-accessible facilities, pull-through sites, a store, and a restaurant are available.

Reservations, fees: Reservations are required; the fee is $9–12 per night. Open June–October.

Directions: From St. Anthony, go north 41 miles on U.S. 20 to Island Park; the campground is on the east side of the highway.

Contact: Targhee National Forest, Island Park Ranger District, HC 65, P.O. Box 975, Island Park, ID 83429; 208/558-7301.

Trip notes: You can fish on the Buffalo River. You can boat, water-ski, and fish for kokanee salmon, whitefish, brook, rainbow, and cutthroat trout in the 7,000-acre Island Park Reservoir. The Box Canyon Trail is a six-mile hike, with a trailhead at Box Canyon Campground.

13 Snowy River Campground

 5

Location: In Island Park; map ID6, grid c7.

Campsites, facilities: There are 57 RV or tent campsites. Propane gas and a sanitary disposal facility are available.

Reservations, fees: No reservations are needed; the fee is $10–14 per night. Open year-round.

Directions: From West Yellowstone, go 30 miles south on U.S. 20; the campground is between mile markers 383 and 384.

Contact: Snowy River Campground, HC 66, P.O. Box 431, 3502 N. Hwy. 20, Island Park, ID 83429; 208/558-7112.

Trip notes: This campground has 10 acres of grassy valley and access to Henry's River Lake. You can boat, water-ski, and fish for kokanee salmon, whitefish, brook, rainbow, and cutthroat trout in the 7,000-acre Island Park Reservoir. The Box Canyon Trail is a six-mile hike, with a trailhead at Box Canyon Campground. Island Park was a collapsed volcano in prehistoric times. The former caldera is 18 miles long and 23 miles wide and marked by a 1,200-foot scarp on the south and west rims. You can golf at Island Park Village Golf Course.

14 Flat Rock

 6

Location: In Targhee National Forest; map ID6, grid c7.

Campsites, facilities: There are 40 RV or tent campsites, which can accommodate a maximum RV length of 32 feet. There are wheelchair-accessible facilities.

Reservations, fees: Reservations are required; the fee is $9–10 per night. Open June–September. The stay limit is 16 days.

Directions: From St. Anthony, go north 41 miles on U.S. 20 to Island Park. At the intersection of A2 (Kilgore-Yale Road) and U.S. 20, take U.S. 20 north 3.5

miles to the Flat Rock campground sign and turn left to the campground.

Contact: Targhee National Forest, Island Park Ranger District, HC 65, P.O. Box 975, Island Park, ID 83429; 208/558-7301.

Trip notes: You can boat, water-ski, and fish for kokanee salmon, whitefish, brook, rainbow, and cutthroat trout in the 7,000-acre Island Park Reservoir. The Box Canyon Trail is a six-mile hike, with a trailhead at Box Canyon Campground. Island Park was a collapsed volcano in prehistoric times. The former caldera is 18 miles long and 23 miles wide and marked by a 1,200-foot scarp on the south and west rims. You can golf at Island Park Village Golf Course.

15 Pond's Lodge

 5

Location: North of Ashton; map ID6, grid c7.

Campsites, facilities: There are 64 RV or tent campsites. Hookups, wheelchair-accessible restrooms, a mini-mart, and a restaurant are available. Pets are allowed on leashes.

Reservations, fees: No reservations are needed; the fee is $6.50–15 per night.

Directions: From St. Anthony, go north on U.S. 20 to Island Park. The campground is on the west side of the highway.

Contact: Pond's Lodge, P.O. Box 258, Island Park, ID 83429; 208/558-7221.

Trip notes: You can boat, water-ski, and fish for kokanee salmon, whitefish, brook, rainbow, and cutthroat trout in the 7,000-acre Island Park Reservoir. The Box Canyon Trail is a six-mile hike, with a trailhead at Box Canyon Campground. Island Park was a collapsed volcano in prehistoric times. The former caldera is 18 miles long and 23 miles wide and marked by a 1,200-foot scarp on the south and west rims. You can golf at Island Park Village Golf Course.

16 Robin's Roost

 6

Location: In Island Park; map ID6, grid c7.

Campsites, facilities: There are 13 RV or tent campsites. Hookups, showers, a restaurant, laundry facilities, propane gas, and a mini-mart are available.

Reservations, fees: No reservations are needed; the fee is $8–12 per night.

Directions: From West Yellowstone, take U.S. 20 south for 22 miles to Island Park; the campground is on the left (it's the only Chevron station in Island Park).

Contact: Robin's Roost, HC 66, P.O. Box 10, Island Park, ID 83429; 208/558-7440.

Trip notes: You can boat, swim, water-ski, canoe, and fish in Hebgen Lake, near West Yellowstone. In Yellowstone National Park, you can fish (with permit), hike, boat, canoe, and see wildlife in their spectacular habitat. You can boat, water-ski, and fish for kokanee salmon, whitefish, brook, rainbow, and cutthroat trout in the 7,000-acre Island Park Reservoir. The Box Canyon Trail is a six-mile hike, with a trailhead at Box Canyon Campground. Island Park was a collapsed volcano in prehistoric times. The former caldera is 18 miles long and 23 miles wide and marked by a 1,200-foot scarp on the south and west rims. You can golf at Island Park Village Golf Course.

17 McCrea Bridge

 5

Location: In Targhee National Forest; map ID6, grid c7.

Campsites, facilities: There are 25 RV or tent campsites, which can accommodate a maximum RV length of 32 feet.

Reservations, fees: Reservations are required; the fee is $8 per night. Open June-September.

Directions: Macks Inn is 45 miles of St. Anthony on U.S. 20. From Macks Inn, go 3.5 miles south on U.S. 20, then 2.2 miles northwest on County Road 30 to the campground.

Contact: Targhee National Forest, Island Park Ranger District, HC 65, P.O. Box 975, Island Park, ID 83429; 208/558-7301.

Trip notes: This is a very popular camping spot, next to the boat ramp. You can fish, float, and swim. Island Park was a collapsed volcano in prehistoric times. The former caldera is 18 miles long and 23 miles wide and marked by a 1,200-foot scarp on the south and west rims. You can golf at Island Park Village Golf Course.

18 Aspen Lodge
 5

Location: Near Yellowstone Park; map ID6, grid c7.

Campsites, facilities: There are eight RV campsites. Laundry facilities, hookups, a restaurant, and a sanitary disposal facility are available. Pets are allowed on leashes.

Reservations, fees: No reservations are needed; the fee is $10 per night.

Directions: From St. Anthony, go north 41 miles on U.S. 20 to Island Park. From Island Park, turn at milepost 397.5 off U.S. 20 to the lodge.

Contact: Aspen Lodge, HC 66, P.O. Box 269, Island Park, ID 83429; 208/558-7407.

Trip notes: You can golf at Island Park Village. There are many hiking trails and fishing streams throughout Targhee National Forest and Yellowstone National Park. You can boat, water-ski, and fish for kokanee salmon, whitefish, brook, rainbow, and cutthroat trout in the 7,000-acre Island Park Reservoir. The Box Canyon Trail is a six-mile hike, with a trailhead at Box Canyon Campground. Island Park was a collapsed volcano in prehistoric times. The former caldera is 18 miles long and 23 miles wide and marked by a 1,200-foot scarp on the south and west rims. You can golf at Island Park Village Golf Course.

19 Box Canyon
 6

Location: In Targhee National Forest; map ID6, grid c7.

Campsites, facilities: There are 19 RV or tent campsites, which can accommodate a maximum RV length of 32 feet.

Reservations, fees: No reservations are needed; the fee is $9 per night. Open June–September.

Directions: From West Yellowstone, go 28 miles south on Highway 20. The campground is one mile south of the Island Park Ranger Station (watch for signs.)

Contact: Targhee National Forest, Island Park Ranger District, HC 65, P.O. Box 975, Island Park, ID 83429; 208/558-7301.

Trip notes: You can boat, water-ski, and fish for kokanee salmon, whitefish, brook, rainbow, and cutthroat trout in the 7,000-acre Island Park Reservoir. The Box Canyon Trail is a six-mile hike, with a trailhead here. Island Park was a collapsed volcano in prehistoric times. The former caldera is 18 miles long and 23 miles wide and marked by a 1,200-foot scarp on the south and west rims. You can golf at Island Park Village Golf Course.

20 Buttermilk
 6

Location: In Targhee National Forest; map ID6, grid c7.

Campsites, facilities: There are 54 RV or tent campsites, which can accommodate a maximum RV length of 32 feet.

Reservations, fees: No reservations are needed; the fee is $10 per night. Open June–September.

Directions: From St. Anthony, go north 41 miles on U.S. 20 to Island Park. At the intersection of A2 (Kilgore-Yale Road) and U.S. 20, take Kilgore-Yale Road west two miles to the campground sign (Forest Service Road 126), turn left and go three miles to the Buttermilk campground sign, turn right to the campground.

Contact: Targhee National Forest, Island Park Ranger District, HC 65, P.O. Box 975, Island Park, ID 83429; 208/558-7301.

Trip notes: You can boat, water-ski, and fish for kokanee salmon, whitefish, brook, rainbow, and cutthroat trout in the 7,000-acre Island Park Reservoir. The Box Canyon Trail is a six-mile hike, with a trailhead at Box Canyon Campground. Island Park was a collapsed volcano in prehistoric times. The former caldera is 18 miles long and 23 miles wide and marked by a 1,200-foot scarp on the south and west rims. You can golf at Island Park Village Golf Course.

21 West End

 6

Location: In Targhee National Forest; map ID6, grid c6.

Campsites, facilities: There are 19 RV or tent campsites, which can accommodate a maximum RV length of 22 feet. Picnic tables, grills, a vault toilet, and a boat ramp are available.

Reservations, fees: No reservations are needed; the fee is $9 per night. Open June 1– September 15.

Directions: From St. Anthony, go north 41 miles on U.S. 20 to Island Park. Three miles before St. Anthony, turn left at the campground sign at Forest Service Road 167, turn right and go 9.5 miles on Forest Service Road 167 to the Y intersection, stay right, and the campground is a mile and a half ahead on the right. Check the road conditions, as Forest Service Road 167 is often rough, with potholes.

Contact: Targhee National Forest, Island Park Ranger District, HC 65, P.O. Box 975, Island Park, ID 83429; 208/558-7301.

Trip notes: You can boat, swim, fish, and hike in Targhee National Forest.

22 Riverside

 6

Location: In Targhee National Forest; map ID6, grid c7.

Campsites, facilities: There are 57 RV or tent campsites. Picnic tables, grills, wheelchair-accessible restrooms, and pull-through sites are available. Pets are allowed on leashes.

Reservations, fees: Reservations are suggested; the fee is $9 per night. Open June 1– September 30.

Directions: From Ashton, go 16.5 miles north on U.S. 20, then one mile southeast on Forest Service Road 304 to the campground.

Contact: Targhee National Forest, Ashton Ranger District, P.O. Box 858, Ashton, ID 83420; 208/652-7442, fax 208/652-7863.

Trip notes: This popular wooded campground is on the river, where you can fish. You can hike in Targhee National Forest.

23 Birch Creek

 4

Location: Near Mud Lake Wildlife Management Area; map ID6, grid d1.

Campsites, facilities: There are 16 RV or tent campsites, which can accommodate a maximum RV length of 25 feet. Wheelchair-accessible restrooms are available.

Reservations, fees: No reservations are needed; the fee is $4 per night. Open May 15– September 30.

Directions: From Idaho Falls, go north on I-15 24 miles to Exit 143, then go west 12 miles to Mud Lake. From Mud Lake, go 25 miles northwest on Highway 28 to the campground.

Contact: Bureau of Land Management, Idaho Falls District Office, 1405 Hollipart Drive, Idaho Falls, ID 83401; 208/524-7500.

Trip notes: To the southeast is Mud Lake Wildlife Management Area, a wetlands habitat for thousands of snow geese that stop over here every March and April. The Camas National Wildlife Refuge covers 10,000 acres of wetlands, with an interpretive center and self-guided trails. You can fish and hike in Targhee National Forest.

24 Warm River

     7

Location: Near Ashton; map ID6, grid d7.

Campsites, facilities: There are 17 RV or tent campsites, which can accommodate a maximum RV length of 24 feet. Vault toilets and water are available. Pets are allowed on leashes.

Reservations, fees: Reservations are accepted; the fee is $6 per night. Open June 1–September 30.

Directions: From St. Anthony, go north 13 miles on U.S. 20 to Ashton. From Ashton, go 10 miles northeast on Highway 47 to the campground.

Contact: Ashton Ranger District, 30 S. Yellowstone Hwy., P.O. Box 858, Ashton, ID 83420; 208/652-7442.

Trip notes: Harriman State Park, north of Ashton, has fishing, hiking, mountain biking, and a variety of wildlife.

25 Jessen's RV & Bed & Breakfast

    5

Location: South of Ashton; map ID6, grid d7.

Campsites, facilities: There are 22 RV or tent sites, some with hookups. There are laundry facilities, showers, propane gas, workout facilities, and a sanitary disposal station available. Pets are allowed on leashes.

Reservations, fees: No reservations are needed; the fee is $14 per night.

Directions: From St. Anthony, go north 13 miles on U.S. 20 to Ashton. The campground is two miles of town.

Contact: Jessen's RV & Bed & Breakfast, 1146 N. 3400 East, Hwy. 20, Ashton, ID 83420; 208/652-3356.

Trip notes: Ashton has two 18-hole golf cours-

es, and there are hiking trails and fishing in Targhee National Forest to the north.

26 Aspen Acres Golf Club & RV Park

    5

Location: Near Ashton; map ID6, grid d7.

Campsites, facilities: There are 40 RV or tent campsites, some with hookups. There are laundry facilities, showers, and a sanitary disposal station available. Pets are allowed on leashes.

Reservations, fees: Reservations are accepted; the fee is $16.50–19.00 per night.

Directions: From St. Anthony, go north 13 miles on U.S. 20 to Ashton. From Ashton, go nine miles southeast on Highway 32 to the campground.

Contact: Aspen Acres Golf Club & RV Park, 4179 E. 1100 North, Ashton, ID 83420; 208/652-3524.

Trip notes: Ashton has two 18-hole golf courses, and there are hiking trails and fishing in the Targhee National Forest, to the north.

27 Haven Motel & Trailer Park

    4

Location: Northwest of Idaho Falls; map ID6, grid e3.

Campsites, facilities: There are 13 RV or tent sites.

Reservations, fees: No reservations are needed; the fee is $8 per night.

Directions: From Rexburg on U.S. 20, go west on Highway 33 to Mud Lake and the campground.

Contact: Haven Motel & Trailer Park, 1079 E. 1500 North, Mud Lake, ID 83450; 208/663-4821.

Trip notes: Mud Lake Wildlife Management Area, north of here, is a bird sanctuary, with songbirds, migrating waterfowl, and raptors. Mule deer and pronghorn antelope frequent the area. You can fish and use small boats here.

28 Rainbow Lake & Campground

 4

Location: In Rexburg; map ID6, grid e5.

Campsites, facilities: There are 60 RV or tent campsites, some with hookups. Wheelchair-accessible restrooms, laundry facilities, showers, and a sanitary disposal station are available. Pets are allowed on leashes.

Reservations, fees: No reservations are needed; the fee is $12–14 per night.

Directions: From Rexburg, go .25 mile west and 1.25 miles south on U.S. 20 to the campground.

Contact: Rainbow Lake & Campground, 2245 S. 2000W, Rexburg, ID 83440; 208/356-3681.

Trip notes: You can boat and fish nearby. The Upper Snake River Valley Historical Society has a museum about the Teton flood and local history.

29 Mountain River Ranch RV Park

 6

Location: East of Rigby; map ID6, grid f5.

Campsites, facilities: There are 27 RV or tent campsites, some with hookups. Showers and a sanitary disposal station are available. Pets are allowed on leashes.

Reservations, fees: Reservations are accepted; the fee is $14–16 per night. Open June 1–October 1.

Directions: From Idaho Falls, take U.S. 26 east to Ririe, where there are signs directing you to Mountain River Ranch, Heise Hot Springs, and Kelly Canyon Ski Area. Take a left at these signs, and follow the road to the RV park.

Contact: Mountain River Ranch RV Park, 95-8 N. 5050, Ririe, ID 83443; 208/538-7337; www.mountainriverranch.com.

Trip notes: You can fish at Ririe Reservoir and hike the Cress Creek Nature Trail. Heise Hot Springs, natural mineral waters, are on the north bank of the Snake River.

30 7N Ranch

 6

Location: East of Rigby; map ID6, grid f5.

Campsites, facilities: There are 28 RV or tent campsites, some with hookups. Showers, laundry facilities, and a sanitary disposal station are available. Pets are allowed on leashes.

Reservations, fees: No reservations are needed; the fee is $7–13 per night.

Directions: From Idaho Falls, go 21 miles on U.S. 26 to the campground.

Contact: 7N Ranch, 5156 E. Heise Rd., Ririe, ID 83443; 208/538-5097.

Trip notes: You can fish at Ririe Reservoir and hike the Cress Creek Nature Trail. Heise Hot Springs, natural mineral waters, are on the north bank of the Snake River.

31 Heise Hot Springs

 6

Location: East of Rigby; map ID6, grid f6.

Campsites, facilities: There are 50 RV or tent campsites, some with hookups. Wheelchair-accessible restrooms, laundry facilities, showers, restaurant, and a swimming pool are available.

Reservations, fees: No reservations are needed; the fee is $10–15 per night. Open December–October.

Directions: From Idaho Falls, go east 22 miles on U.S. 26, turn left at the signs and follow the road for four miles to the resort on the north bank of the Snake River.

Contact: Heise Hot Springs, 5116 Heise Rd., P.O. Box 417, Heise, ID 83443; 208/538-7312.

Trip notes: You can fish at Ririe Reservoir and hike the Cress Creek Nature Trail. The natural mineral waters of the hot springs are on the north bank of the Snake River.

32 Kelly's Island

 6

Location: East of Rigby; map ID6, grid f6.

Campsites, facilities: There are 15 RV or tent campsites, which can accommodate a maximum RV length of 40 feet, some with hookups. Wheelchair-accessible restrooms and water are available.

Reservations, fees: No reservations are needed; the fee is $6 per night. Open May 1–October 31.

Directions: From Idaho Falls, go 22 miles east on U.S. 26 to Heise. From Heise, go two miles east on the access road, and the campground is on the north side of the river.

Contact: Bureau of Land Management, Idaho Falls District Office, 1405 Hollipart Drive, Idaho Falls, ID 83401; 208/524-7500.

Trip notes: You can fish at Ririe Reservoir and hike the Cress Creek Nature Trail. Heise Hot Springs, natural mineral waters, is on the north bank of the Snake River.

33 Pine Creek

 7

Location: In Big Hole Mountains; map ID6, grid f7.

Campsites, facilities: There are nine RV or tent sites, which can accommodate a maximum RV length of 15 feet. A vault toilet is available.

Reservations, fees: No reservation is needed; the fee is $6 per night. Open June 15–September 15.

Directions: From Driggs, go south on Highway 33 to Victor. From Victor, go 6.5 miles west on Highway 31; the campground is on the Victor side of Pine Creek Pass.

Contact: Teton Basin Ranger District, P.O. Box 777, Driggs, ID 83422; 208/354-2312.

Trip notes: You can hike and mountain bike such trails as Patterson Creek Trail and Moose Creek Trail.

34 Mike Harris

 7

Location: In Targhee National Forest; map ID6, grid f8.

Campsites, facilities: There are 12 RV or tent campsites with a maximum RV length of 20 feet. Pull-through sites, drinking water, and vault toilets are available. Pets are allowed on leashes.

Reservations, fees: No reservations are needed; the fee is $6 per night. Open June 15–September 15. The stay limit is 14 days.

Directions: From Victor, Idaho, go four miles southeast on Highway 33 to the campground sign, turn right and go .3 mile to campground.

Contact: Teton Basin Ranger District, P.O. Box 777, Driggs, ID 83422; 208/354-3421 or 208/354-2312.

Trip notes: This campground is in a forested setting close to the Wyoming border and offers fishing and hiking.

35 Juniper Park

 6

Location: At Ririe Reservoir map ID6, grid g5.

Campsites, facilities: There are 49 RV or tent campsites, which can accommodate a maximum RV length of 42 feet, some with hookups and pull-through sites. Restrooms, barrier-free access, showers, a sanitary disposal station, and a playground are available. Pets are allowed on leashes.

Reservations, fees: No reservations are needed; the fee is $9–12 per night. Open May 15–October 15.

Directions: From Idaho Falls, go east on U.S. 26 to Meadow Creek Road, then south on Meadow Creek Road to the Ririe Reservoir.

Contact: Bureau of Reclamation, 1150 N. Curtis Rd., Boise, ID 83706; 208/436-4187, 208/378-5312.

Trip notes: You can hike, boat, fish, and swim at Ririe Reservoir.

36 Sunnyside Acres Park

 4

Location: At Idaho Falls; map ID6, grid g4.

Campsites, facilities: There are 25 RV or tent sites, some with hookups and pull-throughs. There are showers, laundry facilities, and a sanitary disposal station available.

Reservations, fees: No reservations are needed; the fee is $14 per night.

Directions: From I-15 at Idaho Falls, take Exit 118 onto West Broadway if you are southbound, or take Exit 113 onto Jackson Highway if you are northbound, to reach the campground.

Contact: Sunnyside Acres Park, 905 W. Sunnyside Rd., Idaho Falls, ID 83401; 208/523-8403.

Trip notes: Idaho Falls has a 29-acre greenbelt that runs along the Snake River, three golf courses, and all the amenities you'd expect for a city its size (pop. 50,000).

37 Shady Rest Campground

 4

Location: At Idaho Falls; map ID6, grid g4.

Campsites, facilities: There are 55 RV or tent campsites, some with hookups. Laundry facilities and showers are available.

Reservations, fees: No reservations are needed; the fee is $11–12 per night.

Directions: From Pocatello, go north on I-15 to Idaho Falls, take the U.S. 20/Broadway Street exit, and turn right. At North Yellowstone Avenue, turn left and go to the campground.

Contact: Shady Rest Campground, 2200 N. Yellowstone, Idaho Falls, ID 83401; 208/524-0010. This campground is in the city of Idaho Falls.

Trip notes: Idaho Falls has a 29-acre greenbelt that runs along the Snake River, three golf courses, and all the amenities you'd expect for a city its size.

38 South Fork Lodge

 6

Location: Near Swan Valley; map ID6, grid g7.

Campsites, facilities: There are 48 RV or tent campsites, some with hookups. Showers, a restaurant, and a sanitary disposal station are available. Pets are allowed on leashes.

Reservations, fees: No reservations are needed; the fee is $10–17 per night.

Directions: From Idaho Falls, go 45 miles east on U.S. 26 to Swan Valley. The campground is four miles west of Swan Valley on U.S. 26.

Contact: South Fork Lodge, P.O. Box 22, Swan Valley, ID 83449; 208/483-2112.

Trip notes: Palisades Reservoir is nearby, where you can swim, boat, water-ski, and fish for Mackinaw and kokanee trout. There are several hiking trails in the surrounding mountains. Snake River also has good fishing and floating opportunities.

39 Falls

 6

Location: Near Swan Valley; map ID6, grid g7.

Campsites, facilities: There are 23 RV or tent sites, which can accommodate a maximum RV length of 24 feet. Vault toilets and water are available.

Reservations, fees: No reservations are needed; the fee is $6 per night. Open May 21–September 7.

Directions: From Idaho Falls, go 45 miles east on U.S. 26 to Swan Valley. Four miles before Swan Valley, go 2.3 miles south on Forest Service Road 076 to the campground.

Contact: Palisades Ranger District, 3659 E. Ririe Hwy., Idaho Falls, ID 83401; 208/523-1412.

Trip notes: Palisades Reservoir is nearby, where you can swim, boat, water-ski, and fish for Mackinaw and kokanee trout. There are several hiking trails in the surrounding mountains. Snake River also has good fishing and floating opportunities.

40 Falls Group Area

     6

Location: Near Swan Valley; map ID6, grid g7.

Campsites, facilities: There is one group campsite, which can accommodate a maximum RV length of 22 feet. Vault toilets and water are available.

Reservations, fees: Reservations are accepted; the fee is $6 and up per night. Open May 21–September 7.

Directions: From Idaho Falls, go 45 miles east on U.S. 26 to Swan Valley. Four miles before Swan Valley, go 2.3 miles south on Forest Service Road 076 to the campground.

Contact: Palisades Ranger District, 3659 E. Ririe Hwy., Idaho Falls, ID 83401; 208/523-1412.

Trip notes: Palisades Reservoir is nearby, where you can swim, boat, water-ski, and fish for Mackinaw and kokanee. There are several hiking trails in the surrounding mountains. Snake River also has good fishing and floating opportunities.

41 Palisades

       6

Location: Northeast of Palisades; map ID6, grid g8.

Campsites, facilities: There are eight RV or tent campsites, which can accommodate a maximum RV length of 22 feet. Vault toilets and water are available.

Reservations, fees: No reservations are needed; the fee is $6 per night. Open May 21–September 15.

Directions: From Idaho Falls, go 55 miles east on U.S. 26 to Palisades. From Palisades, go two miles northeast on Forest Service Road 225 to the campground.

Contact: Palisades Ranger District, 3659 E. Ririe Hwy., Idaho Falls, ID 83401; 208/523-1412.

Trip notes: Palisades Lakes Trailhead is located here. Palisades Reservoir is nearby, where you can swim, boat, water-ski, and fish for Mackinaw and kokanee trout. There are

several hiking trails in the surrounding mountains. Snake River also has good fishing and floating opportunities.

42 Palisades RV Park & Cabins

    4

Location: At Palisades Dam; map ID6, grid g8.

Campsites, facilities: There are 14 RV or tent campsites, which can accommodate a maximum RV length of 40 feet, some with pull-through sites. Pets are allowed on leashes.

Reservations, fees: Reservations are accepted; the fee is $13.50–17.90. Open April–October.

Directions: From Idaho Falls, go east on U.S. 26 to Palisades, and the RV park is on the highway at mile marker 385, across from gas station.

Contact: Palisades RV Park & Cabins, 3802 Swan Valley Hwy., Palisades, ID 83428; 208/483-4485.

Trip notes: Palisades Reservoir is nearby, where you can swim, boat, water-ski, and fish for Mackinaw and kokanee trout. There are several hiking trails in the surrounding mountains. Snake River also has good fishing and floating opportunities.

43 Calamity

   6

Location: At Palisades Dam; map ID6, grid g8.

Campsites, facilities: There are 41 RV or tent sites, which can accommodate a maximum RV length of 32 feet. Wheelchair-accessible restrooms, a boat ramp, and water are available.

Reservations, fees: Reservations are accepted; the fee is $6 per night. Open May 21–September 15.

Directions: From Idaho Falls, go 55 miles east on U.S. 26 to Palisades. From Palisades, go 2.6 miles south on U.S.

26, then 1.1 miles southwest on Forest Service Road 058 to the campground.

Contact: Palisades Ranger District, 3659 E. Ririe Hwy., Idaho Falls, ID 83401; 208/523-1412.

Trip notes: Palisades Reservoir is nearby, where you can swim, boat, water-ski, and fish for Mackinaw and kokanee trout. There are several hiking trails in the surrounding mountains. The Snake River has good fishing and floating opportunities.

44 Big Elk Creek

 5

Location: At Palisades Reservoir in Targhee National Forest; map ID6, grid g8.

Campsites, facilities: There are 21 campsites, which can accommodate a maximum RV length of 22 feet. Group sites are available. Drinking water and a vault toilet are available.

Reservations, fees: Reservations are accepted for groups, $8 per night; the fee is $35 for groups. Open mid-May–mid-September. The stay limit is 16 days.

Directions: From Palisades, go 5.4 miles southeast on U.S. 26, then 1.4 miles northeast on Forest Road 262 to the campground.

Contact: Palisades Ranger District, 3659 E. Ririe Hwy., Idaho Falls, ID 83401; 208/523-1412.

Trip notes: You can fish Palisades Reservoir for cutthroat and brown trout, kokanee salmon and Mackinaw. You can also swim, boat, and water-ski on this 16,000-acre lake. There is a trailhead here for Little Elk Creek Trail (up the creek) and you can take that into the Snake River Range. Caribou National Forest has numerous backcountry hiking and horseback riding trails.

45 Blowout

 6

Location: At Palisades Reservoir in Targhee National Forest; map ID6, grid g8.

Campsites, facilities: There are 19 RV or tent campsites, which can accommodate a maxi-

mum RV length of 32 feet. Vault toilets, drinking water, and a boat ramp are available.

Reservations, fees: No reservations are needed; the fee is $5 per night. Open June–October. The stay limit is 16 days.

Directions: From Palisades, go nine miles southeast on U.S. 26.

Contact: Palisades Ranger District, 3659 E. Ririe Hwy., Idaho Falls, ID 83401; 208/523-1412.

Trip notes: You can boat, swim, water-ski, or fish in Palisades Reservoir. You can go horseback riding nearby.

46 Graves Creek

 4

Location: On Fort Hall Indian Reservation; map ID6, grid h5.

Campsites, facilities: There are five RV or tent campsites, which can accommodate a maximum RV length of 15 feet. A vault toilet is available.

Reservations, fees: No reservations are needed; the fee is $5 per night. Open May 1–October 31.

Directions: From Blackfoot, go seven miles north on U.S. 91, then 10 miles east on Wolverine Road, right on Cedar Creek Road for 13 miles, right on Trail Creek Bridge Road for six miles, and the road turns into Lincoln Creek Road, and the campground is one mile.

Contact: Bureau of Land Management, Idaho Falls District Office, 1405 Hollipart Drive, Idaho Falls, ID 83401; 208/524-7500.

Trip notes: You can fish in Portneuf River and Reservoir for rainbow and cutthroat trout.

47 Cutthroat Trout

 4

Location: On Fort Hall Indian Reservation; map ID6, grid h5.

Campsites, facilities: There are five RV or tent campsites, which can accommodate a maximum RV length of 15 feet. A vault toilet is available.

Reservations, fees: No reservations are needed; the fee is $5 per night. Open May 1–October 31.

Directions: From Blackfoot, go seven miles north on U.S. 91, then 10 miles east on Wolverine Road, right on Cedar Creek Road for 13 miles, right on Trail Creek Bridge Road for six miles, and the road turns into Lincoln Creek Road, and the campground is three miles.

Contact: Bureau of Land Management, Idaho Falls District Office, 1405 Hollipart Drive, Idaho Falls, ID 83401; 208/524-7500.

Trip notes: You can fish in Portneuf River and Reservoir for rainbow and cutthroat trout.

Falls River

MAP ID7

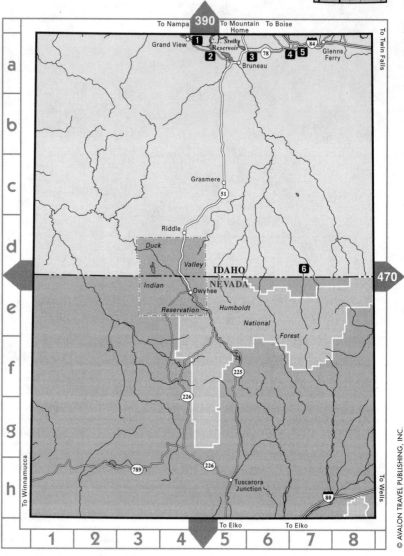

CHAPTER ID7

1 C. J. Strike Parks 467
2 Cove 467
3 Bruneau Dunes
State Park 467
4 Three Island Crossing
State Park 468
5 Trails West RV Park
and Campground 468
6 Desert Hot Springs 468

1 C. J. Strike Parks

 4

Location: Southwest of Mountain Home; map ID7, grid a4.

Campsites, facilities: There are 50 RV or tent campsites, which can accommodate a maximum RV length of 40 feet. Pull-through sites, flush toilets, and water are available.

Reservations, fees: No reservations are needed; the fee is $12 per night. Open year-round.

Directions: From Mountain Home, take Highway 67 to Grandview southeast on Highway 78, turn left at the high school, then go north to C. J. Strike Dam.

Contact: Idaho Fish & Game Department, Bruneau, ID 83604; 208/845-2324.

Trip notes: There are three parks in this area. The Snake River Birds of Prey National Area is 482 acres along 81 miles of the Snake River Canyon, home to the largest number of nesting raptors in the U.S. You can mountain bike or hike the Swans Fall Loop, a 17.5-mile trail that follows the Snake River. You can walk or bike in the C. J. Strike Wildlife Management Area and see deer, raptors, and waterfowl.

2 Cove

 4

Location: South of Mountain Home; map ID7, grid a5.

Campsites, facilities: There are 26 RV or tent campsites, which can accommodate a maximum RV length of 25 feet. Pull-through sites, vault toilets, and water are available.

Reservations, fees: No reservations are needed; the fee is $8 per night. Open April 15–October 31.

Directions: From Mountain Home, go south on Highway 51 to Bruneau, then go two more miles to Highway 78, and go west on Highway 78 to the campground.

Contact: Bureau of Land Management, Boise District Office, 3948 Development Ave., Boise, ID 83705; 208/384-3300.

Trip notes: You can boat, swim, fish, and hike here.

3 Bruneau Dunes State Park

 5

Location: South of Mountain Home; map ID7, grid a6.

Campsites, facilities: There are 48 RV or tent campsites, which can accommodate a maximum RV length of 30 feet. Hookups, showers, wheelchair-accessible restrooms, water, and a sanitary disposal facility are available.

Reservations, fees: Reservations are accepted; the fee is $12 per night. Open year-round. The stay limit is 15 days.

Directions: From Mountain Home, go 18 miles south on Highway 51, then two miles east on Highway 78 to state park.

Contact: Bruneau Dunes State Park, HC 85, P.O. Box 41, Mountain Home, ID 83647; 208/366-7919.

Trip notes: There is a 470-foot-high sand dune at this 4,800-acre park, the largest single-structured sand dune in North America. A variety of waterfowl, coyote, and rabbit frequent the area, and early morning and late evenings are the best times to see them. You can fish for bass and bluegill and hike the five-mile trail.

◪ Three Island Crossing State Park

 5

Location: At Glenns Ferry; map ID7, grid a7.

Campsites, facilities: There are 101 RV or tent campsites. Wheelchair-accessible restrooms, hookups, showers, water, and a sanitary disposal facility are available.

Reservations, fees: Reservations are available; the fee is $12 per night. Open year-round. There is a stay limit of 15 days.

Directions: From Twin Falls, go 52 miles west on I-84 to Exit 121 (Glenns Ferry). From Glenns Ferry, go two miles west on Madison Street to the state park.

Contact: Three Island Crossing State Park, P.O. Box 609, Glenns Ferry, ID 83623, 208/366-2394.

Trip notes: This area was one of the most famous river crossings on the historic Oregon Trail. There is an interpretive center, self-guided tours, and programs. A golf course and Carmela Vineyards are nearby.

◫ Trails West RV Park and Campground

 4

Location: In Glenns Ferry; map ID7, grid a7.

Campsites, facilities: There are 52 RV or tent campsites. Hookups, showers, laundry facilities, and a sanitary disposal station are available. Pets are allowed on leashes.

Reservations, fees: No reservations are needed; the fee is $10–15 per night. Open year-round.

Directions: From Twin Falls, go 52 miles west on I-84 to Exit 121 (Glenns Ferry); the campground is on North Bannock Street.

Contact: Trails West RV Park & Campground, Route 1, Box 400, 510 N. Bannock St., Glenns Ferry, ID 83623; 208/366-2002.

Trip notes: Glenns Ferry has a golf course and a museum. Three Island Crossing State Park was one of the most famous river crossings on the historic Oregon Trail. There is an interpretive center, self-guided tours, and programs. Carmela Vineyards are nearby.

◻ Desert Hot Springs

 3

Location: Southwest of Twin Falls, near Nevada border; map ID7, grid d7.

Campsites, facilities: There are 12 RV sites and several tent campsites, some with hookups. Wheelchair-accessible restrooms, showers, a swimming pool, and restaurant are available. Pets are allowed on leashes.

Reservations, fees: No reservations are needed, but reservations are accepted; the fee is $4.50–15.50 per night. Open year-round.

Directions: From Twin Falls, go 31 miles south on U.S. 93 to Rogerson. From Rogerson, go 50 miles west on Three Creek Road to Desert Hot Springs, on the left.

Contact: Desert Hot Springs, General Delivery, Rogerson, ID 83302; 208/857-2233.

Trip notes: You can kayak, canoe, or fish (Memorial Day–November) at Bruneau River, which goes through the Bruneau Canyon. There are trails for hiking and mountain biking in the area. This is badlands territory, and it is unique and remote.

WAYNE SCHERR

RV camping

MAP ID8

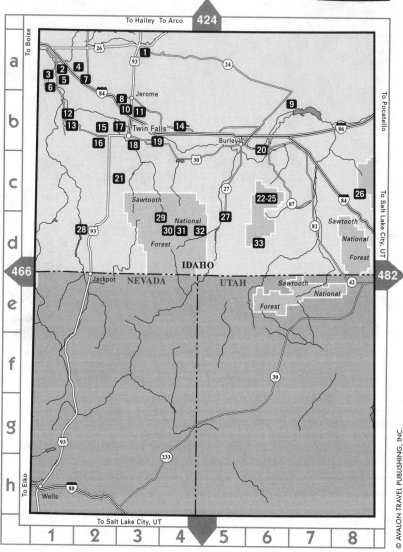

CHAPTER ID8

■1 McFall Hotel and RV Park...471
■2 Rock Lodge Resort
& Creekside RV Park........471
■3 Sligar's 1000 Springs
Resort..........................472
■4 High Adventure River
Tours RV Park & Store.....472
■5 Hagerman RV Village.......472
■6 Sportsman's River
Resort..........................473
■7 Intermountain Motor
Homes and RV Park.........473
■8 Big Tree RV Park.............473
■9 Lake Walcott State Park...473
■10 Twin Falls-Jerome KOA.....474
■11 Quinn's Rainbow Lodge.....474
■12 Miracle Hot Springs.........474
■13 Banbury Hot Springs.......474
■14 R & E Greenwood Store....475
■15 Twin Falls County
Fairgrounds...................475

■16 Curry Trailer Park...........475
■17 Oregon Trail Campground
& Family Fun Center........475
■18 Blue Lakes RV Park..........475
■19 Anderson Camp &
RV Sales and Service........476
■20 PV Travel Stop 216..........476
■21 Nat-soo-pah Hot Springs
& RV Park.....................476
■22 Thompson Flat...............476
■23 Lake Cleveland...............477
■24 Bennett Springs.............477
■25 Brackenbury..................477
■26 Sublett......................477
■27 City of Oakley RV Park.....478
■28 Lud Drexler Park............478
■29 Schipper.....................478
■30 Pettit........................479
■31 Diamondfield Jack..........479
■32 Bostetter....................479
■33 City of Rocks
National Reserve............480

■1 McFall Hotel and RV Park

      4

Location: In Shoshone; map ID8, grid a3.

Campsites, facilities: There are 10 RV or tent campsites. Hookups and showers are available. Pets are allowed on leashes.

Reservations, fees: No reservations are needed; the fee is $8–15 per night. Open year-round.

Directions: The McFall Hotel is on South Rail Street in Shoshone.

Contact: McFall Hotel & RV Park, 210 S. Rail, Shoshone, ID 83352; 208/734-1350.

Trip notes: This campground is behind the famous McFall Hotel, which is listed on the National Register of Historic Places. Guests who visited the hotel in its heyday include three U.S. presidents and Ernest Hemingway. You can fish in the Big Wood River.

■2 Rock Lodge Resort & Creekside RV Park

    4

Location: In Hagerman; map ID8, grid a1.

Campsites, facilities: There are 11 RV or tent campsites. Wheelchair-accessible restrooms, laundry facilities, hookups, a restaurant, and showers are available. Pets are allowed on leashes.

Reservations, fees: No reservations are needed; the fee is $8–15 per night. Open year-round.

Directions: From Twin Falls, go 32 miles west on I-84 to Bliss. From Bliss go 14 miles south on Highway 30 to Hagerman. The resort is on Highway 30 on Billingsley.

Contact: Rock Lodge Resort & Creekside RV Park, P.O. Box 449, 17940 U.S. 30, Hagerman, ID 83332; 208/837-4822.

Trip notes: U.S. 30 is known as Thousand Springs Scenic Route, with waterfalls and wildlife. Hagerman National Fish Hatchery holds rainbow and steelhead trout. There is a self-guided tour available.

3 Sligar's 1000 Springs Resort

 4

Location: In Hagerman; map ID8, grid a1.

Campsites, facilities: There are 60 RV or tent campsites. Wheelchair-accessible restrooms, hookups, showers, and a swimming pool are on-site. Pets are allowed on leashes.

Reservations, fees: No reservations are needed; the fee is $9–14 per night.

Directions: From Twin Falls, go 32 miles west on I-84 to Bliss. From Bliss, go south on U.S. 30 to Hagerman and the resort is right on the highway.

Contact: Sligar's 1000 Springs Resort, 18734 Hwy. 30, Route 1, Box 90, Hagerman, ID 83332; 208/837-4987.

Trip notes: U.S. 30 is known as Thousand Springs Scenic Route, with waterfalls and wildlife. Hagerman National Fish Hatchery holds rainbow and steelhead trout. There is a self-guided tour available.

4 Adventure River Tours RV Park & Store

 4

Location: Northwest of Twin Falls; map ID8, grid a2.

Campsites, facilities: There are 24 RV or tent campsites. Wheelchair-accessible restrooms, hookups, showers, propane gas, and pull-

through sites are available. Pets are allowed on leashes.

Reservations, fees: No reservations are needed; the fee is $12–15 per night.

Directions: From Twin Falls, go west 17 miles on I-84 to Wendell. From Wendell, go six miles northwest on I-84 to the RV park.

Contact: High Adventure River Tours RV Park & Store, I-84 Exit 147, Hagerman, ID 83332; 208/837-9005, 800/286-4123.

Trip notes: The nearby Niagara Springs Area was named for the springs where the waters bubble, then tumble over the cliffs. The Thousand Springs Preserve, owned by the Nature Conservancy, has Sand Springs Falls, a 400-foot waterfall. You can canoe or float the Snake River, and guided tours can be arranged.

5 Hagerman RV Village

 4

Location: In Hagerman; map ID8, grid a1.

Campsites, facilities: There are 53 RV or tent campsites, which can accommodate a maximum RV length of 75 feet. There are pull-through sites, hookups, laundry facilities, showers, an exercise room, and playground. Pets are allowed on leashes.

Reservations, fees: No reservations are needed; the fee is $10–16 per night. Open year-round.

Directions: From Twin Falls, go 32 miles west on I-84 to Bliss. From Bliss, go eight miles south on U.S. 30 and the campground is on the right before town.

Contact: Hagerman RV Village, 18049 Hwy. 30 North, P.O. Box 297, Hagerman, ID 83332; 208/837-4906, 208/837-4412.

Trip notes: The Hagerman Fossil Beds National Monument is not open to the public, but rangers lead free tours of sites throughout the summer. The digs here have produced more than 125 skeletons of prehistoric horses, now considered Idaho's state fossil. The Malad Gorge State Park is northwest of Hagerman. The Malad River runs through the gorge, and you can stand on the footbridge, 175 feet above the Malad River, to view the gorge. The river tumbles 60 feet at the Devils Washbowl, then continues through a spectacular 250-foot gorge on its way to the Snake River, 2.5 miles downstream. There are several good trails in the state park.

6 Sportsman's River Resort

 4

Location: Near Hagerman; map ID8, grid a1.
Campsites, facilities: There are 10 RV and tent campsites. Hookups, showers, and a restaurant are available.
Reservations, fees: No reservations are needed; the fee is $16 per night. Open year-round.
Directions: From Twin Falls, go 32 miles west on I-84 to Bliss. From Bliss go 14 miles south on Highway 30 to Hagerman. From Hagerman, go five miles south on U.S. 30 to the resort.
Contact: Sportsman's River Resort, 5 Gilhooley Lane, Hagerman, ID 83332; 208/837-6202, 208/837-6575.
Trip notes: U.S. 30 is known as Thousand Springs Scenic Route, with waterfalls and wildlife. Hagerman National Fish Hatchery holds rainbow, and steelhead trout. There is a self-guided tour available.

7 Intermountain Motor Homes and RV Park

 4

Location: Northwest of Twin Falls; map ID8, grid a2.
Campsites, facilities: There are 25 RV or tent campsites, which can accommodate a maximum RV length of 60 feet. Wheelchair-accessible restrooms, laundry facilities, pull-through sites, hookups, showers, and a sanitary disposal facility are available.
Reservations, fees: No reservations are needed; the fee is $10 and up per night. Open year-round.

Directions: From Twin Falls, go 16 miles northwest on I-84 to Wendell; the campground is off I-84 between Exits 155 and 157.
Contact: Intermountain Motor Homes and RV Park, 1894 Frontage Rd. North, Wendell, ID 83355; 208/536-2301.
Trip notes: The nearby Niagara Springs Area was named for the Niagara Springs, where the waters bubble, then tumble over the cliffs. The Thousand Springs Preserve, owned by the Nature Conservancy, has Sand Springs Falls, a 400-foot waterfall. You can canoe or float the Snake River, and guided tours can be arranged.

8 Big Tree RV Park

 4

Location: In Jerome; map ID8, grid b3.
Campsites, facilities: There are 25 RV or tent campsites. Hookups, laundry facilities, and showers are available.
Reservations, fees: No reservations are needed; the fee is $12–15 per night. Open year-round.
Directions: This campground is on 1st Avenue in Jerome.
Contact: Big Tree RV Park, 300 1st Ave. West, Jerome, ID 83338; 208/324-8265.
Trip notes: Jerome has an 18-hole golf course and a historical museum.

9 Lake Walcott State Park

 5

Location: Southwest of Pocatello; map ID8, grid b7.
Campsites, facilities: There are 22 RV or tent campsites, which can accommodate a maximum RV length of 60 feet. Wheelchair-accessible restrooms, water, pull-through sites, and a sanitary disposal station are available. Pets are allowed on leashes.
Reservations, fees: No reservations are needed; the fee is $12 per night. Open year-round.

Directions: From Rupert, go six miles northeast on Highway 24, then go east six miles on County Road 400N to the refuge.

Contact: Lake Walcott State Park, 951 E. Minidoka Dam, Rupert, ID 83350; 208/436-1258; Bureau of Reclamation, 208/436-6117.

Trip notes: You can boat, fish, and hike here. The Minidoka National Wildlife Refuge stretches for 25 miles along the shore of the Snake River and includes Lake Walcott.

10 Twin Falls-Jerome KOA

 4

Location: North of Twin Falls; map ID8, grid b3.

Campsites, facilities: There are 112 RV or tent campsites. There are accessible restrooms, a swimming pool, a restaurant, laundry facilities, hookups, showers, water, pull-through sites, a sanitary disposal facility, playground, and miniature golf.

Reservations, fees: No reservations are needed; the fee is $18–25 per night. Open March 15–November 1.

Directions: From I-84 in Twin Falls, take Exit 173, and go one mile north on U.S. 93 to the campground.

Contact: Twin Falls-Jerome KOA, 5431 U.S. 93, Jerome, ID 83338; 208/324-4169.

Trip notes: This campground is near the Snake River Canyon. Twin Falls has golf courses and museums.

11 Quinn's Rainbow Lodge

4

Location: In Twin Falls; map ID8, grid b3.

Campsites, facilities: There are 60 RV or tent campsites. Wheelchair-accessible restrooms, hookups, laundry facilities, showers, a restaurant, and a sanitary disposal facility are available. Pets are allowed on leashes.

Reservations, fees: No reservations are needed; the fee is $8–16 per night. Open year-round.

Directions: From U.S. 93, get off at Addison Avenue East, go to Morningstar and turn right, then to Maple, turn left on Maple to the campground.

Contact: Quinn's Rainbow Lodge, 1972 Maple Ave., Twin Falls, ID 83301; 208/487-2020.

Trip notes: Twin Falls has three golf courses and several museums.

12 Miracle Hot Springs

 5

Location: West of Twin Falls; map ID8, grid b1.

Campsites, facilities: There are 35 RV or tent campsites. Hookups and a swimming pool are available. Pets are allowed on leashes.

Reservations, fees: No reservations are needed; the fee is $8–10 per night. Open year-round.

Directions: ? From Twin Falls, go 18 miles west on U.S. 30 to Buhl. From Buhl, go 10 miles northwest on U.S. 30 to the hot springs.

Contact: Miracle Hot Springs, P.O. Box 171, Buhl, ID 83604; 208/543-6002, 208/543-6091.

Trip notes: There is a natural mineral springs pool here.

13 Banbury Hot Springs

 5

Location: East of Twin Falls; map ID8, grid b1.

Campsites, facilities: There are 22 RV and 30 tent campsites. Wheelchair-accessible restrooms, laundry facilities, hookups, showers, a swimming pool, and a sanitary disposal station are available. Pets are allowed on leashes.

Reservations, fees: No reservations are needed; the fee is $10–14.50 per night. Open May 1–September 2.

Directions: From Twin Falls, go 18 miles west on U.S. 30 to Buhl. From Buhl, go 10 miles northwest on U.S. 30, then 1.5 miles east on Banbury Road to the hot springs.

Contact: Banbury Hot Springs, P.O. Box 348, Buhl, ID 83604; 208/543-4098.

Trip notes: This is the community swimming pool, with water from natural mineral springs.

R & E Greenwood Store
   3

Location: Near the Snake River; map ID8, grid b4.

Campsites, facilities: There are 20 RV and tent campsites. Wheelchair-accessible restrooms, a restaurant, hookups, showers, and a restaurant, and a sanitary disposal facility are available. Pets are allowed on leashes.

Reservations, fees: No reservations are needed; the fee is $15 per night. Open March 1–October 31.

Directions: From I-84 east of Twin Falls, take Exit 194 south; the campground is right there at the exit.

Contact: R & E Greenwood Store, 1015 Ridgeway Rd. South, Hazelton, ID 83335; 208/829-5735.

Trip notes: You can fish in the Snake River.

15 Twin Falls County Fairgrounds
  3

Location: In Filer; map ID8, grid b2.

Campsites, facilities: There are 100 RV or tent campsites. Hookups, restrooms, showers, and a sanitary disposal facility are here. Large groups are welcome.

Reservations, fees: No reservations are needed; the fee is $7 per night.

Directions: From I-84 in Twin Falls, take Exit 173. Just before the light, take the truck route. Follow Poleline Road seven miles and signs will take you to fairgrounds.

Contact: Twin Falls County Fairgrounds, P.O. Box 257, Filer, ID 83328; 208/326-4396.

Trip notes: Twin Falls has golf courses and museums.

16 Curry Trailer Park
   4

Location: South of Twin Falls; map ID8, grid b2.

Campsites, facilities: There are 16 RV or tent campsites, some with hookups. Pets are allowed on leashes.

Reservations, fees: No reservations are needed; the fee is $14 per night.

Directions: From Magic Valley Hospital, 650 Addison Ave. West in Twin Falls, take Highway 30 (Bracken Street South), and go three miles west to the trailer park.

Contact: Curry Trailer Park, 21323 Hwy. 30, Filer, ID 83328; 208/733-3961.

Trip notes: This campground is near the Snake River Canyon. Twin Falls has golf courses and museums.

17 Oregon Trail Campground & Family Fun Center
   4

Location: In Twin Falls; map ID8, grid b3.

Campsites, facilities: There are 50 RV or tent campsites. Wheelchair-accessible restrooms, laundry facilities, hookups, showers, and a sanitary disposal facility are available. Pets are allowed on leashes.

Reservations, fees: No reservations are needed; the fee is $15 per night. Open year-round.

Directions: The campground is on U.S. 30 (Kimberly Road) as it heads east from town.

Contact: Oregon Trail Campground & Family Fun Center, 2733 Kimberly Rd., Twin Falls, ID 83301; 208/733-0853, 800/733-0853.

Trip notes: Twin Falls has three golf courses and several museums.

18 Blue Lakes RV Park
    4

Location: In Twin Falls; map ID8, grid b3.

Campsites, facilities: There are 37 RV or tent campsites. Wheelchair-accessible restrooms, laundry facilities, hookups, showers, and a sanitary disposal facility are available. Pets are allowed on leashes.

Reservations, fees: No reservations are needed; the fee is $14

per night. Open year-round.

Directions: This campground is just east of U.S. 93 (Blue Lakes Boulevard) in Twin Falls.

Contact: Blue Lakes RV Park, 1122 North Blue Lakes Blvd, Twin Falls, ID 83301; 208/734-5782.

Trip notes: Twin Falls has three golf courses and several museums.

19 Anderson Camp & RV Sales and Service

 3

Location: East of Twin Falls; map ID8, grid b3.

Campsites, facilities: There are 150 RV or tent campsites. Hookups, laundry facilities, showers, propane gas, and a swimming pool are available. Pets are allowed on leashes.

Reservations, fees: No reservations are needed; the fee is $17–24 per night. Open year-round.

Directions: From I-84 at Twin Falls, take Exit 182 and go half a mile east on Frontage Road to the campground.

Contact: Anderson Camp & RV Sales and Service, Route 1, Eden, ID 83325; 208/825-9800, fax 208/825-9715.

Trip notes: You can fish in the Snake River.

20 PV Travel Stop 216

 5

Location: In Burley; map ID8, grid b6.

Campsites, facilities: There are 120 RV and 10 tent campsites, some with hookups and pull-throughs. Laundry facilities, showers, a store, and a sanitary disposal station are available. Pets are allowed on leashes. There is a trout pond on-site.

Reservations, fees: Reservations are accepted; the fee is $15–20 per night. Open year-round.

Directions: From I-84 near Burley, take Exit 216 to the campground.

Contact: PV Travel Stop, Route 1, Box 33, Delco, ID 83323; 208/654-2133.

Trip notes: Burley has an 18-hole and a nine-

hole golf course. You can fish, boat, swim, and water-ski on the Snake River.

21 Nat-soo-pah Hot Springs & RV Park

 4

Location: South of Twin Falls; map ID8, grid c3.

Campsites, facilities: There are 75 RV or tent campsites. Hookups, showers, a swimming pool, and a sanitary disposal station are available. Pets are allowed on leashes.

Reservations, fees: No reservations are needed; the fee is $10 per night. Open May–Labor Day.

Directions: From Twin Falls, go 16 miles south on U.S. 93 to Hollister; then go 3.5 miles east at the marked turnoff to Nat-soo-pah Hot Springs.

Contact: Nat-soo-pah Hot Springs & RV Park, 2738 E. 2400 North, Twin Falls, ID 83301; 208/655-4337.

Trip notes: There are three outdoor pools filled with natural mineral water, a slide, and shady picnic area.

22 Thompson Flat

 7

Location: In Sawtooth National Forest; map ID8, grid c6.

Campsites, facilities: There are 16 RV or tent campsites, which can accommodate a maximum RV length of 22 feet. A vault toilet and water are available.

Reservations, fees: Reservations are accepted; the fee is $5 per night. Open June–October. Groups can be accommodated for an additional fee.

Directions: From Burley, go east nine miles on Highway 81, then south on Highway 77 to Albion. From Albion, go 5.5 miles southeast on Highway 77, then eight miles west on Forest Service Road 70549 (Howell Canyon Road) to the campground.

Contact: Burley Ranger District, Route 3, 3650

Overland Ave., Burley, ID 83318; 208/678-0430.

Trip notes: This forested campground is near an alpine meadow. Lake Cleveland, at 8,300 feet elevation, is a little over a mile to the west of Thompson Flat campground, and you can fish here for rainbow trout, but powerboats are prohibited. The Howell Canyon Recreation Area is in Sawtooth National Forest, and you can hike in the Pomerelle Ski Area.

23 Lake Cleveland

    7

Location: In Sawtooth National Forest; map ID8, grid c6.

Campsites, facilities: This campground has tent campsites only; no RVs are allowed. A vault toilet and water are available.

Reservations, fees: No reservations are needed; the fee is $5 per night. Open July–September.

Directions: From Burley, go east nine miles on Highway 81, then south on Highway 77 to Albion. From Albion, go 5.5 miles southeast on Highway 77, then 10 miles west on Forest Service Road 70549 (Howell Canyon Road) to the campground.

Contact: Burley Ranger District, Route 3, 3650 Overland Ave., Burley, ID 83318; 208/678-0430.

Trip notes: Lake Cleveland is at 8,300 feet elevation, and you can fish here for rainbow trout, but powerboats are prohibited. The Howell Canyon Recreation Area is in Sawtooth National Forest, and you can hike in the Pomerelle Ski Area.

24 Bennett Springs

    7

Location: In Sawtooth National Forest; map ID8, grid c6.

Campsites, facilities: There are seven RV or tent campsites. A vault toilet is available.

Reservations, fees: No reservations are needed; the fee is $5 per night. Open May 15–October 31.

Directions: From Burley, go east nine miles on Highway 81, then south on Highway 77 to Albion. From Albion, go 5.5 miles southeast on Highway 77, then five miles southwest on Forest Service Road 70549 (Howell Canyon Road) to the campground.

Contact: Burley Ranger District, Route 3, 3650 Overland Ave., Burley, ID 83318; 208/678-0430.

Trip notes: Lake Cleveland is at 8,300 feet elevation, and you can fish here for rainbow trout, but powerboats are prohibited. The Howell Canyon Recreation Area is in Sawtooth National Forest, and you can hike in the Pomerelle Ski Area.

25 Brackenbury

    7

Location: In Sawtooth National Forest; map ID8, grid c6.

Campsites, facilities: There are nine RV or tent campsites. A vault toilet and water are available.

Reservations, fees: No reservations are needed; the fee is $5 per night. Open July 10–September 30.

Directions: From Burley, go east nine miles on Highway 81, then south on Highway 77 to Albion. From Albion, go 5.5 miles southeast on Highway 77, then 9.6 miles west on Forest Service Road 70549 (Howell Canyon Road) to the campground.

Contact: Burley Ranger District, Route 3, 3650 Overland Ave., Burley, ID 83318; 208/678-0430.

Trip notes: Lake Cleveland is at 8,300 feet elevation, and you can fish here for rainbow trout, but powerboats are prohibited. The Howell Canyon Recreation Area is in Sawtooth National Forest, and you can hike in the Pomerelle Ski Area.

26 Sublett

    4

Location: In Sawtooth National Forest; map ID8, grid c8.

Campsites, facilities: There are seven RV or tent campsites, which can accommodate a maximum RV length of 22 feet. Vault toilets, a boat ramp, and water are available.

Reservations, fees: No reservations are needed; the fee is $5 per night. Open June–November.

Directions: From the junction of I-86 and I-84, take I-84 23 miles south to mile marker or Exit 245 east, and follow Sublett Road to the reservoir.

Contact: Burley Ranger District, Route 3, 3650 Overland Ave., Burley, ID 83318; 208/678-0430.

Trip notes: You can fish, boat, and swim at Sublett Reservoir. The Curlew National Grassland southeast of the reservoir is popular for day hikes by bird lovers.

27 City of Oakley RV Park

 5

Location: In Oakley; map ID8, grid d5.

Campsites, facilities: There are 11 RV sites, some with hookups, and a grassy area for tents. Wheelchair-accessible restrooms, water, showers, and a sanitary disposal station are available. Pets are allowed on leashes.

Reservations, fees: Reservations are accepted; the fee is $5–10 per night. Open May–October.

Directions: From Burley, go south on State Highway 27 for 22 miles to Oakley. From Oakley city center, go .5 mile south on Main Street to the RV park on the left.

Contact: City of Oakley, 200 W. Main, P.O. Box 266, Oakley, ID 83346; tel./fax 208/862-3313.

Trip notes: Goose Creek Reservoir is seven miles to the southwest, and you can swim, boat, and fish there. Oakley Warm Springs is six miles south of town. Mormons settled Oakley in 1878, and today the city is listed on the National Register of Historical Places.

28 Lud Drexler Park

    4

Location: West of Rogerson; map ID8, grid d2.

Campsites, facilities: There are 20 RV or tent campsites, which can accommodate a maximum RV length of 25 feet. There are wheelchair-accessible restrooms, water, a ramp dock, and shaded picnic tables are available.

Reservations, fees: No reservations are needed; the fee is $5 per night. Open year-round.

Directions: From Twin Falls, go 31 miles south on U.S. 93 to Rogerson. From Rogerson, go seven miles west on Three Creek Road to the campground, which is on the left, adjacent to Salmon Falls Dam.

Contact: Bureau of Land Management, Boise District Office, 3948 Development Ave., Boise, ID 83705; 208/384-3300 or 208/678-5514.

Trip notes: You can fish for kokanee, crappie, bass, perch, walleye, rainbow, and brown trout at Salmon Falls Reservoir, and Cedar Creek Reservoir has rainbow trout. You can also fish in Cedar Creek 10 miles west.

29 Schipper

     5

Location: In Sawtooth National Forest; map ID8, grid d3.

Campsites, facilities: There are seven RV or tent campsites, which can accommodate a maximum RV length of 10 feet. Hookups, vault toilets, and water are available.

Reservations, fees: No reservations are needed; no fee is charged. Open June 1–September 30.

Directions: From Twin Falls, go six miles north on U.S. 93 to I-84, then east on I-84 to mile marker 182, then south on G3 two miles to Hansen. From Hansen, go 26 miles south on County Road G3 to the campground.

Contact: Sawtooth National Forest, 2647 Kimberly Rd. E., Twin Falls, ID 83301; 208/737-3200.

Trip notes: There are many miles of trails in

the Sawtooth National Forest, and you can fish for rainbow and cutthroat trout in Goose Creek, as well as in other streams. Ross Falls Trail is a .25-mile interpretive trail; the 2.6-mile Eagle Nature Trail is between Pettit and Diamondfield Jack Campgrounds. Pike Mountain Overlook has outstanding views. You can boat, swim, and fish in Goose Creek Reservoir seven miles southwest of Oakley.

30 Pettit

 5

Location: In Sawtooth National Forest; map ID8, grid d4.

Campsites, facilities: There are nine RV or tent campsites, which can accommodate a maximum RV length of 22 feet. There are hookups, vault toilets, and water available.

Reservations, fees: No reservations are needed; the fee is $6 per night. Open June 1– September 30.

Directions: From Twin Falls, go six miles north on U.S. 93 to I-84, then east on I-84 to mile marker 182, then south on G3 two miles to Hansen. From Hansen, go 27 miles south on County Road G3 to the campground.

Contact: Sawtooth National Forest, 2647 Kimberly Rd. E., Twin Falls, ID 83301; 208/737-3200.

Trip notes: There are many miles of trails in the Sawtooth National Forest, and you can fish for rainbow and cutthroat trout in Goose Creek, as well as other streams. Ross Falls Trail is a .25-mile interpretive trail; the 2.6-mile Eagle Nature Trail is between Pettit and Diamondfield Jack Campgrounds. Pike Mountain Overlook has outstanding views. You can boat, swim, and fish in Goose Creek Reservoir seven miles southwest of Oakley.

31 Diamondfield Jack

 5

Location: In Sawtooth National Forest; map ID8, grid d4.

Campsites, facilities: There are eight RV or tent campsites, which can accommodate a maximum RV length of 32 feet. Hookups, vault toilets, and water are available.

Reservations, fees: No reservations are needed; the fee is $6 per night. Open June 1– October 15.

Directions: From Twin Falls, go six miles north on U.S. 93 to I-84, then east on I-84 to mile marker 182, then south on G3 two miles to Hansen. From Hansen, go 28 miles south on County Road G3 to the campground.

Contact: Sawtooth National Forest, 2647 Kimberly Rd. E., Twin Falls, ID 83301; 208/737-3200.

Trip notes: There are many miles of trails in the Sawtooth National Forest, and you can fish for rainbow and cutthroat trout in Goose Creek, as well as in other streams. Ross Falls Trail is a .25-mile interpretive trail; the 2.6-mile Eagle Nature Trail is between Pettit and Diamondfield Jack Campgrounds. Pike Mountain Overlook has outstanding views. You can boat, swim, and fish in Goose Creek Reservoir seven miles southwest of Oakley. This camping area is heavily used by off-road vehicles.

32 Bostetter

 5

Location: In Sawtooth National Forest; map ID8, grid d4.

Campsites, facilities: There are 18 RV or tent campsites, which can accommodate a maximum RV length of 16 feet. Vault toilets and water are available, but the water is not always drinkable.

Reservations, fees: No reservations are needed; the fee is $6 per night. Open June– October.

Directions: From Burley, go south on Highway 27 for 22 miles to Oakley. From Oakley, go 20 miles west on Forest Service Road 70500 to the campground. This road could be difficult for an RV anytime and impassable, period, when wet.

Contact: Sawtooth National

Forest, 2647 Kimberly Rd. E., Twin Falls, ID 83301; 208/737-3200.

Trip notes: This campground runs along Bostetter Spring. You can hike many miles of trails in the Sawtooth National Forest and you can fish for rainbow and cutthroat trout in Goose Creek, as well as other streams. Ross Falls Trail is a .25-mile interpretive trail; the 2.6-mile Eagle Nature Trail is between Pettit and Diamondfield Jack Campgrounds. Pike Mountain Overlook has outstanding views. You can boat, swim, and fish in Goose Creek Reservoir seven miles southwest of Oakley. This road could be difficult for an RV anytime and impassable, period, when wet.

33 City of Rocks National Reserve

   8

Location: In Sawtooth National Forest; map ID8, grid d6.

Campsites, facilities: There are 89 RV or tent campsites. Vault toilets and water are available.

Reservations, fees: No reservations are needed; the fee is $7 per night. Group sites can be reserved ahead of time. Open March 1–November 30.

Directions: From Burley, go east nine miles on Highway 81, then south on Highway 77 through Albion to Almo. From Almo, go three miles southwest on City of Rocks Road to the campground.

Contact: City of Rocks National Reserve Headquarters, 3010 S. Almo Rd., P.O. Box 169, Almo, ID 83312; 208/824-5519.

Trip notes: This 14,300-acre reserve has granite rock formations rising 600 feet, creating a unique and memorable sight. This area is popular with experienced, technical rock climbers, as the peaks are rated 5.0–5.14, and only for experts. The City of Rocks National Reserve Headquarters in Almo has maps and overnight backpacking permits. You can hike in the Sawtooth National Forest, and nature lovers will see Rocky Mountain bluebirds, various songbirds, and lush meadow wildflowers.

Bean Lake Wildlife Refuge

WAYNE-SCHERR

MAP ID9

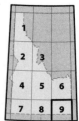

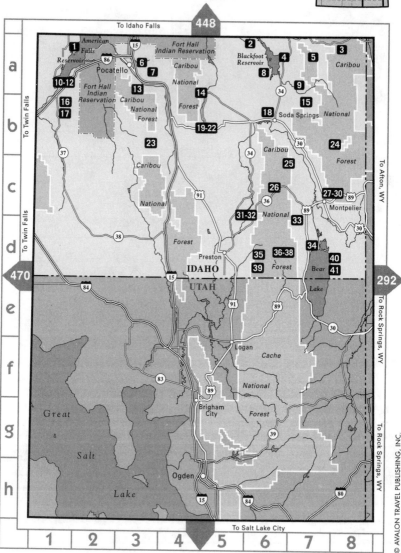

CHAPTER ID9

1 Sportsman Park on
American Falls Reservoir...483
2 Sage Hen Flats 484
3 Pinebar 484
4 White Locks Marina
& RV Park 484
5 Gravel Creek................484
6 Cowboy RV Park 485
7 Pocatello KOA...............485
8 Dike Lake (China Cap) 485
9 Mill Canyon 485
10 Seagull Bay Yacht Club.....486
11 Willow Bay
Recreation Area............486
12 Pipeline.......................486
13 Scout Mountain 486
14 Big Springs 487
15 Diamond Creek 487
16 Indian Springs
Swimming & RV 487
17 Massacre Rocks
State Park 488
18 Trail Motel & Restaurant..488
19 Lava Ranch Inn Motel
& RV Campground 488
20 Cottonwood Family
Campground 488

21 Lava Spa Motel
& RV Park 489
22 Mountain View
Trailer Park...................489
23 Hawkins Reservoir..........489
24 Summit View................490
25 Eight Mile 490
26 Emigration....................490
27 Montpelier Creek KOA.....490
28 Montpelier Canyon 491
29 Elbow...........................491
30 Rendezvous Village
RV Park 491
31 Maple Grove..................491
32 Redpoint 492
33 Paris Springs.................492
34 Cloverleaf.....................492
35 Albert Moser.................492
36 Willow Flat....................493
37 North Canyon Overflow...493
38 Porcupine.....................494
39 Deer Cliff Store,
Cafe, & RV....................494
40 Cedars and Shade
Campground 494
41 Bear Lake State Park.......494

1 Sportsman Park on American Falls Reservoir

 5

Location: On American Falls Reservoir; map ID9, grid a1.

Campsites, facilities: There are 29 RV or tent campsites. There are hookups, restrooms, and water are available.

Reservations, fees: No reservations are needed; the fee is $5–10 per night. Open seasonally; call for specific dates.

Directions: From American Falls, go north on Highway 39 to Aberdeen. From Aberdeen, go three miles on Boat Dock Road to the reservoir.

Contact: Bureau of Reclamation Visitor Center, 2881 Hwy. 39, American Falls, ID 83211; 208/226-2217, 208/397-7111.

Trip notes: This is the largest reservoir on the Snake River and the second largest in the state. You can boat, swim, fish, and windsurf here. The town of American Falls has a nine-hole golf course.

❷ Sage Hen Flats

 4

Location: Northeast of Pocatello; map ID9, grid a6.

Campsites, facilities: There are five RV or tent campsites, which can accommodate a maximum RV length of 15 feet. Vault toilets are provided.

Reservations, fees: No reservations are needed; the fee is $5 per night. Open May 1–October 31.

Directions: From Blackfeet, go seven miles north on U.S. 91, then 10 miles east on Wolverine Road. Take a right on Cedar Creek Road for 13 miles, then right on Trail Creek Bridge Road for six miles. The road turns into Lincoln Creek Road; the campground is six miles.

Contact: Bureau of Land Management, Idaho Falls District Office, 1405 Hollipart Drive, Idaho Falls, ID 83401; 208/524-7500.

Trip notes: You can fish the Blackfoot River and the Blackfoot Reservoir for rainbow and cutthroat trout. You can boat, swim, and water-ski at the reservoir.

❸ Pinebar

 5

Location: In Caribou National Forest; map ID9, grid a8.

Campsites, facilities: There are five RV or tent campsites, which can accommodate a maximum RV length of 20 feet. A vault toilet is available.

Reservations, fees: No reservations are needed; the fee is $6 per night. Open June 1–September 30.

Directions: From Soda Springs, go 45 miles northeast on Highway 34, the campground is approximately 11 miles from Freedom, Wyoming.

Contact: Forest Supervisor, Caribou National Forest, Federal Building, Suite 172, 250 S. 4th Ave., Pocatello, ID 83201; 208/236-7500.

Trip notes: You can hike mountain trails. You can fish Reservoir for rainbow and cutthroat trout in the Blackfoot River and the Blackfoot Reservoir, and you can boat, swim, and water-ski at the reservoir.

❹ White Locks Marina & RV Park

 5

Location: On Blackfoot Reservoir; map ID9, grid a6.

Campsites, facilities: There are 50 RV or tent campsites, some with hookups. Laundry facilities, showers, propane gas, a restaurant, and a sanitary disposal station are available. Pets are allowed on leashes.

Reservations, fees: No reservations are needed; the fee is $7–17.50 per night.

Directions: From Soda Springs, go 18 miles north on Highway 34 to the campground.

Contact: White Locks Marina & RV Park, 3429 Hwy. 34, Henry, ID 83230; 208/574-2208.

Trip notes: You can fish the Blackfoot River and the Blackfoot Reservoir for rainbow and cutthroat trout. You can boat, swim, and water-ski at the reservoir.

❺ Gravel Creek

 5

Location: In Caribou National Forest; map ID9, grid a7.

Campsites, facilities: There are nine RV or tent campsites, which can accommodate a maximum RV length of 20 feet. A vault toilet is available.

Reservations, fees: No reservations are needed; the fee is $6 per night. Open June 1–September 30.

Directions: From Soda Springs, go 31 miles north on Highway 34 to the sign, then south on Wayen Loop, right on Forest Service Road 191 to the campground.

Contact: Forest Supervisor, Caribou National Forest, Federal Building, Suite 172, 250 S. 4th Ave., Pocatello, ID 83201; 208/236-7500.

Trip notes: You can fish the Blackfoot River and the Blackfoot Reservoir for rainbow and cutthroat trout. You can boat, swim, and water-ski at the reservoir.

6 Cowboy RV Park

     4

Location: In Pocatello; map ID9, grid a3.

Campsites, facilities: There are 41 RV sites, some with hookups and pull-throughs, but no tent sites. Showers, laundry facilities, and a sanitary disposal station are available. Pets are allowed on leashes.

Reservations, fees: No reservations are needed; the fee is $18 per night.

Directions: From I-15, go one mile west on Exit 67 in Pocatello to the campground.

Contact: Cowboy RV Park, 845 Barton Rd., Pocatello, ID 83204; 208/232-4587.

Trip notes: The 180-acre Cherry Spring Nature Area has three self-guided nature trails. Additional trails originate up Mink Creek and the surrounding area. American Falls Reservoir is to the west.

7 Pocatello KOA

    4

Location: In Pocatello; map ID9, grid a3.

Campsites, facilities: There are 85 RV or tent campsites, some with hookups. Wheelchair-accessible restrooms, laundry facilities, showers, propane gas, and a sanitary disposal station are available. Pets are allowed on leashes.

Reservations, fees: No reservations are needed; the fee is $18.50–24.50 per night.

Directions: From I-15 at Pocatello, take Exit 71 (Pocatello Creek Road) 1.25 miles to the campground on the right.

Contact: Pocatello KOA, 9815 W. Pocatello Creek Rd., Pocatello, ID 83201; 208/233-6851, 800/562-9175.

Trip notes: The 180-acre Cherry Spring Nature Area has three self-guided nature trails.

Additional trails originate up Mink Creek and the surrounding area. American Falls Reservoir is to the west.

8 Dike Lake (China Cap)

    5

Location: On Blackfoot Reservoir; map ID9, grid a6.

Campsites, facilities: There are 35 RV or tent campsites, which can accommodate a maximum RV length of 25 feet. A vault toilet is available.

Reservations, fees: No reservations are needed; the fee is $5 per night. Open May 1–October 31.

Directions: From Soda Springs, go north for 14 miles on Highway 34 to China Cap Road, then 1.5 miles west to Dike Road and the campground.

Contact: Bureau of Land Management, Idaho Falls District Office, 1405 Hollipart Drive, Idaho Falls, ID 83401; 208/524-7500.

Trip notes: You can fish the Blackfoot River and the Blackfoot Reservoir for rainbow and cutthroat trout. You can boat, swim, and water-ski at the reservoir.

9 Mill Canyon

     4

Location: In Caribou National Forest; map ID9, grid a7.

Campsites, facilities: There are 10 RV or tent campsites, which can accommodate a maximum RV length of 32 feet; some have pull-through sites.

Reservations, fees: No reservations are needed; the fee is $6 per night. Open June 1–September 30.

Directions: From Soda Springs, go 10.1 miles north on Highway 34, then 11.4 miles east on County Road 30C, 1.9 miles east on Forest Service Road 20095, and then take Forest Service Road 20099 west six miles to the campground.

Contact: Forest Supervisor, Caribou National Forest, Federal Building, Suite 172, 250 S. 4th Ave., Pocatello, ID 83201; 208/236-7500.

Trip notes: The 180-acre Cherry Spring Nature Area has three self-guided nature trails. Additional trails originate up Mink Creek and the surrounding area. American Falls Reservoir is to the west.

10 Seagull Bay Yacht Club

    5

Location: On American Falls Reservoir; map ID9, grid a1.

Campsites, facilities: There are 48 RV or tent campsites. Hookups, showers, water, and a sanitary disposal facility are available.

Reservations, fees: No reservations are needed; the fee is $10–15 per night. Open May–Labor Day.

Directions: From American Falls, go east on I-86 to the Seagull Bay exit, cross under I-86, take the first right, and go three miles to the club.

Contact: Bureau of Reclamation, Bureau of Reclamation Visitor Center, 2881 Hwy. 39, American Falls, ID 83211; 208/226-2217, 208/226-2086.

Trip notes: American Falls is the largest reservoir on the Snake River and the second largest in the state. You can boat, swim, fish, and windsurf here. The town of American Falls has a nine-hole golf course.

11 Willow Bay Recreation Area

      5

Location: On American Falls Reservoir; map ID9, grid a1.

Campsites, facilities: There are 26 RV or tent campsites. Wheelchair-accessible restrooms, a restaurant, laundry facilities, hookups, showers, propane gas, water, and a sanitary disposal facility are available. Pets are allowed on leashes.

Reservations, fees: No reservations are needed; the fee is $11–16 per night.

Directions: From American Falls, go north on Highway 39 to Exit 40 (Marina Road. Drive a half mile right on Marina Road to the campground.

Contact: Bureau of Reclamation, 550 N. Oregon Trail, American Falls, ID 83211; 208/226-2688, fax 208/226-2548.

Trip notes: American Falls is the largest reservoir on the Snake River and the second largest in the state. You can boat, swim, fish, and windsurf here. The town of American Falls has a nine-hole golf course.

12 Pipeline

    5

Location: At American Falls Reservoir; map ID9, grid a1.

Campsites, facilities: There are five RV or tent campsites, which can accommodate a maximum RV length of 17 feet.

Reservations, fees: No reservations are needed; the fee is $4 per night. Open year-round.

Directions: From American Falls, go southwest on Frontage Road 1.5 miles parallel to I-86, then turn right at the sign onto a gravel road for .25 mile to the campground.

Contact: Bureau of Land Management, Burley District Office, 15 E. 200 South, Burley, ID 83318; 208/677-6641, 208/236-6860, or 208/766-4766.

Trip notes: American Falls is the largest reservoir on the Snake River and the second largest in the state. You can boat, swim, fish, and windsurf here. The town of American Falls has a nine-hole golf course.

13 Scout Mountain

     4

Location: In Caribou National Forest; map ID9, grid a3.

Campsites, facilities: There are 32 RV or tent campsites, which can accommodate a maximum RV length of 30 feet. Wheelchair-accessible restrooms and water are available.

Reservations, fees: No reservations are needed; the fee is $6 per night. Open May 15–October 1.

Directions: From Pocatello, go south on I-15 to Exit 63 (Portneuf Area Recreation Sign), then take East Fork Road to the left and follow to the campground.

Contact: Forest Supervisor, Caribou National Forest, Federal Building, Suite 172, 250 S. 4th Ave., Pocatello, ID 83201; 208/236-7500.

Trip notes: The 180-acre Cherry Spring Nature Area has three self-guided nature trails. Additional trails originate up Mink Creek and the surrounding area. American Falls Reservoir is to the west.

14 Big Springs

 4

Location: In Caribou National Forest; map ID9, grid a4.

Campsites, facilities: There are 11 RV or tent campsites, which can accommodate a maximum RV length of 30 feet, some with barrier-free access. Vault toilets and water are available. Pets are allowed on leashes.

Reservations, fees: No reservations are needed; the fee is $6 per night. Open May 15–October 1.

Directions: From Soda Springs, go 22 miles west on U.S. 30 to Lava Hot Springs. From Lava Hot Springs, go 10 miles north on Bancroft Highway, then eight miles west on Forest Service Road 036 to the campground.

Contact: Forest Supervisor, Caribou National Forest, Federal Building, Suite 172, 250 S. 4th Ave., Pocatello, ID 83201; 208/236-7500.

Trip notes: The 180-acre Cherry Spring Nature Area has three self-guided nature trails. Additional trails originate up Mink Creek and the surrounding area. American Falls Reservoir is to the west.

15 Diamond Creek

 6

Location: In Caribou National Forest; map ID9, grid b7.

Campsites, facilities: There are 20 RV or tent campsites. A vault toilet is available.

Reservations, fees: No reservations are needed; the fee is $6 per night. Open June 1–September 30.

Directions: From Soda Springs, go 10.1 miles north on Highway 34, then 11.4 miles east on County Road 30C, 4.9 miles northeast on Forest Service Road 95, and finally 12.5 miles southeast on Forest Service Road 102 to the campground.

Contact: Forest Supervisor, Caribou National Forest, Federal Building, Suite 172, 250 S. 4th Ave., Pocatello, ID 83201; 208/236-7500.

Trip notes: There are several trailheads here, and auto tours, but a four-wheel drive is recommended. You can hike in the Caribou National Forest.

16 Indian Springs Swimming & RV

 5

Location: Near American Falls Reservoir; map ID9, grid b1.

Campsites, facilities: There are 125 RV or tent campsites. Hookups, showers, propane gas, laundry facilities, a restaurant, a swimming pool, and a sanitary disposal facility are available. Pets are allowed on leashes.

Reservations, fees: Reservations are accepted; the fee is $11–17 per night. Open April 16–October 10.

Directions: From American Falls, go three miles west on Highway 37 to the campground.

Contact: Indian Springs Swimming & RV, 3249 Indian Springs Rd., American Falls, ID 83211; 208/226-2174 or 208/226-2174.

Trip notes: There are volleyball courts, a game room, and horseshoe pit on site. This campground is not far from

American Falls Reservoir, the largest reservoir on the Snake River and the second largest in the state. You can boat, swim, fish, and windsurf here. American Falls has a nine-hole golf course.

17 Massacre Rocks State Park

     5

Location: Southwest of American Falls Reservoir; map ID9, grid b1.

Campsites, facilities: There are 49 RV or tent campsites, which can accommodate a maximum RV length of 55 feet. Hookups, pull-through sites, showers, restrooms, water, and a sanitary disposal facility are available.

Reservations, fees: No reservations are needed; the fee is $12 per night. Open year-round. The stay limit is 15 days.

Directions: From American Falls on I-86, go 12 miles west; take Exit 28 to the state park.

Contact: Massacre Rocks State Park, 3592 N. Park Lane, American Falls, ID 83211; 208/548-2672.

Trip notes: For many years, Oregon Trail pioneers stopped here to rest. There are 900 acres of sagebrush desert area along the Snake River, making it a prime bird-watching area, and there are hiking trails throughout the park. Rangers offer interpretive programs during the summer. For additional activities, you can go to American Falls Reservoir, the largest reservoir on the Snake River and the second largest in the state. You can boat, swim, fish, and windsurf here. American Falls has a nine-hole golf course.

18 Trail Motel & Restaurant

    4

Location: In Soda Springs; map ID9, grid b6.

Campsites, facilities: There are 17 RV or tent sites, some with hookups. There are wheelchair-accessible facilities and a nearby restaurant.

Reservations, fees: No reservations are needed; the fee is $9–35 per night.

Directions: From Pocatello, go south 25 miles on I-15 miles to McCammon. From McCammon, go east on U.S. 30 to Soda Springs, and the campground is on East 200 South in town.

Contact: Trail Motel & Restaurant, 213 E. 200 South, Soda Springs, ID 83276; 208/547-3909.

Trip notes: The 160-acre Formation Springs Preserve, named because the spring water has been estimated to be 13,000 year old, is nearby. Formation Cave is 20 feet high and 1,000 feet long. There is a nine-hole golf course in town. A short, fun float is on the Portneuf River through town.

19 Lava Ranch Inn Motel & RV Campground

     5

Location: In Lava Hot Springs; map ID9, grid b4.

Campsites, facilities: There are 52 RV or tent campsites, some with hookups. Showers are available. Pets are allowed on leashes.

Reservations, fees: No reservations are needed; the fee is $8 and up per night.

Directions: From Soda Springs, go 22 miles west on U.S. 30 to Lava Hot Springs. From Lava Hot Springs, go one mile west; the campground is on the river.

Contact: Lava Ranch Inn Motel & RV Campground, 9611 Hwy. 30, Lava Hot Springs, ID 83246; 208/776-9917, 208/776-5546.

Trip notes: You can fish on the river, and Lava Hot Springs offers geothermal and swimming pools. Near Grace, to the south, is Niter Ice Cave, a natural lava cave. You can fish for brown, cutthroat, and rainbow trout in the Portneuf River. There is a nine-hole golf course nearby.

20 Cottonwood Family Campground

    5

Location: In Lava Hot Springs; map ID9, grid b4.

Campsites, facilities: There are 111 RV or

tent campsites, which can accommodate a maximum RV length of 40 feet.

Reservations, fees: No reservations are needed; the fee is $17–24 per night. Open May 1–September 30.

Directions: From Pocatello, go south 25 miles on I-15 to Exit 47 (Highway 30); take Highway 30 and pass the pool, pass the Amoco, to reach the campground at the east end of McCammon.

Contact: Cottonwood Family Campground, P.O. Box 307, 100 Bristol Park Lane, Lava Hot Springs, ID 83246; 208/776-5295.

Trip notes: You can fish on the river, and Lava Hot Springs offers geothermal and swimming pools. Near Grace, to the south, is Niter Ice Cave, a natural lava cave. You can fish for brown, cutthroat, and rainbow trout in the Portneuf River. There is a nine-hole golf course nearby.

21 Lava Spa Motel & RV Park

 4

Location: In Lava Hot Springs; map ID9, grid b4.

Campsites, facilities: There are 15 RV or tent campsites, some with hookups. Wheelchair-accessible restrooms are available.

Reservations, fees: No reservations are needed; the fee is $20 per night.

Directions: From Pocatello, go south 25 miles on I-15 to Exit 47 (Highway 30); take Highway 30 and pass the pool. At the stop sign go left on Main Street and the campground is at the east end of McCammon.

Contact: Lava Spa Motel & RV Park, 359 E. Main St., Lava Hot Springs, ID 83246; 208/776-5589.

Trip notes: You can fish on the river, and Lava Hot Springs offers geothermal and swimming pools. Near Grace, to the south, is Niter Ice Cave, a natural lava cave. You can fish for brown, cutthroat, and rainbow trout in the Portneuf River. There is a nine-hole golf course nearby.

22 Mountain View Trailer Park

 4

Location: In Lava Hot Springs; map ID9, grid b5.

Campsites, facilities: There are 80 RV or tent campsites, some with hookups. Showers and propane gas are available. Pets are allowed on leashes.

Reservations, fees: No reservations are needed; the fee is $20–25 per night. Open April 1–September 30.

Directions: From Pocatello, go south 25 miles on I-15 to Exit 47 (Highway 30), go through Lava Hot Springs, and then take a right to the campground.

Contact: Mountain View Trailer Park, Inc., P.O. Box 687, Lava Hot Springs, ID 83246; 208/776-5611.

Trip notes: You can fish on the river, and Lava Hot Springs offers geothermal and swimming pools. Near Grace, to the south, is Niter Ice Cave, a natural lava cave. You can fish for brown, cutthroat, and rainbow trout in the Portneuf River. There is a nine-hole golf course nearby.

23 Hawkins Reservoir

 6

Location: South of Pocatello; map ID9, grid b3.

Campsites, facilities: There are 14 RV or tent sites, which can accommodate a maximum RV length of 20 feet. A vault toilet is available. Pets are allowed on leashes.

Reservations, fees: No reservations are needed; the fee is $6 per night. Open year-round.

Directions: From Pocatello, go 37 miles south on I-15 to Virginia. Take Exit 36 and go .5 mile west on Virginia Road to the campground.

Contact: Bureau of Land Management, Idaho Falls District Office, 1405 Hollipart Drive, Idaho Falls, ID 83401; 208/524-7500.

Trip notes: You can boat and fish

on the reservoir. The 120-acre area is home to mule deer, red fox, coyote, waterfowl, and the occasional moose and elk.

24 Summit View
 6

Location: In Caribou National Forest; map ID9, grid b8.

Campsites, facilities: There are 20 RV or tent campsites, which can accommodate a maximum RV length of 32 feet. Water is available.

Reservations, fees: No reservations are needed; the fee is $5 per night. Open June 15–September 5.

Directions: From Soda Springs go 19 miles south on U.S. 30 to Georgetown. From Georgetown, go 2.4 miles east on County Road 20102, then six miles north on Forest Service Road 20095 to the campground.

Contact: Forest Supervisor, Caribou National Forest, Federal Building, Suite 172, 250 S. 4th Ave., Pocatello, ID 83201; 208/236-7500.

Trip notes: You can hike and fish in the Caribou National Forest.

25 Eight Mile
 6

Location: In Caribou National Forest; map ID9, grid c7.

Campsites, facilities: There are seven RV or tent sites, which can accommodate a maximum RV length of 16 feet, but the road can be rough, so you might not want to bring your RV here. Vault toilets and water are available, but this is a primitive camp.

Reservations, fees: No reservations are needed; the fee is $4. Open May 31–October 30.

Directions: From Soda Springs, go 9.2 miles south on County Road 30025, then four miles south on Forest Service Road 30025 to the campground.

Contact: Forest Supervisor, Caribou National Forest, Federal Building, Suite 172, 250 S. 4th Ave., Pocatello, ID 83201; 208/236-7500.

Trip notes: Near Grace, to the south, is Niter Ice Cave, a natural lava cave. You can fish and hike in the national forest.

26 Emigration
 7

Location: In Caribou National Forest; map ID9, grid c6.

Campsites, facilities: There are 25 RV or tent campsites, which can accommodate a maximum RV length of 22 feet. Restrooms and water are available.

Reservations, fees: No reservations are needed; the fee is $6 per night. Open June–September.

Directions: From Montpelier, go six miles west on U.S. 89 to Ovid. From Ovid, go 10.5 miles west on Highway 36 to the campground.

Contact: Montpelier Ranger District, 431 Clay St., Montpelier, ID 83254; 208/847-0375.

Trip notes: This campground is in a timbered setting and near the trailhead of the 55-mile Bear River Mountain Range Trail.

27 Montpelier Creek KOA
 5

Location: East of Montpelier; map ID9, grid c7.

Campsites, facilities: There are 50 RV or tent campsites, some with hookups. Wheelchair-accessible restrooms, laundry facilities, showers, and a sanitary disposal station are available. Pets are allowed on leashes.

Reservations, fees: No reservations are needed; the fee is $15–18.50 per night. Open April 15–October 31.

Directions: From Soda Springs, go south on U.S. 30 to Montpelier. From Montpelier, go two miles east on Highway 89 to the campground.

Contact: Montpelier Creek KOA, P.O. Box 87, Montpelier, ID 83254; 208/847-0863.

Trip notes: Montpelier has a golf course and a history museum. Montpelier Reservoir is to the east, and you can fish, but no motorboats are allowed.

28 Montpelier Canyon

   6

Location: East of Montpelier; map ID9, grid c7.

Campsites, facilities: There are 13 RV or tent campsites, which can accommodate a maximum RV length of 32 feet. A vault toilet and water are available.

Reservations, fees: No reservations are needed; the fee is $6 per night. Open May–October.

Directions: From Soda Springs, go south on U.S. 30 to Montpelier. From Montpelier, go 3.3 miles east on U.S. 89 to the campground.

Contact: Montpelier Ranger District, 431 Clay St., Montpelier, ID 83254; 208/847-0375.

Trip notes: Montpelier has a golf course and a history museum. Montpelier Reservoir is to the east, and you can fish, but no motorboats are allowed.

29 Elbow

   5

Location: In Caribou National Forest; map ID9, grid c7.

Campsites, facilities: There are 20 RV or tent campsites, which can accommodate a maximum RV length of 32 feet. A vault toilet is available.

Reservations, fees: No reservations are needed; the fee is $6 per night. Open June 1–September 15.

Directions: From Soda Springs, go south on U.S. 30 to Montpelier. From Montpelier, go six miles east on U.S. 89 to the campground.

Contact: Montpelier Ranger District, 431 Clay St., Montpelier, ID 83254; 208/847-0375.

Trip notes: Montpelier has a golf course and a history museum. Montpelier Reservoir is to the east, and you can fish, but no motorboats are allowed.

30 Rendezvous Village RV Park

  3

Location: In Montpelier; map ID9, grid c8.

Campsites, facilities: There are 30 RV or tent campsites, some with hookups. Showers, a restaurant, and a sanitary disposal station are available. Pets are allowed on leashes.

Reservations, fees: No reservations are needed; the fee is $10–15 per night. Open April 15–October 31.

Directions: Montpelier is southeast of Soda Springs on U.S. 30. The campground is on the right just before the junction with U.S. 89. From U.S. 89 in Montpelier, going northeast toward Washington St./U.S. 89, turn left onto U.S. 89/4th St./U.S. 30, drive .3 mile. Stay straight on 4th St./U.S. 30 to the campground.

Contact: Rendezvous Village RV Park, 577 N. 4th St., Montpelier, ID 83254; 208/847-1100.

Trip notes: Montpelier has a golf course and a history museum. Montpelier Reservoir is to the east, and you can fish there, but no motorboats are allowed.

31 Maple Grove

  5

Location: Northeast of Preston; map ID9, grid c5.

Campsites, facilities: There are 20 RV or tent campsites, which can accommodate a maximum RV length of 17 feet. Wheelchair-accessible restrooms are available.

Reservations, fees: No reservations are needed; the fee is $5 per night.

Directions: From Pocatello, go south on U.S. 91 to Preston. From Preston, go 5.5 miles northeast on Highway 36, then three miles northeast on Highway 36, and eight miles north on Oneida Narrows Road to the campground.

Contact: Bureau of Land Management, Idaho Falls District Office, 1405 Hollipark Dr., Idaho Falls, ID 83401; 208/524-7500.

Trip notes: This campground is near the Bear River and Oneida Narrows Reservoir, where you can fish for perch and walleye.

32 Redpoint

    5

Location: Northeast of Preston; map ID9, grid c6.

Campsites, facilities: There are six RV or tent campsites, which can accommodate a maximum RV length of 20 feet. A vault toilet is available.

Reservations, fees: No reservations are needed; the fee is $5 per night.

Directions: From Pocatello, go south on U.S. 91 to Preston. From Preston, go 5.5 miles northeast on Highway 34, then four miles north on Oneida Narrows Road to the campground.

Contact: Bureau of Land Management, Idaho Falls District Office, 1405 Hollipark Dr., Idaho Falls, ID 83401; 208/524-7500.

Trip notes: This campground is near the Bear River and Oneida Narrows Reservoir, where you can fish for perch and walleye.

33 Paris Springs

      6

Location: Near Paris; map ID9, grid d7.

Campsites, facilities: There are 12 RV or tent campsites. A vault toilet and water are available.

Reservations, fees: No reservations are needed; the fee is $6 per night. Open June–September.

Directions: From Montpelier, go west, then south on U.S. 89 to Paris. From Paris, go two miles south on U.S. 89, then 3.8 miles west on Paris Canyon Road; the campground is to the left.

Contact: Montpelier Ranger District, 431 Clay St., Montpelier, ID 83254; 208/847-0375.

Trip notes: This campground is in a timbered setting where you can hike. Bear Lake to the

south is a beautiful turquoise blue, stretching 20 miles in length. You can swim, boat, and fish for cutthroat and lake trout. Bear Lake National Wildlife Refuge is 17,600 acres of nesting ground for mallard, pintail, and canvasback ducks. Sandhill cranes, herons, egrets, Canada geese, and white pelicans frequent the area.

34 Cloverleaf

     6

Location: South of Paris; map ID9, grid d7.

Campsites, facilities: There are 19 RV or tent campsites, which can accommodate a maximum RV length of 22 feet. Flush toilets and water are available.

Reservations, fees: No reservations are needed; the fee is $6 per night. Open June 15–September 5.

Directions: From Paris, go 6.8 miles south on U.S. 89, then west on St. Charles Creek Road (Forest Service Road 412) to the campground. From St. Charles, go 1.2 miles north on U.S. 89, then west on St. Charles Creek Road (Forest Service Road 412) to the campground.

Contact: Montpelier Ranger District, 431 Clay St., Montpelier, ID 83254; 208/847-0375.

Trip notes: Bear Lake, off U.S. 89 on the Idaho/Utah border, is a beautiful turquoise blue, stretching 20 miles in length. You can swim, boat, and fish for cutthroat and lake trout. Bear Lake National Wildlife Refuge is 17,600 acres of nesting ground for mallard, pintail, and canvasback ducks. Sandhill cranes, herons, egrets, Canada geese, and white pelicans frequent the area. A trailhead nearby takes you to Minnetonka Cave, a limestone cave open for tours June–September for a fee.

35 Albert Moser

    6

Location: In Caribou National Forest; map ID9, grid d6.

Campsites, facilities: There are nine RV or

tent campsites, which can accommodate a maximum RV length of 16 feet. Vault toilets and water are available.

Reservations, fees: Reservations are accepted; the fee is $5–10 per night. Open June–September.

Directions: From Preston, go four miles southeast on U.S. 91, then 10 miles northeast on Cub River Road and two miles east on Hillyard Canyon Road to the campground.

Contact: Montpelier Ranger District, 431 Clay St., Montpelier, ID 83254; 208/847-0375.

Trip notes: This campground is in a mountain setting, and a nature trail is nearby. You can fish in the Cub River. The Minnetonka Cave is a geological site with stalagmite and stalactite formations. Guided tours are offered for a fee. You can fish here and a trailhead is nearby. Bear Lake, to the southeast, is a beautiful turquoise blue, stretching 20 miles in length. You can swim, boat, and fish for cutthroat and lake trout. Bear Lake National Wildlife Refuge is 17,600 acres of nesting ground for mallard, pintail, and canvasback ducks. Sandhill cranes, herons, egrets, Canada geese, and white pelicans frequent the area.

36 Willow Flat

 7

Location: In Caribou National Forest; map ID9, grid d6.

Campsites, facilities: There are 52 RV or tent campsites, which can accommodate a maximum RV length of 22 feet. A vault toilet and water are available.

Reservations, fees: No reservations are needed; the fee is $6 per night. Open June 15–September 5.

Directions: From Preston, go four miles southeast on U.S. 91, then 10 miles northeast on Cub River Road and six miles east on Hillyard Canyon Road to the campground.

Contact: Montpelier Ranger District, 431 Clay St., Montpelier, ID 83254; 208/847-0375.

Trip notes: You can fish in the Cub River. The Minnetonka Cave is a geological site with stalagmite and stalactite formations. Guided tours are offered for a fee. You can fish here, and a trailhead is nearby. Bear Lake, to the southeast, is a beautiful turquoise blue, stretching 20 miles in length. You can swim, boat, and fish for cutthroat and lake trout. Bear Lake National Wildlife Refuge is 17,600 acres of nesting ground for mallard, pintail, and canvasback ducks. Sandhill cranes, herons, egrets, Canada geese, and white pelicans frequent the area.

37 North Canyon Overflow

 7

Location: In Caribou National Forest; map ID9, grid d6.

Campsites, facilities: There are six RV or tent campsites, which can accommodate a maximum RV length of 22 feet. A vault toilet is available.

Reservations, fees: No reservations are needed; the fee is $6 per night. Open June–September.

Directions: From Paris, go 6.8 miles south on U.S. 89, then 8.9 miles west on St. Charles Creek Road (Forest Service Road 412) to the campground. From St. Charles, go 1.2 miles north on U.S. 89 to St. Charles Creek Road.

Contact: Montpelier Ranger District, 431 Clay St., Montpelier, ID 83254; 208/847-0375.

Trip notes: You can fish in the Cub River. The Minnetonka Cave is a geological site, with stalagmite and stalactite formations. Guided tours are offered for a fee. You can fish here and a trailhead is nearby. Bear Lake, to the southeast, is a beautiful turquoise blue, stretching 20 miles in length. You can swim, boat, and fish for cutthroat and lake trout. Bear Lake National Wildlife Refuge is 17,600 acres of nesting ground for mallard, pintail, and canvasback ducks. Sandhill cranes, herons, egrets, Canada geese, and white pelicans frequent the area.

38 Porcupine

     7

Location: In Caribou National Forest; map ID9, grid d6.

Campsites, facilities: There are 12 RV or tent campsites, which can accommodate a maximum RV length of 22 feet. A flush toilet and water are available.

Reservations, fees: No reservations are needed; the fee is $6 per night. Open June 10–September 5.

Directions: From St. Charles, go 1.2 miles north on U.S. 89, then 7.6 miles west on St. Charles Creek Road (Forest Service Road 412) campground. From Paris, go 6.8 miles south on U.S. 89 to the St. Charles Creek Road turnoff.

Contact: Montpelier Ranger District, 431 Clay St., Montpelier, ID 83254; 208/847-0375.

Trip notes: You can fish in the Cub River. The Minnetonka Cave is a geological site with stalagmite and stalactite formations. Guided tours are offered for a fee. Bear Lake, to the southeast, is a beautiful turquoise blue, stretching 20 miles in length, and you can swim, boat, and fish for cutthroat and lake trout. Bear Lake National Wildlife Refuge is 17,600 acres of nesting ground for mallard, pintail, and canvasback ducks. Sandhill cranes, herons, egrets, Canada geese, and white pelicans frequent the area.

39 Deer Cliff Store, Cafe, & RV

      4

Location: In Caribou National Forest; map ID9, grid d6.

Campsites, facilities: There are 11 RV or tent campsites, some with hookups. Wheelchair-accessible restrooms, laundry facilities, showers, and a restaurant are available. Pets are allowed on leashes.

Reservations, fees: No reservations are needed; the fee is $5–15 per night. Open year round.

Directions: From Preston, go four miles south on State Street, and then go eight miles up Cub River Canyon.

Contact: Deer Cliff Store, Cafe & RV, 1942 N. Deer Cliff Rd., Preston, ID 83263; 208/852-1736.

Trip notes: This campground is in a mountain setting. A nature trail is nearby, and you can fish here.

40 Cedars and Shade Campground

      5

Location: South of Montpelier; map ID9, grid d8.

Campsites, facilities: There are 100 RV or tent campsites. Pets are allowed on leashes.

Reservations, fees: No reservations are needed; the fee is $8–12 per night.

Directions: From Paris, go south on U.S. 89 to Bear Lake. From the northeast corner of Bear Lake, the campground is two miles south along the lake on Eastside Lake Road.

Contact: Cedars and Shade Campground, P.O. Box 219, Paris, ID 83261; 208/945-2608.

Trip notes: Bear Lake is a beautiful turquoise blue, stretching 20 miles in length. You can swim, boat, and fish for cutthroat and lake trout. Bear Lake National Wildlife Refuge is 17,600 acres of nesting ground for mallard, pintail, and canvasback ducks. Sandhill cranes, herons, egrets, Canada geese, and white pelicans frequent the area.

41 Bear Lake State Park

    6

Location: South of Montpelier; map ID9, grid d8.

Campsites, facilities: There are 48 RV or tent campsites, which can accommodate a maximum RV length of 60 feet. Hookups, pull-through sites, vault toilets, and a sanitary disposal station are available. Pets are allowed on leashes.

Reservations, fees: Reservations are accepted; the fee is $8–11 per night. Open May 1–October 1.

Directions: From Montpelier, go south on U.S. 30 to Pingle Road and take Merkley Lake Road and Eastside Lake Road for 29 miles (past the North Beach Unit, which is day-use only) to Bear Lake State Park, East Beach Unit, on the east side of the lake about a mile and a half from the Idaho-Utah border.

Contact: Bear Lake State Park, P.O. Box 297, 181 S. Main, Paris, ID 83261; 208/945-2790.

Trip notes: Bear Lake is a beautiful turquoise blue, stretching 20 miles in length. You can swim, boat, and fish for cutthroat and lake trout. Bear Lake National Wildlife Refuge is 17,600 acres of nesting ground for mallard, pintail, and canvasback ducks. Sandhill cranes, herons, egrets, Canada geese, and white pelicans frequent the area.

RESOURCE GUIDE

MONTANA

National Forests

BEAVERHEAD-DEERLODGE NATIONAL FOREST
Forest Supervisor's Office, 420 Barrett St., Dillon, MT 59725-3572; 406/683-3900 or 406/683-3913

Dillon Ranger District, 420 Barrett St., Dillon, MT 59725-3572; 406/683-3900

Wise River Ranger District, P.O. Box 100, Wise River, MT 59762; 406/832-3178

Wisdom Ranger District, P.O. Box 238, Wisdom, MT 59761; 406/689-3243

Butte Ranger District, 1820 Meadowlark, Butte, MT 59701; 406/494-2147

Jefferson Ranger District, #3 Whitetail Rd., Whitehall, MT 59759; 406/287-3223 or 800/433-9206 (Montana only)

Pintler Ranger District (Philipsburg Office), P.O. Box 805, Philipsburg, MT 59858; 406/859-3211

Pintler Ranger District (Deer Lodge Office), 1 Hollenback Rd., Deer Lodge, MT 59722; 406/846-1770

Madison Ranger Station, 5 Forest Service Rd., Ennis, MT 59729; 406/682-4253

BITTERROOT NATIONAL FOREST
Forest Supervisor's Office, 1801 N. 1st St., Hamilton, MT 59840-3114; 406/363-7161, fax 406/363-7106; email: mailroom/r1_bitterroot@fs.fed.us

Darby Ranger Station, 712 N. Main, Darby, MT 59829; 406/821-3913, fax 406/821-3675

Stevensville Ranger Station, 88 Main, Stevensville, MT 59870; 406/777-5461, fax 406/777-7423

Sula Ranger Station, 7338 Highway 93 S., Sula, MT 59871; 406/821-3201, fax 406/821-3678

West Fork Ranger Station, 6735 West Fork Rd., Darby, MT 59829; 406/821-3269, fax 406/821-1211

CLEARWATER NATIONAL FOREST
Powell Ranger District, Lolo, MT 59847; 208/942-3113

CUSTER NATIONAL FOREST
P.O. Box 50760, 1310 Main St., Billings, MT 59105; 406/657-6361

DEERLODGE NATIONAL FOREST
Federal Building, Butte, MT 59703; 406/496-3400

Jefferson Ranger District, 3 Whitetail Rd., Whitehall, MT 59759; 406/287-3223

FLATHEAD NATIONAL FOREST
1935 3rd Ave. E., Kalispell, MT 59901; 406/758-5200, fax 406/758-5363

Eureka Ranger Station, 1299 Highway 93 N., Eureka, MT 59917; 406/296-2536 or 800/280-2267

Whitefish Ranger Station, 1335 Highway 93 W., Whitefish, MT 59937; 406/863-5400

GALLATIN NATIONAL FOREST
P.O. Box 130, Federal Building, Bozeman, MT 59771; 406/587-6701

HELENA NATIONAL FOREST
2880 Skyway Drive, Helena, MT 59626; 406/449-5201

KOOTENAI NATIONAL FOREST
506 Highway 2 W., Libby, MT 59923; 406/293-6211

Troy Ranger Station, 1437 N. Highway 2, Troy, MT 59935; 406/295-4693

LEWIS AND CLARK NATIONAL FOREST
P.O. Box 869, 1101 15th St. N., Great Falls, MT 59403; 406/791-7700

Rocky Mountain Ranger District, 1102 N. Main Ave., Choteau, MT 59422; 406/466-5341

LOLO NATIONAL FOREST
Building 24A, Fort Missoula, Missoula, MT 59802; 406/329-3814

Plains Ranger Station, P.O. Box 429, Plains, MT 59859; 406/824-3821

Trout Creek Ranger Station, 2693 Highway 200, Trout Creek, MT 59874; 406/827-3533 or 406/752-5501

National Parks

Big Horn Canyon National Recreation Area, Superintendent,
P.O. Box 458, Fort Smith, MT 59035; 406/666-2412

Glacier National Park, Superintendent, P.O. Box 128, West Glacier,
MT 59936; 406/888-7800; www.nps.gov/glac

Bureau of Land Management

U.S. Bureau of Land Management, Montana State Office,
5001 Southgate Dr., Billings, MT 59101; 406/255-2888, 406/896-5004

Garnet Resource Area (east of Missoula), 3255 Ft. Missoula Rd.,
Missoula, MT 59804; 406/329-3914

Butte District, 106 N. Parkmont, P.O. Box 3388, Butte, MT 59702;
406/494-5059

Dillon Resource Area, 1005 Selway Dr., Dillon, MT 59725; 406/683-2337

Great Falls Resource Area, Great Falls, MT; 406/727-0503

Havre Resource Area, 1704 2nd St. West, Drawer 911, Havre, MT 59501;
406/265-5891

Lewistown District Office, Airport Road, P.O. Box 1160,
Lewistown, MT 59457; 406/538-7461

Billings Resource Area, 5001 Southgate Dr., Billings, MT 59101;
406/238-1540

Headwaters Resource Area, 406/494-5059

Miles City District Office, 111 Garryowen Rd., Miles City, MT 59301;
406/232-4333

Phillips Resource Area, 406/654-1240

Valley Resource Area, 406/228-4316

U.S. Army Corps of Engineers

P.O. Box 208, Fort Peck, MT 59223; 406/526-3411

State and Federal Offices

Bureau of Reclamation, Montana Area Office, P.O. Box 30137,
Billings, MT 59107-0137; 406/247-7313 or 406/654-1776

Bureau of Reclamation, P.O. Box 220, Chester, MT 59522; 406/247-7313,
406/456-3228, fax 406/456-3238

Bureau of Reclamation/Bureau of Land Management, 7661 Canyon
Ferry Rd., Helena, MT 59601; 406/475-3128 (summer/fall), 406/475-3319,
fax 406/475-9147

Bureau of Reclamation, Gibson Reservoir, P.O. Box 871, Great Falls, MT 59403; 406/791-7700

Montana Department of Natural Resources and Conservation, 1625 11th Ave., Helena, MT 59620; 406/444-2074

Montana Department of Transportation, P.O. Box 201001, 2701 Prospect Ave., Helena, MT 59620-1001; 406/444-6200, 800/332-6171, or 800/226-7623; website: mdt.state.mt.us

Travel Montana, Department of Commerce, 1424 9th Ave., P.O. Box 200533, Helena, MT 59620-0533; 800/VISIT-MT (800/847-4868) or 406/444-2654; website: travel.mt.gov

U.S. Fish and Wildlife Service, Mountain Prairie Region, P.O. Box 25486 DFC, Denver, CO 80225; 303/236-7400

MONTANA FISH, WILDLIFE & PARKS

1420 E. 6th Ave., Helena, MT 59620; 406/444-2535. If you are over 18 years of age and willing to pay the $1.50 per minute fee, you can call 900/225-5397, a hotline service that has information on recreation-related topics.

Route 1, Box 210, Fort Peck, MT 59; 406/232-4365, 406/232-0900

P.O. Box 949, Three Forks, MT 59752; 406/287-3541

P.O. 1242, Glendive, MT 59330; 406/365-6256

State Trails Coordinator, 1420 E. 6th Ave., Helena, MT 59620; 406/444-4585
   Region 1, 490 N. Meridian Rd., Kalispell, MT 59901; 406/752-5501
   Region 2, 3201 Spurgin Rd., Missoula, MT 59802; 406/542-5500

Helena Area Resource Office, 930 Custer Ave. West, Helena, MT 59620; 406/444-4720

Butte Area Resource Office (limited hours), 1820 Meadowlark Lane, Butte, MT 59701; 406/494-1953
   Region 3, 1400 S. 19th, Bozeman, MT 59718; 406/994-4042.
   Region 4, P.O. Box 6609, Great Falls, MT 59406; 406/454-5840, 406/454-3441

Havre Area Resource Office (limited hours), 2165 Highway 2 East, Havre, MT 59501; 406/265-6177
   Region 5, 2300 Lake Elmo Dr., Billings, MT 59105; 406/247-2940
   Region 6, Route 1-4210, Glasgow, MT 59230; 406/228-3700
   Region 7, P.O. box 1630, Miles City, MT 59301; 406/232-4368

Other Valuable Resources

Blackfeet Nation, P.O. Box 850, Browning, MT 59417; 406/338-7276

Crow Reservation, Crow Agency, MT 59022; 406/638-2601

Flathead Reservation-Confederated Salish & Kootenai Tribes, P.O. Box 278, Pablo, MT 59855; 406/675-2700

Fort Belknap Reservation, Fort Belknap Tourism Office, Rural Route 1, Box 66, Fort Belknap Agency, Harlem, MT 59526; 406/353-2205

Fort Peck Reservation, Fort Peck Assiniboine & Sioux Tribes, P.O. Box 1027, Poplar, MT 59255; 406/768-5155

Montana Campground Owners Association, 185 Council Way, Missoula, MT 59802; 406/549-0881

Northern Cheyenne Reservation, P.O. Box 991, Lame Deer, MT 59043; 406/477-6284 or 406/477-8844

Rocky Boy's Reservation, The Chippewa-Cree Business Committee, P.O. Box 544, Rocky Boy Route, Box Elder, MT 59521; 406/395-4282

Kilbrennen Lake, 406/295-1064

Howard Lake, McGregor Lake, 406/295-7773

WYOMING

National Forests

BIGHORN NATIONAL FOREST
1425 Fort St., Buffalo, WY 82834; 307/684-1100; www.fs.fed.us

1969 S. Sheridan Ave., Sheridan, WY 82801; 307/672-0751; www.fs.fed.us

Medicine Wheel Ranger District, 604 E. Main, P.O. Box 367, Lovell, WY 82431; 307/548-6541; www.fs.fed.us

Cloud Peak Wilderness Area, Bighorn National Forest, 1969 S. Sheridan Ave., Sheridan, WY 82801; 307/672-0751

Paintrock Ranger District, 1220 N. 8th St., P.O. Box 831, Greybull, WY 82426; 307/765-4435

Tensleep Ranger District, 2009 Big Horn Ave., Worland, WY 82401; 307/347-8291

Tongue Ranger District, 1969 S. Sheridan Ave., Sheridan, WY 82801; 307/672-0751

BLACK HILLS NATIONAL FOREST
Highway 14 E., P.O. Box 680, Sundance, WY 82729; 307/283-1361;
www.fs.fed.us

BRIDGER-TETON NATIONAL FOREST
Forest Supervisor, Forest Service Building, 340 N. Cache,
Jackson, WY 83001; 307/739-5500

Big Piney Ranger District, Highway 189, P.O. Box 218,
Big Piney, WY 83113; 307/276-3375; www.fs.fed.us

Buffalo Ranger District, Black Rock Ranger Station, Highway 26-287,
Moran, WY 83013; 307/543-2386; www.fs.fed.us

Greys River Ranger District, 145 Washington St., P.O. Box 338,
Afton, WY 83110; 307/886-3166; www.fs.fed.us

Jackson Ranger District, 340 N. Cache, P.O. Box 1888,
Jackson, WY 83001; 307/739-5570; www.fs.fed.us

Jackson Ranger District, 25 Rosencrans Lane, Jackson, WY 83001;
307/739-5400; www.fs.fed.us

Kemmerer Ranger District, Highway 189, P.O. Box 31,
Kemmerer, WY 83101; 307/877-4515; www.fs.fed.us

Pinedale Ranger District, 210 W. Pine St., P.O. Box 220,
Pinedale, WY 82941; 307/367-4326; www.fs.fed.us

MEDICINE BOW NATIONAL FOREST
2468 Jackson St., Laramie, WY 82070; 307/745-2300; www.fs.fed.us

S. Highway 130, P.O. Box 249, Saratoga, WY 82331; 307/326-5258;
www.fs.fed.us

Thunder Basin National Grassland, 2250 E. Richards,
Douglas, WY 82633; 307/358-4690; www.fs.fed.us

SHOSHONE NATIONAL FOREST
808 Meadow Lane, Cody, WY 82414; 307/527-6241; www.fs.fed.us

Greybull Ranger District, 2044 State St., Greybull, WY 82433;
307/868-2379; www.fs.fed.us

Wapiti Ranger District, 203 A Yellowstone Ave., P.O. Box 1840,
Cody, WY 82414; 307/527-6921; www.fs.fed.us

Wind River District, 1403 W. Ramshorn, P.O. Box 186, Dubois, WY
82513; 307/455-2466; www.fs.fed.us

Washakie District, 333 E. Main St., Lander, WY 82520; 307/332-5460;
www.fs.fed.us

State Parks

Glendo State Park, P.O. Box 398, Glendo, WY 82213; 307/735-4433

Wyoming Division of State Parks & Historical Sites, 122 W. 25th, Herschler Building, 1-E, Cheyenne, WY 82002; 307/777-6323

National Parks

Big Horn Canyon National Recreation Area, National Park Service, P.O. 7458, Fort Smith, MT 59035; 406/666-2412

Devils Tower National Monument, National Park Service, P.O. 8, Devils Tower, WY 82714; 307/467-5283

Grand Teton National Park, Chief Ranger's Office, P.O. Box 170, Moose, WY, 83012; 307/739-3399, 307/739-3300; www.nps.gov/grte

Yellowstone National Park, P.O. Box 168, Yellowstone, WY 82190; 307/344-7381

Bureau of Land Management

Buffalo Field Office, 1425 Fort St., Buffalo, WY 82834-2436; 307/684-1100, fax 307/684-1122; www.wy.blm.gov

Casper Field Office, 2987 Prospector Dr., Casper, WY 82604; 307/261-7600, fax 307/234-1525; www.wy.blm.gov

Cody Field Office, 1002 Blackburn, P.O. Box 518, Cody, WY 82414-0518; 307/587-2216, fax 307/527-7116; www.wy.blm.gov

Kemmerer Field Office, 312 Highway 189 N., Kemmerer, WY 83101-9710; 307/828-4500, fax 307/828-4539; www.wy.blm.gov

Lander Field Office, 1335 Main St., P.O. Box 589, Lander, WY 82520-0589; 307/332-8400, fax 307/332-8447; www.wy.blm.gov

Newcastle Field Office, 1101 Washington Blvd., Newcastle, WY 82701-4453; 307/746-4453, fax 307/746-4840; www.wy.blm.gov

Pinedale Field Office, 432 E. Mill St., P.O. Box 768, Pinedale, WY 82941-0768; 307/367-5300, fax 307/367-5329; www.wy.blm.gov

Rawlins Field Office, 1300 N. 3rd St., P.O. Box 2407, Rawlins, WY 82301-2407; 307/328-4200, fax 307/328-4224; www.wy.blm.gov

Rock Springs Field Office, 280 Highway 191 N., Rock Springs, WY 82901-0256; 307/352-0256, fax 307/352-0329; www.wy.blm.gov

Worland Field Office, 101 S. 23rd St., P.O. Box 119, Worland, WY 82401-0119; 307/347-5100, fax 307/347-6195; www.wy.blm.gov

Wyoming State Office, 5353 Yellowstone Rd., P.O. Box 1828, Cheyenne, WY 82009-4137; 307/775-6256, fax 307/775-6129; www.wy.blm.gov

State and Federal Offices

Wyoming Department of Transportation, 5300 Bishop Blvd., Cheyenne, WY 82009-3340; 888/996-7623 (in Wyoming) or 307/772-0824 (outside Wyoming); website: wydotweb.state.wy.us

Wyoming Game and Fish, 5400 Bishop Blvd., Cheyenne, WY 82006; 307/777-4600

Other Valuable Resources

Big Horn Basin Resource Area, 101 S. 23rd, P.O. Box 119, Worland, WY 82401-0119; 307/347-5100, fax 307/347-6195; www.wy.blm.gov

Flaming Gorge (near Wyoming), P.O. Box 278, Manila, UT 84046; 801/784-3445

National Recreation Reservation Service, 877/444-6777 (a reservation fee applies); www.reserveusa.com

Wyoming Division of Tourism, I-25 at College Drive, Cheyenne, WY 82002; 800/225-5996

IDAHO

National Forests

BITTERROOT NATIONAL FOREST
Forest Supervisor, 316 N. 3rd St., Hamilton, MT 59840; 406/363-3131

West Fork Ranger District, 6735 West Fork Rd., Darby, MT 59829; 406/821-3269, fax 406/821-3269

BOISE NATIONAL FOREST
Forest Supervisor, 1249 S. Vinnell Way, Boise, ID 83709; 208/373-4100

Emmett Ranger District, 1805 Highway 16 #5, Emmett, ID 83617

Idaho City Ranger District, Highway 21, P.O. Box 129, Idaho City, ID 83631; 208/392-6681, 208/364-4330

Cascade Ranger District, Highway 55, P.O. Box 696, Cascade, ID 83611; 208/382-4271, 208/382-7400

Lowman Ranger District, Highway 21, HC 77, Box 3020, Lowman, ID 83637; 208/259-3361

Mountain Home Ranger District, 2180 American Legion Blvd., Mountain Home, ID 83647; 208/587-7961

CARIBOU NATIONAL FOREST
Forest Supervisor, Federal Building, Suite 172, 250 S. 4th Ave., Pocatello, ID 83201; 208/236-7500

Malad Ranger District, 75 S. 140 E., P.O. Box 142, Malad, ID 83252; 208/766-4743

Montpelier Ranger District, 431 Clay, Montpelier, ID 83254; 208/847-0375

Pocatello Ranger District, Federal Building, Suite 187, 250 S. 4th Ave., Pocatello, ID 83201; 208/236-7500

Soda Springs Ranger District, 421 W. 2nd S., Soda Springs, ID 83246; 208/547-4356

CHALLIS NATIONAL FOREST
Highway 93 N., HC-63, Box 1671, Challis, ID 83226; 208/879-2285

Also, see Salmon and Challis National Forests, below.

CLEARWATER NATIONAL FOREST
Forest Supervisor, 12730 U.S. Highway 12, Orofino, ID 83544; 208/476-4541

Lochsa District, Route 1, Box 398, Kooskia, ID 83539; 208/926-4275

North Fork District, P.O. Box 2139, Orofino, ID 83544; 208/476-3775

Palouse District, Route 2, Box 4, Potlatch, ID 83855; 208/875-1131

Pierce District, Kamiah Ranger Station, P.O. Box 308, Kamiah, ID 83256; 208/935-2513

HELENA NATIONAL FOREST
415 S. Front, Townsend, MT 59644; 406/266-3425

IDAHO PANHANDLE NATIONAL FOREST
Forest Supervisor, 3815 Schreiber Way, Coeur d'Alene, ID 83814-8363; 208/765-7223

Bonners Ferry Ranger District, Route 4, Box 4860, Bonners Ferry, ID 83805; 208/267-5561

Fernan Ranger District, 2502 E. Sherman Ave., Coeur d'Alene, ID 83814; 208/769-3000

Priest Lake Ranger District, HCR 5, Box 207, Priest River, ID 83856; 208/443-2512, 800/280-2267

Sandpoint Ranger District, 1500 Highway 2, Sandpoint, ID 83864; 208/263-5111

St. Joe (Avery) Ranger District, HC Box 1, Avery, ID 83802;
208/245-4517

St. Joe (St. Maries) Ranger District, P.O. Box 407, St. Maries, ID 83861;
208/245-2531

Wallace Ranger District, P.O. Box 14, Silverton, ID 83867; 208/725-1221

NEZ PERCE NATIONAL FOREST
Route 2, Box 475, Grangeville, ID 83530; 208/983-1950

Clearwater Ranger District, Route 2, Box 475, Grangeville, ID 83530;
208/983-1963

Elk City Ranger District, P.O. Box 416, Elk City, ID 83525; 208/842-2245

Moose Creek Ranger District, P.O. Box 464, Grangeville, ID 83530;
208/983-2712

Red River Ranger District, Red River Route, P.O. Box 23,
Elk City, ID 83525; 208/842-2255

Salmon River Ranger District, Slate Creek Ranger Station,
HC 01, P.O. Box 70, White Bird, ID 83554; 208/839-2211

Selway Ranger District, Fenn Ranger Station, HCR 1, P.O. Box 91,
Kooskia, ID 83539; 208/926-4258

PAYETTE NATIONAL FOREST
Forest Supervisor, 800 W. Lakeside Ave., P.O. Box 1026,
McCall, ID 83638; 208/634-0700

Council Ranger District, 500 E. Whitely Ave., P.O. Box 567,
Council, ID 83612; 208/253-0100

Krassel Ranger District, 500 N. Mission, P.O. Box 1026,
McCall, ID 83638; 208/634-0600

McCall Ranger District, 102 Lake St., P.O. Box 1026, McCall, ID 83638;
208/634-0400

New Meadows Ranger District, 700 Virginia, P.O. Box J,
New Meadows, ID 83654; 208/347-0300

Weiser Ranger District, 275 E. 7th, Weiser, ID 83672; 208/549-4200

SALMON AND CHALLIS NATIONAL FORESTS
Forest Supervisor, Highway 93 N., RR 2, Box 600, Salmon, ID 83467;
208/756-5100

Challis Ranger District, Highway 93, HC 63, Box 1669, Challis, ID 83226;
208/879-4321

Leadore Ranger District, Highway 28, P.O. Box 180, Leadore, ID 83464; 208/768-2500

Lost River Ranger District, Highway 93 N., P.O. Box 507, Mackay, ID 83251; 208/588-2224

Middle Fork Ranger District, Highway 93 N., P.O. Box 750, Challis, ID 83226; 208/879-5204

North Fork Ranger District, Highway 93, P.O. Box 180, North Fork, ID 83466; 208/865-2383

Salmon/Colbalt Ranger Districts, Highway 93 S., RR 2, Box 600, Salmon, ID 83467; 208/756-5100

Yankee Fork Ranger District, Highway 75, HC 67, Box 650, Clayton, ID 83227; 208/838-2201

SALMON NATIONAL FOREST
P.O. Box 729, Salmon, ID 83467; 208/756-2215, fax 208/756-5151

SAWTOOTH NATIONAL FOREST
Forest Supervisor, 2647 Kimberly Rd. E., Twin Falls, ID 83301-7976; 208/737-3200

Burley Ranger District, 3650 S. Overland Ave., Burley, ID 83318-3242; 208/678-0430

Fairfield Ranger District, P.O. Box 189, Fairfield, ID 83327; 208/764-2202

Ketchum Ranger District, P.O. Box 2356, Ketchum, ID 83340; 208/622-5371

Twin Falls Ranger District, 2647 Kimberly Rd. E., Twin Falls, ID 83301-7976; 208/737-3200

TARGHEE NATIONAL FOREST
Headquarters, 420 N. Bridge Rd., P.O. Box 208, St. Anthony, ID 83445; 208/624-3451

Ashton Ranger District, 30 S. Yellowstone Highway, P.O. Box 858, Ashton, ID 83420; 208/652-7442

Dubois Ranger District, P.O. Box 46, Dubois, ID 83423; 208/374-5422

State Parks
Island Park Ranger District, P.O. Box 220, Island Park, ID 83429; 208/558-7301

Palisades Ranger District, 3659 E. Ririe Highway, Idaho Falls, ID 83401; 208/523-1412

Priest Lake State Park, Indian Creek Bay #423, Coolin, ID 83821; 208/446-2200

Teton Basin Ranger District, P.O. Box 777, Driggs, ID 83422; 208/354-2312

National Parks

City of Rocks National Reserve, P.O. Box 169, Almo, ID 83312; 208/824-5519

Craters of the Moon National Monument, Superintendent, P.O. Box 29, Arco, ID 83213; 208/527-3267

Hagerman Fossil Beds National Monument, P.O. Box 570, Hagerman, ID 83332; 208/837-4793

Hells Canyon National Recreation Area, Route 1, Box 270A, Enterprise, OR 97828; 503/523-6391

Sawtooth National Recreation Area Headquarters, Star Route (eight miles north of Ketchum on Highway 75), Ketchum, ID 83340; 208/727-5000, 208/727-5013, 208/737-3200

Sawtooth National Recreation Area, Stanley Office, HC 64, P.O. Box 9900, Stanley, ID 83278; 208/774-3001

Nez Perce National Historical Park, P.O. Box 93, Highway 95, Spalding, ID 83551; 208/843-2261

Bureau of Land Management

Idaho State Office, 1387 S. Vinnell Way, Boise, ID 83709; 208/373-4000

Boise District Office, 3948 Development Ave., Boise, ID 83705; 208/384-3300

Burley District Office, 15 East, 200 South, Burley, ID 83318; 208/677-6641

Coeur d'Alene District Office, 1808 N. 3rd St., Coeur d'Alene, ID 83814; 208/769-5000

Idaho Falls District Office, 1405 Hollipart Dr., Idaho Falls, ID 83401; 208/524-7500

Salmon District Office, P.O. Box 430, Highway 93 S., Salmon, ID 83467; 208/756-5400

Shoshone District Office, P.O. Box 2-B, 400 W. F St., Shoshone, ID 83352; 208/886-2206

U.S. Army Corps of Engineers

Army Corps of Engineers, U.S. Highway 2, Oldtown, ID 83822; 208/437-3133

State and Federal Offices

Bureau of Reclamation, 1150 N. Curtis Rd., Boise, ID 83706; 208/436-4187, 208/378-5312

Idaho Department of Fish and Game, 600 Walnut, P.O. Box 25, Boise, ID 83707; 800/ASK-FISH (800/275-3474), 800/554-8685, or 208/334-3700, fax 208/334-2114; www.state.id.us/fishgame/fishgame.html

Idaho Department of Transportation, 3311 W. State St., P.O. Box 7129, Boise, ID 83707-1129; (24-hour road conditions report) 208/376-8028, 800/432-7623; website: www.state.id.us/itd/itdhmpg.htm

Other Valuable Resources

Idaho Department of Commerce, Idaho Travel Council, P.O. Box 83720, Boise, ID 83720-0093; 800/VISIT-ID (800/847-4843); www.visitid.org

Idaho Grape Growers and Wine Producers Commission, P.O. Box 1147, Meridian, ID 83642; 888/223-WINE (888/223-9463). Call for a free tour brochure.

Lucky Peak Nursery, HC33 Box 1085, Boise, ID 83706; 208/343-1977

INDEX

ABC

backcountry camping: 6
bears: 19
Bureau of Land Management: Idaho 507; Montana 498; Wyoming 502
California Trail: 13
campfires: 5, 20-21
camping gear: 26
checklists: 26
children: camping with 14-15, 23; games 14-15; hiking with 15
climate: 23-24
clothing: 26
Cottonwood Creek Dinosaur Trail: 10
Craters of the Moon National Monument: 9

DEF

dinosaurs: 10, 11, 12
Dry Creek Petrified tree Environmental Education Area: 10
ethical camping: 4, 23; keep it wild tips 4, 5, 10, 12, 16, 18, 22
fire: 20-21
fishing/fishing licenses: 6, 16-17
floating: 15-16
fly-fishing: 16-17
Fossil Butte National Monument: 9
fossil fish: 10-11
fossils: 9-13
Frank Church--River of No Return Wilderness: 7-8

G

games: 14-15
gear: 26
geothermal features: 4-5
Glacier National Park: 6-7
Going-to-the-Sun Road: 6
Grand Teton National Park: 7
grizzly bears: 19
guides: 25

HIJ

Hagerman Fossil Beds National Monument: 13
health/safety: general discussion: 17-20; sanitation 16; see also safety
hiking: 7, 15
hot springs: 19-20
Jurassic Digs: 11

KLM

lava flows: 9
Lewis and Clark expedition: 13
Lewis and Clark Highway: 13
Lewis and Clark National Historic Trail Interpretive Center: 13
maps: 25
moose: 19
mountain lions: 18
Museum of the Rockies: 12

NOP

national forests: Idaho 503-506; Montana 496-497; Wyoming 500-501
national parks: general discussion 4-7; Idaho 507; Montana 498; Wyoming 502
Native Americans: 6
noise: 23
Oregon Trail: 13
outfitters: 25
petrified trees/wood: 10, 12
pets: 3, 7, 18, 23
photography: 17
Pompey's Pillar: 13

QRS

Red Gulch Dinosaur Tracksite: 12
resource guide: 496-508
road conditions: 24-25
rules of camping: 23; see also ethical camping

safety: general discussion 17-20;
    backcountry 24-25; bison 17;
    campfires 20-21; floating 16;
    geothermal features 5, 20; grizzly
    bears 19; hiking and climbing 7;
    hot springs 20; lightning 24; moose
    19; mountain lions 19; wildlife 3,
    17-19
sanitation: 16
state parks: Idaho 506-507; Montana
    499; Wyoming 502

TUV
trespassing: 21-22
Tynsky's Fossil Fish: 10

U.S. Army Corps of Engineers: Idaho
    508; Montana 498
Ulrich's Fossil Gallery: 10-11
Vore Buffalo Jump: 9-10

WXYZ
Warfield Fossils: 11
weather: 23-24
weather conditions: 24
wildfires: 20-21
wildlife viewing: 3-4
wine: 13-14
Wyoming Dinosaur Center, The: 11
Yellowstone National Park: 4-5

CAMPGROUND INDEX

MONTANA CAMPGROUNDS

A
Ackley Lake State Park: 174
Afterbay: 202
Alder/Virginia City KOA: 166
Alhambra RV Park: 152
Alta: 137
Angler's Roost: 128
Anita Reservoir: 198
Apgar: 54
Arrowhead Resort: 70
Aspen Grove: 144
Aspen: 185
Avalanche: 53

B
Bad Medicine: 38
Bakers Hole: 227
Bannack: 140
Barretts Park: 169
Barry's Landing: 203
Basin: 189
Basin Canyon: 154
Battlefield Country Market: 201
Battle Ridge: 178
Bear Canyon Campground: 180
Bear Creek: 109, 169
Bear Creek Pass: 130
Beaver Creek: 224
Beaver Creek Park Campground: 95
Beaver Dam: 160
Beaverhead: 136
Beavertail Hill State Park: 124
Beaver Valley Haven: 116
Benchmark: 86
Benton RV Park: 96
Big Arm: 70
Big Arm Resort & Marina: 71
Big Beaver: 184
Big Bend RV Park: 37
Big Creek Campground: 54
Big Horn RV Park: 201

Big Larch: 75
Big Nelson: 88
Big Pine: 77
Big Sky Camp and RV Park: 207
Big Sky Campground: 199
Big Sky RV Park: 157
Big Sky RV Resort & Marina: 69
Big Therriault: 49
Big Timber KOA Campground: 179
Billings Metro KOA: 199
Birdland Bay RV Resort: 42
Bitterroot Family Campground: 130
Bitterroot Flat: 127
Black Bear: 129
Black Sandy Beach: 146
Blodgett Canyon Campground: 127
Blue Mountains RV Park: 33
Bolster Dam Campgrounds: 115
Bone Trail: 102
Boulder: 135
Bowman Lake: 51
Bozeman KOA: 163
Branham Lakes: 164
Bull River: 39
Butte KOA: 158
Buzz In RV Park & Campground: 148

C
Cabin City: 42
Cabin Creek: 224
Cabinet Gorge RV Park & Campground: 39
Cable Mountain: 128
Cameahwait: 221
Cameron Store & Cabins: 169
Camp Creek: 102
Camp Tuffit: 69
Camper Corner: 167
Campfire Lodge Resort: 224
Campground St. Regis: 42
Canyon Ferry RV Park & Storage: 149
Canyon RV & Campground: 59

Canyon: 186
Carbella: 187
Casa Village: 199
Cascade: 189
Cascade: 74
Castle Rock Inn & RV Park: 165
Cave Mountain: 84
Cedar Hills Campground: 179
Chalet Bearmouth Campground: 124
Charles Waters: 125
Chief Joseph: 191
Chief Joseph Park: 177
Chief Looking Glass: 125
Chief Mountain Junction: 49
Chinaman's Gulch: 149
Chippy Park: 185
Chisholm: 182
Choteau KOA: 84
Choteau Park & Campground: 85
City Park Campground: 202
Clark Canyon Reservoir: 221
Cliff Point: 225
Coalbanks Landing: 95
Colter: 191
Columbia Falls RV Park: 61
Conestoga Campground: 176
Cooney: 181
Cooper Creek: 88
Copper Creek: 131
Copper King: 41
Coram RV Park: 56
Cottonwood: 168
Cottonwood Camp: 202
Court Sheriff: 150
Cow Creek: 209
Crazy Creek: 134
Cromwell Dixon: 151
Crooked Creek: 103
Crossroads Motel & RV Park: 73
Crystal Creek: 128
Crystal Lake: 175
Cut Bank: 56

D
Dailey Lake: 186
Dalles: 126
Deadman's Basin: 177
Deer Lick Resort: 68
Deer Lodge KOA: 153
Delmoe Lake: 158
Denton's Point: 129
Departure Point: 144
Devil Creek: 62
Devils Creek: 103
Diamond 'S' RV Park: 73
Dickie Bridge: 134
Dick's RV Park: 87
Dillon KOA: 167
Dinner Station: 166
Divide Bridge: 161
Doris Point: 61
Dorr Skeels: 38
Downstream: 108
Doyle: 210
Dry Wolf: 174

EF
Eagle Creek: 190
Eagle Nest RV Resort: 72
East Bank: 134
East Boulder: 181
East Fork: 129
East Rosebud Lake: 188
Eastwood Estates: 198
Edgewater Motel & RV Resort: 65
Ekstrom Stage Station: 124
Elkhorn Guest Ranch: 125
Emerald Lake: 187
Emery Bay: 60
Ennis: 166
Evergreen Campground: 95
EZ-K RV Park: 33
Fairmont RV Park: 157
Fairweather: 158
Fairy Lake: 178
Falls Creek: 184
Finley Point: 72

Firebrand Pass Campground: 57
Fish Creek: 53
Fishtrap Lake: 40
Flat Lake: 109
Flint Creek: 128
Fort Belknap Rest Area: 101
Fort Ponderosa RV Park: 96
Fort Three Forks Motel & RV Park: 159
Fourchette Creek: 102
Fourth of July: 135
Free Enterprise Health Mine: 156
Fresno Beach: 94

G
Gary Smith Memorial: 81
Glacier Campground: 55
Glacier Peaks RV Park: 60
Glacier Pines RV Park: 64
Glendive Campground: 116
Gold Rush: 42
Good Time Camping & RV Park: 125
Goose Bay Marina: 152
Grandview Campgrounds: 200
Grasshopper: 138
Grasshopper Creek: 176
Great Falls KOA Campground: 88
Great Northern Fair & Campground: 94
Greek Creek: 165
Green Oasis Campground: 208
Green Valley Campground: 115
Greenough Lake: 192
Greenwood Village RV Park: 64
Greycliff: 162
Grizzly: 126

H
H & C RV: 147
Half Moon: 178
Handkerchief Lake: 67
Hap Hawkins: 222
Happy's Inn: 40
Hardin KOA: 200

Harrison Lake: 162
Harry's Flat: 126
Havre KOA Campground: 95
Havre RV Park & Travel Plaza: 94
Helena Campground & RV Park: 147
Hellgate: 150
Hells Canyon: 185
Hicks Park: 185
Hideaway RV Campground: 227
Hilltop: 225
Hilltop Campgrounds: 103
Historic Jersey Lily Campground: 197
Hi-Way Bar & Quick Stop: 94
Holiday Springs: 208
Holland Lake: 73
Holter Lake: 146
Home Gulch: 85
Hood Creek: 182
Hooper Lake: 145
Horse Prairie: 222
Hostel of the Rockies at St. Ignatius Camping: 74
Howard Lake: 39
Humbug Spires: 162
Hunter's Beaverhead Marina & Park: 222
Huntley Diversion Dam: 198

IJ
Ideal Motel & RV Park: 197
Indian Creek Campground: 153
Indian Hill: 175
Indian Road: 154
Indian Trees: 135
Intake: 115
Island Area: 83
Itch-Kep-Pe Park: 179
James Kipp: 102
J & M RV Park: 97
Jellystone RV Park: 122
Jennings Camp: 132
Jerry's RV Park: 50
Jim & Mary's RV Park: 122
Jimmy Joe: 187

JJ's Rough Country: 150
Jo Bonner: 149
Jocko Hollow Campground: 76
Johnson's of St. Mary: 51
Jordan RV Park: 111
Judith Landing: 96
Jumping Creek: 175

K
Kading: 153
Kamp Katie: 110
Kiehns Bay: 93
Kilbrennan Lake: 36
Kim's Marina & RV Resort: 148
Kings Hill: 174
Kintla Lake: 48
Kiwanis Campground: 97
Koocanusa Resort: 36
Kremlin: 93

L
La Rue's Wayside Mobile/RV Park: 209
Ladysmith: 156
Lake Alva: 74
Lake Blaine Resort: 65
Lake Como Lower: 131
Lake Como Upper: 131
Lake Five Resort: 55
Lake Mary Ronan Lodge & Resort: 69
Lake Mary Ronan State Park: 68
Lake Shel-oole Campground: 82
Lake Shore Lodge: 164
Lakeside Resort: 147
Langhor: 181
Lantis Spring: 213
LaSalle RV Park & Campground: 63
Lee Creek: 124
Lewis & Clark: 123, 222
Lewis & Clark Caverns State Park: 161
Lewis & Clark RV Park: 82
Lexley Acres: 162
Lick Creek Campground: 131

Lid Creek: 62
Limber Pine: 192
Lincoln Road RV Park: 148
Lion's Bitterroot Youth Camp: 65
Little Bighorn Camp: 198
Little Bighorn Camp: 201
Little Joe: 222
Little Montana Truck Stop & Café: 103
Little Therriault: 49
L'n Eve Travel Trailer Park: 87
Loch Leven: 183
Lodgepole: 136
Log Gulch: 144
Logan State Park: 40
Logging Creek: 51, 88
Lolo Hot Springs Resort: 123
Lonesomehurst: 226
Lonetree: 223
Lost Creek State Park: 128
Lost Johnny Point: 61
Lowland: 157

M
Madison Arm Resort & Marina: 226
Madison River: 224
Madison River Cabins & RV: 170
Maidenrock: 161
Makoshika State Park: 116
Mallard's Rest: 183
Manhattan Camper Court: 160
Many Glacier: 50
Many Pines: 174
Mariners Haven: 35
Martin Creek: 132
Maverick Mountain RV Park: 139
May Creek: 137
McGillivray: 36
McGregor Lake: 65
McGregor Lake Resort: 66
Mcguire Creek: 110
McLeod Resort: 181
Meadowlark Campground: 37
Medicine Rocks State Park: 213

Merry Widow RV Park: 155
Miles City KOA: 207
Mill Creek: 164
Miner Lake: 139
Mission Meadow Campground: 72
Missoula KOA: 123
Missouri Headwaters State Park: 159
M-K: 193
Mono Creek: 137
Montana Gulch: 102
Moose Creek: 151, 174
Moose Flat: 165
Moosehead Campground, Store, &
    Rock Shop: 133
Mormon Creek: 156
Mortimer Gulch: 85
Mountain Acres RV Park &
    Campground: 97
Mountain Meadow RV Park &
    Campground: 60
Mountain Meadows Resort & Golf
    Course: 69
Mountain Range RV Park: 179
Mountain View RV Park: 158
Mountain View Trailer Court: 122
Mrnak RV Park: 213
Murray Bay: 63
Mussigbrod: 135

NO
Nelson Creek: 110
Nelson Reservoir: 101
North American RV Park &
    Campground: 55
North Bootlegger: 82
North Dickey Lake: 50
North Shore: 41
North Van Houten: 139
Northern Cheyenne: 208
Norton: 126
Old North Trail Campground: 50
Orofino: 155
Osen's Campground: 180
Out Post Campground: 122

Outback Montana: 67
PQ
Painted Rock: 136
Palisades: 188
Paradise Livingston Campground:
    180
Paradise Valley/Livingston KOA: 183
Park Lake: 151
Parkside: 192
Peck Gulch: 35
Pelican Truck Plaza Motel: 200
Perry's RV Park & Campground: 189
Pete Creek: 34
Pigeon Creek: 161
Pine Creek: 183
Pine Grove: 186
Pines Campground, The: 109
Pipestone Campground: 159
Placid Lake State Park: 76
Polson/Flathead Lake KOA: 71
Pondera RV Park: 84
Potosi: 163
Price Creek: 138
Quartz Creek: 51
Quartz Flat: 76

R
Racetrack: 127
Rainbow Point: 226
Rancho Motel & Campground: 108
Ratine: 191
Ravalli Store: 74
Red Cliff: 169
Red Lodge KOA: 187
Red Mountain: 163
Red Shale: 209
Reservoir Lake: 140
Rexford Bench: 34
Richardson Creek: 177
Rising Sun: 53
River Point: 75
River Run: 93
Riverfront Motel & Cabins, The: 41
Riverside: 148

Riverside Park: 201
Riverview Campground: 81
Roadrunner RV Park: 154
Rock Canyon RV Park: 182
Rock Creek Marina: 109
Rocking C Ranch: 72
Rocking J Cabins & Campground: 97
Rocky Gorge: 35
Rocky Mountain Campground: 190
Rocky Mountain "Hi" RV Park &
    Campground: 64
Rombo: 134
Rosebud Battlefield: 208
Ruby Reservoir: 168
Russell Gates Memorial: 77
Rustic Wagon RV Campground &
    Cabins: 227

S
Sacajawea Memorial: 217
Sage Creek: 202
Salmon Lake State Park: 77
Sam Billings Memorial: 133
San-Suz-Ed RV Park & Campground:
    59
Scheer's Trailer Court: 110
Schumaker: 129
Sears Motel & Campground: 56
Seeley Lake: 75
Seymour: 132
Shady Grove Campground: 81
Shady Rest RV Park: 107
Sheridan: 190
Silos RV & Fishing Camp: 152
Silos: 152
Skidway: 154
Skyline RV Park: 163
Slate Creek: 136
Sleeping Wolf Campground & RV
    Park: 54
Sleepy Hollow Mobile Home & RV
    Park: 145
Sloway: 43
Smiley's RV Park: 57

Smith's Mobile Park: 108
Snow Bank: 186
Snowberg Port & Court: 71
Soda Butte: 191
South Bootlegger: 83
South Fork: 86
South Madison: 170
South Van Houten: 139
Spar Lake: 38
Spillway: 130
Spire Rock: 164
Sportsman's RV Park: 37
Spotted Bear: 68
Sprague Creek: 53
Spring Creek: 175
Spring Creek Campground & Trout
    Ranch: 178
Spring Creek RV Park: 145
Spring Grove Trailer Court: 116
Spring Gulch: 132
Spring Hill: 130
Springs Campground: 176
Spruce Park RV Park: 64
Square & Round Dance Center: 123
Squaw Rock: 153
Stanton Creek Lodge: 58
Steel Creek: 137
St. Mary Lake: 52
St. Mary-Glacier Park KOA
    Kampground: 52
St. Regis KOA: 42
St. Regis Riding Stables: 43
Sula Country Store, Campground, &
    RV Park: 133
Summit: 62
Sundance RV Park & Campground:
    56
Sunrise Campground: 180
Sunrise Trailer Court: 84
Sunset Trailer Court: 156
Sunset Village RV: 200
Swan Creek: 165
Swan Lake: 70
Swan Village Market & Campground:
    68

TU
Tally Lake: 58
Terry RV Oasis: 207
Thain Creek: 96
Thompson Falls State Park: 41
Three Forks Campground: 62
Three Forks KOA Campground: 160
Timbers RV Park: 66
Timber Wolf Resort, The: 60
Toll Mountain: 160
Tom Miner: 188
Tongue River Reservoir: 210
Toston Dam: 157
Trafton Park: 101
Trailer Village: 199
Trails West Campground: 107
Trout Creek: 76
Trout Pond: 108
Tuchuck: 49
Tucker Crossin' RV Park
    Campground: 127
Twin Lakes: 138
2 Bar Lazy H RV Park &
    Campground: 159
Two Medicine: 52

VW
Valley Garden: 166
Varney Bridge: 168
VFW Campground: 83
Vigilante: 146
Virginia City Campground: 167
Wade Lake: 225
Wagons West: 86
Wagon Wheel Campground &
    Cabins: 228
Warm Springs: 133
Wayfarers: 67
West Boulder: 184
West Cameahwait: 223
West End: 108
West Fork: 223
West Fork: 84
West Fork Cabins & RV Park: 223

West Glacier KOA: 59
West Madison: 170
West Shore: 66
White Birch RV & Campground: 63
White Buffalo Campground: 209
White Earth: 151
Whitefish KOA: 58
Whitefish Lake State Park: 58
Whitehouse: 155
Whitetail: 34
Wickham Gulch: 213
Williamson Park Campground: 82
Willow Creek: 40, 83
Willow Creek Campground: 73
Windmill Park: 181
Wood Lake: 87
Woodland RV Park: 37
Woods Bay Marina & RV Park: 66

XYZ
Y Lazy R RV Park: 57
Yaak Falls: 36
Yellow Bay: 71
Yellowstone Grizzly RV Park: 228
Yellowstone Holiday Resort: 225
Yellowstone Park KOA: 227
Yellowstone River RV Park and
    Campground: 199
Yellowstone's Edge RV Park: 184

WYOMING CAMPGROUNDS
A
Absaroka Bay RV Park: 242
Alcova Lake Campground: 316
American Presidents Campground:
    309
Antelope Run Campground: 313
Arlington Outpost: 318
Arrowhead RV Camp: 330
Astoria Hot Springs: 255
Atherton Creek: 251
Atlantic City: 308
Ayers Natural Bridge: 315

B

B Q Corral: 327
Bald Mountain: 263
Bearlodge: 287
Belle Fourche River: 287
Bennett Court: 329
Big Atlantic Gulch: 307
Big Game: 241
Big Horn Mountain Campground: 281
Big Horn Mountain KOA
  Campground: 279
Big Sandy Recreation Area: 297
Bobbie Thompson: 322
Boswell Creek: 322
Boulder Lake: 295
Boulder Park: 270
Boysen Marina: 274
Boysen State Park: 274
Bridge Bay: 239
Brooklyn Lake: 319
Brooks Lake: 249
Brown Mountain: 247
Buckboard Crossing: 300
Buffalo Bill State Park: 241
Buffalo Bill Village: 242
Buffalo KOA Campground: 280
Bull Creek: 270

C

Cabin Creek: 256
Cabin Creek Trailer Park: 266
Camp Big Horn RV Park: 262
Camp Cody RV Park: 243
Campbell Creek: 316
Canyon Campground: 238
Carnahan Ranch: 330
Casper KOA: 313
Castle Gardens: 271
Chuckwagon RV & Gifts: 329
Circle Park: 268
Circle-Up Camper Court: 253
Clearwater: 240
Cody KOA: 243
Colter Bay: 247

Colter Bay RV Park: 247
Conner Battlefield State Historic Site:
  262
Cook Lake Campground: 288
Cottonwood: 308
Country Camping RV and Tent Park:
  272
County Market Conoco: 288
Crazy Woman: 282
Crystal Creek: 252
Crystal Park Campground: 289
Curtis Canyon: 252
Curtis Gulch: 316

DE

Dead Swede: 265
Deer Creek: 245
Deer Creek RV Campground: 314
Deer Park: 269
Deer Park Campground: 280
Devils Tower KOA: 287
Diamond Guest Ranch: 318
Dickinson Creek: 304
Double Cabin: 249
Douglas Jackalope KOA: 314
Eagle Creek: 240
Eagle RV Park: 272
East Fork: 265
Elbow: 256
Elk Fork: 241
Elk Country Inn & RV Park: 253
Esterbrook: 317
Esterbrook Lodge: 317

FG

Falls: 250
Fiddlers Campground: 306
Firehole Canyon: 299
Fishing Bridge RV Park: 238
Flagg Ranch Village: 246
Foothills Mobile Home & RV Park:
  298
Foothills Motel & Campground: 262
Forest Park: 295

Fort Caspar Campground: 314
Fountain of Youth RV Park: 272
Fremont Lake: 294
Friend Park: 317
Gateway Campground: 243
Glendo Marina: 328
Glendo State Park: 327
Goshen County Fairgrounds: 331
Grand Teton Park RV Resort: 248
Grandview RV Park: 273
Granite Creek: 254
Grant Village: 245
Green River Lake: 255
Greentrees Crazy Woman
    Campground: 282
Greybull KOA: 266
Gros Ventre: 251
Guernsey State Park: 328

HIJ
Half Moon: 294
Hams Fork: 297
Harper's Park & RV: 297
Hart Ranch Hideout RV Park &
    Campground: 306
Hatchet: 248
Hawk Springs State Recreation Area:
    331
Hells Half Acre Campground: 276
High Plains Campground: 282
Hitching Post Campground: 241
Hoback: 256
Hole in the Wall Campground: 284
Holiday Lodge Campground: 304
Horse Creek: 251
Horseshoe Bend: 261
Hunter Corrals: 268
Indian Campground: 281
Indian Creek: 237
Island Park: 269
Jack Creek: 246, 310
Jenny Lake: 250

KL
Kaycee RV Park #1: 283
Kaycee RV Park #2: 283
Kaycee Town Park: 283
Keyhole State Park: 287
Lake Owen: 322
Lake Viva Naughton: 297
Lakeside Lodge Resort & Marina: 294
Lakeview: 269
Lakeview Motel & Campground: 328
Lander City Park: 304
Laramie KOA: 320
Larson Park Campground: 329
Lazy J Corral RV Park: 255
Lazy R: 262
Leigh Creek: 270
Lewis Lake: 245
Libby Creek/Willow Campground:
    319
Lizard Creek: 246
Lodgepole: 315
Lost Cabin: 282
Louis Lake: 307
Lovell Camper Park: 263
Lyman/Fort Bridger KOA: 299
Lynx Creek: 257

M
Madison: 238
Mammoth Campground: 236
Maverick Mobile Home Park: 304
Meadowlark Resort: 271
Medicine Lodge Lake: 267
Medicine Lodge State Archeological
    Site: 267
Middle Fork: 281
Middle Piney Lake: 296
M/K RV Park: 273
Moose Flat: 293
Mountain View Campground: 288
Mountain View Lodge: 243
Mountain View Motel and
    Campground: 280
Murphy Creek: 258

NO

Narrows: 257
New Fork Lake: 257
New RV Park: 274
Newton Creek: 239
Norris: 237
North Tongue: 264
Oasis Campground: 268
Owen Creek: 265
Owl Creek Kampground: 275

PQ

Pahaska: 239
Paintrock Lakes: 267
Park County Fairgrounds: 263
Pebble Creek: 236
Pelton Creek: 322
Pine Bluffs RV Park: 332
Pinedale Campground: 295
Pinnacles: 249
Pioneer Municipal Park: 331
Pitzer's RV Park: 331
Ponderosa Campground: 244
Pony Soldier RV Park: 330
Popo Agie: 307
Porcupine: 263
Prairie View Campground: 327
Prune Creek: 264

R

Ranger Creek: 265
Rawlins KOA Kampground: 310
Ray Lake Campground & Cafè: 305
Reunion Flat Group Area: 250
Reuter: 288
Rex Hale: 240
Rim Campground: 315
Rimrock RV: 289
River Campground: 308
Riverside Campground: 253, 320
Riverside RV Park: 298
River's View RV Park: 244
Riverton RV Park: 275
Rob Roy Campground: 321

Rock Springs KOA: 298
Rocky Acres Campground: 303
Rose Garden RV Park: 266
Rudy's Camper Court: 275
RV World Campground: 308

S

Sacajawea: 296
Sagebluff RV Park: 283
Saratoga Lake: 318
Scab Creek: 295
Seminoe State Park: 318
7K Motel and RV Park: 242
Shell Campground: 266
Shell Creek: 266
Sheridan RV Park: 279
Sibley Lake: 264
Signal Mountain: 248
Sinks Canyon Campground: 305
Sinks Canyon State Park: 305
Sitting Bull Creek: 269
Sleeping Bear RV Park &
    Campground: 303
Sleeping Giant: 239
Slough Creek: 236
Snake River Park KOA: 254
Snowy Range Trailer Park: 320
South Brush Creek: 319
South Fork: 281
Station Creek: 257
Swift Creek: 296

TUV

Ten Broek RV Park & Cabins: 271
Teton Canyon: 250
Teton Village KOA: 252
Tex's Travel Camp: 299
Three Mile: 239
Tie City: 320
Tie Flume: 264
Tie Hack: 281
Tower Falls: 237
Trail Creek: 252
Trails End: 294

Vedauwoo: 321
Virginian Lodge RV Park: 254

WXYZ
Wagon Box Campground: 279
Wagon Wheel Campground: 254
Wapiti: 240
Warren Bridge: 293
West Tensleep Lake: 268
Western Hills Campground: 309
Wheatland City Park (Lewis Park) : 330
Whiskey Grove: 256
Wind River View Campground: 296
Wood River: 248
Worland Cowboy Campground: 271
Worthen Meadows: 306
Yellow Pine: 321
Yellowstone Valley RV Park: 244

IDAHO CAMPGROUNDS

A
Abbot: 418
Albeni Cove Recreation Area: 350
Albert Moser: 492
Albertini's Carlin Bay Resort: 361
Alpine Country Store & RV Park: 356
Alpine Trailer Park: 349
Alturas Inlet: 437
Amanita: 399
Americana Kampground: 416
Anderson Camp & RV Sales and Service: 476
Anderson Ranch Reservoir Campgrounds: 419
Apgar: 375
Aquarius: 371
Arrowhead RV Park on the River: 402
Aspen Acres Golf Club & RV Park: 457
Aspen Lodge: 455

B
Bad Bear: 411
Baker Creek: 439
Banbury Hot Springs: 474
Basin Creek: 432
Baumgartner: 418
Bayhorse: 430
Bayhorse Lake: 430
Bayview Scenic Motel & RV Park: 354
Bear Lake State Park: 494
Bear Valley: 402
Beaver Creek: 344, 403
Bell Bay: 361
Bennett Springs: 477
Berlin Flats: 356
Beyond Hope Resort: 359
Big Creek: 364
Big Eddy: 407
Big Eight Mile: 428
Big Elk Creek: 462
Big Flat: 401
Big Hank: 356
Big Roaring River Lake and Big Trinity Lake: 417
Big Springs: 452, 487
Big Tree RV Park: 473
Birch Creek: 456
Black Rock: 413
Blind Creek: 432
Blowout: 462
Blue Anchor Trailer & RV Park: 362
Blue Lake Campground: 346
Blue Lakes RV Park: 475
Bonanza: 429
Bonners Ferry Resort: 345
Bonneville: 408
Bostetter: 479
Bottle Bay Resort: 351
Boulder View: 440
Boulevard Motel & RV Park: 358
Boundary Creek: 402
Bounds: 443
Box Canyon: 455
Brackenbury: 477
Broken Arrow: 385
Brownlee: 397

Bruneau Dunes State Park: 467
Brush Lake Campground: 341
Buckhorn Bar: 395
Buffalo Loops A-G: 453
Bull Trout Lake: 406
Bumblebee: 360
Burren West LLC RV/Trailer Park: 446
Buttermilk: 455

C
C. J. Strike Parks: 467
Cabin Creek: 399
Calamity: 461
Caldwell Campground & RV Park: 414
Canyon Creek: 372, 399
Canyon: 442
Capital Mobile Park: 412
Caribou: 439
Carroll's Travel Plaza & RV Park: 444
Castle Creek: 378
Cedar Motel & RV Park: 358
Cedars and Shade Campground: 494
Century II Campground: 387
Challis All Valley RV Park: 429
Challis Hot Springs: 429
Chaparral: 417
Chemeketan: 439
Chinook Bay: 434
City of Oakley RV Park: 478
City of Rocks National Reserve: 480
Cloverleaf: 492
Coeur d'Alene KOA: 358
Coeur d'Alene RV Resort: 358
Cold Springs: 392
Conrad Crossing: 365
Cooper Creek: 340
Copperfield Park: 392
Corn Creek: 386
Cottonwood: 428
Cottonwood Family Campground: 488
Cougar Point: 388
Cove: 467

Cowboy RV Park: 485
Cozy Cove: 406
Crags: 388
Craters of the Moon National Monument: 445
Crystal Gold Mine & RV Park: 362
Cummings Lake Lodge: 385
Curry Trailer Park: 475
Custer: 429
Cutthroat Trout: 462

DE
Deep Creek Resort: 345
Deer Cliff Store, Cafe, & RV: 494
Deer Creek Lodge: 419
Dent Acres: 372
Desert Hot Springs: 468
Devil's Elbow: 356
Diamond Creek: 487
Diamondfield Jack: 479
Dickensheet: 348
Dike Lake (China Cap): 485
Dog Creek: 419
Dworshak State Park: 372
Easley: 440
Ebenezer Bar Campground: 387
Edgewater Resort: 350
Edna Creek: 411
Ed's R & R Shady River RV Park: 363
Eight Mile: 490
Elbow: 491
Elk Creek: 431
Elk Mountain RV Resort: 433
Emerald Creek: 370
Emigration: 490
Evergreen: 395

FG
Fall Creek Resort and Marina: 420
Falls: 460
Falls Group Area: 461
Farragut State Park: 354
Federal Gulch: 443
Fiesta RV Park: 416

Fish Creek: 377
Flat Rock: 432, 453
Fly Flat: 365
Fox Farm RV Resort: 350
French Creek: 402
Frontier Motel & RV Park: 400
Garfield Bay Resort: 352
Gateway RV Park: 404
Geisingers: 342
Giant White Pine: 369
Given's Hot Springs: 418
Glacier View: 435
Golden Gate: 394
Grandjean: 409
Gravel Creek: 484
Graves Creek: 462
Grayback Gulch: 413
Grouse Campground: 382

H
Hagerman RV Village: 472
Hammer Creek: 379
Harpster RV Park: 376
Harrison City RV Park: 362
Haven Motel & Trailer Park: 457
Hawkins Reservoir: 489
Hayfork: 411
Hazard Lake: 381
Heald's Haven: 426
Heise Hot Springs: 458
Helende: 408
Hells Canyon Park: 382
Hells Gate State Park: 373
Hemlock's Country Inn: 344
Henry's Lake State Park: 451
Heyburn State Park: 362
Hi Valley RV Park: 414
Hidden Creek: 371
Hidden Village: 373
High Adventure River Tours RV Park & Store: 472
Holiday Motel & RV: 412
Holman Creek: 433
Honeysuckle: 357

Hot Springs: 409
Hower's: 406
Huckleberry: 364
Huckle Berry Heaven: 371

IJ
Idaho Country Resort: 349
Idyl Acres RV Park: 341
Indian Creek: 346
Indian Hot Springs: 404
Indian Springs Swimming & RV: 487
Indianhead Motel & RV Park: 404
Intermountain Motor Homes and RV Park: 473
Iron Bog: 443
Iron Creek: 434
Iron Lake: 426
Island View Resort: 351
Jessen's RV & Bed & Breakfast: 457
Junction Lodge: 378
Juniper Park: 459

KL
Kaniksu Resort RV & Marina: 346
Kellogg/Silver Valley KOA: 361
Kelly Forks: 372
Kelly's Island: 459
Kelso Lake Resort: 355
Kennally Creek: 397
Killarney Lake: 361
Kirkham Hot Springs: 411
Kit Price: 356
Lafferty: 395
Laird Park: 370
Lake Cleveland: 477
Lake Fork: 394
Lake Walcott State Park: 473
Lakeview: 407
Lakeview Village: 395
Landing Zone RV Park: 444
Last Chance: 382
Lava Ranch Inn Motel & RV Campground: 488
Lava Spa Motel & RV Park: 489

Lazy River RV Park: 409
Lema's Store & RV Park: 428
Lewis Clark Resort: 375
Lionhead: 343
Little Boulder Creek: 371
Littlewood Reservoir: 445
Lodgepole Pine Inn: 380
Lola Creek: 403
Lower Luby Bay: 347
Lud Drexler Park: 478

M
MacDonald's Hudson Bay Resort: 354
Mackay Reservoir: 437
Macks Inn Resort: 451
Mann Creek Campground: 403
Maple Grove: 491
Mason Creek RV Park: 415
Massacre Rocks State Park: 488
McCall Campground: 396
McCormick Park: 396
McCrea Bridge: 454
McFall Hotel and RV Park: 471
McFarland: 427
Meadow Creek: 341
Meadow Lake: 430
Meadows RV Park, The: 442
Meadows RV Park: 393
Mike Harris: 459
Mill Canyon: 485
Mill Creek: 429
Miracle Hot Springs: 474
Miss Lily's Saloon and Buggy Stop: 374
Misty Meadows RV Park & Camping: 363
Mokins Bay: 357
Monroe Creek Campground: 404
Monte Vista Motel & RV Park: 359
Montour Wildlife Area: 412
Montpelier Canyon: 491
Montpelier Creek KOA: 490
Morgan Bar: 427
Mormon Bend: 431

Mosquito Flat Reservoir: 428
Mount Heyburn: 436
Mountain Home KOA: 421
Mountain River Ranch RV Park: 458
Mountain View: 410, 434
Mountain View Mobile Home & RV Park: 377
Mountain View RV Park: 397, 417, 444
Mountain View Trailer Park: 489
Murdock: 440
Murph's RV Park: 396

NO
Nat-soo-pah Hot Springs & RV Park: 476
Navigation: 341
Neat Retreat: 409
Nester's Riverside Campground: 420
New Haven Lodge: 410
Ninemeyer: 414
Noe Creek: 373
North Canyon Overflow: 493
North Fork: 440
North Fork Motel & Campground: 386
North Shore Alturas Lake: 437
O'Hara Bar: 376
On the River RV Park: 416
Oregon Trail Campground & Family Fun Center: 475
Osprey: 343
Outlet: 348, 435

P
Palisades: 461
Palisades RV Park & Cabins: 461
Paradise/Justrite: 400
Paris Springs: 492
Park Creek: 410
Park Creek: 441
Pen Basin: 398
Pettit: 479
Phi Kappa: 441

Pine Bar: 377
Pinebar: 484
Pine Creek: 459
Pine Flats: 410
Pinehurst Resort: 393
Pine Resort: 420
Pines RV Campground: 370
Pinewood Lodge-Motel-RV Park & Storage: 401
Pipeline: 486
Playground Sports & RV Park, The: 415
Plowboy: 342
Pocatello KOA: 485
Point: 436
Poison Creek: 399
Pole Flat: 431
Ponderosa State Park: 394
Pond's Lodge: 454
Porcupine: 494
Power Plant: 414
Prairie Creek: 439
Priest Lake RV Resort & Marina: 347
Priest River Recreation Area: 352
Prospector's Gold RV & Campground: 380
PV Travel Stop 216: 476

QR
Quinn's Rainbow Lodge: 474
Rainbow Lake & Campground: 458
Rainbow Point: 400
R & E Greenwood Store: 475
Rattlesnake: 405
Red River: 379
Redpoint: 492
Redrock RV & Camping Park: 449
Reeder Bay: 346
Rendezvous Village RV Park: 491
Riley Creek Recreation Area: 352
River Delta Resort: 353
River Front Gardens RV Park: 380
River Haven RV Park: 418
River Junction RV Park: 375
River Lake RV Park: 353

River Park Golf Course and RV Campground: 438
River Village RV Park: 380
Riverside RV & Campground: 445
Riverside RV Park: 380
Riverside: 405, 456
Robin Hood RV Park & Campground: 359
Robin's Roost: 454
Robinson Lake: 340
Rock Lodge Resort & Creekside RV Park: 471
Rockford Bay Resort: 360
Round Lake State Park: 352
R-Place RV Park: 349
RV Park Milepost 382: 365
Ryan's Wilderness Inn: 376

S
Sage Hen Flats: 484
Salmon Meadows: 387
Salmon River: 407
Salmon River Campground & RV Park: 427
Sam Owen: 351
Sandy Beach Resort: 353
Scenic Bay Marina: 354
Scenic "6" Park: 370
Schipper: 478
Scout Mountain: 486
Seagull Bay Yacht Club: 486
Seven Devils: 381
7N Ranch: 458
Shadowy St. Joe: 363
Shady Acres Campground: 359
Shady Rest Campground: 460
Shafer Butte: 413
Sheep Trail: 431
Shoreline: 398
Silver Beach Resort: 355
Silver City Lodgings: 420
Silver Creek: 405
Silver Creek Plunge: 404
Silver Leaf Motel & RV Park: 362

Silverwood RV Park: 355
Slate Creek: 379
Sligar's 1000 Springs Resort: 472
Smith Lake: 344
Smokey Bear (Alturas Lake): 437
Smokey Cubs: 427
Snake River RV Resort: 415
Snowy River Campground: 453
Sockeye: 436
Soldier Creek RV Park: 445
South Fork: 378
South Fork Lodge: 460
Southwestern Idaho Senior Citizens
    Recreation Association: 398
Sportsman Park on American Falls
    Reservoir: 483
Sportsman's River Resort: 473
Spring Bar: 381
Spring Creek: 400
Spring Creek Campground: 386
Springy Point Recreation Area: 349
Spruce Tree: 366
Squaw Bay Camping Resort: 360
Staley Springs Lodge: 450
Stanley Lake: 407
Star Hope: 442
Steck: 403
Steel Creek Group Area: 452
St. Joe Lodge & Resort: 364
Stoddard Creek: 452
Sublett: 477
Summit Creek: 433
Summit View: 490
Sun Valley Resort: 442
Sundance Village RV Park: 348
Sundown RV Park: 377
Sunny Gulch: 434
Sunnyside Acres Park: 460
Suntree RV Park: 357
Swift Water RV Park: 379
Swinging Bridge: 408

TUV
Ten Mile: 412

Thompson Flat: 476
Three Island Crossing State Park: 468
Three Rivers Resort: 375
Tie Creek: 408
Timber Creek: 430
Tin Can Flat: 365
Torreys Burnt Creek Inn: 433
Town & Country Motel & RV Park:
    345
Trail Creek: 405
Trail Motel & Restaurant: 488
Trails West RV Park and
    Campground: 468
Trapper Creek: 342
Travel America Plaza: 352
Trestle Creek RV Park: 349
Turner Flat: 364
Twin Creek: 385
Twin Falls County Fairgrounds: 475
Twin Falls-Jerome KOA: 474
Twin Rivers Canyon Resort: 344
Upper and Lower O'Brien: 432
Upper Coffee Pot: 452
Upper Luby Bay: 347
Upper Payette Lake: 393
Valley View General Store & RV Park:
    450
Village Motel & RV: 451

WXYZ
Wagon Wheel, The: 421
Wagon Wheel Motel & RV Park: 438
Wagonhammer Springs Campground:
    386
Wallace Lake: 387
Warm Lake Lodge: 401
Warm River: 457
Warm Springs Resort: 413
Washington Creek: 373
Water's Edge RV Resort: 401
West End: 456
West Mountain: 399
Westside Resort: 357
Westside RV Park: 398

Whiskey Rock: 353
White Knob Motel & RV Park: 438
White Locks Marina & RV Park: 484
Whitebird Motel & RV Park: 378
Wilderness Gateway: 374
Wild Goose: 376
Wildhorse: 441
Wild Rose Ranch: 450
Williams Lake: 426
Williams Lake Resort: 426

Willow Bay Recreation Area: 486
Willow Creek: 417
Willow Flat: 493
Winchester Lake State Park: 374
Windy Saddle: 381
Wolf Lodge Campground: 360
Woodhead Park: 396
Wood River: 440
Yellow Pine: 394
Zim's Hot Springs: 393

ABOUT THE AUTHOR

Judy Kinnaman has traveled extensively throughout the West writing outdoor travel and recreation articles for magazines, newspapers, and visitor guides. Judy, her husband, two daughters, and three dogs have enjoyed camping nearly every weekend during the summer months for the past 10 years, braving rain, snow, and more often, glorious sunshine. With the variety of weather and topography in Montana, Wyoming, and Idaho, camping has always been an adventure. Her first book, *Auto Adventures*, came from the desire to share the experience, and this camping book is designed to encourage others to get out there and find their own fun. In addition to nonfiction writing, Judy Kinnaman has had several short stories published and is completing a mystery novel.

AVALON
TRAVEL
publishing

How far will our travel guides take you? As far as you want.

Discover a rhumba-fueled nightspot in Old Havana, explore prehistoric tombs in Ireland, hike beneath California's centuries-old redwoods, or embark on a classic road trip along Route 66. Our guidebooks deliver solidly researched, trip-tested information—minus any generic froth—to help globetrotters or weekend warriors create an adventure uniquely their own.

And we're not just about the printed page. Public television viewers are tuning in to Rick Steves' new travel series, *Rick Steves' Europe*. On the Web, readers can cruise the virtual black top with *Road Trip USA* author Jamie Jensen and learn travel industry secrets from Edward Hasbrouck of *The Practical Nomad*. With Foghorn AnyWare eBooks, users of handheld devices can place themselves "inside" the content of the guidebooks.

In print. On TV. On the Internet. In the palm of your hand.
We supply the information. The rest is up to you.

Avalon Travel Publishing
Something for everyone

www.travelmatters.com

Avalon Travel Publishing guides are available at your favorite book or travel store.

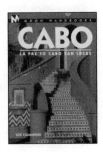

Will you have enough stories to tell your grandchildren?

Yahoo! Travel

DO YOU YAHOO!?